Listening to the Text

ETS Studies
David W. Baker, editor

Listening to the Text

*Oral Patterning
in Paul's Letters*

John D. Harvey

Foreword by
Richard N. Longenecker

Baker Books
A Division of Baker Book House Co
Grand Rapids, Michigan 49516

APOLLOS

Published by Baker Books
a division of Baker Book House Company
P.O. Box 6287, Grand Rapids, MI 49516-6287
United States of America

and

Apollos (an imprint of Inter-Varsity Press)
38 De Montfort Street
Leicester LE1 7GP
England

Printed in the United States of America

Library of Congress Cataloging-in-Publication Data

Harvey, John D., 1951–
    Listening to the text: oral patterning in Paul's letters / John D. Harvey ; foreword by Richard N. Longenecker.
        p.   cm. — (Evangelical Theological Society studies series)
    Includes bibliographical references and indexes.
    ISBN 0-8010-2200-2 (pbk.)
    1. Bible. N.T. Epistles of Paul—Language, style. 2. Rhetoric in the Bible. 3. Rhetorical criticism. I. Title. II. Series.
BS2635.6.L3H37   1998
227' .066—dc21   98-19538

For information about academic books, resources for Christian leaders, and all new releases available from Baker Book House, visit our web site:
http://www.bakerbooks.com

British Library Cataloging-in-Publication Data

A catalogue of this book is available from the British Library.
ISBN: 0-85111-464-4

Contents

FOREWORD

There has recently arisen in the scholarly study of the New Testament the realization that both Greco-Roman society and the world of Judaism were largely oral in nature. Speeches and addresses were composed to be heard, and thus were constructed with various stylistic features and patterns to facilitate their being heard aright. Formal letters were written with many of these oral speech patterns incorporated so that the addressees would understand them when read aloud. Even private letters reflect a large oral component, for they were usually dictated by writers to amanuenses and read aloud by their recipients.

Analyses of Greco-Roman rhetoric and Hellenistic letter writing have been in vogue for twenty or thirty years now. As well, some work has been done on rhetorical and epistolary practices within early Judaism. All of this research is highly significant for the interpretation of the letters of the New Testament, particularly those of Paul. Matters having to do with orality, however, have largely "fallen between the cracks," with attention usually directed to either rhetorical modes or epistolary conventions. Dr. Harvey, however, has sought to rectify this situation by highlighting the various ways in which oral patterning affected both speech and writing in antiquity in general and Paul in particular.

Dr. Harvey's treatment is informed and perceptive. In addition, it is clear, concise, and constructive. In Part 1 he introduces the reader to rhetorical criticism, epistolary analysis, and the study of orality in the first century. In Part 2 he sets out the evidence for oral patterning in the Greco-Roman world and the Septuagint. In the process he discusses categories, definitions, and controls necessary for the evaluation of these features. Then in Part 3 he traces the various forms of oral patterning that appear in seven uncontested letters of Paul, highlighting in the process the exegetical benefits that accrue from "listening to the text" in terms of its oral patterning.

There are, of course, a number of recent articles and monographs that touch on issues of orality in Paul's letters. Almost all of them, however, focus on only one of the apostle's letters or on only a section within a letter. What Dr. Harvey has done is to cast his net more broadly by surveying a wider range of Paul's letters in the light of ancient rhetorical and epistolary practices. In so doing he has provided us with a better picture of oral patterning in the ancient world and a more comprehensive treatment of how oral patterning functions in Paul's letters, pointing out in the process how an understanding of oral patterns aids in the analysis and interpretation of the apostle's letters.

Listening to the Text challenges its readers to analyze and interpret Paul's letters in a new way. It also suggests all sorts of discussions that could be mounted on the basis of what is presented, for the data itself opens up many avenues of research what could be explored. Throughout his study, however, Dr. Harvey has kept his focus sharp, written crisply and concisely, but also left much to be developed by others. Nonetheless, what he has done in highlighting the issues, drawing parallels, identifying certain features of importance in Paul's letters, and making suggestions as to the significance of what he presents, is highly important for interpretation. In many ways Dr. Harvey's work breaks new ground. Biblical exegetes, therefore, need to give serious attention to what he presents—profiting from his research, being challenged by his insights and conclusions, and using his work as a stepping stone toward a better analysis and more faithful interpretation of what Paul has written under the Spirit's guidance for the Church.

Richard N. Longenecker, B.A., M.A., Ph.D., D.D.
Distinguished Professor of New Testament
McMaster Divinity College
McMaster University
       and
Professor Emeritus of New Testament
Wycliffe College
University of Toronto

ACKNOWLEDGMENTS

Seven years is a long time to work on a single project, and such a project cannot be completed without a great deal of assistance. It is my pleasure to acknowledge some of the people who have provided that assistance.

First, the guidance and care of Dr. Richard N. Longenecker made it possible for me to "stay the course." His willingness to listen to my worries and fears encouraged me when I was discouraged, and his patient editorial work strengthened the final product immeasurably.

Second, the gracious forbearance of Dr. Kenneth B. Mulholland, Dean of Columbia Biblical Seminary, and the administration of Columbia International University made it possible for me to research, write, and revise my work while carrying a full teaching load. Their willingness to limit my involvement in certain areas increased the amount of discretionary time available to work on this project and freed me to give it the attention it demanded.

Third, my wife, Anita, has been a constant source of support and encouragement since the days we began discussing the possibility of doctoral studies. Her willingness to continue working during the course of those studies and her uncomplaining patience as the process lengthened beyond expectation demonstrated her love in ways which words could never have done.

Most importantly, all honor must go to our Lord Jesus Christ for granting grace sufficient to the task. He never calls us to a task for which He does not supply the resources. *Soli deo gloria!*

ABBREVIATIONS

AJA	*American Journal of Archaeology*
AJP	*American Journal of Philology*
AJSL	*American Journal of Semitic Languages and Literature*
AnBib	Analecta biblica
ANRW	*Aufstieg und Niedergang der römischen Welt*
ATR	*Anglican Theological Review*
AusBR	*Australian Biblical Review*
AUSS	*Andrews University Seminary Studies*
BA	*Biblical Archaeologist*
BAGD	W. Bauer, W. F. Arndt, F. W. Gingrich, and F. W. Danker, *A Greek-English Lexicon of the New Testament and Other Early Christian Literature*
BETL	Bibliotheca ephemeridum theologicarum lovaniensium
Bib	*Biblica*
BJRL	*Bulletin of the John Rylands University of Manchester*
Bsac	*Bibliotheca Sacra*
BSOAS	*Bulletin of the School of Oriental and African Studies*
BTB	*Biblical Theological Bulletin*
CBQ	*Catholic Biblical Quarterly*
CJ	*Classical Journal*
CompLit	*Comparative Literature*
ContRev	*Contemporary Review*
CP	*Classical Philology*
CQ	*Classical Quarterly*
CTR	*Criswell Theological Review*
CW	*Classical World*
ETR	*Ephemerides theologicae lovanienses*
EvQ	*Evangelical Quarterly*
ExpTim	*Expository Times*
FilNeot	*Filologia Neotestamentaria*
HNT	Handbuch zum Neuen Testament
HSCP	*Harvard Studies in Classical Philology*

HTR	*Harvard Theological Review*
HUCA	*Hebrew Union College Annual*
ICSB	*Institute of Classical Studies Bulletin*
IDBSup	Supplementary volume to G. A. Buttrick (ed.), *Interpreter's Dictionary of the Bible*
IFMJ	*International Folk Music Journal*
Int	*Interpretation*
JAC	Jahrbuch für Antike und Christentum
JAF	*Journal of American Folklore*
JBL	*Journal of Biblical Literature*
JBR	*Journal of Bible and Religion*
JETS	*Journal of the Evangelical Theological Society*
JHS	*Journal of Hellenic Studies*
JQR	*Jewish Quarterly Review*
JR	*Journal of Religion*
JRH	*Journal of Religious History*
JSJF	*Jerusalem Studies in Jewish Folklore*
JSNT	*Journal for the Study of the New Testament*
JSNTSup	Journal for the Study of the New Testament—Supplement Series
JSOTSup	Journal for the Study of the Old Testament—Supplement Series
JTS	*Journal of Theological Studies*
LB	*Linguistica Biblica*
Neot	*Neotestamentica*
NLH	*New Literary History*
NovT	*Novum Testamentum*
NTS	*New Testament Studies*
OJRS	*Ohio Journal of Religious Studies*
OrT	*Oral Tradition*
PEGLMBS	*Proceeding of the Eastern Great Lakes and Midwest Biblical Societies*
PMLA	*Publication of the Modern Language Association*
PQ	*Philological Quarterly*
PTMS	Pittsburgh Theological Monograph Series
PW	Pauly-Wissowa, *Real-Encyclopädie der classischen Altertumswissenschaft*
PWSup	Supplement to Pauly-Wissowa, *Real-Encyclopädie der classischen Altertumswissenschaft*
RAC	*Reallexikon für Antike und Christentum*
RB	*Revue biblique*
RelSRev	*Religious Studies Review*
RHPR	*Revue d'histoire et de philosophie religieuses*

RSPT	*Revue des sciences philosophiques et théologiques*
SBLDS	SBL Dissertation Series
SBLSP	*SBL Seminar Papers*
SNTSMS	Society for New Testament Studies Monograph Series
TAPA	*Transactions of the American Philological Association*
TE	*Theologica Evangelica*
TGl	*Theologie und Glaube*
TLZ	*Theologische Literaturzeitung*
TS	*Theological Studies*
TZ	*Theologische Zeitschrift*
VT	*Vetus Testamentum*
WTJ	*Westminster Theological Journal*
YCS	*Yale Classical Studies*
ZAW	*Zeitschrift für die alttestamentliche Wissenschaft*
ZNW	*Zeitschrift für die neutestamentliche Wissenschaft*
ZTK	*Zeitschrift für Theologie und Kirche*

INTRODUCTION

Paul and his letters have fascinated readers for generations. Scholars have analyzed his theology, his missionary practices, the chronology of his life, the sociology of the churches he planted, the epistolary structure of his letters, the rhetorical structure of his letters, and many other features. Most of this analysis, however, has treated Paul's letters as purely literary compositions and has, by and large, ignored an important aspect of Paul's culture: its orality.

The popular culture of the first century was, technically, a rhetorical culture. In a rhetorical culture, literacy is limited, and reading is vocal. Even the solitary reader reads aloud (Acts 8:30). The normal mode of writing is by dictation, and that which is written down is intended to be read aloud to a group rather than silently by the individual. Such a culture is familiar with writing, but is, in essence, oral. The predominantly oral nature of a rhetorical culture requires speakers to arrange their material in ways that can be followed easily by a listener. Clues to the organization of thought are, of necessity, based on sound rather than on sight.

For Paul, communicating via letters had certain advantages. Letter writing was as close to face-to-face communication as first-century correspondents could come. Paul's use of emissaries also enhanced communication because the emissaries had personal knowledge of the content of the letters they carried. Nevertheless, as Paul Achtemeier observes, clues to the organization of his letters were still essential:

> Such clues are all the more necessary in letters . . . since they have no flow of narrative to aid the listener. It is even more necessary for NT letters which tend to be longer than the other letters of late Western antiquity. While the average length of a letter of Cicero was 295 words, and that of Seneca 955, the average length of a Pauline letter is 2,500 words. Thus what is necessary for letters in general would be the more necessary for Paul: clues to organization so the listener would not simply be lost in a forest of verbiage.[1]

---

[1] P. J. Achtemeier, *"Omne Verbum Sonat*: The New Testament and the Oral Environment of Late Western Antiquity," *JBL* 109 (1990) 22.

Although both epistolary and rhetorical analysis are, to a degree, helpful in following the flow of Paul's argument, neither is completely adequate for the task. On the one hand, the use of epistolary conventions was one way of signaling changes in the flow of the argument. Introducing the letter-body with a disclosure formula, for example, alerted the recipient(s) that the main business of the letter was at hand.[2] Similarly, Paul often used vocatives to signal transitions within the letter-body.[3] It is unlikely, however, that epistolary conventions alone would have been adequate to help listeners find their way through the complex argumentation of Paul's letters.

On the other hand, understanding the rhetorical task of *dispositio* could help listeners identify the macro-scale composition of an argument. As well, understanding the rhetorical task of *elocutio* could help listeners appreciate the use of figures and grand style at the micro-scale. Yet the rhetorical handbooks had little to say regarding intermediate-scale composition. Other, recognizable oral patterns would be needed. Since Paul dictated his letters,[4] these clues would, of necessity, be oral/aural.[5]

Several questions follow naturally: What elements of oral patterning were common in Paul's day? Which of them did Paul use? How did he use them? An exhaustive examination of the rhetoric and literature of antiquity in an attempt to answer the first question would be impractical. Similarly, a detailed study of all the letters attributed to Paul would be an immense task. Nevertheless it is important to survey as much of the literature as possible.

The study that follows will proceed in three parts. Part One will lay theoretical and historical foundations for the examination of oral patterning. It will review scholarly work done in the areas of oral theory, epistolary analysis, and rhetorical

---

[2] Cf. J. T. Sanders, "The Transition From Opening Epistolary Thanksgiving to Body in the Letters of the Pauline Corpus," *JBL* 81 (1962) 348-362; T. Y. Mullins, "Disclosure: A Literary Form in the New Testament," *NovT* 7 (1965) 44-60; J. L. White, "Introductory Formulae in the Body of the Pauline Letter," *JBL* 90 (1971) 17-33.

[3] Cf. J. L. White, *The Form and Function of the Body of the Greek Letter: A Study of the Letter-Body in the Non-Literary Papyri and in Paul the Apostle*, SBLDS 2, (Missoula, MT: University of Montana Press, 1972) 66.

[4] Cf. R. N. Longenecker, "Ancient Amanuenses and the Pauline Epistles," in *New Dimensions in New Testament Study*, ed. R. N. Longenecker and M. C. Tenney (Grand Rapids: Zondervan, 1974) 281-297.

[5] W. H. Kelber: "His letters may in fact accommodate the requirements of oral speech more successfully than is commonly acknowledged . . . the letters, dictated by a speaker and intended for hearers . . . will at least in part have been shaped by oral, prophetic speech patterns" (*The Oral and Written Gospel: The Hermeneutics of Speaking and Writing in the Synoptic Tradition, Mark, Paul and Q* [Philadelpia: Fortress, 1983] 168). M. R. P. McGuire concurs: "A man read even a private letter aloud in a low voice. This practice obviously had great influence on epistolary convention and style. It also helped to make the letter addressed to an individual or a group an easy and natural vehicle for philosophical or religious discussion or exposition" ("Letters and Letter Carriers in Ancient Antiquity," *CW* 53 [1960] 150).

analysis. As well, it will investigate orality and literacy in the first century, with particular attention given to the aural audience of Paul's day.

Part Two will investigate selected Greco-Roman and OT texts to collect examples of oral patterning. These examples will be grouped into general categories, a working definition for each category will be developed, and basic criteria for identifying the phenomena in each category will be established. This discussion will establish a framework for the study of oral patterning in Paul's letters.

Part Three will test for elements of oral patterning in Paul's letters. Seven letters generally considered to be authentic letters of Paul will be surveyed, and readily apparent examples of oral patterning in each letter will be collected; structures suggested by other scholars will also be evaluated.[6] The results of this survey will be synthesized in an attempt to understand the ways in which Paul used oral patterning and to compare his habits with those of other ancient speakers and writers. Exegetical insights drawn from the examination of oral patterning will also be noted.

Parts Two and Three will concentrate on eight specific patterns: chiasmus, inversion, alternation, inclusion, ring-composition, word-chain, refrain, and concentric symmetry. These patterns fit within that aspect of rhetoric known as style (*elocutio*). Not every aspect of style, however, will be examined in detail. Specific rhetorical figures such as anaphora, antistrophe, parechesis, homoeoteleuton, and climax will be mentioned only incidentally. Neither Hebrew parallelism nor the use of link-words will be examined at length. Finally, Paul's use of the diatribe—especially in Romans—will not be addressed, for extensive work has already been done on that particular compositional device.[7] It is not that the above-mentioned aspects of style are unimportant. To include them, however, would broaden the scope of the present study considerably.

As will become obvious in Part Three, other scholars have proposed numerous examples of the patterns that form the focus of this study. The analysis of these phenomena, however, has been approached in a piecemeal fashion. No work has sought to compile and evaluate a comprehensive collection of these patterns in Paul's

---

[6] The database for Part 3 will consist of Romans, 1 and 2 Corinthians, Galatians, Philippians, 1 Thessalonians, and Philemon. The authenticity of 2 Thessalonians, Ephesians, and Colossians is questioned by many scholars, and the Pastoral Epistles present a number of special challenges. None of these latter six letters will be included in this study, but it should be noted that—in each case—the objections to Paul as the author are not insurmountable. In order to make the task of this study manageable, however, it has been necessary to limit the database under consideration. The seven generally accepted Pauline letters have been chosen to make the results of this study accessible to the largest possible audience.

[7] E.g., R. Bultmann, *Der Stil der paulinischen Predigt und die kynische-stoische Diatribe* (Göttingen: Vandenhoeck & Ruprecht, 1910); S. K. Stowers, *The Diatribe and Paul's Letter to the Romans*, SBLDS 57 (Chico, CA: Scholars, 1981).

letters, nor has the exegetical value of such patterns been given much attention. It is hoped that the present study will correct these oversights.

Part One

ORAL PATTERNING IN HISTORICAL PERSPECTIVE

Chapter 1

ORALITY, LETTERS, AND RHETORIC

The study of oral patterning touches on three areas related to biblical research: oral theory, epistolary analysis, and rhetorical analysis. The scholarly work done in each of these areas will be summarized in this chapter.

A. Oral Theory

Modern interest in orality began with the writings of Milman Parry in the 1920s and 1930s.[1] Since that time the literature on the subject has mushroomed. In his annotated bibliography John Foley lists over 1,800 entries related to oral theory, 1,500 of which stem—directly or indirectly—from Parry's pioneering work.[2] Elsewhere Foley identifies three sources of influence on Parry: (1) the Homeric question, (2) philology, and (3) anthropology.[3]

Homer, Philology, and Anthropology. The Homeric question revolved around issues such as "who Homer was, when he composed the poems we conventionally attribute to him, and what implications the answers to these queries have for the edition and interpretation of the *Iliad* and *Odyssey.*"[4] As early as the first century, Josephus suggested that Homer's works were originally compiled from oral songs (*CAp* 1.11-12). In 1767 Robert Wood's *An Essay on the Original Genius of Homer* again suggested that these works were the product of oral, not written, tradition. Three decades later Friedrich Wolf built a solid case for Homer's orality,[5]

---

[1] See below for a discussion of Parry's work.

[2] J. M. Foley, *Oral-Formulaic Theory and Research: An Introduction and Annotated Bibliography* (New York: Garland, 1985).

[3] J. M. Foley, *The Theory of Oral Composition: History and Methodology* (Bloomington, IN: Indiana University Press, 1988) 1.

[4] Ibid.

[5] F. Wolf, *Prolegomena ad Homerum sive (de) Operum Homericorum Prisca et Genuina Forma Variisque Mutationibus et Probabili Ratione Emendande* (Halle: Saxonum, 1795).

and in 1840 Gottfried Hermann connected Homer's formulaic style with oral composition.[6]

Parry was influenced by the work of German and French philologists as well. Johann Ernst Ellendt suggested that the word forms found in Homer were caused by the demands of the meter in which the poems were composed.[7] Similarly, Heinrich Düntzer concluded that the use of hexameter influenced Homer's diction[8] and resulted in "fixed epithets" (*stehende Beiwörter*).[9] Antoine Meillet, who was one of Parry's mentors at the Sorbonne, was convinced that "the Homeric epic is made up entirely of formulas which are transmitted by the poets."[10]

Fieldwork conducted by anthropologists among oral cultures provided analogies to the hypothetical orality of Homer. Vasilii Radlov's work among the Turkish peoples of Central Asia identified the tendency to use stock "idea-parts" in composition.[11] Gerhard Gesemann observed the tendency South Slavic poets had of following set compositional schemes in their stories.[12] Matija Murko, who was present at Parry's thesis defense, noted the way in which South Slavic itinerant poets used clichés, repetition, and formulaic structures in their poems and called for further comparative study of these phenomena.[13]

---

[6] G. Hermann, "De Iteratis apud Homerum" (Leipzig dissertation, 1840).

[7] J. E. Ellendt, *Über den Einfluss des Metrums auf der Gebrauch von Wortformen und Wortverbindungen* (Königberg: Programm Altstädtisches Gymnasaium, 1861).

[8] H. Düntzer, "Über den Einfluss des Metrums auf den homerischen Ausdruck," *Jahrbücher für classische Philologie* 10 (1864) 673-694.

[9] H. Düntzer, "Zur Beurtheilung der stehende homerischen Beiwörter," in *Homerische Abhandlungen* (Leipzig: Hahn'sche Verlagsbuchhandlung, 1872) 507-516.

[10] A. Meillet, *Les Origines indo-européennes des mètres grecs* (Paris: Presses Universitaires de France, 1923) 61.

[11] V. V. Radlov, *Proben der Volksliteratur der nördlichen türkischen Stämme, vol 5: Der Dialect der Kara-Kirgisen* (St. Petersburg: Commissionäre der Kaiserlichen Akademie der Wissenschaften, 1885).

[12] G. Gesemann, *Studien zur südslavischen Volksepik* (Reichenberg: Verlag Gebrüder Stiepel, 1926).

[13] M. Murko, *La Poésie populaire épique en Yougoslavie au début du XXe siècle* (Paris: Librairie Ancienne Honoré Champion, 1929). Other works by Murko include, "Die Volksepik der bosnischen Mohammedaner, *Zeitschrift des Vereins für Volkunde* 19 (1909) 13-30; *Bericht über phonografische Aufnahmen epischer, meist mohammedanischer Volkslieder im nordwestlichen Bosnien im Sommer 1912* (Vienna: Alfred Hölder, 1912); *Bericht über eine Bereisung von Nordwestbosnien und der angrenzenden Gebiete von Kratien und Dalmatien behufs Erforschung der Volksepik der bosnischen Mohammedaner* (Vienna: Alfred Hölder, 1913); *Bericht über eine Reise zum Studium der Volksepik in Bosnien und Herzegowina im Jahre 1913* (Vienna: Alfred Hölder, 1915); *Bericht über phonografische Aufnahmen epischer Volkslieder im mittleren Bosnien und in der Herzegowina im Sommer 1913* (Vienna: Alfred Hölder, 1915); "Neues über südslavische Volksepik," *Neue Jahrbücher für das klassische Altertum, Geschichte und deutsche Literatur* 22 (1919) 273-296; idem, "L'Etat actuel de la poésie populaire épique yougoslave," *Le*

Marcel Jousse. In addition to the influence of Homeric scholars, philologists, and anthropologists, Parry himself states that Marcel Jousse's *Le Style oral rhythmique et mnémotechnique chez les Verbo-moteurs* is "valuable as an attempt to set forth the psychological basis of oral poetic style."[14] Jousse distinguished between spoken style, oral style, and written style. Spoken style is the style of everyday conversation. Oral style is designed to be heard, remembered, and transmitted by memory. Written style is intended to be preserved in print for publication and distribution.

Oral style uses juxtaposition rather than the subordination of written style. It is characterized by simple connectors, verbal association, word-chains, and parallelism. Parallelism is "the automatic repetition of a propositional gesture"[15] and flows out of the fact that mankind is bilateral.

According to Jousse the basic building block of oral style is the "propositional gesture." The propositional gesture is triggered as a reflex to a mental disposition and is complete in itself. It might be as simple as a child saying "no soup" to indicate that he/she does not want to eat soup. An adult might express the same mental disposition by saying "I would prefer not to have soup." In either case the propositional gesture is a unity. Social groups tend to stereotype frequently-used gestures in traditional oral formulas or clichés.

Composition in oral style is heavily dependent on these traditional formulas and makes use of "rhythmic schema." A rhythmic scheme is "the balanced repetition of two, and sometimes three, approximately parallel propositional gestures."[16] Rhythmic schema are grouped into recitatives (stanzas), and recitatives are grouped into longer recitations. Jousse uses 1 Jn 1:1 as an illustrative recitative:

> ὃ ἦν ἀπ' ἀρχῆς,
> ὃ ἀκηκόαμεν,
> ὃ ἑωράκαμεν τοῖς ὀφθαλμοῖς ἡμῶν,
> ὃ ἐθεασάμεθα
> καὶ αἱ χεῖρες ἡμῶν ἐψηλάφησαν,
> περὶ τοῦ λόγου τῆς ζωῆς

Monde slave 5 (1928) 321-351; "Auf den Spuren der Volksepik durch Jugoslavien," *Slavische Rundschau* 3 (1931) 173-183; "Nouvelles observations sur l'état actuel de la poésie épique en Yougoslavie," *Revue des études slaves* 13 (1933) 16-50.

[14] M. Parry, "Studies in the Epic Techinque of Oral Verse-Making, I: Homer and the Homeric Style," *HSCP* 41 (1930) 79. There is a difference of opinion regarding how much influence Jousse's work—published in 1924—had on Parry. The editors of the 1990 reprint of Jousse's book state that it "decisively influenced the work of Milman Parry" (M. Jousse, *The Oral Style* [New York: Garland Publishing, Inc, 1990] vii). Foley sees a less direct influence (*Oral Composition* 13). In either case, Jousse's book is a significant milestone in the modern discussion of orality.

[15] Jousse, *Oral Style* 95.

[16] Ibid. 114.

This verse is not poetry as we often conceive of it. The number of syllables in parallel propositional gestures may—and probably will—vary. Oral style is not characterized by mechanical meter, but by a rhythm that has ease of memorization as its aim. Poetry is a literary development that gathers the techniques of oral style and "transform[s] them into a purely esthetic, sophisticated, difficult stylistic game, *in the manner of* the old utilitarian oral style."[17]

Jousse drew his examples from a wide range of sources, including both OT and NT. He viewed Jesus as the consummate oral teacher and approached him under his anthropological, ethnic aspect as a Galilean rabbi, teaching according to the oral-style method of his milieu and time."[18] He devoted one portion of his book to "Paul's style and its translation," and he explained the "family resemblance" between the NT letters on the basis of their underlying Aramaic oral style.

Milman Parry. Jousse's work was published the year that Milman Parry arrived in Paris to begin work on his doctorate at the Sorbonne (1924). The previous year Parry had completed a master's thesis that focused on diction in Greek epic poetry.[19] Although he still thought of Homer as a traditional poet who wrote his verse, Parry's thesis contained many of the ideas that he would develop in his later work, especially his interest in the ornamental adjective.[20]

It was the ornamental adjective, or "fixed epithet," that was the focus of Parry's doctoral thesis.[21] His starting point was the widely recognized formulary diction in Homer. He defined a formula as "a group of words which is regularly employed under the same metrical conditions to express a given essential idea."[22] Among the common formulae in Homer is the noun-epithet formula in which "the epithet combines with the substantive . . . or with its substantive and a preposition, to make complete formulae which fill the entire space between a caesura and either

---

[17] Ibid. 191 (the emphasis is his).

[18] Introduction to the 1981 edition, ibid. xiv.

[19] M. Parry, "A Comparative Study of Diction as One of the Elements of Style in Early Greek Epic Poetry" (M.A. thesis, University of California, 1923).

[20] Adam Parry: "Almost all of Parry's ideas on Homeric poetry can be found in his M.A. thesis, but his emphasis there is mainly aesthetic" (*The Making of Homeric Verse. The Collected Papers of Milman Parry*, A. Parry, ed. [New York: Oxford University Press, 1987] xxvii). Cf. Foley: "Here are the beginnings, however inchoate, of some of his most persuasive and far-reaching insights: the limitations of form on the expression of thought, the ornamental adjective, the persistence and conservatism of Homeric diction over time, metrical convenience, the 'thrift' or 'economy' of Homeric phraseology, the aesthetic excellence of an epitomized diction" (*Oral Composition* 20).

[21] M. Parry, *L'Epithète traditionnelle dans Homère: Essai sur un problème de style homérique* (Paris: Société Editrice "Les Belles Lettres," 1928). The English translation is found in A. Parry, *Homeric Verse* 2-190.

[22] A. Parry, *Homeric Verse* 13.

the beginning or the end of the line."[23] Certain of these eptithets appear regularly with the same nouns in similar contexts. Rather than its aesthetic effect in a given context, the use of such a fixed epithet is "entirely dependent on its power to facilitate versification."[24] It is the product of the tradition in which the poet finds him/herself. Forced to find combinations of words that fit the demands of hexameter, the poet adopts those noun-epithet formulae that most effectively accomplish the purpose. These combinations are then passed along to the next generation of poets who use and, if possible, improve them.

Subsequent writings further developed the basic idea in his doctoral thesis.[25] The influence of Jousse and Murko, however, soon led Parry to conceive of Homer as an oral poet, rather than simply a traditional one. Two essays on the technique of oral verse-making in epic poetry mark the shift to viewing Homer as an oral poet.[26] In these essays Parry contends that epic poetry such as Homer's was performed by the poet before an audience. The poet actually recomposed the poem each time it was performed. This composition was facilitated by a supply of stereotyped formulae that enabled the poet to tell the story fluently within the parameters of the traditional style. An analysis of the openings of the *Iliad* and *Odyssey* demonstrates the heavily formulaic nature of the poems and suggests their oral origins. Parry spent the summers of 1933 and 1934 in Yugoslavia collecting examples of twentieth century oral poems and comparing them to the model he had developed for Homer.[27] After Parry's accidental death in 1935, the work he had begun was carried on by Albert Lord.

Albert Lord.[28] Albert Bates Lord had accompanied Parry on his 1934 trip to Yugoslavia. He made a trip of his own to Albania in 1937. As a result of these visits he wrote a series of articles dealing with specific problems in Homer that could

---

[23] Ibid. 20.

[24] Ibid. 28.

[25] M. Parry, *Les Formules et la métrique d'Homère* (Paris: Société Editrice "Les Belles Lettres," 1928); idem, "The Homeric Gloss: A Study in Word-sense," *TAPA* 59 (1928) 233-247; idem, "The Distinctive Character of Enjambement in Homeric Verse," *TAPA* 60 (1929) 200-220; idem, "The Traditional Metaphor in Homer," *CPh* 28 (1933) 30-43; idem, "The Traces of the Digamma in Ionic and Lesbian Greek," *Language* 10 (1934) 130-144; idem, "About Winged Words," *CPh* 32 (1937) 59-63.

[26] M. Parry, "Studies in the Epic Technique of Oral Verse-Making, I: Homer and Homeric Style," *HSCP* 41 (1930) 73-147; idem, "Studies in the Epic Technique of Oral Verse-Making, II: The Homeric Language as the Language of an Oral Poetry," *HSCP* 43 (1932) 1-50.

[27] M. Parry, "Whole Formulaic Verses in Greek and Southslavic Heroic Songs," *TAPA* 64 (1933) 179-197. Unpublished works are "Homer and Huso, I: The Singer's Rests in Greek and Southslavic Heroic Songs" and "Cor Huso: A Study of Southslavic Song."

[28] The bibliography in Foley (*Oral Composition* 147-149) lists 54 entries written or co-authored by Lord with three more forthcoming. The focus here will be on his earlier writings, particularly his book *The Singer of Tales*.

be addressed by analogy to the oral tradition he observed in the Balkans.[29] Later fieldwork in Yugoslavia (1950-51) and in Bulgaria (1958-59) led to additional articles on a variety of related topics.[30] It was his book *The Singer of Tales*,[31] however, that "made Oral-Formulaic Theory a discipline of its own."[32]

The express purpose of *The Singer* was "to present [the oral theory of Milman Parry] as fully and yet as simply as possible."[33] The book is divided into two parts: theory and application. The first part examines oral tradition in Yugoslavia: the performance and training of the singers, the use of formulae, the use of typical thematic sequences, the nature of the songs produced, and the interaction between writing and the oral tradition. Part II applies, by analogy, the insights drawn from Southslavic oral composition to Homer's *Odyssey* and *Iliad* and, more briefly, to the medieval epic poems *Beowulf*, *Song of Roland*, and *Digenis Akritas*. Lord's use of the comparative method expanded the foundation begun by Parry and set the stage for further scholarly study of oral-formulaic theory.

Oral-Formulaic Theory. The Parry-Lord theory has been carried forward by a host of scholars and applied to over one hundred language areas. An exhaustive list may be found in Foley's annotated bibliography. A few representative scholars will be noted here.

James Notopoulos was, along with Lord, one of the first scholars sympathetic to Parry's theories. His initial work highlighted such aspects of Homer's poetry as parataxis and ring-composition.[34] He later extended his study to include such areas as modern Greek heroic poetry, geometric art, Hesiod, and the Homeric hymns.[35]

---

[29] Lord, "Homer and Huso I: The Singer's Rests in Southslavic Heroic Song," *TAPA* 67 (1936) 106-113; idem, "Homer and Huso II: Narrative Inconsistencies in Homer and Oral Poetry," *TAPA* 69 (1938) 439-445; idem, "Homer and Huso III: Enjambement in Greek and Southslavic Heroic Song," *TAPA* 79 (1948) 113-124; idem, "Homer, Parry, and Huso," *AJA* 52 (1948) 34-44.

[30] Lord, "Composition by Theme in Homer and Southslavic Epos," *TAPA* 82 (1951) 71-80; idem, "Yugoslav Epic Folk Poetry," *IFMJ* 3 (1951) 57-61; idem, "Homer's Originality: Oral Dictated Texts," *TAPA* 84 (1953) 124-134; idem, "Avdo Medjedović, Guslar," *JAF* 69 (1956) 320-330; idem, "The Role of Sound Patterns in Serbocroatian Epic," in *For Roman Jakobson*, M. Halle, H. G. Lunt, H. McLean, C. H. Van Schooneveld, eds. (The Hague: Mouton, 1956) 301-305; idem, "The Poetics of Oral Creation," *Comparative Literature: Proceedings of the Second Congress of the International Comparative Literature Association*, W. P. Friedrich, ed. (Chapel Hill, NC: University of North Carolina Press, 1959) 1-6.

[31] Lord, *The Singer of Tales* (Cambridge, MA: Harvard University Press, 1960).

[32] Foley, *Oral Composition* 36.

[33] Lord, *Singer* 12.

[34] J. Notopoulos, "Parataxis in Homer," *TAPA* 80 (1949); idem, "Continuity and Interconnexion in Homeric Oral Composition," *TAPA* 82 (1951) 81-101.

[35] J. Notopoulos, "Homer and Cretan Heroic Poetry: A Study in Comparative Oral Poetry," *AJP* 73 (1952) 225-250; idem, "Homer as an Oral Poet in the Light of Modern Greek Heroic Oral Poetry," *Yearbook of the American Philological Society* (Philadelphia: American Philological

Geoffrey Kirk was cautious of pressing the Yugoslav analogy too closely and questioned whether a special "oral poetics" was really necessary to understand Homer.[36] Joseph Russo also raised questions about aspects of the Parry-Lord approach, particularly their analysis of Homer's formulaic style. Initially he was concerned that the Parry-Lord model was too restrictive and argued for a kind of formula that was basically metrical and syntactic rather than verbal.[37] He later questioned the Parry-Lord premise that formularity reveals orality and suggested that Homer's formulaic style might actually be the result of an "aural" style, one that is shaped by and intended to be followed by the ear.[38] Adam and Anne Amory Parry sought to demonstrate that the Homeric poems are both formulaic and aesthetic. They argued that the poet was in control of, rather than controlled by, the formulaic idiom.[39]

Berkeley Peabody's detailed study on Hesiod's *Works and Days* applied five tests of orality to that epic poem: (1) the *phoneme* test requires consistency in the patterns of language-sounds used; (2) the *formulaic* test requires consistency in the patterns of word-forms used; (3) the *enjambment* test requires consistency in the patterns of syntactic periods used; (4) the *thematic* test requires consistency in the patterns of lexical elements used; (5) the *song* test requires consistency in the

Society, 1954) 249-253; idem, "Homer and Geometric Art: A Comparative Study in the Formulaic Technique of Composition," *Athena* 61 (1957) 65-93; idem, "Modern Greek Heroic Oral Poetry and Its Relevance to Homer," text accompanying Folkways Record FE 4468, *Modern Greek Heroic Oral Poetry* (New York: Folkways, 1959); idem, "Homer, Hesiod, and the Achaean Heritage of Oral Poetry," *Hesperia* 29 (1960) 177-197; idem, "The Homeric Hymns as Oral Poetry: A Study of the Post-Homeric Oral Tradition," *AJP* 83 (1962) 337-368.

[36] G. S. Kirk, "Homer and Modern Oral Poetry: Some Confusions," *Classical Quarterly* 10 (1960) 271-281; idem, *The Songs of Homer* (Cambridge: Cambridge University Press, 1962); idem, "Studies in Some Technical Aspects of Homeric Style," *YCS* 20 (1966) 76-152; idem, "Homer: The Meaning of an Oral Tradition," in *Literature and Western Civilization: The Classical World*, D. Daiches and A. Thorlby, eds. (London: Aldus Books, 1972) 155-171; idem, *Homer and the Oral Tradition* (Cambridge: Cambridge University Press, 1976).

[37] J. A. Russo, "A Closer Look at Homeric Formulas," *TAPA* 94 (1963) 235-247; idem, "The Structural Formula in Homeric Verse," *YCS* 20 (1966) 219-240. The first article was critiqued by W. W. Martin, "The Fallacy of the Structural Formula," *TAPA* 96 (1965) 241-253.

[38] J. A. Russo, "Is 'Oral' or 'Aural' Composition the Cause of Homer's Formulaic Style?" in *Oral Literature and the Formula*, B. A. Stolz and R. S. Shannon, eds. (Ann Arbor, MI: Center for the Coördination of Ancient and Modern Studies, 1976) 31-54. In this essay he raised four areas of concern: (1) the definition of a formula, (2) the use of formulas, (3) the formula-analysis of sample Homeric passages, and (4) the significance of Homer's formulaic style.

[39] Adam Parry, "The Language of Achilles," *TAPA* 87 (1956) 1-7; idem, "Have We Homer's *Iliad*?" *YCS* 20 (1966) 177-216; idem, "Language and Characterization in Homer," *HSCP* 76 (1972) 1-22. Anne Amory Parry, "The Gates of Horn and Ivory," *YCS* 20 (1966) 3-57; idem, "Homer as Artist," *CQ* 65 (1971) 1-15; idem, *Blameless Aegisthus: A Study of AMYMΩN and Other Homeric Epithets* (Leiden: Brill, 1973).

patterns of discourse generated.[40] As the result of applying these tests, Peabody concluded that Hesiod's epic poem was indeed the product of oral tradition.

Aside from ancient Greek poetry, the most sustained research has been done on Old English poetry, particularly the epic poem *Beowulf*.[41] The Old French *Song of Roland* has also attracted attention.[42] Growing out of her work on oral cultures in Africa, Ruth Finnegan has sought to broaden perspectives on the nature of "oral literature" and its relationship to written literature.[43] Other scholars have investigated Serbo-Croatian, Hispanic, medieval German, Byzantine, modern Greek, Irish, Arabic, Sumerian, Indian, Chinese, Norwegian, and Russian oral traditions.[44] The application of oral-formulaic theory has been extended even further to include folk

---

[40] B. Peabody, *The Winged Word: A Study in the Technique of Ancient Greek Oral Composition as Seen Principally through Hesiod's "Works and Days"* (Albany, NY: State University of New York Press, 1975) 3.

[41] Two scholars of note in this area are: F. P. Magoun, Jr, "Recurring First Elements in Different Nominal Compounds in *Beowulf* and in the *Elder Edda*," in *Studies in English Philology*, K. Malone and M. B. Ruud, eds. (Minneapolis: University of Minnesota Press, 1929) 73-78; idem, "The Oral-Formulaic Character of Anglo-Saxon Narrative Poetry," *Speculum* 28 (1953) 446-467; idem, "Bede's Story of Caedman: The Case History of an Anglo-Saxon Oral Singer," *Speculum* 30 (1955) 49-63; idem, "The Theme of the Beasts of Battle in Anglo-Saxon Poetry," *Neuphilologische Mitteilungen* 56 (1955) 81-90; and R. P. Creed, "Studies in the Techniques of Composition of the *Beowulf* Poetry in British Museum MS. Cotton Vitellius A. xv," Ph.D. dissertation (Harvard University, 1955); idem, "*Beowulf* 2231a: *sinc-fæt (sõhte)*," *PQ* 35 (1956) 206-208; idem, "The *andswarode*-System in Old English Poetry," *Speculum* 32 (1957) 523-528; idem, "On the Possiblity of Criticizing Old English Poetry," *Texas Studies in Literature and Language* 3 (1961) 97-106; idem, "The Singer Looks at His Sources," *Comparative Literature* 14 (1962) 44-52; idem, "The *Beowulf*-Poet: Master of Sound-Patterning," in *Oral Traditional Literature: A Festschrift for Albert Bates Lord*, J. M. Foley, ed. (Columbus, OH: Slavica, 1981) 194-216. For further discussion, see Foley, *Theory* 65-74.

[42] The most prominent works are: J. Rychner, *La Chanson de geste: Essai sur l'art épique des jongleurs* (Geneva and Lille: E. Droz and Giard, 1955); J. J. Duggan, *The Song of Roland: Formulaic Style and Poetic Craft* (Berkeley: University of California Press, 1973).

[43] R. Finnegan, *Limba Stories and Story-Telling* (Oxford: Clarendon, 1967); idem, *Oral Literature in Africa* (Oxford: Clarendon, 1970); idem, "How Oral is Oral Literature?" *BSOAS* 37 (1974) 52-64; idem, "What Is Oral Literature Anyway? Comments in the Light of Some African and Other Comparative Material," in *Oral Literature and the Fomula*, Stolz and Shannon, eds. (Ann Arbor, MI: Center for the Coördination of Ancient and Modern Studies, 1976) 127-166; idem, *Oral Poetry: Its Nature, Significance, and Social Context* (Cambridge: Cambridge University Press, 1977). Her basic premise is that there is a continuity, rather than a clearcut line between "oral" and "written" literature: "'Oral literature' . . . is not after all a single clear-cut category, nor is it opposed in any absolute way to written literature. 'Oral composition' similarly is not just one kind of process, predictable from some detectable kind of style called 'formulaic' but on the contrary . . . can take a number of different forms" ("What Is Oral Literature Anyway?" 161).

[44] For a summary of each of these traditions, see Foley, *Oral Composition* 74-93.

ballads, country blues singers, and African-American folk-preachers in rural areas of the United States.[45]

Other Directions. Interest in orality has expanded beyond the study of oral cultures and traditions. Eric Havelock, challenged by the idea of Homeric orality, has sought to "demonstrate what may be called the growth of the early Greek mind."[46] While Parry, Lord, and others focused on the mechanics of oral verse-making, Havelock's writings concentrate on the "oral state of mind and oral conditions of culture."[47] His work has a double thrust: (1) the pre-literate nature of Greek culture prior to the introduction of the alphabet around 700 B.C., and (2) the impact of the vocalized alphabet on Greek civilization.[48]

Havelock argues that, prior to the introduction of the alphabet, early Greek culture was neither "primitive" nor "illiterate." It was nonliterate; oral communication dominated all relationships and transactions. The introduction of the alphabet around 700 B.C. was merely the first step in the Greek journey to literacy. This

---

[45] For intriguing reading on the last topic, see B. A. Rosenberg, *The Art of the American Folk Preacher* (New York: Oxford University Press, 1970); idem, "The Formulaic Quality of Spontaneous Sermons," *JAF* 83 (1970) 3-20; idem, "The Psychology of the Spiritual Sermon," in *Religious Movements in Contemporary America*, I. I. Zaretsky and M. P. Leone, eds. (Princeton: Princeton University Press, 1974) 135-149; idem, "The Message of the American Folk Sermon," *OrT* 1 (1986) 695-727.

[46] E. A. Havelock, *Preface to Plato* (Cambridge, MA: Harvard University Press, 1963) vii. Other related works by Havelock include "Preliteracy and the Presocratics," *ICSB* 13 (1966) 44-67; "Thoughtful Hesiod," *YCS* 20 (1966) 61-72; idem, "Dikaiosune: An Essay in Greek Intellectual History," *Phoenix* 23 (1969) 49-70; "Prologue to Greek Literacy," in *University of Cincinnati Classical Studies II* (Norman, OK: University of Oklahoma Press, 1973) 331-391; Origins of Western Literacy (Toronto: Ontario Institute for Studies in Education, 1976); "The Preliteracy of the Greeks," *NLH* 8 (1977) 369-391; "The Alphabetization of Homer," in *Communications Arts in the Ancient World*, E. Havelock and J. P. Hershbell, eds. (New York: Hastings House, 1978) 3-21; "The Ancient Art of Oral Poetry," *Philosopy and Rhetoric* 12 (1979) 187-202; "The Oral Composition of Greek Drama," *Quaderni Urbanati di Cultura Classica* 35 (1980) 61-113; *The Literate Revolution in Greece and Its Cultural Consequences* (Princeton: Princeton University Press, 1982); "The Linguistic Task of the Presocratics," in *Language and Thought in Early Greek Philosophy*, K. Robb, ed. (LaSalle, IL: Monist Library of Philosophy, 1983) 7-82; "The Orality of Socrates and the Literacy of Plato," in *New Essays on Socrates*, E. Kelly, ed. (Washington, DC: University Press of America 1984) 67-93; "Oral Composition in the *Oedipus Tyrannus* of Sophocles," *NLH* 16 (1984) 175-197; "The Alphabetic Mind: A Gift of Greece to the Modern World," *OrT* 1 (1986) 134-150; *The Muse Learns to Write. Reflections on Orality and Literacy from Antiquity to the Present* (New Haven: Yale University Press, 1986); "The Cosmic Myths of Homer and Hesiod," *OrT* 2 (1987) 31-53.

[47] Havelock, *Muse* 52.

[48] The Greek alphabet was an advance on all pre-Greek syllabaries because it included vowels. Havelock: ". . . in the Greek system it became possible for the first time to document all possible forms of linguistic statement with fluency and to achieve fluent recognition, that is fluent reading, of what had been written, on the part of a majority of any population" ("Preliteracy of the Greeks" 369).

journey moved through several stages: craft literacy (seventh and sixth centuries), recitation literacy (sixth and fifth centuries), and scriptorial literacy (fourth century).[49] The writings of Plato (c. 450 B.C.) reflect the tension between the tenacity of orality and the spread of literacy. Those same writings also reflect the beginnings of a shift from concrete to abstract thought.[50]

The philosophical, sociocultural, and psychological implications of different cultural traditions are also the focus of Walter Ong's work on oral theory.[51] His writings are eclectic and wide-ranging. They go far beyond the boundaries initially established by Parry and Lord. Particularly helpful for this study is his analysis of culture developing in three basic stages: oral, alphabet/print, and electronic. Each stage of culture has its own distinct characteristics. The characteristics of orally based thought and expression are: (1) it is additive rather than subordinate; (2) it is aggregative rather than analytic; (3) it is redundant; (4) it is conservative/traditionalist; (5) it is close to the human lifeworld; (6) it is agonistically toned; (7) it is empathetic and participatory rather than objectively distanced; (8) it is homeostatic; and (9) it is situational rather than abstract.[52] Also noteworthy is Ong's view of twentieth century culture as one of "secondary orality." It is "superficially identical with that of primary orality but in depth utterly contrary, planned and self-

---

[49] Cf. Havelock, *Literate Revolution* 59, and "Preliteracy of the Greeks" 372-373. A fuller discussion of the various stages of literacy will be undertaken in Chapter Two.

[50] Havelock: "If we are correct, what Plato is pleading for could be shortly put as the invention of an abstract language of descriptive science to replace a concrete language of oral memory" (*Preface* 237).

[51] The number of entries in Ong's bibliography is enormous. For a complete list, see the Selected Bibliography in *OrT* 2 (1987) 19-30. Works related to oral theory include "Review of *The Singer of Tales* by Albert Lord," *Criticism* 4 (1962) 74-78; "Review of *Preface to Plato* by Eric A. Havelock," *Manuscripta* 7 (1964) 179-181; "Oral Residue in Tudor Prose Style," *PMLA* 80 (1965) 145-154; *The Presence of the Word* (New Haven: Yale University Press, 1967); "Oral Culture and the Literate Mind," in *Minority Language and Literature*, D. Fisher, ed. (New York: Modern Language Association of America, 1977) 134-149; *Interfaces of the Word: Studies in the Evolution of Consciousness and Culture* (Ithaca, NY: Cornell University Press, 1977); "Literacy and Orality in Our Times," *ADE Bulletin* 58 (1978) 1-7; *Orality and Literacy* (London: Mithuen, 1982); "The Psychodynamics of Oral Memory and Narrative: Some Implications for Biblical Studies," in *The Pedagogy of God's Image: Essays on Symbol and the Religious Imagination*, R. Mason, ed. (Chico: Scholars, 1982) 55-73; "Oral Remembering and Narrative Structures," in *Georgetown University Round Table on Languages and Linguistics 1981*, D. Tannen, ed. (Washington, DC: Georgetown University Press, 1982) 12-24; "Orality, Literacy, and Medieval Textualization," *NLH* 16 (1984) 1-12; "Writing is a Technology that Restructures Thought," in *The Written Word: Literacy in Transition*, G. Baumann, ed. (Oxford: Clarendon, 1986) 33-50.

[52] Ong, *Orality and Literacy* 36-57. By "aggregative" Ong means that oral cultures tend to use slogans and cliche's current in everyday speech. By "agonistic" he means that they tend to be polemical in their approach to issues. By "homeostatic" he means that they tend to live in the present.

conscious where primary orality is unplanned and unselfconscious, totally dependent on writing and print for its existence . . . whereas primary orality was not only innocent of writing and print but vulnerable to these media and ultimately destroyed by them."[53]

Biblical Studies. Robert Culley provides an excellent summary of the discussion of oral tradition among biblical scholars prior to 1960.[54] Key figures included: Johann Gottfried Herder, who assumed oral sources for parts of both the OT and the NT;[55] Hermann Gunkel, who suggested that most of the basic genres of Israel's literature were formed during a period of oral tradition;[56] Rudolph Bultmann, who assumed a mixture of oral and written sources for the gospels;[57] H. S. Nyberg, who argued that (a) tradition in the ancient Orient was primarily oral, (b) a period of oral tradition lay behind most written texts, and (c) even after the advent of writing the primary means of transmission was oral;[58] and Eduard Nielsen, who proposed formal criteria pointing to oral tradition.[59] Although he was not a biblical scholar, Marcel Jousse also emphasized the oral background of both the OT and the NT.[60]

The year 1963 marked a significant date for the discussion of orality in OT studies. In that year three works appeared that acknowledged their relationship to the research of Parry and Lord. Stanley Gevirtz suggested that the fixed pairs in both Ugaritic and Israelite poetry were evidence of a traditional diction that facilitated oral composition in much the same way the fixed epithets of Greek poetry did.[61] William Whallon likened Hebrew synonymous parallelism to the Homeric epithet and Anglo-Saxon kenning (alliteration) as evidence of a common stylistic idiom related to oral transmission.[62] Robert Culley sought to describe a range of oral traditions and

---

[53] Ong, *Interfaces* 298.

[54] R. C. Culley, "Oral Tradition and Biblical Studies," *OrT* 1 (1986) 30-41. See also "Oral Tradition and the OT: Some Recent Discussion," *Semeia* 5 (1976) 1-33.

[55] J. G. Herder, "Vom Erlöser der Menschen: Nach unsern drei ersten Evangelien," in *Herders Sämmtliche Werke*, B. Suphan, ed. (Berlin: Weidmannsche Buchhandlung, 1880) XIX: 135-252.

[56] H. Gunkel, *Genesis* (Göttingen: Vandenhoeck & Ruprecht, 1910).

[57] R. Bultmann, *History of the Synoptic Tradition*, J. Marsh, trans. (New York: Harper and Row, 1963), first German edition, 1921.

[58] H. S. Nyberg, *Studien zum Hoseabuche* (Uppsala: Lundequistska Bokhandeln, 1935).

[59] E. Nielsen, *Oral Tradition. A Modern Problem in Old Testament Introduction* (Chicago: Alec R. Allenson, Inc, 1954). The criteria he proposed were: (1) monotonous style, (2) recurrent expressions, (3) paratactic style, (4) rhythm and euphony, (5) anacolutha, (6) repetition, (7) the use of twos and threes, (8) "memory words," (9) representative themes (ibid. 36).

[60] Cf. comments above.

[61] S. Gevirtz, *Patterns in the Early Poetry of Israel* (Chicago: Chicago University Press, 1963).

[62] W. Whallon, "Formulaic Poetry in The Old Testament," *CompLit* 15 (1963) 1-14.

suggested that a number of possibilities existed for the composition and transmission of OT texts.[63]

These initial OT studies were soon followed by more. In 1967 Culley's dissertation identified 177 repeated formulae and formulaic phrases in the OT psalms, located primarily in individual laments, individual thanksgivings, and hymns.[64] These repeated phrases were presented as evidence of traditional oral-formulaic language, although Culley left open the question of whether any of the extant psalms are oral compositions. Whallon followed his initial article with a book comparing Homeric, Old English, and OT poetry.[65] He concluded that parallelism was created to "satisfy a desire for *high style*."[66] Word pairs became formulaic because they enabled the poet to create effective parallelisms. Perry Yoder also argued for the formulaic character of fixed pairs and stressed the utility of those pairs in oral composition.[67]

On the other hand, William Watters specifically criticized the work of Gevirtz, Whallon, and Culley as inadequate.[68] Culley's work, he argued, was misdirected in that he tried to compare Hebrew to other languages before he established the true nature of Hebrew poetry.[69] Gevirtz and Whallon, although on the right track with their study of word pairs,[70] chose isolated examples rather than examining exhaustively entire books of the OT. In an attempt to remedy that shortcoming, Watters analyzed the books of Isaiah, Job, Lamentations, and Ruth. He concluded

---

[63] R. C. Culley, "An Approach to the Problem of Oral Tradition," *VT* 13 (1963) 113-125.

[64] R. C. Culley, *Oral Formulaic Language in the Biblical Psalms* (Toronto: University of Toronto Press, 1967).

[65] W. Whallon, *Formula, Character, and Context: Studies in Homeric, Old English, and Old Testament Poetry* (Cambridge, MA: Harvard University Press, 1969).

[66] Ibid. 148 (the emphasis is his).

[67] P. B. Yoder: "We can thus regard the technique of parallelistic composition by the use of traditional word pairs as a technique developed by oral poetic traditions to meet the needs of oral poets. The needs which this techinque solved for the poet were two: first, it bound cola together to form lines, since two cola sharing a traditional word pair would easily be recognized as a unit; and secondly, it aided the poet in providing a second colon, which would be easily recognizable as such when the second colon contained the second term of a word pair whose first term occurred in the first colon" ("A-B Pairs and Oral Composition in Hebrew Poetry," *VT* 21 [1971] 483).

[68] W. R. Watters, *Formula Criticism and the Poetry of the Old Testament* (Berlin: de Gruyter, 1976).

[69] Watters: "He sought to carry over the characteristics of Indo-European oral techniques to Hebrew poetry. He failed to examine the Hebrew texts and tradition alone and evaluate their own characteristics." (ibid. 18).

[70] Watters: "We would guess that repeated word pairs outnumber repeated phrases 50:1 in the biblical psalms or any other Hebrew poetry. There are simply far more repeated word pairs than there are repeated phrases" (ibid. 42).

that repeated phrases alone are insufficient in determining whether a work is the product of oral tradition. Rather, "the essential value and usefulness of formula criticism lies in its ability to test the uniform diction of a given book or author . . . it can do this even better than it can compare the dictions of two or more books."[71]

In the mid-1970s David Gunn produced three articles on aspects of oral prose style and the OT.[72] Culley also touched on the issue of oral prose in a 1976 monograph.[73] Volume 5 of *Semeia* (1976) focused on "Oral Tradition and Old Testament Studies" and reflected the growing interest in applying oral theory to the OT.[74] More recent works related to the OT have been produced by Everett Fox,[75] Heda Jason,[76] Yehoshua Gitay,[77] Yair Zakovitch,[78] John Van Seters,[79] and Patricia Kirkpatrick.[80]

Until recently there was less written on orality and the NT. In 1961 Birger Gerhardsson produced the first major study on oral and written transmission in the NT period.[81] His approach emphasized verbatim memorization and delivery from memory. Mnemonic techniques used to aid memory included catch-words, acrostics, and "signs."[82] He suggested that Jesus had his disciples memorize specific teaching

---

[71] Ibid. 141.

[72] D. M. Gunn, "Narrative Patterns and Oral Tradition in Judges and Samuel," *VT* 24 (1974) 286-317; idem, "The 'Battle Report: Oral or Scribal Convention?" *JBL* 93 (1974) 513-518; idem, "Traditional Composition in the 'Succesion Narrative'," *VT* 26 (1976) 214-229. A later work is *The Story of King David: Genre and Interpretation.* JSOTSup 6 (Sheffield: JSOT Press, 1978).

[73] R. C. Culley, *Studies in the Structure of Hebrew Narrative* (Missoula, MT: Scholars, 1976).

[74] Essays include: R. C. Culley, "Oral Tradition and the OT: Some Recent Discussion"; B. O. Long, "Recent Field Studies in Oral Literature and the Question of *Sitz im Leben*"; R. B. Coote, "The Application of Oral Theory to Biblical Hebrew Literature"; A. B. Lord, "Formula and Non-Narrative Theme in South Slavic Oral Epic and the OT"; W. J. Urbrock, "Oral Antecedents to Job: A Survey of Formulas and Formulaic Systems"; J. Van Seters, "Oral Patterns or Literary Conventions in Biblical Narrative."

[75] E. Fox, "The Samson Cycle in an Oral Setting," *Alcheringa Ethnopoetics* 4 (1978) 51-68.

[76] H. Jason, "The Story of David and Goliath: A Folk Epic?" *Bib* 60 (1979) 36-70.

[77] Y. Gitay, "Deutero-Isaiah: Oral or Written?" *JBL* 99 (1980) 185-197.

[78] Y. Zakovitch, "From Oral to Written Tale in the Bible," *JSJF* 1 (1981) 9-43.

[79] J. Van Seters, *Abraham in Tradition and History* (New Haven: Yale University Press, 1975); idem, *In Search of History* (New Haven: Yale University Press, 1983).

[80] P. G. Kirkpatrick, "Folklore Studies and the Old Testament" (Ph.D. dissertation, Oxford, 1984).

[81] B. Gerhardsson, *Memory and Manuscript: Oral Tradition and Written Transmission in Rabbinic Judaism and Early Christianity* (Lund: C. W. K. Gleerup, 1961). A concise summary of Gerhardsson's book is found in J. A. Fitzmyer, "Memory and Manuscript: The Origins and Transmission of the Gospel Tradition," *TS* 23 (1962) 442-457.

[82] By "signs" Gerhardsson meant either (1) the use of Scripture to call to mind doctrinal

but gave additional interpretations in less fixed forms. This mix explains many of the differences between the gospels.

In the same year Charles Lohr examined oral techniques in Matthew's Gospel.[83] He determined that Matthew revealed his concern for the continuity and interconnection of his materials by using formulaic language, repetitive devices, and structural devices. Formulaic language includes phrases such as "the law and the prophets," "the gospel of the kingdom," and "when Jesus had finished these words." Important repetitive devices include inclusion, refrain, foreshadowing, retrospection, and thematic development. Key structural devices include grouping of like materials, repetition of key-words, and concentric symmetry. Lohr suggests that Matthew's use of these techniques points to a community that preferred traditional oral communication.

In 1977 Trinity University in San Antonio, Texas held an interdisciplinary dialogue on relationships among the Gospels.[84] One of the seminars in this colloquium was "Oral Traditional Literature and the Gospels." In the invited paper Lord examined the early chapters of the Synoptic Gospels from the perspective of oral traditional literature. He determined that those chapters exhibit certain characteristics of that type of literature.[85] In his response, Leander Keck rejected Lord's suggestions and argued instead for literary relationships among the Synoptic Gospels.[86]

H. Van Dyke Parunak noted the differences between documents produced today and those produced during ancient times.[87] He suggested that the world of antiquity was oriented toward the spoken word and used indicators more attuned to the ear than to the eye. He examined a number of surface structural features in biblical texts and discussed the way in which these features function to signal emphasis, identify peripheral material, mark divisions of argument, and preview

statements, or (2) the use of memory words or sentences formed by taking characteristic letters or decisive key words from longer doctrinal passages.

[83] C. H. Lohr, "Oral Techniques in the Gospel of Matthew," *CBQ* 23 (1961) 403-435.

[84] The Collected papers were later published as *The Relationships Among the Gospels: An Interdisciplinary Dialogue*, W. O. Walker, Jr., ed. (San Antonio: Trinity University Press, 1978).

[85] A. B. Lord, "The Gospels as Oral Traditional Literature," in *Relationships* 33-91. The characteristics he noted were: (1) the texts vary from one another to such an extent as to rule out the possibility that one author could have copied another; (2) the sequence of episodes shows chiastic variations in arrangement; (3) there is a marked tendency toward elaboration and expansion of episodes and sequences; (4) there is a duplication of multiforms.

[86] L. E. Keck, "Oral and Independent or Literary and Interdependent?" in *Relationships* 93-102.

[87] H. V. D. Parunak, "Oral Typesetting: Some Uses of Biblical Structure," *Bib* 62 (1981) 153-168.

coming exposition. He even suggested the need for a "grammar" describing the function of such features as chiasmus, inclusion, and alternation.

Werner Kelber has written more extensively than anyone on orality and the NT, especially the Gospels. His 1979 article on Mark argued that the second Gospel was not the logical extension of oral tradition but, rather, a counter to it.[88] Kelber expanded his discussion in *The Oral and Written Gospel*.[89] The primary focus of this book is oral tradition and its relationship to the Gospels, especially Mark. Kelber decisively rejects both Bultmann's model of "evolutionary progression" and Gerhardsson's model of "passive transmission." Instead he views oral transmission as a process of social identification and preventive censorship. The emphasis on the "living word" led to a de-emphasis on an "original form." Transmission occurred as re-composition and re-creation rather than as rote memorization.

Kelber's interest in the psychodynamics of orality comes to the fore in his chapter on "Orality and Textuality in Paul." He emphasizes Paul's preferences for the oral gospel and personal presence. Evidence of those preferences is found in Paul's prophetic style and his use of letters, especially in the apostolic parousia and the use of παρακαλῶ formulae.

In a later article Kelber extended his field of investigation to John's Gospel.[90] He suggests that the fourth Gospel was written to counteract a perversion of the words (*logoi*) of Jesus. By introducing Jesus as the Word (*Logos*) and by including the numerous saying of Jesus present in the Gospel, the *logoi* are brought under the authority of the incarnate *Logos*.

Recently, scholars in increasing numbers are calling for a consideration of orality in NT studies. C.-B. Amphoux brings the discussion nearly full circle in an article that reviews Jousse's work and challenges scholars to consider the principles of that work in the exegesis of the NT.[91] Joanna Dewey calls for a better understanding of how oral and written media worked together and in opposition to one another in early Christianity.[92] Arthur Dewey writes that little has been done to "bring the recent discussion of orality to the writings of Paul."[93] Pieter Botha notes both the importance and the scarcity of research done on orality, literacy, and interpretation.[94]

---

[88] W. H. Kelber, "Mark and Oral Tradition," *Semeia* 6 (1979) 7-55.

[89] Kelber, *Oral and Written Gospel*.

[90] W. H. Kelber, "The Authority of the Word in St. John's Gospel: Charismatic Speech, Narrative Text, Logocentrism, Metaphysics," *OrT* 2 (1987) 108-131.

[91] C.-B. Amphoux, "Le Style oral dans le Nouveau Testament," *ETR* 63 (1988) 379-384. He contends that an understanding of oral style is the natural and indispensable prelude to all exegesis because it puts us in contact with the world of the NT.

[92] J. Dewey, "Oral Methods of Structuring Narrative in Mark," *Int* 43 (1989) 32-44.

[93] A. J. Dewey, "A Re-Hearing of Romans 10:1-15," *SBLSP* [1990] 273.

[94] P. J. J. Botha, "Mute Manuscripts: Analysing a Neglected Aspect of Ancient Communication," *TE* 23 (1990) 35-47.

Paul Achtemeier also comments on the way in which the "high residual orality" of late Western antiquity has been neglected in NT research.[95]

B. Epistolary Analysis

Adolf Deissmann's comments on Paul's letters mark the beginning of interest in NT epistolary analysis.[96] After comparing Paul's letters with common Greek letters found in the papyri, Deissmann determined that Paul wrote "real" letters. That is, his letters were *ad hoc* documents intended for specific readers in specific situations rather than literary works intended for publication. This insight soon led others to do further study on the form and function of NT letters in general, and Paul's letters in particular.

Early Studies. In 1912 Paul Wendland identified the basic components of the openings and closings of Paul's letters. The openings generally followed the form: salutation and thanksgiving; the basic components of the closings were: doxology, greeting, and benediction.[97] Eleven years later Francis X. J. Exler's dissertation clarified the basic parts of the Hellenistic letter (opening, body, closing) and the conventional phrases present in each part,[98] and Henry Meecham examined papyrus letters from Oxyrhynchus to see what light they shed on NT language and thought.[99]

The years 1927-1935 saw several other scholars explore various aspects of ancient epistolography. Ernst Lohmeyer examined the Pauline greetings.[100] George Boobyer studied the topic of "thanksgiving" in Paul's letters.[101] J. Sykutris developed a system for classifying ancient letters by type and produced a summary of letter

---

[95] P. J. Achtemeier, "*Omne Verbum Sonat*: The New Testament and the Oral Environment of Late Western Antiquity," *JBL* 109 (1990) 3-27.

[96] A. Deissmann, *Light from the Ancient East: The New Testament Illustrated by Recently Discovered Texts of the Graeco-Roman World*, L. R. M. Strachan, trans. (London: Hodder & Stoughton, 1909).

[97] P. Wendland, "Die urchristlichen Literaturformen," in *HNT* 1.3 (Tübingen: Mohr/ Siebeck, 1912) 341-343.

[98] F. X. J. Exler, "The Form of the Ancient Greek Letter: A Study in Greek Epistolography" (Ph.D. dissertation, Catholic University of America, 1923).

[99] H. G. Meecham, *Light from Ancient Letters: Private Correspondence in the Non-Literary Papyri of Oxyrhynchus of the First Four Centuries, and its Bearings on New Testament Language and Thought* (London: George Allen & Unwin, Ltd., 1923). He concluded: (1) that NT Greek was the same as the Greek used elsewhere in the Greco-Roman world; (2) that Paul's letters were identical to secular correspondence in their language and use of formulae; and (3) that the thoughts expressed in the NT bore an intimate relation to the thought currents of the age.

[100] E. Lohmeyer, "Probleme paulinischer Theologie I: Briefliche Grussüberschriften," *ZNW* 26 (1927) 158-173.

[101] G. H. Boobyer, *"Thanksgiving" and the "Glory of God" in Paul* (Borna: Noske, 1929).

theory.[102] Otto Roller sought to define letter structure in Paul's letter as a means of determining the genuineness of those letters.[103] L. Champion investigated benedictions and doxologies in Paul's letters.[104] Clinton Keyes studied the Greek letter of introduction.[105]

Two important works appeared in 1938 and 1939. First, Henry Steen studied the body of papyrus letters and identified recurring phrases that functioned in conjunction with imperatives.[106] These "clichés" served to soften or strengthen the imperatives. Steen's work augmented that done earlier by Exler, who had concentrated primarily on the opening and closing portions of the Hellenistic letter.

Steen's essay was followed by Paul Schubert's book on the Pauline thanksgivings (1939).[107] This latter work is perhaps the best known of the early studies. Schubert proposed two types of thanksgivings. The first (Type Ia) uses one or more participial clauses (usually of time and cause) to modify the principal verb, has a pronominal prepositional phrase (e.g., περὶ ὑμῶν) modifying the participial construction, and concludes with a purpose clause (usually ἵνα or εἰς with an infinitive). Philippians, 1 Thessalonians, and Philemon have this type of thanksgiving. The second (Type Ib) lacks the participial clause(s), has the pronominal prepositional phrase modifying the principal verb, and concludes with a causal ὅτι clause. 1 Corinthians and 2 Thessalonians have this type of thanksgiving. The thanksgiving in Romans is a "mixed type." Schubert's study was the first to concentrate on a single portion of the Pauline letter; it was also the last major study for over a decade.

Increasing Interest. No major works were produced during the 1940s,[108] but the 1950s and 1960s saw increasing interest in epistolary analysis. In 1953 David Bradley studied the paraenetic portions of Paul's letters and compared them to the *topoi* of various extra-biblical writers.[109] In 1956 Heikki Koskenniemi suggested that the primary "idea" behind the Hellenistic letter was that of maintaining personal

---

[102] J. Sykutris, "Epistolographie," in *PW* 186-220.

[103] O. Roller, *Das Formular der paulinischen Briefe: Ein Beitrag zur Lehre vom antiken Briefe* (Stuttgart: Kohlhammer, 1933).

[104] L. Champion, "Benedictions and Doxologies in the Epistles of Paul" (dissertation, Ruprecht-Karls Universität, Heidelberg, 1934).

[105] C. W. Keyes, "The Greek Letter of Introduction," *AJP* 56 (1935) 28-44.

[106] H. A. Steen, "Les clichés epistolaires dan les lettres sur papyrus Greque," *Classica et Mediaevalia* 1 (1938) 119-176.

[107] P. Schubert, *Form and Function of the Pauline Thanksgivings* (Berlin: Topelmann, 1939). The same year he also published an essay reviewing work on the Pauline letter to that date: "Form and Function of the Pauline Letter," *JR* 19 (1939) 365-377.

[108] A. M. Perry compared Paul's letters with papyrus letters and sought to evaluate which were composites ("Epistolary Form in Paul," *Crozer Quarterly* 25 [1948] 48-53).

[109] D. G. Bradley, "The *Topos* as a Form in the Pauline Paraenesis," *JBL* 72 (1953) 238-246.

contact and imparting information, that is, turning absence into presence.[110] In 1960 Martin McGuire addressed the topic of "Letters and Letter Carriers in Christian Antiquity."[111]

Twenty-three years after Schubert's study of the Pauline thanksgiving, Jack Sanders sought to define more precisely the way in which Paul made the transition from the thanksgiving to the letter-body.[112] Also in 1962 Terence Mullins began a series of articles discussing smaller forms within the NT letters.[113] Gordon Bahr took up first the general issue of letter writing in the first century,[114] then the more specific topic of the subscriptions in Paul's letters.[115] William Doty's dissertation surveyed both Hellenistic letters and Paul's letters and proposed the following basic structure: (1) introduction (sender, recipient, greetings, and health wish[es]); (2) body (introduced by stereotyped formulae); (3) conclusion (greetings, wishes, and prayer sentence).[116] Carl Bjerkelund examined the use of παρακαλῶ phrases in Paul's letters.[117]

Robert Funk's writings began the formal study of the body of the Pauline letter. In a chapter of his book *Language, Hermeneutic, and the Word of God*, Funk

---

[110] H. Koskenniemi: " . . . die ἀπουσία zur παρουσία machen." (*Studien zur Idee und Phraseologie des griechischen Briefes bis 400 n. Chr.* [Helsinki: Suomalaisen Kirjallisuuden Kirjapaino Oy, 1956) 38. In this, he anticipates Funk's work on the "apostolic parousia"; see n. 128 below.

[111] M. P. P. McGuire, "Letters and Letter Carriers in Christian Antiquity," *CW* 53 (1960) 150-157.

[112] J. T. Sanders, "The Transition From Opening Epistolary Thanksgiving to Body in the Letters of the Pauline Corpus," *JBL* 81 (1962) 348-362. The primary items he noted were the use of doxological language to close the thanksgiving and the use of certain formal phrases to open the letter-body.

[113] T. Y. Mullins, "Petition as a Literary Form," *NovT* 5 (1962) 46-54. See also "Disclosure: A Literary Form in the New Testament," *NovT* 7 (1964) 44-50; "Greeting as a New Testament Form," *JBL* 87 (1968) 418-426; "Formulas in New Testament Epistles," *JBL* 91 (1972) 380-390; "Ascription as a Literary Form," *NTS* 19 (1973) 194-205; "Visit Talk in the New Testament Letters," *CBQ* 35 (1973) 350-358; "Benediction as a New Testament Form," *AUSS* 15 (1977) 59-64.

[114] G. J. Bahr, "Paul and Letter Writing in the Fifth [*sic*] Century," *CBQ* 28 (1966) 465-477.

[115] G. J. Bahr, "The Subscriptions in the Pauline Letters," *JBL* 87 (1968) 27-41. Bahr's suggestion was that Paul not only dictated his letters, he also regularly closed those letters with an autograph subscription in his own hand.

[116] W. G. Doty, "The Epistle in Late Hellenism and Early Christianity: Developments, Influences, and Literary Form" (Ph.D. dissertation, Drew University, 1966). Doty later published his findings in *Letters in Primitive Christianity* (Philadelphia: Fortress, 1973). Cf. also "The Classification of Epistolary Literature," *CBQ* 31 (1969) 183-199.

[117] C. J. Bjerkelund, *Parakalo: Form, Funktion, und Sinn der parakalo-Sätze in den paulinischen Briefen* (Oslo: Universitetsforlaget, 1967).

identified both a general epistolary substructure and standard elements in the letter-body.[118] Wendland had previously suggested that Paul's letters opened with a salutation and a thanksgiving and closed with a doxology, greetings, and a benediction. Funk took this form as normative and proposed an epistolary substructure of salutation, thanksgiving, body, paraenesis, and closing. The body included: (1) a formal opening, (2) connecting and transitional formulae, (3) a concluding eschatological climax, and (4) a travelogue. In a subsequent essay Funk developed a theoretical construct for the travelogue and renamed it the "apostolic parousia."[119]

Coming of Age. The decade of the 1970s saw the continuing development of epistolary analysis. Early works in this period include Robert Jewett's discussion of the way in which themes in the thanksgiving of Philippians provide evidence supporting the integrity of that letter,[120] Klaus Thraede's study of the basic characteristics and themes of the Greco-Roman letter,[121] and Robert Karris's examination of the paraenetic elements in the Pastoral Epistles.[122] Books by Chan-Hie Kim[123] and John L. White[124] initiated the investigation of specific letter types.

White was instrumental in generating interest in epistolary analysis. In 1971 he identified six formulae Paul used to introduce the body of his letters.[125] That same year he presented a paper at the annual meeting of the Society of Biblical Literature analyzing Paul's letter to Philemon from the perspective of epistolary analysis.[126]

White's dissertation on the body of the Greek letter was published in 1972. In it he wrote, "We must assume . . . that all of the major elements of the Pauline

---

[118] R. W. Funk, *Language, Hermeneutic, and the Word of God* (New York: Harper and Row, 1966).

[119] R. W. Funk, "The Apostolic 'Parousia': Form and Significance," in *Christian History and Interpretation: Studies Presented to John Knox*, W. R. Farmer, C. F. D. Moule, R. R. Niebuhr, eds. (Cambridge: Cambridge University Press, 1967) 249-268.

[120] R. Jewett, "The Epistolary Thanksgiving and the Integrity of Philippians," *NovT* 12 (1970) 53-65. A later essay of his is "Romans as an Ambassadorial Letter," *Int* 36 (1982) 5-20.

[121] K. Thraede, *Gründzuge griechisch-römisher Brieftopik* (Münich: Beck, 1970).

[122] R. J. Karris, "The Function and Sitz im Leben of the Paraenetic Elements in the Pastoral Epistles" (Ph.D. dissertation, Harvard University, 1971).

[123] C.-H. Kim, *Form and Structure of the Familiar Greek Letter of Recommendation*, SBLDS 4 (Missoula, MT: University of Montana Press, 1972). Kim also indexed Greek papyrus letters ("Index of Greek Papyrus Letters," *Semeia* 22 [1981] 107-112).

[124] J. L. White, *The Form and Structure of the Official Petition*, SBLDS 5 (Missoula, MT: University of Montana Press, 1972). Cf. J. L. White and K. A. Kensinger, "Categories of Greek Papyrus Letters," *SBLSP* (1976) 79-92.

[125] J. L. White, "Introductory Formulae in the Body of the Pauline Letter," *JBL* 90 (1971) 17-33.

[126] J. L. White, "The Structural Analysis of Philemon: A Point of Departure in the Formal Analysis of the Pauline Letter," *SBLSP* (1971) 1-48.

letter are now identified."[127] He then began to expand the work on the letter-body begun by his mentor, Robert Funk. Working extensively with papyrus letters, White argued that the Greek letter-body was composed of three sections: the body-opening, the body-middle, and the body-closing. The same basic structure can be found in Paul's letters: the body-opening is introduced by one of several formulae;[128] the body-middle is divided into two parts: a theological argument and a practical section;[129] the body-closing begins with a motivation-for-writing formula and ends with the apostolic parousia. White's examination of the letter-body has been foundational for subsequent work on the form of Paul's letters.

Scholars in the 1970s published a variety of studies focusing on different aspects of the ancient letter. John Hurd proposed a "response-letter" form for 1 Thessalonians.[130] Gordon Wiles,[131] Klaus Berger,[132] and Peter O'Brien[133] all produced works related to the thanksgiving passages and prayer reports found at the beginning of Paul's letters. Hendrickus Boers used 1 Thessalonians as a case study in examining the thanksgiving, "central," apostolic parousia, and exhortation sections of Paul's letters.[134] Geoffrey Cuming examined three common phrases found at the

---

[127] J. L. White, *The Form and Function of the Body of the Greek Letter: A Study of the Letter-Body in the Non-Literary Papyri and in Paul the Apostle*, SBLDS 2 (Missoula, MT: University of Montana Press, 1972) 45. Subsequent works by White include: "Epistolary Formulas and Clichés in Greek Papyrus Letters," *SBLSP* (1978) 289-319; "The Ancient Epistolography Group in Retrospect," *Semeia* 22 (1981) 1-14; "The Greek Documentary Letter Tradition Third Century B.C.E. to Third Century C.E.," *Semeia* 22 (1981) 89-106; "Saint Paul and the Apostolic Letter Tradition," *CBQ* 45 (1983) 433-444; "New Testament Epistolary Literature in the Framework of Ancient Epistolography," *ANRW* Series II.25.2 (1984) 1730-1756; *Light from Ancient Letters*, (Philadelphia: Fortress, 1986); "Ancient Greek Letters," in *Greco-Roman Literature in the New Testament*, D. E. Aune, ed. (Atlanta: Scholars, 1988) 85-106.

[128] Cf. White, "Introductory Formulae." The formulae he identifies are: (1) disclosure formula, (2) request formula, (3) joy expression, (4) expression of astonishment, (5) statement of compliance, and (6) formulaic use of a verb of seeing or hearing.

[129] The exception is the letter to Philemon.

[130] J. C. Hurd, Jr., "Concerning the Structure of 1 Thessalonians," Paper presented at the annual meeting of the Society of Biblical Literature, Los Angeles, CA, 1-5 September 1972.

[131] G. P. Wiles, *Paul's Intercessory Prayers* (Cambridge: Cambridge University Press, 1973).

[132] K. Berger, "Apostelbrief und apostolische Rede: Zum Formular frühchristlicher Briefe," *ZNW* 65 (1974) 190-231. Berger contended that the thanksgiving section was not a regular feature of the Hellenistic letter.

[133] P. T. O'Brien, "Thanksgiving and the Gospel in Paul," *NTS* 21 (1974) 144-155; idem, *Introductory Thanksgivings in the Letters of Paul* (Leiden: Brill, 1977).

[134] H. Boers, "Form Critical Study of Paul's Letters: 1 Thessalonians as a Case Study," *NTS* 22 (1976) 140-158. Of special interest in Boers's article is the identification of an "apostolic apology" that addressed Paul's circumstances and ministry. Such sections appear in Rom 1:14-16; 2 Cor 1:12-17; Gal 1:10-2:21; Phil 1:12-26; 3:2-14; 1 Thess 2:1-12.

end of NT letters and suggested that they also occurred at the end of early Christian worship services.[135] M. Luther Stirewalt, Jr. examined fifteen extra-biblical documents that he believed could be categorized as "letter-essays."[136] Abraham Malherbe provided a summary of ancient epistolary theory and a collection of texts related to that theory.[137] Henry Gamble compared the endings of Paul's letters as a means of addressing the text-critical issues surrounding Romans 14-16.[138]

An Established Discipline. The period since 1980 has seen the widespread adoption of epistolary analysis as an established discipline in NT studies. The number of works produced in recent years is substantial. The following discussion is a concise survey rather than an exhaustive analysis.

Stanley Stowers's dissertation on the diatribe in Romans returned to a topic initially broached by Bultmann.[139] Ronald Russell used the basic approach pioneered by Funk and White to analyze the epistolary structure of Philippians.[140] In two articles, Stanley Olson compared the expressions of confidence in the papyrus letters with those found in NT letters.[141] Wentzel Coetzer examined the paraenetic sections of Paul's letters and determined that no rigid scheme can explain the origin of the "literary genre" of paraenesis.[142] Judith Lieu studied the apostolic greeting "Grace to you and peace," that endured in Christian letters until the fourth century.[143]

In 1986 John Roberts began a series of articles focusing on the transitions to the letter-body in Paul's letters.[144] Linda Belleville used epistolary analysis to provide

---

[135] G. J. Cuming, "Service-endings in the Epistles," *NTS* 22 (1975) 110-113. The phrases he studied were: "The God of peace be with you"; "Greet one another with a holy kiss"; and "The grace of our Lord Jesus Christ be with you."

[136] M. L. Stirewalt, Jr., "The Form and Function of the Greek Letter-Essay," in *The Romans Debate*, K. Donfried, ed. (Minneapolis: Augsburg, 1977) 175-206.

[137] A. J. Malherbe, "Ancient Epistolary Theorists," *OJRS* 5 (1977) 3-77.

[138] H. Y. Gamble, *The Textual History of the Letter to the Romans* (Grand Rapids: Eerdmans, 1977).

[139] S. K. Stowers, *The Diatribe and Paul's Letter to the Romans*, SBLDS 57 (Chico, CA: Scholars, 1981).

[140] R. Russell, "Pauline Letter Structure in Philippians," *JETS* 25 (1982) 295-306.

[141] S. N. Olson, "Epistolary Uses of Expressions of Self-Confidence," *JBL* 103 (1984) 585-597; idem, "Pauline Expressions of Confidence in His Readers," *CBQ* 47 (1985) 282-295. Olson found that NT expressions of self-confidence functioned as thematic statements introducing sections designed to influence the reader's view of the writer and his character. Expressions of confidence in the readers were a persuasive technique designed to increase the likelihood of a favorable hearing rather than a sincere reflection of the writer's view of the addressees.

[142] W. C. Coetzer, "The Literary Genre of Paraenesis in the Pauline Letters," *TE* 17 (1984) 36-42.

[143] J. L. Lieu, "'Grace to you and Peace': The Apostolic Greeting," *BJRL* 68 (1985) 161-175.

[144] J. H. Roberts, "Pauline transitions to the letter-body," *BETL* 73 (1986) 93-99;

positive support for the unity of 1 Corinthians.[145] She later argued that 2 Cor 1:8-7:16 formed a letter of "apologetic self-commendation."[146] Also working in 1 Corinthians, Margaret Mitchell argued that the standard understanding of περὶ δὲ as marking topics raised by the Corinthians in a letter to Paul was faulty.[147] In 1989 Loveday Alexander proposed that Philippians should be understood as a "familiar" letter with its thematic unity focused on the message of reassurance found in 1:12-26.[148] Ann Jervis and Jeffrey Weima, both students of Richard Longenecker and John Hurd, used epistolary analysis to pursue a better understanding of Paul and his letters.[149]

C. Pauline Rhetoric

Paul's "rhetoric" has been frequently discussed, the earliest recorded instance being that of the Christians at Corinth (2 Cor 10:10-11).[150] The Church Fathers considered it appropriate to analyze Paul's letters in terms of classical rhetoric.[151]

"Transitional techniques to the letter-body in the *corpus Paulinum*," in *A South African perspective on the New Testament: Essays by South African New Testament scholars presented to Bruce Manning Metzger during his visit to South Africa in 1985*, J. H. Petzer and P. J. Hartin, eds. (Leiden: Brill, 1986) 187-201; "The Eschatological Transitions to the Pauline Letter-body," *Neotestamentica* 20 (1986) 29-35; "θαυμαζω: An expression of perplexity in some examples from papyri letters," *Neotestamentica* 25 (1991) 109-122; "Paul's expression of perplexity in Galatians 1:6: The force of emotive argumentation," *Neotestamentica* 26 (1992) 329-338.

[145] L. L. Belleville, "Continuity or Discontinuity: A Fresh Look at 1 Corinthians in the Light of First-Century Epistolary Forms and Conventions," *EvQ* 59 (1987) 15-37.

[146] L. L. Belleville, "A Letter of Apologetic Self-Commendation," *NovT* 31 (1989) 142-163.

[147] M. M. Mitchell, "Concerning 'peri de' in 1 Corinthians," *NovT* 31 (1989) 229-256. Mitchell concluded that the only requirement of the new topic introduced by περὶ δὲ was that it was readily known to both author and reader. Although it served to introduce the next subject in a discussion, it was not restricted to a letter of response. Consequently, the composition, structure, and arrangement of 1 Corinthians was determined by Paul's rhetorical purpose, not by a letter from the Corinthians.

[148] L. Alexander, "Hellenistic Letter-Forms and the Structure of Philippians," *JSNT* 37 (1989) 87-101.

[149] L. A. Jervis, *The Purpose of Romans: A Comparative Letter Structure Investigation*, JSNTSup 55 (Sheffield: JSOT Press, 1991); J. A. D. Weima, *Neglected Endings: The Significance of the Pauline Letter Closings*, JSNTSup 101 (Sheffield: JSOT Press, 1994).

[150] The extensive literature on 2 Cor 10-12 does not need to detain us here. A good starting point for further study is C. Forbes, "Comparison, Self-Praise and Irony: Paul's Boasting and the Conventions of Hellenistic Rhetoric," *NTS* 32 (1986) 1-30. A different approach is taken by M. A. Chevallier, "L'Argumentation de Paul dans 2 Corinthiens 10 à 13," *RHPR* 70 (1990) 3-15.

[151] The most notable example is Augustine, *City of God* 11.18 and *On Christian Doctrine* 4.7.11-15; 4.20.39-44. Among others, see Methodius, *The Banquet of the Ten Virgins* 3.2 and Chrysostom, *Homily* 8 and *Homily* 31 on Romans; *Homily* 28 on 1 Corinthians; *Homily* 13 on 2 Corinthians; *Homily* 7 on Colossians.

The Protestant Reformers used rhetorical categories in commenting on his writings.[152] During the seventeenth and eighteenth centuries several scholars continued to note Paul's knowledge and use of rhetoric.[153] The nineteenth and early twentieth centuries saw the production of a number of works that addressed the relation of rhetorical concepts to Paul's writings,[154] culminating in Rudolf Bultmann's study of the diatribe in 1910.[155] Individual scholars continued the investigation during the next five decades;[156] but, on the whole, for about a half-century the search for

---

[152] The most frequently cited scholars from this era are Erasmus, Bucer, Melanchthon, Bullinger, and Calvin. For Melanchthon, see R. Schäfer, "Melanchthons Hermeneutik im Römerbrief-Kommentar von 1532," ZTK 60 (1963) 216-235. For Calvin, see B. Girardin, Rhétorique et théologie: Calvin, Le commentaire de l'Epître aux Romains (Paris: Beauchesne, 1979) esp. 205-273, 369-387. The latter work also interacts extensively with the writings of Erasmus, Bucer, and Bullinger. See also T. H. L. Parker, Commentaries on the Epistle to the Romans 1532-1542 (Edinburgh: T & T Clark, 1986).

[153] E.g., H. Grotius, Annotationes in Novum Testamentum, 3 vols. (Paris, 1641-50) 2:488; M. Poole, Annotations upon the Holy Bible, 2 vols. (London: Parkhurst & others, 1688), see comment on 2 Cor 8:7; J. A. Bengel, Gnomon Novi Testamenti, 2 vols. (1742), see 2:9-503 for the Pauline epistles; S. J. Baumgarten, Auslegung der beiden Briefe St. Pauli an die Corinthier (Halle: Gebauer, 1761). Betz writes of Baumgarten: "Baumgarten's treatment of the Corinthian epistles is remarkable in several respects. In the first place, he employed categories which today would be called literary and rhetorical, though they are neither clearly identified as such nor sufficiently distinguished from considerations of sentence structure and internal logic" (H. D. Betz, 2 Corinthians 8 & 9 [Philadelphia: Fortress, 1985] 4). The capstones to this period are the works by K. L. Bauer on Paul's argumentation (Logica Paullina [Halle, 1774]) and rhetorical technique (Rhetoricae Paullinae [Halle, 1782]).

[154] E.g., C. G. Wilke, Die neutestamentliche Rhetorik: Ein Seitenstück zur Grammatik des neutestamentlichen Sprachidioms (Leipzig: Arnold, 1843); J. Forbes, The Symmetrical Structure of Scripture (Edinburgh: T & T Clark, 1854); idem, Analytical Commentary on the Epistle to the Romans, Tracing the Train of Thought by the Aid of Parallelism (Edinburgh: T & T Clark, 1868); C. F. G. Heinrici, Das zweite Sendschreiben des Apostels Paulus an die Korinthier (Berlin: Hertz, 1887); R. G. Moulton, The Literary Study of the Bible (London: Isbister & Co., 1896) esp. 439-461; J. Weiss, "Beiträge zur paulinischen Rhetorik," in Theologische Studien, C. R. Gregory, et al, eds. (Göttingen: Vandenhoeck & Ruprecht, 1897) 165-247; E. Norden, Die antike Kunstprosa vom VI. Jahrhundert v. Chr. bis in die Zeit der Renaissance, 2 vols. (Leipzig: Teubner, 1898) esp. 2:492-510; E. König, Stylistik, Rhetorik, Poetik in Bezug auf die biblische Literatur (Leipzig: Weicher, 1900); F. Blass, Die Rhythmen der asianischen und römischen Kunstprosa (Leipzig: Deichert, 1905) esp. 42-78, 196-216.

[155] R. Bultmann, Der Stil der paulinischen Predigt und die kynische-stoische Diatribe (Göttingen: Vandenhoeck & Ruprecht, 1910).

[156] Significant works produced between 1911 and 1960 include F. H. Colson, "Μετεσχημάτισα 1 Cor iv 6," JTS 17 (1915-16) 379-384; E. B. Allo, "Le défaut d'éloquence et le style oral de Saint Paul," RSPT 23 (1934) 29-39; E. von Dobschütz, "Zum Wortschatz und Stil des Römerbriefs," ZNW 33 (1934) 51-66; N. W. Lund, Chiasmus in the New Testament (Chapel Hill, NC: University of North Carolina Press, 1942); W. A. Jennrich, "Classical Rhetoric in the New Testament," CJ 44 (1948-49) 30-32; D. Daube, "Rabbinic Methods of Interpretation and Hellenistic Rhetoric," HUCA 22 (1949) 239-264; A. Brunot, La genie littéraire de saint Paul

the rhetorical Paul waned.[157] The 1960s, however, brought renewed interest in rhetorical analysis.

Rhetoric Revived. Several factors contributed to the revival of interest in a rhetorical analysis of Paul's writings. One was the attention given to rhetoric by non-biblical scholars between the mid-1950s and the mid-1970s, with their focus being either on classical rhetoric in its different forms[158] or on the "new" rhetoric with its emphasis on argumentation.[159]

A second factor was the work of the OT scholar James Muilenburg. Starting from an early interest in literary approaches to the Bible, Muilenburg increasingly devoted his attention to matters of structure, style, and "rhetoric."[160] His 1968 presidential address to the annual meeting of the Society of Biblical Literature urged scholars to go beyond the study of biblical form to the study of biblical rhetoric, and has been called "the beginning of modern rhetorical criticism in Biblical studies."[161]

(Paris: Cerf, 1955); J. Jeremias, "Chiasmus in den Paulusbriefen," *ZNW* 49 (1959) 145-156.

[157] Betz suggests that the neglect of rhetorical investigation in the mid-twentieth century was due to criticism by Norden and others, and the rise of the history of religions school (*2 Corinthians 8 & 9* 129, n.2). See also "The Problem of Rhetoric and Theology according to the Apostle Paul," in *L'Apôtre Paul,* A. Vanhoye, ed. [Leuven: Peeters/Leuven University, 1986] 16-48).

[158] Cf. D. L. Clark, *Rhetoric in Greco-Roman Education* (New York: Columbia University Press, 1957); H. Lausberg, *Handbuch der literarischen Rhetorik: Eine Grundlegung der Literaturwissenschaft,* 2 vols. (Munich: Heubner, 1960); idem, *Elemente der Literarischen Rhetorik,* 2nd ed. (Munich: Heubner, 1963); R. F. Howes, *Historical Studies of Rhetoric and Rhetoricians* (Ithaca, NY: Cornell University Press, 1961); G. A. Kennedy, *The Art of Persuasion in Greece* (Princeton: Princeton University Press, 1963); idem, *The Art of Rhetoric in the Roman World: 300 B.C.-A.D. 300* (Princeton: Princeton University Press, 1972); R. A. Lanham, *A Handlist of Rhetorical Terms: A Guide for Students of English Literature* (Berkeley: University of California Press, 1968); R. Stark, ed. *Rhetorika: Schriften zur aristotelischen und hellenistischen Rhetorik* (Hildesheim: Olms, 1968).

[159] The most prominent work was that of C. Perelman and L. Olbrechts-Tyteca, *The New Rhetoric,* trans. J. Wilkinson and P. Weaver (South Bend, IN: Notre Dame University Press, 1971). Other significant writers were K. Burke, *A Rhetoric of Motives* (New York: Braziller, 1955); E. Corbett, *Classical Rhetoric for the Modern Student* (New York: Oxford University Press, 1965); idem, ed. *Rhetorical Analysis of Literary Works* (New York: Oxford University Press, 1969); E. Black, *Rhetorical Criticism: A Study in Method* (New York: Macmillan, 1965); W. J. Brandt, *The Rhetoric of Argumentation* (New York: Bobbs-Merrill, 1970). The work of these scholars was, in fact, a return to the "old" concept of rhetoric as persuasion (cf. B. L. Mack, *Rhetoric and the New Testament* [Minneapolis: Fortress, 1990] 14-16).

[160] For a concise summary of Muilenburg's work, see J. R. Lundbom, *Jeremiah: A Study in Ancient Hebrew Rhetoric,* SBLDS 18 (Missoula, MT: Scholars, 1975) 129, n. 3 and 176-177.

[161] D. F. Watson, "The New Testament and Greco-Roman Rhetoric: A Bibliography," *JETS* 31 (1988) 465. Muilenburg's address was later published as "Form Criticism and Beyond," *JBL* 88 (1969) 1-18.

Although Muilenburg's immediate impact was on OT studies, his challenge to move beyond form criticism had significant implications for biblical studies as a whole.[162]

A third factor was the concern of NT scholars to spell out the relation of Paul to his first-century Greco-Roman context.[163] This concern is prominent, for example, in the work of Edwin Judge.[164] Judge's investigations into the social status of the early Christians led him to suggest that Paul's contemporaries would have identified him with the professional "sophists" of the day.[165] He argued that the circumstances of missionary work forced Paul to adopt the conventions of the traveling philosopher: "For Paul the art was acquired by hard experience rather than by training. It was as his own profession, that of a rabbi, failed him, that he took up the new one."[166] Although he was compelled to use sophistic methods, Paul refused to indulge in rhetorical self-display and was careful to distinguish himself from professionally-trained sophists.[167] The complex first-century situation and twentieth-century ignorance of that situation led Judge to call for a more detailed analysis of NT rhetoric.[168]

Pauline Pioneers. As Vernon Robbins and John Patton have observed, "The interest in rhetorical analysis that began during the 1960s spawned philosophical

---

[162] W. Wuellner notes that the publications of Muilenburg's students "have done much to make the reference to rhetoric acceptable, if not fashionable, again in biblical exegesis" ("Where is Rhetorical Criticism Taking Us?" *CBQ* 49 [1987] 454). For a series of essays by Muilenburg's students designed to reflect the impact of his "rhetorical criticism," see J. J. Jackson and M. Kessler, eds. *Rhetorical Criticism: Essays in Honor of James Muilenburg*, PTMS 1 (Pittsburgh: Pickwick Press, 1974).

[163] V. K. Robbins and J. H. Patton correctly note that "in New Testament study the father of rhetorical analysis is unquestionably Amos N. Wilder" ("Rhetoric and Biblical Criticism," *Quarterly Journal of Speech* 66 [1980] 328). Wilder's treatment, however, emphasized literary forms common to the Gospels: dialogue, story, and parable. See A. N. Wilder, *The Language of the Gospel: Early Christian Rhetoric* (New York: Harper & Row, 1964). Our concern is with the foundational work related to Paul's writings.

[164] E. A. Judge, *The Social Pattern of Christian Groups in the First Century* (London: Tyndale, 1960); idem, "The Early Christians as a Scholastic Community," *JRH* 1 (1960/61) 4-15, 125-137; idem, "Paul's Boasting in Relation to Contemporary Professional Practice," *AusBR* 16 (1968) 37-50; idem, "St. Paul and Classical Society," *JAC* 15 (1972) 19-36.

[165] Judge, "Scholastic Community," 126.

[166] Ibid. 127.

[167] Ibid. 136; "Paul's Boasting" 44-47.

[168] Judge: "If New Testament scholars regard as essential the definitive handbooks of lexicography (e.g., Bauer/Arndt/Gingrich) and of grammar (e.g., Blass/Debrunner), they must equally demand a complete analysis of New Testament rhetoric" ("Paul's Boasting," 45). This analysis is particularly important for certain portions of Paul's writings: "Such is the subtlety of the lost rhetorical art, that until we have it under control we can hardly think we know how to read passages which both by style and content belong to Paul's struggle with rhetorically trained opponents for the support of his rhetorically fastidious converts" (ibid. 48).

elaborations and detailed applications to biblical texts during the 1970s."[169] Included among these elaborations and applications was a growing stream of studies that used rhetorical criticism to analyze Paul's letters.[170] In particular, the writings of Hans Dieter Betz and Wilhelm Wuellner deserve mention.

Betz's work on Paul has been the most significant rhetorical analysis of Paul's writings produced during the late twentieth century.[171] Betz's exegesis of 2 Corinthians led him to conclude that Paul stood in a philosophical tradition that reached back to Socrates.[172] Paul should be viewed as a philosopher and rhetorical "layman" (such as Socrates, the Cynics, and the Stoics); his opponents should be viewed as Sophists and rhetorical "professionals" (such as Cicero).[173] Paul's rejection of "rhetoric," therefore, should be seen as parallel to portrayals of Socrates by his followers, who differentiated between a law-court speech and a philosophical defence speech. 2 Corinthians 10-13, in fact, falls into the latter category and is a fragment of an artfully composed "apology" in letter form.[174]

Betz explored the idea of the "apologetic letter genre" at greater length in his writings on Galatians. His 1975 article sought to analyze Galatians "according to Graeco-Roman rhetoric and epistolography."[175] First, the epistolary prescript (1:1-5)

---

[169] Robbins and Patton, "Rhetoric and Biblical Criticism," 330. Among the "philosophical elaborations" are D. Greenwood, "Rhetorical Criticism and Formgeschichte: Some Methodological Considerations," *JBL* 89 (1970) 418-426; M. Kessler, "A Methodological Setting for Rhetorical Criticism," *Semitics* 4 (1974) 22-36; I. M. Kikawada, "Some Proposals for the Definition of Rhetorical Criticism," *Semitics* 5 (1977) 67-91; M. T. Brown, "The Interpreter's Audience: A Study of Rhetoric and Hermeneutics" (Ph.D. dissertation, Graduate Theological Union, 1978).

[170] See N. Schneider, *Die Rhetorische Eigenart der paulinische Antithese* (Tübingen: Mohr, 1970); R. Scroggs, "Paul as Rhetorician: Two Homilies in Romans 1-11," in *Jews, Greeks, and Christians*, R. Hammerton-Kelly and R. Scroggs, eds. (Leiden: Brill, 1976) 271-298; F. F. Church, "Rhetorical Structure and Design in Paul's Letter to Philemon," *HTR* 71 (1978) 17-33; J. Zmijewski, *Der Stil der paulinischen 'Narrenrede'* (Bonn: Hanstein, 1978); R. A. Humphries, "Paul's Rhetoric of Argumentation in 1 Corinthians 1-4" (Ph.D. dissertation, Graduate Theological Union, 1979).

[171] Major works from the 1970's include H. D. Betz, *Der Apostel Paulus und die sokratische Tradition: Eine exegetische Untersuchung zu seiner 'Apologie' 2 Kor 10-13* (Tübingen: Mohr-Siebeck, 1972); "The Literary Composition and Function of Paul's Letter to the Galatians," *NTS* 21 (1975) 353-379; *Galatians: A Commentary on Paul's Letter to the Churches in Galatia* (Philadelphia: Fortress, 1979). Two later works by Betz are *2 Corinthians 8 and 9* (1985); "The Problem of Rhetoric and Theology According to the Apostle Paul," (1986).

[172] *Sokratische Tradition* 14.

[173] In this conclusion, Betz is close to Judge. Judge, however, finds certain weaknesses in Betz's overall argument ("St. Paul and Classical Society" 35).

[174] *Sokratische Tradition* 14. This conclusion is confirmed both by Demetrius's τοποι ἐπιστολικοι and by the work of Windisch (ibid. 40-41).

[175] "Literary Composition" 353.

and postscript (6:11-18) were identified and separated from the rest of the letter.[176] Then, close comparison with Greco-Roman rhetorical handbooks suggested that the body of Galatians is to be understood in terms of the patterns of classical rhetoric in general and the apologetic letter in particular.[177]

This approach was developed in detail in Betz's 1979 commentary. That commentary focused on the arrangement of Galatians as it relates to the classical handbooks on rhetoric and argued that the apologetic letter form provides the key to its interpretation.[178] As the first major commentary to adopt a consistently "rhetorical" approach to one of Paul's letters, Betz's *Galatians* has provoked extensive response and reaction.[179] Hester suggests that Betz's commentary obliges all NT scholars to become rhetorical critics.[180] At the very least, it compels all commentators on Galatians to interact with his work.[181]

Wilhelm Wuellner approached Pauline rhetoric from a different perspective.[182] Convinced that epistolary analysis cannot solve the problems connected with the body of Paul's letters, Wuellner adopted Perelman and Olbrechts-Tyteca's focus on argumentation.[183] In his 1977 essay on Romans Wuellner sketched a basic rhetorical

---

[176] Ibid. 355.

[177] Ibid. 354.

[178] Betz suggests that Galatians follows a modified form of the juridical address, being divided into exordium (1:6-11), narratio (1:12-2:14), propositio (2:15-21), probatio (3:1-4:31), and exhortatio (5:1-6:10).

[179] See W. Meeks, "Review of H. D. Betz, *A Commentary on Paul's Letter to the Churches in Galatia,*" *JBL* 100 (1981) 304-307; W. D. Davies, "Review of H. D. Betz, *Galatians,*" *RelSRev* 7 (1981) 310-318; P. W. Meyer, Review of H. D. Betz, *Galatians,*" *RelSRev* 7 (1981) 318-323; D. E. Aune, "Review of H. D. Betz, *Galatians,*" *RelSRev* 7 (1981) 323-328; M. Silva, "Betz and Bruce on Galatians," *WTJ* 45 (1983) 371-385; H. Hübner, "Der Galaterbrief und das Verhältnis von antiker Rhetorik und Epistolographie," *TLZ* 109 (1984) 241-250; G. A. Kennedy, *New Testament Interpretation Through Rhetorical Criticism* (Chapel Hill, NC: University of North Carolina Press, 1984) 141-148.

[180] J. D. Hester, "The Use and Influence of Rhetoric in Galatians 2:1-14," *TZ* 42 (1986) 388.

[181] See, e.g., R. N. Longenecker, *Galatians* (Dallas: Word, 1990) ciii-cv, cix-cxiii.

[182] W. Wuellner, "Paul's Rhetoric of Argumentation in Romans: An Alternative to the Donfried-Karris Debate Over Romans," *CBQ* 38 (1976) 330-351; idem, "Greek Rhetoric and Pauline Argumentation," in *Early Christian Literature and the Classical Tradition,* W. R. Schödel and R. L. Wilken, eds. (Paris: Beauchesne, 1979) 177-188. More recent works by Wuellner include "Paul as Pastor: The Function of Rhetorical Questions in First Corinthians," in *L'Apôtre Paul,* A. Vanhoye, ed. (Leuven: Peeters/Leuven University Press, 1986) 49-77; "Where Is Rhetorical Criticism Taking Us?" *CBQ* 49 (1987) 448-463. On the use of rhetorical questions in 1 Corinthians, see also D. F. Watson, "1 Corinthians 10:23-11:1 in the Light of Greco-Roman Rhetoric: The Role of Rhetorical Questions," *JBL* 108 (1989) 301-318.

[183] Wuellner: "Hellenistic-Roman and Near Eastern epistolographic studies, no matter how exacting they will be executed, cannot solve the problems of Romans or that of any other letter

outline of the letter, then investigated the "rhetorical situation" to which the letter was addressed.[184] This approach "help[s] us out of the two impasses created by the fixation with form- and genre-criticism on the one hand, and with specific social or political situations on the other hand."[185]

For Wuellner, argumentation rather than arrangement or style is the key to understanding the rhetorical Paul. In fact, argumentation—specifically the rhetorical situation—*determines* style. One concrete example of this concept is Paul's use of digressions. An analysis of three major digressions in 1 Corinthians leads to the conclusion that Paul frequently adopts methods that are "self-consciously Greek."[186] Wuellner concluded, "Digressions, like other rhetorical devices, must be viewed as more than evidences of Paul's 'style.' Instead we have demonstrated that these stylistic devices are functionally determined by the rhetorical situation."[187]

Rhetoric Rampant. To say that rhetorical analyses are proliferating rapidly, may be something of an understatement. Duane Watson's bibliography lists 73 works produced between 1980 and 1990 on the Pauline letters alone.[188] These studies use a variety of methods to address a wide range of issues. It is impossible here to survey these studies exhaustively, so the discussion must be limited to a representative sampling. For the sake of convenience, scholars will be grouped against a backdrop of the principal divisions of ancient rhetoric.

Ancient rhetoric was generally viewed as having five tasks: invention, arrangement, style, memory, and delivery.[189] Invention (Latin, *inventio*; Greek, *heuresis*) included the planning of the discourse and the arguments to be used in it. Arrangement (Latin, *dispositio*; Greek, *taxis*) was the composition of various parts into an effective whole. Style (Latin, *elocutio*; Greek, *lexis*) was concerned with the choice of words (diction) and the composition of words into sentences (synthesis),

---

of Paul. Such studies will clarify the letter *frame*, and the conventions of letter frames, but they cannot solve the problem of the letter structure, or the problems connected with the 'body' of the Pauline letters" ("Romans" 156).

[184] The basic outline is that of exordium (1:1-15), probatio (1:16-15:13), and peroratio (15:14-16:23). The argumentative situation is defined as "the influence of the earlier stages of the discussion of [sic] the argumentative possibilities open to the speaker" (ibid. 155). The specific question addressed is "to what sort of judgment the piece of argumentation is directed" (ibid. 157).

[185] Ibid. 152.

[186] "Pauline Argumentation" 188. Here Wuellner uses a phrase first suggested by R. M. Grant, "Hellenistic Elements in 1 Corinthians," in *Early Christian Origins*, A. Wikgren, ed. (Chicago: Quadrangle, 1961) 63. The digressions are 1 Cor 1:19-3:21; 9:1-10:13; 13:1-13.

[187] Ibid.

[188] Watson, "Bibliography" (1988) 470-472; idem, "The New Testament and Greco-Roman Rhetoric: A Bibliographical Update," *JETS* 33 (1990) 520-523.

[189] Cicero, *De Inventione* 1.7.9; Quintilian, *Institutio Oratoria* 3.3.1; *Rhetorica ad Herennium* 1.2.3. See also R. A. Lanham, *A Handlist of Rhetorical Terms* (Berkeley, CA: University of California Press, 1969) 106.

including the use of figures. Memory (Latin, *memoria*; Greek, *mneme*) addressed the techniques of fixing speech in the mind before delivery. Delivery (Latin, *pronuntiatio*; Greek, *hypocrisis*) set rules for control of the voice and use of gestures. Only the first three are significant for the rhetorical analysis of Paul's letters.

Wuellner's work, as noted above, has as its primary concern the area of invention. Many scholars have followed in his footsteps, four of whom will be mentioned here.[190] Stanley Stowers's study of the diatribe in Romans concluded that the dialogical character of that letter was central to Paul's self-presentation as a teacher and to the message he sought to convey.[191] Folker Siegert analyzed Paul's argumentation in Romans 9-11, then categorized it according to the work of Perelmann and Olbrechts-Tyteca.[192] Steven Kraftchick's dissertation examined how Paul used ethos and pathos in Galatians 5 and 6 to further his argument.[193] Neil Elliot's dissertation explored Paul's application of topics in the argument of Romans, giving particular attention to the way in which the progression of the argument modified the rhetorical situation.[194] In each case, the writer's primary interest lay in the way Paul's argumentative strategy shaped his presentation of material.

Betz's emphasis on arrangement has been embraced by a large number of scholars, many of whom have applied it to Romans and Galatians.[195] Paul's

---

[190] See also R. M. Berchman, "Galatians (1:1-5): Paul and Greco-Roman Rhetoric," in *Judaic and Christian Interpretation of Texts: Contents and Contexts*, J. Neusner and E. Frerichs, eds. (New York: University of America, 1987) 1-15; J. P. Sampley, "Paul, His Opponents in 2 Corinthians 10-13 and the Rhetorical Handbooks," in *The Social World of Formative Christianity and Judaism*, J. Neusner, *et al*, eds. (Philadelphia: Fortress, 1988) 162-177.

[191] Stowers: "Objections and false conclusions in Romans 3-7 arise when the argumentation has developed to the point where there is a clear and sharp statement of some claim or thesis which is very important to Paul's thought, but which needs qualification and further explanation so that false inferences will not be drawn" (*Diatribe*, 150).

[192] F. Siegert, *Argumentation bei Paulus gezeigt an Römer 9-11* (Tübingen: Mohr, 1985).

[193] S. J. Kraftchick, "Ethos and Pathos in Galatians Five and Six: A Rhetorical Analysis," (Ph.D. dissertation, Emory University, 1985).

[194] N. Elliot: "A meaningful rhetorical-critical analysis of Romans . . . will involve examining Paul's selection and application of topics in the letter with an eye to examining how Paul construes a basis of agreement with his audience and sets about transferring that agreement to new propositions or values" (*The Rhetoric of Romans: Argumentative Strategy and Constraint and Paul's 'Dialogue with Judaism'*, JSNTSup 45, [Sheffield: JSOT Press, 1990] 60).

[195] For example, see R. Jewett, "Romans as an Ambassadorial Letter," *Int* 36 (1982) 5-20; B. H. Brinsmead, *Galatians: Dialogical Response to Opponents*, SBLDS 65 (Chico, CA: Scholars, 1982); J. D. Hester, "Rhetorical Structure of Galatians 1:11-2:14," *JBL* 103 (1984) 223-233; R. G. Hall, "The Rhetorical Outline of Galatians: A Reconsideration," *JBL* 106 (1987) 277-287; F. Vouga, "Römer 1,18-3,20 als narratio," *TGl* 77 (1987) 225-236; B. Fiore, "Romans 9-11 and Classical Forensic Rhetoric," *PEGLMBS* 8 (1988) 117-126; J. Smit, "The Letter of Paul to the Galatians: A Deliberative Speech," *NTS* 35 (1989) 1-26; J. N. Aletti, "La présence d'un modele rhétorique en Romains: Son role et son importance," *Bib* 71 (1990) 1-24.

Thessalonian letters, as objects of rhetorical analysis, have also attracted the attention of Robert Jewett and Frank Hughes.[196] Jewett uses rhetorical analysis as part of an "experimental and interdisciplinary" approach "to provide methodical control of . . . exegetical inferences as well as . . . a more precise grasp of the relationship between the writer and the recipients."[197] Specifically, he examines the issues of rhetorical genre and arrangement.[198] Hughes's method is nearly identical to Betz's in that he seeks to identify the rhetorical genre of 2 Thessalonians by comparing it with a hellenistic model, namely the "deliberative rhetorical letter" exemplified by Demosthenes's first epistle.[199] Once the genre of the letter is recognized, the author's intention in writing and, ultimately, the audience's situation can be determined.[200]

In 1985 Norman Petersen sought to combine literary and sociological analysis, using Philemon as a case study.[201] Petersen's application of rhetorical analysis, however, is incidental and not well-defined. He uses "rhetoric" in two principal ways: Paul's sequence of emplotment (in the literary analysis section), and his use of language (in the sociological analysis section). Petersen's literary analysis section is the shorter of the two, primarily because he is concerned with language as the expression of shared ways of understanding and behavior.[202] This concern leads him to undertake a "sociological exploration of Paul's rhetoric" by examining Paul's metaphorical use of role language to determine the structures underlying his relations with others.[203] His concern with language and metaphor places Petersen within the sphere of "style" in general and of "diction" in particular.[204]

---

[196] R. Jewett, *The Thessalonian Correspondence: Pauline Rhetoric and Millenarian Piety* (Philadelphia: Fortress, 1986); F. W. Hughes, *Early Christian Rhetoric and 2 Thessalonians*, JSNTSup 29, (Sheffield: JSOT Press, 1989). See also C. A. Wanamaker, *Commentary on 1 & 2 Thessalonians* (Grand Rapids: Eerdmans, 1990).

[197] Jewett, *Thessalonian Correspondence* xiv.

[198] Jewett: "We must infer from the genre, rhetorical structure, and content of Paul's epistolary discourse what was going on in the Thessalonian congregation" (ibid. 66). See pages 91-109 for his conclusions.

[199] Hughes: "All of the *partes orationis* which are found in Demosthenes's *Epistle 1* . . . are indeed found in the Second Letter to the Thessalonians" (*2 Thessalonians* 50).

[200] Hughes: "I propose that rhetorical criticism can help scholars to identify the lived situation of letters in the Pauline corpus, primarily because the use of certain rhetorical *genera* and topics seems to presuppose certain situations" (ibid. 30).

[201] N. R. Petersen, *Rediscovering Paul* (Philadelphia: Fortress, 1985).

[202] Petersen adopts Beidelman's understanding of "language" as "total symbolic behavior," including grammar, syntax, vocabulary, gestures, facial expressions, clothing, and furnishings (ibid. 18-20).

[203] Ibid. 102.

[204] This approach has also been adopted by Pheme Perkins, who uses Paul's "rhetorical presentation" to "map" the social world by noting terminology in Philippians ("Christology, Friendship and Status: The Rhetoric of Philippians," in *SBLSP* [1987] 509-520).

Since Josef Zmijewski's 1978 study of 2 Corinthians 11-12, major works on the compositional aspects of Paul's style ("synthesis") have been relatively rare.[205] Charles Robbins analyzed Phil 2:6-11 according to classical principles for composing periodic sentences and concluded that the passage is comprised of two sentences, each consisting of a four-cola unit and a two-cola unit.[206] Aída Spencer used "stylistics" to compare the subconscious choices Paul made in composing three passages and determined that he adopted persuasive tactics that varied according to the historical situation faced.[207] Douglas Campbell's dissertation used Greco-Roman rhetoric to resolve the syntactical difficulties within the central part of Rom 3:21-26.[208]

In contrast to the general tendency to emphasize only one aspect of rhetoric, George Kennedy advocates the use of a comprehensive method for rhetorical analysis. He recommends several stages in the practice of rhetorical criticism; they include: (1) identify the rhetorical unit; (2) define the rhetorical situation and the overriding rhetorical problem; (3) determine the species of rhetoric used; (4) analyze the arrangement, invention, and style of the material in the unit; (5) evaluate the rhetorical effectiveness of the unit.[209] This approach has been generally applauded by reviewers, but it has been fully implemented by only a few other scholars.[210] It is doubly unfortunate that the application of this method—both by Kennedy himself and by others—is too brief to be of much help.[211]

---

[205] J. Zmijewski, *Der Stil der paulinischen 'Narrenrede'*, cited above.

[206] C. J. Robbins, "Rhetorical Structure of Philippians 2:6-11," *CBQ* 42 (1980) 73-82.

[207] A. B. Spencer, *Paul's Literary Style: A Stylistic and Historical Comparison of II Corinthians 11:16-12:13, Romans 8:9-39, and Philippians 3:2-4:13* (Jackson: ETS, 1984). Spencer draws a distinction between style, which is "largely subconscious, unique, felt, but readily observable," and rhetoric, which is "a conscious mode of persuasion" (26).

[208] D. A. Campbell, *The Rhetoric of Righteousness in Romans 3:21-26*, JSNTSup 65 (Sheffield: Academic Press, 1992). Campbell uses rhetorical analysis at the stylistic level to clarify the syntax and determine the mutual relationships and basic functions of the clauses in the passage.

[209] G. A. Kennedy, *New Testament Interpretation* 33-38. It should be noted that Kennedy tends to run the discussion of his "stages" together, so this enumeration is not definitive. A similar understanding may be found in D. F. Watson, *Invention, Arrangement, and Style: Rhetorical Criticism of Jude and 2 Peter*, SBLDS 104 (Atlanta: Scholars, 1988) 8-28. C. C. Black identifies six stages ("Rhetorical Criticism and the New Testament," *PEGLMBS* 8 [1988] 77-80).

[210] For reviews, see V. K. Robbins, "Review of George A. Kennedy, *New Testament Interpretation through Rhetorical Criticism*," *Rhetorica* 3 (1985) 145-149; W. Wuellner, "Rhetorical Criticism," 454; C. C. Black, "Rhetorical Criticism and Biblical Interpretation," *ExpTim* 100 (1989) 254-255; idem, "Rhetorical Questions: The New Testament, Classical Rhetoric, and Current Interpretation," *Dialog* 29 (1990) 62-70. D. F. Watson, one of Kennedy's students, has used this method in his analysis of Philippians ("A Rhetorical Analysis of Philippians and Its Implications for the Unity Question," *NovT* 30 [1988] 57-88).

[211] Chapter 4 of *New Testament Interpretation* uses 2 Corinthians as an example of judicial rhetoric; chapter 7 evaluates 1 Thessalonians and Galatians as deliberative rhetoric and Romans

It should be noted that some scholars have chosen to integrate rhetorical investigation with other critical methods. Michael Bünker argues that rhetorical analysis is not possible without also taking into consideration epistolography.[212] Linda Belleville and Walter Hansen take a similar approach.[213] Elizabeth Schüssler-Fiorenza combines rhetorical criticism with reader-response criticism and evaluative theological criticism.[214] Bruce Johanson uses text-linguistic analysis to delimit and focus text sections as the basis for an analysis of Paul's means of persuasion.[215] It seems likely that the number of such hybrid approaches will continue to increase.

In conclusion, three recent full-scale monographs should be mentioned. Antoinette Wire follows Perelman and Olbrechts-Tyteca in adopting "the New Rhetoric" for her analysis of 1 Corinthians.[216] She first identifies and traces arguments that reappear throughout the text.[217] She then works through one unit of the text at a time, taking into account all the arguments Paul used and the implications of those arguments for the Corinthians.[218] By focusing on one particular portion of Paul's audience, Wire seeks to arrive at an accurate picture of the women prophets who were part of the Corinthian church.

Margaret Mitchell, on the other hand, favors "historical rhetorical criticism" as the appropriate method for studying 1 Corinthians.[219] Through an extensive

---

as epideictic rhetoric. T. H. Olbricht has offered a more extended analysis of 1 Thessalonians from the standpoint of Aristotelian rhetoric ("An Aristotelian Rhetorical Analysis of 1 Thessalonians" in *Greeks, Romans, and Christians*, W. Meeks, D. Balch, E. Ferguson, eds. [Minneapolis: Fortress, 1990] 216-236).

[212] M. Bünker, *Briefformular und rhetorische Disposition im 1. Korintherbrief* (Göttingen: Vandenhoeck & Ruprecht, 1983) 15.

[213] L. L. Belleville, "A Letter of Apologetic Self-Commendation: 2 Cor 1:8-7:16," *NovT* 31 (1989) 142-163; G. W. Hansen, *Abraham in Galatians: Epistolary and Rhetorical Contexts*, JSNTSup 29, (Sheffield: JSOT Press, 1989).

[214] E. Schüssler-Fiorenza, "Rhetorical Situation and Historical Reconstruction in 1 Corinthians," *NTS* 33 (1987) 386-403.

[215] B. C. Johanson, *To All the Brethren: A Text-Linguistic and Rhetorical Approach to 1 Thessalonians* (Stockholm: Almqvist and Wiksell, 1987). Johanson's rhetorical concern is invention, but he rejects commonly used rhetorical procedures—such as determination of genre and analysis of rhetorical disposition—as inadequate for his purposes (36-43).

[216] A. C. Wire, *The Corinthian Women Prophets. A Reconstruction through Paul's Rhetoric* (Minneapolis: Fortress, 1990).

[217] Wire calls this step "textual rhetoric" (ibid. 6). Such arguments include: arguments by dissociation of concepts, quasi-logical arguments, arguments based on the structure of reality, and arguments establishing the structure of reality.

[218] Wire calls this step "structural rhetoric" (ibid. 7). She divides 1 Corinthians into five units: chapters 1-4, 5-7, 8-11, 12-14, and 15-16.

[219] By "historical rhetorical analysis," Mitchell means an "analysis of 1 Corinthians in the light of the literary/rhetorical conventions operative in the first century" (*Paul and the Rhetoric of Reconciliation: An Exegetical Investigation of the Language and Composition of 1 Corinthians*

comparison with ancient speeches, letters, and rhetorical handbooks, she determines that 1 Corinthians conforms to the expectations for deliberative discourse.[220] The thesis statement of the letter (1:10) addresses the issue of factionalism and introduces a theme that may be traced, using political terms and topoi, throughout the entire letter. A compositional analysis confirms that 1 Corinthians is a unified deliberative letter that urges concord within the Corinthian community. Mitchell concludes that her work "consciously present[s] a *constructive* argument for the unity of 1 Corinthians" in the face of various partition theories.[221]

Similarly, Timothy Geoffrion investigates "the coherence of the Apostle Paul's letter to the Philippians by focusing specifically on its rhetorical purpose and composition, using its canonical form as the point of departure."[222] Building on Watson's analysis of the rhetorical structure of Philippians,[223] Geoffrion assumes that the letter fits the genre of deliberative rhetoric, with its purpose stated in the *narratio* (1:27-30). From that foundation he moves first to an analysis of the key concepts found in 1:27-30,[224] then to the analysis of secondary themes and Paul's use of examples,[225] and finally to a compositional analysis of the major rhetorical units of the letter.[226] He concludes that Philippians is a unified letter intended to encourage steadfastness by means of political and military terminology as well as the rhetorical device of exemplification.

D. Summary

All three of the disciplines surveyed in this chapter have gained widespread popularity in scholarly circles. Rhetorical and epistolary analysis have been used

---

[Louisville, KY: Westminster/John Knox, 1993] 8). She is adamant that "appeals to the modern philosophical examinations of the rhetorical forces of all texts should not be put at the service of historical arguments" (ibid. 6).

[220] Mitchell identifies the following characteristics of deliberative rhetoric in 1 Corinthians: a future time frame, an appeal to advantage, the use of examples, the treatment of factionalism and concord.

[221] Ibid. 298.

[222] T. C. Geoffrion, *The Rhetorical Purpose and the Political and Military Character of Philippians: A Call to Stand Firm* (Lewiston, NY: Edwin Mellen Press, 1993) 1.

[223] Watson, "Philippians."

[224] Gioffrion identifies those key concepts as "political identity, Gospel, ambiguity over future events, steadfastness, unity, faith, witness, fear(lessness), adversaries, salvation/destruction, concern for suffering, God's role in the believers' lives, and the values and experiences shared by Paul and the Philippians" (*Philippians* 32).

[225] The specific complementary themes Geoffrion studies are: unity, joy, and κοινωνία.

[226] Geoffrion divides the letter into the following units: epistolary prescript (1:1-2), exordium (1:3-26), narratio (1:27-30), probatio (2:1-3:21), peroratio with epistolary closing (4:1-23).

extensively in the study of Paul's letters. The application of oral theory to the NT, however, has been limited, with most of the work being done in the Gospels. The first step in a comprehensive analysis of oral patterning in Paul's letters would be to examine the degree of orality present in first-century culture. This task will be undertaken in the next chapter.

Chapter 2

ORALITY AND LITERACY IN THE FIRST CENTURY

As noted in the preceding chapter, scholars in increasing numbers are seeking to apply to biblical texts insights gained from the study of oral theory. One important aspect of this work is a fresh interest in the proper understanding of the culture of the first century, in particular the proper approach to the documents produced by that culture. There is both a growing recognition that first century culture was largely oral and a corresponding concern that scholars might be guilty of imposing on ancient texts presuppositions more appropriate to the widespread literacy of modern culture.[1] In fact, Joanna Dewey has suggested that it is necessary to develop a "first-century media model" for early Christianity.[2] Since the discussion has been framed in a variety of ways, it will be necessary first to review more closely the work of several scholars.

A. Differing Perspectives

Literacy. Eric Havelock, as noted above, was concerned primarily with early Greek culture rather than with biblical studies. It is his work, however, that is the starting point for any discussion of the shift from orality to literacy. Havelock argues that the population of Athens did not become "literate" in the commonly accepted sense until the last third of the fifth century B.C. Subsequent to the invention of the Greek alphabet in the eighth century B.C., Greek culture moved through several stages on its way to literacy.

Craft literacy characterized Greek culture through the middle of the sixth century. In a craft-literate culture, reading and writing the alphabet were skills mastered by a restricted portion of the population. *Recitation literacy* developed in the last part of the sixth century and first half of the fifth century but was characterized by decipherment rather than fluent reading: "The use of the written word is very

---

[1] For a concise introduction to these issues, see Botha, "Mute manuscripts."

[2] Dewey, "Oral Methods" 44.

restricted, and any reading of it is regarded as ancillary to the central function of culture, which still is, as it had always been, to memorize and recite the poets."[3]

Scriptorial literacy was not achieved until the last third of the fifth century B.C. It was at that time that the average Athenian was able to pick up a script and read it. According to Havelock, the transition to scriptorial literacy was the major cultural transition of the Hellenistic age. It was a transition "from the word still orally shaped and heard and shared communally to the word read in silence and solitude."[4] Of particular interest for the present study is the fact that Havelock characterizes Palestinian culture at the time of Christ as "only craft-literate."[5]

Havelock, then, would place the shift from orality to literacy in Greek culture around 450 B.C. Tony Lentz, however, suggests that the influence of oral tradition persisted later still. The common appearance of writing around 450 B.C. "marks only the beginning of its interaction with oral culture."[6] He suggests that orality remained strong in Greek culture far beyond the time of Plato. The tension between orality and literacy continued at least to the time of Isocrates (c. 390 B.C.) and was still evident as late as Aristotle (c. 322 B.C.). In fact, Lentz suggests, the "tense" relationship between the two traditions was vital for the development of Greek philosophy and science.[7]

Media. Thomas Boomershine has approached the issue from the perspective of the primary communication medium operative in a given culture.[8] Boomershine's main concern is to urge scholars to consider how biblical interpretation needs to adapt to the media shift from literacy to electronics. As a prelude to that discussion, however, he traces the way in which previous shifts have affected Judeo-Christian communities and their approach to hermeneutics. He identifies four types of cultures and characterizes each by its primary communication medium. They are: oral culture, manuscript culture, print culture, and silent print culture. The late twentieth century is moving toward a fifth culture: electronic culture.

In oral culture, the medium is sound, transmitted by memory. In manuscript culture, writing becomes the dominant communication system; traditions are collected and preserved in manuscripts; public reading of the written manuscript is the primary means of distribution. In print culture, moveable type makes possible widespread duplication and distribution of documents; private study and interpreta-

---

[3] Havelock, "Preliteracy" 372.

[4] Havelock, *Literate Revolution* 10.

[5] Ibid.

[6] T. M. Lentz, *Orality and Literacy in Hellenic Greece* (Carbondale, IL: Southern Illinois University Press, 1989) 176.

[7] Ibid. 175.

[8] T. E. Boomershine, "Biblical Megatrends: Towards a Paradigm for the Interpretation of the Bible in Electronic Media," *SBLSP* (1987) 144-157.

tion becomes common. In silent print culture, texts are entirely dissociated from sound and, in the case of biblical studies, serve as "documentary sources for the establishment of either historical facticity . . . or theological truths or ideas."[9] For the purposes of the present study, the important point to note is that Boomershine places the shift from oral culture to manuscript culture in the late first century A.D. and connects it with the developing hermeneutics of Christianity.

Orality. As noted above, Ong's analysis of the development of culture includes three stages: oral, alphabetic/print, and electronic. These stages correspond roughly to Boomershine's media categories. Perhaps more helpful for the purposes of this study, however, is Ong's comment on the possibility of degrees of orality within different cultures:

> Of course, long after the invention of script and even of print, distinctively oral forms of thought and expression linger, competing with the forms introduced with script and print. Cultures in which this is the case can be referred to as radically oral, largely oral, residually oral, and so on through various degrees . . . of orality.[10]

This approach not only makes Ong's alphabetic/print stage more manageable, it also highlights the fact that the interaction between oral and written cultures continued long after the time of Plato (Havelock), Isocrates, or Aristotle (Lentz). The transition from orality to literacy was, in reality, gradual rather than abrupt, a conclusion that is supported by the findings of other scholars.

Thomas Farrell's study of the Nicene Creed of 325, for example, concludes that the creed was designed to be "remembered by the catechumens who, for the most part, were from a residual form of primary oral culture."[11] M. T. Clanchy's study of the development of literacy in medieval England highlights the tenacity of orality in the middle ages and includes a number of interesting parallels to Lentz's study on Hellenic Greece.[12] Ong himself has examined "oral residue" in Tudor prose[13] and has argued that the eighteenth century is the watershed "dividing residually oral culture from typographical culture."[14]

---

[9] Ibid. 147.

[10] Ong, *Presence* 22.

[11] T. J. Farrell, "Early Christian Creeds and Controversies in the Light of the Orality-Literacy Hypothesis," *OrT* 2 (1987) 138.

[12] M. T. Clanchy, *From Memory to Written Record: England, 1066-1307* (Cambridge, MA: Harvard University Press, 1979).

[13] Ong defines "oral residue" as "habits of thought and expression tracing back to pre-literate situations or practice, or deriving from the dominance of the oral as a medium in a given culture, or indicating a reluctance or inability to dissociate the written medium from the spoken" ("Oral Residue" 146).

[14] Ong, *Presence* 69.

	Havelock (Literacy)	Boomershine (Media)	Ong (Orality)
	Pre-literate	Oral	Oral
600 B.C.	Craft-literate		Radically Oral
500 B.C.	Recitation-literate		
400 B.C.	Script-literate		
			Largely Oral
A.D. 100		Manuscript	
			Residually Oral
A.D. 1400	Type-literate	Print	
A.D. 1700		Silent Print	Minimally Oral
A.D. 2000		Electronic	Secondarily Oral

When these differing approaches to culture are compared, three observations may be made in summary: (1) the transition from primary orality to primary literacy is gradual, proceeding through a number of stages;[15] (2) orality continues its influence long after the introduction of the alphabet and writing;[16] (3) the NT documents were composed during a period of dynamic interaction between orality and literacy.[17]

Synthesis. What, then, was the nature of first century culture? In recent scholarship three terms have been used in an effort to characterize that culture more

---

[15] Cf. Farrell: "The point is that literacy and the development of literate thought proceed by degrees, so to speak. That is, becoming literate involves more that [sic] just acquiring the basic rudiments of reading and writing a vowelized form of phonetic alphabetic literacy" ("Creeds" 135).

[16] Cf. Kelber: "Because the vast majority of people were habituated to the spoken word, much of what was written was meant to be recited and listened to. The practice of writing did thus not immediately make literacy the new model of linguistic behavior, nor were oral speech forms and habits summarily extinguished by literature. The oral medium was tenacious, and literacy by itself slow in undermining the world of oral values. Orality, therefore, which had been humankind's sole or predominant medium for millennia, dominated long after the introduction of writing" (*Oral and Written Gospel* 17). For an extended discussion, see Ong, *Presence* 54-63.

[17] Cf. Kelber: "Overall, the communications world of the first century must have been one of considerable intricacy . . . By itself, literacy will not undermine the world of orality, unless written texts are consciously embraced as models of conceptual conduct. The two media not only co-existed in the first century, they will also have interacted with one another. Oral traditions can fixate into texts, while texts in turn may stimulate oral impulses" ("Mark" 21).

precisely: manuscript culture, scribal culture, and rhetorical culture. In addition to Boomershine, Dewey has referred to first century culture as a manuscript culture;[18] and although not specifically discussing first century culture, Ong mentions manuscript culture as one of the stages in the transition from oral communication to alphabet and print.[19] The problem with using "manuscript" to describe first century culture is that it focuses on a single, literary aspect and fails to take into account the important role oral communication played in the overall make-up of the culture.

A more common approach is to label the culture in which the NT was produced as scribal. Botha defines scribal culture as "culture familiar with writing but in essence still significantly, even predominantly, oral."[20] Kelber in particular distinguishes between oral culture, scribal culture, and print culture.[21]

Recently, however, Vernon Robbins has expressed discontent with "scribal" as the most appropriate term to describe first century culture. He suggests that a more precise series of designations would be: (1) oral culture, (2) rhetorical culture, (3) scribal culture, and (4) print culture. He concludes:

> The phrase 'oral culture' should be used for those environments where written literature is not in view. The phrase 'rhetorical culture', in contrast, should refer to environments where oral and written speech interact closely with one another. It would be best to limit 'scribal culture' to those environments where a primary goal is to 'copy' either oral statements or written texts.[22]

In Robbins's view the first century was a rhetorical culture characterized by the "lively interaction between oral and written composition."[23] This distinction is important for the scholarly discussion of the composition of NT documents, especially the Gospels, because:

---

[18] Dewey, "Oral Methods" 33.

[19] Ong, *Presence* 54.

[20] Botha, "Mute manuscripts" 42. He continues: "In scribal culture reading is largely vocal and illiteracy the rule rather than the exception."

[21] W. H. Kelber, "From Aphorism to Sayings Gospel and from Parable to Narrative Gospel," in *Foundations & Facets Forum* 1 (1985) 23-30.

[22] V. K. Robbins, "Writing as a Rhetorical Act in Plutarch and the Gospels," in *Persuasive Artistry. Studies in New Testament Rhetoric in Honor of George A. Kennedy*, JSNTSup 50, D. F. Watson, ed. (Sheffield: JSOT Press, 1991) 145.

[23] V. K. Robbins, "Progymnastic Rhetorical Composition and Pre-Gospel Traditions: A New Approach," in *The Synoptic Gospels. Source Criticism and the New Literary Criticism*, BETL 110, C. Focant, ed. (Leuven: Leuven University Press, 1993) 116. He thus provides a formal term for first-century Mediterranean culture that Botha had earlier described as a "fusion" or "overlap" between oral and scribal cultures ("Mute manuscripts" 42-43). The term is not new, however, for Ong had used it in his writings: "Basically, rhetorical culture means culture in which, even after the development of writing, the pristine oral-aural modes of knowledge storage and retrieval still dominate" (*Interfaces* 214).

Only during the last half of the second century did a scribal culture that resisted rhetorical composition as it reperformed the gospel traditions begin to dominate the transmission of early Christian literature. For this stage of transmission the prevailing literary-historical methods of analysis are highly informative. To impose such a scribal environment on the context in which the New Testament gospels initially were written and re-written is a fundamental error.[24]

Robbins suggests that a spectrum of writing activities also existed in Mediterranean antiquity. He identifies five kinds of writing: (1) scribal reproduction, (2) progymnastic composition, (3) narrative composition, (4) discursive composition, and (5) poetic composition.[25] Since it is the first of these categories that is in view when discussing Paul and his letters, Robbins's definition is helpful. Scribal reproduction "consisted of making copies of extant texts, transcribing messages and letters from dictation, and reproducing stock documents like receipts."[26]

Robbins's analysis highlights the complex nature of first century Mediterranean culture. It was a culture characterized by the interaction of oral, rhetorical, and scribal environments. It will be necessary, therefore, to explore each of these environments further in order to obtain a clearer picture of the role of oral patterning in that culture.

B. The Oral Environment

Oral Thought and Expression. Ong has done the fullest examination of the characteristics of oral culture. He observes that "the differences between oral-aural culture and our own technological culture are of course so profound as to defy total itemization."[27] He has, however, attempted to identify the most significant aspects of oral culture, particularly as they relate to oral thought and expression.

First, oral culture is oriented to the present.[28] It has no history in the modern sense, for there are no written records. It is possible to ask questions about the past, but "in verbal accounts of the past . . . the items that we should isolate as facts become inextricably entangled with myth."[29]

---

[24] Ibid.

[25] Robbins, "Writing" 145, n.3. The primary focus of Robbins's writings is on progymnastic composition that "consisted of writing traditional materials clearly and persuasively rather than in the oral or written form it came to the writer" (ibid.).

[26] Ibid.

[27] Ong, *Presence* 23.

[28] Elsewhere Ong uses the term "homeostatic" (*Orality and Literacy* 56).

[29] Ong, *Presence* 23.

Second, knowledge is organized in terms of the human lifeworld and is concrete rather than abstract.[30] Havelock, in particular, has traced the development of Greek thought and has discussed at some length the shift from concrete to abstract thinking that accompanied the spread of literacy.[31]

Third, oral culture tends to be ceremonial. "Verbalized learning takes place quite normally in an atmosphere of celebration or play. As events, words are more celebrations and less tools than in literate cultures."[32]

Fourth, oral culture promotes the development of memory skills. These memory skills, however, do not emphasize verbatim recall. Oral memory is "thematic and formulaic, and [the] formulas are prefabricated metrical units."[33] The field-based research done by Parry, Lord, and others highlights the fact that, although oral singers may affirm that they sing the same words, no epic poem is ever performed in precisely the same way twice.[34]

Fifth, the works performed in an oral culture serve to educate as well as entertain.[35] Again, Havelock explores this concept at some length and concludes that the early Greek poets served as a source of instruction and indoctrination in, among other things, ethics and administrative skills.[36] Poetry was "first and last a didactic instrument for transmitting the tradition."[37]

Lord correctly observes that many of Ong's characteristics of orality "go more widely than 'words heard and words seen,' to encompass a psychology of the 'oral mind' and many facets of the world of the unlettered which have little, if anything, to do with oral or written literature."[38] On the other hand, Lord has concentrated his study on the works produced by oral cultures. He has itemized four tendencies characteristic of oral expression: (1) it is additive rather than subordinate; (2) it is

---

[30] Ong, *Presence* 33-34.

[31] Cf. Havelock, *Preface*, Part II.

[32] Ong, *Presence* 30.

[33] Ibid. 24. He continues: "Hearing a new story [the singer] does not try to memorize it by rote. He digests it in terms of its themes . . . which are essentially the themes of all the singers in his tradition. He then verbalizes it in the formulas or formulaic elements he has in stock, which are also essentially those of the other poets in his tradition except that each individual poet will have his own particular twists and turns of style" (ibid. 25).

[34] E.g., Lord, *Singer* 13-29.

[35] Ong: "If the poets were not at large, saying things over and over again, much of the knowledge in an oral-aural culture would evaporate" (ibid. 28).

[36] Havelock, *Preface* 29.

[37] Ibid. 43.

[38] Lord, "Words Heard and Words Seen," in *Oral Tradition and Literacy: Changing Visions of the World*, R. A. Whitaker, E. R. Sienaert, eds. (Durban, South Africa: Natal University Oral Documentation and Research Center, 1986) 5. He is referring specifically to those characteristics itemized in Ong's book *Orality and Literacy*.

aggregative rather than analytic; (3) it is redundant rather than concise; (4) it is conservative rather than creative.[39]

Elsewhere, Lord has noted that oral expression is acoustically-oriented: "One word begins to suggest another by its very sound; one phrase suggests another not only by reason of idea or by a special ordering of ideas, but also by acoustic value."[40] William Stanford, who has written a full-scale monograph on Greek euphony, concurs: "Unlike a modern writer, who may write for the eye and the brain alone, the ancient Greek poet always had to choose *some* kind of sound-group for his compositions, since the silent enjoyment of literature was out of the question in his time."[41] As might be expected, this orientation to sound has a significant impact on the composition that takes place within an oral environment.

Oral Composition. In his discussion of "oral residue" in Tudor prose, Ong makes the point that such habits of composition are, by-and-large, automatically formed rather than consciously introduced.[42] What, then, are the habits automatically favored by oral cultures?

First, the extensive work done in extra-biblical studies on oral theory has pointed out the heavily formulaic nature of oral composition. The extent to which formulaic density can be used as a measure of oral composition has been variously evaluated,[43] but the way in which the use of formulae can assist oral composition has not been questioned. Susan Wittig notes that formulaic style has value for the listener as well: it establishes a psychological anticipation that results in more efficient recognition and enhanced understanding.[44] In terms of its persuasive value, formulaic composition results in the greater likelihood of acceptance and agreement by the listeners.[45]

Lord has given attention to the impact that writing has on oral composition, particularly as it relates to the use of formulas: "One of the changes that comes about in the 'transitional' stage is that gradually *formulas*, no longer being necessary for

---

[39] Lord, "Characteristics of Orality," *OrT* 2 (1987) 54-62. In fact, Ong lists similar characteristics, but he does not discuss them at length (cf. *Orality and Literacy* 37-41).

[40] Lord, *Singer* 33. Cf. Lord, "The Role of Sound Patterns in Serbocroatian Epic."

[41] W. B. Stanford, *The Sound of Greek. Studies in the Greek Theory and Practice of Euphony* (Berkeley, CA: University of California Press, 1967) 77 (the emphasis is his).

[42] Ong, "Oral Residue" 146. J. S. Kselman (quoting D. I. Masson) makes a similar point in the context of discussing chiasmus in Hebrew poetry: "These patterns . . . are seldom consciously worked out by the poet, and even more rarely are they consciously analyzed by the reader or listener. On the other hand, the poet with a good ear is aware that one version of a phrase or line sounds better than another, and the reader is aware to some extent of pleasure in the sound" ("Semantic-Sonant Chiasmus in Biblical Poetry," *Bib* 58 [1977] 223).

[43] E.g., Russo, "'Oral' or 'Aural' Composition?"

[44] S. Wittig, "Formulaic Style and the Problem of Redundancy," *Centrum* 1 (1973) 128.

[45] Ibid. 131.

composition, give place to true *repetitions*, which are repeated for aesthetic or referential reasons rather than for ease in verse-making."[46] In purely oral composition, "formulas do not point to other uses of themselves; they do not recall other occurrences."[47]

What Lord describes as "true repetitions" *are*, however, present in oral composition. Although Finnegan questions the use of repetition as a criterion for separating oral from written poetry,[48] she affirms that "repetition in some form *is* characteristic of oral poetic style; repetition of phrases, lines or verses . . . are common in oral poetry."[49]

Bennison Gray argues that both oral poetry and oral prose are characterized by repetition.[50] According to Gray, the primary difference between oral and written composition is that of duplication versus description. An oral composer would say, "he tried and tried," whereas a literate author would write, "he tried very hard."[51] Repetition in oral composition includes repeated incidents as well as repeated words[52] and may be seen as a second "habit" of oral composition.

As with formulaic style, repetition has a practical value in an oral environment. Ong writes:

> Oral cultures need repetition, redundancy, verboseness for several reasons. First . . . spoken words fly away. A reader can pause over a point he wants to reflect on, or go back a few pages to return to it. The inscribed word is still there. The spoken word is gone. So the orator repeats himself, to help his hearers think it over. Second, spoken words do not infallibly carry equally well to everyone in an audience: synonyms, parallelisms, repetitions, neat oppositions, give the individual hearer a second chance if he did not hear well the first time. If he missed the "not only," he can probably reconstruct it from the "but also." Finally, the orator's thoughts do not always come as fast as he would wish, and even the best orator is at times inclined to repeat what he has just said in order to "mark time" while he is undertaking to find what move to make next.[53]

---

[46] Lord, "Perspectives" 492 (the emphasis is his).

[47] Ibid.

[48] Finnegan, *Oral Poetry* 129-133.

[49] Ibid. 129 (the emphasis is hers).

[50] B. Gray, "Repetition in Oral Literature," *JAF* 84 (1971) 293.

[51] Ibid. 300.

[52] Ibid. 296.

[53] Ong, *Interfaces* 114. Finnegan agrees: "Oral poetry—like anything transmitted through an oral medium—is necessarily ephemeral. Once said, it cannot, for that performance anyway, be recaptured. Repetition has real point in such circumstances: it makes it easier for the audience to grasp what has been said and gives the speaker/singer confidence that it has understood the message he is trying to communicate" (*Oral Poetry* 129).

Ruth Crosby's work makes it clear that, for these reasons, repetition continued as a significant feature of composition and delivery well into the Middle Ages.[54]

A natural correlative to repetition is parallelism. Jousse, in particular, stresses parallelism as characteristic of oral composition. He defines parallelism as "the automatic repetition of a propositional gesture."[55] According to Jousse, parallelism is, in effect, a mental reflex action, an "automatic triggering of a propositional gesture . . . of a type similar [in respect toof its form and meaning] to the one which has immediately preceded."[56]

The use of parallelism is, of course, clearly seen in the Hebrew poetry of which it is characteristic. Most of the discussion of oral theory as it relates to OT texts has focused on the use of word pairs. As with formula density and repetition, the value of word pairs as a criterion for determining the degree of orality present in Hebrew poetry had been questioned.[57] For the purposes of a study that focuses on prose composition (such as the present one), however, a comment by Whallon is helpful in distinguishing between the parallelism of poetry and the parallelism of prose: "The one [that of poetry] is known by its use of synonyms and antonyms, the other [that of prose] by its repetition of the same word."[58]

Whallon's distinction highlights what is one of the common threads found in many scholars' discussions of oral composition: that of verbal or "acoustic" correspondence. Ong uses the term "mnemonic patterns" to refer to the way in which thought is shaped for oral recurrence.[59] Paul Kiparsky uses the term "echoes" to refer to "purely phonological repetition without any necessary lexical or syntactic relationship."[60] Havelock discusses "acoustic echoes" and the "echo-principle" repeatedly in his writings.[61] In biblical studies, Dewey adopts another term from Havelock: "acoustic responses."[62]

---

[54] R. Crosby, "Oral Delivery in the Middle Ages," *Speculum* 11 (1936) 88-110. Cf. Finnegan, *Oral Poetry* 129.

[55] Jousse, *Oral Style* 95.

[56] Ibid. 98. He continues: "This constitutes *parallelism*, a deep-seated, universal principle of psychological automatism that operates in human thought when it is living and spontaneous, not deformed by the conventional rules of *our* written language" (ibid.; the emphasis is his).

[57] See the discussion in Chapter 1.

[58] Whallon, *Formula, Character, and Context* 196. His discussion extends over several pages and includes numerous OT examples.

[59] Ong, *Orality and Literacy* 34.

[60] P. Kiparsky, "Oral Poetry: Some Linguistic and Typological Considerations," in *Oral Literature and the Formula*, B. A. Stolz and R. S. Shannon, eds., (Ann Arbor, MI: Center for the Coordination of Ancient and Modern Studies, 1976) 90-91.

[61] Havelock, *Preface* 187; idem, "Alphabetization" 14-15; idem, *Muse* 72-73.

[62] Dewey, "Oral Methods" 39.

The tendency for sound to lead to sound has already been mentioned above. In his essay on sound-patterning in Serbocroatian epic poetry, Lord notes:

> The predominant vowels or consonants or consonant clusters in one part of the line aid in determining the choice of words or the choice of the formula which will follow. The singer may keep to a given sound pattern for several lines, then shift to another for several more lines, and so on. The story moves onward on these waves of sound as well. Interestingly enough, it is often the sounds of the key word of a passage which dictate the alliteration or assonance of the whole passage; this key word is, as it were, the bridge between idea and sound pattern.[63]

The passage he cites from the "Song of Bagdad" will serve as an example:

> Kud god skita, za Aliju pita.
> Kazaše ga u gradu Kajnidu.
> Kad tatarin pod Kajnidu dode,
> Pa eto ga uz čaršiju prode,
> Pa prilazi novom bazdrdanu,
> Te upita za Alino dvore.
> Bazdrdan mu dvore ukazao.
> Kad tatarin na kapiju dode,
> Pa zadrma halkom na vratima.
> Zveknu halka, a jeknu kapija.[64]

It is evident that, in addition to the rhyming that is present, the consonants *k, g, t, d,* and *z*—as well as the vowel combination *a-i-u*—play an important part in the composition of the passage.

Elsewhere, Stanford notes that the Greek rhetorical techniques of homoiokatarkton, homoioteleuton, parechesis, paromoiosis, and paronomasia are all formalized categories for the repetition of letters and syllables.[65] At times, "such rhymes and assonances seem to have tickled the ears of the Greeks agreeably with little or no reference to their sense."[66] Practically, however, such sound patterns serve to facilitate memory.[67]

The relation of verbal and/or acoustic correspondence to oral patterning will be developed more fully below. It is sufficient now to note the importance given to this phenomenon by scholars whose primary focus is orality and oral theory. Also

---

[63] Lord, "Sound Patterns" 302. Cf. R. P. Creed, "Sound-Patterning in Some Sung and Dictated Performances of Avdo Medjedović," *Canadian-American Slavic Studies* 15 (1981) 116-121.

[64] Ibid.

[65] Stanford, *Sound of Greek* 83.

[66] Ibid. 85.

[67] Stanford notes such English examples as "a stitch in time saves nine," "finders keepers, losers weepers," "waste not, want not," "look before you leap," and "penny wise, pound foolish" (ibid. 84).

to be developed more fully below are the specific means composers in highly oral cultures use to order their material. At this point it is enough simply to note the devices—in addition to parallelism—that have been identified by scholars working in the field of oral theory. The use of stereotyped formulae has been noted by many scholars.[68] As well, Lord has discussed chiasmus[69] and ring-composition;[70] Cedric Whitman has written extensively on ring-composition and geometric structure in Homer;[71] Havelock has discussed "reverse correspondences" as seen in ABA and ABBA patterns;[72] and Jousse has noted the presence of "controlling mnemotechnical frame[s], organized symmetrically from either end of the recitation to the centre."[73] Each of these scholars is convinced that such compositional techniques grew out of the need to order material in such a way as to enhance understanding by the listener.

C. The Rhetorical Environment

Traditional Rhetoric. As noted above, classical Greek rhetorical categories are basically formalizations of the ways in which speech was used in oral cultures. Kennedy calls the preformalized uses of language "traditional" rhetoric,[74] and Lord highlights the relation between the world of orality and this kind of rhetoric:

> There is a tendency for us in the European tradition to forget how extensive and how basic our literary heritage from the world of orality has been, and there is a correponding tendency to believe that the world of literacy invented some of the characteristics of literature, which in reality originated in oral literature. Among them is a sense of form and structure . . . and many devices, later termed "rhetorical" and attributed to the schools, which actually were created in the crucible of the oral world. The world of orality gave us anaphora . . . epiphora . . . alliteration, assonance, rhyme, both internal, medial, and end, and the sense of balanced structure is typified by parallelism in sentences and other forms of parataxis.[75]

---

[68] See the discussion in Chapter 1.

[69] Lord, *Singer* 42.

[70] Lord, "The Merging of Two Worlds: Oral and Written Poetry as Carriers of Ancient Values," in *Current Issues in Oral Literature Research: A Memorial for Milman Parry*, J. M. Foley, ed. (Columbus, OH: Slavica, 1986) 53-64. Cf. Dewey: "Ring composition (inclusio) is endemic in oral narrative, marking the boundaries of individual episodes and of much longer sections" ("Oral Methods" 38).

[71] C. H. Whitman, *Homer and the Heroic Tradition* (Cambridge, MA: Harvard University Press, 1967) 97-98 (ring-composition) and ibid., 252-284 (geometric structure).

[72] Havelock, "Code" 140-143.

[73] Jousse, *Oral Style* 218.

[74] G. A. Kennedy, *Classical Rhetoric and Its Christian and Secular Tradition from Ancient to Modern Times* (Chapel Hill, NC: University of North Carolina Press, 1980) 6.

[75] Lord, "Words Seen" 13. Cf. Stanford's comment above.

Greek culture prior to the introduction of the alphabet was an oral culture. The rhetoric of that culture was traditional rhetoric that utilized the techniques of oral composition discussed above. Kennedy describes the way in which rhetoric is learned in such a culture: "The would-be orator listens to speakers and acquires a sense of oratorical conventions and of what is effective. He does not work out a theory, but he imitates, and sometimes succeeds. He builds up a technique of organizing the subject and a collection of examples, of stock phrases, of themes."[76]

Conceptual Rhetoric. Eventually, the Greeks began to analyze the processes of traditional rhetoric, give names to the techniques used, and organize those techniques into a system that could be formally studied and taught. Kennedy refers to this organized system as "conceptual" rhetoric.[77] Burton Mack sketches the beginning of this conceptualization and concludes that by the end of the fifth century B.C. the foundations were laid for what is commonly referred to as "classical rhetoric" in Greece.[78]

Within classical rhetoric, three traditions of theory and practice developed: sophistic, philosophical, and technical.[79] Sophistic rhetoric may be identified with Gorgias and Isocrates. This tradition "emphasizes the speaker, rather than the speech or audience . . . It is often ceremonial and cultural, rather than active and civic, and though moral in tone, tends not to press for difficult decisions or immediate action."[80]

Philosophical rhetoric began with Socrates and his objections to sophistic rhetoric. It "tends to deemphasize the speaker and to stress the validity of his message and the nature of his effect on an audience. Furthermore, it classifies speeches on the basis of the audience, whether they are only spectators or are judges of past or future events."[81]

Finally, technical rhetoric is the most conceptualized tradition, being described at some length in later handbooks such as Cicero's *De Inventione*, Quintilian's *Institutio Oratio*, and the anonymous *Rhetoric ad Herrennium*. Technical rhetoric "concentrates on the speech . . . [and] is highly pragmatic; it shows how to present a subject efficiently and successfully but makes no attempt to judge the morality of the speaker or his effect on an audience."[82]

---

[76] Ibid. 10.

[77] Ibid. 15-17.

[78] B. L. Mack, *Rhetoric and the New Testament* (Minneapolis: Fortress, 1990) 26. It does not appear that the Jews ever conceptualized rhetoric to any notable extent, although "the importance of speech among them is everywhere evident in the Old Testament, and undoubtedly they learned its techniques by imitation" (Kennedy, *Rhetorical Criticism* 11).

[79] Mack, *Rhetoric* 26.

[80] Kennedy, *Classical Rhetoric* 17.

[81] Ibid.

[82] Ibid. 16.

First Century Rhetoric. By the beginning of the first century conceptualized rhetoric was well established in Greco-Roman culture.[83] Mack states that at least 350 Greek cities were established in the eastern Mediterranean region during the Hellenistic and early Roman periods.[84] These cities had schools in which formal training in rhetoric took place, for rhetoric was held in high regard among educated Greeks.[85]

According to Mack, Greek schools were divided into three levels: elementary, secondary, and professional.[86] Elementary education was offered to children between the ages of 7 and 14 years[87] and included instruction in writing, reading, and counting.[88] Between the ages of 15 and 17 years, secondary education focused on literary studies such as expressive reading and explanation of the text.[89] Mack states that it was at the secondary level that instruction in rhetoric began: "Special handbooks for teachers of the 'first exercises' in rhetoric (later called *progymnasmata*) were written in such a way that a student could move by degrees from the rhetorical analysis of literature that was already familiar to the principles and practice of specifically rhetorical compositions such as speeches."[90]

Professional education began at age 18 and was acquired in either a school of philosophy or a school of rhetoric. The schools of philosophy provided advanced study in the humanities. The schools of rhetoric supplied training for such professions as teacher, lawyer, public official, civic leader, and most forms of literary activity.[91] Technical professions such as medicine were learned by apprenticeship.

---

[83] Mack: "By the first century B.C.E., the practice of rhetoric had been thoroughly enculturated, the system of techniques fully explored, the logic rationalized, and the pedagogy refined. Rhetoric permeated both the system of education and the manner of public discourse that marked the culture of Hellenism on the eve of the Roman age" (*Rhetoric* 28).

[84] Ibid. 29.

[85] H. I. Marrou: "The thing that really showed whether a man was cultivated or not was not whether he had studied science or medicine . . . but whether he had received either of the two rival and allied forms of advanced education which were still the most widespread and characteristic . . . the philosophical and the rhetorical. Of these the dominant member was unquestionably the second, which left a profound impression on all manifestations of the Hellenistic spirit. For the very great majority of students, higher education meant taking lessons from the rhetor, learning the art of eloquence from him" (*A History of Education in Antiquity*, G. Lamb, trans. [New York: Sheed & Ward, 1956] 194).

[86] Mack, *Rhetoric* 30.

[87] This is the age range normally associated with the Greek word παῖς, thus the term παιδεία for the instruction of such children.

[88] Cf. Marrou, *Education* 150-164. Mack lists reading, writing, literature, arithmetic, music, and physical exercises (*Rhetoric* 30).

[89] Marrou, *Education* 165-167.

[90] Mack, *Rhetoric* 30.

[91] Cf. Mack, ibid.

It is, of course, possible to overemphasize the number of people with access to the advanced levels of education. Lentz states that reading and writing was limited to "the more aristocratic and wealthy elements of society."[92] The cost of basic education was high, and secondary education was even more expensive.[93] Lentz also notes that education at the primary level "was limited both in the length of time spent in the study of grammar and in the scope of the overall instruction."[94] Plato recommended three years for the study of letters (*Laws* 809E); Aristotle suggested seven years (*Politics* 1336B). In either case, the time frame was limited.

The schools were not, however, the only venue for exposure to first century rhetoric. Greek cities also had theaters and marketplaces, both of which were traditional places for the active practice of rhetoric. Mack provides a good summary:

> Techniques of rhetoric were tested in the public arena, just as were performances in music, literature, gymnastics, theater, and so on. The agora, the gymnasium, and the city chambers, were all good places to give and hear an interesting speech . .
> All people, whether formally trained or not, were fully schooled in the wily ways of sophists, the eloquence required at civic festivals, the measured tones of the local teacher, and the heated debates where differences of opinion battled for the right to say what should be done. To be engulfed in the culture of Hellenism meant to have ears trained for the rhetoric of speech.[95]

Rhetorical categories and figures were part of the culture of the day.[96] They were "in the air," and everyone, whether formally or informally educated, was influenced by rhetoric.[97]

---

[92] Lentz, *Orality and Literacy* 58.

[93] Lentz: "Socrates, in Plato's *Cratylus* (384B-C), recorded that Prodicus had a price range from fifty drachmas to one drachma for lectures . . . If the drachma represented a day's wages for a workman, going to secondary school could have been quite expensive" (ibid. 59).

[94] Ibid. 61.

[95] Mack, *Rhetoric* 31.

[96] Cf. esp. A. J. Malherbe, whose writings include "The Beasts at Ephesus," *JBL* 87 (1968) 71-80; "'Gentle as a Nurse': The Cynic Background of 1 Thess 2," *NovT* 12 (1970) 203-217; "Medical Imagery in the Pastoral Epistles," in *Texts and Testaments: Critical Essays on the Bible and Early Church Fathers*, ed. W. E. March (San Antonio: Trinity, 1980) 19-35; *Social Aspects of Early Christianity*, 2nd ed. (Baton Rouge: Louisiana State University Press, 1983); "Exhortation in First Thessalonians," *NovT* 25 (1983) 238-256; "Self-Definition among Epicureans and Cynics," in *Self-Definition in the Greco-Roman World, Jewish and Christian Self-Definition*, vol. 3, eds. E. P. Sanders and B. F. Meyer (Philadelphia: Fortress, 1983); "'In Season and Out of Season': 2 Timothy 4:2," *JBL* 103 (1984) 235-243; *Moral Exhortation: A Greco-Roman Sourcebook* (Philadelphia: Fortress, 1986); *Paul and the Thessalonians* (Philadelphia: Fortress, 1987).

[97] A. Stock writes: "From the beginning of the Empire, rhetoric prevailed over all other genres and invaded all the other fields: grammar, drama, history, and philosophy. All ancient writing was meant to be read aloud, which brought it about that the rules of oratorical discourse

D. The Scribal Environment

Writing Systems and Scribes. Writing systems and scribes played an important role in Ancient Near Eastern culture long before the first century. Henri Marrou, for example, summarizes the history of educational development in the period from 1000 B.C. to A.D. 500 as a "progressive transition from a 'noble warrior' culture to a 'scribe' culture."[98] Writing systems existed, of course, before 1000 B.C., and groups of specialists who could work with those systems soon came into existence. These specialists were the scribes.

Jack Goody and Ian Watt note that the first Ancient Near Eastern writing systems arose at the end of the fourth millennium.[99] Initially, these early systems were pictographic, with logograms eventually added in order to permit a wider range of expression.[100] The development of cuneiform writing in Sumeria and hieroglyphics in Egypt led to the growth of scribal classes in both societies.[101] Although little remains of the early Minoan (3000-1000 B.C.) and Mycenaean (1600-1100 B.C.) civilizations, the discovery of Linear A and Linear B scripts on Crete suggests the existence of scribes and an educational system in those cultures as well.[102]

The development of the Semitic syllabaries between 1500 and 1000 B.C. marked a significant advance on earlier writing systems, because they were based on the representation of syllables rather than on the representation of words.[103] These phonetic systems, however, were still incomplete and required a skilled class of specialists to interpret them. Goody and Watt suggest that two factors slowed the diffusion of these writing systems: (1) the intrinsic difficulties of the systems themselves, and (2) the fact that writing was largely used as an aid to memory.[104] With a writing system composed solely of consonants, it was impossible to distinguish, for example, between *ba, be, bi, bo,* and *bu* apart from oral interpretation. The fact that vowel pointing was not added to the Hebrew Scriptures until the time of the Massoretes attests to the heavy reliance on oral tradition in Jewish culture well after the first century. Alongside that reliance on oral tradition, however, was

---

invaded the world of texts" ("Chiastic Awareness and Education in Antiquity," *BTB* 14 [1984] 26).

[98] Marrou, *Education* xiv.

[99] J. Goody and I. Watt, "The Consequences of Literacy," in *Literacy in Traditional Societies*, J. Goody, ed. (New York: Cambridge University Press, 1968) 35.

[100] Ibid.

[101] Marrou, *History* xiv-xvii.

[102] Ibid. xvii-xviii. Cf. Goody and Watt, "Consequences" 36, n.1.

[103] Goody and Watt, "Consequences" 35. Cf. Havelock, *Literate Revolution* 60-76.

[104] Goody and Watt, "Consequences" 39. In support of their argument, they note that the first "generally recognized text"of the Torah was not published until six centuries after the Hebrew writing system was adopted (ibid. 40).

a high regard for the manuscripts that helped preserve it. Kelber has noted the premium placed on the written word by both the Hebrew and Hellenistic branches of Judaism,[105] and both the OT and the NT bear witness to the important role that scribes played in Jewish society.

It was during the middle of the eighth century that the Greeks first took certain of the Semitic signs for consonants and used them as vowels.[106] This new alphabet was "the first comprehensively and exclusively phonetic system for transcribing human speech."[107] Goody and Watt note that "the system was easy, explicit and unambiguous . . . Its great advantage over the syllabaries lay in the reduction of the number of signs and in the ability to specify consonant and vowel clusters."[108]

The Romans soon borrowed the Greek system from the Etruscans and developed their own alphabet.[109] Yet the initial introduction of phonetic alphabets did not eliminate the need for scribes. Bahr,[110] Longenecker,[111] and Achtemeier[112] all have extended discussions of the prominent role played by scribes and dictation—in both Greek and Latin—in the first century. If, as Robbins suggests, the first century was a rhetorical culture, it was nevertheless a culture with a significant scribal component.

Writing and Reading. Papyrus was the most common writing material used, whether in scrolls or in codices.[113] Space was at a premium, and economy took precedence over beauty. Writing was done in columns with similar numbers of

---

[105] Kelber, *Oral and Written Gospel* 16-17. The most significant pieces of evidence he offers are the Qumran manuscripts and the Septuagint project. Cf. C. H. Roberts, "Books in the Graeco-Roman World and in the New Testament," in *The Cambridge History of the Bible*, 3 vols., P. R. Ackroyd, et al, eds. (Cambridge: Cambridge University Press, 1970) 1:49-51.

[106] The earliest extant inscriptions using the new alphabet occur in the last two decades of that century (Goody and Watt, "Consequences" 42).

[107] Ibid. 41.

[108] Ibid. Cf. Havelock, *Literate Revolution* 77-88.

[109] Marrou places this development in the seventh century B.C. (*Education* 250).

[110] Bahr, "Paul and Letter Writing" 468-475.

[111] Longenecker, "Ancient Amanuenses" 282-288.

[112] Achtemeier, "Omne Verbum Sonat" 12-15.

[113] F. G. Kenyon argues that papyrus rolls were completely dominant well into the second century, with codices possible in the second century and probable in the third (*Books and Readers in Ancient Greece and Rome* [Oxford, 1932; repr., Chicago: Ares, 1980] 110-111). The Alands argue that "from all appearances the codex form was used by Christian writers from the very beginning" (K. and B. Aland, *The Text of the New Testament*, E. F. Rhodes, trans. [Grand Rapids: Eerdmans, 1987] 101).

letters, regardless of where words began and ended.[114] Punctuation was occasional at best,[115] and diacritical marks were rare.[116]

Dictation was the normal method of composition,[117] although it was not the only method. Dio Chrysostom maintained that dictation was easier than doing his own writing (18.18). Quintilian, on the other hand, preferred to write out his speeches himself (*Inst Or* 11.2.33). In either case, writing was closely connected to the spoken word.[118]

Similarly, reading was commonly done aloud.[119] According to Dio Chrysostom, authors presented their works publicly (8.9; 12.5). A number of ancient sources provide evidence for the custom of having works read aloud by slaves.[120] Both of these practices were to be expected, but even reading for private study was done aloud.[121] The most commonly cited examples of this latter phenomenon are Philip's encounter with the Ethiopian eunuch (Acts 8:30) and Augustine's

---

[114] Achtemeier: "Suetonius notes as a peculiarity of the emperor Augustus that he did not divide a word at the end of a line, but wrote the remaining letters below the rest of the word and drew a loop around them. Since this was a noteworthy peculiarity, it is clear that the normal practice was simply to continue letters on the following line regardless of the words to which they belonged" ("Omne Verbum Sonat" 10, n.41). Achtemeier also notes a comment by Seneca (*Ep Mor* 40.11) regarding the fact that, in contrast to the practice of the Greeks, some Latin writers separated their words (ibid. n.43).

[115] Kenyon: "Punctuation is often wholly absent, and is never full and systematic . . . Where it exists at all, it is generally either in the form of a single dot . . . or of a blank space, often accompanied by a short stroke (παράγραφος) below the first letters of the line in which the pause in the sense occurs" (*Books and Readers* 65). W. B. Sedgwick notes that a regular system of punctuation in documents did not evolve until well into the Middle Ages ("Reading and Writing in Classical Antiquity," *ContRev* 135 [1929] 93).

[116] Kenyon: "Accents are very rarely used . . . Breathing marks are still more rare, but a square rough breathing is occasionally added, especially with relative pronouns . . . Where accents or breathings do occur, they have, oftener than not, been added subsequently by a different hand" (*Books and Readers* 66).

[117] Achtemeier: "The normal mode of composition of any writing was to dictate it to a scribe—for the wealthy, often one of their slaves . . . The material dictated would then be reviewed by the author, who corrected scribal mistakes" ("Omne Verbum Sonat" 12).

[118] Achtemeier: ". . . *no* writing occurred that was not vocalized. That is obvious in the case of dictation, but it was also true in the case of writing in one's own hand. Even in that endeavor, the words were simultaneously spoken as they were committed to writing, whether one wrote one's own words or copied those of another" (ibid. 15).

[119] Frank Gilliard has questioned the contention that reading and writing were exclusively oral ("More Silent Reading in Antiquity: *Non Omne Verbum Sonabat*," *JBL* 112 (1993) 689-694). He concedes, however, that the predominant method of performing both tasks was to do them aloud.

[120] Achtemeier (ibid. 16) cites Seneca (*Ep Mor* 64.2), Martial (*Epigrams* 2.1, 6), Dio Chrysostom (18.6), and Pliny (*Letters* 3.5; 7.1).

[121] Cf. Stanford, *Sound of Greek* 2.

amazement over Ambrose's ability to read silently (*Confessions* 6.3).[122] G. L. Hendrickson surveys a broad range of evidence and concludes: "Reading silently was not, therefore, impossible (though the degree of silence is still open to debate); but it not only was unusual, it was accounted an imperfect and defective method of reading."[123]

There were three factors that contributed to the practice of reading aloud. First, there was a cultural bias in favor of orality. Seneca, for example, criticizes one author's style because "he was writing those words for the mind rather than for the ear."[124] Second, there was the long-established practice of oral composition and dictation. Third, the very nature of first century documents made the task of reading difficult.[125] Achtemeier notes that "the visual format of the ancient manu-script—words run together, and in addition often abbreviated, no punctuation to indicate sentences or paragraphs—conveyed virtually no information about the organization and development of the content it intended to convey."[126] This lack of visual information made it necessary for the reader to sound out syllables and words and, consequently, reinforced the practice of reading aloud.[127] The most important

---

[122] Augustine writes, ". . . when Ambrose was reading, his eyes travelled over the page, and his mind sought out the meaning, but his voice and tongue were silent . . . thus we saw him reading silently and never otherwise." Stanford places this incident in A.D. 384 and notes that two years later Augustine was also able to read silently (ibid.). He concludes: "But for long after the year A.D. 386 silent reading seems to have remained rare and difficult for most people" (ibid. 3).

[123] G. L. Hendrickson, "Ancient Reading," *CJ* 25 (1929) 192. He continues: "Throughout antiquity and the Middle Ages reading aloud was the general habit of the learned as well as of the unlearned. Silent reading was unusual, but in what degree exceptional or possible the evidence as yet collected does not permit us to say. With the renewed literary activity of the Renaissance and the invention of printing the educated world went over by degrees to the now universal habit of silent reading" (ibid. 193). Sedgwick thinks that the growth of the monastic system with its vows of silence was the reason that reading aloud eventually ceased ("Reading and Writing" 94).

[124] *Ep Mor* 100.2. Cf. Achtemeier ("Omne Verbum Sonat" 11), who also cites Seneca (*Ep Mor* 6.5; 75.1) as well as Papias (Eusebius, *Hist eccl* 3.39.4).

[125] Marrou notes that public reading and recitation (or "expressive reading") was not taught until the secondary school level because of the level of difficulty posed by the documents themselves. He writes: "A proper reading, therefore, required an attentive study of the text; it needed to be thoroughly prepared; and there are sometimes traces of this kind of preparation in the papyri—we can see where the boy has used strokes to separate lines and words and cut up words into syllables for the sake of scansion" (*Education* 166). According to Petronius, the person who could read a book without such prior preparation was worthy of praise (*Satyricon* 75).

[126] Achtemeier, "Omne Verbum Sonat" 17.

[127] Stanford: "Normally, it seems, an ancient Greek or Roman had to pronounce each syllable before he could understand a written word. The written letters informed his voice; then his voice informed his ear; and finally his ear, together with the muscular movements of his vocal organs, conveyed the message to his brain" (*Sound of Greek* 1).

point to note for the purposes of the present study is that both reading and writing were closely tied to oral expression.

Letter Writing and Delivery. Naturally enough, letters shared the characteristics of other documents produced in the first century.[128] The normal method of composition was by dictation,[129] and Bahr suggests that a workable system of Greek shorthand was in place at least as early as the middle of the first century B.C.[130] From Rom 16:22 it is evident that Paul dictated his letter to the Roman church. Paul's comments in 1 Cor 16:21, Gal 6:11, and Phlm 19 suggest that his other letters were dictated as well and that he often added a final note in his own hand.[131]

Because letters were read aloud—as were other documents—they had a kinship with oral communication. Stirewalt observes that letters would have been the natural, if somewhat inadequate, substitute for conversation,[132] and McGuire thinks that they would have been the natural vehicle for the discussion of philosophical and religious topics.[133] For Paul, communicating via letters had the advantage of allowing him "to stay in near-oral touch with his addressees."[134] Funk's work on the apostolic parousia has served to highlight the way in which Paul used letters to establish his "presence" while being physically absent.[135]

Once a letter was written, however, the challenge of delivering it still remained. McGuire notes that although the Roman government established a postal service for official use, "private groups and individuals . . . had to maintain their own letter-carrier service, or rely on 'contacts' in the imperial administration, or on the kindness of traveling friends, or pay merchants or sea captains to deliver their letters."[136] These circumstances bring to the fore the importance of the individuals

---

[128] For an excellent introduction to Greek letter writing, see White, *Ancient Letters* 189-220.

[129] Cicero gives several reasons for dictating letters: (1) a busy schedule (*Ad Quint* 2.16.1; 3.3.1; *Ad Att* 2.23.1; 4.16.1); (2) illness or other physical disabilities (*Ad Att* 6.9.6; 7.2.3; 8.13.1; 10.14.1; 10.17.2; *Ad Quint* 2.2.1); (3) the ability to engage in multiple activities at once (*Ad Quint* 3.1.19; *Ad Att* 5.17.1; 14.21.4; 15.13.5; 15.27.3). Quintilian adds poor handwriting or the inability to write well (*Inst Or* 1.28).

[130] Bahr, "Paul and Letter Writing" 474.

[131] Although Longenecker has suggested that because of the brevity and the personal nature of the letter Paul wrote all of Philemon himself ("Ancient Amanuenses" 291). Bahr's comment is that Paul's use of amanuenses is "beyond doubt" ("Paul and Letter Writing" 468). Cf. also Bahr, "Subscriptions."

[132] M. L. Stirewalt, "Paul's Evaluation of Letter Writing," in *Search the Scriptures*, J. M. Myers, et al, eds. (Leiden: Brill, 1969) 179.

[133] McGuire, "Letters and Letter Carriers" 150.

[134] Kelber, *Oral and Written Gospel* 168.

[135] Cf. Funk, "Apostolic Parousia."

[136] McGuire, "Letters and Letter Carriers" 150.

who served to deliver private letters to their destinations. White notes that "the scribe was sometimes hired to deliver the letter as well as to write it."[137] This method, however, would have been expensive.[138] A more economical method would have been to find a friend who was traveling through or to the destination of the letter and let him serve as the letter carrier.

Paul solved the problem by using co-workers to deliver his letters. His letters are replete with the names of individuals who worked at his side, through whom he maintained contact with the churches he had planted, and who could serve as letter carriers should circumstances demand it.[139] Using such individuals had, for Paul, the added advantage of enhancing his "presence" in the churches. Richard Ward, writing from the perspective of performance history, suggests that "oral performance by a trusted emissary" was part of Paul's design for establishing his apostolic presence, especially in the case of 2 Corinthians 10-13.[140] In fact, oral delivery was the second "act" in creating "Paul-in-the-letter."[141] If, as Ward suggests, Paul selected his emissaries for their rhetorical skill in interpreting his letters,[142] his correspondence is a fascinating window on all three of the environments of the first century: the oral, the scribal, and the rhetorical.

E. Assesssing the Aural Audience

A consideration of the oral, rhetorical, and scribal environments of the first century suggests that a mixture of orality and literacy was present. The culture was no longer a primarily oral culture; yet it was not a fully literate culture either. In Ong's terms, it was largely—or perhaps radically—oral. To use Havelock's

---

[137] White, *Ancient Letters* 216. He continues: "The messenger would have been somewhat more trustworthy in these cases—both as interpreter of the letter's concerns and as letter carrier—than messengers who merely happened to be traveling toward the letter's destination" (ibid.).

[138] Cf. Stirewalt for an extended discussion of the difficulties involved in first century letter delivery ("Paul's Evaluation" 182-186).

[139] The most obvious example is Epaphroditus (Phil 2:25-29). Stirewalt discusses other possible letter carriers at some length (ibid. 186-190). His concluding comment is helpful: "Paul's men were not chance travelers or strangers. They were men devoted to the same task as Paul. They were concerned with the problems and solutions, the doctrine, exhortation, greeting; they themselves were partners in the communication and therefore mediators of it" (ibid. 190).

[140] R. F. Ward, "Pauline Voice and Presence as Strategic Communication," *SBLSP* (1990) 290.

[141] Ibid. 291. He continues: "The embodiment of 'Paul-in-the letter' was the basis for transforming the social structure at Corinth by collapsing the distance between performer and audience; the act of incarnation of the letter's persona transforms the Corinthian audience and establishes a new relationship between the church and Paul" (ibid. 292).

[142] Ibid. 291.

categories, it was either recitation-literate or script-literate. Robbins's suggestion of "rhetorical" as the best term to describe the overall culture seems appropriate.

Despite the introduction of the Greek alphabet and the subsequent spread of literacy, a premium was still placed on the spoken word. Speeches were given aloud; reading was done aloud; even writing was done aloud. Oral composition was the rule, not the exception. Thought and expression were shaped, to a greater or lesser extent, by sound. These facts suggest that an investigation of oral patterning must focus on "acoustic resonances" *heard* by the original audience rather than on conceptual parallels found by silently rereading the texts. What remains to be considered is the audience's ability to process the information that was presented orally.

It might prove helpful in this regard to consider a phenomenon frequently observed in Homer's works. John Myres has called attention to the presence of formal balance in both the *Iliad* and the *Odyssey*.[143] He traces the Greek tendency to create symmetry in geometric art, graphic art, architecture, sculpture, and painting, and argues that this preference for "pedimental composition" also carried over to language—with the result that significant words, phrases, or events were often placed at the center of literary works.[144] When Myres applies this theory to the *Iliad*, the result is a complex diagrammatic analysis with the Achaean embassy to Achilles (Book 9) at its center.[145]

Cedric Whitman has also examined "geometric structure" in Homer's works. He contends that a geometric approach was central to classical Greek art.[146] He notes that in the case of epic poetry, however, the initial impulse for composition of this sort was mnemonic.[147] This mnemonic function may be seen in Homer's use of ring-composition:

> This framing device . . . had its origin undoubtedly in the oral singer's need to bind the parts of his story together for simple coherence. Like the retrospective summaries of preceding action so characteristic of epic, it took both the poet's and

---

[143] J. L. Myres, "The Last Book of the 'Iliad'," *JHS* 52 (1932) 264-296; idem, "The Pattern of the Odyssey," *JHS* 72 (1952) 1-19; idem, "The Structure of the 'Iliad' Illustrated by the Speeches," *JHS* 74 (1954) 122-141.

[144] J. L. Myres, *Who were the Greeks?* (Berkeley, CA: University of California Press, 1930) 511-525. H. R. Immewahr has suggested the term "circular composition" for Myres's approach and defines it as "the exact correspondence between a small number of sections in a [narrative] in such a way that the main section occurs in the center . . . and the preceding and following sections correspond to each other in inverse sequence" (*Form and Thought in Herodotus* [Cleveland, OH: Western Reserve University Press, 1966] 72).

[145] Myres, "Last Book" 280. The diagram is, in fact, circular. This may explain Immerwahr's suggestion.

[146] Whitman: "The tendency is symptomatic of the artistic spirit of the age" (*Homer* 96).

[147] Ibid. 98.

the audience's mind back to a point where the next event was to find its orientation . . . Homer uses this device . . . to give shape and clarity to the sections of his work, which, composed paratactically and with almost equal detail and emphasis in every part, might otherwise fall into an intolerably unarticulated series.[148]

Havelock stresses the oral significance of such verbal correspondences. He argues that what Myres and Whitman have described in visual, geometric terms should, in fact, be interpreted in acoustic, aural terms:

The echo principle . . . is directly acoustic and only indirectly imagistic. It is persistent in both poems and has been well documented by Homeric scholars, but with this difference, that the mechanism is interpreted in visual terms alone . . . as though panels of matching series were arranged in sequences like aba, abba, abcba, and the like in the manner of painted altar-pieces. But it was the ear, not the eye, that had to be seduced and led on by such arrangements, relying on the actual sounds of identical or similar words enclosed in similar sounding formulas and paragraphs.[149]

According to Havelock, the oral psychology of both the composer and his audience demanded such correspondences in order to provide connections between disparate "facts." These facts must be connected in some way and—for the oral composer—this connection is best accomplished by phrasing the facts in such a way that they resemble one another.[150] Since the spoken word is gone as soon as it is uttered, the oral composer works forward in a process of continual anticipation:

The composer has to hint or to warn or to predict what the next thing he says is going to be like, or the next after that, even in the moment when he is saying the thing in front of it. So that the memory as it absorbs statement A is half-prepared to move on to statement B. This produces an effect of continuous recall in the narrative, as names, and adjectives and verbs repeat themselves, evoking situations in series which are partly novel, partly duplicate of each other.[151]

A simple example of this echo-principle is seen in the Raft-building passage from the *Odyssey*:[152]

ὣς ἔφατ᾽· ἠέλιος δ᾽ ἄρ᾽ ἔδυ καὶ ἐπὶ κνέφας ἦλθεν·
ἐλθόντες δ᾽ ἄρα τώ γε μυχῷ σπείους γλαφυροῖο
τερπέσθην φιλότητι, παρ᾽ ἀλλήλοισι μένοντες.

---

[148] Ibid. 252.

[149] Havelock, "The Alphabetization of Homer," in *Communications Arts in the Ancient World* 14.

[150] Havelock: ". . . as an echo resembles its original" (ibid.).

[151] Ibid.

[152] Cf. Peabody, *Winged Word* 203.

ἦμος δ' ἠριγένεια φάνη ῥοδοδάκτυλος 'Ηώς,
αὐτίχ' ὁ μὲν χλαῖνάν τε χιτῶνά τε ἔννυτ' 'Οδυσσεύς,

αὐτὴ δ' ἀργύφεον φᾶρος μέγα ἔννυτο Νύμφη,
λεπτὸν καὶ χαρίεν, περὶ δὲ ζώνην βάλετ' ἰξυῖ
καλὴν χρυσείην, κεφαλῇ δ' ἐφύπερθε καλύπτρην·
καὶ τότ' 'Οδυσσῆϊ μεγαλήτορι μήδετο πομπήν·

δῶκεν μέν οἱ πέλεκυν μέγαν, ἄρμενον ἐν παλάμῃσι,
χάλκεον, ἀμφοτέρωθεν ἀκαχμένον· αὐτὰρ ἐν αὐτῷ
στειλειὸν περικαλλὲς ἐλάϊνον, εὖ ἐναρηρός·

δῶκε δ' ἔπειτα σκέπαρνον ἐΰξοον· ἄρχε δ' ὁδοῖο
νήσου ἐπ' ἐσχατιῆς, ὅθι δένδρεα μακρὰ πεφύκει,
κλήθρη τ' αἴγειρός τ', ἐλάτη τ' ἦν οὐρανομήκης,
αὖα πάλαι, περίκηλα, τά οἱ πλώοιεν ἐλαφρῶς.

αὐτὰρ ἐπεὶ δὴ δεῖξ' ὅθι δένδρεα μακρὰ πεφύκει,
ἡ μὲν ἔβη πρὸς δῶμα Καλυψώ, δῖα θεάων,
αὐτὰρ ὁ τάμνετο δοῦρα· θοῶς δέ οἱ ἤνυτο ἔργον.
εἴκοσι δ' ἔκβαλε πάντα, πελέκκησεν δ' ἄρα χαλκῷ,

ξέσσε δ' ἐπισταμένως καὶ ἐπὶ στάθμην ἴθυνεν.
τόφρα δ' ἔνεικε τέρετρα Καλυψώ, δῖα θεάων·
τέτρηνεν δ' ἄρα πάντα καὶ ἥρμοσεν ἀλλήλοισι,
γόμφοισιν δ' ἄρα τήν γε καὶ ἁρμονίῃσιν ἄρασσεν.   (5.225-248)

In the preceding passage, the echoes occur within a limited context. It seems, however, that the aural audience was capable of recognizing such echoes over a considerable expanse. Whitman cites Odysseus's recognition by Eurycleia as an example: "Between the discovery of the scar and the old woman's instantaneous gesture of surprise, Homer inserts a seventy-five-line episode about the origin of the scar, returning with perfect ease to the moment in hand by the mere repetition of the single verb, 'recognized.'"[153] The pertinent portions of the text are set out below:

νίζε δ' ἄρ' ἄσσον ἰοῦσα ἄναχθ' ἑόν· αὐτίκα δ' ἔγνω
οὐλήν, τήν ποτέ μιν σῦς ἤλασε λευκῷ ὀδόντι
Παρνησόνδ' ἐλθόντα μετ' 'Αυτόλυκόν τε καὶ υἷας,   (19.392-394)

οὐλὴν, ὅττι πάθοι· ὁ δ' ἄρα σφίσιν εὖ κατέλεξεν
ὡς μιν θηρεύοντ' ἔλασεν σῦς λευκῷ ὀδόντι,
Παρνησόνδ' ἐλθόντα σὺν υἱάσιν Αὐτολύκοιο.

τὴν γρηῢς χείρεσσι καταπρηνέσσι λαβοῦσα
γνῶ ῥ' ἐπιμασσαμένη, πόδα δὲ προέηκε φέρεσθαι·   (19.464-468)

---

[153] Whitman, *Homer* 253.

Whitman highlights the repetition of γινώσκω as a means of resuming the main narrative. Also to be noted is the verbal correspondence between the opening and closing lines of the episode about the origin of the scar. Homer thus uses repeated wording to give his listeners a means of following the main story line. The fact that the same words are used, rather than synonyms, confirms Havelock's contention that the listener was aided by acoustic, not conceptual, parallels. Furthermore, Havelock maintains that such echoes may well extend over multiple sections of a given work.[154]

Whitman raises the natural question of "whether the audience, listening to an aural presentation of the poem, could possibly have caught the signs of such 'fearful symmetry,' or whether it would have meant anything to them if they did."[155] He concludes that "the human mind is a strange organ, and one which perceives many things without conscious or articulate knowledge of them, and responds to them with emotions necessarily and appropriately vague. An audience hence might feel more symmetry than it could possibly analyze or describe."[156]

If Whitman's analysis is correct, the aural audience was capable of perceiving—consciously or unconsciously—connections between spoken words separated by considerable time and verbiage.[157] It may be, given our twentieth century literate mindset, that we can never fully appreciate the capabilities of the first century aural audience. What does seem clear, however, is that repeated words and repeated sounds played an important role in facilitating those capabilities. It was the context of the familiar that enabled the listener to connect new ideas with those that had preceded.[158]

With an assessment of the first century aural audience Part 1 is complete. Against this general historical background, Part 2 turns to an examination of selected works that illustrate the use of various oral patterns by speakers and writers prior to and contemporary with Paul.

---

[154] The example Havelock cites extends over nine books of the *Iliad* ("Alphabetization" 14).

[155] Whitman, *Homer* 255.

[156] Ibid.

[157] In fact, Whitman suggests that parallels between the opening and closing books of the *Iliad* might well have been perceptible. That issue will be taken up in the next chapter.

[158] This observation is true even in the case of Hebrew poetry, where synonyms were frequently used to continue a theme over an extended portion of a composition. The structured context established by parallelism of sense permitted the poet "a relatively high degree of freedom, when choosing from among several terms" (Whallon, *Formula, Character, and Context* 157). Furthermore, the fact that scholars have noted the presence of both inclusion and ring-composition in the OT (e.g., Lundbom, *Jeremiah*) suggests that Jewish composers recognized the value of repeated wording to structure longer sections of their compositions.

Part Two

ORAL PATTERNING IN ANTIQUITY

Chapter 3

GRECO-ROMAN PRECEDENTS AND PARALLELS

Paul did not live in a vacuum. Rather, he was in many ways very much a product of his age. He was "an apostle to the Gentiles" (Rom 11:13), but also "a Hebrew of Hebrews" (Phil 3:5). He was able to use, for example, both the Greek diatribe (Rom 3:27-4:3) and Jewish "pearl-stringing" (Rom 3:10-18) with equal effectiveness. He could state unreservedly, "I have become all things to all people, that I may by all means save some" (1 Cor 9:22).

Paul's use of Greek and Jewish rhetorical devices suggests that he drew on both cultures in his thought and expression. It will be necessary, therefore, to examine examples from both sources in order to determine possible influences on his use of oral patterning. The present chapter will examine the use of oral patterning in the Greco-Roman world, with the use of oral patterning in the Hebrew Scriptures being examined in the next chapter. In both chapters the focus will be illustrative rather than exhaustive. The reason for this is twofold: (1) other studies have already confirmed the widespread presence of oral compositional devices in ancient texts, and (2) the volume of texts is such that it would be impossible to examine the phenomenon of oral patterning everywhere that it appears. The concern in these chapters is not how frequently the patterns occur but rather the ways in which authors used them. These findings will, in turn, establish a background against which to analyze oral patterning in Paul's letters.

This chapter will survey selected figures and works in Greco-Roman literature and rhetoric. Homer's *Iliad* and *Odyssey* are closely connected with oral tradition and were, most likely, the first Greek works committed to writing.[1] Similarly, the fifth century historian Herodotus's *Histories* is the first extended historical record preserved in prose form.[2] Plato (d. 347 B.C.), using an "extremely polished oral

---

[1] Although the tradition preserved in the *Iliad* and the *Odyssey* is much older, the written form of these epics is commonly dated in the seventh century B.C.

[2] Herodotus's death is commonly dated c. 420 B.C. Long contends that Herodotus presented readings from his work orally at Athens (T. Long, *Repetition and Variation in the*

style,"[3] was the first ancient thinker to reflect consciously on the issue of the relation between oral tradition and writing. Isocrates (d. 338 B.C.) was the first "modern" writer in the sense that he dictated his orations so that they could be "published" orally by others.[4] Demosthenes (d. 322 B.C.) was perhaps the greatest Athenian orator and left numerous examples of the practice of rhetoric. Aristotle's *"Art" of Rhetoric* was one of the first handbooks on Greek rhetoric.[5] The *Rhetoric to Alexander*, although generally regarded as pseudonymous,[6] is also associated with Aristotle and will be considered as well. Cicero (d. 43 B.C.) and Quintilian (d. A.D. 100) are included because they both produced major works on the theory of rhetoric. Because it is sometimes attributed to Cicero, the anonymous *Rhetorica ad Herennium* is included.[7] Dio Chrysostom (d. A.D. 120), the Cynic Epistles, and the papyri are chosen as representative of literary and non-literary works close to Paul's time.

In each case, the survey will seek to highlight characteristic features of the speaker/writer's uses of oral patterning. In some cases, this means that less characteristic features will be given less space. Although Herodotus, for example, uses formal balance in his *Histories*, the more characteristic feature of his work is ring-composition; consequently, more space will be devoted to this latter feature. Similarly, transposition will be mentioned in surveying Isocrates's works, but the discussion of this pattern will be more extensive in the section on Plato, since he uses it so frequently.

A. Homer: "The Last Thing First"

Numerous oral compositional devices are present in Homer's *Iliad* and *Odyssey*, which were committed to written form c. 600 B.C. Recognition of Homer's

---

Short Stories of Herodotus [Frankfurt am Main: Athenaüm, 1987] 16).

[3] Lentz, *Orality and Literacy* 168. He descibes Plato as being in tension between oral tradition and writing (ibid. 33). Cf. also Havelock, *Preface*.

[4] Lentz, *Orality and Literacy* 123. According to Lentz, Isocrates's works reflect a dynamic interaction between oral and written composition.

[5] Aristotle (d. 322 B.C.) was a contemporary of Demosthenes. His *Rhetoric*, as well as his other major works, was not produced in a "written style" but rather retains connections to the oral tradition of the past (ibid. 167).

[6] *Rhetorica ad Alexandrum* is introduced by a preface in the form of a letter from Aristotle to Alexander during the latter's campaign in the East. Scholars largely reject this ascription of authorship. Some argue that Anaximenes of Lampsacus, one of Alexander's tutors, was the author. For a concise discussion of the issues involved, see the introduction to the edition by H. Rackham (Cambridge, MA: Harvard University Press, 1937).

[7] The *Rhetorica ad Herennium* is commonly dated c. 86-82 B.C. Although it is sometimes attributed to Cicero, most scholars think the real author unknown. For further discussion see the introduction to the edition by H. Caplan (Cambridge: Harvard University Press, 1954).

repeated use of formulae and epithets, in fact, triggered the modern discussion of oral theory.[8] Examples at the end of the preceding chapter highlight Homer's use of the echo-principle and ring-composition.

Perhaps the device for which Homer is best known, however, is that of inversion. Homer's use of this technique was well-known to Cicero, who wrote to his friend Atticus:

> You ask what can have happened about the trial to give such an unexpected ending, and you want to know, too, why I showed less fight than usual. Well! In my answer I'll put the cart before the horse like Homer (respondebo tibi ὕστερον πρότερον ᾿Ομηρικῶς).[9]

Similarly, Aristarchus noted that Homer used the device of "the last thing first."[10] This use of inversion can be seen in both the *Iliad* and the *Odyssey*.[11]

One simple example of inversion occurs in the *Iliad* at the end of the catalogue of Achaean ships and captains. The poet ends his catalogue by saying, "These were the leaders of the Danaans and their lords." When he follows this statement with a question (2.761-762) about the best (ἄριστος) men and horses (ἵππων), the answer is given in reverse order:

<u>ἵπποι</u> μὲν μέγ᾿ ἄρισται ἔσαν . . .   (2.763)

<u>ἀνδρῶν</u> αὖ μέγ᾿ ἄριστος ἔην . . .   (2.768)

Similarly in the *Odyssey*, when the king of the Phaeacians receives Odysseus his wife, Arete, asks a series of questions (7.237-239)

(1)   Who are you among men, and from whence (τίς, πόθεν εἰς ἀνδρῶν)?
(2)   Who gave you this raiment (τίς τοι τάδε εἵματ᾿ ἔδωκεν)?
(3)   Did you not say that you came here wandering over the sea?

Odysseus answers the question about his travels first (7.240-289). He then explains where he got his clothing (7.295-297), repeating verbatim the words of the original question (μοι τάδε εἵματ᾿ ἔδωκε). Much later the questions about his identity (ὄνομα in 8.550) and home (πόλις in 8.555) are repeated and then answered :

νῦν δ᾿ <u>ὄνομα</u> πρῶτον μυθήσομαι . . .   (9.16)

ναιετάω δ᾿ ᾿Ιθάκην ἐυδείελον . . .   (9.21)

---

[8] See the discussion in Chapter 1 above.

[9] *Letters to Atticus* 1.16.1. He then proceeds to discuss first his "lack of fight" (lines 5-39), then the trial (lines 40ff).

[10] Quoted in Bowra, *Homer* 58.

[11] These examples are drawn from Bowra, *Homer* 58-59. See also *Iliad* 14.20-25.

The most intricate instance of inversion in Homer occurs in Book 11 of the *Odyssey*. When Odysseus speaks to his mother's ghost, he asks her a series of questions about the situation at Ithaca:

τίς νύ σε κὴρ ἐδάμασσε τανηλεγέος θανάτοιο;
ἦ δολιχὴ <u>νοῦσος</u>, ἦ Ἄρτεμις <u>ἰοχέαιρα</u>
<u>οἷς ἀγανοῖς βελέεσσιν ἐποιχομένη κατέπεφνεν</u>;   (11.171-173)

εἰπὲ δέ μοι <u>πατρός</u> τε καὶ <u>υἱέος</u>, ὃν κατέλειπον,
ἦ ἔτι πὰρ κείνοισιν ἐμὸν <u>γέρας</u>, ἦέ τις ἤδη
ἀνδρῶν ἄλλος ἔχει, ἐμὲ δ' οὐκέτι φασὶ νέεσθαι.   (11.174-176)

εἰπὲ δέ μοι μνηστῆς ἀλόχου βουλήν τε νόον τε,
ἠὲ <u>μένει</u> παρὰ παιδὶ καὶ ἔμπεδα πάντα φυλάσσει,
ἦ ἤδη μιν ἔγημεν Ἀχαιῶν ὅς τις ἄριστος.   (11.177-179)

Her answers, however, are given in exactly the opposite order and—with the addition of Telemachus's name—using the same key words:

ὣς ἐφάμην, ἣ δ' αὐτίκ' ἀμείβετο πότνια μήτηρ·
καὶ λίην κείνη γε <u>μένει</u> τετληότι θυμῷ
σοῖσιν ἐνὶ μεγάροισιν· ὀϊζυραὶ δέ οἱ αἰεὶ
φθίνουσιν νύκτες τε καὶ ἤματα δάκρυ χεούσῃ.   (11.181-183)

σὸν δ' οὔ πώ τις ἔχει καλὸν <u>γέρας</u>, ἀλλὰ ἔκηλος
<u>Τηλέμαχος</u> τεμένεα νέμεται καὶ δαῖτας ἐΐσας
δαίνυται, ἃς ἐπέοικε δικασπόλον ἄνδρ' ἀλεγύνειν·
πάντες γὰρ καλέουσι. <u>πατὴρ</u> δὲ σὸς αὐτόθι μίμνει
ἀγρῷ οὐδὲ πόλινδε κατέρχεται . . .   (11.184-188)

οὕτω γὰρ καὶ ἐγὼν ὀλόμην καὶ πότμον ἐπέσπον·
οὔτ' ἐμέ γ' ἐν μεγάροισιν ἐΰσκοπος
<u>οἷς ἀγανοῖς βελέεσσιν ἐποιχομένη κατέπεφνεν</u>,
οὔτε τις οὖν μοι <u>νοῦσος</u> ἐπήλυθεν, ἥ τε μάλιστα
τηκεδόνι στυγερῇ μελέων ἐξείλετο θυμόν·
ἀλλά με σός τε πόθος σά τε μήδεα, φαίδιμ' Ὀδυσσεῦ,
σή τ' ἀγανοφροσύνη μελιηδέα θυμὸν ἀπηύρα.   (11.197-203)

Even within the answers, the order of elements is inverted:

Questions: (1)   How did his mother die?
                     (a)   disease?
                     (b)   archer?
              (2)   How are his father and son?
                     (a)   father
                     (b)   son
              (3)   Is his honor still intact?
              (4)   Does his wife still wait for him?

Answers:	(4)	His wife waits for him.
	(3)	His honor is intact.
	(2)	His father and son are still alive.
		(b) Telemachus (son)
		(a) father
	(1)	His mother died of longing for him.
		(b) not archer
		(a) not disease

Here Homer demonstrates great sophistication in his use of "the last thing first." The basic pattern no doubt originated in the mnemonic purpose of helping the singer keep in mind what he had said previously.[12] Homer, however, has taken the pattern and expanded it with considerable artistry. The fact that Homer's use of this pattern was known to Cicero and others suggests that it was a technique firmly established in later rhetorical practice.

B. Herodotus: The Master of "Ring-Composition"

Several studies have attempted to analyze the compositional techniques used by the historian Herodotus (c. 484-424 B.C.). John Myres argues for "pedimental composition" as the main structural feature of Herodotus's writing.[13] Henry Immerwahr agrees that Herodotus used pedimental (or circular) composition on a restricted scale.[14] He rejects it, however, as the main structural feature of the historian's work. Immerwahr proposes instead that "ring composition" was Herodotus's primary compositional technique.

Citing the earlier work of Müller, Pohlenz, and van Otterlo,[15] Immerwahr defines "ring-composition" as the approximate correspondence between the initial and final statements of a section.[16] Van Otterlo suggested two types of ring composition: "inclusive," in which the sentences that frame a section refer to the narrative they bracket, and "anaphoric," in which the sentences that frame a section resume the thread of the narrative interrupted by a digression.[17] According to

---

[12] Cf. Whitman, *Homer* 254.

[13] J. L. Myres, *Herodotus. Father of History* (Oxford: Clarendon, 1953) 81-91.

[14] Immerwahr, *Form and Thought* 71-72. He points to the stories of Arion and the Dolphin (1.23-24), Polycrates and Samos (3.39-60), and the sea skirmishes before the Battle of Artemisium (7.179-195) as examples. Even more convincing are the accounts of the Battle of Thermopylae (7.196-239) and Xerxes's decision to invade Greece (7.8-19).

[15] G. Müller, *De Aeschyli Supplicum temporum atque indole* (Halle, 1908); M. Pohlenz, *Herodot, der erste Geschichtsschreiber des Abendlandes* (Berlin: Teubner, 1937); and W. A. A. van Otterlo, *Untersuchungen über Begriff, Anwendung und Entstehung der Griechischen Ringkomposition* (Amsterdam: N.V. Noord-Hollandsche Uitgevers Maatschappij, 1944).

[16] Immerwahr, *Form and Thought* 55.

[17] Van Otterlo, *Ringkomposition* 7.

Immerwahr, this use of framing sentences derived ultimately from oral composition—in particular, oral transmission related to the epic.[18] Recently, Timothy Long has argued that Herodotus presented readings from his works at Athens and that the use of ring composition would have been appropriate for such oral presentations.[19]

Ring composition is, in fact, quite common in Herodotus's *Histories*. The material enclosed by the framing sentences may be as short as one section or as long as an entire book. An exhaustive catalog of the phenomenon in Herodotus is impossible, but a number of representative instances will be noted below.

One example of "inclusive" composition that frames a single section is found in the Samian stories. Following an extended discussion of the history of Samos, Herodotus comes to a description of its greatness (3.60). The section begins and ends with similar wording:

ἐμήκυνα δὲ περὶ Σαμίων μᾶλλον ὅτι . . .   (3.60.1)

τούτων εἴνεκεν μᾶλλόν τι περὶ Σαμίων ἐμήκυνα.   (3.60.4)

An example of "anaphoric" composition on a slightly larger scale occurs in Herodotus's account of Croesus's reign. Here he concludes a section (1.81) with the dispatch of messengers to announce that Croesus was besieged and to ask for help from the Spartans. The arrival of the messengers is described two sections later (1.83). The intervening section (1.82) describes the Spartans' feud with the Argives over Thyrea and is framed by statements using similar wording:

τούτους δὲ ἐξέπεμπε τὴν ταχίστην δέεσθαι βοηθέειν
ὡς πολιορκεομένου Κροίσου.   (1.81.1)

ἦκε ὁ Σαρδιηνὸς κῆρυξ δεόμενος Κροίσῳ βοηθέειν
πολιορκεομένῳ.   (1.83.1)

This technique of anaphoric composition is often used to frame descriptions of peoples or places that are mentioned in the course of a narrative. For example, it is

---

[18] Immerwahr, *Form and Thought* 12.

[19] Long: "In oral presentations such as we imagine Herodotus might have given, ring composition served to demark the major divisions of a section, almost . . . like spoken paragraph indentations . . . [Otterlo] saw that, without ring composition, the running style of early Greek prose would have struck the listener, or reader, as a disconnected succession of individual clauses lacking any natural conclusion. Instead, with ring composition the repeated words either tell the listener that the one section has ended or alert him that the author is returning to a point he has let drop . . . When a Greek listened to a story, he liked to know where he was going, and ring composition made clear what the destination was . . . the introductory statement tells us where we are heading and its repetition assures us we have arrived" (Long, *Repetition and Variation* 16).

used to describe the distant parts of the earth (3.106-116), the Scythians (4.1-83), the Hellespont (4.85-87), the river Tearus (4.89-91), and the Gatae people (4.93-97).

Anaphoric composition is even used to frame an entire book. At the beginning of Book 2 Herodotus introduces the subject of Cambyses's expedition against Egypt (2.1.1-2):

> τελευτήσαντος δὲ Κύρου παρέλαβε τὴν βασιληίην <u>Καμβύσης, Κύρου</u> ἐὼν παῖς καὶ Κασσανδάνης . . . '῾Ιωνας μὲν <u>καὶ Αἰολέας</u> ὡς δούλους παρτωίους ἐόντας ἐνόμιζε, ἐπὶ δὲ Αἴγυπτον ἐποιέετο <u>στρατηλασίην</u>, ἄλλους τε παραλαβὼν τῶν <u>ἦρχε</u> καὶ δὴ καὶ '<u>ελλήνων</u> τῶν ἐπεκράτεε.

He then embarks on a lengthy history of Egypt that concludes with his depiction of the reign of Amasis, the Egyptian king at the time when Cambyses assumed the throne. This history constitutes the contents of Book 2. Book 3, however, resumes the subject of Cambyses's expedition by repeating key phrases from the beginning of Book 2 (3.1.1):

> ἐπὶ τοῦτον δὴ τὸν '῾Αμασιν <u>Καμβύσης ὁ Κύρου ἐστρατεύετο</u>, ἄγων ἄλλους τε, τῶν <u>ἦρχε</u> καὶ '<u>ελλήνων</u> '῾Ιωνας τε καὶ Αἰολέας, δι' αἰτίην τοιήνδε . . .

One final example is the story of Arion and the dolphin. It is a particularly interesting example in that it uses both anaphoric *and* inclusive framing statements. The account of Alyates's war against the Milesians concludes with a statement about him (1.22.4). The next section introduces the story of Arion and the dolphin (1.23.1), a story which concludes with similar wording (1.24.8). Herodotus then resumes his main narrative by mentioning Alyates's death (1.25.1). The resulting framing statements may be represented as follows:

> κατὰ μὲν <u>τὸν πρὸς Μιλησίους</u> τε καὶ Θρασύβουλον <u>πόλεμον</u> '<u>Αλυάττη</u> ὧδε ἔσχε.

>> τῷ δὴ <u>λέγουσι Κορίνθιοι</u> ὁμολογέουσι δέ σφι <u>Λέσβιοι</u> ἐν τῷ βίῳ θῶμα <u>μέγιστον</u> παραστῆναι, '<u>Αρίονα</u> τὸν Μηθυμναῖον <u>ἐπὶ δελφῖνος</u> ἐξενειχθέντα <u>ἐπὶ Ταίναρον</u>.

>> ταῦτα μέν νυν <u>Κορίνθιοί</u> τε καὶ <u>Λέσβιοι</u> λέγουσι, καὶ '<u>Αρίονος</u> ἐστὶ ἀνάθημα χάλκεον οὐ <u>μέγα ἐπὶ Ταινάρῳ, ἐπὶ δελφῖνος</u> ἐπεὼν ἄνθρωπος.

> '<u>Αλυάττης</u> δὲ ὁ Λυδὸς <u>τὸν πρὸς Μιλησίους πόλεμον</u> διενείκας μετέπειτα τελευτᾷ, βασιλεύσας ἔτεα ἑπτὰ καὶ πεντήκοντα.

Here the inclusive statements about Arion frame the narrative to which they refer, while the final anaphoric statement about Alyates resumes the thread of the narrative that was interrupted by the digression. This method of composition enabled the listener to identify the extent of the digressive material *and* recall the point at which the main train of thought had been abandoned.

Another significant feature of Herodotus's *Histories* is the way in which he handles alternative courses of action.[20] Often when two alternatives are examined, the sequence in which they are discussed involves an inverted or partially inverted arrangement that is reminiscent of Homer's practice. The simplest arrangement follows an ABBA pattern as found in the discussion between Onesilus and his servant.[21] Upon learning that his opponent, Artybius, has a horse trained to fight, Onesilus gives his servant a choice of fighting against the horse (τὸν ἵππον) or against Artybius hmself (αὐτὸν Ἀρτύβιον). The servant's answer addresses the options in reverse order (5.111.4):[22]

> Βασιλέα μὲν <u>καὶ στρατηγὸν</u> χρεὸν εἶναί φημι βασιλέϊ τε καὶ στρατηγῷ προσφέρεσθαι . . .
>
> ἡμέας δὲ τοὺς ὑπηρέτας ἑτέροισί τε <u>ὑπηρέτῃσι</u> προσφέρεσθαι <u>καὶ πρὸς ἵππον</u> .

When Xerxes questions Artabanus about his enemies, Artabanus identifies two enemies (land and sea) and then discusses them in reverse order (7.49.1-3):

> τὰ δύο τοι τὰ λέγω πολλῷ ἔτι πολεμιώτερα γίνεται. τὰ δὲ δύο ταῦτα ἐστὶ <u>γῆ</u> τε καὶ <u>θάλασσα</u>.
>
> οὔτε γὰρ τῆς <u>θαλάσσης</u> ἔστι λιμὴν τοσοῦτος οὐδαμόθι, . . . ὅστις ἐγειρομένου χειμῶνος δεξάμενός σευ τοῦτο τὸ ναυτικὸν φερέγγυος ἔσται διασῶσαι τὰς νέας . . . καὶ δὴ τῶν δύο τοι τοῦ ἑτέρου εἰρημένου τὸ ἕτερον ἔρχομαι ἐρέων. <u>γῆ</u> δὴ πολεμίη τῆδέ τοι κατίσταται . . .

At times this simple pattern is extended to create more intricate arrangements. For example, when Cyrus seeks to instigate a rebellion against the Median king Astyages, the alternatives are discussed in ABABBA order. (1.126.3-4). The first day—on Astyages's orders—Cyrus requires the Persians to clear a thorny tract of 400 square furlongs. The second day—on his own initiative—Cyrus arranges a feast for them. After the feast he asks them whether they prefer the task of yesterday (τὰ τῇ προτεραίῃ) or their present state (τὰ παρεόντα). When the Persians reply that yesterday was evil (κακὰ) but today was good (ἀγαθά), Cyrus makes his case:

---

[20] Cf. M. L. Lang, *Herodotean Narrative and Discourse* (Cambridge, MA: Harvard University Press, 1984) 52-58.

[21] Cf. Lang, *Herodotean Narrative* 56. She also notes a similar discussion between the Cypriotes and the Ionians (5.109).

[22] The fact that in the immediately preceding context Onesilus has been described as βασιλεύς and Artybius has been described as στρατηγός makes the servant's answer clear.

βουλομένοισι μὲν ἐμέο πείθεσθαι ἔστι τάδε τε καὶ ἄλλα μυρία ἀγαθά, οὐδένα πόνον δουλοπρεπέα ἔχουσι· μὴ βουλομένοισι δὲ ἐμέο πείθεσθαι εἰσὶ ὑμῖν πόνοι τῷ χθιζῷ παραπλήσιοι ἀναρίθμητοι.

The verbal relationships in this example are more complex. In the Persians' response, evil (κακός) is associated with the past (πρότερος) and good (ἀγαθός) is associated with the present (πάρειμι). In Cyrus's speech, no toil (οὐδείς πόνος) is connected with the good, so toil (πόνος) is the natural alternative. The progression, however, is quite clear, with identical wording used to introduce the options and, thus, highlight the alternatives discussed.

The presentation of alternatives in Herodotus's writings serves multiple functions. It defines the issues at stake, but it also involves the listener/reader in the decision-making process.[23] Frequently, the first alternative stated is also the concluding element in the discussion so that the material is framed in the same way as it is in ring-composition. In fact, both the way in which Herodotus presents alternatives and his use of ring-composition seem to have been designed to assist and involve the listener. So both techniques may be classified as forms of oral patterning.

C. Plato: Transposition and Contrast

Plato (427-347 B.C.) also used the technique of discussing "the last thing first." Two examples from his epistles will serve to illustrate. The first instance occurs in his third epistle (315c):

ἐγὼ δὲ οὐδὲ ἀνθρώπῳ κλήσει,
μήτι δὴ θεῷ, παρακελευσαίμην ἂν δρᾶν τοῦτο,
θεῷ μὲν ὅτι παρὰ φύσιν προστάττοιμ᾽ ἄν . . .
ἀνθρώπῳ δὲ ὅτι τὰ πολλὰ βλάβην ἡδονὴ καὶ λύπη γεννᾷ

The second occurs in his eleventh epistle (358d):

ἐπέστειλα μέν σοι καὶ πρότερον ὅτι πολὺ διαφέρει πρὸς ἅπαντα ἃ λέγεις αὐτὸν ἀφικέσθαι σε ᾿Αθήναζε· ἐπειδὴ δὲ σὺ φῂς ἀδύνατον εἶναι, μετὰ τοῦτο ἦν δεύτερρον, εἰ δυνατὸν ἐμὲ ἀφικέσθαι ἢ Σωκράτη, ὥσπερ ἐπέστειλας.

νῦν δὲ Σωκράτης μέν ἐστι περὶ ἀσθένειαν τὴν τῆς στραγγουρίας, ἐμὲ δὲ ἀφικόμενον ἐνταῦθα ἄσχημον ἂν εἴη ˋμη διαπράξασθαι ἐφ᾽ ἅπερ σὺ παρακαλεῖς.

---

[23] Lang comments: "In all these speeches the use of alternatives backed by their potential for good and evil serves both to provide arguments for and against the two courses of action and to define the issues at stake so as to clarify the situation" (ibid. 161 n.8).

The more common compositional phenomenon in Plato, however, is the use of transposition at the sentence level. In some instances the same word or words are used to reinforce a point:[24]

ᾧ μηδεὶς <u>ἐναντία πραττέτω</u>·
<u>πράττει</u> δ᾿ <u>ἐναντία</u>, ὅστις θεοῖς ἀπεχθάνεται.   (*Symposium* 193b)

<u>θείῳ</u> δὴ καὶ <u>κοσμίῳ</u> ὅ γε φιλόσοφος ὁμιλῶν
<u>κόσμιός</u> τε καὶ <u>θεῖος</u> εἰς τὸ δυνατὸν ἀνθρώπῳ γίγνεται.   (*Republic* 500c)

More frequently, however, the contrast between opposite ideas is sharpened by the use of transposition:[25]

τῷ μὲν <u>δουλεύειν</u> καὶ <u>ἄρχεσθαι</u> ἡ φύσις προστάττει,
τῇ δὲ <u>ἄρχειν</u> καὶ <u>δεσπόζειν</u>   (*Phaedo* 80a)

ἵνα <u>αὐτὴ</u> <u>δικαιοσύνη</u>
πρὸς <u>ἀδικίαν</u> <u>αὐτὴν</u> κριθείη   (*Republic* 612c)

John Denniston documents numerous additional instances of transposition in Plato, noting that it was a favorite device of earlier Ionian philosophers as well.[26] It may be that speakers and writers who wanted their words to be remembered found this compositional device attractive because of the striking way in which it reinforces comparisons and sharpens contrasts. In any case, transposition appears to have been one important form of oral patterning that was prevalent in the Greek world.

D. Isocrates: The Profession of Rhetoric

As a professional orator, Isocrates (436-338 B.C.) drew on a broad range of oral patterns. In *Panegyricus*, for example, he uses transposition at the sentence level (4.95):[27]

---

[24] Additional examples occur in *Republic* 334a and 552c.

[25] Additional examples occur in *Phaedo* 114c, *Symposium* 185e, *Republic* 410d, and *Laws* 782d.

[26] J. D. Denniston, *Greek Prose Style* (Oxford: Clarendon, 1952) 75-77. Some of his examples are less clear than others. Earlier in his book he writes concerning the Ionian historians and philosophers: "Moreover, chiasmus, which is, generally speaking, much rarer in Greek than some people imagine, is here much favored . . . the alliterations, too, are sometimes arranged chiastically" (3, see also 74-75).

[27] "Transposition" will be used throughout this chapter to describe what some scholars call "chiasmus." Scholars employ differing criteria to describe chiasmus, however, and that term will not be used until it has been defined in the following chapter. In this chapter transposition will be used to refer to the reversal of repeated or contrasting terms in a sentence. See also the discussion of *commutatio* below.

ἀλλ᾽ ὥσπερ τῶν ἀνδρῶν τοῖς καλοῖς καγαθοῖς αἱρετώτερον ἐστιν
<u>καλῶς</u> <u>ἀποθανεῖν</u> ἢ <u>ζῆν</u> <u>αἰσχρῶς</u>, οὕτω καὶ τῶν πόλεων ταῖς
ὑπερεχούσαις λυσιτελεῖν ἐξ ἀνθρώπων ἀφανισθῆναι μᾶλλον ἢ
δούλαις ὀφθῆναι γενομέναις.

In the same work he inverts the order of topics he is addressing (4.67-68):

ἔστι γὰρ ἀρχικώτατα μὲν τῶν γενῶν καὶ μεγίστας δυναστείας ἔχοντα
<u>Σκύθαι</u> καὶ <u>Θρᾷκες</u> καὶ <u>Πέρσαι</u> . . .

ἐπιφανέστατος μὲν οὖν τῶν πολέμων ὁ <u>Περσικὸς</u> γέγονεν, οὐ μὴν ἐλάττω
τεκμήρια τὰ παλαιὰ τῶν ἔργων ἐστὶ τοῖς περὶ τῶν πατρίων
ἀμφισβητοῦσιν. ἔτι γὰρ ταπεινῆς οὔσης τῆς ᾽ελλάδος ἦλθον εἰς τὴν
χώραν ἡμῶν <u>Θρᾷκες</u> μὲν μετ᾽ εὐμόλπου τοῦ Ποσειδῶνος,
<u>Σκύθαι</u> δὲ μετ᾽ ᾽Αμαζόνων . . .

Elsewhere, Isocrates uses the conjuctions μὲν and δὲ as part of his inverted
structures. One example from *Antidosis* (15.180) discusses the body (σῶμα) and
the soul (ψυχή):

ὁμολογεῖται μὲν γὰρ τὴν φύσιν ἡμῶν ἔκ τε <u>τοῦ σώματος</u> συγκεῖσθαι καὶ
<u>τῆς ψυχῆς</u> . . .

<u>τῆς μὲν</u> γὰρ ἔργον εἶναι βουλεύσασθαι καὶ περὶ τῶν ἰδίων καὶ περὶ τῶν
κοινῶν, <u>τοῦ δὲ σώματος</u> ὑπηρετῆσαι τοῖς ὑπὸ τῆς ψυχῆς γνωσθεῖσιν.

That same oration, in fact, has a longer section on masters and pupils that uses μὲν
. . . δὲ to structure an ABBAAB pattern (15.188):[28]

εἶναι δὲ τούτων προσῆκον ἑκατέροις,
<u>τοῖς τε διδάσκουσι</u>
καὶ <u>τοῖς μανθάνουσιν</u>,
ἴδιον μὲν <u>τοῖς μὲν</u> εἰσενέγκασθαι τὴν φύσιν οἵαν δεῖ,
<u>τοῖς δὲ</u> δύνασθαι <u>παιδεῦσαι</u> τοὺς τοιούτους,
κοινὸν δ᾽ ἀμφοτέρων τὸ περὶ τὴν ἐμπειρίαν γυμνάσιον·
δεῖν γὰρ <u>τοὺς μὲν</u> ἐπιμελῶς ἐπιστατῆσαι τοῖς <u>παιδευομένοις</u>
<u>τοὺς δ᾽</u> ἐγκρατῶς ἐμμεῖναι τοῖς προσταττομένοις.

His relatively brief ethical dissertation *To Nicocles* contains a significant
concentration of oral patterning features. Three times he uses inversion:

<u>τὰς μὲν ἐργασίας</u> αὐτοῖς καθίστη κερδαλέας,
<u>τὰς δὲ πραγματείας</u> ἐπιζημίους,
ἵνα <u>τὰς μὲν</u> φεύγωσι,
πρὸς <u>δὲ τὰς</u> προθυμότερον ἔχωσιν.   (2.18)

---

[28] The basic order is: masters, pupils, pupils, masters, masters, pupils. Although the text
is prose, it has been laid out in parallel lines in order to make the structure clear.

ἀστεῖος εἶναι πειρῶ
καὶ σεμνός·
τὸ μὲν γὰρ τῇ τυραννίδι πρέπει,
τὸ δὲ πρὸς τὰς συνουσίας ἁρμόττει. (2.34)

ὅ τι ἂν ἀκριβῶσαι βουληθῇς ὧν ἐπίστασθαι προσήκει τοὺς
βασιλεῖς, ἐμπειρίᾳ μέτιθι καὶ φιλοσοφίᾳ·
τὸ μὲν γὰρ φιλοσοφεῖν τὰς ὁδούς δείξει,
τὸ δ' ἐπ' αὐτῶν τῶν ἔργων γυμνάζεσθαι δύνασθαί σε χρῆσθαι
τοῖς πράγμασι ποιήσει. (2.35)

Elsewhere in this same oration, his advice on the superiority of a good name (δόξαν καλὴν) over great riches (πλοῦτον μέγαν) uses μὲν . . . δὲ in a precise ABBAABBA pattern (2.32):

περὶ πλείονος ποιοῦ δόξαν καλὴν
ἢ πλοῦτον μέγαν τοῖς παισὶ καταλιπεῖν·
ὁ μὲν γὰρ θνητός,
ἡ δ' ἀθάνατος,
καὶ δόξῃ μὲν χρήματα κτητά,
δόξα δὲ χρημάτων οὐκ ὠνητή,
καὶ τὰ μὲν καὶ φαύλοις παραγίγνεται,
τὴν δ' οὐχ οἷόν τ' ἀλλ' ἢ τοὺς διενεγκόντας κτήσασθαι. (2.32)

Isocrates himself describes the writing of *To Nicocles* in this way (15.68): "I detach one part from another, and breaking up the discourse, as it were, into what we call general heads, I strive to express in a few words each bit of counsel which I have to offer." The compositional techniques itemized above reinforce the orator's stated purpose by making the "few words of counsel" both concise and memorable.

E. Demosthenes: The Practice of Rhetoric

Demosthenes (384-322 B.C.), who was born a half-century later than Isocrates, was perhaps the greatest Athenian orator and left numerous examples of the practice of rhetoric. There are several instances of transposition in his speeches:[29]

ἵν' ὥσπερ ἐκεῖνος ἕτοιμον ἔχει δύναμιν
τὴν ἀδικήσουσαν καὶ καταδουλωσομένην ἅπαντας τοὺς Ἕλληνας,
οὕτω τὴν σώσουσαν ὑμεῖς καὶ βοηθήσουσαν ἅπασιν
ἕτοιμον ἔχητε. (8.46)

αὐτὸς μεν πολεμεῖν ὑμῖν,
ὑφ' ὑμῶν δὲ μὴ πολεμεῖσθαι. (9.9)

---

[29] Other examples occur in 8.70, 18.48, and 18.158. Denniston notes three other instances (2.29; 7.22; 18.163), although they are somewhat less clear (*Style* 75-77).

There are also a few cases where Demosthenes inverts the order of the topics he is discussing. The clearest example of this is in *De Corona* (18.123):[30]

ἐγὼ <u>λοιδορίαν κατηγορίας</u> τούτῳ διαφέρειν ἡγοῦμαι,
τῷ τὴν <u>μὲν κατηγορίαν</u> ἀδικήματ᾽ ἔχειν, ὧν ἐν τοῖς νόμιος εἰσὶν αἱ
τιμωρίαι, τὴν <u>δὲ λοιδορίαν</u> βλασφημίας, ἃς κατὰ τὴν αὐτῶν φύσιν τοῖς
ἐχθροῖς περὶ ἀλλήλων συμβαίνει λέγειν.[31]   (18.123)

Earlier in the same speech, Demosthenes picks up the wording used immediately before an acknowledged digression (18.62) when resuming his main argument (18.66):[32]

ἐν τοιαύτῃ δὲ καταστάσει καὶ ἔτ᾽ ἀγνοίᾳ τοῦ συνισταμένου καὶ φυομένου
κακοῦ τῶν ἁπάντων ᾽ελλήνων ὄντων, δεῖ σκοπεῖν ὑμᾶς, ἄνδρες
᾽Αθηναῖοι, <u>τί προσῆκον</u> ἦν ἐλέσθαι πράττειν καὶ <u>ποιεῖν τὴν πόλιν</u>;

ἀλλ᾽ ἐκεῖσ᾽ ἐπανέρχομαι. <u>τί τὴν πόλιν</u>, Αἰσχίνη, <u>προσῆκε ποιεῖν</u> ἀρχὴν
καὶ τυραννίδα τῶν ᾽ελλήνων ὁρῶσαν ἑαυτῷ κατασκευαζόμενον
Φίλιππον;

These compositional techniques found in Demosthenes's orations correspond to the forms of oral patterning used by Homer, Herodotus, and Plato: inversion, framing sentences, and transposition. He also drew on a range of oral patterns in structuring his speeches, much as did Isocrates. It seems fair, therefore, to infer that these rhetorical features were common among early Greek speakers and writers, and furthermore, that they were part of the rhetorical inventory on which later Greek speakers and writers drew.[33]

F. Aristotle: The Theory of Rhetoric

Aristotle's *The "Art" of Rhetoric* is one of the first handbooks on Greek rhetoric. In it Aristotle (384-322 B.C.) devotes considerable space to the three species of rhetoric (i.e., forensic, deliberative, and epideictic), to invention, and to arrangement (the way in which an argument is constructed). His discussion of style focuses largely on the three levels of style (i.e., plain, middle, and grand), the use

---

[30] See also 9.61.

[31] "The difference between <u>railing</u> and <u>accusation</u> I take to be thus: <u>accusation</u> implies crimes punishable by law; <u>railing</u>, such abuse as quarrelsome people vent upon one another according to their disposition."

[32] See also 18.40-42. In that case, however, the correspondence of wording is less exact.

[33] This conclusion appears to be confirmed by the works of Epicurus (341-270 B.C.). The extant evidence is fragmentary and so will simply be itemized in this note: *Vatican Fragments* 4, 25, 37; *Letter to Herodotus* 45, 46, 52, 60, 72.

of figures, and the composition of individual sentences. There is very little in the
Rhetoric on oral patterning, simply because Aristotle's attention was focused
elsewhere. The compositional techniques that Aristotle used in setting out his
teaching, however, are instructive.

In discussing periodic style, Aristotle notes that clauses are either divided or
opposed. When clauses are opposed, one contrary idea is brought close to another,
or the same word is coupled with two contrary ideas. He uses the following as an
example (1410a):

> ἀμφοτέρους δ᾽ ὤνησαν, καὶ <u>τοὺς ὑπομείναντας</u> καὶ <u>τοὺς ἀκολουθήσαντας</u>·
> <u>τοῖς μὲν</u> γὰρ πλείω τῆς οἴκοι προσεκτήσαντο,
> <u>τοῖς δὲ</u> ἱκανὴν τὴν οἴκοι κατέλιπον.

A similar example occurs earlier in the *Rhetoric* (1362a):

> ἀκολουθεῖ δὲ διχῶς· ἢ γὰρ <u>ἅμα</u> ἢ <u>ὕστερον</u>,
> οἷον τῷ μὲν μανθάνειν τὸ ἐπίστασθαι <u>ὕστερον</u>,
> τῷ δὲ ὑγιαίνειν τὸ ζῆν <u>ἅμα</u>.

Aristotle comments that this kind of style is pleasing because "Contraries are easily
understood and even more so when placed side by side, because antithesis resembles
a syllogism" (1410a).

Another common device in the *Rhetoric* is the use of the same word or words
to begin and end the discussion of a specific topic. This pattern occurs in several
forms. In some cases a single word, repeated throughout the discussion, begins and
ends the section:

> <u>πλούτου</u> δὲ μέρη νομίσματος, πλῆθος <καὶ> γῆς χωρίων κτῆσις . . .

> . . . καὶ γὰρ ἡ ἐνέργειά ἐστι τῶν τοιούτων καὶ χρῆσις <u>πλοῦτος</u>.   (1361a)

> <u>εὐτυχία</u> δέ ἐστίν ὧν ἡ τύχη ἀγαθῶν αἰτία . . .

> . . . πάντα γὰρ τὰ τοιαῦτα <u>εὐτυχήματα</u> δοκεῖ εἶναι.   (1362a)

In other cases, two or more words are used. They may occur in the same order:

> <u>πολυφιλία</u> δὲ καὶ <u>χρηστοφιλία</u> οὐκ ἄδηλα τοῦ φίλου . . .

> . . . ᾧ δὴ πολλοὶ τοιοῦτοι, <u>πολύφιλος</u>, ᾧ δὲ καὶ ἐπιεικεῖς ἄνδρες,
> <u>χρηστόφιλος</u>.   (1361b)

Or they may be inverted:

> αἱ δὲ <u>βάσανοι</u> μαρτυρίαι τινές εἰσιν, ἔχειν δὲ δοκοῦσι τὸ <u>πιστόν</u> . . .

> . . . ὥστε οὐδέν ἐστι <u>πιστόν</u> ἐν <u>βασάνοις</u>.   (1376b)

This practice of bracketing a discussion is not limited to Aristotle's *Rhetoric*. It is also found, for example, in his treatise on *Politics*. In particular, it appears quite clearly in his discussion of the three aspects of government, viz. the deliberative (τὸ βουλευόμενον), the executive (ἡ ἀρχή), and the judicial (τὸ δικαστικὸν):[34]

κύριον δ᾽ ἐστὶ τὸ βουλευόμενον περὶ πολέμου καὶ εἰρήνης καὶ
συμμαχίας καὶ διαλύσεως . . . (1298a)

περὶ μὲν οὖν τοῦ βουλευομένου καὶ τοῦ κυρίου δὴ τῆς πολιτείας
τοῦτον διωρίσθω τὸν τρόπον. (1299a)

ἐχομένη δὲ τούτων ἐστὶν ἡ περὶ τὰς ἀρχὰς διαίρεσις . . . πόσαι τε
ἀρχαὶ καὶ κύριαι τίνων, καὶ περὶ χρόνου . . . (1299a)

οἱ μὲν οὖν τρόποι τῶν περὶ τὰς ἀρχὰς τοσοῦτοι τὸν ἀριθμόν εἰσι, καὶ
διῄρηνται κατὰ τὰς πολιτείας οὕτως. (1300b)

λοιπὸν δὲ τῶν τριῶν τὸ δικαστικὸν εἰπεῖν . . . (1300b)

ὅσους μὲν οὖν ἐνδέχεεται τρόπους εἶναι τὰ δικαστήρια εἴρηται. (1301a)

In one portion of Aristotle's *Politics*, his use of similar words to begin and end sections is reminiscent of Herodotus's use of ring-composition. That portion is his discussion of the destruction and preservation of various forms of governments, and the technique seems to have been considered admirably suited for helping listeners/readers follow the basic structure of a long and involved argument.

Aristotle begins by stating the questions to be answered in the course of the discussion: (1) What causes lead to revolutions and the destruction of governments? and (2) What safeguards lead to the preservation of governments? These questions contain many of the key words that are repeated at the beginnings and endings of individual sections (1301a):

ἐκ τίνων δὲ μεταβάλλουσιν αἱ πολιτεῖαι καὶ πόσων καὶ ποίων, καὶ τίνες
ἑκάστης πολιτείας φθοραί . . . ἔτι δὲ σωτηρίαι τίνες καὶ κοινῇ καὶ χωρὶς
ἑκάστης εἰσίν, ἔτι δὲ διὰ τίνων ἂν μάλιστα σῴζοιτο τῶν πολιτειῶν
ἑκάστη σκεπτέον ἐφεξῆς τοῖς εἰρημένοις.

The sections that follow discuss the sources and the causes of revolutions in democracies, oligarchies, and aristocracies. In every case except the last, the discussion is bracketed by sentences similar to the inclusive framing statements seen in Herodotus. The last section has no closing parallel. It does, however, end with a summary statement on the causes of revolutions and party factions.

δεῖ δὲ πρῶτον ὑπολαβεῖν τὴν ἀρχήν . . . (1301a)

---

[34] See also 1253b-1255b, 1264b-1266a, 1276b-1277b, and 1277b-1279a.

ἀρχαὶ μὲν οὖν ὡς εἰπεῖν αὗται καὶ πηγαὶ τῶν στάσεών εἰσιν ὅθεν
στασιάζουσιν . . .   (1301b)

ἐπεὶ δὲ σκοποῦμεν ἐκ τίνων αἵ τε στάσεις γίγνονται καὶ αἱ
μεταβολαὶ περὶ τὰς πολιτείας ληπτέον καθόλου πρῶτον τὰς
ἀρχὰς καὶ τὰς αἰτίας αὐτῶν.   (1302a)

γίγνονται μὲν οὖν αἱ στάσεις οὐ περὶ μικρῶν ἀλλ᾽ ἐκ μικρῶν,
στασιάζουσι δὲ περὶ μεγάλων.   (1303b)

ἁπλῶς μὲν οὖν περὶ πάσας τὰς πολιτείας ἐκ τῶν εἰρημένων
συμβέβηκε γίγνεσθαι τὰς μεταβολάς.   (1304b)

αἱ μὲν οὖν δημοκρατίαι μάλιστα μετάβαλλουσι διὰ τὴν τῶν
δημαγῶγων ἀσέλγειαν . . .   (1304b)

τῶν μὲν οὖν δημοκρατιῶν αἱ μεταβολαὶ, γίγνονται πᾶσαι σχεδὸν
διὰ ταύτης τὰς αἰτίας.   (1305a)

αἱ δ᾽ ὀλιγαρχίαι μεταβάλλουσι διὰ δύο μάλιστα τρόπους τοὺς
φανερωτάτους . . .   (1305a)

αἱ μὲν οὖν ὀλιγαρχίαι μεταβάλλουσι καὶ στασιάζουσι διὰ
τοιαύτας αἰτίας . . .   (1306b)

ἐν δὲ ταῖς ἀριστοκρατίαις γίγνονται αἱ στάσεις . . .   (1306b)

ὅθεν μὲν οὖν αἱ μεταβολαὶ γίγνονται τῶν πολιτειῶν καὶ αἱ
στάσεις, εἴρηται σχεδόν.   (1307b)

The next, shorter, group of sections discusses the stability of governments and the factors that safeguard monarchies and tyrannies (1307b-1315b). It also uses framing statements to mark off the various sections, but the statements are not as closely parallel as those noted above. As in the first group, the final section ends with a summary statement that closes the discussion.

So characteristic of Aristotle's composition was this rhetorical technique that the author of the pseudonymous work *Rhetoric to Alexander* adopted it as well, repeatedly beginning and ending his discussion of various topics with the same word or words. Three examples are offered without comment, since the parallels are quite clear. It is also interesting to note the stylized phraseology with which most of the topics are introduced and concluded.[35]

τὸ μὲν οὖν δίκαιον οἷον αὐτό ἐστιν πρότερον ἡμῖν δεδήλωται.   (1422a)
τὸ μὲν οὖν δίκαιον οὕτω μετιὼν πολλαχῶς λήψῃ.   (1422b)

---

[35] Additional examples occur in 1424b-1425a, 1427b, and 1429b-1430a.

τὸ δὲ νόμιμον αὐτὸ μὲν οἰόν ἐστιν ὥρισται ἡμῖν . . .   (1422b)
τὸ μὲν οὖν νόμιμον οὕτω μετιόντες πολλαχῶς δείξομεν.   (1422b)

τὸ δὲ συμφέρον αὐτὸ μὲν οἰόν ἐστιν τοῖς πρότερον ὥρισται . . .   (1422b)
συμφέρειν σφίσιν ᾠήθησαν περιποιῆσαι Λακεδαιμονίους.   (1423a)

Although Aristotle devotes little space to specific instruction on techniques of oral composition, he uses certain devices with skill and regularity. In particular, it appears that the practice of framing portions of a discourse with repeated words or phrases was a form of oral patterning well known to Aristotle and his contemporaries.

G. Roman Rhetoric: Cicero, Quintilian, and *Rhetoric ad Herennium*

Both Cicero (106-43 B.C.) and Quintilian (A.D. 35-95) produced major works on the theory of rhetoric, although, like Aristotle, their writings focused on either very broad or very narrow aspects of the subject. As its name suggests, Cicero's *De Inventione* is concerned with developing "invention" (the planning of the discourse and the arguments to be used in it). In *De Oratore* he notes that the repetition of individual words can produce an impression of force or of grace (9.1.33); in *Orator* he says that sentences can begin and end with the same word or phrase (9.1.38). Other than acknowledging Homer's fondness for inversion, however, there is little in Cicero's writings that is helpful for our purpose in establishing precedents for oral patterning in Paul's letters.

Quintilian's *Institutio Oratoria* has several statements that may have a bearing on oral patterning. One suggestion for improving a child's powers of speech was to make him tell his story from the end to the beginning or start in the middle and go backwards or forwards" (2.4.15). Stock observes that this practice "could not help but contribute to chiastic awareness."[36]

Quintilian stressed the importance of summary reminders to close one section of an extended argument before beginning another (4.2.50-51). Similarly, repetition and grouping of facts served to refresh the memory of the listener(s) and to enhance the cumulative effect of the argument (6.1.1). When an orator breaks away from his main argument in a digression, counsels Quintilian, "he should not be long in returning to the point from which he departed" (4.3.17). The "worst fault of all" was to treat the points in an order different from that assigned to them (4.5.28). On one occasion, however, Quintilian consciously reverses the order of topics that he has just announced (12.2.10a):

> And since philosophy falls into three divisions, physics, ethics, and dialectic, which,
> I ask you, of these departments is not closely connected with the task of the

---

[36] A. Stock, "Chiastic Awareness" 24.

orator? Let us reverse the order just given and deal with the third department which is entirely concerned with words.

He then proceeds to discuss dialectic (2.10b-14), followed by ethics (2.15-20a), and finally physics (2.20b-23a). The way in which this discussion is structured appears to be a conscious appropriation of the principle "the last thing first" used by Homer centuries before.

The anonymous *Rhetorica ad Herennium* is significant here primarily because it comes closest to defining the figure of transposition.[36] As part of a long list of rhetorical figures, the writer discusses "commutatio" or "reciprocal change." This figure is said to exist when two contrasting thoughts are expressed by transposition. Four examples are given (4.39):[37]

1. You must eat to live,
    not live to eat.

2. What can be told of that man is not being told;
    what is being told of him cannot be told.

3. A poem should be a picture that speaks;
    a picture should be a silent poem.

4. If you are a fool, for that reason, you should be silent;
    and yet, although you should be silent, you are not for that reason a fool.

The writer concludes with the statement, "One cannot deny that the effect is neat when in juxtaposing contrasted ideas the words are transposed."

Admittedly, examples of oral patterning are not frequent in these Roman works on rhetoric. There is some evidence, however, that the compositional patterns seen in Greek oratory and literature were operative in Roman rhetoric as well. Marrou has argued persuasively that the Romans adopted much of the Greek educational system by direct transfer.[38] It may be assumed, then, that although their textbooks on rhetorical theory did not highlight matters related to oral patterning, this feature of Greek rhetoric was embraced by Roman orators as well.

---

[36] Although this work is sometimes attributed to Cicero, most scholars think the real author unknown. For further discussion see the introduction to the Loeb Classical Library edition by H. Caplan (Cambridge: Harvard University Press, 1954).

[37] The Latin for each of the above examples is:
   1. Esse oportet ut uiuas, non uiuere ut edas.
   2. Quae de illo dicuntur duci non possunt, quae dici possunt non dicuntur.
   3. Poema loquens pictura, pictura taciturn poema debet esse.
   4. Si stultus es, ea re taces; non tamen si taces, ea re stultus es.

[38] Marrou, *History* 265.

H. Dio Chrysostom

Dio Chrysostom (c. A.D. 40-117), a Greek philosopher born at Prusa in Bithynia, traveled widely in Egypt and the northern areas of the Roman empire, finally settling in Rome. His discourses, like those of Isocrates and Demosthenes before him, reveal a wide range of compositional techniques, including several forms of oral patterning. In a number of places he uses transposition:[39]

φεύγειν δὲ ἀπὸ μὲν τῶν ἀνόπλων πρὸς τοὺς ὡπλισμένους,
ἀπὸ δὲ τῶν ὡπλισμένων πρὸς τοὺς ἀνόπλους.   (6.38)

τοιγαροῦν πολέμου μὲν ὄντος εἰρήνης ἐρῶσιν,
εἰρήνης δὲ γενομένης εὐθὺς μηχανῶνται πόλεμον.   (6.51)

Once he uses an argument constructed on the pattern ABABBABA (3.62):

ὁρᾷς γὰρ ὅτι πανταχοῦ τὸ βέλτιον τοῦ ἥττονος ἔταξεν ὁ θεὸς προνοεῖν
τε καὶ ἄρχειν,
οἷον τέχνην μὲν ἀτευχίας,
ἀσθενείας δὲ δύναμιν,
τοῦ δὲ ἀνοήτου τὸ φρόνιμον προνοεῖν καὶ προβουλεύειν ἐποίησεν.[40]

Furthermore, three times—after acknowledged digressions—he resumes his main argument with words or phrases reminiscent of those that began or preceded the digression. One example will suffice:[41]

ἐγὼ καὶ πρότερον μὲν ὑμᾶς ἠγάπων, ὦ ἄνδρες . . .   (50.1)

(Dio then digresses to discuss his concern for the common people. He
returns to his main topic where he departed from it.)

ὃ δὲ ἔφην, ὅτι καὶ πρότερον ὑμᾶς ἠγάπων . . .   (50.4)

Dio also quotes from other sources. In one of these quotations, that from Hesiod, an ABBAAB pattern appears (12.24):

ῥέα μὲν γὰρ βριάει, ῥέα δὲ βριάοντα χαλέπτει,
ῥεῖα δ᾽ ἀρίζηλον μινύθει καὶ ἄδηλον ἀέξει,
ῥεῖα δέ τ᾽ ἰθύνει σκολιὸν καὶ ἀγήνορα κάρφει.[42]

---

[39] See also 14.2 and 15.29.

[40] "For you see that God has everywhere appointed the superior (A) to care for and rule over the inferior (B); skill (A) for instance over unskillfulness (B); over weakness (B), strength (A); and for the foolish (B), he has made the wise (A) to have care and thought."

[41] The other two instances are 20.13-26 and 36.1-7.

[42] "For lightly this one he strengthens (A), and strength to that one denies (B),

It seems reasonable to infer from a study of Dio's discourses that (1) he used techniques of oral patterning, and (2) such techniques were rooted in earlier Greco-Roman speech and literature. Although Dio Chrysostom was neither a predecessor nor a contemporary of Paul, his works are significant for a study of oral patterning in Paul's letters because he was, at most, only one generation removed from the apostle.

I. The Papyri Letters

It is not surprising to find a few instances of oral patterning in the papyri letters. These letters are generally brief and deal with a single item of business. Nevertheless, a survey of several papyri collections indicates that these materials are not completely devoid of such phenomena. For instance, the Letter of Polemon to Harimouthes opens and closes the "letter-body" with the same wording (P.Hib. 1.41):

διεγγυησας αὐτον παραμονης δραχμων 'A . . .

. . . διεγγυησεις αὐτον των 'A δραχμων.

Similarly, the fragment "Oration against Demosthenes" includes an instance of transposition (P.Oxy. 858):

ἐστω δημηγορος και στρατηγος ὁ αὐτος,
και Δημοσθενης ἀσπιδα και ψηφισμα ἐχων ἀγορευ.[43]

J. The Cynics

Malherbe has edited a collection of writings that date from about 200 B.C. to A.D. 200 and preserve cynic traditions.[44] These letters are generally recognized as being pseudonymous. Most of them are brief, and several are cast in the form of dialogues. Nevertheless, instances of transposition, inclusion, and inversion may be found in them. For example, both Epistle 1 of Anacharsis and Epistle 25 of Crates use transposition in aphorisms:

'Αναχαρσις παρ' 'Αθηναιοις σολοικιζει,
'Αθηνιοι δε παρα Σκυθαις.

Lightly the haughty he abases (B), the lowly he magnifies (A),
Lightly he straightens the crooked (A), and the pride of the proud he withers (B)."

[43] "Let the same man be both orator and general, and let Demosthenes harangue with a shield in his hands as well as a decree."

[44] A. J. Malherbe, *The Cynic Epistles* (Missoula, MT: Scholars Press, 1977).

οὐ γεγονασιν <u>οἱ ἀνθρωποι</u> <u>των ἱππων</u> χαριν,
ἀλλ᾿ <u>οἱ ἱπποι</u> <u>των ἀνθρωπων</u>.

The brief Epistle 41 of Diogenes begins and ends with similar wording:

οὐ δοκει μοι πας το καθ᾿ ἡμας ἐν <u>ἀρετῃ δυνασθαι</u> . . .

. . . ταυτα οὐν ὁ κυων μονα <u>δυνησεται</u> ἃ κατ᾿ <u>ἀρετην</u> ἐνεργειται.

And two of the Epistles of Socrates and the Socratics use inversion in their discussion of topics:

το δε <u>μειζονα</u> ἢ <u>ἐλαττω</u> πραττειν οὐκ ἐπ᾿ αὐτῳ ἐστιν·
ἀλλα <u>του μεν</u> ἑτερα ἐχει την αἰτιαν <u>του δε</u> καθαπαξ αὐτος.   (Ep.Soc. 1)

ἰσθι δε, ὡς δυοιν τουτοιν παλιστα προσδειται πολεμος,
<u>κατεριας</u> τε και <u>ἀφιλοχρηματιας</u>·
δι᾿ <u>ἐκεινην</u> μεν γαρ τοις οἰκειοις φιλοι,
δια <u>καρτεριαν</u> δε φοβεροι τοις ἀντιπαλοις γιννομεθα.   (Ep.Soc. 5)

These examples, of course, are limited in number and scope. They suggest, however, that oral patterning was operative in Paul's day, even at the level of popular thinking and correpondence.

K. Summary

The preceding survey, covering a span of seven centuries, has examined representative works of selected figures in Greco-Roman rhetoric and literature. The object was to determine (1) what examples of "oral patterning" were present in those works, and (2) how the patterns were used. The results of this survey suggest that oral and compositional patterning was a common phenomenon in Greco-Roman culture.

Several types of patterning have been observed, ranging from those used in pithy maxims to those used in organizing discussions on a much larger scale: (1) Brief sentences are made memorable by the use of transposition. (2) Longer sentences invert the topics under discussion in order to deal with what is most readily remembered. (3) Inversion occurs in longer passages as well, listing a number of items and then addressing the items in reverse order. (4) The discussion of alternative courses of action occurs in inverted or partially-inverted order. (5) One or more words are used to mark the beginning and the end of a topic under discussion. (6) "Inclusive" framing sentences are used to mark out blocks of material of varying length. (7) "Anaphoric" framing sentences are used to resume a narrative or an argument that has been interrupted by a digression.

A number of these patterns can be identified in the works of various speakers or writers of antiquity. It may be concluded, therefore, that there were numerous precedents in Greco-Roman culture for Paul's use of oral patterning in his letters. The next task is to investigate the use of oral patterning in the OT.

Chapter 4

SAMPLES FROM THE SEPTUAGINT

Paul knew the OT; of that fact there can be no question. Earle Ellis notes that "the writings of the apostle Paul reveal a person immersed in the content and teaching of the OT."[1] For Paul, the OT writings were "the holy Scriptures" spoken through the prophets (Rom 1:2). They were a source of instruction (Rom 15:4; 1 Cor 10:11) and encouragement (Rom 15:4). They were, in fact, "the oracles of God" (Rom 3:2).

Paul's "immersion" in the OT is reflected in the fact that approximately one-third of the OT quotations in the NT appear in his letters.[2] The *Hauptbriefe* alone contain 88 OT quotations and 58 OT allusions.[3] Although they contain no quotations, Philippians and 1 Thessalonians contain 17 additional allusions.[4] Only Philemon lacks any OT reminiscences, a fact which is understandable given the nature of that letter. Paul's OT quotations are concentrated primarily in the Pentateuch (32), Isaiah (25) and the Psalms (18).[5] Within the Pentateuch, he draws most heavily on Genesis (12) and Deuteronomy (10).[6] His allusions reveal a similar pattern.[7]

Paul's OT was, without doubt, the LXX. In only one of his quotations does he appear to follow the MT against the LXX (1 Cor 3:19a). In contrast, he follows the LXX against the MT twenty-two times. Fifty-one of his quotations agree with

---

[1] E. E. Ellis, *Paul's Use of the Old Testament* (Grand Rapids: Eerdmans, 1957) 10.

[2] Ibid. 11, n. 4.

[3] These figures and those that follow are derived from Appendix I of Ellis's book (ibid. 150-154). Two of the quotations combine two OT references, as do seven of the allusions.

[4] Two of the allusions combine more than one OT reference.

[5] There are 15 quotations from other OT books.

[6] Five quotations come from Exodus, five from Leviticus, and none from Numbers.

[7] Pentateuch (25, distributed as follows: 9 Genesis, 5 in Exodus, 1 in Leviticus, 2 in Numbers, and 8 in Deuteronomy); Isaiah (18); Psalms (15); other books (26, including 4 from Wisdom of Solomon and 1 from Sirach).

the LXX verbatim or with only slight variation. Ellis notes that "even where the quotations vary from the LXX, parallel phraseology is often apparent."[8]

The above facts are suggestive for examining oral patterning in the OT as a background to Paul's letters. It will be necessary to work from the LXX, since that was the version of the OT that Paul used. Furthermore, the pattern of Paul's quotations and allusions suggests that Genesis, Deuteronomy, and Isaiah are a reasonable "database" from which to work. The purpose in this chapter, like that of the previous, is to be illustrative rather than exhaustive, and such a limitation will not be detrimental to this purpose.

Although Paul frequently quotes from the Psalms, two considerations weigh against their inclusion in this chapter. First, their poetic genre is quite different from the overall genre of Paul's letters. Paul does include poetic and/or hymnic passages in his letters (e.g., Phil 2:5-11),[9] and his style often betrays a fondness for Hebrew parallelism (e.g., Rom 10:9-10). In general, however, he writes discursive prose. It seems advisable, therefore, to work with OT writings that are closer to that genre than the Psalms are. Second, the rhetorical features of Hebrew poetry—especially chiasmus—have been studied extensively by others,[10] and it seems unnecessary to rehearse the results of those studies here. On the other hand, considerably less work has been done on the rhetorical features of the other writings selected. Genesis and Deuteronomy, in particular, have been somewhat neglected.

A. Genesis

The most widely recognized compositional device in Genesis is the use of the so-called "toledot" statements.[11] The first occurs in 2:4: αὕτη ἡ βίβλος γενέσεως. The phrase is repeated verbatim in 5:1 and in modified form (αὗται δὲ αἱ γενέσεις) in 6:9; 10:1; 11:10; 11:27; 25:12, 19; 36:1; 37:2. These statements are used repeatedly to begin new sections of the narrative. The account of Noah's life, for example, is clearly delimited by the toledot statements in 6:10 and 10:1. Similarly, the account of Abraham's life is framed by the statements naming his father, Terah (11:27), and his sons, Ishmael (25:12) and Isaac (25:19). The toledot statements,

---

[8] Ibid. 12.

[9] The question of whether Phil 2:5-11 is Pauline or pre-Pauline has generated considerable literature. The important point here is that the passage is generally agreed to be poetic/hymnic, although the precise reconstruction of the poetry/hymn is a topic of dispute.

[10] Cf., e.g., A. Ceresko, "The Chiastic Word Pattern in Hebrew," *CBQ* 38 (1976) 303-311; idem, "The Function of Chiasmus in Hebrew Poetry," *CBQ* 40 (1978) 1-10; N. W. Lund, "Chiasmus in the Psalms," *AJSL* 49 (1933) 281-312. See also the work done on orality in the Psalms (Chapter 1 above).

[11] So named because they have in common the Hebrew word תולדות.

then, fulfill a function similar to that of ring-composition in the Greco-Roman works previously surveyed.

As noted in Chapter 2, both formulaic language and repetition are characteristic of oral style. Gordon Wenham has noted six recurrent formulaic elements in 1:1-2:3:[12]

καὶ εἶπεν ὁ θεός + third person imperative	(1:3, 6, 9, 11, 14, 20, 24)
καὶ ἐγένετο οὕτως	(1:6, 9, 11, 15, 24, 30)
καὶ ἐποίησεν ὁ θεὸς . . .	(1:7, 16, 21, 25, 27)
καὶ εἶδεν ὁ θεὸς ὅτι καλόν . . .	(1:4, 8, 10, 12, 18, 21, 25, 31)
καὶ ἐκάλεσεν/εὐλόγησεν ὁ θεὸς . . .	(1:5, 8, 10, 22, 28; 2:3)
καὶ ἐγένετο ἑσπέρα καὶ ἐγένετο πρωί, ἡμέρα . . .	(1:5, 8, 13, 19, 23, 31)

Inclusion and ring-composition frequently delimit episodes or portions of episodes within the narrative.[13] The confusion of languages in 11:1-9 is one example:

καὶ ἦν πᾶσα ἡ γῆ χεῖλος ἕν, καὶ φωνὴ μία πᾶσιν.

διὰ τοῦτο ἐκλήθη τὸ ὄνομα αὐτῆς Σύγχυσις, ὅτι ἐκεῖ συνέχεεν κύριος τὰ χείλη πάσης τῆς γῆς, καὶ ἐκεῖθεν διέσπειρεν αὐτοὺς κύριος ὁ θεὸς ἐπὶ πρόσωπον πάσης τῆς γῆς.

Abraham's rescue of Lot is a second instance, one which uses proper names (14:13-24):

παραγενόμενος δὲ τῶν ἀνασωθέντων τις ἀπήγγειλεν ᾿Αβρὰμ τῷ περάτῃ· αὐτὸς δὲ κατῴκει πρὸς τῇ δρυὶ τῇ Μαμβρῇ ὁ ῾ Αμορις τοῦ ἀδελφοῦ ᾿εσχὼλ καὶ ἀδελφοῦ Αὐνάν, οἳ ἦσαν συνωμόται τοῦ ᾿Αβράμ.

πλὴν ὧν ἔφαγον οἱ νεανίσκοι καὶ τῆς μερίδος τῶν ἀνδρῶν τῶν συμπορευθέντων μετ᾿ ἐμοῦ, ᾿εσχὼλ, Αὐνάν, Μαμβρῇ, οὗτοι λήμψονται μερίδα.

The preceding examples both use inclusive ring-composition, but the episode of Judah and Tamar, inserted within the Joseph narrative, is framed by anaphoric ring-composition in 37:36 and 39:1:

οἱ δὲ Μαδιηναῖοι ἀπέδοντο τὸν ᾿Ιωσὴφ εἰς Αἴγυπτον τῷ Πετεφρῇ τῷ σπάδοντι Φαραώ, ἀρχιμαγείρῳ.

᾿Ιωσὴφ δὲ κατήχθη εἰς Αἴγυπτον, καὶ ἐκτήσατο αὐτὸν Πετεφρῆς ὁ εὐνοῦχος Φαραώ, ἀρχιμάγειρος, ἀνὴρ Αἰγύπτιος, ἐκ χειρὸς ᾿Ισμαηλιτῶν, οἳ κατήγαγον αὐτὸν ἐκεῖ.

---

[12] G. J. Wenham, *Genesis 1-15* (Waco: Word, 1987) 6.

[13] In addition to the examples noted in the text, see 21:22-32; 26:6-17; 35:1-7.

Within individual sections, a variety of phenomena occur. Inversion is present in 3:9-20 where the consequences of the Fall are invoked on the participants in an order that reverses the way in which the participants are initially named:[14]

καὶ ἐκάλεσεν κύριος ὁ θεὸς τὸν ᾿Αδὰμ καὶ εἶπεν αὐτῷ ᾿Αδάμ, ποῦ εἶ; . . .
καὶ εἶπεν ὁ ᾿Αδάμ ῾Η γυνή, ἣν ἔδωκας μετ᾿ ἐμοῦ . . . ἔδωκεν . . . καὶ ἔφαγον.
καὶ εἶπεν ἡ γυνή, ῾Ο ὄφις ἠπάτησέν με, καὶ ἔφαγον.

καὶ εἶπεν κύριος ὁ θεὸς τῷ ὄφει . . .
καὶ τῇ γυναικὶ εἶπεν . . .
τῷ δὲ ᾿Αδὰμ εἶπεν . . .

The early verses of the Cain and Abel story (4:1-5) follow the pattern ABBAABBA, beginning and ending with Cain, who is the focus of the account:[15]

᾿Αδὰμ δὲ ἔγνω εὔαν . . . καὶ συλλαβοῦσα ἔτεκεν τὸν Κάιν . . .
καὶ προσέθηκεν τεκεῖν τὸν ἀδελφὸν αὐτοῦ τὸν ῎Αβελ·
καὶ ἐγένετο ῎Αβελ ποιμὴν προβάτων,
Κάιν δὲ ἦν ἐργαζόμενος τὴν γῆν.
καὶ ἐγένετο μεθ᾿ ἡμέρας ἤνεγκεν Κάιν ἀπὸ τῶν καρπῶν τῆς γῆς . . .
καὶ ῎Αβελ ἤνεγκεν καὶ αὐτὸς ἀπὸ τῶν πρωτοτόκων τῶν προβάτων αὐτοῦ . . .
καὶ ἐπεῖδεν ὁ θεὸς ἐπὶ ῎Αβελ, καὶ ἐπὶ τοῖς δώροις αὐτοῦ,
ἐπὶ δὲ Κάιν καὶ ἐπὶ ταῖς θυσίαις αὐτοῦ οὐ προσέσχεν.

The number of days in the flood episode (7:1-8:14) follows an inverted pattern, beginning with seven days (7:4, 10) and moving through 40 days (7:17) to 150 days (7:24). Then, the sequence is reversed, beginning with 150 days (8:3) and moving through 40 days (8:6) to 7 days (8:10, 12).[16] This same account also has a number of smaller-scale items present in it. The description of the earth's corruption (6:11-13) is emphasized by the repetition of φθείρω and its cognate καταφθείρω (4x). Noah's obedience is emphasized by variations of the statement καὶ ἐποίησεν Νῶε πάντα, ὅσα ἐνετείλατο αὐτῷ κύριος ὁ θεὸς (6:22; 7:5, 9, 16). At the height of the flood (7:18-19) transposition highlights the fact that the waters prevailed over the earth:

καὶ ἐπεκράτει τὸ ὕδωρ καὶ ἐπληθύνετο σφόδρα ἐπὶ τῆς γῆς, καὶ ἐπεφέρετο ἡ κιβωτὸς ἐπάνω τοῦ ὕδατος.
τὸ δὲ ὕδωρ ἐπεκράτει σφόδρα σφοδρῶς ἐπὶ τῆς γῆς, καὶ ἐπεκάλυψεν πάντα τὰ ὄρη τὰ ὑψηλά, ἃ ἦν ὑποκάτω τοῦ οὐρανοῦ·

---

[14] Similarly in 10:1-21, Noah's sons are introduced in one order (Σήμ, Χάμ, ᾿Ιάφεθ) and discussed in the opposite order (᾿Ιάφεθ, Χάμ, Σήμ). The list of opponents in the battles of Gen 14:1-2 is inverted in 14:8-9.

[15] Note also the transposition of subject and verb in verses 3-4. A few verses later God's question to Cain also includes an instance of transposition (4:10-11).

[16] Cf., Wenham, *Genesis 1-15* 157.

The account of the establishment of the covenant between God and Abraham in 17:1-27 contains a number of features of interest. It is loosely framed by the mention of Abraham's age in 17:1 (ἐγένετο δὲ ᾿Αβρὰμ ἐτῶν ἐνενήκοντα ἐννέα) and 17:24 (᾿Αβραὰμ δὲ ἦν ἐνενήκοντα ἐννέα ἐτῶν). The key words διαθήκη (12x), περιτέμνω (9x), and ἀκροβυστία (5x) appear frequently in this chapter, but relatively infrequently elsewhere in the book.[17] The concluding paragraph (17:23-27) is framed by ring-composition which serves to emphasize the first act of circumcision:

καὶ ἔλαβεν ᾿Αβραὰμ ᾿Ισμαὴλ τὸν υἱὸν αὐτοῦ καὶ πάντας τοὺς οἰκογενεῖς αὐτοῦ καὶ πάντας τοὺς ἀργυρωνήτους καὶ πᾶν ἄρσεν τῶν ἀνδρῶν τῶν ἐν τῷ οἴκῳ ᾿Αβραάμ, καὶ περιέτεμεν τὰς ἀκροβυστίας αὐτῶν ἐν τῷ καιρῷ τῆς ἡμέρας ἐκείνης, καθὰ ἐλάλησεν αὐτῷ ὁ θεός.

ἐν τῷ καιρῷ τῆς ἡμέρας ἐκείνης περιετμήθη ᾿Αβραὰμ καὶ ᾿Ισμαὴλ ὁ υἱὸς αὐτοῦ· καὶ πάντες οἱ ἄνδρες τοῦ οἴκου αὐτοῦ καὶ οἱ οἰκογενεῖς καὶ οἱ ἀργυρώνητοι ἐξ ἀλλογενῶν ἐθνῶν, περιέτεμεν αὐτούς.

Elsewhere in the book oral patterns serve to highlight important divine declarations. For example, the summary of creation in 5:1b-2 is framed by ring-composition:

ἦ ἡμέρα ἐποίησεν ὁ θεὸς τὸν ᾿Αδάμ, κατ᾿ εἰκόνα θεοῦ ἐποίησεν αὐτόν· ἄρσεν καὶ θῆλυ ἐποίησεν αὐτοὺς καὶ εὐλόγησεν αὐτούς. καὶ ἐπωνόμασεν τὸ ὄνομα αὐτῶν ᾿Αδάμ, ἦ ἡμέρα ἐποίησεν αὐτούς.

The divine declaration of 9:6 uses transposition:

ὁ ἐκχέων αἷμα ἀνθρώπου ἀντὶ τοῦ αἵματος αὐτοῦ ἐκχυθήσεται, ὅτι ἐν εἰκόνι θεοῦ ἐποίησα τὸν ἄνθρωπον.

The call of Abraham in 12:1-3 includes a double inclusion using ἡ γῆ, is carefully structured using parallelism, and contains an instance of the transposition of verb and object that is often found in Hebrew poetry:

καὶ εἶπεν κύριος τῷ ᾿Αβράμ
᾿ εξελθε ἐκ τῆς γῆς σου
καὶ ἐκ τῆς συγγενείας σου
καὶ ἐκ τοῦ οἴκου τοῦ πατρός σου
εἰς τὴν γῆν, ἣν ἄν σοι δείξω.

καὶ ποιήσω σε εἰς ἔθνος μέγα
καὶ εὐλογήσω σε
καὶ μεγαλυνῶ τὸ ὄνομά σου,
καὶ ἔση εὐλογητός·

---

[17] The exception is chapter 9, which has seven occurrences of διαθήκη..

καὶ εὐλογήσω τοὺς εὐλογοῦντάς σε,
καὶ τοὺς καταρωμένους σε καταράσομαι·
καὶ ἐνευλογηθήσονται ἐν σοὶ πᾶσαι αἱ φυλαὶ τῆς γῆς.

God's promise to Abraham in 13:15-17 is framed by ring-composition and has at
its center a double instance of transposition:[18]

ὅτι πᾶσαν τὴν γῆν, ἣν σὺ ὁρᾷς, σοὶ δώσω αὐτὴν καὶ τῷ σπέρματί σου . . .
καὶ ποιήσω τὸ σπέρμα σου ὡς τὴν ἄμμον τῆς γῆς·
εἰ δύναταί τις ἐξαριθμῆσαι τὴν ἄμμον τῆς γῆς,
καὶ τὸ σπέρμα σου ἐξαριθμηθήσεται.
ἀναστὰς διόδευσον τὴν γῆν . . . ὅτι σοὶ δώσω αὐτήν.

The number and variety of oral compositional devices that are present in
Genesis undoubtedly reflect its origin in and transmission by the oral culture of early
Israel.

B. Deuteronomy

Since George E. Mendenhall's article on "Covenant Forms in Israelite Tradi-
tion,"[19] there has been a widespread acceptance that the overall structure of
Deuteronomy conforms, to a large degree, to the ancient Near Eastern vassal treaty.[20]
On this understanding of the book, its basic structure is:

Preamble		1:1-5
First Discourse: Historical Prologue		1:6-4:43
Second Discourse: The Law		4:44-26:19
Introduction	4:44-49	
Basic Commandments	5:1-11:32	
Specific Legislation	12:1-26:15	
Conclusion	26:16-19	
Third Discourse: Blessings and Curses		27:1-28:69

---

[18] The primary transposition is that of seed . . . dust . . . dust . . . seed. There is, however,
a secondary transposition of number . . . dust . . . seed . . . number.

[19] G. E. Mendenhall, "Covenant Forms in Israelite Tradition," *BA* 17 (1954) 50-76; see
also D. M. McCarthy, *Threat and Covenant: A Study of Form in the Ancient Oriental Documents
and in the Old Testament* (Rome: Pontifical Biblical Institute, 1963, 1978); idem., "Covenant in
the Old Testament: The Present State of Inquiry," *CBQ* 27 (1965) 217-240; idem., *The Old
Testament Covenant: A Survey of Current Opinions* (Oxford: Blackwell, 1972); M. G. Kline, *The
Treaty of the Great King. The Covenant Structure of Deuteronomy* (Grand Rapids: Eerdmans,
1963); D. R. Hillers, *Covenant: The History of a Biblical Idea* (Baltimore: Johns Hopkins, 1969).

[20] Agreement that Deuteronomy fits the vassal treaty form does not mean that scholars are
agreed on the date of the book. For a concise discussion, see P. C. Craigie, *The Book of
Deuteronomy* (Grand Rapids: Eerdmans, 1976) 24-29. The argument about the date of the book,
however, does not affect the understanding of its overall structure.

Fourth Discourse: Concluding Charge 29:1-30:20
Continuity of the Covenant 31:1-34:12

Since Deuteronomy consists of a series of discourses, it is not surprising to find a number of instances of oral patterning in it. Each of the major sections of the book, for example, opens and/or closes with a formulaic statement:

οὗτοι οἱ λόγοι, οὓς ἐλάλησεν Μωυσῆς παντὶ Ἰσραήλ ... (1:1)

οὗτος ὁ νόμος, ὃν παρέθετο Μωυσῆς ἐνώπιον υἱῶν Ἰσραήλ ... (4:44)

καὶ προσέταξεν Μωυσῆς καὶ ἡ γερουσία Ἰσραὴλ λέγων ... (27:1)

οὗτοι οἱ λόγοι τῆς διαθήκης, οὓς ἐνετείλατο κύριος Μωυσῇ
στῆσαι τοῖς υἱοῖς Ἰσραὴλ ἐν γῇ Μωάβ, πλὴν τῆς διαθήκης,
ἧς διέθετο αὐτοῖς ἐν Χωρήβ ... (29:1)

καὶ συνετέλεσεν Μωυσῆς λαλῶν πάντας τοὺς λόγους τούτους
πρὸς πάντας υἱοὺς Ἰσραήλ· καὶ εἶπεν πρὸς αὐτοὺς ... (31:1)

Ring-composition frames the preamble (1:1-5) that, in itself, may be seen as the first member of a frame around 1:1-29:1:

οὗτοι οἱ λόγοι, οὓς ἐλάλησεν Μωυσῆς παντὶ Ἰσραὴλ πέραν τοῦ
Ἰορδάνου ἐν τῇ ἐρήμῳ πρὸς δυσμαῖς πλησίον τῆς ἐρυθρᾶς ἀνὰ
μέσον Φαράν, Τόφολ καὶ Λοβὸν καὶ Αὐλῶν καὶ Καταχρύσεα. (1:1)

ἐν τῷ πέραν τοῦ Ἰορδάνου ἐν γῇ Μωὰβ ἤρξατο Μωυσῆς διασαφῆσαι
τὸν νόμον τοῦτον λέγων ... (1:5)

οὗτοι οἱ λόγοι τῆς διαθήκης, οὓς ἐνετείλατο κύριος Μωυσῇ στῆσαι
τοῖς υἱοῖς Ἰσραὴλ ἐν γῇ Μωάβ, πλὴν τῆς διαθήκης, ἧς διέθετο αὐτοῖς
ἐν Χωρήβ. (29:1)

Ring-composition occurs frequently within the major sections of Deuteronomy.[21] For example, the first portion of the second discourse is framed by 5:1 and 11:32:

καὶ ἐκάλεσεν Μωυσῆς πάντα Ἰσραὴλ καὶ εἶπεν πρὸς αὐτοὺς Ἄκουε,
Ἰσραήλ, τὰ δικαιώματα καὶ τὰ κρίματα, ὅσα ἐγὼ λαλῶ ἐν τοῖς ὠσὶν ὑμῶν
ἐν τῇ ἡμέρα ταύτῃ, καὶ μαθήσεσθε αὐτὰ καὶ φυλάξεσθε ποιεῖν αὐτά.

καὶ φυλάξεσθε τοῦ ποιεῖν πάντα τὰ προστάγματα ταῦτα καὶ τὰς κρίσεις
ταύτας, ὅσας ἐγὼ δίδωμι ἐνώπιον ὑμῶν σήμερον.

---

[21] In addition to the examples of ring-composition noted in the text, see 4:1-40; 8:1-18. As well, the blessings and curses of chapter 28 are introduced using similar wording (28:1-2, 15).

Similarly, the second portion of the same discourse is framed by 12:1 and 26:16:

> καὶ <u>ταῦτα τὰ προστάγματα καὶ αἱ κρίσεις</u>, ἃς <u>φυλάξεσθε ποιεῖν</u> ἐπὶ τῆς γῆς, ἧς κύριος ὁ θεὸς τῶν πατέρων ὑμῶν δίδωσιν ὑμῖν ἐν κλήρῳ, πάσας τὰς ἡμέρας, ἃς ὑμεῖς ζῆτε ἐπὶ τῆς γῆς.

> ἐν τῇ ἡμέρᾳ ταύτῃ κύριος ὁ θεός σου ἐντέλλεταί σοι ποιῆσαι πάντα <u>τὰ δικαιώματα ταῦτα καὶ τὰ κρίματα</u>, καὶ <u>φυλάξεσθε καὶ ποιήσετε</u> αὐτὰ ἐξ ὅλης τῆς καρδίας ὑμῶν καὶ ἐξ ὅλης τῆς ψυχῆς ὑμῶν.

Within the sub-sections of the book a variety of patterns occurs. Ring-composition brackets 5:12-15:

> <u>φύλαξαι τὴν ἡμέραν τῶν σαββάτων ἁγιάζειν αὐτήν</u> . . .

> . . . ὥστε <u>φυλάσσεσθαι τὴν ἡμέραν τῶν σαββάτων καὶ ἁγιάζειν αὐτήν</u>.

And inclusion frames 25:17-19:

> μνήσθητι ὅσα ἐποίησέν σοι ᾿<u>Αμαλὴκ</u> ἐν τῇ ὁδῷ ἐκπορευομένου   σου ἐξ Αἰγύπτου . . .

> . . . <u>ἐξαλείψεις τὸ ὄνομα</u> ᾿<u>Αμαλὴκ</u> ἐκ τῆς ὑπὸ τὸν οὐρανὸν καὶ οὐ μὴ ἐπιλάθῃ.

Although transposition is rare, two examples occur in chapter 32:

> <u>θεὸν τὸν γεννήσαντά σε ἐγκατέλιπες</u>
> καὶ <u>ἐπελάθου θεοῦ τοῦ τρέφοντός σε</u>.   (32:18)

> κἀγὼ <u>παραζηλώσω αὐτοὺς ἐπ᾿ οὐκ ἔθνει</u>,
> <u>ἐπ᾿ ἔθνει ἀσυνέτῳ παροργιῶ αὐτούς</u>.   (32:21)

Formulaic combinations of words is another oral feature of Deuteronomy. An introductory refrain using the name of Israel (ἄκουε, ᾿Ισραήλ), for example, is repeated four times within chapters 5-11 to introduce sub-sections (5:1; 6:3, 4; 9:1).[22] In chapters 19-26, the combination ἐὰν δὲ + subjunctive occurs twenty-four times as an introductory formula. Elsewhere throughout the book, the following (or similar) phrases occur repeatedly:

> πρόσεχε σεαυτῷ . . .

> . . . ἣν ὤμοσεν κύριος τοῖς πατράσιν σου

---

[22] A variant (καὶ νῦν, ᾿Ισραήλ) occurs in 10:12. The only other places in which "Hear, Israel . . ." is used are 20:3 and 27:1; the only other place in which "Now, Israel . . ." is used is 4:1.

καὶ ἐνετειλάμην ὑμῖν ἐν τῷ καιρῷ ἐκείνῳ λέγων . . .

. . . τὰ δικαιώματα αὐτοῦ καὶ τὰς ἐντολὰς αὐτοῦ

. . . ὅσας ἐγὼ ἐντέλλομαί σοι σήμερον

. . . ἐν τῇ γῇ εἰς ἣν ὑμεῖς εἰσπορεύεσθε ἐκεῖ κληρονομῆσαι αὐτήν

The range of oral patterns found in Deuteronomy is more limited than in Genesis. As in Genesis, ring-composition and inclusion play important roles. Somewhat more prominent in Deuteronomy is the use of formulaic statements to introduce sections of the discourses. Inverted patterns are not used, but formulaic language is. Instances of transposition are rare.

C. Isaiah

The book of Isaiah is generally accepted as consisting of two major sections: chapters 1-39 and chapters 40-66.[23] It is interesting to note that this analysis is supported by four references to the divine word that serve to bracket both sections:[24]

ἀκούσατε λόγον κυρίου . . .   (1:10)

ἄκουσον τὸν λόγον κυρίου σαβαωθ . . .   (39:5)

τὸ δὲ ῥῆμα τοῦ θεοῦ ἡμῶν μένει εἰς τὸν αἰῶνα.   (40:8)

ἀκούσατε τὸ ῥῆμα κυρίου . . .   (66:5)

Also interesting is the appearance of three relatively rare words in both chapter 1 and chapter 66, forming an inclusion around the entire book:[25]

| 1:13 | σεμίδαλις | 66:3 |
| 1:13 | σάββατον | 66:23 (twice) |

---

[23] For arguments against unity, see S. R. Driver, *Introduction to the Literature of the Old Testament*, 6th ed., (New York: Scribner's 1897) 236-243 (two Isaiahs); A. Weiser, *Introduction to the Old Testament*, trans. D. M. Barton (London: Darton, Longman & Todd, 1961) 197-208 (three Isaiahs). For arguments supporting unity, see G. L. Archer, *A Survey of Old Testament Introduction*, revised edition (Chicago: Moody, 1974) 339-359. Even scholars who maintain that Isaiah is a unity, however, acknowledge that the prose narrative of chapters 36-39 marks a transition between chapters 1-35 and 40-66.

[24] The only other place where ἀκούω appears in a similar combination with λόγος or ῥῆμα is 28:14.

[25] These are the only two occurrences of σεμίδαλις in Isaiah. σάββατον occurs a total of six times (1:13; 56:2; 58:13 [twice]; 66:23 [twice]). κῆπος occurs a total of five times (1:29; 58:11; 61:11; 65:3; 66:17).

1:29   κῆπος   66:17

Chapters 40-66 have been divided in a number of ways, perhaps the most common being 40-55 (Deutero-Isaiah) and 56-66 (Trito-Isaiah). Leon Liebreich has suggested an alternate division into 40-49 (based on the frequent occurrence of ברא and יצר) and 50-66 (based on the frequent occurrence of עבד), with the latter section being sub-divided into 50-55 and 56-66.[26] Perhaps the best understanding, however, takes into account the twice-repeated refrain that closes chapters 48 and 57 and suggests a grouping of 40-48, 49-57, and 58-66: οὐκ ἔστι χαίρειν τοῖς ἀσεβέσι, λέγει κύριος (48:22; 57:21).[27]

By far the most common compositional device used in Isaiah is inclusion. Liebreich has compiled an exhaustive list of instances of inclusion (what he calls the "envelope figure").[28] His list is based on the MT, and some of his examples are clearer than others. It is unnecessary to reproduce his entire list here, but several of the clearest examples will be noted.[29]

The title "faithful city of Zion" and the word "righteousness" bracket 1:21-26:

πῶς ἐγένετο πόρνη πόλις πιστὴ Σιων πλήρης κρίσεως, ἐν ᾗ δικαιοσύνη ἐκοιμήθη ἐν αὐτῇ, νῦν δὲ φονευταί.

καὶ ἐπιστήσω τοὺς κριτάς σου ὡς τὸ πρότερον καὶ τοὺς συμβούλους σου ὡς τὸ ἀπ᾿ ἀρχῆς· καὶ μετὰ ταῦτα κληθήσῃ Πόλις δικαιοσύνης, μητρόπολις πιστὴ Σιων·

In the same way the title "root of Jesse" and the word "rest" frame 11:1-10:

καὶ ἐξελεύσεται ῥάβδος ἐκ τῆς ῥίζης Ιεσσαι, καὶ ἄνθος ἐκ τῆς ῥίζης ἀναβήσεται. καὶ ἀναπαύσεται ἐπ᾿ αὐτὸν πνεῦμα τοῦ θεοῦ.

καὶ ἔσται ἐν τῇ ἡμέρᾳ ἐκείνῃ ἡ ῥίζα τοῦ Ιεσσαι καὶ ὁ ἀνιστάμενος ἄρχειν ἐθνῶν, ἐπ᾿ αὐτῷ ἔθνη ἐλπιοῦσι, καὶ ἔσται ἡ ἀνάπαυσις αὐτοῦ τιμή.

Although the name "Jacob" is common in chapters 1-48 (33x), it is rare in chapters 49-66 (8x). Two occurrences frame chapter 58:[30]

---

[26] L. J. Liebreich, "The Compilation of the Book of Isaiah," *JQR* 46 (1956) 259-277. In support of his suggestion, Liebreich has identified a number of connecting links between the first and last chapters of each grouping (Liebreich, "The Compilation of the Book of Isaiah" *JQR* 47 [1956] 114-127).

[27] Cf., e.g., J. D. W. Watts, *Isaiah 34-66* (Waco: Word, 1987) 71-72.

[28] Liebreich, "Compilation" 129-138.

[29] See also 14:29-31; 22:1-5; 23:1-14; 35:1-10; 40:1-11; 63:13-64:12; 65:1-10.

[30] The other occurrences in chapters 49-66 are: 49:5, 6, 26; 59:20; 60:16; 65:9.

ἀναβόησον ἐν ἰσχύι καὶ μὴ φείσῃ, ὡς σάλπιγγα ὕψωσον τὴν φωνήν σου καὶ ἀνάγγειλον τῷ λαῷ μου τὰ ἁμαρτήματα αὐτῶν καὶ τῷ οἴκῳ Ιακωβ τὰς ἀνομίας αὐτῶν.

καὶ ἔσῃ πεποιθὼς ἐπὶ κύριον, καὶ ἀναβιβάσει σε ἐπὶ τὰ ἀγαθὰ τῆς γῆς καὶ ψωμιεῖ σε τὴν κληρονομίαν Ιακωβ τοῦ πατρός σου· τὸ γὰρ στόμα κυρίου ἐλάλησε ταῦτα.

Similarly, although words built on the σωζ- root are rare in chapters 58-66, two of them frame 59:1-11:[31]

μὴ οὐκ ἰσχύει ἡ χεὶρ κυρίου τοῦ σῶσαι; ἢ ἐβάρυνε τὸ οὖς αὐτοῦ τοῦ μὴ εἰσακοῦσαι;

ὡς ἄρκος καὶ ὡς περιστερὰ ἅμα πορεύσονται· ἀνεμείναμεν κρίσιν, καὶ οὐκ ἔστι σωτηρία μακρὰν ἀφέστηκεν ἀφ᾽ ἡμῶν.

Another compositional device commonly encountered in Isaiah is that of repeating key words in certain paragraphs. The Song of the Vineyard (5:1-7) is a good example. More than one-half of Isaiah's uses of ἀμπελών (8 of 14) occur in this paragraph. The only two uses of σταφυλή occur here, and two of the three uses of φραγμός in Isaiah are in 5:1-7.

Naturally enough, nine of ten uses of Μωάβ and eight of nine uses of Μωαβεῖτις occur in the oracle directed against Moab (15:1-16:14). In the same way, Isaiah's vision against Egypt (19:1-20:6) contains three-fourths of the uses of Αἰγύπτιος (17 of 20) and Αἴγυπτος (14 of 22).

The announced content of the preceding examples is good reason to expect the repetitions noted. There are other instances, however, where cognate words cluster together in a similar manner. In 24:1-6, cognates of φθείρω (4x) and οἰκέω (6x) are prominent. In 48:1-16, ὄνομα (6x) and cognates of ἀκούω (9x) appear repeatedly—as do, to a lesser extent, καλέω (4x) and cognates of ἀναγγέλλω (3x). Interestingly, ὄνομα and ἀκούω occur only once each in the chapters on either side of Isaiah 48. καλέω and ἀναγγέλλω are equally rare in the immediate context.

On a smaller scale, δικ- words appears four times in 51:1-8, but only once (50:8) in the more immediate context. In 65:18-19 ἀγαλλίαμα/ἀγαλλιάω occurs three times, εὐφροσύνη/εὐφραίνω occurs three times, and Ιερουσαλημ occurs twice. There are other examples of the repetition of key words in Isaiah,[32] but those noted above are sufficient for illustrative purposes.

One passage that combines both the use of inclusion and the repetition of key words is 60:1-22. It is framed in verses 1 and 19 by the verb φωτίζω:

---

[31] The verb σώζω also appears in 60:16; 63:9; 66:19. The noun σωτηρία appears in 63:1, 8. The noun σωτήρ appears only in 62:11.

[32] E.g., in 14:9-19; 14:24-27; 19:16-24; 30:2-7; 42:18-24; 45:11-14; 66:7-9.

φωτίζου φωτίζου, Ιερουσαλημ, ἥκει γάρ σου τὸ φῶς, καὶ ἡ δόξα κυρίου
ἐπὶ σὲ ἀνατέταλκεν.

καὶ οὐκ ἔσται σοι ὁ ἥλιος εἰς φῶς ἡμέρας, οὐδὲ ἀνατολὴ σελήνης φωτιεῖ
σοι τὴν νύκτα, ἀλλ᾿ ἔσται σοι κύριος φῶς αἰώνιον καὶ ὁ θεὸς δόξα σου.

Also present in these verses are φῶς and δόξα. These two words are used repeatedly
throughout the passage, both occurring five times.[33] In addition, the cognate verb
δοξάζω occurs twice,[34] and the verb συνάγω occurs three times.[35]

On a smaller scale, one of the verses cited most frequently as an example of
chiasmus is Isa 6:10, in which the heart-ears-eyes order in the first half of the verse
is inverted in the second half:[36]

ἐπαχύνθη γὰρ ἡ καρδία τοῦ λαοῦ τούτου,
καὶ τοῖς ὠσὶν αὐτῶν βαρέως ἤκουσαν
καὶ τοὺς ὀφθαλμοὺς αὐτῶν ἐκάμμυσαν,
μήποτε ἴδωσι τοῖς ὀφθαλμοῖς
καὶ τοῖς ὠσὶν ἀκούσωσι
καὶ τῇ καρδίᾳ συνῶσι καὶ ἐπιστρέψωσι
καὶ ἰάσομαι αὐτούς.

A comparable example of inversion is seen in the order of Zion and Jerusalem in
52:1-2:

ἐξεγείρου ἐξεγείρου, Σιων,
ἔνδυσαι τὴν ἰσχύν σου, Σιων,
καὶ ἔνδυσαι τὴν δόξαν σου, Ιερουσαλημ πόλις ἡ ἁγία·
οὐκέτι προστεθήσεται διελθεῖν διὰ σοῦ ἀπερίτμητος καὶ ἀκάθαρτος.
ἐκτίναξαι τὸν χοῦν καὶ ἀνάστηθι
κάθισον, Ιερουσαλημ·
ἔκδυσαι τὸν δεσμὸν τοῦ τραχήλου σου, ἡ αἰχμάλωτος θυγάτηρ Σιων.

Transposition of two items at the sentence level, however, is more frequent.
In 5:20, for example, it occurs four times:

οὐαὶ οἱ λέγοντες τὸ πονηρὸν καλὸν καὶ τὸ καλὸν πονηρόν,
οἱ τιθέντες τὸ σκότος φῶς καὶ τὸ φῶς σκότος,
οἱ τιθέντες τὸ πικρὸν γλυκὺ καὶ τὸ γλυκὺ πικρόν.
οὐαὶ οἱ συνετοὶ ἐν ἑαυτοῖς καὶ ἐνώπιον ἑαυτῶν ἐπιστήμονες.

---

[33] φῶς in 60:1, 3, 19 (twice), 20. δόξα in 60:1, 2, 13, 19, 21.

[34] 60:7, 13

[35] 60:4, 7, 22

[36] E.g., M. Dahood, "Chiasmus," in *IDBSup* (Abingdon: Nashville, 1976) 145.

At times, the transposition is that of subject and verb:[37]

ὁ λαὸς ὁ πορευόμενος ἐν σκότει, ἴδετε φῶς μέγα·
οἱ κατοικοῦντες ἐν χώρᾳ καὶ σκιᾷ θανάτου, φῶς λάμψει ἐφ' ὑμᾶς.   (9:2)

At other times the verb and its object are transposed:[38]

ἀνελεῖ δὲ λιμῷ τὸ σπέρμα σου
καὶ τὸ κατάλειμμά σου ἀνελεῖ.   (14:30)

Or the transposition may involve larger portions of the sentence:[39]

καὶ ἐξελεύσεται ῥάβδος ἐκ τῆς ῥίζης Ιεσσαι,
καὶ ἄνθος ἐκ τῆς ῥίζης ἀναβήσεται.   (11:1)

Other examples of transposition that use word-pairs might be cited (e.g., 60:20), as might those that use synonyms (e.g., 60:2). It is clear, however, that the variations of this pattern in Isaiah are comparable to those found elsewhere in the Hebrew Scriptures, especially in the poetic books.

D. Summary

Genesis, Deuteronomy, and Isaiah are three of the books on which Paul drew most heavily for his OT quotations and allusions. The preceding survey has tested for examples of "oral patterning" in these important books. The results of this survey suggest that oral and compositional patterning was common in the OT, as it was in Greco-Roman rhetoric and literature.

Most of the patterns observed in the Greco-Roman works surveyed in the preceding chapter were seen also in the OT. Transposition makes brief sentences memorable. The order in which topics are introduced and then discussed is, at times, inverted. One or more words often frame the beginning and end of passages of various lengths. One new pattern that appears in the OT, however, is the tendency of key words to cluster together in certain passages, thereby emphasizing the topic under discussion. Furthermore, the use of formulaic language seems to be somewhat more common in the OT than in the Greco-Roman works surveyed.[40]

It may be concluded, therefore, that there were numerous precedents in both Greco-Roman and Jewish culture for Paul's use of oral patterning in his letters, thus justifying the study of the phenomenon. Before actually beginning a study of oral

---

[37] See also 27:11.

[38] See also 29:14; 32:6; 42:15-16.

[39] See also 29:17; 40:14; 43:20; 44:21; 55:8.

[40] This observation must be tempered by the fact that no Greek epic poetry was surveyed. As earlier studies on Homer and Hesiod have shown, this type of literature is heavily formulaic.

patterning in Paul's letters, however, it is necessary first to group the Greco-Roman and OT data surveyed into their respective categories, then to develop working definitions for each category, and finally to establish basic criteria for identifying the phenomena in each category. These tasks will be undertaken in the next chapter.

Chapter 5

CATEGORIES AND CONTROLS

Definition of terms is necessary in any scholarly undertaking, and precise definitions are particularly important for the present study. "Chiasmus," for example, has been used in biblical studies to describe everything from the organization of single sentences to the structure of entire books[1]—and, to add to the confusion, such terms as "introverted parallelism,"[2] "inverted parallelism,"[3] "envelope structure,"[4] "concentric symmetry,"[5] "concentric structure,"[6] "circular construction,"[7] and "pedimental symmetry"[8] have been applied to the same phenomenon. In the specific instance of chiasmus, the extent of the structure may well prove useful as a means of defining the phenomenon, since it seems somewhat incongruous to use the same term to describe both the structure of a single sentence and a structure that encompasses several paragraphs.

Equally challenging is the process of establishing some sort of controls to apply to material being considered in such a study. Again, the example of chiasmus will serve to highlight this need, for the absence of clear criteria for detecting "extended chiasmus" in the NT has led to proposals that are judged to be either

---

[1] For an extensive catalog of proposed chiastic constructions of all sizes, see A. di Marco, "Der Chiasmus in der Bibel," *Linguistica Biblica* 36 (1975) 21-97; 37 (1976) 49-68; 39 (1976) 37-85; 44 (1979) 3-70.

[2] J. Jebb, *Sacred Literature* (London: Cadell & Davies, 1820) 53; J. Forbes, *Symmetrical Structure* (Edinburgh: T & T Clark, 1854) 35.

[3] J. Breck, "Biblical Chiasmus: Exploring Structure for Meaning," *BTB* 17 (1987) 71.

[4] R. G. Moulton, *The Literary Study of the Bible* (Boston: Heath, 1889) 56.

[5] P. Rolland, "La structure littéraire de la Deuxième Epître aux Corinthiens," *Bib* 71 (1990) 73.

[6] N. Lohfink, "Darstellungskunst und Theologie in Dtn 1,6-3,29," *Bib* 41 (1960) 122.

[7] H. Immerwahr, *Form and Thought in Herodotus* (Cleveland, OH: Western Reserve University Press, 1966) 72.

[8] J. Myres, *Who were the Greeks?* (Berkeley, CA: University of California Press, 1930) 523.

"highly likely" on one end of the spectrum or "painfully forced and hopelessly elaborate" on the other.[9] Here a consideration of verbal/acoustic correspondences may prove helpful.

This chapter, therefore, is an attempt to establish a degree of order for further study by systematizing the material surveyed in Chapters 3 and 4.[10] The primary tasks will be (1) to categorize the evidence gathered, (2) to develop working definitions for various devices used in oral composition, and (3) to identify key criteria for the phenomena in each category. These categories and criteria will then later be used as the starting points for cataloging instances of oral patterning in Paul's letters.

A. Chiasmus

The term "chiasmus" first appeared in Hermogenes's writings to refer to reversed clauses in a sentence.[11] Although there were a few scholars who addressed the issue of chiasmus before the twentieth century,[12] it was not until Nils Lund's work in the 1930s and 1940s that this compositional technique became widely recognized.[13] Lund not only inaugurated scholarly interest in chiasmus, he also broadened the scope of the term by applying it to the correspondence of multiple elements in longer passages.[14] Since Lund, the identification of chiastic structures has become commonplace in any literary study of the NT.[15]

---

[9] C. L. Blomberg, "The Structure of 2 Corinthians 1-7," *CTR* 4 (1989) 8.

[10] Numerous instances of each type of structure could be cited from the material set out in Chapters 3 and 4. To avoid needless duplication, however, in this chapter only the references will be cited.

[11] *On Invention* 4.3. The noun form (χιασμός) occurs only once, but the verb form (χιάζω) occurs repeatedly.

[12] For the history of the study of chiasm, see R. E. Man, "Chiasm in the New Testament," Th.M. Thesis, Dallas Theological Seminary, 1982.

[13] N. W. Lund, "The Presence of Chiasmus in the New Testament," *JR* 10 (1930) 74-93; "The Presence of Chiasmus in the Old Testament," *AJSLL* 46 (1930) 104-126; "The Influence of Chaismus upon the Literary Structure of the Gospels," *ATR* 13 (1931) 27-48; "The Influence of Chaismus upon the Structure of the Gospel according to Matthew," *ATR* 13 (1931) 405-433; "The Literary Structure of Paul's Hymn to Love," *JBL* 50 (1931) 266-276; "Chiasmus in the Psalms," *AJSLL* 49 (1933) 281-312; *Chiasmus in the New Testament* (1942); "The Significance of Chiasmus for Interpretation," *Crozer Quarterly* 20 (1943) 105-123.

[14] Lund notes that "chiasmus as a principle of literary construction is applied far more extensively than the ordinary four-lined specimens would lead us to believe" (*Chiasmus* 35). For instance, he applies it to the entirety of 1 Cor 11:34-14:40 (ibid. 163-171).

[15] I. H. Thomson's book, *Chiasmus in the Pauline Letters*, JSNTSup 111 (Sheffield: Academic Press, 1995) is the latest work to follow the path that Lund blazed. Unfortunately, it was published too late to be discussed at length in this study. Although Thomson shares with the

Chiasmus has been defined in a variety of ways. The basic concept, however, is that of a symmetrical structure involving an inverted order of corresponding elements.[16] A simple example at the sentence level is found in *Rhetorica ad Herennium* 4.39 under the definition of *commutatio*: "You must eat to live, not live to eat." When the two halves of this maxim are placed in parallel to each other and lines are drawn connecting the corresponding words, the lines form a shape resembling the Greek letter χ (chi) from which the figure derives its name:

<u>Esse</u> oportet ut <u>vivas</u>   a   b

or   ×

non <u>vivere</u> ut <u>edas</u>.   b   a

Chiasmus serves to make ideas memorable. In so doing, it may perform any of three functions: (1) emphasis, (2) comparison, or (3) contrast. An author can emphasize a point by using the same words in both lines (Plato, *Symposium* 193b; *Republic* 500c; Gen 7:18-19; 9:6; 13:16; Isa 11:1) or by using synonyms (P.Oxy 858; Deut 32:21; Isa 27:11; 29:14). Comparison of complementary ideas can be made by using different words (Demosthenes, 8.70; Plato, *Republic* 334a; Isa 55:8). Chiasmus can also sharpen the contrast between opposite ideas by using the same words (Plato, *Phaedo* 80a; Dio 15.29; Isa 5:20; 22:22) or by using antonyms (Isocrates 4.95; Epicurus, Frg 25; Gen 12:3).

One final example—not previously cited—from Herodotus's *Histories* will serve to highlight the way in which chiasmus functions to make sayings memorable. Xerxes, hearing the report of Artemisia's exploits during the otherwise disastrous Battle of Salamis (8.88.3), is reported to have exclaimed:

οἱ μὲν <u>ἄνδρες</u> γεγόνασί μοι <u>γυναῖκες</u>,
αἱ δὲ <u>γυναῖκες</u> <u>ἄνδρες</u>.

---

present writer a concern for tighter controls and a more carefully-refined method of analysis, his book and the present study differ in three significant ways: (1) As regards scope, Thomson focuses on a single compositional device ("extended chiasmus") of a specific length (8-23 verses), while the present study investigates eight different patterns of varying lengths. (2) As regards extent, Thomson examines only five passages (one in Romans, one in Galatians, two in Ephesians, and one in Colossians), while the present study seeks to compile a more nearly comprehensive collection of patterns. (3) As regards results, Thomson's limited database means that he can draw no generalized conclusions regarding Paul's tendencies and habits. The present study, because of it broader scope and extent, is able to present a more fully developed profile of Paul's compositional strategies.

[16] See Breck, "Biblical Chiasmus" 71. Lund defines it as "a rhetorical figure according to which words and ideas are placed crosswise in a sentence" (Lund, "The Presence of Chiasmus in the New Testament" 74). Dahood calls it "a rhetorical term designating a reversal of the order of words in two otherwise parallel clauses" (M. Dahood, "Chiasmus," *IDBSup* 145). Man defines it as "a stylistic literary figure which consists of a series of two or more elements followed by a presentation of corresponding elements in reverse order" (R. E. Man, "Value of Chiasm" 146).

It is interesting to note that each of the examples cited above involves four elements,[17] with only one (Gen 7:18-19) extending beyond the bounds of a single sentence. Traditionally, this is the kind and size of construction to which the term chiasmus has been applied. For the purposes of this study, then, chiasmus will be defined as *the transposition of corresponding words or phrases at the sentence level*. Identification of this pattern is made relatively simple by the fact that identical, synonymous, or antonymous words or phrases are used.

B. Inversion

It is clear from the material set out in the preceding chapters that speakers and writers frequently reversed the order of items they were discussing.[18] It is also clear that (1) the total number of items involved often exceeded four, and (2) the scope of material in which this reversal occurred often encompassed more than one sentence. The most complex example is Odysseus's discussion with his mother's ghost, encompassing five major (and two minor) items on each side of the construction and occupying thirty-three lines in the Loeb edition (*Odyssey* 11.171-203).

Quintilian's discussion of physics, ethics, and dialectic is another example (*Institutio Oratoria*, 12.2.10-23). It is simpler than the structure found in Homer, encompassing only three items on each side of the reversal. It is longer, however, occupying ninety-two lines in the Loeb edition. The introduction of the topics is accomplished in a single sentence. Each topic is then developed at some length in the paragraphs that follow.

This latter example from Quintilian highlights a feature of many of the instances of oral patterning that were cited in the preceding chapters: the corresponding elements are grammatically unequal. Whereas in chiasmus similar (or dissimilar) words and phrases are transposed, in what may be called "inversion," a word or phrase on one side of the construction is developed in a sentence or a paragraph on the other. This device was used by numerous Greco-Roman speakers and writers, including Homer (*Iliad*, 2.761-762; 2.763; 2.768), Herodotus (*Histories* 7.49.2),

---

[17] Against Breck, who argues that chiasmus presupposes a center element that serves as a pivotal theme ("Biblical Chiasmus" 71). He thus distinguishes chiasmus (A-B-C-B'-A') from "direct parallelism" (A-B-A'-B') and "inverted parallelism" (A-B-B'-A').

[18] As noted above, Whitman suggests that the pattern of "the last things first" originated in the singer's need to keep in mind what he had said previously (*Homer* 254). Another perspective is provided by the primacy-recency effect observed in cognitive psychology. When subjects are presented with a list of items and asked to recall them in any order, they remember most accurately those items mentioned first (primacy) and last (recency). Cf. J. P. Houston, *Fundamentals of Learning and Memory*, 4th ed. (New York: Harcourt, Brace, Jovanovich, 1991) 290-291; M. M. Matlin, *Cognition* (New York: Holt, Rinehart and Winston, 1983) 60-62.

Plato (*Epistles*, 315c; 358d), Isocrates (4.67; 4.68), Demosthenes (9.61; 18.123), and Aristotle (*Rhetoric* 1362a; 1410a). It may also be found in the Hebrew Scriptures—specifically, in the works surveyed, in Genesis (3:9-19; 7:1-8:14; 10:1-32; 14:1-9).

Lacking a separate designation for these longer, more complex patterns, many scholars describe them as instances of "extended chiasmus."[19] The rationale for using that term to cover such patterns is that "chiastic" constructions of six, eight, and even ten elements are proposed for a number of OT passages. It is questionable, however, whether such a use of the term is appropriate for defining the nature of the examples above. The OT examples commonly cited are taken largely from poetic or prophetic passages, consisting of relatively short lines common to Hebrew poetry. The examples cited above, however, are prose sections, with the underlying structure of those sections being neither short nor parallel. Furthermore, because of the parallelism inherent in Hebrew poetry, the OT examples commonly cited usually exhibit a grammatical balance between the members (e.g., Isa 6:10). The examples cited above, however, are much less likely to have such a balance; their correspondence is often between a single word and a much longer grammatical unit.

A term other than chiasmus, therefore, seems required to describe this type of oral pattern. Denniston has suggested the term "inversion."[20] For the purposes of this study, his term will be adopted and used to refer to *the reversal of the order in which two or more topics are introduced and subsequently discussed*. In this pattern, as in chiasmus, each element in the first half of the construction is balanced by a corresponding element in the second half. In most cases of inversion, however, the topics are reintroduced by name, and in many instances of paired items the particles μὲν and δὲ are also used in the subsequent discussion. There are a few cases in the Greco-Roman literature where the plural article is used with μὲν and δὲ to reintroduce paired topics not mentioned by name, but in these instances the correspondence between the topics and their development can always be discerned from statements made in the second half of the construction.

C. Alternation

The discussion of alternate courses of action often results in an inverted or partially inverted arrangement. In its simplest form the discussion follows an ABBA pattern and may be seen as a variation of inversion. Herodotus's *Histories* contains numerous instances of this simple form. Onesilus's question to his servant (5.111.2-

---

[19] E.g., K. Grobel, who uses the term "extended chiasmus" for his analysis of Rom 2:6-11 ("A Chiastic Retribution-Formula in Romans 2," in *Zeit und Geschichte: Dankesgabe an Rudolf Bultmann zum 80. Geburtstag*, ed. E. Dinkler [Tübingen: Mohr, 1964] 255, n.3).

[20] Denniston, *Style* 77.

4), for example, lists two options; the servant addresses the options in reverse order, repeating key words from the question to make the connection. More intricate patterns can also be found in Herodotus (1.126.3-4 = ABABBA), Isocrates (2.32 = ABBAABBA), and Dio Chrysostom (3.62 = ABABBABA). The only comparable OT passage is Gen 4:1-5, where the names of Cain and Abel follow the pattern ABBAABBA. In each case, it is verbal connections that make the pattern readily identifiable.

This pattern is sufficiently different from both chiasmus and inversion to warrant a separate category. For the purposes of this study, it will be designated "alternation."[21] Alternation has as its central characteristic *an interplay between two alternate choices or ideas.* This interplay may involve considerable complexity. References to an alternative may repeat the same word, use synonyms, discuss potential results, or give examples. When the first alternative stated is also the concluding element in the discussion, the entire unit is set off as distinct.

D. Inclusion

"Inclusion" is *the use of the same word(s) to begin and end a discussion.*[22] The term itself can be traced back to D. H. Müller,[23] with the pattern that it describes being often highlighted in the analysis of OT literature.[24] It is present in all three of the OT books surveyed in Chapter 4, being more prominent in Isaiah (1:21-26; 11:1-10; 14:29-31; 22:1-5; 35:1-10; 40:1-11; 58:1-14; 59:1-11; 60:1-22; 63:15-64:11; 65:1-10) than in Genesis (11:1-9; 12:1-3; 14:13-24; 21:22-32) or Deuteronomy (25:15-17).

As Chapter 3 made clear, however, Hellenistic speakers and writers used inclusion as well. Aristotle, for example, used it repeatedly in his *Rhetoric* (1361a; 1361b; 1362a; 1376b) and his *Politics* (1253b; 1255b; 1279a). The author of

---

[21] The pattern discussed here may be considerably more intricate than a simple repetition of two or more items in the same order; consequently, this use of "alternation" should not be confused with Parunak's use of the same term. Parunak uses it to refer to an A-B-C-A'-B'-C' pattern of correspondence (Parunak, "Oral Typesetting" 155). This latter pattern is probably better described using Breck's designation "direct parallelism" ("Biblical Chiasmus" 71).

[22] The word "inclusio" is sometimes used instead of inclusion. Parunak uses this word and defines it as "a three-membered (ABA) chiasm whose outer members are short, compared with the center member" ("Oral Typesetting" 188). It is clear from his discussion, however, that what is at issue is the repetition of specific words at the beginning and end of a passage.

[23] D. H. Müller, *Die Propheten in ihrer ursprünglichen Form* (Wien: Hölder, 1896).

[24] See S. Mowinckel, "Die Komposition des deuterojesajanischen Buches," *ZAW* 49 (1931) 87-112; S. E. McEvenue, *The Narrative Style of the Priestly Writer,* AnBib 50 (Rome: Pontifical Biblical Institute, 1971). J. R. Lundbom uses the pattern in his study of Jeremiah and also lists others who have used it elsewhere (*Jeremiah,* esp. 16-17).

Rhetoric to Alexander also used it (1422a; 1422b; 1424b; 1427b; 1429a), as did Epicurus in his *Epistle to Herodotus* (45, 46).

The primary purpose of inclusion seems to have been to delimit discrete topics in an extended discussion. This delimitation takes different forms. The simplest form uses one key word at both the beginning and the end of a discussion (e.g., Aristotle, *Rhetoric* 1361a; Deut 25:17-19). Often, however, two or more words are used (e.g., Isa 1:21-26; 11:1-10). When multiple words are used they may appear in the same order (e.g., P.Hib. 1.41) or their order may be varied (e.g., Aristotle, *Rhetoric* 1376b; Gen 14:13-24). It needs to be stressed, however, that in this pattern it is an *exact* correspondence that must be sought: the same word or words must be used; synonyms or antonyms are not acceptable. The only exception is a nominal form of a word in one place and a cognate verbal form in the other. Particularly significant is the recurrence of a word or phrase that the speaker/author otherwise seldom uses (e.g., Isa 22:1-5; 65:1-10).[25]

E. Ring-Composition

The term "ring-composition" describes a pattern in which a speaker or writer returns to a previous point in the discussion, either concluding or resuming his train of thought. Ring-composition is similar to inclusion in that it frames sections of a discussion. It differs from inclusion in that the framing is done with sentences rather than single words. Ring-composition may be defined, then, as *a correspondence in wording between sentences that frame a section*. The extent of the section framed varies from a few lines (Gen 5:1-2; 13:15-17; Deut 5:12-15) to many pages (Herodotus 2.1-3.1; Demosthenes 18.62-66; Dio Chrysostom 20.13-14; 36.1-7; 50.1-4; Deut 1:1-28:69; 5:1-11:32; 12:1-26:16).

Within this basic pattern there are two types of framing that occur: inclusive and anaphoric. Inclusive framing uses the sentences to begin and end the section to which they belong (Herodotus 3.60.1-4; Gen 21:22-32; 35:1-7; Isa 23:1-14). Anaphoric framing stands outside the section and serves to resume a discussion interrupted by that section (Herodotus 1.81.1-1.83.1; Dio Chrysostom 50.1-4; Gen 37:36-39:1). In either type, however, the correspondence involved is precise: both sentences use some form of the same words.

F. Word-Chain

The frequent repetition of a given word and its cognates within a clearly delimited context is a pattern that is seen in Hebrew literature but is not as readily

---

[25] D. E. Garland makes this point in a NT context ("The Composition and Unity of Philippians. Some Neglected Literary Factors," *NovT* 27 [1985] 160-161).

apparent in Greco-Roman rhetoric and literature. The announced content of a given passage may provide ample reason for such a clustering of words (Isa 5:1-7; 15:1-16:14; 19:1-20:6). At other times, however, the repetition emphasizes or gives color to the topic under discussion, whether that topic is judgment (Isa 24:1-6), obstinacy (Isa 48:1-16), or glory (Isa 60:1-22). This use of word-chains in the OT is not surprising, and it accords well with two elements of oral composition: repetition and the echo-principle.

G. Refrain

Also more readily apparent in Hebrew literature than in Greco-Roman rhetoric and literature was *the repetition of formulaic phrases to open and close sections of a discussion.*[26] The "toledot" statements of Genesis are the most widely-recognized example (2:4; 5:1; 6:10; 10:1; 11:10; 11:27; 25:12, 19; 36:1; 37:2). Similar statements also open and/or close the major sections of Deuteronomy (1:1; 4:44; 27:1; 28:69; 29:1; 31:1). Although the phrase "Hear, O Israel" most often brings to mind the Shema of Deut 6:4, it is actually an introductory refrain repeated four other times in Deuteronomy 5-11 (5:1; 6:3; 9:1; 10:12). Similarly, although the reader would expect to find the command "Hear the Word of the Lord" repeatedly in a prophet such as Isaiah, the phrase is actually used sparingly to open and close the two major sections of the book (1:10; 39:5; 40:8; 66:5). This pattern is actually quite close to ring-composition, but the fact that an opening statement may not be balanced by a closing statement—and vice versa—sets it apart.

H. Concentric Symmetry

Perhaps the most challenging—and the least frequently seen—pattern in the works surveyed is the one Rolland has called "concentric symmetry." Often labeled "extended chiasmus" by scholars, this pattern involves *multiple, inverse correspondences that extend over a considerable expanse of material and have a single element at the center.* Because of the frequency with which this pattern is proposed in all sorts of ancient literature,[27] it will be necessary to examine it at some length. Four test cases will be examined, two from Greco-Roman literature and two from the OT. Each of these examples has been chosen because of its apparent symmetry.

---

[26] This use of formulaic language differs from the formulaic language of, say, the Homeric epic. The latter uses "stock" epithets (e.g., "rosy-fingered dawn," "Odysseus of many wiles," "ox-eyed Hera," "Achilles of swift feet") to fill out lines of a given number of syllables. The former uses the repeated phrases as section markers.

[27] E.g., Welch, *Chiasmus in Antiquity*; Lund, *Chiasmus in the New Testament.*

Four Test Cases. Myres has proposed the following structure for Herodotus's account of Xerxes's decision to invade Europe in *Histories* 7.8-19:[28]

The First Council: Xerxes will fight.	7.8
Mardonius encourages him.	7.9
Artabanus opposes.	7.10
Xerxes still intends to fight.	7.11
The First Dream.	7.12
Second Council: Xerxes will stay at home.	7.13
The Second Dream threatens Xerxes if he does so.	7.14
Xerxes still intends to fight.	7.15
Artabanus protests again.	7.16
Third Dream converts Artabanus to Mardonius's policy.	7.17
Third Council: Xerxes will fight.	7.18
Fourth Dream removes last obstacle.	7.19

Cecil Bowra also has noted "a certain formality of design" to Homer's *Iliad*, especially as it relates to the opening and closing books.[29] This formal balance between the opening and closing books may be seen in a comparison of Books 1-4 and 21-24, perhaps including Books 5 and 20 as well. The following table identifies the principal parallels.

Book 1
A   The Achaeans burn their dead.
B   Nine days pass.
C   Chryseis is returned to Chryses.
D   Achilles sulks for 12 days.
E   Thetis travels to Olympus to visit Zeus.
F   Zeus decides to honor Achilles and trouble the Trojans.

Book 24
D   Achilles weeps for 12 days.
F   Zeus decides to have Achilles return Hector's body.
E   Thetis travels from Olympus to visit Achilles.
C   Hector is returned to Priam.
B   Nine days pass.
A   The Trojans burn Hector's body.

Book 2
A   Zeus appears to Agamemnon in a dream.
B   The Achaean council decides to attack the Trojans.
C   Catalogue of Achaean captains and their ships

Book 23
A   Patroclus appears to Achilles in a dream.
B   Achilles decides to bury Patroclus.
C   Catalogue of Achaean funeral games

Book 3
A   Menelaus and Paris fight to a draw.
B   Aphrodite delivers Paris.

Book 22
B   Athena deceives Hector.
A   Hector and Achilles fight to the death.

---

[28] Myres, *Herodotus* 126.

[29] C. M. Bowra, *Homer* (London: Duckworth, 1972) 106.

Book 4		Book 21	
A	Athena intervenes to incite the Achaeans to fight.	B	The Trojans retreat.
B	The Achaeans advance.	A	Apollo intervenes to save the Trojans from destruction.

Book 5		Book 20	
A	Aphrodite delivers Aeneas from Diomedes.	A	Poseidon delivers Aeneas from Achilles.

Yehuda Radday has proposed the following structure for the story of the Flood in Gen 6:3-9:16:[30]

Divine monologue	6:4-8
It grieved Him to His heart.	6:7
"I will establish my covenant."	6:19
Four stages of entering the ark "as commanded"	6:23-7:16
"Go into the ark."	7:1
The fountains of the deep burst forth.	7:11
Seven verbs of "ascent"	7:17-19
God remembered Noah.	8:1
Seven verbs of "descent"	8:1-5
The fountains of the deep were closed.	8:2
"Go forth from the ark."	8:15
Four stages of leaving the ark	8:7-12
The Lord said in His heart.	8:21
"I established my covenant."	9:9
Divine monologue	9:12-16

Finally, Lund has analyzed the "Song of the Vineyard" in Isa 5:1-7 in the following manner:[31]

Beloved and vineyard are introduced	1
God's constructive work on the vineyard	2
Search for grapes yields only wild grapes	3a
Call to judge between the prophet and his vineyard	3b
Search for grapes yields only wild grapes	4
Question: what to do with the vineyard	5a
God's destructive work with the vineyard	5b-6
Beloved and vineyard are identified	7a
Meaning of the expected and wild grapes	7b

---

[30] Y. T. Radday, "Chiasmus in Hebrew Biblical Narrative," in *Chiasmus in Antiquity* 99. The numbering has been adjusted to reflect that found in the LXX.

[31] Lund, *Chiasmus* 76-79. Lund's analysis involves setting out the entire passage in English. In order to make it comparable with the other examples included, a summary is provided here. The entire passage is set out below. Other passages could have been selected, but—since it has been discussed in Chapter 4—Isa 5:1-7 will serve for illustrative purposes.

Evaluative Criteria. It is clear from these examples that this type of pattern is more conceptual in nature than the others. Narrative material, in particular, often has correspondences that involve similarities in speaker, setting, or action rather than similarities in wording. The conceptual nature of this pattern raises an important question: What controls are to be used in identifying instances of this compositional pattern?

Joanna Dewey, in her analysis of the controversy stories in Mark's Gospel, uses five criteria to support her proposed concentric arrangement for Mk 2:1-3:6: (1) parallelism in content, (2) parallelism of form, (3) repetition of language (especially catchwords), (4) similarity of setting (place or time), and (5) similarity of theology.[32] All five of these proposed criteria are discussed in David Clark's article, "Criteria for Identifying Chiasm."[33] The last two may be handled briefly. Clark notes correctly that setting is actually a restricted type of content.[34] In fact, the type of content involved is specific to narrative genre and, so, cannot be applied to Paul's letters. Regarding Dewey's fifth criterion, Clark comments that "theology is perhaps the least redaily [*sic*] tractable," for "the theological interpretation of many passages will be open to debate."[35]

Although the remaining three criteria hold more potential, all of them have varying degrees of persuasiveness. "Content," Clark writes, "is never totally identical."[36] There is always a degree of abstraction involved in comparing content, and "the point must come where scholars will disagree as to whether the pericopes are truly parallel or not."[37]

Form is, perhaps, more quantifiable. Dewey is able to characterize both 2:1-12 and 3:1-6, for example, as "a controversy apophthegm . . . imbedded into a healing miracle."[38] Nevertheless, Clark notes that different sections "may be completely or almost completely identical, or may have *various degrees of similarity*."[39] In Paul's

---

[32] J. Dewey, "The Literary Structure of the Controversy Stories in Mark 2:1-3:6," *JBL* 92 (1973) 394-401. Her proposed structure is:

A	Healing the paralytic	2:1-12
B	Eating with sinners	2:13-17
C	Question on fasting	2:18-22
B'	Plucking grain on the Sabbath	2:23-28
A'	Healing on the Sabbath	3:1-6

[33] D. J. Clark, "Criteria for Identifying Chiasm," *LB* 35 (1975) 63-72.

[34] Ibid.

[35] Ibid. 66.

[36] Ibid.

[37] Ibid.

[38] Dewey, "Literary Structure" 395.

[39] Clark, "Criteria" 65; emphasis his.

letters, similarities in the sequence of argumentation may well be more helpful than the use of form-critical categories.

Regarding the use of language and catchwords, Clark's comments are particularly helpful:

> Rarer words are more significant than commoner words. Identical forms are more significant than similar forms. The same word class is more significant than different word classes formed from the same root. Identical roots are more significant than suppletive roots.[40]

He goes on to give examples of each variant as it relates to Mark 1-3; one of them will suffice. Some form of the verb ἐξέρχομαι occurs 11 times in Mark 1-3. In contrast, the verb παράγω occurs twice in the first three chapters (1:16; 2:14) and only once elsewhere in Mark (15:21). A proposed correspondence involving παράγω would, therefore, be more convincing than one involving ἐξέρχομαι.[41]

In sum, it may be said that Dewey's five criteria are suggestive. They are not, however, of equal weight. Of the five items that she proposes, form and language appear to be the most readily quantifiable and, thus, to have the greatest potential for use in analyzing Paul's letters.

Elsewhere, Craig Blomberg has suggested nine criteria for identifying instances of "extended chiasmus":[42]

(1) There must be a problem in perceiving the structure of the text in question that more conventional outlines have failed to resolve.

(2) There must be clear examples of parallelism between the two "halves" of the structure.

(3) In addition to conceptual parallelism, verbal and grammatical parallelism should characterize most of the corresponding pairs in the structure.

(4) Verbal parallelism should involve central/dominant terminology.

(5) Verbal and conceptual parallelism should involve words and ideas not regularly found elsewhere within the proposed structure.

(6) Multiple sets of correspondences are desirable.[43]

---

[40] Ibid.

[41] Clark: ". . . to try to use [ἐξέρχομαι] as a catchword would be . . . absurd" (ibid.).

[42] Blomberg, "2 Corinthians" 5-7; he calls this pattern "extended chiasmus."

[43] Blomberg: "A simple ABA or ABBA pattern is so common to so many different forms of rhetoric that it usually yields few startlingly profound insights. Three or four members repeated in inverse sequence may be more significant. Five or more elements paired in sequence usually resist explanations which invoke subconscious or accidental processes" ("2 Corinthians" 6).

(7)   The structure should divide the text at natural breaks that are agreed on in different proposals.

(8)   The central element should have theological or ethical significance.

(9)   Deviations in the order of elements in the "halves" of the structure should be minimal.

In evaluating Blomberg's first criterion, it does not seem necessary, given the precedent in ancient literature of "the last thing first," to limit occurrences of this pattern to material with a perceived structural difficulty. Furthermore, Blomberg's second and third proposals can easily be combined into a single criterion, as can his fourth and fifth items. Although multiple sets of correspondences are indeed desirable (6), they are presupposed in this pattern—as are natural breaks in the text (7) and minimal deviations in the order of elements (9). As for Blomberg's eighth proposal, the question of the theological/ethical significance of a central element is somewhat lessened in narrative material. More properly stated, it should be said that material at the center of a structure often has special importance. Thus Blomberg's nine criteria for identifying "concentric symmetry" (or "extended chiasmus") can be reduced to three:

(1)   There should be examples not only of conceptual parallelism but also of verbal and grammatical parallelism between elements in the two "halves" of the proposed structure.

(2)   Verbal parallelism should involve central/dominant terminology and words/ideas not regularly found elsewhere within the proposed structure.

(3)   The central element should have some degree of significance within the structure.

Herodotus's Histories 7.8-19. What are the results when these criteria are applied to the four proposed test cases? The apparent symmetry of Myres's scheme is certainly attractive. It will be helpful to investigate it more closely.

It is difficult to determine the way in which Myres sees 7.19 relating to the overall scheme. He has designated 7.8-19 as "The Decision of Xerxes," but his layout of 7.1-19 places 7.19 parallel to 7.7. This choice is unfortunate, for references to the conquest of Egypt (Αἰγύπτου ἅλωσις) in 7.8.1 and 7.20.1 appear to frame sections 7.8 through 7.19. In addition, the phrase σύλλογον Περσέων in 7.8.3 corresponds to Περσέων τῶν συλλεχθέντων in 7.19.9 and suggests that the narrative passages of 7.8.1-5 and 7.19.9-14 open and close the section.[44]

---

[44] The verb συλλέγω occurs only three other times in the context of 7.8-19, twice in 7.8 (7.8.6, 24) and once in 7.13 (7.13.4). A further point of correspondence between sections 7.8 and

The entire episode is somewhat more complex than Myres's scheme suggests. If the action, the characters, and the attitudes toward the expedition are isolated, the order is as follows:

Narrative			7.8.1-5
Speech by	Xerxes	Go	7.8.6-64
Speech by	Mardonius	Go	7.9
Speech by	Artabanus	Stay	7.10
Speech by	Xerxes	Go	7.11
Dream to	Xerxes	Stay/Go	7.12
Speech by	Xerxes	Stay	7.13
Dream to	Xerxes	Go	7.14
Speech by	Xerxes	Go	7.15
Speech by	Artabanus	Stay	7.16
Dream to	Artabanus	Go	7.17
Speech by	Artabanus	Go	7.18
Dream to	Xerxes	Go	7.19.1-8
Narrative			7.19.9-14

The first difficulty that arises is that there appears to be an even, rather than an odd, number of elements present, thus disrupting Myres's neat, concentric scheme. Second, there is no consistent pattern to the actions, the characters, or the attitudes expressed by the characters. Mardonius, for example appears only once and is not balanced by a "return appearance" later in the action. Third, 7.12 poses a particular challenge, since it combines Xerxes's decision to stay with a dream encouraging him to go. Should this passage be considered with the "stay" elements or with the "go" elements? Fourth, the turning point in the action seems to occur in 7.14 rather than in 7.13, for it is in 7.14 that a dream convinces Xerxes conclusively to proceed with the invasion. Alternatively, 7.12-14 might, possibly, be considered the center of the structure, because of the crucial decision-making that takes place in those sections. Certainly, the fact that 7.13 is bracketed by dreams in 7.12 and 7.14 is suggestive. Indeed, it could be argued that if 7.17 and 7.18 were combined, a concentric pattern with 7.13 at its center would be the result. Both 7.17 and 7.18 pertain to Artabanus, and his speech in support of the expedition may been seen as the counterpart to Mardonius's earlier speech. It is difficult to understand, however, why Xerxes's decision *not* to invade would be given special prominence in a description of events that explains precisely why Xerxes decided *to* invade.

If the three criteria set out above are applied to this scheme, the results are not favorable. (1) The primary verbal parallels exist between the opening and closing sections (7.8.3 and 7.19.9). The fact that συλλέγω also occurs in 7.13.4 could be viewed as support for 7.13 as the center of the structure. (2) The verbal parallels do

---

7.19 is the promise of gifts (7.8.59) and the desire to receive the gifts (7.19.12), although the word for gifts differs (τιμιώματα is used in 7.8.59; δῶρα is used in 7.19.12).

not involve central or dominant terms. A positive point is the fact that the words involved are not found regularly elsewhere within the section. This latter consideration, however, could be viewed as an argument for the presence of inclusion or ring-composition rather than concentric symmetry. (3) If 7.13 is understood as being at the center of the structure, the significance of that central element is questionable. If on the other hand, the structure is understood as having seven elements on each side (in accordance with the analysis above), there are no elements to balance either Xerxes's speech declaring his intent to stay (7.13) or the dream that convinces Artabanus to change his mind (7.17).

It is at least as easy to view this episode in terms of standard plot development. Longacre suggests a seven-stage understanding of plot development: (1) setting or exposition, (2) inciting moment, (3) developing conflict, (4) climax, (5) denouement (6) final suspense, and (7) conclusion.[45] Using this approach the episode could be analyzed as follows:

Setting/Exposition:	Opening narrative and speeches	7.8-9
Inciting Moment:	Artabanus's speech	7.10
Developing Conflict:	Xerxes's speech and dreams	7.11-14
Climax:	Xerxes's speech and Artabanus' reply	7.15-16
Denouement:	Artabanus's dream	7.17
Final Suspense:	Artabanus's speech	7.18
Conclusion:	Xerxes's dream; closing narrative	7.19

It might be suggested that this analysis resembles an ABCDCBA pattern. It has been demonstrated, however, that narratives of this sort tend to be somewhat symmetrical in any case.[46] If that assessment is accurate, the question naturally arises as to why this particular episode should be singled out as different from others that follow the same plot development.

Homer's Iliad, Books 1 and 24. The correspondence between events in Books 1 and 24 of Homer's *Iliad* has more to commend it.[47] Using the first of the three suggested criteria, it may be observed that verbal and grammatical parallels occur in four of the six pairs. The first two pairs may be examined together: in Book 1 the Achaeans burn their dead on funeral pyres (πυραὶ νεκρῶν) for nine days (ἐννῆμαρ) after being troubled by Apollo; in Book 24 the Trojans burn Hector's body on a funeral pyre (ἐν πυρῇ ὑπάτῃ νεκρὸν) after gathering wood during nine

---

[45] R. E. Longacre, *The Grammar of Discourse* (New York: Plenum, 1983) 21.

[46] Cf. T. Longman, III, *Literary Approaches to Biblical Interpretation* (Grand Rapids: Zondervan, 1987) 92-93.

[47] These parallels will be tested even though they do not form a true instance of concentric symmetry. Because they are so far apart, there is no central element, and the third criterion cannot be applied. If, however, there is evidence that they conform to the first two criteria despite being at opposite ends of the work, such evidence would support the contention that the resulting inverse correspondence was a conscious choice on Homer's part.

days of mourning (ἐννῆμαρ). Admittedly, specific verbal parallels are few. Nevertheless, they are significant. The only other places where funeral pyres for the dead appear in the *Iliad* are in Books 7 and 23.[48] Similarly, a specific nine day time span occurs elsewhere only in Book 12 where it is unrelated to the course of the narrative.[49]

The twelve days of Achilles's sulking in Book 1 are paralleled by twelve days of Achilles's weeping in Book 24. At the end of each time span Homer uses the same phrase to move his narrative forward (ἀλλ᾿ ὅτε δή ῥ᾿ ἐκ τοῖο δυωδεκάτη γένετ᾿ ἠώς, καὶ τότε . . .). This phrase is used only these two times in the *Iliad* (1.493; 24.31). Furthermore, the word δυωδέκατος occurs only six times in the work.[50]

A further parallel involves Achilles's mother, Thetis. In Book 1 she ascends to Mt. Olympus to appeal to Zeus on behalf of Achilles (1.493-530); in Book 24 she is summoned to Mt. Olympus to carry a message from Zeus to Achilles (24.77-137). In this case, as well, there are several verbal parallels. Similar wording opens each passage:

Θέτις . . . ἀνεδύσετο <u>κῦμα θαλάσσης</u>, ἠερίη δ᾿ <u>ἀνέβη</u> μέγαν
<u>οὐρανὸν</u> Οὔλυμπόν τε. <u>εὗρεν δ᾿ εὐρύοπα Κρονίδην</u> . . .   (1.495)

ἀμφὶ δ᾿ ἄρα σφι λιάζετο <u>κῦμα θαλάσσης</u>. ἀκτὴν δ᾿ ἐξαναβᾶσαι
ἐς <u>οὐρανὸν</u> ἀϊχθήτην, <u>εὗρον δ᾿ εὐρύοπα Κρονίδην</u> . . .   (24.96)

Thetis has an active role only in Books 1, 18-19, and 24. Although she is mentioned several times elsewhere in the narrative,[51] unlike Zeus, Apollo, and others her involvement in the action of the narrative is limited. This fact makes her parallel appearances in Books 1 and 24 that much more significant.

Thus, verbal and grammatical parallels occur in four of the six pairings set out in Books 1 and 24 of Homer's *Iliad*. These verbal/grammatical parallels, coupled with the correlation of the order of the six pairs, suggest that Homer designed Book 24 of his *Iliad* to parallel—in reverse order—Book 1. This inverse correspondence

---

[48] The word pyre (πυρή) occurs 22 times in the *Iliad*. Three of the uses are in the passages noted (1.52; 24.787, 789). In Book 7 the Achaeans burn their dead during a cease fire (7.336, 434). In Book 23 the word is used 13 times in describing Patroclus's funeral (23.141-256). The other uses of the word (4.99; 9.546; 18.336) are incidental to the narrative.

[49] In Book 12 the reference is to a nine day span many years in the future when Poseidon and Apollo would destroy the wall around the Achaean ships (12.24). The nine days mentioned in 24.107 are part of the twelve days during which Achilles weeps over Patroclus; the nine days in 24.610 are incidental to the narrative; and the nine days of 24.664 are anticipatory of the days of mourning over Hector (24.784).

[50] In addition to 1.493 and 24.31, it appears in 21.46; 24.81; 24.413; and 24.667. In three of these instances (21.46; 24.81; 24.667) its use is incidental to the main narrative. The fourth instance (24.413) refers to the same time period as does 24.31.

[51] Cf. 6.136; 9.410; 15.76; 16.34; 16.222; 23.14.

between multiple elements on a large scale, then, may be seen as a grand example of concentric symmetry.

The Flood Story of Gen 6:3-9:16. It has already been noted that the sequence of days in the flood story is inverted. There are several additional points of correspondence between the two "halves" of the story. In both 6:6 and 8:21 the verb διανοέω is used in conjunction with God. The only other use of this verb in Genesis is in 6:5 (in conjunction with mankind), with this latter use corresponding to the noun διάνοια in 8:21 (also in conjuction with mankind). The noun διαθήκη in 6:18 corresponds to the seven uses of the same word in 9:9-17. The command to enter the ark (7:1) is balanced by a similarly worded command to leave the ark (8:15-16):

καὶ εἶπεν κύριος ὁ θεὸς πρὸς Νῶε εἴσελθε σὺ καὶ πᾶς ὁ οἶκός σου εἰς τὴν κιβωτόν . . .

καὶ εἶπεν κύριος ὁ θεὸς τῷ Νῶε λέγων ᾿εξελθε ἐκ τῆς κιβωτοῦ, σὺ καὶ ἡ γυνή σου καὶ οἱ υἱοί σου καὶ αἱ γυναῖκες τῶν υἱῶν σου . . .

The statement about the fountains and floodgates in 7:11 corresponds to a similar statement in 8:2:

τῇ ἡμέρᾳ ταύτῃ ἐρράγησαν πᾶσαι αἱ πηγαὶ τῆς ἀβύσσου, καὶ οἱ καταρράκται τοῦ οὐρανοῦ ἠνεῴχθησαν.

καὶ ἐπεκαλύφθησαν αἱ πηγαὶ τῆς ἀβύσσου καὶ οἱ καταρράκται τοῦ οὐρανοῦ, καὶ συνεσχέθη ὁ ὑετὸς ἀπὸ τοῦ οὐρανοῦ.

The chiasmus of 7:17-19[52] is balanced by a similar chiasmus in 8:3-5:

καὶ ἐνεδίδου τὸ ὕδωρ πορευόμενον ἀπὸ τῆς γῆς, ἐνεδίδου καὶ ἠλαττονοῦτο τὸ ὕδωρ μετὰ πεντήκοντα καὶ ἑκατὸν ἡμέρας.

καὶ ἐκάθισεν ἡ κιβωτὸς ἐν μηνὶ τῷ ἑβδόμῳ, ἑβδόμῃ καὶ εἰκάδι τοῦ μηνός, ἐπὶ τὰ ὄρη τὰ ᾿Αραράτ. τὸ δὲ ὕδωρ πορευόμενον ἠλαττονοῦντο ἕως τοῦ δεκάτου μηνός

And the word used for "remembered" in 8:1 (μιμνήσκομαι) occurs only in the final (outer) element of the pattern (9:15-16).[53]

Radday's proposal regarding the structure of Gen 6:3-9:16, however, is not without its difficulties. There are a number of places in which he interpolates elements to fit his scheme. First, the opening "divine monologue" (6:4, 8) actually combines statements from two paragraphs (6:2-5 and 6:6-8). Second, he extracts 6:6 from the first element and makes it a separate item. Third, he extracts the command

---

[52] See Chapter 4 above.

[53] The other occurrences in the book are: 19:29; 30:22; 40:13, 14 (2x), 20, 23; 42:9.

to enter the ark (7:1) from "The four stages of entering the ark 'as commanded'" (6:22; 7:5, 9, 16) in order to make it a separate item. Fourth, he interpolates the command to "Go forth from the ark" (8:15) so that it precedes the "Four stages of leaving the ark" (8:7, 8, 10, 12). Finally, it is difficult to see how the releasing of the raven and the dove (8:7-12) corresponds to the entering of the ark (7:7-16). The more natural parallel is the actual exiting from the ark (8:18-19).

After making a number of modifications, a scheme emerges that seems to hold more promise:

a	God considers (ὁ θεὸς . . . διενοήθη) mankind's wickedness	6:5-8
b	God promises covenant (διαθήκη) with Noah	6:9-22
c	Command to enter the ark (εἴσελθε . . . εἰς τὴν κιβωτόν)	7:1-5
d	Seven day period (ἑπτὰ ἡμέρας)	7:6-10
e	Fountains opened (αἱ πηγαὶ τῆς ἀβύσσου . . . ἠνεῴχθησαν)	7:11
f	Forty days (τεσσαράκοντα ἡμέρας) . . . flood on earth	7:12-17
g	Waters prevail for 150 days	7:18-24
	(chiasmus + ἡμέρας ἑκατὸν πεντήκοντα)	
h	God remembers (μιμνήσκομαι) Noah	8:1
e	Fountains closed (ἐπεκαλύφθησαν αἱ πηγαὶ τῆς ἀβύσσου)	8:2
g'	Waters subside for 150 days	8:3-5
	(chiasmus + πεντήκοντα καὶ ἑκατὸν ἡμέρας)	
f'	Forty days (τεσσαράκοντα ἡμέρας) . . . sent dove	8:6
d'	Two seven day periods (ἡμέρας ἑπτὰ)	8:10-14
c'	Command to exit the ark (ἔξελθε ἐκ τῆς κιβωτοῦ)	8:15-20
a'	God considers (ὁ θεὸς διανοηθεὶς) Noah's offering	8:21-22
b'	God makes covenant (διαθήκη) with Noah	9:1-17

The most glaring break in this scheme occurs at 8:2. This disruption is necessary, however, for the logic of the narrative demands that the fountains of the earth and the floodgates of the heavens be closed before the waters can subside. The only other disruption is in the order of the final two elements. The frequent points of verbal correspondence, the use of a rare word at the center of the structure, the significance of the element at the center of the structure, and the high correlation between the two halves of the structure all point to a carefully crafted concentric structure.

The Song of the Vineyard of Isa 5:1-7. In order to analyze Lund's scheme for Isa 5:1-7, it will be necessary to set out the text in its entirety:[54]

A   Ἄισω δὴ τῷ ἠγαπημένῳ   (5:1)
ᾆσμα τοῦ ἀγαπητοῦ τῷ ἀμπελῶνί μου.
ἀμπελὼν ἐγενήθη τῷ ἠγαπημένῳ
ἐν κέρατι ἐν τόπῳ πίονι·

[54] Lund's original scheme is printed in English. This representation uses the text of the LXX, which—with the few modifications noted below—is an accurate translation of the MT.

B   καὶ φραγμὸν περιέθηκα   (5:2)
      καὶ ἐχαράκωσα
      καὶ ἐφύτευσα ἄμπελον σωρηχ
      καὶ ᾠκοδόμησα πύργον ἐν μέσῳ αὐτοῦ
      καὶ προλήνιον ὤρυξα ἐν αὐτῷ·

C   καὶ ἔμεινα τοῦ ποιῆσαι σταφυλήν,
      ἐποίησε δὲ ἀκάνθας.
        καὶ νῦν, ἄνθρωπος τοῦ Ιουδα,   (5:3)
        καὶ οἱ ἐνοικοῦντες ἐν Ιερουσαλημ,

D   κρίνατε ἐν ἐμοὶ
            καὶ ἀνὰ μέσον τοῦ ἀμπελῶνός μου.

C'   τί ποιήσω ἔτι τῷ ἀμπελῶνί μου   (5:4)
      καὶ οὐκ ἐποίησα αὐτῷ;
      διότι ἔμεινα τοῦ ποιῆσαι σταφυλήν,
      ἐποίησε δὲ ἀκάνθας.

D'   νῦν δὲ ἀναγγελῶ ὑμῖν   (5:5)
            τί ποιήσω τῷ ἀμπελῶνί μου·

B'   ἀφελῶ τὸν φραγμὸν αὐτοῦ καὶ ἔσται εἰς διαρπαγήν,
      καὶ καθελῶ τὸν τοῖχον αὐτοῦ καὶ ἔσται εἰς καταπάτημα,
        καὶ ἀνήσω τὸν ἀμπελῶνά μου   (5:6)
        καὶ οὐ μὴ τμηθῇ οὐδὲ μὴ σκαφῇ,
      καὶ ἀναβήσεται εἰς αὐτὸν ὡς εἰς χέρσον ἄκανθα·
      καὶ ταῖς νεφέλαις ἐντελοῦμαι τοῦ μὴ βρέξαι εἰς αὐτὸν ὑετόν.

A'   ὁ γὰρ ἀμπελὼν κυρίου σαβαωθ   (5:7)
      οἶκος τοῦ Ισραήλ ἐστί
      καὶ ἄνθρωπος τοῦ Ιουδα
      νεόφυτον ἠγαπημένον·

C"   ἔμεινα τοῦ ποιῆσαι κρίσιν,
      ἐποίησε δὲ ἀνομίαν
      καὶ οὐ δικαιοσύνην
      ἀλλὰ κραυγήν.

Lund offers the following arguments in support of his proposal (based on the MT): (1) The beloved and the vineyard are the subjects of A and A'. (2) The constructive work of the husbandman in B is balanced by his destructive work in B'. (3) Both the central lines of B and B' deal with the cultivation of the vineyard. (4) The protection of the watchtower in B is balanced by the protection of the wall and hedge in B'. (5) The removal of stones (hindrance to growth) in B is balanced by the growth of briers and thorns (hindrance to growth) in B'. (6) The trenches that are dug in B are intended to carry away the rains that are withheld in B'. (7) The contrast between the grapes expected and the wild grapes produced is evident in C, C', and

C". (8) The phrase "I pray" (Heb = נא) is repeated in both D and D'. (9) The question raised in D is answered in D'.

Before continuing, four items must be noted about the LXX translation of this passage: (1) In 5:2, planting a hedge (φραγμός) has been substituted for the clearing of stones. (2) In 5:3b and 5:5, the phrase "I pray" has not been translated, although it is present in the MT. (3) In 5:5b "It shall be a spoil" (καὶ ἔσται εἰς διαρπαγήν) has been substituted for burning, and (4) in 5:6 "I will forsake my vineyard" (καὶ ἀνήσω τὸν ἀμπελῶνά μου) has been substituted for laying it waste.

The first point to note in analyzing Lund's proposal is that little can be built on the use of the word vineyard (ἀμπελών), for it is the key word in this passage, occurring eight times. There is, nevertheless, good correspondence between 5:1 and 5:7 because the participle ἠγαπημένος is present in both verses. Second, the correspondence between 5:2a and 5:5b-6 has been made even more explicit in the LXX by the double use of φραγμός. Third, the correspondence between 5:2b and 5:4b is readily apparent and contains the only two uses of σταφυλή in Isaiah. The correspondence of 5:7b with these verses is made even more explicit in the LXX, which adds τοῦ ποιῆσαι and ἐποίησεν. Fourth, it seems better to view 5:4a (rather than 5:3b) as parallel with 5:5a, for both use the same wording to ask and answer the question raised.[55] Finally, it might have been preferable if Lund had been more consistent in following the line divisions in the MT when he developed his scheme. This point applies to 5:7b but is a particular problem in 5:2a and 5:5b-6 where a consistent approach would have resulted, respectively, in four and six lines. A revised layout might be:

A   Ἄισω δὴ τῷ <u>ἠγαπημένῳ</u>   (5:1)
ᾆσμα τοῦ ἀγαπητοῦ τῷ ἀμπελῶνί μου.
ἀμπελὼν ἐγενήθη τῷ <u>ἠγαπημένῳ</u>
ἐν κέρατι ἐν τόπῳ πίονι.

B   καὶ <u>φραγμὸν</u> περιέθηκα καὶ ἐχαράκωσα   (5:2)
καὶ ἐφύτευσα ἄμπελον σωρηχ
καὶ ᾠκοδόμησα πύργον ἐν μέσῳ αὐτοῦ
καὶ προλήνιον ὤρυξα ἐν αὐτῷ·

C   <u>καὶ ἔμεινα τοῦ ποιῆσαι σταφυλήν,</u>
<u>ἐποίησε δὲ ἀκάνθας.</u>

D   καὶ νῦν, ἄνθρωπος τοῦ Ιουδα,   (5:3)
καὶ οἱ ἐνοικοῦντες ἐν Ιερουσαλημ,
κρίνατε ἐν ἐμοὶ
καὶ ἀνὰ μέσον τοῦ ἀμπελῶνός μου.

---

[55] This comment also applies to the MT, in which עתה לצרמי seems a stronger parallel than the use of נא.

E   <u>τί ποιήσω ἔτι τῷ ἀμπελῶνί μου</u>   (5:4)
       καὶ οὐκ ἐποίησα αὐτῷ;

C'   διότι <u>ἔμεινα τοῦ ποιῆσαι σταφυλήν</u>,
       <u>ἐποίησε δὲ ἀκάνθας</u>.

E'   νῦν δὲ ἀναγγελῶ ὑμῖν   (5:5)
       <u>τί ποιήσω τῷ ἀμπελῶνί μου</u>·

B'   ἀφελῶ τὸν <u>φραγμὸν</u> αὐτοῦ καὶ ἔσται εἰς διαρπαγήν,
       καὶ καθελῶ τὸν τοῖχον αὐτοῦ καὶ ἔσται εἰς καταπάτημα,
       καὶ ἀνήσω τὸν ἀμπελῶνά μου   (5:6)
       καὶ οὐ μὴ τμηθῇ οὐδὲ μὴ σκαφῇ,
       καὶ ἀναβήσεται εἰς αὐτὸν ὡς εἰς χέρσον ἄκανθα·
       καὶ ταῖς νεφέλαις ἐντελοῦμαι
       τοῦ μὴ βρέξαι εἰς αὐτὸν ὑετόν.

A   ὁ γὰρ ἀμπελὼν κυρίου σαβαωθ   (5:7)
       οἶκος τοῦ Ισραήλ ἐστί
       καὶ ἄνθρωπος τοῦ Ιουδα
       νεόφυτον <u>ἠγαπημένον</u>·

C "   <u>ἔμεινα τοῦ ποιῆσαι</u> κρίσιν, <u>ἐποίησε δὲ</u> ἀνομίαν
       καὶ οὐ δικαιοσύνην ἀλλὰ κραυγήν.

In summary, there are several points of verbal correspondence present in this passage, with the most balanced being those at the beginning (5:1-2a) and end (5:5b-7a). It is difficult, however, to rationalize the balance of the central section (5:3b-5a), although it seems clear that this is the heart of the passage in that it calls the listener to evaluate the situation and make a judgment on what the husbandman's appropriate response should be. The final line in 5:7b applies the parable directly to Israel by using the identical wording that was used in the central section.

     The preceding test cases have explored the use of the proposed criteria in evaluating four suggested examples of concentric symmetry. The examples have fared unevenly. Myres's proposal for the account of Xerxes's decision to invade Greece was found to be, perhaps, better explained on the basis of standard plot development than on the basis of concentric symmetry. Bowra's suggestion regarding the opening and closing books of Homer's *Iliad* was found to have much to commend it. Although Radday's suggested structure for the Flood episode in Genesis had some weaknesses, a revised approach suggests a strong probability that the construction was intentional. Lund's suggested understanding of Isaiah 5:1-7 was evaluated as having a low probability of intentionality, and a revised approach fared little better, although the basic framing of the center portion of the parable must be acknowledged. These test cases support the suggestion that the proposed criteria provide a valid means of distinguishing between more- and less-likely examples of concentric symmetry.

I. Summary

Chapters 3 and 4 surveyed both Greco-Roman literature and rhetoric and the LXX for uses of oral patterning in antiquity. This chapter has sought to organize the results of that survey. Eight categories of compositional patterns have been identified. In each category, an attempt was made to identify the characteristic feature(s) of the pattern and to establish criteria by which additional examples may be recognized. These categories and criteria will serve as starting points for cataloging the appearances of oral patterning in Paul's letters.

Part Three

ORAL PATTERNING IN PAUL'S LETTERS

Chapter 6

ROMANS

The Pauline authorship of Romans is undisputed. C. E. B. Cranfield writes: "Today no responsible criticism disputes its Pauline authorship."[1] It is generally agreed that Paul wrote the letter shortly before he left Corinth to return to Jerusalem with the collection.[2] Although the words "in Rome" are absent from a few manuscripts, this textual variant is probably the result of a later omission,[3] and a Roman destination is generally assumed. The integrity of chapters 1-15 is also generally accepted,[4] but the relationship of chapter 16 to the rest of the letter has been questioned.[5] Harry Gamble has argued convincingly that chapter 16 was part of the original letter,[6] and for the purposes of this study the integrity of Romans will be presupposed. Various suggestions have been made concerning the purpose of the letter,[7] but that issue does not bear on this study.

Even before the current interest in rhetoric, Romans was examined for insight into Paul's preaching style.[8] This quest has increased with the advent of rhetorical criticism. Curiously—except for 11:33-36—Lund ignores Romans in his study of

---

[1] C. E. B.Cranfield, *The Epistle to the Romans* (Edinburgh: T & T Clark, 1975) 1:2.

[2] Cf. W. G. Kümmel, *Introduction to the New Testament*, trans. H. C. Kee (Nashville: Abingdon, 1975) 311.

[3] Cf. B. M. Metzger, *A Textual Commentary on the Greek New Testament* (New York: United Bible Societies, 1971) 505.

[4] Although contrast W. Schmithals, *Der Römerbrief als historisches Problem* (Gütersloh: Mohn, 1975) and J. Kinoshita, "Romans—Two Writings Combined," *NovT* 7 (1964) 258-277.

[5] Cf. Kümmel, *Introduction* 314-320.

[6] H. Y. Gamble, *The Textual History of the Letter to the Romans* (Grand Rapids: Eerdmans, 1977). The integrity of 16:24 and the authenticity of 16:25-27 are notoriously complex questions that are outside the scope of this study. For an overview, see Gamble; cf. J. A. Fitzmyer, *Romans* (New York: Doubleday, 1993) 48-50; Weima, *Neglected Endings*, 142-144, 217-219.

[7] Cf. Jervis, *Romans* 11-26 for a summary.

[8] E.g., Bultmann, *Stil der paulinischen Predigt* (1910); Scroggs, "Paul as Rhetorician" (1976).

chiasmus. Similarly, Welch thinks that Romans contains little in the way of chiastic structure.[9] On the other hand, Jouette Bassler identifies instances of ring-composition in her analysis of Romans 1:16-2:29;[10] and Peter Ellis analyzes the entire letter using ABA' and "chiastic" formats.[11]

A. Epistolary Structure

Since the opening and closing sections of Romans conform to the epistolary conventions of the day, it seems that the most natural way to approach the overall structure of Romans is as a personal letter. Vocatives, verbs of knowing, and rhetorical questions (most often τί οὖν ἐροῦμεν;) abound in Romans, frequently occurring in combinations which mark transitions in Paul's argument.[12] Three major clusters of epistolary conventions, however, establish the basic contours of the letter:

1:1-13	Sender (1:1), recipients (1:7), greeting (1:7), thanksgiving (1:8), attestation (1:9), visit wish (1:10-11), disclosure formula (1:13)
11:25-12:3	Disclosure formula (11:25), doxology (11:33-36), request formula (12:1), verb of saying (12:3)
15:13-16:27	Peace-wish (15:13), confidence formula (15:14), writing statement (15:15), visit wish (15:22), intention to visit (15:23-25), intention to visit (15:28-29), request formula (15:30), peace-wish (15:33), greetings (16:3-16), request formula (16:17), peace-wish (16:20), grace benediction (16:20), greetings (16:21-23), doxology (16:25-27)

The first cluster is easily recognizable as the letter opening. The second cluster marks a major turning point within the letter-body. The third cluster closes the letter. If the peace wish of 15:33 is seen as concluding the letter-body, the resulting epistolary structure is:

---

[9] Welch: "With Romans, the absence of an overriding stylistic structure is also not surprising. Paul writes in Romans with a sense of doctrinal sophistication. His attention appears to turn to substance and content rather than form or style" ("Chiasmus" 219). Such a statement, taken to its logical conclusion, implies that in the letters where Welch finds elaborate chiastic structures, Paul's concern was with form or style rather than substance and content!

[10] J. M. Bassler, *Divine Impartiality* (Chico, CA: Scholars, 1982) 121-154.

[11] Ellis: "Each part and section can be divided into lesser A-B-A' or A-B-C-B'-A' formats" (*Letters* 203). A. Brunot takes a more cautious approach (*S. Paul* [Paris: Cerf, 1955] 46).

[12] E.g., 6:1-3: Τί οὖν ἐροῦμεν; ἐπιμένωμεν τῇ ἁμαρτίᾳ, ἵνα ἡ χάρις πλεονάσῃ; μὴ γένοιτο· οἵτινες ἀπεθάνομεν τῇ ἁμαρτίᾳ, πῶς ἔτι ζήσομεν ἐν αὐτῇ; ἢ ἀγνοεῖτε ὅτι ὅσοι ἐβαπτίσθημεν εἰς Χριστὸν Ἰησοῦν εἰς τὸν θάνατον αὐτοῦ ἐβαπτίσθημεν;

Letter-opening		1:1-12
Salutation	1:1-7	
Thanksgiving	1:8-12	
Letter-body		1:13-15:33
Body opening	1:13-17	
Body middle	1:18-15:13	
Theological section	1:18-11:36	
Practical section	12:1-15:13	
Body closing	15:14-33	
Letter-closing		16:1-27

Three items in this outline require elaboration. First, many have concluded that 1:15 is the end of the thanksgiving section and that 1:16 is the beginning of the letter-body.[13] It is difficult, however, to ignore the disclosure formula (οὐ θέλω δὲ ὑμᾶς ἀγνοεῖν, ἀδελφοί, ὅτι . . .) at 1:13.[14] Belleville makes the attractive suggestion that Romans, like 2 Corinthians, follows the sequence: letter opening (1:1-7) → thanksgiving section (1:8-12) → full disclosure formula (1:13-15) → thematic summary statement (1:16-17).[15] This approach gives full weight to the disclosure formula and, at the same time, recognizes that 1:16-17 introduces the topic that is central to the letter-body.

Second, the body closing is often designated the "apostolic parousia." Analyses of the structure of a typical apostolic parousia range from (1) Funk's detailed outline (disposition in writing + basis of apostolic relation to recipients + implementation of apostolic parousia + invocation of divine approval + benefits from the apostolic parousia),[16] to (2) Jervis's simpler understanding (writing unit + emissary unit + visit unit),[17] to (3) Mullins's thematic approach ("visit talk").[18] Funk is able to identify the portion that he designates "an elaboration of the basis of his apostolic relation to the recipients" only in Romans (15:15b-21) and 1 Corinthians (1:15-16).[19] Jervis includes 15:15b-21 within the "writing unit."[20] In fact, Rom 15:14-

---

[13] Cf. e.g., Jervis, *Romans* 105-107, who summarizes the options and so argues.

[14] White, for example, considers 1:13-15 to be the body-opening, with the body-middle beginning at 1:16 (*Body* 52-53, 56-59).

[15] L. L. Belleville, *Reflections of Glory: Paul's Polemical Use of the Moses-Doxa Tradition in 2 Corinthians 3.1-18*, JSNTSup 52 (Sheffield: JSOT Press, 1991) 119, n.2.

[16] R. W. Funk, "The Apostolic Parousia: Form and Significance," in *Christian History and Interpretation: Studies Presented to John Knox*, W. R. Farmer, C. F. D. Moule, R. R. Niebuhr, eds. (Cambridge: University Press, 1967) 249-268.

[17] Jervis, *Romans* 113-114.

[18] T. Y. Mullins, "Visit Talk in the New Testament Letters," *CBQ* 35 (1973) 350-358.

[19] Funk, "Apostolic Parousia" 253-254.

[20] Jervis, *Romans* 121-124.

21 has much in common with portions of other letters in which Paul discusses the gospel, his credentials, and his ministry.[21] Although it is not crucial to the understanding of the epistolary structure of Romans, it is possible to view 15:14-32 as consisting of an "apostolic apologia" (15:14-21) and an "apostolic parousia" (15:22-32).

Finally, Weima examines the letter closing and arrives at the following, more detailed, outline:[22]

15:33	Peace benediction
16:1-2	Letter of commendation
16:3-16	First greeting list
16:17-20a	Hortatory section (Autograph)
16:20b	Grace benediction
16:21-23	Second greeting list (Non-autograph)
16:25-27	Doxology

B. Readily Apparent Oral Patterns

With this understanding of the letter's epistolary structure, it is now possible to proceed to an investigation of the oral patterns that appear within Romans.

The Salutation — 1:1-7. Paul expands the salutation considerably in Romans. Interestingly, he also uses inclusion to frame it (1:1, 6-7):

Παῦλος δοῦλος Χριστοῦ ᾿Ιησοῦ, <u>κλητὸς</u> ἀπόστολος . . .

. . . ἐν οἷς ἐστε καὶ ὑμεῖς <u>κλητοὶ</u> ᾿Ιησοῦ Χριστοῦ, πᾶσιν τοῖς
οὖσιν ἐν ῾Ρώμῃ ἀγαπητοῖς θεοῦ, <u>κλητοῖς</u> ἁγίοις· χάρις ὑμῖν
καὶ εἰρήνη ἀπὸ θεοῦ πατρὸς ἡμῶν καὶ κυρίου ᾿Ιησοῦ Χριστοῦ.

The Body: Part 1 — 1:13-4:25. A number of small-scale oral patterns are present in 1:13-32. In 1:17-18 the contrast between God's righteousness and his wrath is heightened by means of a chiasmus:

<u>δικαιοσύνη</u> γὰρ <u>θεοῦ</u> ἐν αὐτῷ <u>ἀποκαλύπτεται</u> . . .
<u>ἀποκαλύπτεται</u> γὰρ <u>ὀργὴ θεοῦ</u> . . .

Another instance of chiasmus occurs in 1:19:

διότι τὸ γνωστὸν τοῦ θεοῦ <u>φανερόν</u> ἐστιν <u>ἐν αὐτοῖς·</u>
ὁ θεὸς γὰρ <u>αὐτοῖς ἐφανέρωσεν.</u>

A third occurs in 1:21:

---

[21] Cf. 1 Cor 1:10-4:21; 2 Cor 1:12-6:10; Gal 1:11-2:21; Phil 1:12-26; 1 Thess 2:1-10.
[22] Weima, *Neglected Endings* 222.

διότι γνόντες τὸν θεὸν
οὐχ ὡς θεὸν ἐδόξασαν . . .

Perhaps the best-known feature of 1:18-32 is the repeated refrain παρέδωκεν αὐτοὺς ὁ θεὸς (1:24, 26, 28). Closely connected with this refrain is the repetition of ἤλλαξαν . . . μετήλλαξαν . . . μετήλλαξαν that occurs in 1:23, 25, 26. The verb πράσσω serves as a link-word connecting 1:32 (2x) to 2:1-3 (3x),[23] with a further instance of chiasmus occurring in 2:1:

ἐν ᾧ γὰρ κρίνεις τὸν ἕτερον,
σεαυτὸν κατακρίνεις . . .

Rom 2:7-10 comprises an inverted structure, contrasting the divine recompense given to the evil with blessings given to the good:

ὃς ἀποδώσει ἑκάστῳ κατὰ τὰ ἔργα αὐτοῦ,

A   τοῖς μὲν καθ᾿ ὑπομονὴν ἔργου ἀγαθοῦ δόξαν καὶ τιμὴν
        καὶ ἀφθαρσίαν ζητοῦσιν, ζωὴν αἰώνιον·

B   τοῖς δὲ ἐξ ἐριθείας καὶ ἀπειθοῦσι τῇ ἀληθείᾳ
        πειθομένοις δὲ τῇ ἀδικίᾳ, ὀργὴ καὶ θυμός—

B'   θλῖψις καὶ στενοχωρία ἐπὶ πᾶσαν ψυχὴν ἀνθρώπου τοῦ
        κατεργαζομένου τὸ κακόν, Ἰουδαίου τε πρῶτον καὶ Ἕλληνος·

A'   δόξα δὲ καὶ τιμὴ καὶ εἰρήνη παντὶ τῷ ἐργαζομένῳ τὸ
        ἀγαθόν, Ἰουδαίῳ τε πρῶτον καὶ Ἕλληνι·

Although the verbal parallels are few, the syntax reinforces the inversion:

τοῖς μὲν . . . ζητοῦσιν   ζωὴν αἰώνιον
τοῖς δὲ . . . πειθομένοις   ὀργὴ καὶ θυμός
θλῖψις καὶ στενοχωρία   ἐπὶ πᾶσαν . . . κατεργαζομένου
δόξα δὲ καὶ τιμὴ καὶ εἰρήνη   παντὶ τῷ ἐργαζομένῳ

And the basic antithetical pattern is clear:[24]

---

[23] For a discussion of the importance of link-words in Paul's letters, see J. A. Fischer, "Pauline Literary Forms and Thought Patterns," *CBQ* 39 (1977) 209-223. Unfortunately, Fischer approaches the topic from the perspective of literary rather than oral composition.

[24] This basic structure has been noted repeatedly; cf. Forbes, *Romans* 7; Jeremias, "Chiasmus" 149; E. Jüngel, "Ein paulinischer Chiasmus" 173-174 (cited by DiMarco, "Chiasmus" 12); Cranfield, *Romans* 149; Dunn, *Romans 1-8* 78; Moo, *Romans 1-8* 134; Fitzmyer, *Romans* 302. Grobel ("Retribution Formula") proposes a more detailed pattern, with conjectural restorations, but Dunn's comment on this proposal is apt: "Grobel's suggestion of a larger chiasmus, vv 6-11, becomes less persuasive with its greater complexity" (*Romans 1-8* 78).

A   Eternal life to those who are seeking good
B   Wrath and anger to those who are seeking evil
B'   Tribulation and distress to those who are doing evil
A'   Glory, honor, and peace to all who are doing good

Two additional examples of chiasmus occur in 2:25 and 3:19b:[25]

περιτομὴ μὲν γὰρ ὠφελεῖ   ἐὰν νόμον πράσσῃς·
ἐὰν δὲ παραβάτης νόμου ᾖς,   ἡ περιτομή σου ἀκροβυστία γέγονεν.

Οἴδαμεν δὲ ὅτι ὅσα ὁ νόμος λέγει τοῖς ἐν τῷ νόμῳ λαλεῖ,
      ἵνα πᾶν στόμα   φραγῇ
      καὶ ὑπόδικος γένηται   πᾶς ὁ κόσμος τῷ θεῷ·

The nouns περιτομή (6x) and ἀκροβυστία (4x) dominate 2:25-27, with the former serving as a link-word to 3:1 (τί οὖν τὸ περισσὸν τοῦ ᾿Ιουδαίου, ἢ τίς ἡ ὠφέλεια τῆς περιτομῆς;). The same word reappears in 3:30, anticipating the return of the word-chain in 4:9-12 (περιτομή = 6x; ἀκροβυστία = 6x).

Although members of the δικαι- (8x) and πιστ- (8x) word-groups are not totally absent from 1:18-3:20, they assume special prominence beginning in 3:21-31 (δικαι- = 9x; πιστ- = 10x) and continuing into 4:1-25 (δικαι- = 10x; πιστ- = 16x). Similarly, λογίζομαι appears in 3:26 and 3:28, anticipating its repeated use in 4:1-25 (11x).

Quotations of Gen 15:6 (ἐπίστευσεν δὲ ᾿Αβραὰμ τῷ θεῷ, καὶ ἐλογίσθη αὐτῷ εἰς δικαιοσύνην) in 4:3 and 4:22 frame the Abraham argument of 4:1-25. This verse, which is also referred to in 4:9, is the key verse for Paul's understanding of Abraham's righteousness. The argument itself may be divided into three sections, based on the cluster of key words present in each: ἐργάζομαι (3x) and ἔργον (1x) in 4:1-8; περιτομή (6x) and ἀκροβυστία (6x) in 4:9-12; and νόμος (5x) and ἐπαγγελία (5x) in 4:13-25.

The Body: Part 2 — 5:1-8:39. Commentators differ on the relationship of chapter 5 to what precedes and what follows. Joseph Fitzmyer identifies four main views: (1) chapter 5 concludes the section that began at 1:16; (2) chapter 5 introduces the section that extends through 8:39; (3) 5:1-11 concludes the the preceding section, while 5:12-21 introduces the subsequent section; and (4) chapter 5 is an isolated unit.[26] It is, of course, often difficult, if not impossible, to identify

---

[25] On 3:19b, cf. Fitzmyer, *Romans* 337.

[26] Fitzmyer, *Romans* 96-97. He then proceeds to give six reasons for relating chapter 5 to what follows: (1) 5:12-21 would be a strange beginning for a new section; (2) 5:1-11 announces what 8:1-39 will develop; (3) 1:16-4:25 centers on Jews and Greeks, who are not mentioned in chapters 5-8; (4) the topic of the Holy Spirit—mentioned in 5:4—is developed in chapter 8; (5) "love" replaces "righteousness" as the most prominent divine attribute; (6) 1:16-4:25 is dominated by the juridical, but 5:1-8:39 emphasizes the ethical.

sharp breaks in Paul's argumentation. The oral patterns found in and around Romans 5 highlight the care with which Paul develops his argument, and suggest that the search for a sharp break in this part of the letter is destined to fail. Paul's use of word-chains will serve as a convenient starting point.

Words of the δικαι- stem form the predominant word-group in Romans, occurring repeatedly throughout chapters 1-11. There is, however, a more distinctive distribution of other words:

	1-4	5	6	7	8	9-11
δικαι-	29	8	6	1	4	13
πιστ-	33	2	1	0	0	14
ζω-	2	4	8	5	7	2
ἁμαρτ-	9	11	17	16	5	1
θανατ-	1	6	7	6	5	0

It is evident from this table that words of the πιστ- group are concentrated in chapters 1-4 and 9-11, while words of the ζω-, ἁμαρτ-, and θανατ- groups occur primarily in chapters 5-8. It is also evident that chapter 5 shares word-chains with both the chapters that precede and those that follow. In effect, Romans 5 looks both backward to chapters 1-4 and forward to chapters 6-8.

Perhaps the stronger oral pattern, however, is the use of ring-composition to tie chapter 5 to the discussion of the life of faith that follows. Running throughout chapters 5-8 is a repeated refrain that gives unity to the section and is suggestive for identifying divisions within the text: διὰ τοῦ κυρίου ἡμῶν 'Ιησοῦ Χριστοῦ. This phrase (and a variation using ἐν + dative) occurs in 5:1, 5:11, 5:21, 6:23, 7:25, and 8:39. Although the title 'Ιησοῦ Χριστοῦ τοῦ κυρίου ἡμῶν (and variations) is used elsewhere in Romans, the only other place it is used in a similar manner is 15:30 (διὰ τοῦ κυρίου ἡμῶν 'Ιησοῦ Χριστοῦ).[27] The repetition of the phrase in 5:1 and 8:39 is probably best seen as an instance of ring-composition.

Furthermore, there are a number of verbal parallels in 5:1-11 that correspond to 8:18-39:[28]

5:5, 8	ἀγάπη	8:35, 39
5:1, 9	δικαιόω	8:30, 33
5:2	δόξα/δοξάζω	8:18, 21, 30
5:2, 4, 5	ἐλπίς/ἐλπίζω	8:20, 24

[27] Other uses of the title occur in 1:4; 4:24; 15:6; 16:18, 20, 24. It is also interesting to note the textual variant in 6:11 that reads ἐν Χριστῷ 'Ιησοῦ τῷ κυρίῳ ἡμῶν.

[28] Cf. D. J. Moo, *Romans 1-8* (Chicago: Moody, 1991) 323.

5:3	θλῖψις	8:35
5:9, 10	σώζω	8:24
5:3, 4	ὑπομονή	8:25

Cues from oral patterning, then, suggest that it is better not to pursue a sharp break at Romans 5. Although chapter 5 is closely linked to chapters 6-8 through Paul's use of refrain, it also shares word-chains with chapters 1-4. Paul's discussion of the life of faith flows naturally out of his discussion of justification by faith. Rhetorically, at least, the transition that takes place in Romans 5 is a smooth one.

Within Romans 5-8, the unity of 5:1-11 is clear. It is framed by the prepositional phrases of 5:1 and 5:11,[29] the repetition of δικαιωθέντες in 5:1 and 5:9, and similar statements at the beginning of 5:3 and 5:11:

οὐ μόνον δέ, ἀλλὰ καὶ καυχώμεθα ἐν ταῖς θλίψεσιν . . .

οὐ μόνον δέ, ἀλλὰ καὶ καυχώμενοι ἐν τῷ θεῷ . . .

Word clusters divide 5:1-11 into three sections: 5:1-5 (ἐλπίς = 3x), 5:6-8 (ἀποθνήσκω = 4x), and 5:9-11 (καταλλάσσω = 2x; καταλλαγή = 1x). Verses 6-8 seem to be worded with special care:

A   ἔτι γὰρ Χριστὸς ὄντων ἡμῶν ἀσθενῶν ἔτι κατὰ καιρὸν
    ὑπὲρ ἀσεβῶν ἀπέθανεν.

B   μόλις γὰρ ὑπὲρ δικαίου τις ἀποθανεῖται·

B' ὑπὲρ γὰρ τοῦ ἀγαθοῦ τάχα τις καὶ τολμᾷ ἀποθανεῖν·

A' συνίστησιν δὲ τὴν ἑαυτοῦ ἀγάπην εἰς ἡμᾶς ὁ θεὸς ὅτι
    ἔτι ἁμαρτωλῶν ὄντων ἡμῶν Χριστὸς ὑπὲρ ἡμῶν ἀπέθανεν.

In particular, the repetition of ὑπέρ phrases drive home the point that Christ died, not on behalf of the righteous or the good, but on behalf of the ungodly—specifically, on behalf of us.

The argument of 5:12-21 is disjointed in that Paul breaks off the thought of 5:12 in an anacoluthon.[30] He appears, however, to resume his initial train of thought

---

[29] E. Käsemann also notes the thematic parallel between εἰρήνην ἔχομεν in verse 1 and τὴν καταλλαγὴν ἐλάβομεν in verse 11 (*Commentary on Romans*, G. Bromiley trans. [Grand Rapids: Eerdmans, 1980] 132).

[30] Some scholars see a chiastic construction in 5:12 (e.g., Feuillet, "Mort et Vie" 490; Dunn, *Romans 1-8* 273):

ὥσπερ δι' ἑνὸς ἀνθρώπου ἡ ἁμαρτία εἰς τὸν κόσμον εἰσῆλθεν
    καὶ διὰ τῆς ἁμαρτίας ὁ θάνατος,
    καὶ οὕτως εἰς πάντας ἀνθρώπους ὁ θάνατος διῆλθεν,
ἐφ' ᾧ πάντες ἥμαρτον—

in 5:18. This repetition might be an instance of anaphoric ring-composition, even though the wording is not exact:

ὥσπερ δι' ἑνὸς ἀνθρώπου ἡ ἁμαρτία εἰς τὸν κόσμον εἰσῆλθεν καὶ διὰ τῆς ἁμαρτίας ὁ θάνατος, καὶ οὕτως εἰς πάντας ἀνθρώπους ὁ θάνατος διῆλθεν ἐφ' ᾧ πάντες ἥμαρτον—

ὡς δι' ἑνὸς παραπτώματος εἰς πάντας ἀνθρώπους εἰς κατάκριμα, οὕτως καὶ δι' ἑνὸς δικαιώματος εἰς πάντας ἀνθρώπους εἰς δικαίωσιν ζωῆς·

The "digression" between these verses explains the concept of universal sin and contrasts with it the gift of grace offered in Christ. As a result of that discussion, "through one man" (5:12) has changed to "through one transgression" (5:18) and "into the world" (5:12) has changed to "to all men" (5:18). Concepts have been developed, but enough of the wording is repeated to make the resumption clear. The resulting structure is a loose ABA' pattern.[31]

Within the digression of 5:13-17 another ABA' pattern appears to be present (5:15-17):[32]

A   ἀλλ' οὐχ ὡς τὸ παράπτωμα, οὕτως καὶ τὸ χάρισμα· εἰ γὰρ τῷ τοῦ ἑνὸς παραπτώματι οἱ πολλοὶ ἀπέθανον, πολλῷ μᾶλλον ἡ χάρις τοῦ θεοῦ καὶ ἡ δωρεὰ ἐν χάριτι τῇ τοῦ ἑνὸς ἀνθρώπου Ἰησοῦ Χριστοῦ εἰς τοὺς πολλοὺς ἐπερίσσευσεν.

B   καὶ οὐχ ὡς δι' ἑνὸς ἁμαρτήσαντος τὸ δώρημα· τὸ μὲν γὰρ κρίμα ἐξ ἑνὸς εἰς κατάκριμα, τὸ δὲ χάρισμα ἐκ πολλῶν παραπτωμάτων εἰς δικαίωμα.

A'   εἰ γὰρ τῷ τοῦ ἑνὸς παραπτώματι ὁ θάνατος ἐβασίλευσεν διὰ τοῦ ἑνός, πολλῷ μᾶλλον οἱ τὴν περισσείαν τῆς χάριτος καὶ τῆς δωρεᾶς τῆς δικαιοσύνης λαμβάνοντες ἐν ζωῇ βασιλεύσουσιν διὰ τοῦ ἑνὸς Ἰησοῦ Χριστοῦ.

Again, similarities of wording are striking, although they are not quite identical. Verse 16 draws a contrast between the κρίμα (resulting in κατάκριμα) and the χάρισμα (resulting in δικαίωμα) in such a way as to highlight both universal sin and individual responsibility.[33] In fact, verse 16 contains six words ending in -μα, the dominant ending in 5:15-19.[34]

Käsemann rejects this analysis for theological and grammatical reasons (*Romans* 147), but the verbal links are at least suggestive.

[31] A (5:12); B (5:13-17); A' (5:18-21)

[32] Cf. Feuillet, "Mort et Vie" 500.

[33] See Dunn, *Romans 1-8* 279-282, for a good analysis of Paul's train of thought.

[34] δώρημα . . . κρίμα . . . καράκριμα . . . χάρισμα . . . παράπτωμα . . . δικαίωμα.

Also likely to have caught the listeners' attention is the parallelism of 5:19:

ὥσπερ γὰρ διὰ τῆς <u>παρακοῆς</u> τοῦ ἑνὸς ἀνθρώπου
<u>ἁμαρτωλοὶ</u> κατεστάθησαν οἱ πολλοί,
οὕτως καὶ διὰ τῆς <u>ὑπακοῆς</u> τοῦ ἑνὸς
<u>δίκαιοι</u> κατασταθήσονται οἱ πολλοί.

In this instance, the similarity of expression highlights the differences in specific words. The paragraph concludes with a chiastic construction that contrasts sin and grace (5:21):

| ἵνα ὥσπερ | ἐβασίλευσεν | ἡ ἁμαρτία | ἐν τῷ θανάτῳ, |
| οὕτως καὶ | ἡ χάρις | βασιλεύσῃ | διὰ δικαιοσύνης . . . |

This contrast, in turn, becomes the starting point for 6:1-11 (τί οὖν ἐροῦμεν; ἐπιμένωμεν τῇ ἁμαρτίᾳ, ἵνα ἡ χάρις πλεονάσῃ;).

The unity of 6:1-11 is reinforced by the sixfold repetition of ἀποθνήσκω.[35] Also worthy of note is the repeated use of the preposition σύν, both in compounds (συνετάφημεν, σύμφυτοι, συνεσταυρώθη, συζήσομεν) and alone (σὺν Χριστῷ). Within 6:1-11 are four examples of chiasmus, representing different degrees of orality:

6:3	ἐβαπτίσθημεν		εἰς Χριστὸν ᾿Ιησοῦν
	εἰς τὸν θάνατον αὐτοῦ		ἐβαπτίσθημεν
6:5	σύμφυτοι γεγόναμεν		τῷ ὁμοιώματι τοῦ θανάτου αὐτοῦ
	τῆς ἀναστάσεως		ἐσόμεθα
6:6	ὁ παλαιὸς ἡμῶν ἄνθρωπος		συνεσταυρώθη,
	ἵνα καταργηθῇ		τὸ σῶμα τῆς ἁμαρτίας
6:10	ὃ γὰρ ἀπέθανεν,	τῇ ἁμαρτίᾳ	ἀπέθανεν ἐφάπαξ·
	ὃ δε ζῇ,	ζῇ	τῷ θεῷ.

Although ἁμαρτία occurs in both 6:12 and 6:14, and although the synonyms βασιλεύω (6:12) and κυριεύω (6:14) also appear in those verses, it is probably best not to consider this repetition an instance of inclusion. For ἁμαρτία occurs sixteen times in chapter 6, including 6:13. Although Forbes proposes a concentric

---

[35] 6:2, 7, 8, 9, 10 [twice]. Dunn correctly notes the *thematic* correspondence between verses 2 and 11 (*Romans 1-8* 305), but this correspondence does not constitute an inclusion as defined in this study. As Forbes has pointed out (*Romans* 24-25), the basic construction is "parallel" rather than "chiastic":

v.2-4	died → knowing → baptized → new life
v.5-7	death → knowing → crucified → justified
v.8-10	died → knowing → raised → alive

arrangement for 6:12-14,[36] a parallel structure seems more natural, particularly when verse 13 is taken into account:

μηδὲ παριστάνετε   τὰ μέλη ὑμῶν   ὅπλα ἀδικίας   τῇ ἁμαρτίᾳ,
ἀλλὰ παραστήσατε   ἑαυτοὺς   τῷ θεῷ . . .
καὶ   τὰ μέλη ὑμῶν   ὅπλα δικαιοσύνης   τῷ θεῷ

As well, as with 5:21, the final contrast in 6:14 (οὐ γάρ ἐστε ὑπὸ νόμον ἀλλὰ ὑπὸ χάριν) becomes the starting point for 6:15-23 (τί οὖν; ἁμαρτήσωμεν ὅτι οὐκ ἐσμὲν ὑπὸ νόμον ἀλλὰ ὑπὸ χάριν;), thereby moving the argument forward and persuasively drawing the listener along with it.

Members of the δουλ- word-group dominate 6:15-23.[37] This concentration of words related to slavery gives the paragraph a perspective that is subtly different than that of 6:1-14, even though the basic theme is the same. The use of βασιλεύω (6:12) and κυριεύω (6:9, 14) in 6:1-14 presents the topic of sanctification from "the top down": sin is no longer king/master. The use of δοῦλος and δουλόω in 6:15-23 presents the same topic from "the bottom up": Christians are now to present themselves as slaves to righteousness.

Although the refrain in 6:23 (ἐν Χριστῷ ᾿Ιησοῦ τῷ κυρίῳ ἡμῶν) appears to mark the end of a section, 7:1-6 functions much as 5:1-11 does. The use of κυριεύω in 7:1 suggests a connection to 6:1-14,[38] and the disclosure formula of that verse (ἢ ἀγνοεῖτε, ἀδελφοί, . . . ὅτι) could be read as introducing a second argument parallel to that of 6:15-23.[39] There is a marked shift in the word-chain, with νόμος appearing six times in 7:1-6 and seventeen times in 7:7-25.[40] Yet 7:1-6 contains a number of verbal connections to 6:1-23, including καταργέω (7:2, 6; cf. 6:6), ἀποθνήσκω (7:2, 3, 6; cf. 6:2, 7, 8, 9, 10), ἐλεύθερος (7:3; cf. 6:18, 20, 22), and δουλεύω (7:6; cf. 6:6, 16, 17, 18, 19, 20, 22). The use of the antithetical word pair σάρξ (7:5) and πνεῦμα (7:6) anticipates the dominance of that word-chain in 8:1-30.[41]

The rhetorical questions of 7:7 (τί οὖν ἐροῦμεν; ὁ νόμος ἁμαρτία;) and Paul's emphatic rejection of the sentiments expressed in them (μὴ γένοιτο) mark

---

[36] Forbes, *Romans* 26. His arrangement is: a (v. 12 = sin) b (v. 13a = members/instruments) c (v. 13b = yield) b' (v. 13d = members/instruments) a' (v. 14 = sin).

[37] δοῦλος (6x); δουλόω (2x). Other key words are ἐλεύθερος (1x), ἐλευθερόω (3x), ὑπακοή (2x), and ὑπακούω (2x).

[38] κυριεύω appears only four times in Romans (6:9; 6:14; 7:1; 14:9) and only twice in other letters ascribed to Paul (2 Cor 1:24; 1 Tim 6:15).

[39] Cf. 6:3, where a similar disclosure formula introduces an alternate understanding of what immediately precedes.

[40] As opposed to three uses in chapter 5, two in chapter 6, and five in chapter 8.

[41] σάρξ occurs 11 times in 8:1-17; πνεῦμα occurs 22 times in 8:1-30.

the beginning of a new paragraph (7:7-12) that focuses on the key word ἐντολή (5x) and uses ring-composition to frame the heart of Paul's teaching (7:8-11):

ἀφορμὴν δὲ λαβοῦσα ἡ ἁμαρτία διὰ τῆς ἐντολῆς κατειργάσατο ἐν ἐμοὶ πᾶσαν ἐπιθυμίαν· χωρὶς γὰρ νόμου ἁμαρτία νεκρά. ἐγὼ δὲ ἔζων χωρὶς νόμου ποτέ· ἐλθούσης δὲ τῆς ἐντολῆς ἡ ἁμαρτία ἀνέζησεν, ἐγὼ δὲ ἀπέθανον, καὶ εὑρέθη μοι ἡ ἐντολὴ ἡ εἰς ζωὴν αὕτη εἰς θάνατον· ἡ γὰρ ἁμαρτία ἀφορμὴν λαβοῦσα διὰ τῆς ἐντολῆς ἐξηπάτησέν με καὶ δι' αὐτῆς ἀπέκτεινεν.

The fifth use of ἐντολή is in the affirmation of 7:12 (καὶ ἡ ἐντολὴ ἁγία καὶ δικαία καὶ ἀγαθή). It reappears in 7:13 as a link-word between the paragraphs.

Yet another rhetorical question (τὸ οὖν ἀγαθὸν ἐμοὶ ἐγένετο θάνατος;) and emphatic rejection (μὴ γένοιτο) mark the beginning of a new paragraph (7:13-25). As in 7:1-6, the adjectives πνευματικός and σάρκινος (7:14) anticipate the word-chain of chapter 8. One half of the letter's uses of κατεργάζομαι (5 of 11) and οἰκέω (3 of 5) appear in this paragraph, with a particularly heavy cluster being found in 7:17-20, where—as in 7:8-11—ring-composition appears to frame a central concept in Paul's discussion:

νυνὶ δὲ οὐκέτι ἐγὼ κατεργάζομαι αὐτὸ ἀλλὰ ἡ οἰκοῦσα ἐν ἐμοὶ ἁμαρτία. οἶδα γὰρ ὅτι οὐκ οἰκεῖ ἐν ἐμοί, τοῦτ' ἔστιν ἐν τῇ σαρκί μου, ἀγαθόν· τὸ γὰρ θέλειν παράκειταί μοι, τὸ δὲ κατεργάζεσθαι τὸ καλὸν οὔ· οὐ γὰρ ὃ θέλω ποιῶ ἀγαθόν, ἀλλὰ ὃ οὐ θέλω κακὸν τοῦτο πράσσω. εἰ δὲ ὃ οὐ θέλω ἐγὼ τοῦτο ποιῶ, οὐκέτι ἐγὼ κατεργάζομαι αὐτὸ ἀλλὰ ἡ οἰκοῦσα ἐν ἐμοὶ ἁμαρτία.

The refrain of 7:24 (διὰ Ἰησοῦ Χριστοῦ τοῦ κυρίου ἡμῶν), the strong affirmation of 8:1 (οὐδεν ἄρα νῦν κατάκριμα τοῖς ἐν Χριστῷ Ἰησοῦ), and a shift in the word-chain all mark a turning point in the argument at the beginning of Romans 8. The word-chain using σάρξ and πνεῦμα is the dominant oral feature in this section of the letter, as the following chart makes clear:

	1-4	5	6	7	8	9-11	12-16
σάρξ	4	0	1	3	11	4	1
πνεῦμα	3	1	0	1	22	1	7

Other notable features include (1) the cluster of four φρον- cognates in 8:5-7, (2) the cluster of four συν- compounds in 8:16-17, (3) the cluster of eight ἀπο-compounds in 8:18-25, and (4) the use of climax in 8:16-17 and 8:29-30.[42]

42 8:16-17 τέκνα . . . κληρονόμοι . . . συγκληρονόμοι
8:29-30 προέγνω . . . προώρισεν . . . ἐκάλεσεν . . . ἐδικαίωσεν . . . ἐδόξασεν

A triumphant statement of God's faithfulness in 8:31-39 concludes chapters 5-8. After a series of questions and brief answers (8:31-34), Paul asks the question that he answers at greater length: τίς ἡμᾶς χωρίσει ἀπὸ τῆς ἀγάπης τοῦ Χριστοῦ; (8:35). He concludes with a confession echoing that question (8:38-39):

> πέπεισμαι γὰρ ὅτι οὔτε θάνατος οὔτε ζωὴ οὔτε ἄγγελοι οὔτε ἀρχαὶ οὔτε ἐνεστῶτα οὔτε μέλλοντα οὔτε δυνάμεις οὔτε ὕψωμα οὔτε βάθος οὔτε τις κτίσις ἑτέρα δυνήσεται ἡμᾶς χωρίσαι ἀπὸ τῆς ἀγάπης τοῦ θεοῦ τῆς ἐν Χριστῷ Ἰησοῦ τῷ κυρίῳ ἡμῶν.

The ring-composition framing 8:35-39 is clear, as is the tenfold use of οὔτε. It is helpful to note as well that 8:39 contains the last of the confessional uses of the title Ἰησοῦ Χριστοῦ τοῦ κυρίου ἡμῶν, the first of which occurred in 5:1. These verses, therefore, serve as a double conclusion, both to 8:31-39 and to chapters 5-8.

The Body: Part 3 — 9:1-11:36. Chapters 9-11 comprise "a carefully composed and rounded unit with a clear beginning (9:1-5) and end (11:33-36)."[43] The relation of these chapters to their context—as well as, of course, their purpose—has been the subject of a great deal of scholarly discussion.[44] They are, however, most naturally understood as an explanation of how the Jews relate to the gospel that is "the power of God for salvation to all who believe, to the Jew first and to the Greek."[45] The unity of these chapters, however, is such that care is needed in subdividing them.

The confessional statement in 9:5 marks the end of an introductory paragraph in which Paul expresses his concern for Israel. Paul regularly uses rhetorical questions to change topics in this letter.[46] Such is the case in 9:30. This question also coincides with a shift in Paul's word-chain from ἔλεος and ἐλεέω to δικαιοσύνη, πίστις, and πιστεύω:[47]

	1-4	5-8	9:1-29	9:30-10:21	11:1-39	12-16
ἔλεος/ἐλεέω	0	0	5	0	4	2
δικαιοσύνη	14	8	0	11	0	1
πίστις/πιστεύω	33	3	0	13	1	10
χάρις	5	10	0	0	5	5

---

[43] Dunn, *Romans 9-16* (Dallas: Word, 1988) 518.

[44] Cf. Fitzmyer, *Romans* 540-541.

[45] See Käsemann, *Romans* 253-260; Cranfield, *Romans* 2:445-450; Fitzmyer, *Romans* 541-543, for good discussions.

[46] Cf. 4:1; 6:1; 7:7; 9:14. See also Dunn's discussion (*Romans* 9-16 579).

[47] The fourfold repetition of δικαιοσύνη in 9:30-31 makes the shift especially apparent.

A saying formula (λέγω οὖν) serves to introduce another rhetorical question (μὴ ἀπώσατο ὁ θεὸς τὸν λαὸν αὐτοῦ;) that performs a similar function in 11:1.[48] Again, there is a shift in the word-chain; this time it is a return to ἔλεος and ἐλεέω with the addition of χάρις.[49] The hymn and doxology of 11:33-36 bring the entire section to a close. If 9:1-5 and 11:33-36 are viewed as introduction and conclusion, the intervening material—especially when the shift in word-chains is taken into account—may be seen as forming an ABA' pattern: 9:6-29 (A); 9:30-10:21 (B); 11:1-32 (A').[50]

The δικαι- and πιστ- word-groups take center stage in Rom 9:30-10:21, this time at the center of an ABA' pattern. Here, as in other places, Paul uses the ABA' pattern to look at an issue from different perspectives. First, Israel's plight is placed against the backdrop of God's sovereignty in 9:6-29. Then in 9:30-10:21 he addresses the heart of the problem: Israel's rejection of the gospel of righteousness by faith. Finally, Paul returns in 11:1-32 to a consideration of Israel's plight in light of God's character, with God's mercy and grace being particularly in focus. The discussion of righteousness by faith at the heart of chapters 9-11 demonstrates that these chapters are not an appendix or excursus but are, in fact, directly related to what precedes—especially chapters 1-4. It would be helpful to have the same sort of repeated refrain as in chapters 5-8, but that is not the case here in chapters 9-11. The kind of specific verbal cues that would have helped the listener are few, but it is possible to give tentative approval to an overall ABA' pattern in these chapters.

---

[48] Dunn: "The opening question (11:1) is a natural conclusion (οὖν) to the preceding answers" (*Romans 9-16* 634); cf. Cranfield (*Romans* 2:543).

[49] Another piece of lexical evidence that needs to be taken into consideration is the presence of six related words: ὑπόλειμμα (9:27), ἐγκαταλείπω (9:29), ὑπολείπω (11:3), καταλείπω (11:4), λεῖμμα (11:5), and λοιπός (11:7). Except for λοιπός (which also appears in 1:3), these words are used nowhere else in Romans. In the other letters ascribed to Paul, ἐγκαταλείπω is found three times (2 Cor 4:9; 2 Tim 4:10, 16); καταλείπω is found three times (1 Thess 3:1; Eph 5:31 [OT quotation]; Tit 1:5); and λοιπός is found fourteen times. The first four words appear in OT quotations, and it is likely that the OT language has influenced Paul to use λεῖμμα and λοιπός in 11:5 and 11:7. Nevertheless, the distribution of these words also supports the ABA pattern proposed for chapters 9-11.

[50] A number of scholars have identified an ABA' or chiastic pattern in these chapters; see Collins ("Chiasmus" 577) for bibliography on early suggestions. Ellis (*Letters* 240) has a related, but less attractive scheme:
A   9:1-5 - The Jews' rejection of the gospel seems to contradict God's promises to Israel
B   9:6-29 - God's promises are fulfilled through the remnant of believing Jews
C   9:30-10:21 - The Jews' misguided zeal for righteousness has led them to reject the gospel
B'   11:1-10 - God's promises are fulfilled through the remnant of believing Jews
A'   11:11-36 - The Jews' rejection of the gospel is only temporary
It seems unnatural to combine 11:11-36 into a single panel and then "pair" it with 9:1-5. Unfortunately, 9:1-5 and 11:33-36 have little in common, so an alternative ABCB'A' scheme that would make these paragraphs parallel must also be regarded as questionable.

The conclusion that Paul reaches in 9:18 (ἄρα οὖν ὃν θέλει ἐλεεῖ, ὃν δὲ θέλει σκληρύνει) raises possible questions about God's fairness in acting as he does (9:19). As an illustration of God's sovereignty in his dealings, Paul turns to the potter who has the authority to create "vessels for honor and for dishonor" (9:20-21). The vessels are then taken up in reverse order in 9:22-23:

ὃ μὲν εἰς τιμὴν σκεῦος
ὃ δὲ εἰς ἀτιμίαν {σκευος} ·
σκεύη ὀργῆς . . . εἰς ἀπώλειαν
σκεύη ἐλέους . . . εἰς δόξαν

The wording varies, but the thought is inverted. The repeated use of σκεῦος and εἰς would probably have served as verbal cues for the listener.

A similar use of inversion occurs in 9:24-29. The order "Jew . . . Gentile" (9:24) is inverted conceptually in the scriptural proofs of 9:25-29:[51]

οὓς καὶ ἐκάλεσεν ἡμᾶς   οὐ μόνον ἐξ Ἰουδαίων
                            ἀλλὰ καὶ ἐξ ἐθνῶν

ὡς καὶ ἐν τῷ Ὡσηὲ λέγει, Καλέσω τὸν οὐ λαόν μου λαόν μου . . .

Ἡσαΐας δὲ κράζει ὑπὲρ τοῦ Ἰσραήλ . . .

The idea of "Gentiles" is picked up with Hosea's reference to "not my people" as the focus of God's gracious activity. The idea of "Jews" is picked up with Isaiah's reference to "Israel" out of whom God will preserve a remnant. The wording, of course, varies. Yet the thought is clearly inverted. Just how apparent this particular instance of inversion would have been to the listener is uncertain.

The chiasmus of 10:3— reinforced by the homoeoteleuton of ἀγνοοῦντες and ζητοῦντες— brings into sharp relief Israel's problem:

	ἀγνοοῦντες γὰρ	τὴν τοῦ θεοῦ δικαιοσύνην,
καὶ	τὴν ἰδίαν δικαιοσύνην	ζητοῦντες στῆσαι,
	τῇ δικαιοσύνῃ τοῦ θεοῦ	οὐχ ὑπετάγησαν·

Jeremias has accurately observed a chiasmus in 10:9-10.[52] Forbes, however, has gone further and pointed out that the words στόμα and καρδία first appear in verse 8 and that the quotations of verses 11 and 13 continue the ideas of believing

---

[51] Cf. Jeremias, "Chiasmus" 150; Käsemann, *Romans* 274.

[52] Jeremias, "Chiasmus" 149. He also points out the way in which Paul has inverted the order of ὁμολογέω/στόμα and πιστεύω/καρδία. The usual understanding of the inverted order of verses 9 and 10 is that verse 9 follows the order of the Deut 30:14 quotation in verse 8b, while verse 10 restores the natural order of belief → confession (e.g. Dunn, *Romans 9-16* 615-616, but contrast Käsemann who rejects this analysis [*Romans* 291]).

and confessing.[53] The result is a combination of chiasmus and alternation that is similar to structures found elsewhere in Romans:[54]

	ἐγγύς σου τὸ ῥῆμά ἐστιν,
A/B	ἐν τῷ <u>στόματί</u> σου καὶ ἐν τῇ <u>καρδίᾳ</u> σου . . .
A	ἐὰν <u>ὁμολογήσῃς</u> ἐν τῷ <u>στόματί</u> σου κύριον Ἰησοῦν,
B	καὶ <u>πιστεύσῃς</u> ἐν τῇ <u>καρδίᾳ</u> σου . . .
B	<u>καρδίᾳ</u> γὰρ <u>πιστεύεται</u> εἰς δικαιοσύνην,
A	<u>στόματι</u> δὲ <u>ὁμολογεῖται</u> εἰς σωτηρίαν.
B	πᾶς ὁ <u>πιστεύων</u> ἐπ᾽ αὐτῷ οὐ καταισχυνθήσεται.
A	πᾶς γὰρ ὃς ἂν <u>ἐπικαλέσηται</u> τὸ <u>ὄνομα</u> κυρίου σωθήσεται.

The ἐπικαλέω that concludes this structure becomes both the link word to 10:14-21 and the beginning of an instance of climax (10:14-15).

Paul has retained the chiastic structure of all three of the OT quotations in 10:19, 11:3, and 11:10:

ἐγὼ παραζηλώσω ὑμᾶς	ἐπ᾽ οὐκ ἔθνει,	
ἐπ᾽ ἔθνει ἀσυνέτῳ	παροργιῶ ὑμᾶς.	(Deut 32:21)

τοὺς προφήτας σου	ἀπέκτειναν,	
τὰ θυσιαστήριά σου	κατέσκαψαν . . .	
καὶ ζητοῦσιν	τὴν ψυχήν μου.	(1 Ki 19:10)

σκοτισθήτωσαν	οἱ ὀφθαλμοὶ αὐτῶν . . .	
τὸν νῶτον αὐτῶν . . .	διὰ παντὸς σύγκαμψον.	(Ps 69:23)

As might be expected, agricultural terms dominate 11:11-24.[55] In addition, a chiasmus is present in 11:18 and an example of alternation in 11:22:[56]

οὐ	<u>σὺ</u>	<u>τὴν ῥίζαν</u> βαστάζεις
ἀλλὰ	<u>ἡ ῥίζα</u>	<u>σέ.</u>

A/B	ἴδε οὖν <u>χρηστότητα</u> καὶ <u>ἀποτομίαν</u> θεοῦ·
B	ἐπὶ μὲν τοὺς πεσόντας <u>ἀποτομία,</u>
A	ἐπὶ δὲ σὲ <u>χρηστότης</u> θεοῦ,

---

[53] Forbes (*Romans* 45): c (mouth) d (heart) c (mouth) d (heart) d (heart/believe) c (mouth/confess) d (believe) c (heart). His analysis relies on equating ἐπικαλέω with ὁμολογέω.

[54] E.g., 2:10-17.

[55] ἐλαία (11:17, 24), ἀγριέλαιος (11:17, 24), καλλιέλαιος (11:24), ἐκκόπτω (11:22, 24), ἐκκλάζω (11:17, 19, 20), ἐγκεντρίζω (11:17, 19, 23 [twice], 24 [twice])

[56] Jeremias notes part of the inversion in 11:22, but he overlooks the fact that ἐκκόπτω serves as a metonymy for ἀποτομία ("Chiasmus" 147, 150). Dunn mentions "the neat chiastic structure of v.24" (*Romans 9–16* 652), but the structure is more naturally understood as "parallel":
σὺ . . . κατὰ φύσιν . . . ἐνεκεντρίσθης εἰς καλλιέλαιον . . .
οὗτοι . . . κατὰ φύσιν . . . ἐγκεντρισθήσονται τῇ ἰδίᾳ ἐλαίᾳ.

A   ἐὰν ἐπιμένῃς τῇ χρηστότητι,
B   ἐπεὶ καὶ σὺ ἐκκοπήσῃ.

Dunn and Käsemann both note the complex chiasmus in 11:30-31:[57]

ὥσπερ γὰρ	ὑμεῖς	ποτε	ἠπειθήσατε	τῷ θεῷ,
	νῦν δὲ	ἠλεήθητε	τῇ τούτων ἀπειθείᾳ,
οὕτως καὶ	οὗτοι	νῦν	ἠπείθησαν	τῷ ὑμετέρῳ ἐλέει
ἵνα καὶ	αὐτοὶ	νῦν	ἐλεηθῶσιν·

There is a less complex chiasmus in 11:32 as well:

συνέκλεισεν γὰρ ὁ θεὸς   τοὺς πάντας εἰς ἀπείθειαν
ἵνα τοὺς πάντας   ἐλεήσῃ

And there is general agreement that an inverted structure is present in 11:33-35:[58]

ὦ βάθος	πλούτου	(riches) A
καὶ	σοφίας	(wisdom) B
καὶ	γνώσεως θεοῦ . . .	(knowledge) C
τίς γὰρ ἔγνω νοῦν κυρίου;		(knowledge) C'
ἢ τίς σύμβουλος αὐτοῦ ἐγένετο;		(wisdom) B'
ἢ τίς προέδωκεν αὐτῷ, καὶ ἀνταποδοθήσεται αὐτῷ;		(riches) A'

It should be noted, however, that (1) the verbal links for this analysis are tenuous, and (2) it is uncertain how apparent this particular instance of inversion would have been to the listener.

The Body: Part 4 — 12:1-15:13. The request formula in 12:1 (παρακαλῶ οὖν ὑμᾶς, ἀδελφοί, διὰ τῶν οἰκτιρμῶν τοῦ θεοῦ) introduces a new section of the letter that extends through 15:13. This section serves as the paraenesis of the letter. The first two verses of chapter 12 function to recall themes developed earlier in the letter and to introduce the application of those themes in daily life.[59] A saying statement in 12:3 (λέγω γὰρ . . .) introduces the first in a series of "practical" issues related to the Christian life.

The oral patterns in chapters 12:1-13:14 are all small in scale, in keeping with the paraenetic nature of the material. The repetition ὑπερφρονεῖν . . . φρονεῖν . . . φρονεῖν . . . σωφρονεῖν in 12:3 would certainly have caught the attention of the listener, as would the repetition of εἴτε . . . ἐν in 12:6-8:

---

[57] Dunn: "This is the most contrived or carefully constructed formulation which Paul ever produced in such a tight epigrammatic form . . . set within a basic chiastic structure" (*Romans 9-16* 687; cf. further discussion and interaction with Cranfield on 688); cf. Käsemann, *Romans* 316

[58] Cf. Forbes, *Romans* 51; Lund, *Chiasmus* 222; Jeremias, "Chiasmus" 150; Dunn, *Romans 9-16* 698.

[59] See Dunn, *Romans 9-16* 707-708, for a good summary of these verses.

εἴτε προφητείαν κατὰ τὴν ἀναλογίαν τῆς πίστεως,
εἴτε διακονίαν ἐν τῇ διακονίᾳ,
εἴτε ὁ διδάσκων ἐν τῇ διδασκαλίᾳ,
εἴτε ὁ παρακαλῶν ἐν τῇ παρακλήσει,
     ὁ μεταδιδοὺς ἐν ἁπλότητι,
     ὁ προϊστάμενος ἐν σπουδῇ,
     ὁ ἐλεῶν ἐν ἱλαρότητι

As would the repeated use of the dative and the participle in 12:10-13:[60]

τῇ φιλαδελφίᾳ εἰς ἀλλήλους φιλόστοργοι,
τῇ τιμῇ ἀλλήλους προηγούμενοι,
τῇ σπουδῇ μὴ ὀκνηροί,
τῷ πνεύματι ζέοντες,
τῷ κυρίῳ δουλεύοντες,
τῇ ἐλπίδι χαίροντες,
τῇ θλίψει ὑπομένοντες,
τῇ προσευχῇ προσκαρτεροῦντες,
ταῖς χρείαις τῶν ἁγίων κοινωνοῦντες,

The larger blocks of instruction move forward by stages, using link-words: ἐκδικέω, ἐκδίκησις, and ὀργή in 12:19 lead to ἔκδικος and ὀργή in 13:4; ὀφειλή in 13:7 leads to ὀφείλω in 13:8; and ἐπιθυμέω in 13:8 leads to ἐπιθυμία in 13:14.

The paragraph on submitting to authority (13:1-7) is loosely framed by the repetition of ὑποτάσσω in 13:1 and 13:5, and it contains a chiasmus in 13:2:

ὥστε ὁ ἀντιτασσόμενος τῇ ἐξουσίᾳ
      τῇ τοῦ θεοῦ διαταγῇ ἀνθέστηκεν,
      οἱ δὲ ἀνθεστηκότες ἑαυτοῖς κρίμα λήμψονται.

The subsequent paragraph—that on love—is held together by the repetition of ἀγάπη (2x) and ἀγαπάω (3x). It also contains a chiasmus (13:10):[61]

ἡ ἀγάπη τῷ πλησίον κακὸν οὐκ ἐργάζεται·
πλήρωμα οὖν νόμου ἡ ἀγάπη.

The argument of 14:1-15:13 is more sustained than that of 12:3-13:14 and, consequently, has somewhat wider scope for oral patterning. A form of inclusion occurs in 14:1 and 15:1.[62] By repeating forms of the ἀσθεν- word group to begin parallel sections, Paul cues the listener to the resumption of a topic addressed earlier:

---

[60] Cf. D. A. Black's analysis of these verses below.

[61] Cf. Dunn, *Romans 9-16* 775.

[62] Dunn: "The chapter break is poorly located in this instance, since 15:1-6 clearly continues the theme of chap. 14. The effect is to summarize the primary responsibilities of 'the strong,' an emphasis which brackets the whole discussion (14:1; 15:1-2)" (*Romans 9-16* 836).

τὸν δὲ ἀσθενοῦντα τῇ πίστει προσλαμβάνεσθε, μὴ εἰς διακρίσεις διαλογισμῶν. ὃς μὲν πιστεύει φαγεῖν πάντα, ὁ δὲ ἀσθενῶν λάχανα ἐσθίει.

ὀφείλομεν δὲ ἡμεῖς οἱ δυνατοὶ τὰ ἀσθενήματα τῶν ἀδυνάτων βαστάζειν, καὶ μὴ ἑαυτοῖς ἀρέσκειν.

This and other instances of resumptive/inclusive wording in 14:1-15:13 may be set out as follows:

ἀσθεν-	14:1		15:1
προσλαμβάνω	14:1, 3		15:7 (2x)
πρόσκομμα/προσκόπτω	14:13	14:20, 21	
πίστις/πιστεύω	14:1, 2	14:22, 23	15:13

From this analysis, a possible ABA' pattern begins to emerge.[63] Additional support for such a pattern is found in the distribution of key word-groups: (1) words for "weak," "strong," and "accept" occur predominantly in 14:1-12 and 15:1-13; (2) words for "stumble" occur exclusively in 14:13-23.[64]

Serving to frame Rom 14:1-12 is an inclusion using ἐξουθενέω and κρίνω:

14:3 ὁ ἐσθίων τὸν μὴ ἐσθίοντα μὴ ἐξουθενείτω, ὁ δὲ μὴ ἐσθίων τὸν ἐσθίοντα μὴ κρινέτω . . .

14:10 σὺ δὲ τί κρίνεις τὸν ἀδελφόν σου; ἢ καὶ σὺ τί ἐξουθενεῖς τὸν ἀδελφόν σου;

This paragraph may be further divided into three sections: 14:1-3; 14:4-9; and 14:10-12. The first (14:1-3) is framed by an inclusion using προσλαμβάνω. The second

---

[63] Cf. Ellis, *Letters* 256:

A	14:1-12	The strong and the weak
B	14:13-23	Obedience and sacrificing the use of one's rights for others
A'	15:1-13	The strong and the weak and the example of Christ

[64] The word distribution may be set out as follows:

	14:1-12	14:13-23	15:1-13
ἀδύνατος	0	0	1
ἀσθενέω	2	0	0
ἀσθένημα	0	0	1
δυνατός	1	0	1
προσλαμβάνω	2	0	2
πρόσκομμα	0	2	0
προσκόπτω	0	1	0
σκανδαλίζω	0	1	0
σκάνδαλον	0	1	0

(14:4-9) contains heavy concentrations of ζάω (5x), ἀποθνήσκω (5x), and κύριος (8x); as well, it features an example of alternation in 14:7-9:[65]

A	οὐδεὶς γὰρ ἡμῶν ἑαυτῷ <u>ζῇ</u>,
B	καὶ οὐδεὶς ἑαυτῷ <u>ἀποθνήσκει</u>·
A	ἐάν τε γὰρ <u>ζῶμεν</u>, τῷ κυρίῳ <u>ζῶμεν</u>,
B	ἐάν τε <u>ἀποθνήσκωμεν</u>, τῷ κυρίῳ <u>ἀποθνήσκομεν</u>.
A	ἐάν τε οὖν <u>ζῶμεν</u>
B	ἐάν τε <u>ἀποθνήσκωμεν</u>, τοῦ κυρίου ἐσμέν.
B	εἰς τοῦτο γὰρ Χριστὸς <u>ἀπέθανεν</u>
A	καὶ <u>ἔζησεν</u>
B	ἵνα καὶ <u>νεκρῶν</u>
A	καὶ <u>ζώντων</u> κυριεύσῃ.

The link-word κρίνω (14:10) is used twice in 14:13. This double use is actually a play on words (μηκέτι οὖν ἀλλήλους κρίνωμεν· ἀλλὰ τοῦτο κρίνατε μᾶλλον), with the second use having the sense of "determine" rather than "judge." κρίνω and its cognate κατακρίνω reappear in 14:22-23, effectively framing the paragraph.

On a smaller scale, in 14:11 and 15:9 Paul again retains the chiastic structure of the OT quotations:

ζῶ ἐγώ, λέγει κύριος,		(Isa 45:23)
ὅτι ἐμοὶ	κάμψει πᾶν γόνυ,	
καὶ πᾶσα γλῶσσα ἐξομολογήσεται	τῷ θεῷ.	

| διὰ τοῦτο | ἐξομολογήσομαί σοι | ἐν ἔθνεσιν, | (Ps 18:49) |
| | καὶ τῷ ὀνόματί σου | ψαλῶ. | |

The Body: Part 5 — 15:14-15:33. There are strong verbal connections between 1:8-15 and 15:14-33. These connections serve to bracket the body of the letter, as Dunn observes: "The restatement of themes covered in 1:8-15 is not simply the result of Paul's using a standard mix of sentiments . . . but is intended to reinforce the bracketing effect of the two sections on the main body of the letter."[66] The strongest points of verbal correspondence are:

1:5	δι᾽ οὗ ἐλάβομεν χάριν	15:15	διὰ τὴν χάριν τὴν δοθεῖσάν μοι
1:5	εἰς ὑπακοὴν πίστεως	15:18	εἰς ὑπακοὴν ἐθνῶν
1:5	ἐν πᾶσιν τοῖς ἔθνεσιν	15:16	εἰς τὰ ἔθνη
1:9	ᾧ λατρεύω . . . τῷ εὐαγγελίῳ	15:16	λειτουργὸν . . . τὸ εὐαγγέλιον
1:10	ἐπὶ τῶν προσευχῶν μου	15:30	ἐν ταῖς προσευχαῖς ὑπερ ἐμοῦ
1:10	ἐν τῷ θελήματι τοῦ θεοῦ	15:32	διὰ θελήματος θεοῦ
1:11	ἐπιποθῶ γὰρ ἰδεῖν ὑμᾶς	15:23	ἐπιποθίαν . . . τοῦ ἐλθεῖν πρὸς ὑμᾶς

---

[65] Cf. Jeremias, "Chiasmus" 147; Käsemann, *Romans* 359.

[66] Dunn, *Romans 9-16* 857.

1:14	ὀφειλέτης εἰμί	15:27	ὀφείλουσιν
1:15	εὐαγγελίσασθαι	15:20	εὐαγγελίζεσθαι

There are other, less exact, parallels as well.[67] Such parallels between a letter-body's opening and closing are to be expected. These portions are intended to re-establish and maintain personal relations with the recipients. It is only natural that similar language will appear in them both, for the overall structure of ancient letters is ABA'.[68] The letter closing of 16:1-27, however, contains no examples of oral patterning.

C. Other Suggested Structures.

Peter Ellis divides Romans into three parts, each arranged in an ABA' pattern:[69]

Part I (1:1-4:25): Paul's thesis: Faith in Jesus is the sole source of salvation for all.

A	(1:1-17)	Greetings, thanksgiving, and statement of thesis
B	(1:18-3:20)	Apparent digression: The Gentiles' system and the Jews' system cannot justify. All need God's justice because all have sinned.
A'	(3:21-4:25)	Thesis summarized (3:21-31) and objection concerning the law answered with an argument from Scripture (4:1-25)

Part II (5:1-11:36): Paul's thesis in another form: God's love for humanity is the foundation of man's hope for salvation.

A	(5:1-11)	Thesis stated: God loves humanity and has proved his love by sending his Son to die for sinners.
B	(5:12-7:25)	Apparent digression: Paul's faith system versus the system of law. Experience proves that all need God's saving love and those who believe have experienced it.
A'	(8:1-11:36)	Thesis of 5:1-11 summarized (8:1-39) and concluded by argument from Scripture showing that God's love does not exclude the Jews (9:1-11:36).

Part III (12:1-16:27): Exhortation, Paul's plans, conclusion

A	(12:1-13:14)	Exhortations
B	(14:1-15:13)	Apparent digression: the strong and the weak
A'	(15:14-16:27)	Conclusion, Paul's plans, final greetings

---

[67] Cf. J. A. D. Weima, "Preaching the Gospel in Rome: A Study of the Epistolary Framework of Romans," in *Gospel in Paul: Studies on Corinthians, Galatians and Romans for Richard N. Longenecker*, L. A. Jervis and P. Richardson, eds., JSNTSup 108 (Sheffield: Academic Press, 1994) 355.

[68] Cf. J. C. Hurd, "Good News and the Integrity of 1 Corinthians," in *Gospel in Paul* 57.

[69] Ellis, *Letters* 204

There are, however, a number of drawbacks to this scheme: (1) It is curious to find key portions of the argument labelled "apparent digressions" (particularly 1:18-3:20 and 14:1-15:13). (2) It is difficult to see how 3:31-4:25 balances 1:1-17. (3) Regarding 12:1-16:27 Ellis himself writes, "The final section . . . (15:14-16:27) forms more of a parallel with section A (1:1-17) of Part I than with section A (12:1-13:14) of Part III and may be intended as an overall inclusion-conclusion."[70] Furthermore, (4) Adding 9:1-11:36 to 8:1-39 and making the combination parallel to 5:1-11 is particularly awkward. It is possible that smaller-scale aspects of Ellis's analysis will prove helpful, but the overall scheme is not particularly persuasive.

It is generally thought that 1:3-4 is an older confession incorporated into the salutation.[71] Jervis sees "a carefully crafted chiastic form" in these verses:[72]

> ἐκ σπέρματος . . .
>   κατὰ σάρκα
>   κατὰ πνεῦμα . . .
> ἐξ ἀναστάσεως νεκρῶν

Furthermore, Angelico DiMarco thinks this confessional bit was inserted in such a way as to result in an ABCC' B' A' scheme for the entire salutation.[73] Unfortunately, DiMarco's scheme requires 1:1 to be "balanced" by 1:5-7 and breaks 1:3 in an unnatural manner. In fact, the chiasmus Jervis identifies is not nearly as apparent as she suggests. It would be more natural to set the aorist participles in parallel:[74]

> περὶ τοῦ υἱοῦ αὐτοῦ
>   τοῦ γενομένου
>   ἐκ σπέρματος Δαυὶδ
>   κατὰ σάρκα,
>
>   τοῦ ὁρισθέντος υἱοῦ θεοῦ
>   ἐν δυνάμει
>   κατὰ πνεῦμα ἁγιωσύνης
>   ἐξ ἀναστάσεως νεκρῶν,
> ᾿Ιησοῦ Χριστοῦ τοῦ κυρίου ἡμῶν

---

[70] Ibid. 260. See J. D. G. Dunn for a list of parallels between 1:8-15 and 15:14-33 (*Romans 9-16* [Dallas: Word, 1988] 857).

[71] Cf. Dunn, *Romans 1-8* (Dallas: Word, 1988) 5; Cranfield, *Romans* 1:57.

[72] Jervis, *Romans* 74.

[73] DiMarco: "Röm 1,1-7 . . . ist chiastisch in den Prolog des Römerbriefes eingefügt, der ingesamt das Schema A 1,1; B 1,2-3a; C 1,3b; C' 1,4ab; B' 1,4c; A' 1,5-7 hat" ("Chiasmus" 11).

[74] See Dunn on whether or not ἐν δυνάμει is an insertion (*Romans 1-8* 6). See Cranfield for the thicket of exegetical problems surrounding verse 4 (*Romans* 1:61).

Clearly, there are parallels within these verses. Yet when *all* the elements of these two verses are taken into consideration, the search for a neat symmetrical arrangement seems destined to fail.

Wuellner suggests that Paul treats the issues in 1:1-15 in "chiastic" order:[75]

A	Paul's interpretation of the gospel, of Christ, of faith	1:1-5
B	His apostolic relation to the church(es) in Rome	1:6
B'	His relation to the church(es) in Rome	1:9-12
A'	The interpretation of his gospel ministry, but with one significant addition: the reference to his having been hindered or frustrated.	1:13-15

Although this analysis may well reflect the topics that Paul addresses in 1:1-15, there are no specific verbal parallels to support it. Furthermore, it is only natural that—in the opening of a letter—Paul would address his relation to the churches. In fact, it is difficult to imagine a significantly different description of the opening of, say, Galatians, where Paul also addresses his understanding of his ministry, the gospel, Christ, and faith as well as his relation to the churches in Galatia. It may be conceded that the order of the topics and the content of these two letters might differ, but the fairly general descriptions that Wuellner uses—with the exception of Paul being hindered from visiting—could be applied as easily to Galatians as to Romans.

Often considered the "theme" of Romans,[76] all or part of 1:16-17 figures in several "inverted" schemes for the letter. John Forbes suggests that 1:17-18 forms an "introverted parallelism" with 3:26:[77]

A	Saving aspect of God's righteousness	1:17
B	Condemning aspect of God's righteousness	1:18
B'	Condemning aspect of God's righteousness ("might be just . . .")	3:26
A'	Saving aspect of God's righteousness (". . . and justifier")	3:26

Michel Bouttier thinks that the themes of salvation (1:16) and righteousness (1:17) are chiastically developed in 1:18-4:25 (righteousness) and 5:1-21 (salvation).[78] James Dunn sees 1:16b tying chapters 1-15 together and 1:17 providing the text for all of Romans 1-11:[79]

God's righteousness to faith:		
"the righteous by faith . . .	1:18-5:21	
. . . shall live"	chaps. 6-8	

---

[75] Wuellner, "Paul's Rhetoric" 338.

[76] E.g., Dunn: "Vv 16-17 is clearly the thematic statement for the entire letter" (*Romans 1-8* 37).

[77] Forbes, *Romans* 118.

[78] Cited by DiMarco, "Chiasmus" 11, n.306.

[79] Dunn, *Romans 1-8* 37.

God's righteousness from faith:
    "the righteous by God's faithfulness"   chaps. 9-11

Of these three proposals, Dunn's holds the most promise based on the use of word-chains.[80] There are concentrations of δίκαιος, δικαιοσύνη, and δικαιόω in chapters 3-4 and chapters 9-10; concentrations of πιστεύω and πίστις occur in the same chapters. With some exceptions, the uses of ζάω and ζωή occur predominantly in chapters 5-8. Unfortunately, however, 1:18-2:29 is conspicuously lacking in the use of any of these words. The overall scheme is quite general, and although it might reflect important themes in Paul's argument, it is does not qualify as an example of oral patterning.

Bouttier's scheme has the same problem with 1:18-2:29 as does Dunn's. In addition, σωτηρία is entirely absent from chapter 5.[81] Forbes's "introverted parallelism" is unlikely to have been apparent to the ear in precisely the form he proposes. Given the concentration of δικαι- and πιστ- word groups in 3:21-26, however, the listener probably would have recalled the combination of the same words in 1:16-17.

Using word-chains and the repetition of the phrase Ἰουδαίῳ τε πρῶτον καὶ Ἕλληνι in 1:16 and 2:10 as key pieces of evidence, Jouette Bassler has argued that the central theme of chapters 1-2 is God's impartiality toward all persons.[82] According to Bassler, this portion of the letter may be divided into two paragraphs. The first (1:16-2:11) is framed by 1:16 and 2:10:

οὐ γὰρ ἐπαισχύνομαι τὸ εὐαγγέλιον, δύναμις γὰρ θεοῦ ἐστιν εἰς σωτηρίαν <u>παντὶ τῷ πιστεύοντι, Ἰουδαίῳ τε πρῶτον καὶ Ἕλληνι·</u>

. . . δόξα δὲ καὶ τιμὴ καὶ εἰρήνη <u>παντὶ τῷ ἐργαζομένῳ τὸ ἀγαθόν,</u> Ἰουδαίῳ τε πρῶτον καὶ Ἕλληνι·

It is rounded off by the statement about God's impartiality in 2:11 (οὐ γάρ ἐστιν προσωπολημψία παρὰ τῷ θεῷ). Included in this first paragraph are four sections (1:22-24; 1:25-27; 1:28-31; 1:32-2:3) that develop the initial statement of divine

---

[80] A summary table of the distribution of key words is useful:

	1-2	3-4	5	6-8	9-11	12-16
δίκαιος	1	2	2	1	0	0
δικαιοσύνη	1	13	2	6	13	1
δικαιόω	1	8	2	4	0	0
πιστεύω	1	8	0	6	8	3
πίστις	5	19	2	0	6	5
ζάω	1	0	0	12	2	7
ζωή	1	0	4	8	1	0

[81] It occurs only in 1:16; 10:1, 10; 11:11; and 13:11.

[82] Bassler, *Divine Impartiality* 121-154.

retribution (1:18-21) and the chiastic retribution formula of 2:6-11 as identified by Grobel.[83] In addition, Bassler has proposed a "ring-structure" for 1:16-2:10:[84]

A	σωτηρίαν παντὶ τῷ πιστεύοντι, ᾿Ιουδαίῳ τε πρῶτον καὶ ῞ελληνι	1:16
B	ἀποκαλύπτεται γὰρ ὀργὴ θεοῦ	1:18a
C	ἐπὶ πᾶσαν ἀσέβειαν καὶ ἀδικίαν ἀνθρώπων	1:18b
D	ὀργή, ἀδικία, ἀλήθεια	1:18
E	εἰς τὸ εἶναι αὐτοὺς ἀναπολογήτους	1:20
E'	διὸ ἀναπολόγητος εἶ	2:1
B'	ἐν ἡμέρᾳ ὀργῆς καὶ ἀποκαλύψεως	2:5
D'	ἀληθείᾳ, τῇ ἀδικίᾳ, ὀργὴ	2:8
C'	ἐπὶ πᾶσαν ψυχὴν ἀνθρώπου	2:9
A'	δόξα δὲ καὶ τιμὴ καὶ εἰρήνη παντὶ τῷ ἐργαζομένῳ τὸ ἀγαθόν, ᾿Ιουδαίῳ τε πρῶτον καὶ ῞ελληνι·	2:10

The second paragraph (2:12-29) develops the theme of divine impartiality (2:12-13) through the use of four case studies arranged in a "ring-like" fashion:[85]

General statement (οὐκ . . . ἀλλά)	vv. 12-13
Conditional Case A (ὅταν)	14-16
Conditional Case B (εἰ δὲ)	17-24
Conditional Case B (ἐὰν)	25
Conditional Case A (ἐὰν)	26
General statement (οὐκ . . . ἀλλά)	28-29

Although lexical links are few,[86] Bassler can point to the word chain ἀνόμος-νόμος-περιτομή-ἀκροβυστία as a unifying factor for the argument of 2:12-29.[87]

Bassler's basic approach has much to commend it. She seeks to work with the text as it is rather than proposing interpolations or emendations. Her use of word-chains is instructive.[88] She is alert to verbal cues present in the text and has sought to build her argument on "formal"[89] evidence rather than on content. Her work serves to highlight many of the verbal interrelationships within chapters 1-2.[90] It remains

---

[83] Grobel, "Retribution Formula" 255-261.

[84] Bassler, *Divine Impartiality* 199.

[85] Ibid. 139.

[86] Regarding 2:28-29, Bassler herself concedes that "there are no linguistic links with 2:11" (ibid. 139).

[87] Ibid. 137.

[88] Although her suggestion that πᾶς is the key word in 1:16-2:10 is less helpful, since it occurs 68 times in Romans alone.

[89] This is her term (ibid. 123).

[90] She does, however, omit two items. (1) The genitive form ᾿Ιουδαίου τε πρῶτον καὶ ῞ελληνος occurs in 2:9. Bassler does not address this verse, perhaps because Grobel has bracketed it as one of Paul's "footnotes." (2) The triple repetition of (μετ)ηλλαξαν (1:23, 25,

to be seen, however, whether her suggestions should be allowed to stand as examples of oral patterning.

Fitzmyer identifies three weaknesses in Bassler's analysis: (1) it ignores the obvious division in the text at 1:32; (2) it does not take into consideration the stylistic shift from third person plural to second person singular in 2:1; and (3) 3:21 echoes 1:17 and so marks the end of the unit more clearly than does 2:11.[91]

Still, the concentric pattern that Bassler suggests for 2:14-27 is attractive, but the fact that νόμος occurs uniformly across all of 2:12-27 makes it difficult to draw the fine distinctions she does in verses 24-27. There does, however, appear to be some merit in her suggestion of alternation in 2:10-17:[92]

A	Ἰουδαίῳ τε πρῶτον	2:10
B	καὶ Ἕλληνι . . .	
B	ὅσοι γὰρ ἀνόμως ἥμαρτον, ἀνόμως καὶ ἀπολοῦνται·	2:12
A	καὶ ὅσοι ἐν νόμῳ ἥμαρτον, διὰ νόμου κριθήσονται·	
A	οὐ γὰρ οἱ ἀκροαταὶ νόμου δίκαιοι παρὰ τῷ θεῷ,	2:13
B	ἀλλ' οἱ ποιηταὶ νόμου δικαιωθήσονται.	
B	ὅταν γὰρ ἔθνη τὰ μὴ νόμον ἔχοντα φύσει τὰ τοῦ νόμου ποιῶσιν . . .	2:14
A	εἰ δὲ σὺ Ἰουδαῖος ἐπονομάζῃ καὶ ἐπαναπαύῃ νόμῳ . . .	2:17

Although some of the above parallels are more conceptual than verbal, the general antithetical pattern is readily apparent. Verses 12 and 13 seem worded in such a way as to make them particularly memorable.

This alternating structure would appear to undermine Forbes's inverted structure for 2:12-15:[93] a (v.12), b (v.13a), b' (v.13b), a' (v.14-15). First, it is difficult to see the way in which verses 14-15 are parallel to verse 12. Furthermore, it is difficult to understand why Forbes has treated verse 12 as a single element while dividing verse 13 into two elements. The οὐ . . . ἀλλά contrast in verse 13 has at least as much unity as the two ὅσοι clauses of verse 12. In keeping with the alternating scheme above, a more natural arrangement would be:

A	ὅσοι γὰρ ἀνόμως ἥμαρτον, ἀνόμως καὶ ἀπολοῦνται·	2:12
B	καὶ ὅσοι ἐν νόμῳ ἥμαρτον, διὰ νόμου κριθήσονται·	
B'	οὐ γὰρ οἱ ἀκροαταὶ νόμου δίκαιοι παρὰ [τῷ] θεῷ,	2:13
A'	ἀλλ' οἱ ποιηταὶ νόμου δικαιωθήσονται.	

---

26) and παρέδωκεν αὐτοὺς ὁ θεὸς εἰς . . . (1:24, 26, 28) is difficult to miss either visually or orally, and seems to work against the four subsections Bassler proposes for 1:18-2:3. See G. Bowman for a different analysis of 1:21-32 ("Noch einmal Römer 1,21-32," *Bib* 54 [1973] 413-414).

[91] Fitzmyer, *Romans* 298.

[92] Bassler, *Divine Impartiality* 144. She does not call it alternation, but it is similar to examples of alternation seen in extrabiblical works.

[93] Forbes, *Romans* 7.

Ernst Käsemann finds "an effective chiasmus" in 2:28-29,[94] but his explanation has more to do with the grammatical function of Ἰουδαῖος and περιτομή in the elliptical syntax than with oral patterning. The natural understanding of the verses is a parallel structure: (a) 2:28a = outward Jew, (b) 2:28b = outward circumcision, (a) 2:29a = inward Jew, (b) 2:29b = inward circumcision.

Fitzmyer argues that the repetition of τί οὖν in 3:1 and 3:9 is an instance of inclusion that joins 3:9 to 3:1-8 rather than to 3:10-20.[95] Although such an understanding is possible, Paul's frequent use of τί οὖν in Romans weighs against it, for he repeatedly uses the phrase to mark the beginning of new sections that draw implications from the preceding discussion.[96]

Jeremias's suggestion that 3:4-8 is chiastically arranged has found widespread support.[97] If, as is likely, πᾶς δὲ ἄνθρωπος ψεύστης is an allusion to or quotation of Ps 116:11 (LXX 115:2), then it is the first of two such OT references in verse 4.[98] Jeremias sees Paul taking up these scriptural references in reverse order in 3:5-8: verses 5-6 address God's righteousness in judging (Ps 51:4); verses 7-8 contrast God's truth with man's lie (Ps 116:11). The verbal links are apparent,[99] and Jeremias's basic scheme may be accepted, although it is uncertain just how apparent the verbal links would have been to the listener.

It is widely suggested that 3:24-26a contains pre-Pauline material, although the extent of that material has caused much disagreement.[100] Its canonical form, Forbes believes is inverted: (a) 3:24-25a = justified, (b) 3:25b = declaration, (b') 3:26a = declaration, (a') 3:26b = justified.[101] Forbes's proposal, however, combines verses 24 and 25a into one element that is considerably longer than the others. It also breaks the relative clause at an awkward place. A more natural arrangement would be to keep the relative clause together:

---

[94] Käsemann, *Romans* 74.

[95] Fitzmyer, *Romans* 326.

[96] E.g., 4:1; 6:1, 15; 7:7; 8:31; 9:30.

[97] Jeremias, "Chiasmus" 154-155. Cf. Dunn, *Romans* 1-8 130; Moo, *Romans 1-8* 192.

[98] Cf. Dunn, *Romans 1-8* 133.

[99] ἀλήθεια and ψεύστης from 3:4a are echoed by ἀλήθεια and ψεῦσμα in 3:7. δικαιόω and κρίνω in 3:4b are echoed by δικαιοσύνη in 3:5 and κρίνω in 3:6.

[100] There are three positions on this issue: (1) the pre-Pauline material begins at verse 24; cf. J. Reumann, "The Gospel of the Righteousness of God: Pauline Interpretation in Rom 3:21-31," *Int* 20 (1966) 432-452; (2) the pre-Pauline tradition begins at verse 25; cf. B. F. Meyer, "The Pre-Pauline Formula in Rom 3:25-26a," *NTS* 29 (1983) 198-208; (3) none of the material in 3:24-26a is pre-Pauline; cf. H. Schlier, *Der Römerbrief* (Freiberg: Herder, 1977). For additional bibliography, see Fitzmyer, *Romans* 354-358.

[101] Forbes, *Romans* 13.

δικαιούμενοι δωρεὰν τῇ αὐτοῦ χάριτι διὰ τῆς ἀπολυτρώσεως τῆς ἐν
Χριστῷ Ἰησοῦ·

ὃν προέθετο ὁ θεὸς ἱλαστήριον διὰ [τῆς] πίστεως ἐν τῷ αὐτοῦ αἵματι
    εἰς ἔνδειξιν τῆς δικαιοσύνης αὐτοῦ
        διὰ τὴν πάρεσιν τῶν προγεγονότων ἁμαρτημάτων ἐν τῇ ἀνοχῇ τοῦ θεοῦ,
        πρὸς τὴν ἔνδειξιν τῆς δικαιοσύνης αὐτοῦ ἐν τῷ νῦν καιρῷ,
            εἰς τὸ εἶναι αὐτὸν δίκαιον καὶ δικαιοῦντα τὸν ἐκ πίστεως Ἰησοῦ.

This arrangement has several advantages: (1) it results in sense lines of relatively similar length; (2) it maintains the parallelism between the ἔνδειξις phrases; and (3) it highlights the importance of πίστις as the basis of God's justifying action. The repetition of ἔνδειξιν τῆς δικαιοσύνης αὐτοῦ almost certainly was apparent to the ear.

John Forbes proposes three structures of varying complexity in 4:11-18.[102] First, he suggests that the idea of Abraham as father in 4:11-12 and 4:17-18 serves to frame the passage. Unfortunately, however, Abraham does not appear by name in 4:17-18, although he is named repeatedly in 4:1-16. The word πατήρ occurs six times in 4:11-18, but it is used more as a link-word than as an element of inclusion.

Second, Forbes suggests that 4:13-16 consists of a inverted pattern:[103]

A   οὐ γὰρ διὰ νόμου ἡ ἐπαγγελία τῷ Ἀβραὰμ ἢ τῷ σπέρματι αὐτοῦ,
B   τὸ κληρονόμον αὐτὸν εἶναι κόσμου,
C   ἀλλὰ διὰ δικαιοσύνης πίστεως·
D   εἰ γὰρ οἱ ἐκ νόμου κληρονόμοι,
E   κεκένωται ἡ πίστις καὶ κατήργηται ἡ ἐπαγγελία·
F   ὁ γὰρ νόμος ὀργὴν κατεργάζεται·
F'   οὗ δὲ οὐκ ἔστιν νόμος οὐδὲ παράβασις.
E'   διὰ τοῦτο ἐκ πίστεως,
D'   ἵνα κατὰ χάριν,
C'   εἰς τὸ εἶναι βεβαίαν τὴν ἐπαγγελίαν παντὶ τῷ σπέρματι,
B'   οὐ τῷ ἐκ τοῦ νόμου μόνον
A'   ἀλλὰ καὶ τῷ ἐκ πίστεως Ἀβραάμ ὅς ἐστιν πατὴρ πάντων ἡμῶν,

The verbal parallels in A and A' (Abraham) and in E through E' (faith-law-law-faith), are clear. But other aspects of the arrangement are weak: (1) the correspondence between B and B' is not at all obvious; (2) a connection between C and C' is possible, but must be inferred; (3) the correspondence between D and D' appears to be antithetical rather than parallel; and (4) several words are repeated within the passage (e.g., ἐπαγγελία [3x], σπέρμα [2x]) but are not taken into consideration in Forbes's proposal—for example, the similarities between A (ἡ ἐπαγγελία τῷ

---

[102] Ibid. 17-18.

[103] Although Forbes's original scheme is in English, it has been set out in Greek here in order to evaluate verbal parallels more effectively.

Ἀβραὰμ ἢ τῷ σπέρματι αὐτοῦ) and C' (τὴν ἐπαγγελίαν παντὶ τῷ σπέρματι). These considerations suggest that the arrangement set out above might not have been readily apparent to the first readers.

Third, he suggests that 4:17-18 also comprises an inverted pattern:

A   καθὼς γέγραπται ὅτι πατέρα πολλῶν ἐθνῶν τέθεικά σε
B   κατέναντι οὗ ἐπίστευσεν θεοῦ
C   τοῦ ζῳοποιοῦντος τοὺς νεκροὺς

C'   καὶ καλοῦντος τὰ μὴ ὄντα ὡς ὄντα·
B'   ὃς παρ' ἐλπίδα ἐπ' ἐλπίδι ἐπίστευσεν
A'   εἰς τὸ γενέσθαι αὐτὸν πατέρα πολλῶν ἐθνῶν κατὰ τὸ
     εἰρημένον, οὕτως ἔσται τὸ σπέρμα σου·

The verbal correspondence between A and A' is particularly strong, and the parallel between B and B' is a good one. The parallel between C ("quickened") and C' ("called") is somewhat less obvious, although it is possible to point to the homoeoteleuton of the participles as an instance of acoustic resonance. The greater difficulty, however, is the fact that the first part of verse 17 (καθὼς γέγραπται ὅτι πατέρα πολλῶν ἐθνῶν τέθεικά σε) may be a parenthetical comment,[104] and so less likely to be part of a tightly-constructed inversion as proposed.

Rudolf Bultmann notes that the themes of death, life, sin, and "sanctity" dominate chapters 5-8. In fact, he sees an inversion in the order in which these themes are developed:[105]

A	Death and life	5:1-21
B	Sin and "sanctity"	6:1-7:6
B'	Freedom from sin	8:1-11
A'	Freedom from death	8:12-29

Nils Dahl has pointed out the thematic parallels between 5:1-11 and chapter 8:[106]

Apart from the climactic chain in Rom. 5:3-4 and the aside in Rom. 5:7, all major themes in Rom. 5:1-11 reappear in Romans 8: Justification and a restored relationship to God as the basis for the hope of future salvation and glory, in spite of present sufferings; the gift of the Holy Spirit, the death of Christ, and the love of God as warrants for this hope; a note of exaltation.

---

[104] The number of punctuation variants offered for verses 16-17 point out the difficulty of determining exactly how the syntax is to be understood.

[105] R. Bultmann, *Existence & Faith. Shorter Writings of Rudolf Bultmann*, trans., S. M. Odgen (New York: Meridian, 1960) 152-153. Funk notes Bultmann's analysis, but he reverses the order of the themes in 5:1-7:6 (*Language, Hermeneutic, and the Word of God* [New York: Harper & Row, 1966] 261).

[106] N. A. Dahl, *Studies in Paul* (Minneapolis: Augsburg, 1977) 88-89.

Douglas Moo has taken these insights, added to them points of verbal correspondence, and proposes "a 'ring composition' or chiasm" for the main development of chapters 5-8:[107]

A	Assurance of future glory	5:1-11
B	Basis for this assurance in work of Christ	5:12-21
C	The problem of sin	6:1-23
C'	The problem of the law	7:1-25
B'	Ground of assurance in the work of Christ, mediated by Spirit	8:1-17
A'	Assurance of future glory	8:18-39

He offers a number of verbal parallels between 5:1-11 and 8:18-39 in support of his proposal.[108] Furthermore, there are particularly high concentrations of key words in certain portions of this section:[109]

ἁμαρτία	6:1-23; 7:1-25	31 times
νόμος	7:1-25	23 times
σάρξ	8:1-17	11 times
πνεῦμα	8:1-17	18 times

Finally, Moo suggests that chapters 6 and 7 are, in a sense, parenthetical.[110] When all of this evidence is taken into consideration, it seems likely that at least an ABA' pattern is present in chapters 5-8. Moo's pattern of inversion certainly cannot be dismissed lightly.

---

[107] Moo, *Romans 1-8* 303.

[108] Ibid. 323; cf. the discussion above.

[109] Cf. Dunn, *Romans 1-8* 301.

	1-4	5:1-11	5:12-21	6:1-23	7:1-25	8:1-17	8:18-39	9-16
ἁμαρτία	4	0	6	16	15	5	0	2
θάνατος	1	1	5	7	5	2	1	0
νόμος	33	0	3	2	23	5	0	6
σάρξ	4	0	0	1	3	11	0	5
σῶμα	2	0	0	2	2	3	1	36
δικαιοσύνη	14	0	2	5	0	1	0	14
δικαιόω	9	2	0	1	0	0	3	0
ζάω	1	0	0	5	4	3	0	7
ζωή	1	1	3	3	1	3	1	1
πιστεύω	9	0	0	1	0	0	0	11
πίστις	24	2	0	0	0	0	0	13
πνεῦμα	3	1	0	0	1	18	4	8

Dunn's columns have been altered slightly to reflect Moo's divisions of the text. His original table included only the information in the first five rows.

[110] Moo: "In a certain sense, 6:1-7:25 is parenthetical to the main points of the section" (*Romans 1-8* 303).

Forbes has proposed an inverted order for 5:12-21:[111] (a) 5:12 = sin/death, (b) 5:13a-14 = law, (c) 5:14b = Adam, (d) 5:15-16a = grace/gift), (d') 5:16b-17 = grace/gift, (c') 5:18-19 = Christ, (b') 5:20 = law, (a') 5:21 = sin/death. The repeated phraseology within 5:12-21 multiplies the number of verbal relationships[112] and increases the likelihood that such an arrangement accurately reflects the structure of the passage. Forbes correctly recognizes the repeated use of such words as ἁμαρτία (5:12 [twice], 13, 20, 21), θάνατος (5:12, 14, 17, 21), νόμος (5:13 [twice], 20), χάρις (5:15 [twice], 17, 20, 21), and χάρισμα (5:15,16). His analysis, however, is weak in other ways: (1) The strong verbal parallels noted above between 5:12 and 5:18 are ignored in his scheme. (2) The correlations that he notes involving ἁμαρτία and θάνατος (5:12 and 5:21) and νόμος (5:13 and 5:20) are good, but they ignore the fact that ἁμαρτία is also present in 5:13 and 5:20. The repetition of βασιλεύω in 5:14 and 5:21 suggests that 5:12-14 might better be seen as a single element, unified by ἁμαρτία . . . θάνατος . . . νόμος . . . βασιλεύω and parallel to 5:20-21 at the very least. (3) Grouping all of 5:12-14 together also avoids the awkward division of 5:14 in Forbes's arrangement. (4) The cluster of χάρις, χάρισμα, and δώρημα that he notes in 5:15-17 is good, but the natural question that arises is why these verses must be divided into two elements rather than being kept together as one. Furthermore, what is the criterion by which verse 16 is divided? If it is on the basis of the τὸ μὲν . . . τὸ δὲ construction, to what, then, is the first part of the verse (καὶ οὐχ ὡς δι᾽ ἑνὸς ἁμαρτήσαντος τὸ δώρημα) parallel?

The cluster of ten words ending in -μα do, indeed, suggest that verses 15-17 constitute at unit, but it is a unit that could just as easily be understood as an A-B-A' pattern (A = v.15, B = v.16, A' = v.17). In fact, an alternate, concentric arrangement of the paragraph is equally possible:

A	διὰ τοῦτο ὥσπερ δι᾽ ἑνὸς . . . ἁμαρτία . . . ἁμαρτίας . . .	5:12-14
	θάνατος . . . καὶ οὕτως . . . θάνατος . . . ἥμαρτον . . . νόμου . . .	
	ἁμαρτία . . . ἁμαρτία . . . νόμου . . . ἐβασίλευσεν . . .	
	θάνατος . . . ἁμαρτήσαντας	
B	εἰ γὰρ τῷ τοῦ ἑνὸς παραπτώματι . . . πολλῷ μᾶλλον . . . χάρις . . .	5:15
	δωρεὰ . . . χάριτι . . . Ἰησοῦ Χριστοῦ . . . ἐπερίσσευσεν	
C	καὶ οὐχ ὡς δι᾽ ἑνὸς ἁμαρτήσαντος τὸ δώρημα· τὸ μὲν γὰρ	5:16
	κρίμα ἐξ ἑνὸς εἰς κατάκριμα, τὸ δὲ χάρισμα ἐκ πολλῶν	
	παραπτωμάτων εἰς δικαίωμα.	
B'	εἰ γὰρ τῷ τοῦ ἑνὸς παραπτώματι . . . πολλῷ μᾶλλον . . .	5:17
	περισσείαν . . . χάριτος . . . δωρεᾶς . . . Ἰησοῦ Χριστοῦ	

[111] Forbes, *Romans* 22-23.

[112] See Dunn, *Romans 1-8* 271, for a list of rhetorical elements present in these verses.

A'   ἄρα οὖν ὡς δι' ἑνὸς . . . οὕτως καὶ. . . ἁμαρτωλοὶ . . .   5:18-21
        νόμος . . . ἁμαρτία, . . . ἐβασίλευσεν . . . ἁμαρτία . . .
        θανάτῳ . . . βασιλεύσῃ

Forbes has proposed yet another inverted arrangement for 8:28-39:[113] (a) v.28a = love, (b) v.28b = purpose, (b') 8:29-34 = purpose, (a') v.35-39 = love. Again, Forbes has correctly identified important parallels, this time involving ἀγαπάω (8:28) and ἀγάπη (8:35, 39), that tend to frame 8:28-39. The decision to take 8:35-39 as a unit is also a good one, since—as was noted above—those verses are framed by a form of ring-composition. The decision to subdivide verse 28, however, is questionable, as is taking verses 29-34 together under the heading of "purpose." Surely the more natural approach is to take all of verse 28 together. And although 8:29-30 certainly fits the theme of purpose, 8:31-34 seems less directly related to it. In fact, the stronger connection between verse 28 and verses 29-30 might very well be that of "calling," since κλητοῖς (8:28) is echoed by ἐκάλεσεν (8:30). The climactic chain-reasoning of 8:29-30 clearly pulls those verses together as a unit. The five rhetorical questions of 8:31-34, however, seem more closely related to the sixth question in 8:35 than to the staccato assertions of 8:30.

Angelico DiMarco has suggested a concentric structure for 8:35-39:[114]

A   wer uns von der Liebe zu Christus abhält   8:35a
B   die Bedrängnis, die Angst . . .   8:35b
C   Zitat: "deinetwegen . . ."   8:36
B'   weder Tod, noch Leben . . .   8:38-39a
A'   wird us von der Liebe zu Gott abhalten . . .   8:39b

The ring-composition of question (v.35a) and answer (v.39) offers nearly identical correspondence between A and A'. A case can be made for a loose correspondence between the opposing forces itemized in verse 35b and verses 38-39. Unfortunately 8:38-39 is a single grammatical unit and is difficult to divide—in contrast to verse 35, which is easily divided into two questions. And if, as most scholars believe, the center of a concentric structure is the focal point, it is difficult to determine why the quotation from Psalm 44 was chosen as the central element in this passage. This scriptural proof seems, rather, to relate most naturally to the list of distresses that precedes it. In fact, DiMarco's scheme omits verse 37 altogether, and it is this verse that may, arguably, be viewed as the primary point of the passage—a suggestion that is reinforced by the repetition of the verb ἀγαπάω.

James Dunn sees a "chiastic" structure to 9:6-29:

vv. 6-9   λόγος, Ἰσραήλ, κληθήσεσθαι, σπέρμα, τέκνα (θεοῦ)
vv. 10-13   καλεῖν, ἀγαπᾶν

---

[113] Forbes, *Romans* 37-38.
[114] DiMarco, "Chiasmus" 14.

vv. 14-18	ἐλεεῖν, θέλων
vv. 19-23	θέλων, ἔλεος
vv. 24-25	καλεῖν, ἀγαπᾶν
vv. 26-29	κληθήσεσθαι, υἱοί (θεοῦ), Ἰσραήλ, λόγος, σπέρμα

This suggestion is certainly possible, for the verbal parallels are impressive.[115] Several of the words Dunn uses to draw parallels, however, are found frequently throughout chapters 9-11. Ἰσραήλ, for example, occurs uniformly in all three chapters, while καλέω is one of the characteristic words in chapter 9 (9:7, 12, 24, 25, 26). The apparent break at 9:14 (τί οὖν ἐροῦμεν; μὴ ἀδικία παρὰ τῷ θεῷ; μὴ γένοιτο·) must also be taken into consideration. A less complex approach to the passage simply divides it into three sections based on word-chains: 9:9-13 (σπέρμα, ἐπαγγελία, τέκνον, καλέω); 9:14-23 (ἐλεέω, ἔλεος, θέλω); 9:24-29 (καλέω).

Benjamin Fiore has suggested a "chiastic arrangement" for 9:30-10:14:[116]

A	Gentiles and Jews pursue righteousness differently	9:30-32a
B	Jews stumble over Christ	9:32b-33
C	Jews are zealous but unsure of God's righteousness	10:2-3
D	Christ is the end of the law	10:4
C'	Righteousness from faith is within you	10:5-8
B'	Belief in Christ brings salvation	10:9-11
A'	No distinction between Gentile and Jew	10:12-13

Fiore offers no evidence to support his suggestion; he simply sets it out as a given. As presented, his scheme has two significant weaknesses: (1) it has no verbal parallels to support it; and (2) although Fiore himself affirms 9:30-10:21 as a unit, his proposal accounts for only part of the section. A further curiosity is the omission of 10:1.

Dunn has found "a rough and unbalanced abcdcba structure" for the issues addressed in 12:1-15:6:

A	The basis for responsible living, by implication, other than the law	12:1-2
B	(The body of) Christ as the social expression of God's people	12:3-8
C	Love as the fundamental moral imperative in human relationships	12:9-21
D	Christians and the powers that be	13:1-7
C'	Love of neighbor as the fulfilling of the law in human relationships	13:8-10
B'	Christ as the pattern of Christian living	13:11-14
A'	The basis for social intercourse, by implication, other than the law	14:1-15:6

His structure, however, is too generalized to be persuasive. It is difficult to see how 12:1-2 "balances" 14:1-15:6, or how 12:3-8 "balances" 13:11-14. Furthermore, although Dunn sees 15:7-13 as "a coda . . . evidently intended to round off the body

---

[115] Dunn, *Romans 9-16* 537.

[116] Fiore, "Romans 9-11" 122.

of the letter,"[117] it is difficult to ignore its close connection with the immediately preceding discussion in 14:1-15:6.

Ellis chooses to accept the more natural division of the text at 14:1. He then proposes an ABCB'A' pattern for 12:1-13:14:[118]

A	Our bodies are for spiritual worship	12:1-2
B	The community, charismatic gifts, and the love command	12:3-21
C	Submission to civil authority	13:1-7
B'	The love command	13:8-10
A'	Our bodies are not for depravity	13:11-14

Ellis's outline is better than Dunn's, but he must combine 12:3-8 with 12:9-21 and set it parallel to 13:8-10. Ellis uses the theme of "love" in 12:9-10 and 13:8-10 as the primary point of correspondence. "The community, charismatic gifts, and the love command," however, is such a general heading for 12:3-21 that it could "match" any number of topics. It seems better to accept an *ad seriatim* approach to Paul's exhortations in 12:1-13:14 than to force them into a concentric pattern.

Black has proposed the following concentric structure for 12:9-13:[119]

A	ἀποστυγοῦντες τὸ πονηρόν, κολλώμενοι τῷ ἀγαθῷ·
B	τῇ φιλαδελφίᾳ εἰς ἀλλήλους φιλόστοργοι τῇ τιμῇ ἀλλήλους προηγούμενοι, τῇ σπουδῇ μὴ ὀκνηροί,
C	τῷ πνεύματι ζέοντες, τῷ κυρίῳ δουλεύοντες,
B'	τῇ ἐλπίδι χαίροντες, τῇ θλίψει ὑπομένοντες, τῇ προσευχῇ προσκαρτεροῦντες,
A'	ταῖς χρείαις τῶν ἁγίων κοινωνοῦντες, τὴν φιλοξενίαν διώκοντες.

---

[117] Dunn, *Romans 9-16* 844.

[118] Ellis, *Letters* 253. His proposed ABA' pattern for 14:1-15:13 has been noted above.

[119] D. A. Black: "The chiastic pattern is . . . the ally of meaning both in heightening the aesthetic impact of the passage in general and in serving as a mnemonic device for the hearers. Such a structure also afforded a means of internal organization in ancient writings which did not make extensive use of punctuation, paragraphs, capitalization, and other devices for indicating unity and transition of thought" ("The Pauline Love Command: Structure, Style, and Ethics in Romans 12:9-21," *FilNeot* 2 [1989] 9).

There are no points of verbal correspondence in this collection of ethical commands, but isocolon, asyndeton, homoeoarcton, and homoeoteleuton create a series of sound patterns that "delight the ear and provide points of contact between lines."[120] Black's arrangement accurately reflects one of Paul's most euphonious oral compositions.

Dunn suggests that the structure of 14:13-23 is "roughly chiastic." Although he does not present any evidence for his suggestion, a number of items support this analysis: (1) the paragraph is framed by the repetition of κρίνω (14:13 [twice]; 14:22) and its cognate κατακρίνω (14:23), as well as the repetition of πρόσκομμα (14:13; 14:20) and its cognate προσκόπτω (14:21); (2) occurrences of the words βρῶμα (3x) and βρῶσις (1x) are clustered in 14:15-20; (3) the basic principles of 14:14-15 are repeated in inverted order in 14:20:

14:14 οἶδα καὶ πέπεισμαι ἐν κυρίῳ   πάντα μὲν καθαρά, ἀλλὰ   14:20b
     Ἰησοῦ ὅτι οὐδὲν κοινὸν δι'   κακὸν τῷ ἀνθρώπῳ τῷ διὰ
     ἑαυτοῦ· εἰ μὴ τῷ λογιζομένῳ   προσκόμματος ἐσθίοντι.
     τι κοινὸν εἶναι, ἐκείνῳ κοινόν.

14:15 εἰ γὰρ διὰ βρῶμα ὁ ἀδελφός
     σου λυπεῖται, οὐκέτι κατὰ
     ἀγάπην περιπατεῖς. μὴ τῷ   μὴ ἕνεκεν βρώματος κατάλυε   14:20a
     βρώματί σου ἐκεῖνον ἀπόλλυε   τὸ ἔργον τοῦ θεοῦ.
     ὑπερ οὗ Χριστὸς ἀπέθανεν.

The structure, however, breaks down somewhat in the center (v.16-19) where it is difficult to propose parallels between the statements comprising Paul's argument.[121] Perhaps the best solution is to see the passage as loosely concentric—recognizing the verbal parallels that frame the paragraph and unify it, but not seeking to draw any fine parallels that would not have been readily apparent to the ear.

Finally, Ellis sees a chiastic construction in 15:18-19:[122]

οὐ γὰρ τολμήσω τι λαλεῖν ὧν οὐ κατειργάσατο Χριστὸς δι' ἐμοῦ
εἰς ὑπακοὴν ἐθνῶν,
         λόγῳ   A
   καὶ   ἔργῳ,   B
         ἐν δυνάμει σημείων καὶ τεράτων,   B'
         ἐν δυνάμει πνεύματος θεοῦ·   A'

---

[120] Ibid.

[121] Verse 16 seems most naturally to be the conclusion to verse 15. Verse 17 seems to be worded with some attention given to euphony (βρῶσις καὶ πόσις . . . δικαιοσύνη καὶ εἰρήνη καὶ χαρά). Verse 18 uses two words (εὐάρεστος and δόκιμος) that figure prominently in Paul's ethical arguments throughout the letter. The ἄρα οὖν of verse 19 reinforces Paul's application.

[122] E. E. Ellis, *Pauline Theology: Ministry and Society* (Grand Rapids: Eerdmans, 1989) 36.

This arrangement, however, has no verbal links to support it, and it depends on the interpretation of ἐν δυνάμει πνεύματος θεοῦ as "the power of the [prophetic] Spirit."[123] It is probable that the listener would have caught the homoeoteleuton of λόγῳ καὶ ἔργῳ and the repetition of ἐν δυνάμει. What Ellis proposes appears to be more a product of literary analysis than of oral composition, and so is not to be seen as an example of oral patterning.

D. Summary

All the oral patterns identified in Chapter 5 are present, to a greater or lesser extent, in Romans. Paul uses repetition, word-chain, and link-words repeatedly. There are also frequent instances of chiasmus, often occurring in OT quotations. Inversion on a small scale is present in several places, as is alternation. Inclusion and ring-composition frame passages of varying lengths, and refrain undergirds all of Romans 5-8. Instances of concentric symmetry are rare, but the ABA' pattern—a simpler variation of the same principle—occurs repeatedly.

---

[123] Ibid.

Chapter 7

1 CORINTHIANS

It is generally agreed that Paul wrote 1 Corinthians during his stay in Ephesus and sent it to Corinth. Although there is continuing discussion over the *absolute* dating of Pauline chronology,[1] the *relative* position of 1 Corinthians in that chronology is not seriously affected. Some scholars have questioned the integrity of the letter,[2] but as John Hurd notes, "Most scholars . . . do not believe that this evidence is strong enough to support the burden of proof which this kind of theory must always bear."[3] The occasion of the letter is generally agreed to be the receipt of news from Corinth to which Paul wished to respond. John Hurd notes three sources of information: (1) from Chloe's people (1:11) come the oral reports to which Paul responds in (at least) chapters 1-3; (2) a letter from Corinth (7:1) sets the agenda for chapters 7-16; and (3) Stephanus, Fortunatus and Achaicus (16:17) probably delivered the letter to Paul in Ephesus.[4]

Lund devotes more space to 1 Corinthians than he does to Ephesians, Colossians, Philippians, Philemon, and Romans combined.[5] Nearly one-half of the NT examples of chiasmus that Jeremias cites come from 1 Corinthians.[6] Welch gives more space to 1 Corinthians than to any other NT book except Matthew and

---

[1] Cf. G. Lüdemann, *Paul, Apostle to the Gentiles: Studies in Chronology*, trans. F. S. Jones (Philadelphia: Fortress, 1984).

[2] E.g., J. Héring, *The First Epistle of Saint Paul to the Corinthians*, trans. A. W. Heathcote, P. J. Allcock (London: Epworth, 1962) xli-xv. H. Conzelmann recites the arguments against integrity, but finds them unconvincing (*1 Corinthians*, trans. J. W. Leitch [Philadelphia: Fortress, 1975] 2-4).

[3] J. C. Hurd, *The Origin of I Corinthians* (London: SPCK, 1965) 47; cf. esp. 42-47.

[4] Ibid. 47-50. Hurd concludes: ". . . it is improbable that Paul had any further sources of information. The information implied, for example, by 11.18 . . . and by 5.1 . . . should be identified as coming either from Chloe's people or from Stephanas and his companions" (ibid. 50).

[5] Lund, *Chiasmus*. 1 Corinthians receives 42 pages while the other five letters receive a total of 28 pages.

[6] Jeremias, "Chiasmus." Jeremias cites 29 examples; 13 of them are from 1 Corinthians.

Revelation.[7] Chiasmus, inclusion, ring-composition, and the ABA' pattern figure prominently in Charles Talbert's work on the Corinthian correspondence.[8] The writings of these scholars, therefore, alert us to expect numerous examples of oral patterning in 1 Corinthians.

A. Epistolary Structure

Verbs of saying, verbs of knowing, and vocatives appear frequently throughout 1 Corinthians. The major clusters of epistolary conventions in the letter, however, are:

1:1-14	Sender (1:1), recipients (1:2), greeting (1:3) thanksgiving (1:4), request formula (1:10), thanksgiving (1:14)
4:14-19	Writing statement (4:14), request formula (4:16), dispatch of emissary (4:17), intention to visit (4:18-19)
12:1-3	περὶ δὲ (12:1), disclosure formula (12:1), disclosure formula (12:3)
16:1-24	περὶ δὲ (16:1), intention to visit (16:5-8), dispatch of emissary (16:10), περὶ δὲ (16:12), request formula (16:15), joy expression (16:17), greetings (16:19-20), autograph (16:21), grace-benediction (16:23), love-wish (16:24)

After a conventional salutation (1:1-3) and thanksgiving (1:4-9), Paul moves into the letter-body of 1:10-4:21, which begins with the request formula παρακαλῶ δὲ ὑμᾶς, ἀδελφοί, διὰ τοῦ ὀνόματος τοῦ κυρίου ἡμῶν Ἰησοῦ Χριστοῦ (1:10) and ends with a body closing (4:14-21).[9] As is often the case at major transition

---

[7] Welch, "Chiasmus." Revelation receives six pages; 1 Corinthians and Matthew receive five pages each.

[8] C. H. Talbert: "No close reading of the text is possible without an awareness of the ancient techniques of inclusion, or ring composition, and of chiasmus, or concentric patterning. In a culture that was oral, there was a need for some technique to signal the beginning and ending of a thought unit. Whereas in a literary culture such boundaries are designated by paragraphs, chapters, subheadings, or even enumeration, in an oral culture the signals had to be heard. It was customary to repeat key words, phrases, and ideas at the start and finish of a thought unit to indicate its boundaries. This we call inclusion, or ring composition . . . Another device used not only to signal the beginning and end of a thought unit but to indicate the arrangement within the unit was chiasmus, or concentric patterning . . . Recognition of this principle of organization in the Corinthian correspondence often allows one to avoid the cliché that Paul's thought is disjointed when it does not seem to follow a linear line of argument" (*Reading Corinthians* [New York: Crossroads, 1987] xv).

[9] Contrast, however, J. C. Hurd: "I suggest that the Body of 1 Corinthians does not end at 4:21 but that 5:1-13 and 6:1-11 are two additional Body units each marked by an opening expression of amazement and reaching a theological climax in 6:11. Paul's three separate pieces

points, there is a cluster of epistolary formulae in 1:10-14. In addition to the request formula in 1:10, other conventions include: vocative (1:11), verb of saying (1:12), and thanksgiving (1:14). The body closing or "apostolic parousia" in 4:14-21 is also marked by a cluster of formulae, including: writing (4:14), request (4:16), sending (4:17), visit (4:18-19).[10]

The closing of the letter is also clearly signaled by the cluster of epistolary conventions in chapter 16. The precise extent of the letter closing is open to some debate, with Weima[11] and Jervis[12] arguing for 16:13-24, and Belleville limiting it to 16:19-24.[13] Surely Weima is correct in connecting 16:1-12 with the περὶ δὲ units of 7:1-15:58.[14] As well, the request formula of 16:15 seems to mark a clear turning point. Whether the five commands of 16:13-14 are to be considered the last element in the paraenesis or the first element in the letter closing is disputed. What is evident, however, is that everything from 16:15 (at least) is directed toward maintaining Paul's relationship with the church. The resulting epistolary structure is:[15]

Letter-opening		1:1-9
Salutation	1:1-3	
Thanksgiving	1:4-9	

---

of unfavorable news are responsible for the unusual structure" ("Concerning the Structure of 1 Thessalonians," Paper presented at the annual meeting of the Society of Biblical Literature, Los Angeles, CA, 1-5 September 1972, 49, n.95).

[10] For a more complete analysis, see Funk, "Apostolic Parousia" 252-254; cf. also Jervis, *Romans* 116-117.

[11] Weima, *Neglected Endings* 201.

[12] Jervis, *Romans* 142-143.

[13] L. L. Belleville, "Continuity or Discontinuity: A Fresh Look at 1 Corinthians in the Light of First-Century Epistolary Forms and Conventions," *EvQ* 59 (1987) 35-37.

[14] Weima, *Neglected Endings* 201.

[15] Belleville's analysis is nearly identical. Although she does not categorize it as such, her basic structure is that of request-response ("Continuity" 23-24):
   Letter-opening (1:1-3)
   Thanksgiving (1:4-9)
   Petition body (1:10-4:21)
   Response sections (5:1-16:14)
   Emissary petition (16:15-18)
   Letter-closing (16:19-24)
Hurd has arrived at an alternate "response letter" form ("1 Thessalonians" 35-36):
   Letter-opening (1:1-3)
   Thanksgiving (1:4-9)
   Comments on oral reports (1:10-6:11)
   Transitional section (6:12-20)
   Responses to written questions (7:1-16:12)
   Letter-closing (16:13-24)

Letter-body		1:10-4:21
Body opening	1:10-13	
Body middle	1:14-4:13	
Body closing	4:14-21	
Paraenesis		5:1-16:14
Letter-closing		16:15-24

Within 5:1-16:14 a number of epistolary conventions mark transitions:[16]

5:1	ὅλως ἀκούεται ἐν ὑμῖν προνεία . . .
6:2	ἢ οὐκ οἴδατε ὅτι . . .
7:1	περὶ δὲ ὧν ἐγρααψατε . . .
7:25	περὶ δὲ τῶν παρθένων . . .
8:1	περὶ δὲ τῶν εἰδωλοθύτων, οἴδαμεν ὅτι . . .
10:1	οὐ θέλω γὰρ ὑμᾶς ἀγνοεῖν, ἀδελφοί, ὅτι . . .
11:3	θέλω δὲ ὑμᾶς εἰδέναι ὅτι . . .
11:18	ἀκούω σχίσματα ἐν ὑμῖν ὑπάρχειν . . .
12:1	περὶ δὲ τῶν πνευματικῶν, ἀδελφοί, οὐ θέλω ὑμᾶς ἀγνοεῖν . . .
15:1	γνωρίζω δὲ ὑμῖν, ἀδελφοί . . .
16:1	περὶ δὲ τῆς λογείας τῆς εἰς τοὺς ἁγίους . . .
16:12	περὶ δὲ 'Απολλῶ τοῦ ἀδελφοῦ . . .

This understanding of the letter's epistolary structure provides a basic framework within which the oral patterns in 1 Corinthians may be examined.

B. Readily Apparent Oral Patterns

The material within the letter-body of 1 Corinthians has been divided in several ways.[17] The most interesting approach, at least for a study of oral patterning, is to view 1:13-4:13 as an example of inversion similar to that seen in Quintilian 12.2.10-23.[18] In 1:13 Paul asks three questions: (1) μεμέρισται ὁ Χριστός; (2) μὴ Παῦλος ἐσταυρώθη ὑπὲρ ὑμῶν; (3) εἰς τὸ ὄνομα Παύλου ἐβαπτίσθητε; In 1:14-4:13, then, he answers these questions in reverse order.

In 1:14 Paul turns first to the issue of baptism. Beginning with an expression of thanksgiving (εὐχαριστῶ τῷ θεῷ), Paul reminds the Corinthians that he baptized few of them. The verb βαπτίζω occurs six times in 1:13-17, accounting for more

---

[16] Cf. Belleville, "Continuity" 24.

[17] See the discussion below for suggestions by Welch, Brunot, and Ellis. More conventional analyses may be found in C. K. Barrett, *A Commentary on the First Epistle to the Corinthians* (New York: Harper and Row, 1968) and G. D. Fee, *The First Epistle to the Corinthians* (Grand Rapids: Eerdmans, 1987).

[18] Cf. Funk, *Language* 261-262, and Talbert, *Corinthians* 4-9. Fee rejects such a scheme: "This [analysis] seems doubtful, especially since 1:18-2:16 scarcely *responds* to the question, 'Was Paul crucified for you?'" (*First Corinthians* 60, n.61).

than one-half of the uses of that word in this letter.[19] Verse 17 is a transitional statement between the issue of baptism—Paul can address that concern relatively succinctly—and the more substantive issue of the significance of Christ's crucifixion. The presence of σταυρός in 1:17 anticipates its repeated use in 1:18-2:16.

Four epistolary conventions occur in 1:17-4:13: (1) a vocative in 1:26 (ἀδελφοί); (2) mention of a past visit in 2:1 (κἀγὼ ἐλθὼν πρὸς ὑμᾶς, ἀδελφοί, ἦλθον οὐ καθ' ὑπεροχὴν); (3) a vocative in 3:1 (ἀδελφοί); and (4) a vocative in 4:6 (ἀδελφοί). Of these four conventions, the strongest is that found in 2:1. It is, however, a mention of a past visit and seems to be more a continuation of Paul's line of thought than a transition point. Although he does not respond directly to the second question in 1:17-2:16, Paul uses σταυρός and σταυρόω five times in these verses.[20] In addition, σοφία and σοφός occur nineteen times in 1:17-2:16, with μωρία and μωρός occurring six times.[21]

Vocatives sometimes mark transition points within a letter-body,[22] and this seems to be the case in 3:1. The subsequent discussion addresses the party factions within the Corinthian church, with the claims of 1:12 (ἐγὼ μέν εἰμι Παύλου, ἐγὼ δὲ ᾿Απολλῶ, ἐγὼ δὲ Κηφᾶ, ἐγὼ δὲ Χριστοῦ.)[23] reappearing in 3:4 (ἐγὼ μέν εἰμι Παύλου, ἕτερος δέ, ἐγὼ ᾿Απολλῶ) and 3:22 (εἴτε Παῦλος εἴτε ᾿Απολλῶς εἴτε Κηφᾶς). Also prominent in 3:1-4:5 is the repeated use of οἰκέω and its cognates.[24] Paul brings his discussion to a close in 4:6 by drawing specific points of application from the analogy of himself and Apollos (ταῦτα δέ, ἀδελφοί, μετεσχημάτισα εἰς ἐμαυτὸν καὶ ᾿Απολλῶν).[25] As mentioned above, it is probably best to view 4:14-21 as a body-closing and therefore distinct from the main line of argument.

In sum, there seems to be support for viewing 1:13-4:13 as an instance of inversion. The distribution of epistolary conventions suggests a threefold division of 1:14-4:13 that corresponds to the three questions in 1:13. As well, "link-words" are used to tie the individual sections together, and significant verbal parallels exist between the questions in 1:13 and the responses in 1:14-4:13.

---

[19] 1:13, 14, 15, 16 (twice), 17; 10:2; 12:13; 15:29 (twice).

[20] 1:17, 18, 23; 2:2, 8. The question in 1:13 is the only other use of either of these words in the letter.

[21] These four words also occur in 3:1-4:13, but with lesser frequency.

[22] White includes vocatives in his list of nonformulaic major transitions within the letter-body (*Body* 66).

[23] Jeremias's suggestion that the names in 1:12 form an inversion with the names in 1:13 seems remote, if for no other reason than that Apollos and Cephas are omitted in 1:13 (cf. "Chiasmus" 151).

[24] οἰκέω (3:16), οἰκοδομή (3:9), ἐποικοδομέω (3:10 [twice]; 3:11; 3:14), οἰκονόμος (4:1 [twice]).

[25] Paul frequently uses ταῦτα to summarize preceding discussions (cf. 1 Cor 4:14; 9:8, 15; 10:6, 11; 12:11). Here is another use of the vocative at a point of transition.

Three smaller-scale oral patterns are present within 1:13-4:13. First, 1:19 retains the chiastic arrangement of the OT quotation:

	ἀπολῶ	τὴν σοφίαν τῶν σοφῶν,
καὶ	τὴν σύνεσιν τῶν συνετῶν	ἀθετήσω.	(Isa 29:14)

Second, there is an example of alternation in 1:22-25 that is rounded off by the inversion observed by Jeremias:[26]

A/A'	ἐπειδὴ καὶ ᾿Ιουδαῖοι σημεῖα αἰτοῦσιν
B/B'	καὶ ῞ελληνες σοφίαν ζητοῦσιν,
	ἡμεῖς δὲ κηρύσσομεν Χριστὸν ἐσταυρωμένον,
A	᾿Ιουδαίοις μὲν σκάνδαλον
B	ἔθνεσιν δὲ μωρίαν,
	αὐτοῖς δε τοῖς κλητοῖς,
A	᾿Ιουδαίοις τε
B	καὶ ῞ελλησιν,
A'	Χριστὸν θεοῦ δύναμιν
B'	καὶ θεοῦ σοφίαν·
B'	ὅτι τὸ μωρὸν τοῦ θεοῦ σοφώτερον τῶν ἀνθρώπων ἐστίν,
A'	καὶ τὸ ἀσθενες τοῦ θεοῦ ἰσχυρότερον τῶν ἀνθρώπων.

Third, another instance of alternation occurs in 4:10:[27]

A	ἡμεῖς μωροὶ διὰ Χριστόν,
B	ὑμεῖς δὲ φρόνιμοι ἐν Χριστῷ·
A	ἡμεῖς ἀσθενεῖς,
B	ὑμεῖς δὲ ἰσχυροί·
B	ὑμεῖς ἔνδοξοι,
A	ἡμεῖς δὲ ἄτιμοι.

After the apostolic parousia of 4:14-21, Paul introduces a new topic with a verb of hearing (ὅλως ἀκούεται ἐν ὑμῖν πορνεία). Although the reference to writing in 5:9 (ἔγραψα ὑμῖν ἐν τῇ ἐπιστολῇ μὴ συναναμίγνυσθαι πόρνοις) suggests a new topic, it is a reference to Paul's previous letter and serves to continue his line of argument.[28] πορνεία and its cognates form the dominant word-chain in 5:1-13. The entire paragraph is held together by inclusion (5:2, 13):[29]

ἵνα ἀρθῇ ἐκ μέσου ὑμῶν ὁ τὸ ἔργον τοῦτο πράξας;

ἐξάρατε τὸν πονηρὸν ἐξ ὑμῶν αὐτῶν.

---

[26] Jeremias, "Chiasmus" 150.

[27] Cf. Jeremias, who classifies it as a chiasmus (ibid. 140).

[28] See Hurd for the relation of 5:9-13a to what precedes and follows (*I Corinthians* 77-78). Note also the second writing formula in 5:11: νῦν δὲ ἔγραψα ὑμῖν μὴ συναναμίγνυσθαι.

[29] Cf. Talbert, *Corinthians* 12.

A new topic begins at 6:1 when Paul introduces the problem of lawsuits. Paul has already prepared the listener for this topic with his triple use of κρίνω in 5:12-13. This new section (6:1-11) is held together by nine uses of κρίνω and its cognates. Asyndeton and anaphora at 6:12, however, mark a return to the topic of immorality, as does the renewed use of πορνεία and its cognates (5x). Again, Paul prepares for the transition by using πόρνοι in 6:9 to begin the list of "the unrighteous" who will not inherit the kingdom.

So there exists an ABA' pattern for chapters 5 and 6.[30] Inclusion and anaphora establish the basic division of the chapters; link-words unify the different sections; and the theme of immorality begun in 5:1-13 is resumed in 6:12-20. The careful way in which Paul makes his transitions from one section to another serves to pull the apparently disparate topics together into a unified discussion.

A number of chiastic patterns can also be seen in 6:13-17. In verse 13a Paul appears to quote a slogan of the Corinthians ("Foods for the stomach, and the stomach for foods").[31] In verse 14a he coins a new slogan appropriate to the issue at hand ("The body is not for fornication but for the Lord, and the Lord for the body"). After each slogan he gives his evaluation of it. The result is a tightly-constructed argument against fornication:[32]

A/B	<u>τὰ βρώματα</u> <u>τῇ κοιλίᾳ</u>,
B/A	καὶ <u>ἡ κοιλία</u> <u>τοῖς βρώμασιν·</u>
B/A	ὁ δὲ θεὸς καὶ <u>ταύτην</u> καὶ <u>ταῦτα</u> καταργήσει.
C/D	<u>τὸ δὲ σῶμα</u> οὐ τῇ πορνείᾳ ἀλλὰ <u>τῷ κυρίῳ</u>,
D/C	καὶ <u>ὁ κύριος τῷ σώματι·</u>
D/C	ὁ δὲ θεὸς καὶ <u>τὸν κύριον</u> ἤγειρεν καὶ <u>ἡμᾶς</u> ἐξεγερεῖ διὰ τῆς δυνάμεως αὐτοῦ.

In the first construction, ταύτην refers to ἡ κοιλία while ταῦτα refers to τὰ βρώματα. In the second, τὸ σῶμα may be taken as a synecdoche for ἡμᾶς.

Paul then adds an additional argument pertaining to the "body" in 6:15-17. Fee is probably correct in his observation that this argument is inverted as well:[33]

E	οὐκ οἴδατε ὅτι τὰ σώματα ὑμῶν μέλη <u>Χριστοῦ</u> ἐστιν;
F	ἄρας οὖν τὰ μέλη τοῦ Χριστοῦ ποιήσω <u>πόρνης</u> μέλη; μὴ γένοιτο.
F	ἢ οὐκ οἴδατε ὅτι ὁ κολλώμενος τῇ <u>πόρνῃ</u> ἓν σῶμά ἐστιν; ἔσονται γάρ, φησίν, οἱ δύο εἰς σάρκα μίαν.
E	ὁ δὲ κολλώμενος <u>τῷ κυρίῳ</u> ἓν πνεῦμά ἐστιν.

---

[30] A = 5:1-13, B = 6:1-11, A' = 6:12-20; cf. Brunot, *S. Paul* 43-44; Ellis, *Letters* 59; Talbert, *Corinthians* 12.

[31] See Hurd's summary of scholarly opinion on possible quotations (*I Corinthians* 68).

[32] Cf. Lund, *Chiasmus* 145; Jeremias, "Chiasmus" 147, n. 7; Fee, *First Corinthians* 253.

[33] Fee, *First Corinthians* 257.

The subtle change from σῶμα and Χριστός in the first line to πνεῦμα and κύριος in the last line serves to remind the Corinthians of the special spiritual relationship they have with Christ.

An abrupt change in 1 Corinthians is signaled at 7:1 by the use of περὶ δὲ ὧν ἐγράψατε. The περὶ δὲ formula is characteristic of chapters 7-16 as Paul moves from issue to issue in response to a letter he had received from the Corinthians.[34] The presence of περὶ δὲ with the genitive at 7:25 marks a transition to a related topic.

In 7:2-4 there is an example of alternation similar to that found in 4:10:[35]

A	ἕκαστος τὴν ἑαυτοῦ γυναῖκα ἐχέτω,
B	καὶ ἑκάστη τὸν ἴδιον ἄνδρα ἐχέτω.
A	τῇ γυναικὶ ὁ ἀνὴρ τὴν ὀφειλὴν ἀποδιδότω,
B	ὁμοίως δὲ καὶ ἡ γυνὴ τῷ ἀνδρί.
B	ἡ γυνὴ τοῦ ἰδίου σώματος οὐκ ἐξουσιάζει ἀλλὰ ὁ ἀνήρ·
A	ὁμοίως δὲ καὶ ὁ ἀνὴρ τοῦ ἰδίου σώματος οὐκ ἐξουσιάζει ἀλλὰ ἡ γυνή.

Paul's instructions in 7:12-16 to Christians married to unbelievers set up a complex combination of chiastic inversions:[36]

A	εἴ τις ἀδελφὸς γυναῖκα ἔχει ἄπιστον, καὶ αὕτη συνευδοκεῖ οἰκεῖν μετ' αὐτοῦ, μὴ ἀφιέτω αὐτήν·
B	καὶ γυνὴ εἴ τις ἔχει ἄνδρα ἄπιστον, καὶ οὗτος συνευδοκεῖ οἰκεῖν μετ' αὐτῆς, μὴ ἀφιέτω τὸν ἄνδρα.
B	ἡγίασται γὰρ ὁ ἀνὴρ ὁ ἄπιστος ἐν τῇ γυναικί,
A	καὶ ἡγίασται ἡ γυνὴ ἡ ἄπιστος ἐν τῷ ἀδελφῷ· ἐπεὶ ἄρα τὰ τέκνα ὑμῶν ἀκάθαρτά ἐστιν, νῦν δὲ ἅγιά ἐστιν.
A	εἰ δὲ ὁ ἄπιστος χωρίζεται, χωριζέσθω· οὐ δεδούλωται ὁ ἀδελφὸς
B	ἢ ἡ ἀδελφὴ ἐν τοῖς τοιούτοις· ἐν δὲ εἰρήνῃ κέκληκεν ὑμᾶς ὁ θεός.
B	τί γὰρ οἶδας, γύναι, εἰ τὸν ἄνδρα σώσεις;
A	ἢ τί οἶδας, ἄνερ, εἰ τὴν γυναῖκα σώσεις;

---

[34] Cf. Hurd, *I Corinthians* 63-65. Contrast Mitchell, "Concerning 'peri de'" 234.

[35] Cf. Jeremias, "Chiasmus" 149. Fee correctly notes the alternation, but he misses the inversion in verse 4 (*First Corinthians* 277).

[36] Cf. Fee, *First Corinthians* 299, but he misses both the overall pattern and the continuation in 7:15-16.

The overarching pattern is:	Believing brother	A
	Believing sister	B
	Believing sister	B
	Believing brother	A
	Believing brother	A
	Believing sister	B
	Believing sister	B
	Believing brother	A

Within 7:12-14 the pattern is:	Believing brother	a
	Unbelieving wife	b
	Believing sister	c
	Unbelieving husband	d
	Unbelieving husband	d
	Believing sister	c
	Unbelieving wife	b
	Believing husband	a

There are verbal parallels between 7:7 and 7:17, and it is interesting to observe how Paul adds to and builds on those parallels so as to structure 7:17-24 in terms of a threefold repetition:

7:7   ἀλλὰ ἕκαστος ἴδιον ἔχει χάρισμα ἐκ θεοῦ, ὁ μεν οὕτως, ὁ δὲ οὕτως.

7:17   εἰ μὴ ἑκάστῳ ὡς ἐμέρισεν ὁ κύριος, ἕκαστον ὡς κέκληκεν ὁ θεός, οὕτως περιπατείτω·

7:20   ἕκαστος ἐν τῇ κλήσει ᾗ ἐκλήθη ἐν ταύτῃ μενέτω.

7:24   ἕκαστος ἐν ᾧ ἐκλήθη, ἀδελφοί, ἐν τούτῳ μενέτω παρὰ θεῷ.

By the use of chiasmus in 7:22 Paul explains why each person should remain in the calling in which he/she was called by God:[37]

ὁ γὰρ ἐν κυρίῳ κληθεὶς δοῦλος   ἀπελεύθερος κυρίου ἐστίν·
ὁμοίως ὁ ἐλεύθερος κληθεὶς   δοῦλός ἐστιν Χριστοῦ.

Another use of περὶ δὲ with the genitive (περὶ δὲ τῶν εἰδωλοθύτων) at 8:1 marks a new topic in Paul's letter. This introductory formula is linked to the disclosure formula οἴδαμεν ὅτι. The entire combination is repeated in 8:4 (περὶ τῆς βρώσεως οὖν τῶν εἰδωλοθύτων οἴδαμεν ὅτι). Although some have argued

---

[37] Cf. Jeremias, "Chiasmus" 148. Naturally enough, καλέω is the key word in 7:17-24, occurring nine times.

for a partitioning of chapters 8-10, most see these chapters as a unit.[38] This unity is supported by a concern for edification (οἰκοδομέω) in both chapter 8 (vv.1, 10) and chapter 10 (v.23) and by the repeated occurrence of the εἰδωλ- word group.[39]

The fact that this latter word group—with one exception (10:7)—occurs exclusively in 8:1-13 and 10:14-28 suggests the possibility that an ABA' pattern is present.[40] Further support is provided by the clusters of συνείδησις in 8:7-13 (3x) and 10:23-29 (5x). Such an analysis sees 8:1-13 and 10:14-11:1 as the outer panels, and views 9:1-10:13 as giving examples of how the principles of liberty should and should not be applied. The abrupt introduction of four rhetorical questions at 9:1 and the combination of a vocative and an imperative at 10:14 serve to set off this central application section.

The presence of a major disclosure formula at 10:1 (οὐ θέλω γὰρ ὑμᾶς ἀγνοεῖν, ἀδελφοί) makes it possible to divide the central panel into two sections (9:1-27 and 10:1-13), and so to argue for an ABB'A' pattern.[41] The presence of differing word chains in the two paragraphs lends credence to viewing them as two distinguishable sections.[42] Yet there is no clear correspondence between 9:1-27 and 10:1-13 that would suggest that they are intended to be anything other than two extended illustrations. It is, therefore, best to see 8:1-11:1 as a loose ABA' pattern.

Within 8:1-11:1 there are several readily-apparent oral patterns. Both 8:12 and 8:13 contain instances of chiasmus. In both cases the inversion in the last clause seems to be for emphasis:

οὕτως δὲ ἁμαρτάνοντες εἰς τοὺς ἀδελφοὺς . . .
εἰς Χριστὸν ἁμαρτάνετε.

διόπερ εἰ βρῶμα σκανδαλίζει τὸν ἀδελφόν μου,
οὐ μὴ φάγω κρέα . . . ἵνα μὴ τὸν ἀδελφόν μου σκανδαλίσω.

Jeremias has suggested that the first two questions of 9:1 ("Am I not free? Am I not an apostle?")[43] are answered in reverse order in 9:1b-27—that is, in 9:1b-18

---

[38] See Hurd for a summary of partition theories (*I Corinthians* 45) and an examination of the integrity of 8:1-11:1 (ibid. 115-149). Also on 11:1: "The verse logically belongs with 10:22-33 as the climax of Paul's argument, yet it clearly serves to introduce 11:2" (ibid. 89, n.1).

[39] εἰδωλόθυτον (8:1, 4, 7, 10; 10:19, 28), εἰδωλολατρία (10:14), εἰδωλολάτρης (10:7), εἴδωλον (8:4, 7; 10:19), εἰδωλεῖον (8:10).

[40] Both Brunot (*S. Paul* 43-44) and Ellis (*Letters* 76) adopt such an analysis.

[41] Cf. Collins, "ABA Pattern" 581-582; Talbert, *Corinthians* 58. Talbert actually makes a break at 9:23. The disclosure formula at 10:1, however, seems to weigh against his analysis.

[42] 9:1-17 - ἐξουσία (6x), εὐαγγέλιον (6x), εὐαγγελίζομαι (3x)
10:1-13 - πορνεύω (4x), πειράζω (5x)

[43] A few manuscripts reverse the order of these questions, but the present reading is preferred. Cf. Héring, *First Epistle* 75; Fee *First Corinthians* 394, n.9.

Paul addresses his apostleship; in 9:19-27 he addresses his freedom.[44] Primary support for this analysis seems to be the statement ἐλεύθερος γὰρ ὢν ἐκ πάντων πᾶσιν ἐμαυτὸν ἐδούλωσα of 9:19. Three other factors, however, must be considered as well: (1) that three of the four uses of ἀπόστολος/ἀποστολή in chapter 9 occur in 9:1-2;[45] (2) that the emphatic ἡ ἐμὴ ἀπολογία τοῖς ἐμε ἀνακρίνουσίν ἐστιν αὕτη seems to be the beginning of a new idea;[46] and (3) that when he used a similar question-and-answer style in 1:13-4:13, Paul dealt with the last (less important) question succinctly and with the first (more important) questions at greater length. It seems preferable, therefore, to modify Jeremias's proposal somewhat. Although 9:1-27 can still be understood as an example of inversion, it is probably better to see Paul answering the "apostleship" question in 9:1b-2 and the "freedom" question in 9:3-27.[47] In fact, Paul's discussion of his "rights" in 9:3-18 simply prepares the way for his primary point in 9:19-23: that he limits his freedom for the sake of the gospel.

The parallelism, repetition, and word-play in 9:20-22 would have been difficult for any ancient hearer or reader to ignore:

τοῖς Ἰουδαίοις ὡς Ἰουδαῖος,
  ἵνα Ἰουδαίους κερδήσω·

τοῖς ὑπὸ νόμον ὡς ὑπὸ νόμον, μὴ ὢν αὐτὸς ὑπὸ νόμον,
  ἵνα τοὺς ὑπὸ νόμον κερδήσω·

τοῖς ἀνόμοις ὡς ἄνομος, μὴ ὢν ἄνομος θεοῦ ἀλλ' ἔννομος Χριστοῦ,
  ἵνα κερδάνω τοὺς ἀνόμους·

τοῖς ἀσθενέσιν ἀσθενής,
  ἵνα τοὺς ἀσθενεῖς κερδήσω·

τοῖς πᾶσιν γέγονα πάντα,
  ἵνα πάντως τινὰς σώσω.

As well, the unity of 10:22-33 would have been readily observable—not only because of the fivefold use of συνείδησις, but also because of the inclusion of 10:22-23 and 10:33:

---

[44] Jeremias, "Chiasmus" 155-156. A number of commentators follow this analysis, e.g., J. Murphy-O'Connor, 1 Corinthians (Dublin: Veritas, 1979) 85; Fee, First Corinthians 393. It is interesting to find Fee endorsing this approach since he rejects a similar analysis of 1:13-4:13 (see above); the evidence here seems less compelling.

[45] The third use is in 9:5.

[46] Charles Hodge, in particular, ties verse 3 with what precedes (An Exposition of the First Epistle to the Corinthians, reprint (Grand Rapids: Eerdmans, 1972) 154; cf. L. Morris, 1 Corinthians (Grand Rapids: Eerdmans, 1985) 129.

[47] Cf. Talbert, Corinthians 61.

πάντα ἔξεστιν, ἀλλ' οὐ πάντα <u>συμφέρει</u>.
πάντα ἔξεστιν, ἀλλ' οὐ πάντα οἰκοδομεῖ.
μηδεὶς <u>τὸ ἑαυτοῦ ζητείτω</u> ἀλλὰ τὸ τοῦ ἑτέρου.

καθὼς κἀγὼ πάντα πᾶσιν ἀρέσκω, μὴ <u>ζητῶν τὸ ἐμαυτοῦ</u>
<u>σύμφορον</u> ἀλλὰ τὸ τῶν πολλῶν, ἵνα σωθῶσιν.

Although Paul departs from the περί δέ formula at the beginning of chapter 11, the disclosure formula in 11:3 (θέλω δὲ ὑμᾶς εἰδέναι ὅτι) suggests a transition point, as do the use of ἐπαινῶ δὲ ὑμᾶς ὅτι (cf. 11:7) and παρέδωκα ὑμῖν τὰς παραδόσεις (cf. 15:3) in 11:2.[48] Talbert finds an inclusion in 11:2 and 11:16:[49]

ἐπαινῶ δὲ ὑμᾶς ὅτι πάντα μου μέμνησθε καί, καθὼς παρέδωκα ὑμῖν, τὰς παραδόσεις κατέχετε.

εἰ δέ τις δοκεῖ φιλόνεικος εἶναι, ἡμεῖς τοιαύτην συνήθειαν οὐκ ἔχομεν οὐδὲ αἱ ἐκκλησίαι τοῦ θεοῦ.

Although this analysis may be true conceptually, there are no verbal links usually present in such a pattern. There are, however, other verbal links within the passage that serve to unify it: (1) the only two uses in the NT of ἀκατακάλυπτος occur in 11:5 and 11:13; (2) the only three uses in the NT of κατακαλύπτω occur in 11:6 (twice) and 11:7; (3) ἀνήρ is used fourteen times; (4) γυνή is used sixteen times; and (5) κεφαλή is used nine times.

The frequency of verbal repetitions in 11:2-16 has led to conflicting chiastic arrangements for the passage. It is probably best, therefore, to lay out the entire passage before discussing it in detail:

11:2 ἐπαινῶ δὲ ὑμᾶς ὅτι πάντα μου μέμνησθε καὶ καθὼς παρέδωκα
ὑμῖν τὰς παραδόσεις κατέχετε.

11:3 θέλω δὲ ὑμᾶς εἰδέναι ὅτι παντὸς ἀνδρὸς ἡ κεφαλὴ ὁ Χριστός ἐστιν,
κεφαλὴ δὲ γυναικὸς ὁ ἀνήρ,
κεφαλὴ δὲ τοῦ Χριστοῦ ὁ θεός.

11:4 <u>πᾶς ἀνὴρ προσευχόμενος ἢ προφητεύων</u> κατὰ <u>κεφαλῆς</u> ἔχων
<u>καταισχύνει τὴν κεφαλὴν αὐτοῦ·</u>

11:5 <u>πᾶσα δὲ γυνὴ προσευχομένη ἢ προφητεύουσα ἀκατακαλύπτῳ</u>
<u>τῇ κεφαλῇ καταισχύνει τὴν κεφαλὴν αὐτῆς·</u>
ἐν γάρ ἐστιν καὶ τὸ αὐτὸ τῇ ἐξυρημένῃ.

---

[48] Hurd takes 11:2 to refer to the Corinthians' letter to Paul (*I Corinthians* 182-183). C. E. Faw suggests that δέ is an abbreviated form of the περί δέ convention ("On the Writing of First Thessalonians" *JBL* 71 (1952) 221; cf. Hurd, *I Corinthians* 90, n.2).

[49] Talbert, *Corinthians* 66.

11:6 εἰ γὰρ οὐ <u>κατακαλύπτεται γυνή</u>, καὶ <u>κειράσθω</u>·
   εἰ δὲ <u>αἰσχρὸν γυναικὶ</u> τὸ <u>κείρασθαι</u> ἢ ξυρᾶσθαι, <u>κατακαλυπτέσθω</u>.

11:7 <u>ἀνὴρ</u> μὲν γὰρ οὐκ ὀφείλει <u>κατακαλύπτεσθαι</u> τὴν κεφαλήν,
   εἰκὼν καὶ <u>δόξα</u> θεοῦ ὑπάρχων·
 ἡ <u>γυνὴ</u> δὲ <u>δόξα</u> ἀνδρός ἐστιν.

11:8 οὐ γάρ ἐστιν   <u>ἀνὴρ ἐκ γυναικός</u>,
   ἀλλὰ   <u>γυνὴ ἐξ ἀνδρός</u>·
11:9 καὶ γὰρ οὐκ ἐκτίσθη <u>ἀνὴρ διὰ τὴν γυναῖκα</u>,
   ἀλλὰ   <u>γυνὴ διὰ τὸν ἄνδρα</u>.

11:10 διὰ τοῦτο ὀφείλει <u>ἡ γυνὴ</u> ἐξουσίαν ἔχειν ἐπὶ τῆς <u>κεφαλῆς</u>
   διὰ τοὺς ἀγγέλους.

11:11 πλὴν   οὔτε <u>γυνὴ χωρὶς ἀνδρὸς</u>
       οὔτε <u>ἀνὴρ χωρὶς γυναικὸς ἐν κυρίῳ</u>·
11:12 ὥσπερ γὰρ   <u>ἡ γυνὴ ἐκ τοῦ ἀνδρός</u>,
   οὕτως καὶ   <u>ὁ ἀνὴρ διὰ τῆς γυναικός</u>·
   τὰ δὲ πάντα ἐκ τοῦ θεοῦ.

11:13 ἐν ὑμῖν αὐτοῖς κρίνατε· πρέπον ἐστὶν <u>γυναῖκα ἀκατακάλυπτον</u>
   τῷ θεῷ <u>προσεύχεσθαι</u>;
11:14 οὐδὲ ἡ φύσις αὐτὴ διδάσκει ὑμᾶς ὅτι
   <u>ἀνὴρ μὲν ἐὰν κομᾷ ἀτιμία αὐτῷ ἐστιν</u>,
11:15   <u>γυνὴ δὲ ἐὰν κομᾷ δόξα αὐτῇ ἐστιν</u>;
   ὅτι <u>ἡ κόμη</u> ἀντὶ περιβολαίου δέδοται αὐτῇ.

11:16 εἰ δέ τις δοκεῖ φιλόνεικος εἶναι, ἡμεῖς τοιαύτην συνήθειαν
   οὐκ ἔχομεν, οὐδὲ αἱ ἐκκλησίαι τοῦ θεοῦ.

Several points in the above passage immediately stand out: (1) the tightly-constructed argument of 11:8-12 related to the creation order; (2) the verbal links within 11:4-7; (3) the verbal links within 11:13-15; (4) the repetition of ἀκατακάλυπτον . . . προσεύχομαι . . . δόξα in 11:4-7 and 11:13-15; and (5) the way in which 11:10 and 11:16 differ from the strongly parallelistic structure of the rest of the passage.

The basic overall structure of 11:2-16 may be seen as:[50]

	Introduction	11:2-3
A	Prayer/Prophecy and Covering the Head	11:4-7
B	Creation Order	11:8-12
A'	Prayer and Covering the Head	11:13-15
	Conclusion	11:16

---

[50] Talbert (*Corinthians* 66) proposes a similar pattern: A = 11:3-10; B = 11:11-12; A' = 11:13-15.

Within 11:8-12 there is a pattern of concentric symmetry:[51]

A	Origin of man and woman	11:8
B	Relationship between man and woman	11:9
C	Application to prayer and covering the head	11:10
B'	Relationship between man and woman	11:11
A'	Origin of man and woman	11:12

So the entire passage serves to develop the relationship of authority set forth in 11:3: God → Christ → man → woman.[52]

A new, but related, topic is introduced at 11:17 with the use of ἐπαινῶ (cf. 11:2). The presence of ἀκούω in 11:18 suggests that this information came to Paul by oral report.[53] The issue addressed arises when the church "comes together" (συνέρχομαι, 11:17, 18, 20). Paul's double use of this word in 11:33-34 closes the section with an inclusion. Within the section itself, 11:17-22 is framed by an inclusion using ἐπαινῶ:[54]

τοῦτο δὲ παραγγέλλων οὐκ ἐπαινῶ ὅτι . . .

ἐπαινέσω ὑμᾶς; ἐν τούτῳ οὐκ ἐπαινῶ.

Also within the section, it is apparent from the phrase ἐγὼ γὰρ παρέλαβον ἀπὸ τοῦ κυρίου, ὃ καὶ παρέδωκα ὑμῖν that a piece of church tradition is introduced in 11:23a. It is generally accepted that this piece of tradition extends from 11:23b through 11:25, with Paul's concluding comment in 11:26.[55] The section therefore breaks into three paragraphs that seem to suggest an ABA' pattern:[56]

---

[51] Cf. Lund, *Chiasmus* 148. T. P. Shoemaker has a similar—but more detailed—analysis ("Unveiling Equality. 1 Corinthians 11:2-16," *BTB* 17 [1987] 62).

[52] M. Crumpacker ("Headship and the Equality of the Sexes [1 Cor 11:2-16]," Paper presented at the annual meeting of the Evangelical Theological Society, Washington, D.C., 16-18 November, 1993) proposes a six-part analogy in these verses that emphasizes covenantal love rather than hierarchical authority:

Christ	Husband	Father
Believers	Wife	Son

[53] Cf. Hurd, *I Corinthians* 78.

[54] Cf. Talbert, *Corinthians* 73.

[55] E.g., Barrett, *First Corinthians* 264-270; H. Conzelmann, *1 Corinthians*, trans. J. W. Leitch, (Philadelphia: Fortress, 1975) 196-201; Fee, *First Corinthians* 545-556.

[56] Cf. Ellis, *Letters* 88. Brunot also has an ABA' pattern but divides it 11:17-22; 11:23-32; 11:33-34 (*S. Paul* 43-44). Fee (*First Corinthians* 532) prefers an ABB' A' pattern:

A	11:17-22	The statement of the problem
B	11:23-26	The repetition of the "tradition"
B'	11:27-32	"So then"—in response to vv. 23-26
A'	11:33-34	"So then"—in response to vv. 17-22

Although this arrangement correctly reflects the inclusion of 11:17-22 and 11:33-34 and the

A	The Problem Stated	11:17-22
B	The Tradition Invoked	11:23-26
A'	The Problem Corrected	11:27-34

The shift to a new topic is marked at 12:1-3 by the use of περί δέ in combination with a cluster of three disclosure formulae:[57]

12:1	περὶ δὲ τῶν πνευματικῶν, ἀδελφοί, οὐ θέλω ὑμᾶς ἀγνοεῖν.
12:2	οἴδατε ὅτι . . .
12:3	διὸ γνωρίζω ὑμῖν ὅτι . . .

The discussion of τῶν πνευματικῶν extends through the end of chapter 14, and a new topic is introduced in chapter 15 with a disclosure formula (15:1) and a "tradition" saying (15:3). The ABA' structure of chapters 12-14 is widely recognized:[58]

A	Criteria for evaluating the gifts	12:1-31
B	Love is the fundamental criterion	13:1-13
A'	Advice for exercising the gifts	14:1-40

On a more detailed level, it is possible to see 12:1-3 and 14:37-40 serving as "frame-passages" for the entire section. Support for this position may be found in the repetition of πνευματικός (12:1; 14:37), ἀγνοέω (12:1; 14:38), and κύριος (12:3; 14:37). The anaphora in 12:4-6 (διαιρέσεις) suggests the beginning of a rhetorical section separate from 12:1-3. Furthermore, the writing statement in 14:37

---

vocative at 11:33, it seems an unnecessary division of 11:27-34, especially given the cluster of κρίνω cognates (7) in 11:29-34. It is simpler to see Paul using 11:33-34 to round off the discussion by reminding his listeners of its beginning.

[57] This break works against Talbert (*Corinthians* 81), who views chapters 11-14 as an ABA' structure:

A	Prayer and prophecy	(11:2-16)
B	The Lord's Supper	(11:17-34)
A'	Prayer and prophecy	(chaps. 12-14)

[58] Cf. Brunot, S. Paul 43-44; Collins, "ABA Pattern" 582-583; Murphy-O'Connor, *1 Corinthians* 104; Welch, "Chiasmus" 217; Ellis, *Letters* 91; Talbert, *Corinthians* 81; Fee, *First Corinthians* 571. This analysis is not universal, however. E. L. Titus thinks chapter 13 is a non-Pauline interpolation ("Did Paul Write I Corinthians?" *JBR* 27 [1959] 299-302). Héring (*First Corinthians* 134) and J. T. Sanders ("First Corinthians 13, Its Interpretation Since the First World War," *Int* 20 [1966] 181-187) think it is Pauline but inserted by an unknown redactor. Barrett sees it as a "ready-made piece" that Paul inserted at its present location (*First Corinthians* 297). Conzelmann cites Weiss that "chap. 13 is here not in its original place," but he leaves open the question of authorship (*1 Corinthians* 217-220). It is possible, as Lund has done (*Chiasmus* 164), to see an inclusion consisting of διατάξομαι in 11:34b and τάξιν in 14:40. Paul anticipates and smooths the change of topic with a transitional sentence in 11:34 and brings the overall discussion of church order (11:2-14:40) to a close with a summary statement in 14:40.

and the vocative in 14:39 tend to set 14:37-40 off from the rest of the chapter. The result is an instance of concentric symmetry:[59]

A	Introduction: the gifts and those who have them	12:1-3
B	The diversity and unity of the spiritual gifts: the principle	12:4-31
C	The gifts and the graces	13:1-13
B'	The diversity and unity of the spiritual gifts: the application	14:1-36
A'	Conclusion: the leaders and the gifts	14:37-40

The first section in Paul's discussion of spiritual gifts is readily divided into three paragraphs. The triple use of διαιρέσεις in 12:4-6 forms an inclusion with διαιροῦν in 12:11.[60] The link-words σῶμα (18 times) and μέλη (13 times) unify 12:12-27. In 12:28-31 the triple use of χάρισμα (12:28, 30, 31) suggests that Paul has returned to the topic begun in 12:4-12 where the same word appeared twice (12:4, 9). Once again it appears that an ABA' pattern is present:[61]

A	Varieties of gifts (χάρισμα)	12:4-11
B	Variety within the body (σῶμα)	12:12-27
A'	Varieties of gifts (χάρισμα)	12:28-31

Two examples of chiasmus occur in 12:8 and 12:12. The second sets up the discussion that follows in 12:13-27.[62]

ᾧ μὲν γὰρ διὰ τοῦ πνεύματος δίδοται λόγος σοφίας,
ἄλλῳ δὲ λόγος γνώσεως κατὰ τὸ αὐτὸ πνεῦμα

καθάπερ γὰρ
τὸ σῶμα ἕν ἐστιν καὶ μέλη πολλὰ ἔχει,
πάντα δὲ τὰ μέλη τοῦ σώματος πολλὰ ὄντα ἕν ἐστιν σῶμα,
οὕτως καὶ ὁ Χριστός·

The transitions at the beginning and end of chapter 13 are worthy of note. Conzelmann finds them "harsh,"[63] and Barrett thinks them "awkward."[64] Such characterizations, however, are merely personal opinions. There is nothing inherently

---

[59] Cf. Lund, *Chiasmus* 164. Differences in transition points between Lund's outline and that proposed here may be attributed to the way in which Paul makes those transitions.

[60] Talbert notes an inclusion in 12:4 and 12:11 based on the repetition of τὸ αὐτὸ πνεῦμα (*Corinthians* 82). It is questionable, however, to base an inclusion in part on a word (πνεῦμα) that occurs twelve times in the chapter. On the other hand, the only NT occurrences of διαίρεσις are in 12:4-6, and the only other NT occurrence of διαιρέω is in Lk 15:12.

[61] Cf. Talbert *Corinthians* 82; Ellis, *Letters* 91.

[62] Cf. Fee, *First Corinthians* 601.

[63] Conzelmann, *1 Corinthians* 215, 233.

[64] Barrett, *First Corinthians* 297.

impossible about the transitions, and, in fact, they appear to exhibit a careful choice of words:

12:31 ζηλοῦτε δὲ τὰ χαρίσματα τὰ μείζονα . . .

14:1 διώκετε τὴν ἀγάπην, ζηλοῦτε δὲ τὰ πνευματικά, μᾶλλον δὲ ἵνα προφητεύητε.

The repetition of the command using ζηλοῦτε functions as anaphoric ring-composition. The change from τὰ χαρίσματα to τὰ πνευματικά marks a return to the wording in 12:1 and 14:37.[65]

The chapter breaks naturally into three paragraphs (13:1-3; 13:4-7; 13:8-13), the last two of which begin asyndetically with ἡ ἀγάπη. There is widespread scholarly support for an ABA' pattern in this chapter as well.[66] The primary evidence for such a pattern is the repetition of the three gifts (γλῶσσαι, προφητεία, γνῶσις), first in 13:1-3 and then in 13:8. The central paragraph is a listing of the characteristics of love, the first two of which are chiastically arranged (13:4):

ἡ ἀγάπη	μακροθυμεῖ,
χρηστεύεται	ἡ ἀγάπη

So, although the evidence is not quite as compelling for 13:1-13 as it is for 12:3-31, the ABA' structure for the chapter should probably be allowed to stand:[67]

A	Comparison of love with the gifts: love gives them value	13:1-3
B	The characteristics of love: love stands the test of time	13:4-7
A'	Comparison of love with the gifts: love abides while the gifts cease	13:8-13

Paul resumes his discussion of χαρίσματα/πνευματικά in 14:1 where he left it in 12:31 with a command using ζηλόω. The command in 14:1 is, in turn, echoed in 14:39 as inclusive ring-composition:

ζηλοῦτε δὲ τὰ πνευματικά, μᾶλλον δὲ ἵνα προφητεύητε.

ζηλοῦτε τὸ προφητεύειν, καὶ τὸ λαλεῖν μὴ κωλύετε γλώσσαις·

---

[65] Fee: "Some have argued for more significant differences between these two words; more likely it is a matter of emphasis. At the end of chap. 12, where he had been speaking specifically of the *gifts* themselves as charismatic endowments, he told them, 'eagerly desire the greater *charismata.*' Now in a context where the emphasis will be on the activity of the Spirit in the community at worship, he says, 'eagerly desire the things of the Spirit.'" (*First Corinthians* 655).

[66] Cf. Lund, *Chiasmus* 175-176; Brunot, *S. Paul* 43-44; J. Dupont (cited in DiMarco, "Chiasmus" 18); Murphy-O'Connor, *1 Corinthians* 125; Ellis, *Letters* 97; Talbert, *Corinthians* 86.

[67] Cf. Lund, *Chiasmus* 176; Ellis, *Letters* 91.

In his second statement, Paul shifts the focus of the command to the specific pursuit of prophecy as foremost among the πνευματικά. This shift serves to reflect and summarize the immediately preceding discussion.

It is instructive to review the way in which Paul has made his transitions from 11:34 through 14:40:

11:34   τὰ δὲ λοιπὰ ὡς ἂν ἔλθω <u>διατάξομαι</u>.

12:31   <u>ζηλοῦτε δὲ τὰ χαρίσματα</u> τὰ μείζονα.

14:1   <u>ζηλοῦτε δὲ τὰ πνευματικά</u>, μᾶλλον δὲ ἵνα <u>προφητεύητε</u>.

14:39   <u>ζηλοῦτε τὸ προφητεύειν</u>, καὶ . . . μὴ κωλύετε γλώσσαις·

14:40   πάντα δὲ εὐσχημόνως καὶ κατὰ <u>τάξιν</u> γινέσθω.

By repeating key words and phrases, Paul has given unity to his far-ranging discussion. At the same time, by carefully modifying the relationships among these words and phrases he has alerted his listener to the progress of his line of argument.

In an example of inclusive ring-composition on a smaller scale, the repetition of the phrase μᾶλλον δὲ ἵνα προφητεύητε frames 14:1-5:

διώκετε τὴν ἀγάπην, ζηλοῦτε δὲ τὰ πνευματικά, <u>μᾶλλον δὲ ἵνα</u> <u>προφητεύητε</u>.

θέλω δὲ πάντας ὑμᾶς λαλεῖν γλώσσαις, <u>μᾶλλον δὲ ἵνα</u> <u>προφητεύητε</u>·

An interesting construction, combining word play, repetition, and chiasmus, occurs in 14:20:[68]

μὴ	παιδία <u>γίνεσθε</u>	<u>ταῖς φρεσίν,</u>
ἀλλὰ	τῇ κακίᾳ	νηπιάζετε,
	<u>ταῖς δὲ φρεσὶν</u>	τέλειοι <u>γίνεσθε</u>.

A more common example of chiasmus occurs in 14:22:[69]

αἱ γλῶσσαι εἰς σημεῖόν εἰσιν οὐ <u>τοῖς πιστεύουσιν</u> ἀλλὰ <u>τοῖς ἀπίστοις</u>, ἡ δὲ προφητεία οὐ <u>τοῖς ἀπίστοις</u> ἀλλὰ <u>τοῖς πιστεύουσιν</u>.

A new section begins at 15:1 with the disclosure formula γνωρίζω δὲ ὑμῖν, ἀδελφοί and the "tradition" saying ὃ καὶ παρελάβετε. The tradition saying of 15:1

---

[68] Fee characterizes it as an ABA' pattern at the sentence level (*First Corinthians* 678).

[69] Cf. Jeremias, "Chiasmus" 147; Johanson, "Tongues, A Sign for Unbelievers?: A Structural and Exegetical Study of I Corinthians XIV.20-25," *NTS* 25 (1979) 186; Fee, *First Corinthians* 677.

is reinforced by another at 15:3: παρέδωκα γὰρ ὑμῖν ἐν πρώτοις, ὃ καὶ παρέλαβον. There are few epistolary conventions or oral patterns to help organize the chapter. Rather, it seems to follow a logical progression from the reliability of the gospel witness to the resurrection (15:1-11) through the certainty of the resurrection (15:12-34) and the nature of the resurrection (15:35-49) to the promise of the resurrection (15:50-58).

Talbert correctly notes the symmetrical way in which Paul enumerates the witnesses of the resurrection in 15:5-8:[70]

A	ὤφθη Κηφᾷ,
B	εἶτα τοῖς δώδεκα·
C	ἔπειτα ὤφθη ἐπάνω πεντακοσίοις ἀδελφοῖς ἐφάπαξ . . .
C'	ἔπειτα ὤφθη ᾿Ιακώβῳ,
B'	εἶτα τοῖς ἀποστόλοις πᾶσιν·
A'	ἔσχατον δὲ πάντων ὡσπερεὶ τῷ ἐκτρώματι ὤφθη κἀμοί.

The logic of Paul's argument concerning the resurrection is reinforced by two inverted structures.[71] The first is in 15:12-13. The second instance occurs slightly later in 15:15-16:

A	εἰ δὲ Χριστὸς κηρύσσεται ὅτι ἐκ νεκρῶν ἐγήγερται,
B	πῶς λέγουσιν ἐν ὑμῖν τινες ὅτι ἀνάστασις νεκρῶν οὐκ ἔστιν;
B'	εἰ δὲ ἀνάστασις νεκρῶν οὐκ ἔστιν,
A'	οὐδὲ Χριστὸς ἐγήγερται·

A	ἤγειρεν τὸν Χριστόν ὃν οὐκ ἤγειρεν,
B	εἴπερ ἄρα νεκροὶ οὐκ ἐγείρονται.
B'	εἰ γὰρ νεκροὶ οὐκ ἐγείρονται,
A'	οὐδὲ Χριστὸς ἐγήγερται

As Paul expands the basic principle stated in 15:38, he produces two passages that would be readily apprehended by the ear. The two passages, however, are structured quite differently. The first, 15:39-41, is structured using inversion, with the turning point in the middle of verse 40:[72]

A	οὐ πᾶσα σὰρξ ἡ αὐτὴ σάρξ,
B	ἀλλὰ ἄλλη μὲν ἀνθρώπων,
	ἄλλη δὲ σὰρξ κτηνῶν,
	ἄλλη δὲ σὰρξ πτηνῶν,
	ἄλλη δὲ ἰχθύων.

---

[70] Talbert, *Corinthians* 97.

[71] Cf. Fee, *First Corinthians* 739.

[72] Ibid. 783.

C καὶ σώματα ἐπουράνια,
   καὶ σώματα ἐπίγεια·

C' ἀλλὰ ἑτέρα μὲν ἡ τῶν ἐπουρανίων δόξα,
    ἑτέρα δὲ ἡ τῶν ἐπιγείων.

B'   ἄλλη δόξα ἡλίου,
  καὶ ἄλλη δόξα σελήνης,
  καὶ ἄλλη δόξα ἀστέρων·

A' ἀστὴρ γὰρ ἀστέρος διαφέρει ἐν δόξῃ.

Although lines A and A' have no verbal parallels, they are conceptually parallel and summarize the two halves of the passage. The relationship between B and B' is readily apparent as examples of the summary statements. The verbal parallels in C and C' are also clear. The first half of the structure is held together by the word pair σάρξ-σῶμα; the second half uses the link-word δόξα. The transition between the two sections is made by the double use of ἐπουράνια and ἐπίγεια in 15:40. Also apparent, especially in verses 39 and 40, is the use of homoeoteleuton.

The second passage, 15:42-44, is arranged in strict antithesis that relies heavily on anaphora and homoeoteleuton. The basic oral pattern is that of alternation, although a variety of words are used to make the contrast:

οὕτως καὶ ἡ ἀνάστασις τῶν νεκρῶν.

A σπείρεται ἐν φθορᾷ,
B ἐγείρεται ἐν ἀφθαρσίᾳ·
A σπείρεται ἐν ἀτιμίᾳ,
B ἐγείρεται ἐν δόξῃ·
A σπείρεται ἐν ἀσθενείᾳ,
B ἐγείρεται ἐν δυνάμει·
A σπείρεται σῶμα ψυχικόν,
B ἐγείρεται σῶμα πνευματικόν.
A εἰ ἔστιν σῶμα ψυχικόν,
B ἔστιν καὶ πνευματικόν.

The conclusion of Paul's instruction on the resurrection is introduced with a saying statement (τοῦτο δέ φημι, ἀδελφοί). The discussion is brought to a close with the statement of thanksgiving in 15:57 (τῷ δὲ θεῷ χάρις τῷ διδόντι ἡμῖν τὸ νῖκος διὰ τοῦ κυρίου ἡμῶν Ἰησοῦ Χριστοῦ). Within this passage, Jeremias has proposed an inverted structure for 15:50-54, based on the antithesis of "alive" and "dead."[73]

Before commenting further on the passage, it is probably best to lay out 15:50-57 in its entirety:

---

[73] Jeremias, "Chiasmus" 148; idem, "Flesh and Blood" 152-154.

15:50 σὰρξ καὶ αἷμα βασιλείαν θεοῦ <u>κληρονομῆσαι</u> οὐ δύναται,
οὐδὲ ἡ φθορὰ τὴν ἀφθαρσίαν <u>κληρονομεῖ</u>.

15:51 ἰδοὺ μυστήριον ὑμῖν λέγω·
πάντες οὐ κοιμηθησόμεθα, πάντες δὲ <u>ἀλλαγησόμεθα</u>,
15:52 ἐν ἀτόμῳ, ἐν ῥιπῇ ὀφθαλμοῦ, ἐν τῇ ἐσχάτῃ <u>σάλπιγγι</u>·
<u>σαλπίσει</u> γάρ, καὶ οἱ νεκροὶ ἐγερθήσονται ἄφθαρτοι
καὶ ἡμεῖς <u>ἀλλαγησόμεθα</u>.

15:53	δεῖ γὰρ	τὸ φθαρτὸν τοῦτο	ἐνδύσασθαι	ἀφθαρσίαν
	καὶ	τὸ θνητὸν τοῦτο	ἐνδύσασθαι	ἀθανασίαν.
15:54	ὅταν δὲ	τὸ φθαρτὸν τοῦτο	ἐνδύσηται	ἀφθαρσίαν
	καὶ	τὸ θνητὸν τοῦτο	ἐνδύσηται	ἀθανασίαν,

τότε γενήσεται ὁ λόγος ὁ γεγραμμένος,
κατεπόθη ὁ θάνατος εἰς <u>νῖκος</u>.
15:55 ποῦ σου, θάνατε, <u>τὸ νῖκος</u>;
ποῦ σου, θάνατε, <u>τὸ κέντρον</u>;
15:56 <u>τὸ δὲ κέντρον</u> τοῦ θανάτου <u>ἡ ἁμαρτία</u>,
ἡ δὲ δύναμις <u>τῆς ἁμαρτίας</u> ὁ νόμος·
15:57 τῷ δὲ θεῷ χάρις τῷ διδόντι ἡμῖν <u>τὸ νῖκος</u> διὰ τοῦ κυρίου ἡμῶν
Ἰησοῦ Χριστοῦ.

As can be seen from the above arrangement, verse 50 stands alone and is held together by structural parallelism and the repetition of κληρονομέω. Verses 51 and 52 form a unit in which it is possible to see an ABA' (or an ABB'A') pattern based on the repetition of ἀλλάσσω and σάλπιγξ/σαλπίζω. Parallelism and verbal repetition are apparent in 15:53-54a. Although 15:54b is grammatically part of the sentence that begins in 15:54a, it has strong verbal links to what follows in 15:55-57. The triple use of νίκη and the use of climax in 15:56 tie at least 15:54b-57 together.

Again, it is possible to see in the passage an ABA' pattern with 15:54b-55 and 15:57 serving as the outer members and 15:56 serving as the central member. If 15:54-55a is joined to 15:55b (as it should be grammatically) the result is a double ABA' pattern:

A	The change at the resurrection	15:51
B	The trumpet of the resurrection	15:52a
A'	The change at the resurrection	15:52b
A	Future triumph over death	15:53-55
B	Present disarming of death	15:56
A'	Total triumph over death in Christ	15:57

The entire chapter is then rounded off with a combination of an inferential conjunction, a vocative, an imperative, and a disclosure formula in 15:58. There are no oral patterns in chapter 16.

C. Other Suggested Structures

Welch has suggested that all of 1 Corinthians can be outlined using an inverted arrangement, with each of the major sections following either a concentric or an ABA' pattern:[74]

A	Introduction	1:1-9
B	Divisions in the church regarding leadership	1:10-2:5
	a	Division over men's authority and Paul's approach to baptism (1:10-17)	
	b	God has promised that he will destroy the wisdom of the wise (1:18-21)	
	c	Jews require a sign, Greeks seek wisdom (1:22)	
	d	We preach Christ crucified (1:23a)	
	c'	To the Jews a stumblingblock, to the Greeks foolishness (1:23b)	
	b'	Christ, the power and wisdom which destroys the wisdom of the wise (1:24-31)	
	a'	Paul's cautious approach to preaching (2:1-5)	
C	Man is led by the Spirit of God	2:6-4:21
	a	The will of God is imparted by the Spirit to those who will receive it (2:6-3:9)	
	b	Jesus Christ: the only Foundation (3:10-23)	
	a'	All we have is imparted by apostles dedicated to giving their all (4:1-21)	
D	Sexual problems within the Church	5:1-7:40
	a	Excommunication of Fornicators (5:1-8)	
	b	The Power to Judge (5:9-6:20)	
	a'	Advice concerning proper sexual relations (7:1-40)	
D'	Idolatry within the Church	8:1-11:34
	a	Eating meat offered to idols (8:1-8)	
	b	Avoiding the Abuse of the Power to Judge (8:9-10:23)	
	a'	Advice concerning proper worship and eucharist (11:1-34)	
C'	Man is led by the gifts of the Spirit	12:1-14:40
	a	Different gifts are given to all: unity in theory (12:1-34)	
	b	Love: the greatest of all (13:1-13)	
	a'	All gifts have a place in the congregation: unity in practice (14:1-40)	
B'	Divisions in the church regarding the Resurrection	15:1-58
A'	Conclusion	16:1-24

Central to Welch's arrangement are the claims (1) that 1:10-2:5 and 15:1-58 are the only portions of the letter that deal with divisions over points of doctrine, and (2) that 5:1-11:34 addresses the two issues—as outlined in the Jerusalem Decree—that "define the central message of the gospel as it was taken to the Gentiles . . . keeping oneself free from fornication and avoiding idolatry."[75] With regard to Welch's first claim, it is unclear how "leadership" is a matter of doctrine on the same level as that of the resurrection.

---

[74] Welch, "Chiasmus" 216-217.

[75] Ibid 219.

With regard to Welch's second claim, Hurd has argued cogently that (1) Paul's attempt to enforce the Jerusalem Decree lay behind his previous letter,[76] (2) two of the major concerns of that earlier letter were the dangers of immorality and idolatry,[77] (3) Paul's instructions on these topics in the previous letter differed from his original preaching in Corinth,[78] (4) the letter from the Corinthians to Paul raised specific questions about his inconsistency,[79] and (5) Paul's response to those questions is found in 1 Corinthians 7-16.[80] Such an analysis, of course, lends some credence to Welch's proposal, for it highlights the importance of the Jerusalem Decree in the Corinthian correspondence—particularly as that decree relates to issues addressed in 1 Corinthians. Hurd's analysis also, however, points out a weakness in Welch's proposal, for it connects chapter 7 with the material that follows rather than with what precedes it. Formal support connecting chapter 7 to what follows is found not only in the repeated use of περὶ δὲ in 7:1-16:12, but also in the ABA' structure of 5:1-6:20. The transition from sexual immorality to marital fidelity is a natural one,[81] but formal considerations weigh against taking chapters 5-7 as a unit. In any event, it is unclear how the content of D "corresponds" to that of D'. Once chapter 7 is separated from chapters 5 and 6, Welch's scheme begins to unravel.

Also weakening Welch's arrangement is his failure to take into account the ABA' structure of 8:1-11:1. Such an understanding separates 11:2-34 from chapters 8-10 and creates further imbalance in Welch's scheme. Furthermore, although 11:2-34 deals with issues related to worship, it is unclear that "idolatry" is the best heading for all of the material of this section. Nor is the suggested parallel between 8:1-8 and 11:1-34 clear.

Welch correctly identifies the ABA' structure of chapters 12-14, but the correspondence between these chapters and 2:6-4:21 is apparent only in the titles he has given to each. It is true that πνεῦμα occurs repeatedly in 2:4-14 (9x) and in 12:3-14:32 (19x), but a similar cluster appears in chapters 5-6 (7x). Finally, Welch's decision to lump all of chapter 16 together as the "conclusion" fails to do justice to 16:1-14, which is, most naturally, to be taken as part of the περὶ δὲ sections that began in chapter 7. Epistolary analysis indicates that 16:15-24 forms the letter closing. So if any section is to be set parallel to the letter opening of 1:1-9, it seems most natural that it should be this letter closing.

---

[76] Hurd, *I Corinthians* 260.

[77] Ibid. 259. The other issues Hurd identifies are (3) Resurrection of believers, and (4) Announcement of the Collection (ibid. 241).

[78] Ibid. 244-245.

[79] Ibid. 274.

[80] Ibid. 65-82.

[81] The transition is assisted by the use of πορνεία in 7:2 as a link-word.

It is instructive to compare Welch's arrangement of 1:10-4:21 with the suggestion of Brunot:[82]

1:1-3:4 - Folly and Wisdom
A   Wisdom of the world and wisdom of God   1:18-2:5
        a   God's wisdom is superior (1:18-25)
        b   Proof of the opposition of the two wisdoms (1:26-31)
        a'   Paul's preaching is inspired by God's wisdom (2:1-5)
B   The true wisdom of God   2:6-16
A'   Return to the question of Paul's preaching   3:1-4

3:5-4:16 - The Apostolic Ministry
A   Paul and Apollos are only God's workmen   3:5-10
B   Serious responsibilities of cooperators of God   3:11-23
A'   True merits of God's workmen   4:1-15

And that of Ellis:[83]

A   The problem: teachers, the cross, and wisdom   1:10-2:5
        a   Reputedly wise teachers are causing disunity (1:10-17)
        b   But true wisdom is found only in the cross (1:18-25)
        a'   When Paul taught, he taught the wisdom of God (1:26-2:5)
B   Apparent digression   2:6-16
        a   The wisdom Paul teaches (2:6-7)
        b   Description of wisdom (2:8-12)
        a'   The wisdom Paul teaches (2:13-16)
A'   Advice concerning teachers   3:1-4:21
        a   The function of teachers (3:1-17)
        b   A reprise of the wisdom-folly of the cross (3:18-23)
        a'   A reprise of the function of teachers (4:1-21)

These three schemes all have breaks in thought at 1:18, 2:6, and 4:1. All three agree that 4:1 forms a second-level transition within the argument. They do not, however, agree on the significance of the the breaks at 2:6 and 1:18. Welch, for example, sees 2:6 as the major break in the argument. Ellis agrees that it is a major break, but only one of two (the other being at 3:1). Brunot sees the primary break in the passage happening at 3:5, with 2:6 as a minor transition point within 1:18-3:4. Nor do they agree on the secondary breaks within sections.

The number and variety of disagreements among these three schemes point up the difficulties inherent in trying to subdivide 1:10-4:21. The section is, in fact, a relatively seamless argument, without such clear indicators as seen elsewhere in the letter (e.g., 5:1-6:20; 8:1-11:1; 12:1-14:40). Although it is probable that the listener would have recognized the cohesiveness of the argument in 1:10-4:13, it

---

[82] Brunot, *S. Paul* 43-44.

[83] Ellis, *Letters* 45.

seems less likely that the complex schemes suggested by Welch, Brunot, and Ellis would have been readily apparent to the ear. The inverted pattern suggested earlier in this chapter seems at least as likely.

Both Kenneth Bailey and Talbert have proposed concentric structures for the end of chapter 1 and the beginning of chapter 2—Bailey for 1:17-2:2 and Talbert for 1:17-2:5.[84] These two proposals are virtually identical in 1:21-24:

E   εὐδόκησεν ὁ θεὸς διὰ τῆς μωρίας τοῦ κηρύγματος   1:21
     σῶσαι τοὺς πιστεύοντας

F   ἐπειδὴ καὶ Ἰουδαῖοι σημεῖα αἰτοῦσιν   1:22
     καὶ Ἕλληνες σοφίαν ζητοῦσιν,

G   ἡμεῖς δὲ κηρύσσομεν   1:23a
     Χριστὸν ἐσταυρωμένον,

F'   Ἰουδαίοις μὲν σκάνδαλον   1:23b
     ἔθνεσιν δὲ μωρίαν,

E'   αὐτοῖς δὲ τοῖς κλητοῖς, (Ἰουδαίοις τε καὶ Ἕλλησιν,)   1:24
     Χριστὸν θεοῦ δύναμιν καὶ θεοῦ σοφίαν·

Beyond agreement on these verses, however, the two schemes diverge. Talbert views 1:18-21a and 1:25-31 as parallel units. Bailey divides both 1:18-21a and 1:25-31 into three subsections, continuing his concentric structure to three more levels. Both writers recognize conceptual similarities between 1:17 and 2:1-2 (2:1-5 in Talbert).

It can readily be seen that the strongest verbal parallels in 1:21-24 are the repetition of Ἰουδαῖοι and Ἕλληνες.[85] Other than those similarities, however, there are few oral parallels. Neither Bailey nor Talbert takes into account the way in which 1:25 seems to round off the thought of 1:19-24, and both ignore the break at 1:26 that consists of a combination of imperative and vocative (βλέπετε γὰρ τὴν κλῆσιν ὑμῶν, ἀδελφοί).[86]

Fee proposes inverted constructions for both 2:15-16 and 3:10-11.[87] The first of these suggestions is, perhaps, possible:

---

[84] K. E. Bailey, "Recovering the Poetic Structure of I Cor i.17-ii.2," *NovT* 17 (1975) 265-296; Talbert, *Corinthians* 4. The structure shown is that by Bailey; Talbert's is similar.

[85] Neither scheme works with the third occurrence of Ἰουδαίοις τε καὶ Ἕλλησιν in verse 24. Bailey views it as a redactor's addition ("Poetic Structure" 287).

[86] Bailey removes the problem by attributing the phrase to a redactor ("Poetic Structure" 280-283). Perhaps the least attractive aspect of Bailey's scheme is his tendency to remove "comments" in his effort to find the form of the "original" poem. Such an exercise will always involve conjectures that detract from the credibility of the analysis

[87] Fee, *First Corinthians* 117, 137.

ὁ δὲ πνευματικὸς ἀνακρίνει [τὰ] πάντα,
αὐτὸς δὲ ὑπ' οὐδενὸς ἀνακρίνεται.
τίς γὰρ ἔγνω νοῦν κυρίου, ὃς συμβιβάσει αὐτόν;
ἡμεῖς δὲ νοῦν Χριστοῦ ἔχομεν.

Unfortunately, it takes Fee almost three pages to explain what he sees as an inverted construction, and then the explanation is largely conceptual.[88] In terms of oral patterning it is far more likely that the listener would have noticed the triple use of ἀνακρίνω in 2:14-15. Fee's second suggestion, however, is strongly supported by the verbal parallels that occur within 3:10-11:

. . . ὡς σοφὸς ἀρχιτέκτων θεμέλιον ἔθηκα,
   ἄλλος δὲ ἐποικοδομεῖ.
   ἕκαστος δὲ βλεπέτω πῶς ἐποικοδομεῖ·
   θεμέλιον γὰρ ἄλλον οὐδεὶς δύναται θεῖναι παρὰ τὸν κείμενον . . .

Jeremias has observed the inversion of noun and modifying genitive in 4:13b, but it seems unlikely that this shift would have been readily apparent to the ear:[89]

| ὡς | περικαθάρματα | τοῦ κόσμου | (ab) | ἐγενήθημεν, |
| | πάντων | περίψημα, | (ba) | ἕως ἄρτι |

Lund proposed the following concentric structure for 5:2-6:[90]

A   καὶ ὑμεῖς πεφυσιωμένοι ἐστέ, καὶ οὐχὶ μᾶλλον ἐπενθήσατε,

B   ἵνα ἀρθῇ ἐκ μέσου ὑμῶν ὁ τὸ ἔργον τοῦτο πράξας;
    ἐγὼ μεν γάρ, ἀπὼν τῷ σώματι παρὼν δὲ τῷ πνεύματι,
    ἤδη κέκρικα ὡς παρὼν
    τὸν οὕτως τοῦτο κατεργασάμενον

C   ἐν τῷ ὀνόματι τοῦ κυρίου ἡμῶν Ἰησοῦ,
    συναχθέντων ὑμῶν
    καὶ τοῦ ἐμοῦ πνεύματος
    σὺν τῇ δυνάμει τοῦ κυρίου ἡμῶν Ἰησοῦ,

B' παραδοῦναι τὸν τοιοῦτον τῷ Σατανᾷ
    εἰς ὄλεθρον
    τῆς σαρκός,
    ἵνα τὸ πνεῦμα
    σωθῇ
    ἐν τῇ ἡμέρᾳ τοῦ κυρίου.

A' οὐ καλὸν τὸ καύχημα ὑμῶν.

[88] Ibid. 117-120.
[89] Jeremias, "Chiasmus" 146.
[90] Lund, *Chiasmus* 147.

This scheme has some strengths, especially the repetition of παρὼν in verse 3 and the similarities between τῷ ὀνόματι τοῦ κυρίου [ἡμῶν] Ἰησοῦ and τῇ δυνάμει τοῦ κυρίου ἡμῶν Ἰησοῦ in verse 4. There are, however, certain weaknesses. The parallel suggested between A and A' is conceptual rather than verbal, and that between B and B' is tenuous at best. The natural grammatical structure is, at times, discarded in favor of the conceptual scheme. Furthermore, the handling of verse 5 appears forced: it has no support from verbal parallels, and phrases that normally would be taken together are split to fit the scheme. Lund has, it seems, over-analyzed this passage, and so reached conclusions that are neither readily inferred from the available evidence nor readily apparent to the ear.

Lund takes thirteen pages to develop a complex scheme for chapter 7, with various subsections nearly all arranged chiastically.[91] Portions of chapter 7 have been analyzed above, and the details of Lund's elaborate argument need not detain us in this study. His overall scheme, however, may be examined:

A	Introduction: A man is not to touch a woman	7:1
B	The Sexual Problem in the Married State and its Solution	7:2-5
C	Rules Governing Married Couples and Some Unmarried	7:6-17
D	Circumcision and Uncircumcision	7:18-20
D'	Bond or Free	7:21-24
C	Rules Governing Virgins and Some Married Couples	7:25-23
B'	The Sexual Problem in the Virgin State and its Solution	7:36-39
A'	Conclusion: A woman is happier as she is	7:40

Lund's basic analysis of this chapter is certainly correct: "It will be seen at a glance that the first three parts and the last three deal with the sexual problem, while parts [D] and [D'] deal with classes in the church, and what their attitude ought to be."[92] This appraisal suggests that at least an ABA' pattern is present.[93] Nonetheless, the further question remains: How finely can this basic pattern be refined?

Natural divisions in the text occur at 7:8 (λέγω δὲ τοῖς ἀγάμοις καὶ ταῖς χήραις), 7:12 (τοῖς δὲ λοιποῖς λέγω ἐγώ, οὐχ ὁ κύριος), and 7:25 (περὶ δὲ τῶν παρθένων ἐπιταγὴν κυρίου οὐκ ἔχω). The internal coherence of 7:12-16 has been noted above, as has that of 7:17-24.[94] There seems to be an additional shift in the argument at 7:39.[95] The resulting sections and their word-chains are:

---

[91] Lund, *Chiasmus* 151-163.

[92] Ibid. 151.

[93] Cf. Ellis, *Letters* 66: A = 7:1-17; B = 7:17-24; A' = 7:25-40.

[94] The entire section is unified by the repetition of the verb καλέω (9x) and by the similar phraseology of 7:17, 7:20, and 7:24. Lund's decision to divide 7:17-24 is, therefore, at least open to question.

[95] Although γυνή occurs repeatedly in 7:25-40, ἀνήρ is used only once in 7:25-38. The discussion in 7:39-40 returns—specifically—to marital relations between husband and wife.

7:1-7	γυνή, ἀνήρ
7:8-11	γαμέω (and cognates)
7:12-16	ἄπιστος
7:17-24	καλέω
7:25-38	γαμέω (and cognates), παρθένος, μεριμνάω (and cognates)
7:39-40	γυνή, ἀνήρ

The points of correspondence are immediately obvious: 7:1-7 and 7:39-40 focus on the duties and responsibilities of those who are married, while 7:8-11 and 7:25-38 give instructions to those who are not married (ἄγαμος). 7:17-24 steps back from the marriage context to set out the basic principle that Paul wishes to drive home: ἕκαστος ἐν τῇ κλήσει ᾗ ἐκλήθη ἐν ταύτῃ μενέτω. Unfortunately, 7:12-16 is an anomaly in that it seems to have no "balancing" section. This fact results in three possibilities: (1) 7:12-16 and 7:17-24 are to be understood as corresponding sections; (2) 7:8-11 and 7:12-16 are to be understood as one section; or (3) an intentional concentric structure is not present.

The first suggestion is possible, for the burden of 7:12-16 is that the believing partner should remain with an unbelieving spouse rather than seek a change in marital status. The principle enunciated in 7:17-24, however, seems to have broader application than simply to 7:12-16.[96] The second suggestion is also possible, for both 7:8-11 and 7:12-16 address believers in "unusual" marital states. The fact that Paul makes a clear distinction in 7:12, however, weighs against this understanding. So, without denying the existence of structural relationships within the chapter, it is perhaps best to view Paul's argument here as following a loose ABA' pattern rather than a more detailed concentric structure:[97]

A	Instructions for the Married (or Formerly Married)	7:1-16
B	The Guiding Principle: Remain as you are	7:17-24
A'	Instructions for the Unmarried	7:25-40

Talbert has proposed a concentric structure for 7:2-5:[98]

A	Possible acts of immorality	7:2
B	Sexual union is all right	7:3
C	Woman is dependent on man	7:4a
C'	Man is dependent on woman	7:4b
B'	Sexual union is encouraged	7:5a
A'	Temptation to immorality	7:5b

---

[96] The distribution of μένω in the chapter supports this contention (7:8, 11, 20, 24, 40).

[97] Cf. Ellis, *Letters* 67.

[98] Talbert, *Corinthians* 38; cf. W. Bühlmann and K. Scherer, *Stilfiguren de Bibel* (Freiberg: Herder, 1973) 29.

As noted above, the strongest verbal relationships occur in 7:2-4. There is little, however, to relate verse 5 to verse 2, as Talbert suggests. A natural question is, Why are the two parallel clauses of verse 4 treated separately, whereas the similar parallel clauses in verses 2 and 3 are not? If the text were handled consistently, either verse 4 would be treated as a single element, or verses 2 and 3 would be subdivided. The latter choice makes the alternation described above more apparent than Talbert's scheme.

Talbert also proposes a concentric structure for 7:7-24, based on Paul's saying statements in 7:8, 7:10, and 7:12:[99]

A	Each has his or her own special gift from God and so lives	7:7b
B	*I say* to the unmarried and widows	7:8-9
C	*The Lord commands* to the married	7:10-11
B'	*I say* to those married to unbelievers	7:12-16
A'	Live in terms of the gifts assigned to you and in terms of your Christian calling	7:17-24

Talbert is correct in working, as he does, with the saying statements as internal transitions. As well, verbal parallels in 7:17 suggest that what Paul says here is related to what he said in 7:7.[100] Talbert's scheme, however, has several disadvantages: (1) it is awkward to see half of one verse (7:7b) "balanced" by eight verses (7:17-24); (2) there are no verbal parallels between 7:8-9 and 7:12-16; and (3) the content of 7:8-9 bears little similarity to that of 7:12-16. It is questionable whether the change in saying statements alone is adequate for identifying a pattern of concentric symmetry.

Lund has suggested the following inverted structure for 9:19-22:[101]

A   ἐλεύθερος γὰρ ὢν ἐκ πάντων
      πᾶσιν ἐμαυτὸν ἐδούλωσα,
      ἵνα τοὺς πλείονας κερδήσω·

B   καὶ ἐγενόμην
      τοῖς Ἰουδαίοις
      ὡς Ἰουδαῖος,
      ἵνα Ἰουδαίους κερδήσω·

C   τοῖς ὑπὸ νόμον
      ὡς ὑπὸ νόμον,
      μὴ ὢν αὐτὸς ὑπὸ νόμον,
      ἵνα τοὺς ὑπὸ νόμον κερδήσω·

---

[99] Talbert, *Corinthians*, 40.

[100] The verbal parallels are primarily οὕτως and ἕκαστος.

[101] Lund, *Chiasmus* 147.

C'   τοῖς ἀνόμοις
ὡς ἄνομος,
μὴ ὢν ἄνομος θεοῦ
ἀλλ' ἔννομος Χριστοῦ,
ἵνα κερδάνω τοὺς ἀνόμους·

B'   ἐγενόμην
τοῖς ἀσθενέσιν
ἀσθενής,
ἵνα τοὺς ἀσθενεῖς κερδήσω·

A'   τοῖς πᾶσιν
γέγονα πάντα,
ἵνα πάντως τινὰς σώσω.

Once again, however, this seems to be a case of over-analysis, for apart from the obvious affinities between C and C', significant verbal parallels are few, and a conceptual relationship between B and B' is difficult to discern. Fee's comment regarding the possibility of an inverted structure in these verses is apt: ". . . if so, it is in form only, not in content."[102] As Fee demonstrates, the form can be explained just as readily in terms of parallelism:[103]

Intro.: Being free from all, I became a slave to all,
        in order to win the many.
1)   to the Jews, as a Jew
        in order to win the Jews;
2)   to those under the law, as under the law (although not really myself under the law)
        in order to win those under the law;
3)   to those not under the law, as not under the law (although not lawless)
        in order to win those not under the law;
4)   to the weak, weak
        in order to win the weak.
Concl.: I have become all things to all people,
        in order by all means to save some.
Reason: I do all things
        for the sake of the gospel,
        in order to share its blessings.

Jeremias notes an example of chiasmus using verbs and objects in 10:3-4:[104]

| καὶ πάντες τὸ αὐτὸ πνευματικὸν | βρῶμα | ἔφαγον, |
| καὶ πάντες τὸ αὐτὸ πνευματικὸν | ἔπιον | πόμα· |

---

[102] Fee, *First Corinthians* 423, n.9.
[103] Ibid.
[104] Jeremias, "Chiasmus" 146.

Although the parallelism of these lines is readily apparent, it is difficult to judge how much of an impact the inversion in 10:4a would have made, especially with the anaphora of 10:1-3 preceding it[105] and the phrase ἔπινον γὰρ ἐκ πνευματικῆς ἀκολουθούσης πέτρας following it.

Similarly, Fee suggests an inverted construction for 10:17:[106]

A   because there is one loaf
B   we who are many are one body
B'   for we all partake
A'   of the one loaf

Such a chiasmus, however, is more apparent in his English translation than it is in the Greek, which reads:

ὅτι εἷς ἄρτος,
ἓν σῶμα οἱ πολλοί ἐσμεν,
οἱ γὰρ πάντες
    ἐκ τοῦ ἑνὸς ἄρτου μετέχομεν.

The correspondence between εἷς ἄρτος and ἑνὸς ἄρτου is, of course, obvious. Less obvious, however, is the correspondence between B and B', and the decision to divide the third clause leads, naturally, to the question: Why was the second clause not handled in the same way? A more consistent handling of the text would suggest that the inverted structure Fee proposes is more a product of his own analysis than of Paul's composition.

Fee also proposes a concentric structure for 10:23-33:[107]

A   Criterion: the good of others   10:23-24
B   Personal freedom re: food   10:25-27
C   Illustration   10:28-29a
B'   Personal freedom defended   10:29b-30
A'   Criterion generalized: all might be saved: 10:31-33

The inclusion of 10:23-24 and 10:33 has been noted above. Otherwise, the scheme lacks verbal parallels to support it. Rather, the internal coherence of the passage is highlighted by the uniform distribution of συνείδησις (5x) and ἐσθίω (4x) throughout verses 25-31. So although there is nothing inherently impossible about

---

[105] οἱ πατέρες ἡμῶν πάντες ὑπὸ τὴν νεφέλην ἦσαν
                        καὶ   πάντες διὰ τῆς θαλάσσης διῆλθον,
                        καὶ   πάντες εἰς τὸν Μωϋσῆν ἐβαπτίσθησαν ἐν τῇ νεφέλῃ καὶ
                               ἐν τῇ θαλάσσῃ,

[106] Fee, *First Corinthians* 469.

[107] Fee, *First Corinthians* 478.

Fee's arrangement,[108] there is little to suggest that it reflects an oral pattern, whether intentional or unintentional.

Talbert proposes an inverted structure for 11:3-9:[109]

A	Origin of woman (appeal to creation)	11:3
B	Man/head not covered	11:4
C	Woman/head covered	11:5
C'	Woman/head covered	11:6
B'	Man/head not covered	11:7
A'	Origin of woman (appeal to creation)	11:8-9

The strength of this arrangement is in verse 4-7 where the argument clearly moves from the man (11:4), to the woman (11:5-6), and then back to the man (11:7). So at least an ABA' structure is present. But whether the central panel (11:5-6) should be divided into two parts is a matter of dispute. On the one hand, of course, both verses deal with the woman; on the other, however, verse 5 has close verbal connections to the preceding verse, while verse 6 has connections with what follows. Probably, the verbal repetitions should be given more weight. Also, it needs to be noted that the parallel between 11:3 and 11:8-9 is not as close as Talbert's headings would suggest, since verse 3 has more to do with an authority structure than with the "origin of woman." Yet it cannot be denied that both elements state general principles applicable to the creation order as they pertain to the relationship of men and women.

Talbert offers an ABA' pattern for 11:27-32:[110]

A	Danger in wrong behavior	11:27
B	Exhortation to proper behavior	11:28
A'	Danger in wrong behavior	11:29-32

Although this outline correctly reflects the argument of the paragraph, it lacks the sort of formal support found in ABA' patterns elsewhere in the letter. A closer examination of the passage reveals that ἐσθίω, πίνω, ἄρτος, and ποτήριον occur uniformly across verses 27-29, thereby depriving Talbert of the sort of shift in the word-chains that would be expected in an ABA' pattern. Classifying every instance in which Paul moves back and forth between positive and negative statements as an example of the ABA' pattern certainly highlights the antithetical nature of his thinking, but it also trivializes the basic concept of the ABA' structural pattern—a pattern that is quite useful in understanding the sometimes seemingly disjointed nature of Paul's argumentation.

---

[108] Although he might well have included verse 27 in his "illustration" section.

[109] Talbert, *Corinthians* 66.

[110] Ibid. 79.

Lund proposes quite a detailed arrangement for 12:4-30.[111] One example will serve to illustrate. He arranges 12:4-6 concentrically:

> διαιρέσεις δὲ χαρισμάτων εἰσίν,
> τὸ δὲ αὐτὸ πνεῦμα·
>   καὶ διαιρέσεις διακονιῶν εἰσιν,
>   καὶ ὁ αὐτὸς κύριος·
> καὶ διαιρέσεις ἐνεργημάτων εἰσίν,
> ὁ δὲ αὐτὸς θεός, ὁ ἐνεργῶν τὰ πάντα ἐν πᾶσιν.

A parallel arrangement, however, would be far more natural:

> διαιρέσεις δὲ χαρισμάτων εἰσίν,
>   τὸ δὲ αὐτὸ πνεῦμα·
> καὶ διαιρέσεις διακονιῶν εἰσιν,
>   καὶ ὁ αὐτὸς κύριος·
> καὶ διαιρέσεις ἐνεργημάτων εἰσίν,
>   ὁ δὲ αὐτὸς θεός, ὁ ἐνεργῶν τὰ πάντα ἐν πᾶσιν.

Lund's overall arrangement for 12:4-30 has few points of verbal correspondence, most commonly using σῶμα as the key word. But the fact that σῶμα occurs eighteen times in chapter 12 suggests that it is part of the word-chain rather than the key to a concentric structure. Furthermore, Lund's outline includes a section (12:14-19) that is arranged sequentially (A-B-C-D-E-A'). As well, it has opening (12:4-11) and closing (12:28-30) sections that do not match well (A-B-C vs. C-A-B).

Belleville suggests that 12:3-6 is an inverted structure:[112]

A	οὐδεὶς ἐν πνεύματι θεοῦ λαλῶν λέγει, ᾿Ανάθεμα ᾿Ιησοῦς,
B	καὶ οὐδεὶς δύναται εἰπεῖν, Κύριος ᾿Ιησοῦς,
C	εἰ μὴ ἐν πνεύματι ἁγίῳ.
C'	διαιρέσεις δὲ χαρισμάτων εἰσίν, τὸ δὲ αὐτὸ πνεῦμα·
B'	καὶ διαιρέσεις διακονιῶν εἰσιν, καὶ ὁ αὐτὸς κύριος·
A'	καὶ διαιρέσεις ἐνεργημάτων εἰσίν, ὁ δὲ αὐτὸς θεός . . .

Although this arrangement is attractive, the outer members (A and A') are not truly parallel, and B and C most naturally belong together as a single element.

Similarly, she sees an inverted structure in 12:12-14:[113]

A	καθάπερ γὰρ τὸ σῶμα ἕν ἐστιν καὶ μέλη πολλὰ ἔχει,
B	πάντα δὲ τὰ μέλη τοῦ σώματος πολλὰ ὄντα ἕν ἐστιν σῶμα . . .

---

[111] Lund, *Chiasmus* 165-167.

[112] Belleville, "Continuity" 26, n.24. The entirety of the Greek text is provided.

[113] Ibid. 27; cf. Fee, *First Corinthians* 601. Again, the full Greek text is provided.

B'   καὶ γὰρ ἐν ἑνὶ πνεύματι ἡμεῖς πάντες εἰς ἓν σῶμα ἐβαπτίσθημεν . . .

A'   καὶ γὰρ τὸ σῶμα οὐκ ἔστιν ἓν μέλος ἀλλὰ πολλά.

The repeated uses of σῶμα and μέλος in these verses obscure, to a degree, the arrangement Belleville proposes, but it may be represented as: many members-one body-one body-many members. Although such a structural schema is not inherently impossible, her outline is not readily apparent.

Lund[114] and Welch[115] both propose similar arrangements for 13:4-7:

A   ἡ ἀγάπη μακροθυμεῖ,
       χρηστεύεται ἡ ἀγάπη,
B   οὐ ζηλοῖ,
         οὐ περπερεύεται,
         οὐ φυσιοῦται,
         οὐκ ἀσχημονεῖ,
         οὐ ζητεῖ τὰ ἑαυτῆς,
         οὐ παροξύνεται,
         οὐ λογίζεται τὸ κακόν,
         οὐ χαίρει ἐπὶ τῇ ἀδικίᾳ,
         συγχαίρει δὲ τῇ ἀληθείᾳ·
A'   πάντα στέγει,
      πάντα πιστεύει,
      πάντα ἐλπίζει,
      πάντα ὑπομένει.

The only obvious oral features in these verses are (1) the chiasmus in verse 4a, (2) the repetition of οὐ in verse 4b-6, and (3) the fourfold repetition of πάντα in verse 7. These items are accurately reflected in the arrangement set out above. It is unlikely, however, that this passage can be considered a true example of the ABA' pattern, for there are no points of verbal correspondence between A and A'.

Lund takes two pages to explain another proposed concentric structure for 13:8-13:[116]

A   ἡ <u>ἀγάπη</u> οὐδέποτε πίπτει.

B   εἴτε δὲ προφητεῖαι, καταργηθήσονται·
      εἴτε γλῶσσαι, παύσονται·
      εἴτε γνῶσις, καταργηθήσεται.

---

[114] Lund, *Chiasmus* 176.

[115] Welch, "Chiasmus" 215.

[116] Lund, *Chiasmus* 176.

C   ἐκ μέρους γὰρ γινώσκομεν
     καὶ ἐκ μέρους προφητεύομεν·
     ὅταν δὲ ἔλθῃ τὸ τέλειον,
     τὸ ἐκ μέρους καταργηθήσεται.

D   ὅτε ἤμην νήπιος,
     ἐλάλουν ὡς νήπιος,
     ἐφρόνουν ὡς νήπιος,
     ἐλογιζόμην ὡς νήπιος·
     ὅτε γέγονα ἀνήρ, κατήργηκα τὰ τοῦ νηπίου.

C'   βλέπομεν γὰρ ἄρτι δι᾿ ἐσόπτρου ἐν αἰνίγματι,
     τότε δὲ πρόσωπον πρὸς πρόσωπον·
     ἄρτι γινώσκω ἐκ μέρους,
     τότε δὲ ἐπιγνώσομαι καθὼς καὶ ἐπεγνώσθην.

B'   νυνὶ δὲ μένει πίστις, ἐλπίς, ἀγάπη, τὰ τρία ταῦτα·

A'   μείζων δὲ τούτων ἡ ἀγάπη.

His primary pieces of evidence are: (1) ἀγαπή creates an inclusion around the paragraph, (2) B discusses three gifts, while B' discusses three graces, and (3) both C and C' deal with the concepts of imperfection and perfection. Two additional items may be added: the fivefold repetition of νήπιος in 13:11, and the prepositional phrase ἐκ μέρους that occurs three times in C and once in C'. The cumulative weight of this evidence suggests that Lund's arrangement accurately reflects the structure of the passage.

Ellis sees an ABA' structure in 14:1-40:[117]

A	Better to prophesy than to speak in tongues	14:1-5
B	Tongue-speaking does not build up the community	14:6-25
A'	Better to prophesy than to speak in tongues	14:26-40

The ring-composition that frames 14:1-5 has been noted above. Further transition points within the chapter, however, are difficult to pinpoint with precision, the most likley possibilities being the vocatives at 14:20 and 14:26. Neither are shifts in the word-chain of much help, for προφητεύω and its cognates (14x), γλῶσσα (16x), and ἐκκλησία (9x) are distributed evenly throughout the passage. The type of formal clues that are present in ABA' patterns elsewhere in the letter, therefore, are largely absent here. This fact suggests that Ellis's arrangement is open to question.

---

[117] Ellis, *Letters* 92.

Lund also proposes a structure that encompasses nearly all of chapter 14.[118] As is so often the case, Lund's structure is quite elaborate, and space does not permit an exhaustive evaluation. One of the simpler sections is 14:14-19:

Λ ἐὰν γὰρ προσεύχωμαι γλώσσῃ, 14:14
  τὸ πνεῦμά μου προσεύχεται,
   ὁ δὲ νοῦς μου ἄκαρπός ἐστιν.
    τί οὖν ἐστιν;

B   προσεύξομαι τῷ πνεύματι,
    προσεύξομαι δὲ καὶ τῷ νοΐ·
   ψαλῶ τῷ πνεύματι,
    ψαλῶ δὲ καὶ τῷ νοΐ.

B'   ἐπεὶ ἐὰν εὐλογῇς ἐν πνεύματι,
    ὁ ἀναπληρῶν τὸν τόπον τοῦ ἰδιώτου
    πῶς ἐρεῖ τὸ 'Αμήν ἐπὶ τῇ σῇ εὐχαριστίᾳ,
    ἐπειδὴ τί λέγεις οὐκ οἶδεν;
    σὺ μὲν γὰρ καλῶς εὐχαριστεῖς,
    ἀλλ' ὁ ἕτερος οὐκ οἰκοδομεῖται.

A'   εὐχαριστῶ τῷ θεῷ, πάντων ὑμῶν μᾶλλον γλώσσαις λαλῶ·
    ἀλλὰ ἐν ἐκκλησίᾳ θέλω πέντε λόγους τῷ νοΐ μου λαλῆσαι,
    ἵνα καὶ ἄλλους κατηχήσω,
    ἢ μυρίους λόγους ἐν γλώσσῃ.

As is true throughout the chapter, the argument is relatively seamless, with πνεῦμα (4x) and νοῦς (4x) occurring repeatedly and, therefore, making it difficult to argue persuasively for either an inverted or a concentric structure. Lund's arrangement is possible, but it is not readily apparent.

  Talbert believes that chapter 15 is held together with the inclusion "brethren/in vain" in 15:1-2 and 15:58:[119]

γνωρίζω δὲ ὑμῖν, <u>ἀδελφοί</u>, τὸ εὐαγγέλιον ὃ εὐηγγελισάμην ὑμῖν, ὃ καὶ παρελάβετε, ἐν ᾧ καὶ ἑστήκατε, δι' οὗ καὶ σῴζεσθε, τίνι λόγῳ εὐηγγελισάμην ὑμῖν εἰ κατέχετε, ἐκτὸς εἰ μὴ <u>εἰκῇ</u> ἐπιστεύσατε.

ὥστε, <u>ἀδελφοί</u> μου ἀγαπητοί, ἑδραῖοι γίνεσθε, ἀμετακίνητοι, περισσεύοντες ἐν τῷ ἔργῳ τοῦ κυρίου πάντοτε, εἰδότες ὅτι ὁ κόπος ὑμῶν οὐκ ἔστιν <u>κενὸς</u> ἐν κυρίῳ.

---

[118] Lund, *Chiasmus* 183-186.

[119] Talbert, *Corinthians* 96.

This analysis is unlikely, however, since the Greek words he translates "in vain" are different (εἰκῇ and κενὸς) and fail to conform to the verbal repetition normally found in inclusion. Furthermore, ἀδελφοί also appears in verses 6 and 50, the latter verse being an instance of direct address comparable to the uses in verses 2 and 58.

Ellis has proposed an ABA' structure for chapter 15:[120]

A   Argumentation for the bodily resurrection of Christ (15:1-11); implications of this common preaching and tradition (15:12-19); first apocalyptic scenario (15:20-28)

B   *Ad hominem* arguments for the resurrection (15:29-34)

A'   Argumentation for a bodily resurrection (15:35-49) and second apocalyptic scenario (15:50-58)

To make the ABA' pattern work, however, Ellis must combine 15:1-19 with 15:20-28 to make A. He then must combine 15:35-49 with 15:50-58 to make A'. The more natural understanding of his analysis is:[121]

A	Argumentation . . .	15:1-19
B	Apocalyptic scenario	15:20-28
C	*Ad hominem* arguments for the resurrection	15:29-34
A'	Argumentation . . .	15:35-49
B'	Apocalyptic scenario	15:50-58

Welch sees chapter 15 as an example of concentric symmetry:[122]

A   Witnesses to the resurrection of Christ (15:1-11)

B   Dispute over the reality of the resurrection (15:12)

C   Explanation that without the resurrection our preaching is vain, we are false witnesses and we are most miserable (15:13-19)

D   Christ and Adam (15:20-23)

C'   Explanation that without the resurrection our baptizing is vain, our tribulations are worthless, and we may as well gratify ourselves (15:29-34)

B'   Possible dispute over the nature of the resurrection and the problem discovered (15:35-44)

D'   Christ and Adam (15:45-49)

A'   Testimony of the mystery of the resurrection and of all mankind (15:50-58)

There are, however, few verbal parallels to support this arrangement. Verse 12 seems unnaturally separated from 15:13-19, and 15:45-49 seems to continue the argument

---

[120] Ellis, *Letters* 106.

[121] This analysis is quite close to that of Murphy-O'Connor, *1 Corinthians* 137-151.

[122] Welch, "Chiasmus" 218.

of 15:35-44.[123] Furthermore, although it is possible that a pattern of concentric symmetry might have one element out of order, such a displacement renders the scheme less convincing than simpler approaches.

Jeremias has suggested that 15:35-57 is another instance of inversion. He argues that the first question in 15:35 (πῶς ἐγείρονται οἱ νεκροί;) is answered in 15:50-58, while the second question (ποίῳ δὲ σώματι ἔρχονται;) is answered in 15:36-49.[124] The break at 15:50 is obvious (τοῦτο δέ φημι, ἀδελφοί). And certainly the suggestion is attractive, especially after finding similar patterns in 1:13-4:13 and 9:1-27. There are, however, problems with such an analysis here. First, the word chains fail to support it. It is true that key words in the second question (σῶμα, οἷος) occur exclusively in 15:35-49.[125] But key words in the first question (νεκρός, ἐγείρω) are also to be found largely in 15:35-49 rather than in 15:50-57, as might be expected if an inversion were present.[126] Furthermore, it is questionable that 15:50-57 answers the question as to the *way* in which the resurrection will occur. It might be, instead, that the second question makes the first more specific.[127] The evidence here, in fact, is less convincing than for the earlier passages, and so it seems better not to see 15:35-57 as an instance of inversion.

D. Summary

As was the case in Romans, all eight oral patterns appear in 1 Corinthians. Chiasmus is quite frequent, occurring no fewer than twelve times. Inversion of various scales is present, ranging from what occurs within paragraphs to what occurs in the structuring of a number of chapters (e.g., 1:14-4:13). Several examples of alternation are present, as are several instances of inclusion. Ring-composition is a key factor in the transitions that link stages of Paul's argument in chapters 12-14. Word-chains are readily apparent in numerous places, often helping to give definition to ABA' patterns. Refrain is not common in 1 Corinthians, although the saying statements within 7:7-24 might be an example. Concentric symmetry and the related ABA' pattern occur with some frequency, often bringing clarity to Paul's apparently digressive argumentation.

---

[123] A fact supported by the continuation of ψυχικός and πνευματικός across Welch's suggested break at 15:44.

[124] Jeremias, "Chiasmus" 155-156; idem, "'Flesh and Blood Cannot Inherit the Kingdom of God' 1 Cor 15:50," *NTS* 2 (1956) 156-157. Talbert follows Jeremias (*Corinthians* 100).

[125] σῶμα in 15:37, 37, 38 (twice), 40, 44 (twice); οἷος in 15:48 (twice).

[126] νεκρός in 15:32, 35, 42, 52; ἐγείρω in 15:32, 35, 42, 43 (twice), 44, 52.

[127] So Fee: "The two questions are probably to be understood as corresponding to one another." (*First Corinthians* 780). Cf. Conzelmann, *1 Corinthians* 280; esp. n.6.

Chapter 8

2 CORINTHIANS

Pauline authorship of 2 Corinthians is generally accepted, as are the Corinthian destination and the general date of composition. Even those scholars who argue for a composite letter believe that the extant Corinthian correspondence was written by Paul within a relatively short period, generally A.D. 54-56. If 2 Cor 6:14-7:1 is a fragment of Paul's "Previous Letter" (1 Cor 5:9-11), as some suggest,[1] then the *terminus a quo* may be pushed earlier, perhaps to A.D. 51. There is, however, a small but growing number of scholars who, following the lead of John Knox, are re-thinking Pauline chronology.[2] The tendency among these scholars is toward an earlier dating scheme in general. Gerd Lüdemann, for instance, would move the Corinthian correspondence to A.D. 49-50.[3]

The integrity of the letter, however, is hotly disputed. Talbert itemizes positions ranging from acceptance of 2 Corinthians as a single letter to a nine-letter hypothesis that involves the partitioning of both 1 and 2 Corinthians.[4] Martin[5] and Furnish[6] both discuss the issue at length and conclude that chapters 10-13 are a separate letter written later than chapters 1-9. Betz argues for chapters 8 and 9 as separate letters.[7] Kümmel concludes that canonical 2 Corinthians is a single letter, written amid interruptions.[8]

---

[1] Cf. Hurd, *1 Corinthians* 235-239.

[2] Cf. J. Knox, *Chapters in a Life of Paul* (Nashville: Abingdon, 1950).

[3] G. Lüdemann, *Paul, Apostle to the Gentiles*, trans. F. S. Jones (Philadelphia: Fortress, 1984) 262-263.

[4] Talbert, *Corinthians* xviii-xix.

[5] R. P. Martin, *2 Corinthians* (Waco: Word, 1986) xxxviii-lii.

[6] V. P. Furnish, *II Corinthians* (Garden City: Doubleday, 1984) 29-55.

[7] H. D. Betz, *2 Corinthians 8 and 9* (Philadelphia: Fortress, 1985) 129-144.

[8] Kümmel, *Introduction* 287-293.

Jervis provides a review of the issues and an introduction to the bibliography.[9] She notes four major points at which the integrity of 2 Corinthians might be questioned (2:14-7:4; 6:14-7:1; chapters 8-9; and chapters 10-13) and summarizes the major arguments on both sides in each instance. Oral patterns observed in the letter appear to bear on two of the passages in question (2:14-7:4 and 6:14-7:1), but relationships among chapters 1-7, 8-9, and 10-13 are outside the scope of this study.

Abrupt changes of topic, Paul's preoccupation with his travel plans and the Corinthians' attitude toward him, his emotional defense of his apostleship, and the lack of a central doctrinal conflict all serve to set 2 Corinthians apart. The canonical version of 2 Corinthians is, from the perspective of rhetorical and epistolary analysis, one of Paul's most challenging writings.

A. Epistolary Structure

In analyzing the structure of 2 Corinthians, it is most appropriate to begin with its epistolary conventions.[10] A survey of the major epistolary formulae yields the following clusters:

1:1-16	Sender (1:1a), recipients (1:1b), greeting (1:2), blessing (1:3), disclosure formula (1:8), writing statement (1:13), confidence statement (1:15a), intention to visit (1:15b-16)
2:3-14	Writing statement (2:3), confidence formula (2:3), writing statement (2:4), request formula (2:8), writing statement (2:9), statement of thanks (2:14)
8:1-9	Disclosure formula (8:1), attestation (8:3), disclosure formula (8:9)
8:16-22	Statement of thanks (8:16-17), dispatch of emissary (8:18), dispatch of emissary (8:22)
9:1-5	περὶ μὲν (9:1), writing statement (9:1), dispatch of emissary (9:3), dispatch of emissary (9:5)
9:15-10:2	Statement of thanks (9:15), request formula (10:1), request formula (10:2)
12:14-13:13	Intention to visit (12:14), intention to visit (12:20), intention to visit (12:21), intention to visit (13:1), intention to visit (13:2), writing statement (13:10), peace-wish (13:11), greetings (13:12), grace-benediction (13:13)

The salutation is clearly established by the sequence: sender-recipients-greeting in 1:1-2. In place of his more common thanksgiving, Paul follows the

---

[9] Jervis, *Romans* 59-65.

[10] The question of whether or not 2 Corinthians is a single letter will be left open in the analysis that follows.

salutation with a *berakah* section in 1:3-7.[11] A disclosure formula (οὐ γὰρ θέλομεν ὑμᾶς ἀγνοεῖν, ἀδελφοί) in 1:8 marks the letter-opening, which extends through 1:11. The body-middle begins with a thematic statement in 1:12-14,[12] followed by a confidence statement and the start of a discussion of Paul's travel plans in 1:15-16. That discussion of travel plans continues through the cluster of formulae in 2:3-13, with the statement of thanks in 2:14 marking an abrupt shift of topics to his ministry as an apostle.

The disclosure formula in 8:1-2 (γνωρίζομεν δὲ ὑμῖν, ἀδελφοί) marks a clear transition point. Although some scholars have argued that a new letter begins at 8:1,[13] Paul uses comparable disclosure formulae at 1 Cor 12:3, 1 Cor 15:1, and Gal 1:11. An argument for the beginning of a separate letter, therefore, must be made on other grounds. Funk analyzes 8:16-23 and 9:1-5 as secondary examples of the apostolic parousia,[14] but Jervis correctly observes that these sections deal with a visit for the sake of the collection and are, therefore, not comparable to passages such as Rom 15:14-33 or 1 Cor 4:14-21.[15]

Another statement of thanks occurs in 9:15, and the double request formula at 10:1-2 (αὐτὸς δὲ ἐγὼ Παῦλος παρακαλῶ ὑμᾶς . . . δέομαι δὲ) marks a major transition point. Paul uses a comparable request formula at 1 Thess 4:1, however, and—as was the case at 8:1—the argument for the beginning of a separate letter must be made on other grounds.[16] Multiple instances of "visit talk"[17] in 12:14-13:2 suggest the beginning of an apostolic parousia at 12:14,[18] although—given the close connection of 12:14-21 to what precedes—it might be preferable to limit the apostolic parousia to 13:1-10; 13:11-13 comprises a fairly complete letter-closing.[19]

---

[11] Compare Galatians, where a rebuke section (1:6-10) replaces the thanksgiving.

[12] Cf. Belleville, *Reflections* 119-120.

[13] E. g., Betz maintains that these two chapters are separate letters (*2 Corinthians 8 and 9*, esp 129-144). Chapter 8 is a letter fragment of mixed type with two aims: 8:1-15 is advisory (deliberative rhetoric); 8:16-23 is administrative (juridical rhetoric). Chapter 9 is an advisory letter (deliberative rhetoric). The collection had been suspended during the crisis between Paul and the Corinthian church; these letters were written subsequent to the rest of 2 Corinthians (which Betz sees as a composite of three other letter fragments) and were intended to make a new beginning on the collection. See Martin (*2 Corinthians* 249-250) and Furnish (*II Corinthians* 408-409, 429-433) for counter-arguments.

[14] Funk, "Apostolic Parousia" 254.

[15] Jervis, *Romans* 112.

[16] On the issue of whether a fragment of a new letter begins at this point, see (pro) Furnish (*II Corinthians* 35-41) and (con) Kümmel (*Introduction* 290-291).

[17] A phrase proposed by T. Y. Mullins, "Visit Talk in the New Testament Letters," *CBQ* 35 (1973) 350-358.

[18] Cf. Funk, "Apostolic Parousia" 254. See also his comments in *Language* (265) where he refers to 12:14-13:10 as the "travel section."

[19] The elements present are: summary advice (13:11a), peace-wish (13:11b), greetings

The basic epistolary form of canonical 2 Corinthians may therefore be set out as follows:

Letter-opening		1:1-7
Salutation	1:1-2	
Blessing section	1:3-7	
Letter-body		1:8-13:10
Body opening	1:8-11	
Body middle	1:12-12:21	
Body closing	13:1-10	
Letter-closing		13:11-13

B. Readily Apparent Oral Patterns

After the salutation of 1:1-2, Paul replaces the customary thanksgiving with a blessing section in 1:3-7.[20] This carefully crafted eulogy is unified by the repetition of παρακαλέω and its cognates. The overall structure uses both inversion and alternation:[21]

A	εὐλογητὸς <u>ὁ θεὸς</u>
B	καὶ <u>πατὴρ</u> τοῦ κυρίου ἡμῶν Ἰησοῦ Χριστοῦ,
B'	ὁ <u>πατὴρ</u> τῶν οἰκτιρμῶν
A'	καὶ <u>θεὸς</u> πάσης παρακλήσεως,
C	<u>ὁ παρακαλῶν ἡμᾶς</u>
D	<u>ἐπὶ πάσῃ τῇ θλίψει</u> ἡμῶν,
D'	εἰς τὸ δύνασθαι ἡμᾶς παρακαλεῖν τοὺς <u>ἐν πάσῃ θλίψει</u>
C'	διὰ τῆς παρακλήσεως ἧς <u>παρακαλούμεθα</u> αὐτοὶ ὑπὸ τοῦ θεοῦ·
D	ὅτι καθὼς περισσεύει <u>τὰ παθήματα</u> τοῦ Χριστοῦ εἰς ἡμᾶς,
C	οὕτως διὰ τοῦ Χριστοῦ περισσεύει καὶ <u>ἡ παράκλησις</u> ἡμῶν.
D	εἴτε δὲ <u>θλιβόμεθα</u>, ὑπὲρ τῆς ὑμῶν παρακλήσεως . . .
C	εἴτε <u>παρακαλούμεθα</u>, ὑπὲρ τῆς ὑμῶν παρακλήσεως . . .

(13:12), grace-benediction (13:13). Cf. Weima, *Neglected Endings* 209; Jervis *Romans* 132-133, 143.

[20] Talbert calls it a *berakah* (*Corinthians* 134); Belleville, a "eulogy period" (*Reflections* 108-114). Although some scholars argue that this section extends through verse 11, it is better to see the disclosure formula (οὐ γὰρ θέλομεν ὑμᾶς ἀγνοεῖν, ἀδελφοί, ὑπὲρ τῆς θλίψεως ἡμῶν τῆς γενομένης ἐν τῇ Ἀσίᾳ) in verse 8 as introducing the letter-body; cf. ibid. 115-119.

[21] Cf. Belleville, *Reflections* 111. Lund correctly notes the inversion in 1:3-4 but incorrectly extends it to include 1:5 (*Chiasmus*, 150). Martin misses the pattern in 1:3-4 and argues for an inversion in 1:5 (*2 Corinthians* 8); cf. Furnish: "[this verse] has certain characteristics of a formal *chiasmus* without being, strictly speaking chiastic" (*II Corinthians* 118). Lund, Martin, and Furnish all miss the alternation in 1:5-7. See the discussion below.

καὶ ἡ ἐλπὶς ἡμῶν βεβαία ὑπὲρ ὑμῶν,

D   εἰδότες ὅτι ὡς κοινωνοί ἐστε τῶν <u>παθημάτων</u>,
C   οὕτως καὶ τῆς <u>παρακλήσεως</u>.

The link-word θλῖψις connects 1:3-7 to 1:8-11, and the contrast between suffering/tribulation and encouragement/comfort sets the tone for chapters 1-7. The opening inversion reminds the readers that God is a compassionate Father who is the source of all encouragement.

The body-middle begins with a thematic summary statement in 1:12-14.[22] This statement is framed by inclusion:[23]

1:12   ἡ γὰρ <u>καύχησις ἡμῶν</u> αὕτη ἐστίν . . .

1:14   ὅτι <u>καύχημα ὑμῶν</u> ἐσμεν . . .

The subtle shift from Paul's boast in his conduct (1:12) to the Corinthians' boast in Paul (1:14) sets the stage for the subsequent discussion of Paul's integrity in his dealings with the Corinthians (1:15-2:11).

It is at 2:13 that the integrity question first arises.[24] Paul abruptly shifts topics from his travel plans (1:15-2:13) to a discussion of his ministry as an apostle (2:14-7:4). Just as abruptly at 7:5, he returns to the subject of his travel plans (7:5-7). These sudden changes of topic, coupled with the apparent continuity between 2:12-13 and 7:5,[25] have led some scholars to suggest that 2:14-7:4 is an interpolation.[26] It is possible, however, that 2:12-13 and 7:5-6 represent an instance of anaphoric ring-composition:

<u>ἐλθὼν</u> δὲ εἰς τὴν Τρῳάδα εἰς τὸ εὐαγγέλιον τοῦ Χριστοῦ, καὶ θύρας μοι ἀνεῳγμένης ἐν κυρίῳ, <u>οὐκ ἔσχηκα ἄνεσιν</u> τῷ πνεύματί μου τῷ μὴ εὑρεῖν με <u>Τίτον</u> τὸν ἀδελφόν μου, ἀλλὰ ἀποταξάμενος αὐτοῖς <u>ἐξῆλθον εἰς Μακεδονίαν</u>.

---

[22] Cf. Belleville, *Reflections* 119-120.

[23] Cf. Martin, *2 Corinthians* 19. Note also the confidence expression in 1:15 (καὶ ταύτῃ τῇ πεποιθήσει) that suggests the beginning of a new section.

[24] See Belleville for a further discussion of this issue (*Reflections* 84-94).

[25] Martin: "In fact, if 2:14-7:4 were extracted from the text, Paul's mentioning of Titus and Macedonia in 2:12, 13 would flow perfectly into the mention of Paul's rendezvous with Titus in Macedonia as explained in 7:5-16" (*2 Corinthians* xliii).

[26] E.g., W. Schmithals who sees 1:1-2:13 + 7:5-16 as "a coherent piece of the 'letter of joy' which Paul writes from Macedonia not long before his arrival in Corinth" (*Gnosticism in Corinth*, trans. J. E. Steely [Nashville: Abingdon, 1971] 97). He believes that 2:14-6:13 + 7:2-4 is the body of a letter sent to Corinth between the "painful visit" (2 Cor 2:1) and the "sorrowful letter" (2 Cor 2:3-4, 9; 7:8, 12) in which Paul communicated his original travel plans (ibid. 100). He also believes that 6:14-7:1 is an interpolated portion of the "previous letter" (ibid. 96).

καὶ γὰρ ἐλθόντων ἡμῶν εἰς Μακεδονίαν οὐδεμίαν ἔσχηκεν ἄνεσιν ἡ σὰρξ ἡμῶν, ἀλλ᾽ ἐν παντὶ θλιβόμενοι—ἔξωθεν μάχαι, ἔσωθεν φόβοι. ἀλλ᾽ ὁ παρακαλῶν τοὺς ταπεινοὺς παρεκάλεσεν ἡμᾶς ὁ θεὸς ἐν τῇ παρουσίᾳ Τίτου·

Having expressed his confidence despite adverse circumstances, Paul returns to the account of his travels and the way in which that confidence was borne out when he met Titus in Macedonia. It is only natural that he would resume his account at the point at which he had abandoned it.[27]

There is an instance of inversion in 2:15-16:[28]

	ὅτι Χριστοῦ εὐωδία ἐσμεν τῷ θεῷ
A	ἐν <u>τοῖς σῳζομένοις</u>
B	καὶ ἐν <u>τοῖς ἀπολλυμένοις,</u>
B'	<u>οἷς μὲν</u> ὀσμὴ ἐκ θανάτου εἰς θάνατον,
A'	<u>οἷς δὲ</u> ὀσμὴ ἐκ ζωῆς εἰς ζωήν.

The internal coherence of 3:1-11 is confirmed by the repeated uses of ἐπιστολή (2x), γράμμα (3x), γράφω (2x), πνεῦμα (4x), δόξα (8x), δοξάζω (2x), διάκονος (1x), and διακονία (3x). πνεῦμα (2x) and δόξα (3x) carry over into 3:12-18, where they are joined by κάλυμμα (4x) and ἀνακαλύπτω (2x). Within the latter paragraph is an instance of chiasmus that uses homoeoteleuton in the verbs (3:15-16):

ἀλλ᾽ ἕως σήμερον ἡνίκα ἂν ἀναγινώσκηται
    Μωϋσῆς <u>κάλυμμα</u> ἐπὶ τὴν καρδίαν αὐτῶν <u>κεῖται·</u>
ἡνίκα δὲ ἐὰν ἐπιστρέψῃ πρὸς κύριον,
    περιαιρ<u>εῖται</u> τὸ <u>κάλυμμα.</u>

Two examples of chiasmus occur in chapter 4. The first (4:3) uses two periphrastic participles and pushes them to the outside of the construction for emphasis:

εἰ δὲ καὶ <u>ἔστιν κεκαλυμμένον</u> τὸ εὐαγγέλιον ἡμῶν,
ἐν τοῖς ἀπολλυμένοις <u>ἐστὶν κεκαλυμμένον.</u>

The second (4:14) uses the more common transposition of verb and object:

	ὁ <u>ἐγείρας</u>	τὸν κύριον Ἰησοῦν
καὶ	ἡμᾶς σὺν <u>Ἰησοῦ</u>	<u>ἐγερεῖ</u> . . .

---

[27] Martin (2 *Corinthians* xliii) and Ellis (*Letters* 145) both offer plausible explanations for Paul's sudden change of topic.

[28] Cf. Furnish, *II Corinthians* 177.

Statements that Paul does not lose heart bracket the entire chapter (4:1, 16):[29]

διὰ τοῦτο, ἔχοντες τὴν διακονίαν ταύτην, καθὼς ἠλεήθημεν, οὐκ
ἐγκακοῦμεν . . .

διὸ οὐκ ἐγκακοῦμεν . . .

In 5:1-10 there is an example of alternation that is reminiscent of Paul's discussion of living and dying in Phil 1:18b-26.[30] In 5:1-5 Paul uses the metaphor of being clothed/unclothed (ἐνδύω/ἐκδύω) to continue the contrast between temporal and eternal values begun in 4:16-18. After a combined confidence/disclosure formula in 5:6 (θαρροῦντες οὖν πάντοτε καὶ εἰδότες), he shifts to the idea of being "at home" (ἐνδημέω) in the body and "absent" (ἐκδημέω) from the Lord in 5:6-10:

	θαρροῦντες οὖν πάντοτε καὶ εἰδότες ὅτι
A	ἐνδημοῦντες ἐν τῷ σώματι
B	ἐκδημοῦμεν ἀπὸ τοῦ κυρίου—
	διὰ πίστεως γὰρ περιπατοῦμεν οὐ διὰ εἴδους—

	θαρροῦμεν δὲ καὶ εὐδοκοῦμεν μᾶλλον
B	ἐκδημῆσαι ἐκ τοῦ σώματος
A	καὶ ἐνδημῆσαι πρὸς τὸν κύριον.

	διὸ καὶ φιλοτιμούμεθα,
A	εἴτε ἐνδημοῦντες
B	εἴτε ἐκδημοῦντες,
	εὐάρεστοι αὐτῷ εἶναι.

The words καταλλάσσω (3x) and καταλλαγή (3x) give coherence to 5:16-21, a paragraph in which two instances of chiasmus occur. The first appears designed to contrast the Christian's old life with new life in Christ. This contrast is accentuated by the placement of the adjectives in their respective clauses (5:17):

ὥστε εἴ τις ἐν Χριστῷ, καινὴ κτίσις·
    τὰ ἀρχαῖα   παρῆλθεν,
    ἰδοὺ γέγονεν   καινά

The second chiasmus not only contrasts sin with righteousness, it emphasizes the fact that Christ was made sin in our place by moving the second use of ἁμαρτία forward in its clause (5:21):

---

[29] Cf. Belleville, *Reflections* 142.

[30] See discussion on Philippians below. Within the passage itself it is interesting to note Paul's repetition of θαρροῦμεν (5:6; cf. 5:5) after the parenthetical interruption of διὰ πίστεως γὰρ περιπατοῦμεν οὐ διὰ εἴδους.

τὸν μὴ γνόντα   ἁμαρτίαν
ὑπὲρ ἡμῶν ἁμαρτίαν   ἐποίησεν,
ἵνα ἡμεῖς γενώμεθα   δικαιοσύνη θεοῦ ἐν αὐτῷ.

In addition to these smaller-scale items within 2:14-5:21, a number of other features may be noted: (1) the phrase "commend ourselves" (συνίστημι + ἑαυτοῦς) is repeated in 3:1; 4:2; and 5:12;[31] (2) a recurring pattern using ἔχω appears in 3:4; 3:12; 4:1; 4:7; and 4:13;[32] and (3) phrases using a form of οἶδα occur in 5:1; 5:6; 5:11; and 5:16.[33] All of these features lend unity to the section.

Various explanations have been given for the relation of 6:14-7:1 to its context. Although the literature on this issue is enormous, four basic solutions have been proposed: (1) it is an anti-Pauline fragment that a redactor inserted into the present context;[34] (2) it is a fragment of the "Previous Letter" interpolated into the present context;[35] (3) it is a non-Pauline fragment used by Paul in support of his argument;[36] (4) it is a Pauline digression.[37]

Belleville calls the passage an ethical topos within the "request section" (6:1-7:2) of chapters 1-7.[38] Part of her analysis touches on matters related to oral patterning.[39] She points out that the range of meaning of χωρέω in 7:2 includes the

---

[31] Cf. Talbert, *Corinthians* 133. Thus:
3:1   ἀρχόμεθα πάλιν ἑαυτοὺς συνιστάνειν;
4:2   ἀλλὰ τῇ φανερώσει τῆς ἀληθείας συνιστάνοντες ἑαυτοὺς πρὸς πᾶσαν συνείδησιν ἀνθρώπων ἐνώπιον τοῦ θεοῦ.
5:12   οὐ πάλιν ἑαυτοὺς συνιστάνομεν ὑμῖν . . .

[32] Cf. Belleville, *Reflections* 142. Thus:
3:12   ἔχοντες οὖν τοιαύτην ἐλπίδα πολλῇ παρρησίᾳ χρώμεθα . . .
4:1   διὰ τοῦτο, ἔχοντες τὴν διακονίαν ταύτην . . .
4:7   ἔχομεν δὲ τὸν θησαυρὸν τοῦτον ἐν ὀστρακίνοις σκεύεσιν . . .
4:13   ἔχοντες δὲ τὸ αὐτὸ πνεῦμα τῆς πίστεως . . .

[33] Ibid. 152. Thus:
5:1   οἴδαμεν γὰρ ὅτι ἐὰν ἡ ἐπίγειος ἡμῶν οἰκία τοῦ σκήνους καταλυθῇ
5:6   θαρροῦντες οὖν πάντοτε καὶ εἰδότες ὅτι ἐνδημοῦντες ἐν τῷ σώματι ἐκδημοῦμεν ἀπὸ τοῦ κυρίου . . .
5:11   εἰδότες οὖν τὸν φόβον τοῦ κυρίου ἀνθρώπους πείθομεν . . .
5:16   ὥστε ἡμεῖς ἀπὸ τοῦ νῦν οὐδένα οἴδαμεν κατὰ σάρκα·

[34] Cf. H. D. Betz, "2 Cor 6.14-7.1: An Anti-Pauline Fragment?" *JBL* 92 [1973] 88-108.

[35] Cf. Hurd, *I Corinthians* 235-237.

[36] Cf. Dahl, *Studies in Paul* 62-69; Furnish, *II Corinthians* 371-383; Martin, *2 Corinthians* 190-195.

[37] Cf. Talbert, *Corinthians* 171-177.

[38] Belleville, *Reflections*. See pages 94-103 for a discussion of the integrity issue; see pages 156-160 for the line of argument in the Request Section; see pages 167-169 for a structural outline of chapters 1-7.

[39] Ibid. 98-99.

idea of "give way, withdraw," and so might be a reference to the preceding injunctions to "come out from their midst" (ἐξέλθατε ἐκ μέσου αὐτῶν) and "be separate" (ἀφορίσθητε). She also notes the repeated ideas of 6:11-13 and 7:2-3:

τὸ στόμα ἡμῶν ἀνέῳγεν πρὸς ὑμᾶς, Κορίνθιοι, ἡ καρδία ἡμῶν πεπλάτυνται· οὐ στενοχωρεῖσθε ἐν ἡμῖν, στενοχωρεῖσθε δὲ ἐν τοῖς σπλάγχνοις ὑμῶν· τὴν δὲ αὐτὴν ἀντιμισθίαν, ὡς τέκνοις λέγω, πλατύνθητε καὶ ὑμεῖς.

χωρήσατε ἡμᾶς· οὐδένα ἠδικήσαμεν, οὐδένα ἐφθείραμεν, οὐδένα ἐπλεονεκτήσαμεν. πρὸς κατάκρισιν οὐ λέγω, προείρηκα γὰρ ὅτι ἐν ταῖς καρδίαις ἡμῶν ἐστε εἰς τὸ συναποθανεῖν καὶ συζῆν.

The points of verbal correspondence are not strong, but the repetition of the cognate verbs στενοχωρέω and χωρέω is at least suggestive. The possibility that this is an instance of anaphoric ring-composition cannot be ruled out.

It is interesting, as well, to note the connections between 7:4 and 7:5-6:

πολλή μοι παρρησία πρὸς ὑμᾶς, πολλή μοι καύχησις ὑπὲρ ὑμῶν· πεπλήρωμαι τῇ παρακλήσει, ὑπερπερισσεύομαι τῇ χαρᾷ ἐπὶ πάσῃ τῇ θλίψει ἡμῶν.

καὶ γὰρ ἐλθόντων ἡμῶν εἰς Μακεδονίαν οὐδεμίαν ἔσχηκεν ἄνεσιν ἡ σὰρξ ἡμῶν, ἀλλ᾽ ἐν παντὶ θλιβόμενοι—ἔξωθεν μάχαι, ἔσωθεν φόβοι. ἀλλ᾽ ὁ παρακαλῶν τοὺς ταπεινοὺς παρεκάλεσεν ἡμᾶς ὁ θεὸς ἐν τῇ παρουσίᾳ Τίτου·

Not only does Paul here resume the discussion of 1:15-2:13, he also refers back to the intervening material as a good public speaker was wont to do.[40]

It is, in fact, difficult to identify a clear break in 7:2-16. Although much has been made of the "seam" at 7:5, there are other features that cut across that seam. Belleville, for example, has shown how 7:3-16 could be understood as the body-closing, beginning with πρὸς κατάκρισιν οὐ λέγω (7:3) that "functions as a surrogate for the customary writing/responsibility formula."[41] Both Martin and Furnish comment on the way in which 7:4 "has set the model for what follows."[42] The verbal links between 7:4 and 7:5-6 have been noted above. Furnish suggests that 7:4-16 is framed by expressions of confidence in 7:4 (πολλή μοι παρρησία πρὸς ὑμᾶς, πολλή μοι καύχησις ὑπὲρ ὑμῶν) and 7:16 (χαίρω ὅτι ἐν παντὶ θαρρῶ

---

[40] A similar instance occurs in 1 Cor 14:1. See the discussion above.

[41] Belleville, *Reflections* 119; cf. ibid. 160-163. To this could be added the saying expression in the same verse: προείρηκα γὰρ ὅτι . . .

[42] Martin, *2 Corinthians* 216; cf. Furnish: "7:4; reads almost like the topic sentence of what follows" (*II Corinthians* 392).

ἐν ὑμῖν).[43] Martin suggests that the repeated use of παρεκαλέω in 7:6 and 7:13 constitutes an instance of inclusion.[44]

All of these considerations highlight the fact that Paul's letters cannot always be divided into neat, clearly identifiable sections. Παρακαλέω and παράκλησις occur seven times in these verses; χαίρω and χαρά occur six times; θλῖψις and θλίβω occur twice; and καύχησις and καυχάομαι occur three times. This passage, in fact, seems to be a good example of the way in which Paul sometimes uses "catch-words" to hold a paragraph together.

The clusters of epistolary conventions within chapters 8 and 9 serve to highlight a basic structure of 8:1-15; 8:16-24; 9:1-15, with the entire section being bound together by the words χάρις, ἁπλότης, and περισσεύω.[45] The distribution of these words suggests the presence of an ABA' pattern:[46]

	8:1-15	8:16-24	9:1-15
χάρις	5	2	3
ἁπλότης	1	0	2
περισσεύω	3	0	3

The only readily evident instance of chiasmus in chapters 8-9 occurs in 9:6—being technically an example of epanadiplosis:

ὁ σπείρων <u>φειδομένως</u>   <u>φειδομένως</u> καὶ θερίσει,
καὶ ὁ σπείρων <u>ἐπ' εὐλογίαις</u>   <u>ἐπ' εὐλογίαις</u> καὶ θερίσει.

The double request formula at 10:1-2 marks another transition point. A number of verbal links may be noted that lend unity to all of 10:1-13:10. First, forms of ἄφρων and ἀφροσύνη occur eight times in 11:1-12:11.[47] Second, the phrase

---

[43] Ibid.

[44] Martin, *2 Corinthians* 216.

[45] Χάρις is used ten times in chapters 8-9 as opposed to six times in chapters 1-7 and twice in chapters 10-13. Ἁπλότης is used three times in these chapters but only five times in the rest of Paul. Περισσεύω is used six times as opposed to four other times in the rest of canonical 2 Corinthians.

[46] Cf. Ellis, *Letters* 160. It may be noted that these sections agree with Betz's basic analysis of letter and rhetoric types as well (*2 Corinthians 8 and 9* 139):
8:1-15 Advisory letter; deliberative rhetoric
8:16-24 Administrative letter; juridical rhetoric
9:1-15 Advisory letter; deliberative rhetoric

[47] 11:1, 16 [twice], 17, 19, 21; 12:6, 11. Cf. Talbert, *Corinthians* 115.

ὑστερηκέναι τῶν ὑπερλίαν ἀποστόλων appears in 11:5 and 12:11.[48] Third, the phrase εἰς οἰκοδομὴν καὶ οὐκ εἰς καθαίρεσιν is repeated in 10:8 and 13:10. An inclusion using the verbs ἄπειμι and πάρειμι brackets 10:1-11:

> αὐτὸς δὲ ἐγὼ Παῦλος παρακαλῶ ὑμᾶς διὰ τῆς πραΰτητος καὶ ἐπιεικείας τοῦ Χριστοῦ, ὃς κατὰ πρόσωπον μὲν ταπεινὸς ἐν ὑμῖν, <u>ἀπὼν</u> δὲ θαρρῶ εἰς ὑμᾶς· δέομαι δὲ τὸ μὴ <u>παρὼν</u> θαρρῆσαι . . .

> τοῦτο λογιζέσθω ὁ τοιοῦτος, ὅτι οἷοί ἐσμεν τῷ λόγῳ δι' ἐπιστολῶν <u>ἀπόντες</u>, τοιοῦτοι καὶ <u>παρόντες</u> τῷ ἔργῳ.

The subsequent paragraph is framed by the phrase "commend ourselves" (συνίστημι + ἑαυτούς) in 10:12 and 10:18:

> οὐ γὰρ τολμῶμεν ἐγκρῖναι ἢ συγκρῖναι ἑαυτούς τισιν τῶν <u>ἑαυτοὺς συνιστανόντων</u> . . .

> οὐ γὰρ ὁ <u>ἑαυτὸν συνιστάνων</u>, ἐκεῖνός ἐστιν δόκιμος, ἀλλὰ ὃν ὁ κύριος συνίστησιν.

An interesting chain of link-words occurs in 10:1-6:

> αὐτὸς δὲ ἐγὼ Παῦλος παρακαλῶ ὑμᾶς . . . ὃς κατὰ πρόσωπον μὲν ταπεινὸς ἐν ὑμῖν, <u>ἀπὼν</u> δὲ <u>θαρρῶ</u> εἰς ὑμᾶς· δέομαι δὲ τὸ μὴ <u>παρὼν</u> <u>θαρρῆσαι</u> τῇ πεποιθήσει ᾗ <u>λογίζομαι</u> τολμῆσαι ἐπί τινας τοὺς <u>λογιζομένους</u> ἡμᾶς ὡς κατὰ σάρκα <u>περιπατοῦντας</u>. ἐν σαρκὶ γὰρ <u>περιπατοῦντες</u> οὐ κατὰ σάρκα <u>στρατευόμεθα</u>, τὰ γὰρ ὅπλα τῆς <u>στρατείας</u> ἡμῶν οὐ σαρκικὰ ἀλλὰ δυνατὰ τῷ θεῷ πρὸς <u>καθαίρεσιν</u> ὀχυρωμάτων, λογισμοὺς <u>καθαιροῦντες</u> καὶ πᾶν ὕψωμα <u>ἐπαιρόμενον</u> κατὰ τῆς γνώσεως οῦ θεοῦ, καὶ αἰχμαλωτίζοντες πᾶν νόημα εἰς τὴν <u>ὑπακοὴν</u> τοῦ Χριστοῦ, καὶ ἐν ἑτοίμῳ ἔχοντες ἐκδικῆσαι πᾶσαν <u>παρακοήν</u>, ὅταν πληρωθῇ ὑμῶν ἡ <u>ὑπακοή</u>.

In this paragraph, Paul moves the argument forward by repeating a form of the key word found in the immediately preceding thought.[49] The listener is drawn ever forward by the combination of anticipation and echo.

The contrasting statement of 10:11 is chiastically worded:[50]

οἷοί ἐσμεν	τῷ λόγῳ δι' ἐπιστολῶν	ἀπόντες,
τοιοῦτοι καὶ	παρόντες	τῷ ἔργῳ.

The condemnation in 10:12 of the approach used by Paul's opponents is carefully worded as well, with the fourfold use of ἑαυτοὺς heightening the impact:

---

[48] Cf. ibid.

[49] θαρρέω . . . λογίζομαι . . . περιπατέω . . . στρατεύομαι . . . καθαιρέω . . . ὑπακοή

[50] Cf. Martin, *2 Corinthians* 301.

ἀλλὰ αὐτοὶ   ἐν <u>ἑαυτοῖς</u>   <u>ἑαυτοὺς</u>   μετροῦντες
καὶ   συγκρίνοντες   <u>ἑαυτοὺς</u>   <u>ἑαυτοῖς</u>   οὐ συνιᾶσιν.

The carefully worded statement in 12:7 is an example of inversion:[51]

A   διό, <u>ἵνα μὴ ὑπεραίρωμαι</u>,
B   ἐδόθη <u>μοι</u>
C   σκόλοψ τῇ σαρκί,
C'   ἄγγελος Σατανᾶ,
B'   ἵνα <u>με</u> κολαφίζῃ,
A'   <u>ἵνα μὴ ὑπεραίρωμαι</u>.

A construction similar to that of 10:12 occurs in 12:9, although it is uncertain how apparent the pattern would have been to the ear:[52]

ἀρκεῖ   σοι   ἡ χάρις μου·
ἡ γὰρ δύναμις   ἐν ἀσθενείᾳ   τελεῖται.

Within 12:14-13:10 the repetition of τρίτον τοῦτο ἔρχομαι πρὸς ὑμᾶς at 12:14 and 13:1 may be seen either as inclusion or as parallel beginnings of separate paragraphs. It is probably the latter, although 13:1-10 is set off by an inclusion using ἄπειμι and πάρειμι:

προείρηκα καὶ προλέγω ὡς <u>παρὼν</u> τὸ δεύτερον καὶ <u>ἀπὼν</u> νῦν . . .

διὰ τοῦτο ταῦτα <u>ἀπὼν</u> γράφω, ἵνα <u>παρὼν</u> μὴ ἀποτόμως χρήσωμαι . . .

Two final instances of chiasmus occur in 12:20 and 13:3. In the latter verse, as is frequently the case, chiasmus sharpens a contrast:[53]

φοβοῦμαι γὰρ μή πως ἐλθὼν
    <u>οὐχ οἵους θέλω</u>   <u>εὕρω ὑμᾶς</u>,
    κἀγὼ <u>εὑρεθῶ ὑμῖν</u>   <u>οἷον οὐ θέλετε</u>

ἐπεὶ δοκιμὴν ζητεῖτε τοῦ ἐν ἐμοὶ λαλοῦντος Χριστοῦ·
    ὃς <u>εἰς ὑμᾶς</u>   οὐκ ἀσθενεῖ
    ἀλλὰ δυνατεῖ   <u>ἐν ὑμῖν</u>.

C. Other Suggested Structures

Brunot and Ellis argue for the unity of 2 Corinthians based on an overall ABA' pattern in which chapters 1-7 constitute A, chapters 8-9 constitute B, and chapters

---

[51] Cf. Zmijewski, *Narrenrede* 366; Martin, *2 Corinthians* 393.

[52] Cf. Martin *2 Corinthians* 393.

[53] Ibid. 453, 456; see also Furnish, *II Corinthians* 570.

10-13 constitute A'.[54] Such an approach correctly identifies the three major sections of the letter but is rather over generalized. Although chapters 1-7 and chapters 10-13 both deal with Paul's apostolic ministry, neither Brunot nor Ellis offers evidence that moves beyond the level of general content or that treats specific points of correspondence between these two sections of the letter.

Craig Blomberg and Philippe Rolland have proposed that 1:12-7:16 should be understood as an "extended chiasmus." Blomberg's arrangement has five elements on either side of the center panel:[55]

A	The Corinthians can rightfully boast in Paul	1:12-22
B	Grief and comfort over the painful letter	1:23-2:11
C	Looking for Titus in Macedonia	2:12-13
D	A series of contrasts	2:14-4:6
E	Surviving and triumphing despite every hardship	4:7-5:10
F	The ministry of reconciliation	5:11-21
E'	Surviving and triumphing despite every hardship	6:1-10
D'	A series of contrasts	6:11-7:4
C'	Finding Titus in Macedonia	7:5-7
B'	Grief and comfort over the painful letter	7:8-13a
A'	Paul can rightfully boast in the Corinthians	7:13b-16

Rolland's arrangement is somewhat simpler:[56]

A	Explanations by Paul of his change of itinerary	1:12-2:13
B	The ministry of the new covenant	2:14-3:18
C	The hope of overcoming tribulations	4:1-5:10
B'	The ministry of reconciliation	5:11-6:10
A'	Benefits resulting from the change of itinerary	6:11-7:16

Ellis, however, suggests that an ABA' pattern is the more appropriate understanding of these chapters:[57]

A	Consolation and reconciliation	1:1-2:13
B	The ministry of the new covenant	2:14-7:3
A'	Conciliation and reconciliation	7:4-16

---

[54] The two arrangements differ only in their headings. Brunot (*S. Paul* 44):

A	1:1-7:16	Paul's apology for the apostolic ministry
B	8:1-9:15	The collection
A'	10:1-13:10	Paul's apology

Ellis (*Letters* 139-140):

A	1:1-7:16	Signs of a true apostle
B	8:1-9:15	The collection
A'	10:1-13:10	The signs of a true apostle

[55] Blomberg, "2 Corinthians" 8-9.

[56] Rolland, "Deuxième Epître" 77-78.

[57] Ellis, *Letters* 140.

Belleville also proposes an ABA' pattern:[58]

A	Defensive apology vis-á-vis the Corinthians	1:12-2:11
B	Offensive polemic aimed at an outside opponent	2:12-5:21
A'	Defensive apology vis-á-vis the Corinthians	6:1-7:2

With respect to major rhetorical shifts, all four arrangements agree that a break occurs somewhere in 2:12-14. Blomberg, Ellis, and Belleville also see such a break somewhere in 7:3-5. When identifying *minor* turning points, all four agree as well on breaks at 4:1 and 5:11; three agree on breaks at 1:23,[59] 3:4,[60] 6:1,[61] and 6:11.[62] Ellis' scheme is the simplest, with its center panel being the often-discussed "interpolation" of 2:14-7:4. Rolland and Belleville, however, both offer schemes that bridge the supposed break at 7:5. Blomberg's treatment is the most comprehensive and most plausible, in that he measures his scheme against the criteria he proposes for detecting "extended chiasmus,"[63] and so it is his presentation that will here be evaluated.

The similarities between 2:12-13 and 7:5-7 are, of course, well known. As well, Blomberg notes these additional verbal parallels:[64]

1:12-22	καύχησις, καύχημα, καυχάομαι	7:13b-16
1:23-2:11	λύπη, λυπέω	7:8-13a
2:14-4:6	καρδία, παρρησία, θεοῦ ζῶντος, φῶς, σκότος	6:11-7:4
4:7-5:10	θλίβω, θλῖψις, στενοχωρέομαι, στενοχωρία	6:1-10

With regard to the dominant terminology of these passsages, Blomberg comments: "Only superficial familiarity with this epistle is required to recognize that the terminology identified as parallel in each case epitomizes central concerns of Paul rather than peripheral issues."[65] Regarding the frequency of the terms involved, he continues:

---

[58] Belleville works within what she has defined as the body-middle (1:12-7:3) of a letter of apologetic commendation in chapters 1-7 (*Reflections* 165). It is somewhat confusing to find that she breaks the pattern of argumentation at 2:12 when she elsewhere proposes three major divisions in the "Background Period" of 1:12-5:21: 1:12-3:3; 3:4-4:18; 5:1-21 (ibid. 136-156). See the discussion below.

[59] Blomberg, Rolland, and Belleville.

[60] Blomberg, Ellis, and Belleville.

[61] Blomberg, Ellis, and Belleville.

[62] Blomberg, Rolland, and Belleville.

[63] In Chapter 5, Blomberg's nine criteria were reduced to three.

[64] Blomberg, "2 Corinthians" 11-12.

[65] Ibid. 12.

> Not all of these terms and phrases are entirely unparalleled in 2 Cor 1:12-7:16, but
> overall their frequency in the sections paired as opposites is significant. Paul's only
> other boasting [outside of chapters 10-13] comes in 5:12 and 7:4 . . . The grief
> which dominates 1:23-2:11 and 7:8-13 never recurs elsewhere in chaps. 1-7, and
> only once in the rest of the entire epistle (9:7) . . . the specific expressions for
> "boldness" and "the living God" are unique. "Darkness" occurs nowhere else in
> 2 Corinthians; "light," only in 11:14. "Tribulations" and "distresses," . . . occur
> elsewhere separately, but never together[66]

Finally, he addresses the significance of 5:11-21: "The center of the chiasmus certainly creates a fitting climax. Paul has already proclaimed to the Corinthians 'Jesus Christ and him crucified' as the heart of his gospel (1 Cor 2:2). No more appropriate center for 2 Cor 1-7 could be found."

Blomberg has certainly made a strong case in support of his analysis. Admittedly, the weakest parallel is that proposed between 2:14-4:6 and 6:11-7:4.[67] Nevertheless, even those sections—both rather loosely entitled "A series of contrasts"—have points of verbal correspondence.

A further consideration is the relation of this particular arrangement to the epistolary conventions and readily-apparent oral patterns discussed above. Although a number of epistolary conventions are scattered throughout 1:12-7:16—writing (1:13), confidence (1:15), confidence (3:4), knowing (5:1), confidence (5:6), knowing (5:6, 11), request (6:1), vocative (6:11), saying (7:3)—the only major cluster of formulae occurs in the vicinity of the acknowledged break at 2:14 (2:3-14). As well, the ring-composition proposed for 6:11 and 7:2 in the earlier analysis lends indirect support to Blomberg's suggestion that 6:11-7:4 is a unit. Furthermore, the internal coherence created by word-chains in 3:1-11 and 3:12-18 poses no problem, and the word-chains and alternation present in 5:1-10 support Blomberg's suggested break at 5:10, although there are a number of elements that lend unity to all of 2:14-5:21.[68]

Perhaps the greatest challenge to Blomberg's structure is posed by the numerous catch-words in 7:2-16. As noted above, definitive breaks in Paul's argument are often difficult to establish.[69] Blomberg's paragraph divisions must, therefore, be held lightly. Nevertheless, there is insufficient evidence from the investigation of epistolary analysis and readily apparent oral patterns to overturn

---

[66] Ibid.

[67] Blomberg himself acknowledges, "The least obvious pair matches 2:14-4:6 with 6:11-7:4" (ibid. 11).

[68] See the discussion above.

[69] Blomberg concurs: "Much of the disagreement stems from the fact that Paul's logic contains regular transitional paragraphs which can easily be taken as either concluding a previous thought or beginning a new thought, unless an overarching structure makes it clear what must fit where" (ibid. 14).

Blomberg's overall arrangement. Although it seems doubtful that all of the details of his arrangement would have been readily apparent to the original listeners, it may well represent the concentric nature of Paul's argument.

Within chapters 1-7 a variety of structures have been suggested. Martin and Lund both find "chiastic" patterns in 1:3-11. Martin's proposal for 1:5 must rearrange the Greek wording in order to work:[70]

Martin's scheme	Greek text
overflow (περισσεύει)	καθὼς περισσεύει
Christ's sufferings	τὰ παθήματα τοῦ Χριστοῦ εἰς ἡμᾶς
encouragement through Christ	οὕτως διὰ τοῦ Χριστοῦ
overflows (περισσεύει)	περισσεύει καὶ ἡ παράκλησις ἡμῶν.

The same is true of his proposal for 1:11:[71]

Martin's scheme	Greek text
ἐκ πολλῶν προσώπων	ἵνα ἐκ πολλῶν προσώπων
χάρισμα	τὸ εἰς ἡμᾶς χάρισμα
εὐχαριστηθῇ	διὰ πολλῶν
διὰ πολλῶν	εὐχαριστηθῇ ὑπὲρ ἡμῶν.

Lund's arrangement for 1:3-5 retains the order of the Greek text, but handles it awkwardly:[72]

	εὐλογητὸς ὁ θεὸς
	καὶ πατὴρ
A	τοῦ κυρίου ἡμῶν Ἰησοῦ Χριστοῦ,
	ὁ πατὴρ τῶν οἰκτιρμῶν
	καὶ θεὸς
	πάσης παρακλήσεως, ὁ παρακαλῶν ἡμᾶς
	ἐπὶ πάσῃ τῇ θλίψει ἡμῶν,
B	εἰς τὸ δύνασθαι ἡμᾶς παρακαλεῖν τοὺς
	ἐν πάσῃ θλίψει
	διὰ τῆς παρακλήσεως ἧς παρακαλούμεθα αὐτοὶ ὑπὸ τοῦ θεοῦ·
	ὅτι καθὼς περισσεύει τὰ παθήματα
	τοῦ Χριστοῦ
A'	εἰς ἡμᾶς,
	οὕτως διὰ τοῦ Χριστοῦ
	περισσεύει καὶ ἡ παράκλησις ἡμῶν.

---

[70] Martin, *2 Corinthians* 8.

[71] Ibid. 14.

[72] Lund, *Chiasmus* 150.

Particularly awkward are his decisions to take the last two words of verse 3 (πάσης παρακλήσεως) with verse 4 and to separate τοὺς from ἐν πάσῃ θλίψει in verse 4. Furthermore, verse 5 seems more naturally understood in parallel than in chiastic form. Lund's arrangement, however, seems somewhat forced. The combination of inversion and alternation suggested in the earlier analysis of 1:3-7 seems more natural than Lund's scheme.

Talbert proposes an ABA' structure for 1:12-2:13:[73]

A	Paul's afflictions in Asia	1:8-11
B	Paul's justification for his changed travel plans	1:12-2:2
A'	Paul's afflictions in Macedonia and Troas	2:3-13

Talbert does well in working with an identifiable section of the letter, bounded by the disclosure formula of 1:8 and the statement of thanks in 2:14. As noted in the epistolary analysis earlier, 1:8-11 forms the body-opening. The writing statement and confidence formula in 2:3 make that verse a likely transition point.[74]

The strongest oral feature in 1:12-2:13, however, is the repetition of λυπή (3x) and λυπέω (5x) that occurs in 2:1-7, and bridges Talbert's suggested break between 2:2 and 2:3. Furthermore, there are no points of verbal correspondence between 1:8-11 and 2:3-13 that might suggest the presence of an ABA' pattern. Given these weaknesses, it seems less than certain that the structure Talbert proposes would have been readily apparent to the original listeners.

Belleville proposes 1:12-3:3 as a distinct unit, framed by inclusion.[75] There is some merit to this suggestion because of the repetition of (ἐγ)γράφω, ἀναγινώσκω, and (ἐπι)γινώσκω in 1:13 and 3:2:[76]

οὐ γράφομεν ὑμῖν ἀλλ' ἢ ἃ ἀναγινώσκετε ἢ καὶ ἐπιγινώσκετε . . .

ἡ ἐπιστολὴ ἡμῶν ὑμεῖς ἐστε, ἐγγεγραμμένη ἐν ταῖς καρδίαις ἡμῶν, γινωσκομένη καὶ ἀναγινωσκομένη ὑπὸ πάντων ἀνθρώπων·

The confidence statement at 3:4 also makes that verse a transition point. Yet if this is indeed an instance of inclusion, the section delimited bridges the supposed break at 2:14.[77]

---

[73] Talbert, *Corinthians* 134.

[74] Belleville, however, argues for the attestation statement of 1:23 (ἐγὼ δὲ μάρτυρα τὸν θεὸν ἐπικαλοῦμαι ἐπὶ τὴν ἐμὴν ψυχήν) as a conventional transitional construction (*Reflections* 137).

[75] Belleville, *Reflections* 136.

[76] The verb ἀναγινώσκω is particularly important in this regard, since it occurs only three times in the entire canonical letter (1:13; 3:2, 15).

[77] As well as arguing against her proposed ABA' pattern discussed above.

Curiously, Belleville also proposes an inverted structure for 2:14-4:15, which would seem to nullify the "distinct unit" of 1:12-3:3. "Five themes," she argues, "are introduced in 2:14-17 that Paul treats in reverse order in 3:1-4:15":[78]

A	τῷ δὲ θεῷ χάρις τῷ πάντοτε θριαμβεύοντι ἡμᾶς ἐν τῷ Χριστῷ καὶ τὴν <u>ὀσμὴν τῆς γνώσεως αὐτοῦ</u> φανεροῦντι δι᾿ ἡμῶν ἐν παντὶ τόπῳ·	2:14
B	ὅτι Χριστοῦ εὐωδία ἐσμεν τῷ θεῷ ἐν τοῖς σῳζομένοις καὶ ἐν τοῖς ἀπολλυμένοις, οἷς μὲν ὀσμὴ ἐκ <u>θανάτου</u> εἰς <u>θάνατον</u>, οἷς δὲ ὀσμὴ ἐκ ζωῆς εἰς ζωήν.	2:15-16a
C	<u>καὶ πρὸς ταῦτα τίς ἱκανός;</u>	2:16b
D	οὐ γάρ ἐσμεν ὡς οἱ πολλοὶ καπηλεύοντες τὸν λόγον τοῦ θεοῦ,	2:17a
E	ἀλλ᾿ ὡς ἐξ εἰλικρινείας, ἀλλ᾿ ὡς ἐκ θεοῦ κατέναντι θεοῦ ἐν Χριστῷ λαλοῦμεν.	2:17b
E'	ἀρχόμεθα πάλιν ἑαυτοὺς συνιστάνειν;	3:1a
D'	ἢ μὴ χρῄζομεν ὥς τινες συστατικῶν ἐπιστολῶν πρὸς ὑμᾶς ἢ ἐξ ὑμῶν; . . .	3:1b-3
C'	<u>οὐχ ὅτι ἀφ᾿ ἑαυτῶν ἱκανοί ἐσμεν</u> . . .	3:4-6
B'	εἰ δὲ ἡ διακονία τοῦ <u>θανάτου</u> . . . ἡ διακονία τοῦ πνεύματος . . .	3:7-18
A'	τὸν φωτισμὸν τοῦ εὐαγγελίου τῆς δόξης τοῦ Χριστοῦ . . . <u>φωτισμὸν τῆς γνώσεως τῆς δόξης τοῦ θεοῦ</u> ἐν προσώπῳ Ἰησοῦ Χριστοῦ.	4:1-15

The strongest verbal parallels in this scheme occur in 2:14 and 4:6 and in 2:16b and 3:5. The first set of parallels appears in the use of γνῶσις, a noun that is found only six times in 2 Corinthians. Given the similarities of phraseology, its usage suggests either inclusion or ring-composition. The second set uses ἱκανός, a word that appears only three times in 2 Corinthians. This latter parallel is strengthened by the presence of the cognate words ἱκανότης in 3:5 and ἱκανόω in 3:6. Another parallel is suggested by the use of θάνατος in 2:16 (2x) and 3:7. The context, however, is not truly parallel,[79] and the double use of θάνατος in 4:11-12 weakens the connection between 2:16 and 3:7. Furthermore, 3:7 seems closely tied

---

[78] Ibid. 144-145. She describes it as "a broad chiasm of thought."

[79] 2:16 speaks of Christians as being the "aroma of death to death" to those who are perishing; 3:7 speaks of the "ministry of death" resulting from the Mosaic law.

to 3:3 with its contrast between tablets of stone and tablets of flesh and to 3:6 with its statement that the law, which is engraved in letters on stones, kills.[80]

The parallels that Belleville suggests between 2:17 and 3:1-3 are not obvious *as parallels.* Although the discussion of letters of recommendation in 3:1-3 flows naturally out of Paul's desire that the Corinthians understand his sincerity in 2:17, it is not necessary to view the former verses as inverting two separate aspects of 2:17. There are no points of verbal correspondence to suggest an inverted structure, and it appears that here Belleville has over-analyzed the text. It may be conceded with regard to her overall arrangement that 2:14-4:15 is bracketed by inclusion or ring-composition, and that a degree of internal coherence exists within the section. That these verses form an inverted structure on the order of those seen elsewhere in Paul, however, is open to question.

Martin suggests that 2:14-17 forms inclusive ring-composition with 4:1-6:[81]

2:14	τῆς γνώσεως αὐτοῦ	4:6	τῆς γνώσεως τῆς δόξης τοῦ θεοῦ
2:15	ἐν τοῖς ἀπολλυμένοις	4:3	ἐν τοῖς ἀπολλυμένοις
2:17	ἐξ εἰλικρινείας	4:2	τῇ φανερώσει τῆς ἀληθείας
2:17	κατέναντι θεοῦ	4:2	ἐνώπιον τοῦ θεοῦ

Of the four parallels that Martin suggests, the first two are the strongest; the latter two seem less readily-apparent to the ear. His analysis reinforces Belleville's suggestion that 2:14-4:18 forms a unit.

Within the ring-composition of 2:14-17 and 4:1-6, Martin argues that 2:17-3:18 is constructed in "chiastic" form:[82]

A	Negative assessment of opponents	2:17
B	Positive assessment of Paul's ministry	3:1-6
B'	Positive defense of new covenant	3:7-11
A'	Negative contrast between old and new covenant	3:12-18

Much that has been said already about Belleville's arrangement of 2:14-4:18 applies to this scheme as well. In addition, it may be noted (1) that verbal parallels are entirely lacking; (2) that 2:17 is more an affirmation of Paul's ministry than a negative assessment of his opponents; (3) that the break at 3:7 runs counter to the ἔχω echo that marks the beginning of paragraphs in 3:4-4:18; and (4) that the "negative contrast" between the old and new covenants is not limited to 3:12-18.[83]

---

[80] Grounds for viewing 3:4-11 as a unit are provided by the use of the verb ἔχω in 3:4 and 3:12, apparently to mark the beginning of paragraphs.

[81] Martin, *2 Corinthians* 75.

[82] Ibid. 46.

[83] E.g., 3:6.

Blomberg has identified a "careful chiastic pattern" for 2:14-4:6:[84]

A	Death vs. life	2:14-16a
B	False vs. true approaches to ministry	2:16b-3:3
C	Old covenant vs. new covenant	3:4-18
B'	False vs. true approaches to ministry	4:1-2
A'	Darkness vs. light	4:3-6

This arrangement—which could be more accurately categorized as concentric symmetry—has more to commend it than Martin's. First, there is a repetition of phrases using γνῶσις in 2:14 and 4:6. Second, ἐν τοῖς ἀπολλυμένοις appears in both 2:15 and 4:3. Third, ἑαυτοὺς συνιστάνειν in 3:1 is echoed by συνιστάνοντες ἑαυτοὺς in 4:2. Fourth, the scheme acknowledges the transition at 3:4. And fifth, the scheme does not attempt to make an artificial division within the unified discussion about the old and new covenants (3:4-18).

If 2:14-16a were combined with 2:16b-3:3 and 4:1-2 combined with 4:3-6, the result would be an ABA' pattern. Some might prefer such a simplified analysis. Blomberg's concentric arrangement, however, appears to have merit. One lingering issue, which will not be addressed in this study, is the impact that the inclusion framing 4:1-18 (οὐκ ἐγκακοῦμεν) has on Blomberg's understanding of the overall structure of these chapters.

Martin notes two instances of chiasmus in 6:6-8. The first is in 6:6b-7a:[85]

A	ἐν πνεύματι ἁγίῳ,
B	ἐν ἀγάπῃ ἀνυποκρίτῳ,
B'	ἐν λόγῳ ἀληθείας,
A'	ἐν δυνάμει θεοῦ

Such an understanding is possible based on the inversion: divine-human-human-divine. It seems more likely, however, that the repetition of ἐν plus the dative throughout 6:4-7 would have attracted greater attention than the specific transposition that Martin identifies.

Martin's second example is in 6:8a:

διὰ δόξης (+)   καὶ ἀτιμίας (-)
διὰ δυσφημίας (-)   καὶ εὐφημίας (+)

This arrangement correctly reflects the transposition of positive and negative qualities. It is not, however, an example of chiasmus as that term has been defined in this study. Yet in terms of oral features, it may well have appealed to the ear because it uses similar sounding words.

---

[84] Blomberg, "2 Corinthians" 13.

[85] Martin, 2 Corinthians 162.

Blomberg and Ellis propose nearly identical ABA' patterns for 6:11-7:4:[86]

A	Widen your hearts	6:11-13
B	Separate yourselves from uncleanness	6:14-7:1
A'	Open your hearts	7:2-4

This approach is similar to that of Philip Hughes, who contends that Paul cushions the sharp warning of 6:14-7:1 with loving passages on either side of it.[87] The verbal parallels between 6:11-13 and 7:4-6 have been noted above. Whether 6:11-7:4 is to be seen as an instance of ring-composition or an example of the ABA' pattern, the framing effect of 6:11-13 and 7:2-4 is obvious.[88]

Rolland views chapters 8 and 9 as a case of inversion:[89]

A	Spiritual riches put to the proof in Macedonia	8:1-6
B	Spontaneity of the gift; generosity of Christ	8:7-15
C	Sending of Titus and the brothers	8:16-24
C'	Meaning of the mission of the brothers	9:1-5
B'	Invitation to generosity without constraint	9:6-9
A'	Spiritual riches expected at Corinth	9:10-15

In support of such an arrangement he notes the following verbal parallels:[90]

8:1	τὴν χάριν τοῦ θεοῦ	9:14	χάριν τοῦ θεοῦ
8:2	δοκιμῇ	9:13	δοκιμῆς
8:2	πλοῦτος . . . ἁπλότητος	9:11	πλουτιζόμενοι . . . ἁπλότητα
8:4	δεόμενοι	9:14	δεήσει
8:4	κοινωνίαν	9:13	κοινωνίας
8:7	περισσεύετε	9:8	περισσεύητε
8:9	χάριν	9:8	χάριν
8:15	καθὼς γέγραπται	9:9	καθὼς γέγραπται

---

[86] Blomberg, "2 Corinthians" 13; Ellis, *Letters* 158.

[87] P. E. Hughes, *Paul's Second Epistle to the Corinthians* (Grand Rapids: Eerdmans, 1962) 244. Cf. M. E. Thrall, "The Problem of II Cor. VI.14-VII.1 in Some Recent Discussion," *NTS* 24 (1977) 146.

[88] It may be argued, of course, that the framing effect is caused by the fact that 6:13 originally followed 7:2 and was dislocated by a redactor. The wording, however, suggests a resumption rather than a continuation. Belleville's comment is helpful in this regard: "It is important to observe in Paul's letters that where material prior to a resumption is not merely digressive but connects with the main line of thought, there is usually an addition or modification that refers back to the intervening material. Such a resumption is found in 7.2. For Paul chooses a verb that picks up the call in vv. 17-18 to 'come out (ἐξέλθατε) from their midst' and to 'separate themselves' (ἀφορίσθητε). Moreover, the qualification πρὸς κατάκρισιν οὐ λέγω in 7.3a refers more naturally back to the ethical injunctions in 6.14, 17-18 and 7.1 than to the call for reciprocal affection in vv. 11-13 and 7.2" (*Reflections* 99).

[89] Rolland, "Deuxième Epître" 84.

[90] Ibid. 76.

8:18	συνεπέμψαμεν	9:3	ἔπεμψα
8:23	ἀδελφοὶ ἡμῶν	9:3	τοὺς ἀδελφούς
8:24	ἡμῶν καυχήσεως	9:2	καυχῶμαι

Of the items that Rolland notes, the least helpful is χάρις for it is one of the key words in chapters 8-9, occurring a total of ten times. This frequency of use is a help in highlighting the coherence of these chapters, but it is a hindrance in seeking to establish specific parallels within the chapters. The same may be said of περισσεύω and its cognates. As well, the parallel that Rolland identifies between 8:7 and 9:8 is accurate, but περισσεύω also occurs in 8:1 and 9:12. In addition, περισσεία occurs in 8:2, περίσσευμα in 8:14 (2x), and περισσός in 9:1.

This distribution—with the word group being entirely absent from 8:16-24—suggests the presence of an ABA' structure. The distribution of ἀπλότης (8:2; 9:11, 13), κοινωνία (8:4; 9:13), δέομαι // δέησις (8:4; 9:14), and πλοῦτος // πλουτίζω // πλουτέω // πλούσιος (8:2, 9 [2x], 9:11) also supports an ABA' pattern with 8:16-24 as the center panel. On the other hand, five of the six uses of ἀδελφός are concentrated in 8:16-9:5; the only uses of (συμ)πέμπω are in 8:18, 22; 9:3; and the only four uses of καυχάομαι and its cognates are in 8:16-9:5. The distribution of these latter words lends support to Rolland's analysis that 8:16-24 and 9:1-5 are related.

It is possible to view the asyndetic saying statement of 8:8 (οὐ κατ᾽ ἐπιταγὴν λέγω) as a transition point, but it is much more difficult to identify a break in 9:6-15.[91] The relatively seamless argument of 9:6-15 suggests that Rolland has somewhat over-analyzed the passage. The evidence for an ABA' or an ABBA pattern is a bit stronger than for the more detailed inversion he suggests.[92]

Talbert sees 8:16-23 as being arranged concentrically:[93]

A	Titus	8:16-17
B	The first brother	8:18-19
C	Paul's aim	8:20-21
B'	The second brother	8:22
A'	Titus	8:23

Talbert's analysis seems well-founded, given the repetition of Titus' name in 8:16 and 8:23 and the similarity in wording of 8:18 and 8:22:

συνεπέμψαμεν δὲ μετ᾽ αὐτοῦ τὸν ἀδελφὸν οὗ ὁ ἔπαινος ἐν τῷ εὐαγγελίῳ
διὰ πασῶν τῶν ἐκκλησιῶν . . .

---

[91] Note the distribution of σπείρω // σπόρος (9:6 [2x], 10 [3x]) and of περισσεύω (9:8 [2x], 12).

[92] ABA':   A = 8:1-15; B = 8:16-24; A' = 9:1-15
    ABB'A':   A = 8:1-15; B = 8:16-24; B' = 9:1-5; A' = 9:6-15

[93] Talbert, *Corinthians* 185.

συνεπέμψαμεν δὲ αὐτοῖς τὸν ἀδελφὸν ἡμῶν ὃν ἐδοκιμάσαμεν ἐν πολλοῖς
πολλάκις σπουδαῖον ὄντα . . .

Rolland views chapters 10-13 as an instance of concentric symmetry:[94]

A	Paul claims his authority although absent	10:1-11
B	Polemic against the false apostles	10:12-11:15
C	Paul praises himself in an foolish manner	11:16-12:10
B'	Paul, authentic apostle of the Corinthians	12:11-21
A'	Paul does not wish to use his authority when present	13:1-10

In support of his arrangement, he notes the following verbal parallels:[95]

10:1-2	ἀπὼν, παρὼν	13:2	παρὼν, ἀπὼν
10:11	ἀπόντες, παρόντες	13:10	ἀπὼν, παρὼν
10:12	συνιστανόντων	12:11	συνίστασθαι
11:3	φοβοῦμαι	12:20	φοβοῦμαι
11:3	πανουργίᾳ	12:16	πανοῦργος
11:5	μηδὲν ὑστερηκέναι τῶν ὑπερλίαν ἀποστόλων	12:11	οὐδὲν . . . ὑστέρησα τῶν ὑπερλίαν ἀποστόλων
11:9	κατενάρκησα	12:13	κατενάρκησα
11:11	ἀγαπῶ ὑμᾶς	12:15	ὑμᾶς ἀγαπῶν
11:13	δόλιοι	12:16	δόλῳ

These verbal parallels are significant, for none of the words—except συνίστημι (4:2; 6:4; 7:11) and ἀγαπάω (9:7)—occurs outside of chapters 10-12 in 2 Corinthians. Two additional items may be added: (1) that forms of ἄφρων and ἀφροσύνη occur eight times in chapters 11-12, and (2) that the sixteen occurrences of the verb καυχάομαι are evenly distributed across chapters 10-12.

The inclusions framing 10:1-11 and 13:1-10 have been noted previously. The delimitation of the other sections, however, is less apparent. Rolland suggests that the second section (10:12-11:15) is delimited by the denunciation of the false apostles in 10:12 and 11:13, and that the fourth section (12:11-21) is unified by references to Paul's coming visit (12:14, 20). The central section (11:16-12:10) is what is more or less left over, although Rolland notes that 11:30-12:10 is framed by the idea of boasting in weakness in 11:30 (εἰ καυχᾶσθαι δεῖ, τὰ τῆς ἀσθενείας μου καυχήσομαι) and 12:10 (καυχήσομαι ἐν ταῖς ἀσθενείαις μου).[96]

Clearly, 10:12-18, as noted earlier, is framed by the phrase "commend ourselves."[97] The reappearance of συνίστημι in 12:11 suggests the presence of an

---

[94] Rolland, "Deuxième Epître" 84.

[95] Ibid. 74-75.

[96] Ibid.

[97] Although Ellis (*Letters* 163) and M.-A. Chevallier ("L'argumentation de Paul dans 2 Corinthiens 10 à 13," *RHPR* 70 [1990] 11) connect 10:12-18 with 10:11, the fourfold repetition of καυχάομαι in 10:13-17 suggests that 10:12-18 should be taken with what follows.

inclusion that frames all of 10:12-12:13. For surely 12:14 (not 12:11) begins the discussion of Paul's impending visit. Within 10:12-12:13, verse 11:16 (verb of saying + ἄφρων [2x]) seems to be the other most likely transition point. Although it is possible to suggest additional breaks, there is little formal evidence on which to build.

On the one hand, given the points of verbal correspondence that he identifies, there is nothing inherently impossible about the concentric arrangement that Rolland suggests. On the other hand, however, given the uniform distribution of ἄφρων, ἀφροσύνη, and καυχάομαι across chapters 11 and 12, it is probably best to opt for a simpler arrangement:[98]

10:1-11	Appeal for proper perspective	
10:12-12:13	Foolish boasting	
	10:12-18	The problem with self-commendation
	11:1-15	The danger of self-commendation
	11:16-12:13	Boasting according to the flesh
12:14-21	Appeal for proper understanding	

D. Summary

All of the oral patterns that were identified in the extrabiblical writings and in the OT are present in 2 Corinthians. Chiasmus occurs repeatedly, as does the use of word-chains and link-words. Inclusion is used frequently to delimit portions of the argument, and several times ring-composition is used to resume a discussion after a digression. Although appearing less frequently than inclusion and ring-composition, inversion and alternation occur on a limited scale. Refrain is rare, but similar words sometimes begin successive paragraphs. The number of instances of concentric symmetry may be debated, for concentric structures proposed by some scholars can often be resolved into simpler ABA' patterns.

---

[98] Cf. Talbert: A = 10:1-11, B = 10:12-12:13, A' = 12:14-13:10 (*Corinthians* 111). Similarly, Ellis: A = 10:1-18, B = 11:1-12:10, A' = 12:11-13:14 (*Letters* 163).

Chapter 9

GALATIANS

The Pauline authorship of Galatians is undisputed,[1] as is its integrity. The identity of "the churches of Galatia" (1:2), however, is a matter of considerable discussion. Does the phrase refer to the ethnic region of the Gauls in the north or to the Roman province of Galatia, including the cities in the southern part of that province?[2] Closely tied to the question of destination is that of date. Is Galatians one of Paul's earliest letters, written around A.D. 49-50?[3] Or should it be dated later, say between A.D. 53 and 58?[4] Longenecker notes that "without a doubt, the date of Galatians is one of the knottiest problems in Pauline studies."[5] Fortunately, the destination and date of the letter do not bear on the present study, so detailed discussions of those issues may be left to others.

The structure of Galatians has been analyzed in a variety of ways. In addition to analyses based on content, three approaches are worthy of note. Funk, White, and Doty all include Galatians in their discussions of epistolary analysis.[6] Betz's analysis

---

[1] Longenecker: "The most uncontroverted matter in the study of Galatians is that the letter was written by Paul" (*Galatians* lvii).

[2] For arguments in support of a North Galatian destination, see J. B. Lightfoot, *The Epistle of St. Paul to the Galatians* (London: Macmillan, 1865; repr. Peabody, MA: Hendrickson, 1981) 18-35; J. Moffatt, *An Introduction to the Literature of the New Testament*, 3rd ed. (Edinburgh: T & T Clark, 1918) 83-107; Betz, *Galatians* 4-5. For arguments in support of a South Galatian destination, see W. M. Ramsay, *A Historical Commentary on St. Paul's Epistle to the Galatians*, 2nd ed. (London: Hodder & Stoughton, 1900) 315-316; E. deW. Burton, *A Critical and Exegetical Commentary on the Epistle to the Galatians* (Edinburgh: T & T Clark, 1921) xxi-xliv; F. F. Bruce, *Commentary on Galatians* (Grand Rapids: Eerdmans, 1982) 3-18.

[3] E.g., Bruce, *Galatians* 55-56.

[4] E.g., Lightfoot, *Galatians* 36-56. Betz posits a date between A.D. 50 and 55 (*Galatians* 11-12).

[5] Longenecker, *Galatians* lxxiii.

[6] Funk, *Language* 250-274; idem, "Apostolic Parousia" 249-268; White, *Body* 49-68; Doty, *Letters* 43.

of Galatians as an apologetic letter conforming to the requirements of forensic rhetoric launched a wave of similar rhetorical analyses.[7] Hansen and Longenecker use a combination of epistolary and rhetorical analysis to arrive at a rebuke-request structure for the letter in which both forensic and deliberative rhetoric are prominent.[8] The logical starting point in Galatians, as is true elsewhere in Paul, is a consideration of epistolary structure.

A. Epistolary Structure

The major clusters of epistolary conventions (disregarding vocatives and verbs of "hearing" or "saying") are:

1:1-11	Salutation (1:1-2), greeting (1:3), doxology (1:5), rebuke formula (1:6), disclosure formula (1:11)
3:1-7	Rebuke (3:1), disclosure formula (3:7)
4:12-20	Request formula (4:12), disclosure formula (4:13), attestation (4:15), visit wish (4:20)
5:3-10	Attestation (5:3), confidence formula (5:10)
6:11-18	Writing statement (6:11), peace-wish (6:16), grace-blessing (6:18)

The opening and closing portions of the letter are clearly defined. An extended salutation (1:1-5) closes with the doxology of 1:5. A rebuke section (1:6-10) replaces the thanksgiving section commonly found in Paul's letters. The disclosure formula in 1:11 marks the beginning of the letter-body. The writing statement of 6:11 marks the beginning of the letter closing (6:11-18), which includes a peace-wish (6:16) and a grace-benediction (6:18), but lacks the greetings common at the end of Paul's other letters.

The body of the letter, however, is less easily handled. The clusters of epistolary conventions at 3:1; 4:12; and 5:3 suggest major turning points in the letter. Some scholars have identified 4:12-20 as the apostolic parousia—or, at least, a surrogate for one.[9] Longenecker, however, disagrees: "The closest thing we get to

---

[7] Betz, "Literary Composition"; idem, *Galatians*. Longenecker criticizes Betz on three counts: "Betz must be faulted for (1) trying to make all of Galatians fit the model of forensic rhetoric or conform to the genre of 'apologetic letter,' (2) drawing hard genealogical lines between this one model and Galatians, without taking sufficiently into account other epistolary and rhetorical influences on Paul, and (3) understanding the impact of classical rhetoric on Paul in too scholastic and rigid a fashion" (*Galatians* cxiii).

[8] Hansen, *Abraham in Galatians* 53-54; Longenecker, *Galatians* cix.

[9] Funk, "Apostolic Parousia" 250; White, *Body* 61; Doty, *Letters* 36; Jervis, *Romans* 119.

such talk about a visit in Galatians, however, is in 4:20, where Paul expresses a desire to be with his converts in the present. But a wish to be with his addressees in the present is hardly the same as announcing a planned visit for the future."[10]

Hansen has, perhaps, suggested the best understanding of the letter-body. By comparing the first half of Galatians with Hellenistic θαυμάζω letters and the second half with request formulae found elsewhere in Paul's letters, he arrives at a rebuke-request letter form. A modified version of his outline follows:[11]

Salutation		1:1-5
Rebuke section		1:6-4:11
Rebuke #1 (deserting the gospel)	1:6-2:21	
Rebuke #2 (foolishness about the gospel)	3:1-4:11	
Request section		4:12-6:10
Request #1 (personal and scriptural)	4:12-5:1	
Request #2 (ethical)	5:2-6:10	
Autograph subscription		6:11-18

This outline makes good sense of the turning points marked by the clusters of epistolary conventions. It also accords well with the major thematic sections of the letter, as is apparent from the distribution of key words.

	1:6-2:21	3:1-4:11	4:12-5:1	5:2-6:10
εὐαγγέλ-	13	0	0	0
νόμος	6	17	2	6
πίστις/πιστεύω	6	16	0	4
σπέρμα	0	5	0	0
ἐπαγγελία	0	9	2	0
πνεῦμα	0	5	0	10
σάρξ	3	1	4	7

B. Readily Apparent Oral Patterns

Chiasmus is the most frequently used oral pattern in Galatians, repeatedly serving to heighten the contrast between two opposites. For example, the second half of 2:16 contrasts justification by faith and by works of law:

ἵνα δικαιωθῶμεν ἐκ πίστεως Χριστοῦ καὶ οὐκ ἐξ ἔργων νόμου,
ὅτι ἐξ ἔργων νόμου οὐ δικαιωθήσεται πᾶσα σάρξ.

---

[10] Longenecker, *Galatians* 188.

[11] Cf. Hansen, *Abraham in Galatians* 53-54.

The second part of 2:20 also contains a chiasmus, for in clarifying what he means by ζῇ δὲ ἐν ἐμοὶ Χριστός, Paul continues:

ὃ δὲ νῦν <u>ζῶ ἐν σαρκί</u>,
<u>ἐν πίστει ζῶ</u> τῇ τοῦ υἱοῦ τοῦ θεοῦ . . .

The prepositional phrase ἐν πίστει is brought forward for emphasis to contrast with ἐν σαρκί, thereby highlighting the argument that salvation—and life after salvation—is by faith, not by works done in the flesh.

Similar patterns contrasting πνεῦμα and σάρξ occur in 3:3; 5:17; and 5:25:

ἐναρξάμενοι <u>πνεύματι</u>
νῦν   <u>σαρκὶ</u> ἐπιτελεῖσθε;

ἡ γὰρ <u>σὰρξ</u>   ἐπιθυμεῖ   κατὰ τοῦ <u>πνεύματος</u>,
τὸ δὲ <u>πνεῦμα</u>   κατὰ τῆς <u>σαρκός</u>·

εἰ ζῶμεν <u>πνεύματι</u>,
<u>πνεύματι</u> καὶ στοιχῶμεν.

A double chiasmus in 6:8 uses the same contrast:

ὅτι ὁ σπείρων   εἰς <u>τὴν σάρκα</u> ἑαυτοῦ
ἐκ <u>τῆς σαρκὸς</u>   θερίσει φθοράν,
ὁ δὲ σπείρων   εἰς <u>τὸ πνεῦμα</u>
ἐκ <u>τοῦ πνεύματος</u>   θερίσει ζωὴν αἰώνιον.

A less polemical instance in 4:17 also serves to reinforce Paul's point:

<u>ζηλοῦσιν ὑμᾶς</u> οὐ καλῶς, ἀλλὰ ἐκκλεῖσαι ὑμᾶς θέλουσιν,
<u>ἵνα αὐτοὺς ζηλοῦτε</u>.

One final instance of chiasmus occurs in 6:14:

δι' οὗ ἐμοὶ κόσμος   ἐσταύρωται
κἀγὼ κόσμῳ.

In the first line, the order is dative-nominative; in the second, that order is reversed. It is probable, however, that the homoeoteleuton of κἀγὼ κόσμῳ was more readily apparent to the ear.

Word-chain is also apparent in several passages within Galatians. The noun εὐαγγέλιον and its cognate verb εὐαγγελίζομαι figure prominently in 1:6-10:

Θαυμάζω ὅτι οὕτως ταχέως μετατίθεσθε ἀπὸ τοῦ καλέσαντος ὑμᾶς ἐν χάριτι Χριστοῦ εἰς ἕτερον <u>εὐαγγέλιον</u>, ὃ οὐκ ἔστιν ἄλλο· εἰ μή τινές εἰσιν οἱ ταράσσοντες ὑμᾶς καὶ θέλοντες μεταστρέψαι τὸ <u>εὐαγγέλιον</u> τοῦ Χριστοῦ. ἀλλὰ καὶ ἐὰν ἡμεῖς ἢ ἄγγελος ἐξ οὐρανοῦ <u>εὐαγγελίζηται</u> ὑμῖν παρ' ὃ <u>εὐηγγελισάμεθα</u> ὑμῖν, ἀνάθεμα ἔστω. ὡς προειρήκαμεν, καὶ ἄρτι πάλιν λέγω, εἴ τις ὑμᾶς εὐαγγελίζεται παρ' ὃ παρελάβετε, ἀνάθεμα ἔστω. ἄρτι γὰρ ἀνθρώπους πείθω ἢ τὸν θεόν; ἢ ζητῶ ἀνθρώποις ἀρέσκειν; εἰ ἔτι ἀνθρώποις ἤρεσκον, Χριστοῦ δοῦλος οὐκ ἂν ἤμην.

Paul then provides a link to the letter-body by using the same words in the disclosure formula of 1:11:

γνωρίζω γὰρ ὑμῖν, ἀδελφοί, τὸ εὐαγγέλιον τὸ εὐαγγελισθεν ὑπ' ἐμοῦ . . .

This use of link words to connect successive paragraphs is similar to that seen in the raft-building passage in Homer.

Other more extended examples of word-chains appear in 3:1-4:11. The antithetical pair πίστις (8x) and νόμος (7x) dominate 3:1-14. In the final clause of 3:14, however, ἐπαγγελία appears for the first time in the letter, anticipating a shift in the word chain to ἐπαγγελία (7x), ἐπαγγέλλομαι (1x), and σπέρμα (4x) in 3:15-22. νόμος (8x) reappears in 3:17-24, being joined by the antithetical terms πίστις (6x) and πιστεύω (1x) in 3:22-26. The final occurrences in this section of ἐπαγγελία and σπέρμα are in 3:29, effectively closing a portion of the letter contrasting "faith" and "promise" with "law" and "seed." As well, the nouns δοῦλος (3:28; 4:1, 7) and κληρονόμος (3:29; 4:1, 7) provide the link to 4:1-11, the latter word having been anticipated by its cognate κληρονομία in 3:18 and the former word forming part of the word chain in 4:1-11.

There is no clear word-chain in 4:12-20. In 4:22-5:1, however, ἐλευθερός (5x), ἐλευθερία (1x), and ἐλευθερόω (1x) are contrasted with παιδίσκη (5x), and in 5:13 ἐλευθερία reappears (2x) in conjunction with σάρξ (1x). The latter word begins a new word chain (5:16-26) involving the antithetical word pair πνεῦμα (7x) and σάρξ (5x). This extended use of word-chains and word pairs gives Paul's argumentation a distinctively Jewish flavor.

A related use of oral patterning to sharpen the contrasts of Paul's polemic is that of alternation found in 5:16-25:

A	λέγω δέ, πνεύματι περιπατεῖτε	5:16
B	καὶ ἐπιθυμίαν σαρκὸς οὐ μὴ τελέσητε.	
B	ἡ γὰρ σὰρξ ἐπιθυμεῖ κατὰ τοῦ πνεύματος,	5:17
A	τὸ δὲ πνεῦμα κατὰ τῆς σαρκός . . .	
A	εἰ δὲ πνεύματι ἄγεσθε, οὐκ ἐστε ὑπὸ νόμον.	5:18
B	φανερὰ δέ ἐστιν τὰ ἔργα τῆς σαρκός, ἅτινά ἐστιν . . .	5:19
A	ὁ δὲ καρπὸς τοῦ πνεύματός ἐστιν . . .	5:22
B	οἱ δὲ τοῦ Χριστοῦ ᾿Ιησοῦ τὴν σάρκα ἐσταύρωσαν σὺν τοῖς παθήμασιν καὶ ταῖς ἐπιθυμίαις.	5:24
A	εἰ ζῶμεν πνεύματι, πνεύματι καὶ στοιχῶμεν.	5:25

Paul concludes this section in 5:25 with a chiastically-framed summary statement that makes his point in a memorable way and encourages the behavior he wants the Galatians to adopt:

εἰ ζῶμεν   πνεύματι,
πνεύματι   καὶ στοιχῶμεν.

Flesh and Spirit might be in conflict (5:17), but Christ's death on the cross (5:24) has made them alive to follow the Spirit.

It is possible that a similar instance of alternation occurs in 3:1-14:

A	ἐξ ἔργων νόμου τὸ πνεῦμα ἐλάβετε	3:2
B	ἢ ἐξ ἀκοῆς πίστεως;	
B	ἐναρξάμενοι πνεύματι	3:3
A	νῦν σαρκὶ ἐπιτελεῖσθε;	
A	ὁ οὖν ἐπιχορηγῶν ὑμῖν τὸ πνεῦμα . . . ἐξ ἔργων νόμου	3:5
B	ἢ ἐξ ἀκοῆς πίστεως;	
B	γινώσκετε ἄρα ὅτι οἱ ἐκ πίστεως, οὗτοι υἱοί εἰσιν 'Αβραάμ.	3:7
B	προϊδοῦσα δὲ ἡ γραφὴ ὅτι ἐκ πίστεως δικαιοῖ τὰ ἔθνη ὁ θεὸς . . .	3:8
B	ὥστε οἱ ἐκ πίστεως εὐλογοῦνται σὺν τῷ πιστῷ 'Αβραάμ.	3:9
A	ὅσοι γὰρ ἐξ ἔργων νόμου εἰσὶν ὑπὸ κατάραν εἰσίν . . .	3:10
A	ὅτι δὲ ἐν νόμῳ οὐδεὶς δικαιοῦται παρὰ τῷ θεῷ δῆλον,	3:11
B	ὅτι 'Ο δίκαιος ἐκ πίστεως ζήσεται·	
B	ὁ δὲ νόμος οὐκ ἔστιν ἐκ πίστεως . . .	3:12
A	ἀλλ' 'Ο ποιήσας αὐτὰ ζήσεται ἐν αὐτοῖς.	
B	ἵνα τὴν ἐπαγγελίαν τοῦ πνεύματος λάβωμεν διὰ τῆς πίστεως.	3:14

In this section, the contrast is between life lived in the Spirit according to faith and life lived in the flesh according to the law.

C. Other Suggested Structures

Perhaps the most idiosyncratic structural understanding of Galatians is that proposed by John Bligh.[12] He sees the letter as a series of complex, interlocking chiasms. The "primary chiasm" embraces the entire letter:

A	Prologue	1:1-12
B	Autobiographical section	1:13-2:10
C	Justification by faith	2:11-3:4
D	Arguments from Scripture	3:5-3:29
E	Central chiasm	4:1-10
D'	Argument from Scripture	4:11-4:31
C'	Justification by faith	5:1-10
B'	Moral section	5:11-6:11
A'	Epilogue	6:12-18

According to Bligh, secondary and tertiary chiasms exist within the primary chiasm:

---

[12] J. Bligh, *Galatians in Greek: A Structural Analysis of Paul's Epistle to the Galatians* (Detroit: University Press, 1966); idem, *Galatians—A Discussion of St. Paul's Epistle* (London: St. Paul, 1969).

Primary Chiasm	Secondary Chiasm	Tertiary Chiasm
		1:1-12
	1:1-3:4	1:6-2:10
		2:11-3:4
		3:5-29
1:1-6:18	3:5-4:31	4:1-10
		4:11-31
		5:1-13a
	5:1-6:18	5:13b-6:2
		5:22-6:18

The heart of Bligh's system is the "central chiasm" (4:1-10), which is an expansion of the chiasm Lightfoot noted in 4:4-5. It is not within the scope of this study to undertake an exhaustive investigation of Bligh's analysis, but it is possible to examine his central chiasm and draw some conclusions from it:[13]

A   Λέγω δέ, ἐφ' ὅσον χρόνον ὁ κληρονόμος νήπιός ἐστιν,
B   οὐδὲν διαφέρει δούλου κύριος πάντων ὤν,
C   ἀλλὰ ὑπὸ ἐπιτρόπους ἐστὶν καὶ οἰκονόμους ἄχρι τῆς
    προθεσμίας τοῦ πατρός.
D   οὕτως καὶ ἡμεῖς, ὅτε ἦμεν νήπιοι, ὑπὸ τὰ στοιχεῖα
    τοῦ κόσμου ἤμεθα δεδουλωμένοι·
E   ὅτε δὲ ἦλθεν τὸ πλήρωμα τοῦ χρόνου, ἐξαπέστειλεν
    ὁ θεὸς τὸν υἱὸν αὐτοῦ,
F   γενόμενον ἐκ γυναικός,
G   γενόμενον ὑπὸ νόμον,
G'   ἵνα τοὺς ὑπὸ νόμον ἐξαγοράσῃ,
F'   ἵνα τὴν υἱοθεσίαν ἀπολάβωμεν.
E' ὅτι δέ ἐστε υἱοί, ἐξαπέστειλεν ὁ θεὸς τὸ πνεῦμα τοῦ
    υἱοῦ αὐτοῦ εἰς τὰς καρδίας ἡμῶν, κρᾶζον, Αββα ὁ πατήρ.
D' ὥστε οὐκέτι εἶ δοῦλος ἀλλὰ υἱός· εἰ δὲ υἱός,
    καὶ κληρονόμος διὰ θεοῦ.
C' ἀλλὰ τότε μὲν οὐκ εἰδότες θεὸν ἐδουλεύσατε τοῖς φύσει
    μὴ οὖσιν θεοῖς·
B' νῦν δὲ γνόντες θεόν, μᾶλλον δὲ γνωσθέντες ὑπὸ θεοῦ,
A' πῶς ἐπιστρέφετε πάλιν ἐπὶ τὰ ἀσθενῆ καὶ πτωχὰ στοιχεῖα,
    οἷς πάλιν ἄνωθεν δουλεύειν θέλετε; ἡμέρας παρατηρεῖσθε
    καὶ μῆνας καὶ καιροὺς καὶ ἐνιαυτούς.

The strongest verbal parallels occur in 4:4-6 where the paired participles and ἵνα clauses are prominent. Lightfoot apparently saw 4:4-5 arranged in this way:[14]

ἐξαπέστειλεν ὁ θεὸς τὸν υἱὸν αὐτοῦ, γενόμενον ἐκ γυναικός,
γενόμενον ὑπὸ νόμον,

---

[13] Bligh, *Galatians* 37.

[14] Lightfoot, *Galatians* 168. Cf. Longenecker, *Galatians* 166.

ἵνα τοὺς ὑπὸ νόμον ἐξαγοράσῃ,
ἵνα τὴν υἱοθεσίαν ἀπολάβωμεν.

Bligh correctly notes the parallels between 4:4a and 4:6 and revises the scheme to include 4:6:

A   ὅτε δὲ ἦλθεν τὸ πλήρωμα τοῦ χρόνου, <u>ἐξαπέστειλεν ὁ θεὸς</u>
        <u>τὸν υἱὸν αὐτοῦ,</u>
B   γενόμενον ἐκ γυναικός,
C   γενόμενον <u>ὑπὸ νόμον,</u>
C'   ἵνα τοὺς <u>ὑπὸ νόμον</u> ἐξαγοράσῃ,
B'   ἵνα τὴν υἱοθεσίαν ἀπολάβωμεν.
A'   Ὅτι δέ ἐστε υἱοί, <u>ἐξαπέστειλεν ὁ θεὸς</u> τὸ πνεῦμα <u>τοῦ υἱοῦ</u>
        <u>αὐτοῦ</u> εἰς τὰς καρδίας ἡμῶν, κρᾶζον, Αββα ὁ πατήρ.

In this case the verbal parallels between the outer members are strong, and the repetition of ὑπὸ νόμον at the center is obvious. In addition, there is a conceptual connection between Jesus being "born of a woman" and the adoption conferred on others (born of women) because of Jesus's life and ministry. Yet it is difficult to judge whether the repetition of γενόμενον and ἵνα or the repetition of ὑπὸ νόμον would have been more evident to the listener. Nonetheless, these verses appear to be a carefully-crafted summary of Jesus's saving activity on behalf of the Christian.[15]

Beyond these limits, however, difficulties arise. Bligh originally linked 4:3 with 4:7. This is possible because of the parallel of δουλόω (4:3) and δοῦλος (4:7)—although it is unclear as to why δοῦλος in 4:7 is to be preferred over δουλεύω in 4:8. Bligh's proposed linking of C with C', however, is tenuous, and there are no parallels at all between B and B' or between A and A'. Later he altered this subsection to encompass 4:3-10.[16] In so doing, he shifted the center of the structure to 4:7b (εἰ δὲ υἱός, καὶ κληρονόμος διὰ θεοῦ), ignoring the obvious parallels in 4:4-6. He also inverted 4:9b and 4:10 to make the scheme work, but it is better to work with the text as it is than to propose interpolations to fit a preconceived system. There is also a problem with 4:11, in that it seems to belong with 4:1-10 rather than with 4:12-20. These problems suggest that Bligh's approach is flawed and that his chiastic structure for the entire letter is questionable.[17]

---

[15] Longenecker argues for the presence of a confessional portion in these verses (*Galatians* 169-170). Contrast R. B. Hays *The Faith of Jesus Christ: An Investigation of the Narrative Substructure of Galatians 3:1-4:11*, SBLDS 56 (Chico, CA: Scholars, 1983) 85-137.

[16] Bligh, *Galatians—A Discussion* 342.

[17] Two comments may be made in passing: (1) The links he observed between the prologue (1:1-12) and the epilogue (6:11-18) are to be expected in the portions of a letter concerned with maintaining relations with the readers. In this sense, all letters are "chiastic" or at least loosely-related to the ABA' pattern. (2) Bligh himself notes, "The correspondence between the

Although instances of similar patterns are present in Galatians, it is unlikely that chiasmus or inversion is the basic organizing principle of the letter.

In a related approach, Jeremias suggested that all of Galatians may be seen as an instance of inversion.[18] According to Jeremias, 1:11-12 introduces Paul's two primary lines of argument: the gospel is neither κατὰ ἄνθρωπον (1:11) nor παρὰ ἀνθρώπου (1:12). The remainder of the letter elaborates these lines of argument in reverse order: the gospel is not παρὰ ἀνθρώπου (1:13-2:21), nor is it κατὰ ἄνθρωπον (3:1-6:10). This proposal is intriguing because of the examples of inversion observed in Greco-Roman literature, but what is missing are the clear verbal connections that would have given the listeners a clue to the inversion.[19]

Ellis proposes an ABBA arrangement for the entire book:[20]

A	Freedom from the law and circumcision		1:1-3:5
	a	Paul's surprise at the Galatians leaving the only true gospel (1:1-2:10)	
	b	Peter at Antioch did not observe the Mosaic food laws (2:11-21)	
	a'	"O foolish Galatians"—leaving the only true gospel (3:1-5)	
B	The true sons of Abraham		3:6-29
	a	Sons of Abraham by faith (3:6-9)	
	b	Faith and the law (3:10-22)	
	a'	Sons of God and the posterity of Abraham by faith (3:23-29)	
B'	The true sons of Abraham		4:1-31
	a	Slaves versus sons (4:1-11)	
	b	The Galatians are Paul's "children" in Christ (4:12-20)	
	a'	Sons of the slave girl versus sons of the freeborn wife (4:21-31)	
A'	Freedom from the law and circumcision		5:1-6:18
	a	Freedom from the law and circumcision (5:1-12)	
	b	Freedom for works of love, not for self-indulgence (5:13-6:10)	
	a'	Freedom from the law and circumcision (6:11-18)	

Autobiographical Section [1:13-2:10] and the Moral Section [5:11-6:11] is not immediately obvious . . ." (*Galatians—A Discussion* 39).The explanation that follows is no more obvious than the correspondence it is intended to clarify. Hansen provides an extended critique of Bligh's analysis (*Abraham in Galatians* 75-79).

[18] Jeremias, "Chiasmus" 152-153. He actually uses the term "chiasmus," but "inversion" is more accurate. Hansen notes that F. Mussner (*Der Galaterbrief* [Freiberg: Herder, 1974] 77) and J. C. Beker (*Paul the Apostle: The Triumph of God in Life and Thought* [Philadelphia: Fortress, 1980] 44-45) adopt Jeremias's analysis (*Abraham in Galatians* 74).

[19] Longenecker succinctly summarizes the weaknesses of this approach: "The attempt to see the body of Galatians as one large chiasmus, however, falters on several grounds: (1) the inability of its proponents to identify significant repetitions between its parts; (2) the difficulty of laying out a well-balanced structure between its parts; and (3) uncertainties as to where one theme ends and another begins. It can even be debated, in fact, whether κατὰ ἄνθρωπον and παρὰ ἀνθρώπου are really set out by Paul in balanced fashion, or whether the latter is not an explication of the former and to be paired with ἐδιδάχθην that immediately follows" (*Galatians* 21).

[20] Ellis, *Letters* 175-176.

Much of the apparent balance in this scheme is produced by the wording of the headings given to the four major sections. Those headings, however, are rather general, and it might appear to some readers that the wording was chosen precisely to create the impression of symmetry.

Unfortunately, there is little in the way of verbal correspondence to support Ellis's proposed arrangement—unlike Romans 9-11 or 1 Corinthians 8-11, where the clear shifts in the word-chain support an ABA' understanding of the chapters. Furthermore, the headings of the subsections appear to be somewhat selective. For example, the heading "Faith and the law" assigned to 3:10-22 ignores both the fact that the same antithesis is also present in 3:1-9 and the fact that the emphasis in 3:15-22 shifts from faith to promise. Another example is 4:12-20, where it is questionable that "The Galatians are Paul's 'children' in Christ" accurately summarizes the primary thrust of 4:12-20.

Perhaps the most glaring weakness in Ellis's proposal is the fact that he proposes major divisions in the text at 3:6 and 4:1. The division at 3:6 ignores several considerations: (1) that 1:6-2:21 most naturally constitutes one of the two rebuke sections in the letter; (2) that the word-chain involving πίστις and νόμος (3:1-14) bridges the suggested division, as does the repeated use of πνεῦμα in 3:2-14; and (3) that if an internal division were to be made within 3:1-14, the more natural break would be at the disclosure formula in 3:7. Similarly, the break at 4:1 is not the best. Again, the extent of the rebuke sections and their word-chains argues against this division. Furthermore, Hansen has persuasively demonstrated the unity of 3:1-4:11.[21]

Brunot suggests an ABA' arrangement for 2:15-6:10:[22]

A	There is no liberty except in faith	2:15-4:7
	a Faith makes Christ alive in us (2:15-21)	
	b The law is powerless (3:1-25)	
	a' Faith makes us one in Christ (3:26-4:7)	
B	Are you going to return to slavery?	4:8-31
	a Don't return to slavery (4:8-11)	
	b Become free as I, Paul, am (4:12-20)	
	a' Don't put yourself under the slavery of Hagar (4:21-31)	
A'	There is no liberty except in Christ	5:1-6:10
	a Christ has stamped us for liberty (5:1)	
	b Circumcision makes everything lost (5:2-12)	
	a' Triumph of Christian liberty (5:13-6:10)	

Many of the comments made above in connection with Ellis's scheme also, however, apply to Brunot's, for there are few verbal parallels to support the arrangement. Furthermore, placing 2:15-21 with what follows rather than with what precedes ignores the turning point suggested by the cluster of epistolary formulae in 3:1-7, and

---

[21] Hansen, *Abraham in Galatians* 78. See the discussion below.

[22] Brunot, *S. Paul* 74.

placing a break at 4:8 ignores the basic rebuke-request form of the letter as well as the word-chain that unites 4:1-11.

On a smaller scale, Welch has suggested an inverted structure in 4:1-7:[23]

A	The heir remains a child and servant	4:1
B	Until the time appointed of the father	4:2
C	When that time came, God sent forth his Son	4:4
D	Made under the law	4:4
D'	To redeem those under the law	4:5
C'	Because you are sons, God sent forth the Spirit of his Son	4:6
B'	That you cry, Abba, Father	4:6
A'	That you are no more a servant but a son and heir	4:7

On the positive side, (1) several points of verbal correspondence support this arrangement, and (2) it acknowledges the careful balance of 4:4-6. Negatively, however, verse 3 is omitted altogether from Welch's proposal. The omission of 4:3 raises the further question of the way in which the parallel between 4:3 (ὑπὸ τὰ στοιχεῖα τοῦ κόσμου ἤμεθα δεδουλωμένοι) and 4:8 (ἐδουλεύσατε τοῖς φύσει μὴ οὖσιν θεοῖς)—if it were acknowledged—might affect the understanding of the passage's structure.

Kenneth Bailey has proposed a chiastic structure for 3:5-14 that is centered on the quotation of Hab 2:4 in 3:11b:[24]

A	Spirit, faith, righteousness	3:5-6
B	Gentiles, blessing of Abraham	3:7-9
C	Curse	3:10
D	Law	3:11a
E	Righteousness by faith	3:11b
D'	Law	3:12
C'	Curse (Christ)	3:13
B'	Gentiles, blessing of Abraham (Christ)	3:14a
A'	Spirit, faith, promise.	3:14b

This proposal is attractive because of the evident verbal parallels, but there are some difficulties as well. Verses 5-6 actually belong with the thought unit begun with the vocative in 3:1 and the verb of hearing in 3:2. As well, this unit is reinforced by the repetition of ἐξ ἔργων νόμου ἢ ἐξ ἀκοῆς πίστεως in 3:2 and 3:5. Furthermore, the disclosure formula of 3:7 (γινώσκετε ἄρα ὅτι) suggests that 3:7-14 should be taken together.[25] The unity of this latter section is reinforced by (1) the repeated use of πίστις, νόμος, and κατάρα; (2) the framing statements about Gentiles receiving the blessing of Abraham (3:8-9; 3:14); (3) two quotes from Deuteronomy, both of

---

[23] Welch, *Chiasmus* 214.

[24] K. E. Bailey, *Poet and Peasant* (Grand Rapids: Eerdmans, 1976) 54-55.

[25] Contra Longenecker, (*Galatians* 98).

which begin with the word ἐπικατάρατος (3:10; 3:13); and (4) the use of two
quotations contrasting living ἐκ πίστεως (3:11) and ἐξ ἔργων νόμου (3:2).[26]

Bailey's scheme should probably be seen, rather, as an instance of inversion:

A   γινώσκετε ἄρα ὅτι οἱ ἐκ πίστεως, οὗτοι υἱοί εἰσιν Ἀβραάμ.
      προϊδοῦσα δὲ ἡ γραφὴ ὅτι ἐκ πίστεως δικαιοῖ τὰ ἔθνη ὁ
      θεὸς προευηγγελίσατο τῷ Ἀβραὰμ ὅτι ἐνευλογηθήσονται
      ἐν σοὶ πάντα τὰ ἔθνη. ὥστε οἱ ἐκ πίστεως εὐλογοῦνται σὺν
      τῷ πιστῷ Ἀβραάμ.

B   ὅσοι γὰρ ἐξ ἔργων νόμου εἰσὶν ὑπὸ κατάραν εἰσίν·
      γέγραπται γὰρ ὅτι ἐπικατάρατος πᾶς ὃς οὐκ ἐμμένει
      πᾶσιν τοῖς γεγραμμένοις ἐν τῷ βιβλίῳ τοῦ νόμου τοῦ
      ποιῆσαι αὐτά.

C   ὅτι δὲ ἐν νόμῳ οὐδεὶς δικαιοῦται παρὰ τῷ θεῷ δῆλον, ὅτι
      Ὁ δίκαιος ἐκ πίστεως ζήσεται·

C'   ὁ δὲ νόμος οὐκ ἔστιν ἐκ πίστεως, ἀλλ' Ὁ ποιήσας αὐτὰ
      ζήσεται ἐν αὐτοῖς.

B'   Χριστὸς ἡμᾶς ἐξηγόρασεν ἐκ τῆς κατάρας τοῦ νόμου
      γενόμενος ὑπὲρ ἡμῶν κατάρα, ὅτι γέγραπται,
      ἐπικατάρατος πᾶς ὁ κρεμάμενος ἐπὶ ξύλου,

A'   ἵνα εἰς τὰ ἔθνη ἡ εὐλογία τοῦ Ἀβραὰμ γένηται ἐν Χριστῷ
      Ἰησοῦ, ἵνα τὴν ἐπαγγελίαν τοῦ πνεύματος λάβωμεν διὰ
      τῆς πίστεως.

At the center of this structure is, again, the contrast between life lived by faith and
life lived in the flesh according to the law.

Longenecker adopts Bligh's analysis of 1:1 as chiastic with an understood ἀπό
before θεοῦ πατρὸς:[27]

      οὐκ ἀπ' ἀνθρώπων
      οὐδὲ δι' ἀνθρώπου
      ἀλλὰ διὰ Ἰησοῦ Χριστοῦ
      καὶ [ἀπὸ] θεοῦ πατρὸς

This construction makes good sense of the unusual order of "Jesus Christ and God
the Father"[28] and sees God the Father as the ultimate source of Paul's apostleship
rather than the co-agent with Christ. It is, however, unlikely that this construction
would have been readily apparent to the ear.

---

[26] The antecedent for αὐτὰ and αὐτοῖς must be understood as ἔργων νόμου in 3:10.

[27] Longenecker, *Galatians* 5; cf. Bligh, *Galatians—A Discussion* 62.

[28] Paul's usual order places God first; e.g.,. Rom 1:7; 1 Cor 1:3; 2 Cor 1:2; Phil 1:2.

The clear contrast in 4:25-26 between Hagar = Mt. Sinai = slavery = earthly Jerusalem and Sarah = freedom = heavenly Jerusalem leads Longenecker to propose a chiasm in 4:25-26 with a "lacuna" in the second part:[29]

A	Hagar	4:25
B	Mt. Sinai	
C	Slavery	
D	The present city of Jerusalem	
D'	The Jerusalem that is above	4:26
C'	Freedom	
B'	(Mt. Zion)	
A'	Our mother	

This scheme is less apparent than the contrast that prompts it. Not only is there the lacuna Longenecker mentions, but his proposal inverts the elements of 4:25 to make the scheme work. The verse actually reads:

τὸ δὲ ᾿Αγὰρ	(Hagar)
Σινᾶ ὄρος ἐστὶν ἐν τῇ ᾿Αραβίᾳ,	(Mt. Sinai)
συστοιχεῖ δὲ τῇ νῦν ᾿Ιερουσαλήμ,	(earthly Jerusalem)
δουλεύει γὰρ μετὰ τῶν τέκνων αὐτῆς.	(slavery)

Longenecker also notes a number of parallels between 1:6-10 and 5:1-12 and argues that these sections "form an *inclusio* for Paul's arguments and exhortations regarding [the judaizing] threat in the body of his Galatian letter."[30] The thematic parallels are helpful, but the verbal parallels are weak. Although these paragraphs might well perform the function Longenecker suggests, they do not fit the oral pattern of "inclusion" as defined in this study. The same may be said for his suggested inclusios around 5:13- 6:10 and 5:26-6:3.[31]

Hansen has suggested that the basic structure of 3:1-4:11 can be understood as a "chiastic pattern of thought," which may be outlined as follows:[32]

a	rebuking questions	3:1-5
b	bestowal of the Spirit	3:2, 5
c	faith—sonship	3:6-9
d	faith—law	3:10-14
e	promise—law	3:15-18
e'	law—promise	3:19-22
d'	law—faith	3:23-25
c'	sonship—faith	3:26-29
b'	bestowal of the Spirit	4:1-7
a'	rebuking question	4:8-11

[29] Longenecker, *Galatians* 213.

[30] Ibid. 222.

[31] Ibid. 236, 276.

[32] Hansen, *Abraham in Galatians* 78.

Leaving aside the issue of the rebuking questions—which are prominent in 3:1-5 (5 questions) but less so in 4:8-11 (1 question)—the rest of the structure may be examined in light of oral patterning. First, Hansen has correctly noted the correspondence between 3:2 (τὸ πνεῦμα ἐλάβετε ... ἐξ ἀκοῆς πίστεως) and 4:6 (ἐξαπέστειλεν ὁ θεὸς τὸ πνεῦμα). He has, however, overlooked the presence of wording in 3:14 (τὴν ἐπαγγελίαν τοῦ πνεύματος λάβωμεν διὰ τῆς πίστεως) that is nearly identical to that of 3:2. Second, he has correctly noted the strong conceptual and verbal correspondence between 3:7 (οὗτοι υἱοί εἰσιν 'Αβραάμ) and 3:29 (τοῦ 'Αβραὰμ σπέρμα ἐστέ). Third, he has correctly identified the elements of the word-chains in 3:6-29, although he has established their limits somewhat arbitrarily. A better representation might be: faith—law (3:2-14); promise—seed—law (3:15-22); faith—law (3:23-25). Although the symmetry might not be quite as precise as Hansen's outline suggests, he has—without doubt—established the unity of this section of Paul's letter.

Finally, Weima has identified a concentric structure in 6:12-16:[33]

C	ὅσοι—negative judgment on opponents of Paul	6:12
B	οὐδὲ γὰρ ... ἀλλὰ (circumcision vs. non-circumcision)	6:13
A	ἐμοὶ δὲ μὴ γένοιτο καυχᾶσθαι εἰ μὴ ἐν τῷ σταυρῷ τοῦ κυρίου ἡμῶν 'Ιησοῦ Χριστοῦ	6:14
B'	οὔτε γὰρ ... ἀλλὰ (circumcision vs. non-circumcision)	6:15
C'	ὅσοι—positive judgment on supporters of Paul	6:16

Basing parallels on words used as frequently as ὅσοι, οὐδὲ, and ἀλλὰ is rather tenuous. There is, however, the further verbal correspondence of περιτέμνω in 6:13 (twice) with περιτομή in 6:15 and the parallel use of substantival participles in 6:12 (θέλουσιν) and 6:16 (στοιχήσουσιν). So although Weima himself raises problems with the proposal, it is at least as likely as a number of other suggestions.

D. Summary

Paul uses chiasmus frequently in Galatians. Antithetical word pairs play a prominent role in the frequent word-chains. Link-words repeatedly connect one paragraph to another. Alternation is present in at least one extended passage. There are a limited number of examples of inversion within the letter, but the attempt to find an inverted or concentric structure for the entire letter cannot be sustained. Instances of inclusion and ring-composition—if present at all—are rare.

---

[33] Weima, *Neglected Endings* 157.

Chapter 10

PHILIPPIANS

That Paul wrote Philippians is seldom challenged.[1] Likewise, the Philippian destination of the letter is generally accepted. The traditional approach to the place and date of composition is to locate Paul in Rome c. A.D. 60-62.[2] Other places and dates have been suggested, however, including Corinth (A.D. 50),[3] Ephesus (A.D. 54-55),[4] and Caesarea (A.D. 57-59).[5]

Much of the scholarly discussion on Philippians has focused on the issue of the letter's integrity: is it a single letter or a composite?[6] Recent efforts in support of Philippians as a single letter have used a variety of approaches. Watson, for example, uses rhetorical analysis to argue for the unity of the letter;[7] David Black uses discourse analysis to support his contention that Philippians is "an integral composition . . . directed toward solving the issue of disunity";[8] Boyd Luter and

---

[1] A recent exception is A. Q. Morton and L. McLeman, *Christianity in the Computer Age* (New York: Harper & Row, 1965). Several scholars have criticized Morton and McLeman's work; cf. H. K. McArthur, "Computer Criticism," *ExpTim* 76 (1965) 367-370; idem, "Καὶ Frequency in Greek Letters," <u>NTS</u> 15 (1969) 339-349; M. Whittaker, "A. Q. Morton and J. McLeman," *Theology* 69 (1966) 567-568.

[2] E.g., F. W. Beare, *A Commentary on the Epistle to the Philippians* (New York: Harper & Row, 1959) 15-24.

[3] E.g., S. Dockx, "Lieu et date de l'épître aux Philippiens," *RB* 80 (1973) 230-246.

[4] E.g., J. -F. Collange, *The Epistle of St. Paul to the Philippians*, trans. A. W. Heathcote (London: Epworth, 1979) 15-19.

[5] E.g., G. F. Hawthorne, *Philippians* (Waco: Word, 1983) xli-xliv.

[6] D. E. Garland has an excellent summary of the arguments for and against the integrity of Philippians ("Composition" 144-159). Additional discussion revolves around the Christ-hymn of 2:6-11; cf. R. P. Martin, *Carmen Christi: Philippians ii.5-11 in Recent Interpretation and in the Setting of Early Christian Worship* (Cambridge: University Press, 1967).

[7] Watson, "Rhetorical Analysis."

[8] D. A. Black, "The Discourse Structure of Philippians: A Study in Textlinguistics," *NovT* 37 (1995) 16-49.

Michelle Lee argue that chiasmus is the key to solving the questions of structure, unity, and theme.[9] Nevertheless, Philippians is unquestionably a personal letter, and epistolary analysis seems the most appropriate method to use in defining its basic contours.[10]

A. Epistolary Structure

A survey of the major epistolary conventions of Philippians (disregarding vocatives and verbs of "saying") yields the following clusters of formulae:

1:1-2	Salutation (sender to addressees) and greeting
1:3-12	Thanksgiving (1:3), confidence formula (1:6), prayer (1:9), disclosure formula (1:12)
2:19-3:1	Dispatch of emissary (2:19), dispatch of emissary (2:23), confidence formula (2:24), visit wish (2:24), dispatch of emissary (2:25), dispatch of emissary (2:28), writing statement (3:1)
4:2-10	Request formula (4:2), request formula (4:3), peace-wish (4:7), peace-wish (4:9), joy expression (4:10)
4:20-23	Benediction (4:20), greetings (4:21-22), grace-blessing (4:23)

The salutation (1:1-2), thanksgiving (1:3-11), apostolic parousia (2:19-30), and closing (4:21-23) are clearly identifiable units. The formulae at the end of each cluster generally signify turning points in the letter: the disclosure formula at 1:12 introduces the first major section of the letter; the writing statement at 3:1 introduces another major section; and the joy expression at 4:10 introduces a final note of thanks, that is then closed by the benediction in 4:20.[11] The resulting epistolary structure is:

Salutation	1:1-2
Thanksgiving	1:3-11

---

[9] A. B. Luter and M. V. Lee, "Philippians as Chiasmus: Key to the Structure, Unity and Theme Questions," *NTS* 41 (1995) 89-101.

[10] Previous work on the epistolary structure of Philippians includes P. Schubert, *Form and Function of the Pauline Thanksgivings* (Berlin: Töpelmann, 1939) 4, 73-80; Funk, *Language* 264, 271-272; idem, "Apostolic Parousia" 254, 261-262; G. J. Bahr, "The Subscriptions in the Pauline Letters," *JBL* 87 (1968) 27-41; R. Jewett, "The Epistolary Thanksgiving and the Integrity of Philippians," *NovT* 12 (1970) 40-53; W. G. Doty, *Letters* 43; R. P. Martin, *Philippians* (Greenwood, SC: Attic Press, 1976); R. Russell, "Pauline Letter Structure in Philippians," *JETS* 25 (1982) 295-306; F. B. Craddock, *Philippians* (Atlanta: John Knox, 1985) 4-9; L. Alexander, "Hellenistic Letter-Forms and the Structure of Philippians," *JSNT* 37 (1989) 87-101.

[11] This note of thanks (4:10-20) is often seen as a third letter. E.g., White, *Body* 45.

The most clearly defined epistolary sections occur at the beginning and the end of the letter. Likewise, most of the epistolary formulae occur in these same sections.

B. Readily Apparent Oral Patterns

The verb εὐχαριστῶ, which is the principle verb of the opening thanksgiving section, is modified in 1:3-5 by a series of adverbial phrases. These adverbial phrases can be seen as being arranged in a micro-scale inversion, the key element being the repetition of ἡ δέησις:

	εὐχαριστῶ τῷ θεῷ μου
A	ἐπὶ πάσῃ τῇ μνείᾳ ὑμῶν,
B	πάντοτε ἐν πάσῃ δεήσει μου ὑπὲρ πάντων ὑμῶν
B'	μετὰ χαρᾶς τὴν δέησιν ποιούμενος,
A'	ἐπὶ τῇ κοινωνίᾳ ὑμῶν εἰς τὸ εὐαγγέλιον

The entire first paragraph of the thanksgiving (1:3-8) is undergirded by the word-chain πάσῃ . . . πάντοτε . . . πάσῃ . . . πάντων . . . πάντων . . . πάντας . . . πάντας.

A combination of oral patterns is helpful in understanding 1:12-26. The limits of this section are well-defined by what precedes and what follows. The thanksgiving reaches a definite conclusion with the eschatological climax of 1:11 (πεπληρωμένοι καρπὸν δικαιοσύνης τὸν διὰ ᾽Ιησοῦ Χριστοῦ εἰς δόξαν καὶ ἔπαινον θεοῦ). The disclosure formula of 1:12 (γινώσκειν δὲ ὑμᾶς βούλομαι, ἀδελφοί, ὅτι) marks the transition to a new topic. There is no formulaic indicator at 1:27, but the change to second person exhortation suggests the start of a new section. An inclusion using ὁράω and ἀκούω confirms that 1:27-30 functions as a discrete paragraph.

The disclosure formula at 1:12 signals the start of the Philippian letter-body. Epistolary analysis commonly views the "standard" Pauline letter-body as having three parts: the body-opening, the body-middle, and the body-closing.[12] The body-opening is introduced by a steriotyped formula and identifies a matter of mutual concern. The body-middle carries forward the information introduced and usually consists of a tightly structured theological argument and a loosely structured practical application.[13] The body-closing finalizes the motivation for writing and invokes the

---

[12] White, *Body* 9.

[13] Ibid. 74.

"apostolic parousia." Scholars who apply this model to Philippians are nearly unanimous in their conclusion that 1:12-2:30 is the letter-body:[14]

Body	1:12-2:30
Body-opening	1:12-18a
Body-middle	1:18b-2:18
Theological argument	1:18b-26
Practical application	1:27-2:18
Body-closing	2:19-30

The result is a division of 1:12-26 either in the middle or at the end of verse 18. This analysis is understandable, for 1:12-18 begins with a disclosure formula (1:12) and is organized around the antithesis of pretense and truth, while 1:19-26 begins with a confidence formula (1:19) and is organized around the antithesis of life and death.

Yet a consideration of oral patterning suggests that such an analysis might not be the best approach. Of primary importance here is the fact that the opening disclosure section of 1:12-14 contains elements of inclusion with the closing confidence section of 1:25-26:[15]

Γινώσκειν δὲ ὑμᾶς βούλομαι, ἀδελφοί, ὅτι τὰ κατ᾽ ἐμὲ μᾶλλον εἰς προκοπὴν τοῦ εὐαγγελίου ἐλήλυθεν, ὥστε τοὺς δεσμούς μου φανεροὺς ἐν Χριστῷ γενέσθαι ἐν ὅλῳ τῷ πραιτωρίῳ καὶ τοῖς λοιποῖς πάσιν, καὶ τοὺς πλείονας τῶν ἀδελφῶν ἐν κυρίῳ πεποιθότας τοῖς δεσμοῖς μου περισσοτέρως τολμᾶν ἀφόβως τὸν λόγον λαλεῖν.

καὶ τοῦτο πεποιθὼς οἶδα ὅτι μενῶ καὶ παραμενῶ πᾶσιν ὑμῖν εἰ τὴν ὑμῶν προκοπὴν καὶ χαρὰν τῆς πίστεως, ἵνα τὸ καύχημα ὑμῶν περισσεύῃ ἐν Χριστῷ Ἰησοῦ ἐν ἐμοὶ διὰ τῆς ἐμῆς παρουσίας πάλιν πρὸς ὑμᾶς.

Paul's repetition of προκοπή is particularly significant because the word appears only one other place in the entire Pauline corpus (1 Tim 4:15).

As well, two instances of alternation are present in this passage. One occurs in 1:15-17:

A   τινὲς μὲν καὶ διὰ φθόνον καὶ ἔριν,
B   τινὲς δὲ καὶ δι᾽ εὐδοκίαν τὸν Χριστὸν κηρύσσουσιν·
B'   οἱ μὲν ἐξ ἀγάπης,
      εἰδότες ὅτι εἰς ἀπολογίαν τοῦ εὐαγγελίου κεῖμαι,
A'   οἱ δὲ ἐξ ἐριθείας τὸν Χριστὸν καταγγέλλουσιν, οὐχ ἁγνῶς,
      οἰόμενοι θλῖψιν ἐγείρειν τοῖς δεσμοῖς μου.

---

[14] This outline is White's (ibid. 73-91); cf. Doty, *Letters* 43; Martin, *Philippians* 7; and Russell, "Letter Structure."

[15] Garland has noted two of these elements: προκοπή in 1:12, 25 and πεποιθότας/πεποιθὼς in 1:14, 25 ("Composition" 160). A third item is περισσοτέρως/περισσεύῃ in 1:14, 26.

The other in 1:21-24:

C ἐμοὶ γὰρ <u>τὸ ζῆν</u> Χριστὸς
D καὶ <u>τὸ ἀποθανεῖν</u> κέρδος.
C εἰ δὲ <u>τὸ ζῆν</u> ἐν σαρκί, τοῦτό μοι καρπὸς ἔργου·
   καὶ τί αἱρήσομαι οὐ γνωρίζω.
D συνέχομαι δὲ ἐκ τῶν δύο, τὴν ἐπιθυμίαν ἔχων εἰς <u>τὸ ἀναλῦσαι</u>
      <u>καὶ σὺν Χριστῷ εἶναι</u>, πολλῷ [γὰρ] μᾶλλον κρεῖσσον·
C <u>τὸ δε ἐπιμένειν [ἐν] τῇ σαρκὶ</u> ἀναγκαιότερον δι' ὑμᾶς.

So rather than seeing a break somewhere in 1:18-20, these verses should probably be viewed as the heart of the passage. They summarize the alternatives discussed, connect those alternatives with the ultimate results, and highlight Paul's joy in God's sovereign control of circumstances:

τί γάρ; πλὴν ὅτι παντὶ τρόπῳ, <u>εἴτε προφάσει εἴτε ἀληθείᾳ, Χριστὸς</u> <u>καταγγέλλεται</u>, καὶ ἐν τούτῳ <u>χαίρω·</u> ἀλλὰ καὶ <u>χαρήσομαι</u>, οἶδα γὰρ ὅτι τοῦτό μοι ἀποβήσεται εἰς σωτηρίαν διὰ τῆς ὑμῶν δεήσεως καὶ ἐπιχορηγίας τοῦ πνεύματος Ἰησοῦ Χριστοῦ, κατὰ τὴν ἀποκαραδοκίαν καὶ ἐλπίδα μου ὅτι ἐν οὐδενὶ αἰσχυνθήσομαι, ἀλλ' ἐν πάσῃ παρρησίᾳ ὡς πάντοτε καὶ νῦν <u>μεγαλυνθήσεται Χριστὸς ἐν τῷ σώματί μου, εἴτε διὰ</u> <u>ζωῆς εἴτε διὰ θανάτου</u>.

In fact, as the underlined portions in the above quotation of 1:18-20 indicate, the order of these elements is inverted:

pretext or truth	Christ proclaimed	joy
joy	Christ magnified	life or death.

It is probably going too far to say that Paul's listeners/readers would have "caught" all of the details of the above rhetorical-structural arrangement. Yet it seems reasonable to think that the elements in the outer panels of the passage would have focused their attention on the center panel. A structural-conceptual skeleton of 1:12-26, then, would look like this:

	προκοπὴν . . . πεποιθότας . . . περισσοτέρως	1:12-14
A	διὰ φθόνον καὶ ἔριν	1:15
B	δι' εὐδοκίαν	
B	ἐξ ἀγάπης	1:16
A	ἐξ ἐριθείας	1:17
A	<u>εἴτε</u> προφάσει	1:18-19
B	<u>εἴτε</u> ἀληθείᾳ . . . <u>Χριστὸς</u> καταγγέλλεται,	
	καὶ ἐν τούτῳ <u>χαίρω</u>.	
	ἀλλὰ καὶ <u>χαρήσομαι</u>,	

C   μεγαλυνθήσεται <u>Χριστὸς</u> . . . <u>εἴτε</u> διὰ ζωῆς   1:20
D   <u>εἴτε</u> διὰ θανάτου.

C   τὸ ζῆν   1:21
D   τὸ ἀπεθανεῖν
C   τὸ ζῆν   1:22
D   τὸ ἀναλῦσαι καὶ σὺν Χριστῷ εἶναι   1:23
C   τὸ ἐπιμένειν   1:24

           πεποιθὼς . . . προκοπὴν . . . περισσεύῃ   1:25-26

The recognition of the oral patterns present in 1:12-26, therefore, reinforces the passage's unity and leads to a better understanding of its structure and focus.

There are no formulaic indicators at 1:27. Nonetheless, the change to second person exhortation suggests the start of a new paragraph. This paragraph is delimited by the pairing of ὁράω with ἀκούω in 1:27 and 1:30:[16]

Μόνον ἀξίως τοῦ εὐαγγελίου τοῦ Χριστοῦ πολιτεύεσθε, ἵνα εἴτε ἐλθὼν καὶ <u>ἰδὼν</u> ὑμᾶς εἴτε ἀπὼν <u>ἀκούω</u> τὰ περὶ ὑμῶν . . .

τὸν αὐτὸν ἀγῶνα ἔχοντες, οἷον <u>εἴδετε</u> ἐν ἐμοὶ καὶ νῦν <u>ἀκούετε</u> ἐν ἐμοί.

So here is another use of inclusion by Paul. There is also an instance of chiasmus in 1:27b that serves to emphasize the unity that Paul is encouraging:[17]

ὅτι στήκετε ἐν <u>ἑνὶ πνεύματι</u>,
<u>μιᾷ ψυχῇ</u> συναθλοῦντες τῇ πίστει τοῦ εὐαγγελίου

Phil 2:1-4 shows evidence of careful structuring. Reading the passage aloud gives the impression that it was composed with rhetorical intent.[18] Watson has

---

[16] Cf. Garland, "Composition" 160.

[17] Cf. M. Silva, *Philippians* (Chicago: Moody, 1988) 92.

[18] D. A. Black goes so far as to propose a threefold strophic arrangement for these verses ("Paul and Christian Unity: A Formal Analysis of Philippians 2:1-4," *JETS* 28 [1985] 299-308):

(1)   A   εἴ τις οὖν παράκλησις ἐν Χριστῷ,
       B   εἴ τι παραμύθιον ἀγάπης,
       C   εἴ τις κοινωνία πνεύματος,
       D   εἴ τις σπλάγχνα καὶ οἰκτιρμοί,
(2)   A   πληρώσατέ μου τὴν χαρὰν ἵνα τὸ αὐτὸ φρονῆτε,
       B   τὴν αὐτὴν ἀγάπην ἔχοντες,
       B   σύμψυχοι,
       A   τὸ ἓν φρονοῦντες,
(3)   A   μηδὲν κατ' ἐριθείαν μηδὲ κατὰ κενοδοξίαν,
       B   ἀλλὰ τῇ ταπεινοφροσύνῃ ἀλλήλους ἡγούμενοι ὑπερέχοντας ἑαυτῶν,
       A   μὴ τὰ ἑαυτῶν ἕκαστος σκοποῦντες,
       B   ἀλλὰ καὶ τὰ ἑτέρων ἕκαστοι.

identified three rhetorical features Paul used to drive home his point:[19] (1) *epanaphora*, the use of the same word to form successive beginnings of phrases expressing like and/or different ideas; (2) *regressio*, the use of repetition to reiterate and draw distinctions simultaneously; and (3) *amplification*, the accumulation of a number of characteristics to a single referent. Within the paragraph, 2:2 is structured by inversion and, as in 1:27b, emphasizes Christian unity:[20]

	πληρώσατέ μου τὴν χαρὰν
A	ἵνα τὸ αὐτὸ φρονῆτε,
B	τὴν αὐτὴν ἀγάπην ἔχοντες,
B'	σύμψυχοι,
A'	τὸ ἓν φρονοῦντες

The imperative of 2:5 follows verses 1-4 closely. It introduces the Christ-hymn and should be taken with it. A great deal of scholarly work has been done on the hymn itself.[21] A variety of arrangements have been suggested. The most common approach is strophic.[22] Charles Robbins has analyzed the passage based on the principles of the Greek periodic sentence.[23] Other scholars have proposed different chiastic structures that will be examined below.

There is little in the hymn itself that shows evidence of oral patterning. The three genitives in 2:10 (ἐπουρανίων καὶ ἐπιγείων καὶ καταχθονίων) are examples of homoeoteleuton. There is repetition in the triple use of ὄνομα in 2:9-10. The line ἐταπείνωσεν ἑαυτὸν γενόμενος ὑπήκοος μέχρι θανάτου, θανάτου δε σταυροῦ (2:8) uses both repetition and homoeoteleuton. The only longer section that has some relationship to oral patterning is 2:7-8a with its repeated use of ἑαυτὸν, the three "backward" participial phrases, and the double use of ἄνθρωπος:

Although his basic analysis of the passage's structure is persuasive, it seems unnecessary to view 2:1-4 as hymnic, or even strophic.

[19] Watson, "Rhetorical Analysis" 69.

[20] Cf. W. Schenk, *Die Philipperbriefe des Paulus: Kommentar* (Stuttgart: Kohlhammer, 1984) 178; Black, "Unity" 301; O'Brien, *Commentary on Philippians* (Grand Rapids: Eerdmans, 1991) 165.

[21] See Hawthorne, *Philippians* 71-75, and O'Brien, *Philippians* 186-188, for bibliographies.

[22] E.g., E. Lohmeyer, *Kyrios Jesus: Eine Untersuchung zu Phil. 2,5-11* (Heidelberg: Winter, 1928); J. Jeremias, "Zur Gedankenführung in den paulinischen Briefen," in *Studia Paulina in Honorem J. de Zwaan*, ed. J. N. Sevenster and W. C. van Unnik (Haarlem: E. F. Bonn, 1953) 146-154; Martin, *Carmen Christi* 36-38; C. H. Talbert, "The Problem of Pre-existence in Philippians 2.6-11," *JBL* 86 (1967) 141-153; Collange, *Philippians* 83-86. See O'Brien for a good summary discussion of "literary form" (*Philippians* 182-192).

[23] Robbins, "Rhetorical Structure" 73-82.

ἀλλὰ ἑαυτὸν ἐκένωσεν
μορφὴν δούλου λαβών,
ἐν ὁμοιώματι ἀνθρώπων γενόμενος·
καὶ σχήματι εὑρεθεὶς ὡς ἄνθρωπος
ἐταπείνωσεν ἑαυτὸν

This section, with the addition of the subsequent participial phrase, can be seen as arranged in a micro-scale inversion:

A   ἀλλὰ <u>ἑαυτὸν ἐκένωσεν</u> μορφὴν δούλου λαβών,
B   ἐν ὁμοιώματι <u>ἀνθρώπων</u> γενόμενος·
B'   καὶ σχήματι εὑρεθεὶς ὡς <u>ἄνθρωπος</u>
A'   <u>ἐταπείνωσεν ἑαυτὸν</u> γενόμενος ὑπήκοος μέχρι θανάτου,
          θανάτου δὲ σταυροῦ.

Even this suggestion, however, must be taken as somewhat tentative. To go further and propose an overall chiastic structure for 2:6-11 is speculative.

Likewise, although Lund has proposed an arrangement that encompasses all of 2:12-18,[24] there is little in this paragraph that shows evidence of oral patterning. Second person instruction resumes with the vocative ἀγαπητοί μου in 2:12. But although the conjunction ὥστε indicates a close connection to what precedes, there are no other formulaic indicators in the paragraph. The mention of the "day of Christ" in 2:16 closes the section with a typically Pauline eschatological climax. Inversion on a micro-scale occurs in 2:12:[25]

ὥστε, ἀγαπητοί μου, καθὼς πάντοτε ὑπηκούσατε,
μὴ ὡς <u>ἐν τῇ παρουσίᾳ μου</u> μόνον
ἀλλὰ νῦν πολλῷ μᾶλλον <u>ἐν τῇ ἀπουσίᾳ μου</u>,
μετὰ φόβου καὶ τρόμου τὴν ἑαυτῶν σωτηρίαν κατεργάζεσθε·

The apostolic parousia of 2:19-30 falls naturally into two parts.[26] The first part (2:19-24) deals with the dispatch of Timothy; and is framed both by an inclusion using ταχέως[27] and by inclusive ring-composition:

<u>ἐλπίζω</u> δὲ ἐν κυρίῳ ᾿Ιησοῦ Τιμόθεον <u>ταχέως</u> <u>πέμψαι</u> ὑμῖν, ἵνα κἀγὼ εὐψυχῶ γνοὺς τὰ περὶ ὑμῶν.

τοῦτον μὲν οὖν <u>ἐλπίζω</u> <u>πέμψαι</u> ὡς ἂν ἀφίδω τὰ περὶ ἐμὲ ἐξαυτῆς· πέποιθα δὲ ἐν κυρίῳ ὅτι καὶ αὐτὸς <u>ταχέως</u> ἐλεύσομαι.

---

[24] Lund, *Chiasmus* 221. His arrangement will be examined below.

[25] Cf. Silva, *Philippians* 135.

[26] See Funk, *Language* 264, 271-272; idem, "Apostolic Parousia" 254, 261-262; White, *Body* 77-79, 85; and Jervis, *Romans* 117-119 for detailed discussions of these verses as the apostolic parousia.

[27] Garland notes the inclusion ("Composition" 160).

The second part (2:25-30) discusses the return of Epaphroditus to Philippi and is framed by an inclusion using λειτουργὸν (2:25) and λειτουργίας (2:30):[28]

ἀναγκαῖον δὲ ἡγησάμην 'επαφρόδιτον τὸν ἀδελφὸν καὶ συνεργὸν καὶ συστρατιώτην μου, ὑμῶν δὲ ἀπόστολον καὶ λειτουργὸν τῆς χρείας μου, πέμψαι πρὸς ὑμᾶς . . .

ὅτι διὰ τὸ ἔργον Χριστοῦ μέχρι θανάτου ἤγγισεν, παραβολευσάμενος τῇ ψυχῇ ἵνα ἀναπληρώσῃ τὸ ὑμῶν ὑστέρημα τῆς πρός με λειτουργίας.

These latter verses also contain a possible instance of inversion. The verbal parallels to support an inversion are few, but they are suggestive:

A   ἀναγκαῖον δὲ ἡγησάμην 'επαφρόδιτον τὸν ἀδελφὸν καὶ συνεργὸν καὶ συστρατιώτην μου, ὑμῶν δε ἀπόστολον καὶ λειτουργὸν τῆς χρείας μου, πέμψαι πρὸς ὑμᾶς, ἐπειδὴ ἐπιποθῶν ἦν πάντας ὑμᾶς, καὶ ἀδημονῶν διότι ἡκούσατε ὅτι ἠσθένησεν.

B   καὶ γὰρ ἠσθένησεν παραπλήσιον θανάτῳ·

C   ἀλλὰ ὁ θεὸς ἠλέησεν αὐτόν, οὐκ αὐτὸν δὲ μόνον ἀλλὰ καὶ ἐμέ, ἵνα μὴ λύπην ἐπὶ λύπην σχῶ.

C'   σπουδαιοτέρως οὖν ἔπεμψα αὐτὸν ἵνα ἰδόντες αὐτὸν πάλιν χαρῆτε κἀγὼ ἀλυπότερος ὦ.

B'   προσδέχεσθε οὖν αὐτὸν ἐν κυρίῳ μετὰ πάσης χαρᾶς, καὶ τοὺς τοιούτους ἐντίμους ἔχετε, ὅτι διὰ τὸ ἔργον Χριστοῦ μέχρι θανάτου ἤγγισεν,

A'   παραβολευσάμενος τῇ ψυχῇ ἵνα ἀναπληρώσῃ τὸ ὑμῶν ὑστέρημα τῆς πρός με λειτουργίας.

Second person instruction, which is so evident in 2:1-18, resumes at 3:1. Much of the scholarly discussion of 3:1-4:9 has focused on the question of whether or not a self-contained letter has been inserted into Philippians at this point.[29] Three basic

---

[28] Cf. ibid.

[29] The precise limits of this letter are disputed. B. D. Rahtjen, for example, sees the letter beginning at 3:1 ("The Three Letters of Paul to the Philippians," *NTS* 6 [1959-60] 167-173); Collange places the beginning at 3:1b (*Philippians* 4-6); and W. Schmithals, places it at 3:2 (*Paul & the Gnostics*, trans. J. E. Steely [Nashville: Abingdon, 1972] 67-76). The ending is likewise disputed, with suggestions including 4:1 (Beare, *Philippians* 4), 4:3 (W. Marxsen, *Introduction to the New Testament. An Approach to its Problems*, trans. G. Buswell [Philadelphia: Fortress, 1968] 60-62), 4:7 (P. Benoit, *Les épîtres de saint Paul aux Philippiens, a Philémon, aux Colossiens, aux Ephésiens* [Paris: Cerf, 1956]), and 4:9 (Rahtjen). Still others extend the letter to 4:9, but extract 4:2-7 (Collange) or 4:4-7 (Schmithals) and attach those verses to the original.

arguments have been traditionally offered in support of such an insertion: (1) that there is a drastic change in the tone from the first part of the letter; (2) that the opponents in chapter 3 differ from those in chapters 1-2; and (3) that "finally" in 3:1 suggests that the end of the letter has been reached. Additional arguments based on epistolary considerations are: (1) that τὸ λοιπόν . . . χαίρετε is a farewell formula similar to that found in 2 Cor 13:11; (2) that the position of the apostolic parousia (2:19-30) suggests that the end of the letter-body has been reached; and (3) that 3:1-4:1 does not conform to the expected paraenetic section of the "typical" Pauline letter. Issues regarding the integrity of 3:1-4:9, however, will be less in view in this study than will questions regarding relationships within the section.

Paul's opening exhortation in 3:1 is repeated with emphasis in 4:4, and one argument offered for viewing Philippians as a composite is that "verses 3:1 and 4:4 fit together so exactly that upon sober reflection one must come to the conclusion that a later hand has pulled the two verses apart."[30]

Τὸ λοιπόν, ἀδελφοί μου, χαίρετε ἐν κυρίῳ.

Χαίρετε ἐν κυρίῳ πάντοτε· πάλιν ἐρῶ, χαίρετε.

This understanding, however, is by no means certain,[31] for it demands that 3:1b be taken with what precedes it, so that τὰ αὐτὰ refers to Paul's repeated admonitions to rejoice in 1:25; 2:18; and 2:28-29.[32] Otherwise the original letter read: "Finally, my brothers, rejoice in the Lord; rejoice in the Lord always; again I will say rejoice"—which is redundant in the extreme, even for Paul. An alternate view is that Paul used a modified form of ring-composition in 4:4 to bring his listeners back to where he had broken off at 3:1.[33] Such a use of repeated wording would be in keeping with the rhetorical practices seen elsewhere in his letters.

Garland suggests that "the three insults in 3:2 are balanced chiastically by the three statements about Christians in 3:3."[34] Apart from κατατομή (3:2) and περιτομή (3:3), however, verbal parallels are absent, although the three imperatives of 3:2 are notable for their use of anaphora and homoeoarcton:

βλέπετε τοὺς κύνας,
βλέπετε τοὺς κακοὺς ἐργάτας,
βλέπετε τὴν κατατομήν.

A more likely oral construction occurs in 3:3-4:

---

[30] Schmithals, *Gnostics* 72.

[31] Hawthorne: "In reality, v 1b is quite enigmatic, and one cannot be absolutely certain about its meaning." (ibid.). Cf. Silva, *Philippians* 171; O'Brien, *Philippians* 350-352.

[32] E.g., Schmithals, *Gnostics* 71; Hawthorne, *Philippians* 124.

[33] Some proponents of Philippians as a composite letter, in fact, identify 3:2-4:3 as a unit framed by 3:1 and 4:4. Schmithals: "The thread of the epistle which is interrupted in 3:1 is again taken up abruptly in 4:4" (*Gnostics* 72).

[34] Garland, "Composition" 169.

ἡμεῖς γάρ ἐσμεν ἡ περιτομή,
οἱ πνεύματι θεοῦ λατρεύοντες καὶ καυχώμενοι ἐν Χριστῷ ᾿Ιησοῦ
καὶ οὐκ ἐν σαρκὶ πεποιθότες,
καίπερ ἐγὼ ἔχων πεποίθησιν καὶ ἐν σαρκί.
εἴ τις δοκεῖ ἄλλος πεποιθέναι ἐν σαρκί, ἐγὼ μᾶλλον·

The first line of the relative clause exhibits an example of grammatical chiasmus similar to those Jeremias discusses.[35] The second and third lines are an example of chiasmus, using πειθ- and σάρξ. The final sentence extends the word-chain to a new idea.[36]

Paul's discussion in 3:7-11 of the way in which Christ reoriented his thinking is a tightly-knit passage with numerous verbal parallels and conceptual antitheses:

ἀλλὰ ἅτινα ἦν μοι κέρδη,
ταῦτα ἥγημαι διὰ τὸν Χριστὸν ζημίαν.
ἀλλὰ μενοῦνγε καὶ ἡγοῦμαι πάντα ζημίαν εἶναι
διὰ τὸ ὑπερέχον τῆς γνώσεως Χριστοῦ ᾿Ιησοῦ τοῦ κυρίου μου,
δι᾿ ὃν τὰ πάντα ἐζημιώθην,
καὶ ἡγοῦμαι σκύβαλα
ἵνα Χριστὸν κερδήσω καὶ εὑρεθῶ ἐν αὐτῷ,
μὴ ἔχων ἐμὴν δικαιοσύνην τὴν ἐκ νόμου ἀλλὰ τὴν διὰ πίστεως Χριστοῦ,
τὴν ἐκ θεοῦ δικαιοσύνην ἐπὶ τῇ πίστει,
τοῦ γνῶναι αὐτὸν καὶ τὴν δύναμιν τῆς ἀναστάσεως αὐτοῦ
καὶ τὴν κοινωνίαν τῶν παθημάτων αὐτοῦ,
συμμορφιζόμενος τῷ θανάτῳ αὐτοῦ,
εἴ πως καταντήσω εἰς τὴν ἐξανάστασιν τὴν ἐκ νεκρῶν.

It is these parallels and antitheses that have led many scholars to propose a variety of chiastic arrangements in the passage.[37]

Yet as tempting as it might be to see a larger system at work in 3:7-11, the actual relationships in these verses are relatively modest. The antithetic parallelism of 3:7 is evident:[38]

| ἅτινα | ἦν | μοι | κέρδη, |
| ταῦτα | ἥγημαι | διὰ τὸν Χριστὸν | ζημίαν. |

Chiasmus is present in 3:8b-9a, although the homoeoteleuton of the clause is perhaps the more prominent oral feature:[39]

---

[35] Cf. Jeremias, "Chiasmus" 145-146.

[36] Hawthorne, *Philippians* 123; Schenk, *Philipperbriefe* 250; and O'Brien, *Philippians* 363, all note part of the system, but none of them extends it to 3:4.

[37] The most ambitious, encompassing 3:7-10a, is proposed by Lund; see below.

[38] Cf. O'Brien, *Philippians* 383, who notes that διὰ τὸν Χριστὸν has no parallel, "for Christ is the decisive difference" (ibid. 385).

[39] Cf. Schenk, *Philipperbriefe* 250; O'Brien *Philippians* 392.

ἵνα   Χριστὸν   κερδήσω
καὶ   εὑρεθῶ   ἐν αὐτῷ

And word-chains are clearly present: (1) three of the six uses of ἡγέομαι in Philippians occur in 3:7-8; (2) the only two uses of ζημία in Paul's letters occur in 3:7-8, while ζημιόω (3:8) occurs only twice elsewhere in Paul's letters; (3) both κερδός and κερδαίνω are relatively rare in Paul's letters;[40] and (4) the only use of ἀνάστασις in Philippians (3:10) occurs in conjunction with ἐξανάστασις (3:11)—the latter word, of course, being a hapax legomenon.

Relations within 3:10-11, however, are variously evaluated. Hawthorne and Schenk accept these verses as chiastic;[41] Jeremias, Silva, and O'Brien reject them as a chiasmus.[42] The arguments for and against a chiastic structure are evenly divided. It is sufficient here to present the suggested structure without further comment:

τοῦ γνῶναι αὐτὸν   καὶ τὴν δύναμιν τῆς <u>ἀναστάσεως</u> αὐτοῦ
                     καὶ τὴν κοινωνίαν τῶν <u>παθημάτων</u> αὐτοῦ,
                     συμμορφιζόμενος τῷ <u>θανάτῳ</u> αὐτοῦ,
                     εἰ πως καταντήσω εἰς τὴν <u>ἐξανάστασιν</u> τὴν ἐκ νεκρῶν.

The word-chain shifts in 3:12-14, with the verb καταλαμβάνω being repeated three times in a pair of sentences framed by διώκω:

οὐχ ὅτι ἤδη ἔλαβον ἢ ἤδη τετελείωμαι, <u>διώκω</u> δὲ εἰ καὶ <u>καταλάβω</u>, ἐφ' ᾧ καὶ <u>κατελήμφθην</u> ὑπὸ Χριστοῦ Ἰησοῦ. ἀδελφοί, ἐγὼ ἐμαυτὸν οὐ λογίζομαι <u>κατειληφέναι·</u> ἐν δέ, τὰ μὲν ὀπίσω ἐπιλανθανόμενος τοῖς δὲ ἔμπροσθεν ἐπεκτεινόμενος, κατὰ σκοπὸν <u>διώκω</u> εἰς τὸ βραβεῖον τῆς ἄνω κλήσεως τοῦ θεοῦ ἐν Χριστῷ Ἰησοῦ.

Paul's use of πολίτευμα in 3:20 recalls the verb πολιτεύομαι in 1:27 and is the first of three words in 3:20-4:3 that appeared in 1:27. Garland argues that these words form an inclusion that marks out 1:27-4:3 as a unit,[43] which is a suggestion more plausible than it might first appear. The words used are:

1:27	πολιτεύομαι	3:20	πολίτευμα
1:27	στήκω	4:1	στήκω
1:27	συναθλέω	4:3	συναθλέω

In letters ascribed to Paul, the πολιτευ- root appears only in these two verses and in Eph 2:12. στήκω occurs only seven times in the letters ascribed to Paul, and these

---

[40] κερδός (Phil 1:21; 3:7; Tit 1:11); κερδαίνω (Phil 3:9; 1 Cor 9:19-22 [6x])

[41] Hawthorne, *Philippians* 145; Schenk, *Philipperbriefe* 250-251.

[42] Jeremias, "Chiasmus" 147; Silva, *Philippians* 195; O'Brien, *Philippians* 407.

[43] Garland, "Composition" 160; cf. Black, "Discourse Structure" 34.

are the only two uses in Philippians. Phil 1:27 and 4:3 are the only two occurrences of συναθλέω in the NT. So this repetition of uncommon words—in the same order—is at least suggestive, especially in light of the way in which Paul frames the body of Philemon with ἀναπαύω and τὰ σπλάγχνα in verses 7 and 20.

In light of the immediately preceding discussion, and given the internal cohesiveness of 1:12-26, it is worth asking whether 1:27-4:9 should be seen as being more carefully structured than is sometimes suggested. An inclusion using ὁράω and ἀκούω confirms the limits of 1:27-30. There are no formulaic indicators in this paragraph, but the use of μόνον[44] and the change to second person exhortation suggests the start of a new section. Interestingly, the paired words ὁράω and ἀκούω also appear in 4:9, suggesting an inclusion around all of 1:27-4:9.[45]

Although second person instruction continues in 2:1, the use of οὖν marks a transition in the argument. Also distinguishing 2:1-18 from 1:27-30 is an inclusion, consisting of χαρά in 2:2 and the cognate verbs χαίρω and συγχαίρω in 2:17-18. The material of 2:1-18 is made up of three sub-sections: 2:1-4; 2:5-11; and 2:12-18. The first (2:1-4) consists of a single sentence that has as its main verb the second person imperative verb πληρώσατε. The second (2:5-11), apart from 2:5, is comprised of the Christ-hymn with its primary verbs in the indicative. This second sub-section is closely linked to the first by the repetition of φρονέω in 2:2 (twice) and 2:5. The third sub-section (2:12-18) returns to second person exhortation with its primary verbs κατεργάζεσθε and ποιεῖτε in the imperative. The use of a third person example sandwiched between two hortatory passages reflects a common practice in Paul's argumentation and is, in effect, a miniature ABA' structure.

Both Funk and White have examined the apostolic parousia of 2:19-30. It is enough here to note briefly the features they have identified: (1) the dispatch of an emissary in 2:19, 2:23, and 2:25-28; (2) the anticipation of a visit by Paul in 2:24; (3) the benefits to Paul are mentioned in 2:19 and 2:28; and (4) the benefits to the Philippians are stated in 2:28. The unusual positioning of the apostolic parousia remains to be explained. Watson suggests that this section is a *digressio* and that it uses Timothy and Epaphroditus as examples of the conduct desired.[46] Swift concurs and comments, "Timothy and Epaphroditus were worthy examples of the

---

[44] Black: "Paul opens this text-sequence with μόνον . . . a rare adverb that marks a shift from explanation to exhortation and indicates what is of central importance in the letter: Paul's fear that the community might fall away from its commitment to wholehearted allegiance to the gospel" ("Discourse Structure" 33).

[45] Although ὁράω also appears in 2:26 and 2:28 and ἀκούω also appears in 2:26, the combination of these two words appears only in 1:27; 1:30; and 4:9.

[46] Watson: "The *digressio* is the handling of some theme, which must however have some bearing on the case, in a passage that involves digression from the logical order of our speech . . . The *digressio* in Philippians . . . is also exemplification, serving to embellish, clarify, and vivify the topics used in 2:1-18" ("Rhetorical Analysis" 71).

courageous, humble, others-serving mind of Christ."[47] It seems reasonable, therefore, to view 2:19-30 as fulfilling the double function of advising the Philippians of Paul's travel plans and setting before them two examples of those who have the attitude "which was also in Christ Jesus."

Second person instruction resumes in 3:1. As in 2:1-18, 3:1-4:1 is delimited by an inclusion using χαίρω in 3:1 and χαρά in 4:1.[48] Also as in 2:1-18, 3:1-4:1 consists of three sub-sections: 3:1-4a; 3:4b-14; and 3:15-4:1. The sequence within these sub-sections is second person exhortation (3:1-4a), first person indicative example (3:4b-14), and second person imperative (3:15-4:1). Here, again, Paul uses the ABA' pattern in his argumentation. The paired request formulae in 4:2 and 4:3 suggest the start of a new section of the letter.

Pollard, Dalton, and Garland have done extensive work on the points of correspondence between 2:1-18 and 3:1-4:1.[49] It will be enough here to note the primary points of verbal correspondence between the two sections:

2:1	κοινωνία	3:10
2:2, 17-18	χαίρω, χαρά, συγχαίρω	3:1; 4:1
2:3, 8	ταπεινωφροσύνη, ταπεινόω, ταπείνωσις	3:21
2:3	ἡγέομαι	3:7, 8
2:5	τοῦτο φρονέω	3:15
2:6	ὑπάρχω	3:20
2:7	μορφή, συμμορφίζομαι, σύμμορφος	3:10, 21
2:7	εὑρίσκω	3:9
2:7	σχῆμα, μετασχηματίζω	3:21
2:8	σταυρός	3:18

Pollard summarizes the conceptual relations:[50]

> As Christ had "emptied himself" (ii.7), so Paul had been emptied of everything that, as a Jew, he had counted as his assets [iii.7-8]. As Christ gave up all pretension to equality with God (ii.7), so Paul had been despoiled of all pretension to a right relationship with God (iii.9). As Christ was exalted by God (ii.9-11), so Paul hopes that he will receive the exaltation of "resurrection from the dead" (iii.11).

The preceding analysis suggests an ABA' arrangement in 2:1-4:1 that may be outlined as follows:

A		Exhortation to a right attitude		2:1-18
	a	Challenge to a right attitude	2:1-4	
	b	Christ as the example	2:5-11	
	a'	Exhortation to respond properly	2:12-18	

---

[47] R. C. Swift, "The Theme and Structure of Philippians," *BSac* 141 (1984) 246.

[48] An alternate approach would be to see χαίρετε in 4:4 as marking the end of the section.

[49] Pollard, "Integrity" 62-65; Dalton, "Integrity" 99-100; Garland, "Composition" 157-159.

[50] Pollard, "Integrity" 62.

B	Two examples (Apostolic Parousia)		2:19-30
A'	Exhortation to a right perspective		3:1-4:1
	a Challenge to a right perspective	3:1-4a	
	b Paul as the example	3:4b-14	
	a' Exhortation to respond properly	3:15-4:1	

Furthermore, the repetition of συναθλέω (1:27; 4:3), εὐαγγέλιον (1:27; 4:3), and ὁράω . . . ἀκούω (1:27, 30; 4:9) suggest a possible parallel between 1:27-30 and 4:2-9. This latter suggestion is somewhat more tentative because πολίτευμα and στήκω appear in 3:20 and 4:1 respectively, rather than in 4:2-9.

Schubert was the first to note the important verbal parallels between the opening thanksgiving (1:3-11) and the closing note of thanks (4:10-20).[51] The clearest points of verbal correspondence are:[52]

1:4	χαρά, χαίρω	4:10
1:5	κοινωνία, κοινωνέω	4:15
1:5, 7	εὐαγγέλιον	4:15
1:7	συγκοινωνός, συγκοινωνέω	4:14
1:7	φρονέω . . . ὑπέρ	4:10
1:9	περισσεύω	4:12
1:11	καρπός	4:17
1:11	δόξα	4:19, 20

Within 4:10-20 the only readily-apparent oral pattern is alternation in 4:12:[53]

A	. . . καὶ ταπεινοῦσθαι,
B	. . . καὶ περισσεύειν·
B	. . . καὶ χορτάζεσθαι
A	καὶ πεινᾶν,
B	καὶ περισσεύειν
A	καὶ ὑστερεῖσθαι.

C. Other Suggested Structures

Although it was Welch's conclusion that Philippians "contains no overall chiastic structure,"[54] Luter and Lee have proposed a chiastic outline for the letter:[55]

---

[51] Schubert, *Thanksgiving* 77; cf. Jewett, "Thanksgiving" 53; Dalton, "Integrity" 101; Black, "Discourse Structure" 24.

[52] Another commonly-cited parallel is ἀπὸ τῆς πρώτης ἡμέρας (1:5) with ἐν ἀρχῇ τοῦ εὐαγγελίου (4:15).

[53] Cf. Jeremias, "Chiasmus" 146.

[54] Welch, "Chiasmus" 226. He continues: "Shorter chiastic patterns, of course, may be observed . . . but these structures are for the most part relatively insignificant and unremarkable" (ibid.).

[55] Luter and Lee, "Philippians as Chiasmus" 92.

	(1:1-2) Opening Greetings	
A	(1:3-11) Prologue	(κοινωνία, συγκοινωνός)
B	(1:12-26) Comfort/Example	(δέησις)
C	(1:27-2:4) Challenge	(συναθλέω, παράκλησις, στήκω)
D	(2:5-16) Example/Action	(τοῦτο φρονεῖτε)
E	(2:17-3:1a) Midpoint	
D'	(3:1b-21) Example/Action	(τοῦτο φρονῶμεν)
C'	(4:1-5) Challenge	(συναθλέω, παρακαλέω, στήκω)
B'	(4:6-9) Comfort/Example	(δέησις)
A'	(4:10-20) Epilogue	(κοινωνέω, συγκοινωνέω)
	(4:21-23) Closing Greetings	

This arrangement has much to commend it, especially the recognition of the points of verbal correspondence. Also to be commended is the authors' use of Blomberg's criteria in evaluating their proposed outline. This scheme has much in common with what was proposed above for 1:27-4:9 (although it divides the text differently). As well, it highlights the parallels between 1:3-11 and 4:10-20, as have just been noted.

The weak point in Luter and Lee's outline is the way in which they handle 4:1-9 (elements B' and C'), for there is nothing in the text to suggest that a major break occurs at verse 6. Stronger candidates for such a break are to be found at 4:4 (χαίρετε ἐν κυρίῳ πάντοτε· πάλιν ἐρῶ, χαίρετε) and at 4:8 (τὸ λοιπόν, ἀδελφοί). Furthermore, the proposed outline fails to address the possible inclusion created by the presence of ὁράω and ἀκούω in both 1:27 and 4:9.

The sole verbal parallel between B (1:12-26) and B' (4:6-9) is the word δέησις. Luter and Lee, however, propose another point of correspondence:[56]

> Perhaps Paul's time in prison gave him the idea of having the peace of God 'guard' (φρουρέω; i.e., in a military or custodial manner) their hearts and minds (4.7), since he was constantly aware of the presence of the guards attached to the Praetorium where he was being held (1.13).

The military terminology found within Philippians has been discussed at length by Gioffrion,[57] and the fact that Paul was under military guard undoubtedly had an influence on his use of φρουρέω. It is questionable, however, whether the presence of this verb in 4:7 is an adequate basis for proposing that 1:12-26 is parallel to 4:6-9.

It may be noted in passing that 4:6-9 actually has stronger verbal connections to 1:3-11 than to 1:12-26, for not only does δέησις appear twice in 1:4, but the only uses in Philippians of ἔπαινος are in 1:11 and 4:8. As well, the verb εὐχαριστέω occurs in 1:3, while the noun εὐχαριστία occurs in 4:8. Similarly, the verb προσεύχομαι appears in 1:9 and the noun προσευχή in 4:6.

---

[56] Ibid. 93.

[57] Gioffrion, *Rhetorical Purpose*.

The internal structure of 1:27-4:9 is symmetrically centered around 2:19-30. The parallels between 1:3-11 and 4:10-20 are readily apparent. Yet as tempting as it may be to seek a way in which 1:12-26 can be worked into an overall "chiastic" structure, it is probably best to acknowledge that this "apostolic apologia" has no parallel later in the letter.

Ellis has proposed an overall ABA' structure for Philippians:[58]

A	(1:1-3:1) Spreading the gospel and growth in Christ
a	Fighting the good fight for the sake of the gospel (1:1-30)
b	Life in Christ (2:1-18)
a'	Fighting the good fight for the sake of the gospel (2:19-3:1)
B	(3:2-16) Apparent digression: Growth in Christ depends on faith in Christ and not on observance of the law
A'	(3:17-4:23) Spreading the gospel and growth in Christ

Ellis supports his proposal by noting that the "parallels between A and A' are numerous and, we believe, intentional."[59] In particular, he calls attention to the following items: (1) κοινωνία in 1:5 and 4:15; (2) "at the day of Christ" (1:6,10; 3:20; 4:5); (3) πολιτευ- cognates in 1:27 and 3:20; (4) τοῦτο φρονέω in 2:5 and 4:2; (5) the sending of Epaphroditus (2:25 and 4:18); (6) the reference to the Philippians as "saints" (1:2 and 4:21-22); (7) the reference to "sacrifice" (2:17 and 4:18b); and (8) exhortations in both sections to "rejoice in the Lord."

These parallels, however, vary in significance. Three of the first four items (#1, 3, 4) have been noted in the discussion above. The references to the "day of Christ" (#2) are not equivalent. The first two (1:6, 10) use the words ἡμέρα and Χριστός; those in 3:20 and 4:5 are allusions to the event, but they do not use the actual phrase "day of Christ." The references to Epaphroditus (#5) differ in their content: the first refers to Paul's sending of Epaphroditus *to* Philippi; the second to the gift Paul received *from* Philippi when Epaphroditus arrived. Since Paul consistently refers to Christians as "saints" and since the salutation and closing of letters commonly used similar language, the parallel between 1:2 and 4:21-22 (#6) cannot be given much weight. The references to "sacrifice" in 2:17 and 4:18b (#7) both use the word θυσία, which is relatively rare in Paul's letters.[60] The repeated use of χαρά, χαίρω, and συγχαίρω in the letter dilute the value of the eighth parallel.

Clearly, Ellis's scheme is more general than that proposed by Luter and Lee, and that generality is its greatest weakness, for he fails to give adequate attention to the epistolary and textlinguistic aspects of the letter. Furthermore, his titles for

---

[58] Ellis, *Letters* 117.

[59] Ibid.

[60] Elsewhere only in Rom 12:1 and 1 Cor 10:18.

various portions of the outline could just as easily be applied to any other Pauline letter.

A number of scholars have proposed chiastic structures for the Christ-hymn of 2:6-11. The similarities between them make it possible to examine the arrangements together. Bligh, for example, proposes a series of four " overlapping chiasms," in which the last clause of each chiasm is used as the beginning of the next:[61]

A	ὃς ἐν μορφῇ θεοῦ ὑπάρχων
B	οὐχ ἁρπαγμὸν ἡγήσατο
C	τὸ εἶναι ἴσα θεῷ,
B'	ἀλλὰ ἑαυτὸν ἐκένωσεν
A'	μορφὴν δούλου λαβών,

D	ἑαυτὸν
E	ἐκένωσεν
F	μορφὴν δούλου λαβών,
G	ἐν ὁμοιώματι ἀνθρώπων γενόμενος·
F'	καὶ σχήματι εὑρεθεὶς ὡς ἄνθρωπος
E'	ἐταπείνωσεν
D'	ἑαυτὸν

H	ἐταπείνωσεν
I	ἑαυτὸν
J	γενόμενος ὑπήκοος
K	μέχρι θανάτου,
K'	θανάτου δὲ σταυροῦ.
J'	διὸ καὶ
I'	ὁ θεὸς αὐτὸν
H'	ὑπερύψωσεν

L	διὸ καὶ ὁ θεὸς αὐτὸν ὑπερύψωσεν
M	καὶ ἐχαρίσατο αὐτῷ τὸ ὄνομα τὸ ὑπὲρ πᾶν ὄνομα,
N	ἵνα ἐν τῷ ὀνόματι Ἰησοῦ πᾶν γόνυ κάμψῃ ἐπουρανίων
O	καὶ ἐπιγείων καὶ καταχθονίων,
N'	καὶ πᾶσα γλῶσσα ἐξομολογήσηται
M'	ὅτι κύριος Ἰησοῦς Χριστὸς
L'	εἰς δόξαν θεοῦ πατρός.

Frédéric Manns has proposed three chiastically arranged strophes. His first and third strophes are virtually identical to those of Bligh, but the center section differs:[62]

---

[61] J. Bligh, "Review of R. P. Martin, *Carmen Christi, Philippians ii.5-11 in Recent Interpretation and in the Setting of Early Christian Worship*," *Bib* 49 (1968) 127-129.

[62] F. Manns, "Un hymne judéo-chrétien: Philippiens 2,6-11," *Euntes Docete* 29 (1976) 259-290.

a	ὃς ἐν μορφῇ θεοῦ ὑπάρχων	2:6
b	οὐχ ἁρπαγμὸν ἡγήσατο	
c	τὸ εἶναι ἴσα θεῷ,	
b'	ἀλλὰ ἑαυτὸν ἐκένωσεν	2:7
a'	μορφὴν δούλου λαβών,	

a	ἐν ὁμοιώματι ἀνθρώπων γενόμενος·	
b	καὶ σχήματι εὑρεθεὶς ὡς ἄνθρωπος	
c	ἐταπείνωσεν ἑαυτὸν	2:8
b'	γενόμενος ὑπήκοος μέχρι θανάτου,	
a'	θανάτου δὲ σταυροῦ.	

a	διὸ καὶ ὁ θεὸς αὐτὸν ὑπερύψωσεν	2:9
b	καὶ ἐχαρίσατο αὐτῷ τὸ ὄνομα τὸ ὑπὲρ πᾶν ὄνομα,	
c	ἵνα ἐν τῷ ὀνόματι Ἰησοῦ πᾶν γόνυ κάμψῃ	2:10
d	ἐπουρανίων καὶ ἐπιγείων καὶ καταχθονίων,	
c'	καὶ πᾶσα γλῶσσα ἐξομολογήσηται	2:11
b'	ὅτι κύριος Ἰησοῦς Χριστὸς	
a'	εἰς δόξαν θεοῦ πατρός.	

Morna Hooker arrives at line divisions very similar to those of Manns, although she groups them differently.[63] She suggests that the macro-structure is "chiastic":[64]

A six-line statement about Christ's *kenosis* in becoming a man is followed by a four-line section continuing this theme in terms of his earthly life. The second part of the 'hymn' reverses the form as well as the theme; a four-line statement of Christ's exaltation and receipt of the Name is followed by a six-line expansion of this theme.

Her scanning of the hymn is as follows:

ὃς ἐν μορφῇ θεοῦ ὑπάρχων
οὐχ ἁρπαγμὸν ἡγήσατο
τὸ εἶναι ἴσα θεῷ,
ἀλλὰ ἑαυτὸν ἐκένωσεν
μορφὴν δούλου λαβών,
ἐν ὁμοιώματι ἀνθρώπων γενόμενος·

καὶ σχήματι εὑρεθεὶς ὡς ἄνθρωπος
ἐταπείνωσεν ἑαυτὸν
γενόμενος ὑπήκοος μέχρι θανάτου,
θανάτου δὲ σταυροῦ.

---

[63] M. Hooker, "Philippians 2:6-11" in *Jesus und Paulus: Festscrift für Werner Georg Kümmel zum 70. Geburtstag*, ed. E. E. Ellis and E. Grässer (Göttingen: Vandenhoeck & Ruprecht, 1978) 158. The primary differences are in 2:9-10a.

[64] Ibid. 159. Using the terms defined in Chapter 5 of this study, her ABBA macro-analysis would be an instance of inversion.

διὸ καὶ ὁ θεὸς
αὐτὸν ὑπερύψωσεν
καὶ ἐχαρίσατο αὐτῷ τὸ ὄνομα
τὸ ὑπὲρ πᾶν ὄνομα,

ἵνα ἐν τῷ ὀνόματι ᾿Ιησοῦ
πᾶν γόνυ κάμψῃ
ἐπουρανίων καὶ ἐπιγείων καὶ καταχθονίων,
καὶ πᾶσα γλῶσσα ἐξομολογήσηται
ὅτι κύριος ᾿Ιησοῦς Χριστὸς
εἰς δόξαν θεοῦ πατρός.

Hooker's explanation, however, is fairly general, and it reads more nearly as an afterthought to her primary concern: the poetic form of the hymn. Her suggested "chiastic" arrangement, therefore, may be set aside without further comment.

The fact that both Bligh and Mann have analyzed 2:9-11 in the same way is suggestive. The conceptual parallel between πᾶν γόνυ κάμψῃ and πᾶσα γλῶσσα ἐξομολογήσηται is strong and is reinforced by the repetition of πᾶς. The proposed parallel between τὸ ὄνομα τὸ ὑπερ πᾶν ὄνομα and ὅτι κύριος ᾿Ιησοῦς Χριστὸς, however, lacks points of verbal correspondence, although the explanation behind it is probably that "Lord Jesus Christ" is the "name above every name."

Wolfgang Schenk has proposed what seems to be a more natural understanding of the structure of 2:9-11 in that the actual names of Jesus are set parallel:[65]

ἵνα ἐν τῷ ὀνόματι ᾿Ιησοῦ
πᾶν γόνυ κάμψῃ . . .
καὶ πᾶσα γλῶσσα ἐξομολογήσηται
ὅτι κύριος ᾿Ιησοῦς Χριστὸς . . .

The outer lines of the arrangements proposed by Bligh, Mann, and Schenk have a point of verbal correspondence in their use of θεός, but the ideas expressed in the two lines, however, are quite different. The best comment Bligh can offer is: "Since the Father glorifies Christ (L), his glorification is no infringement of the Father's honour (L')."[66]

It is also interesting that Bligh and Manns have arranged 2:6-7a similarly. This arrangement relies on the presence of μορφή in the first and last lines. Unfortunately, the suggested parallel between οὐχ ἁρπαγμὸν ἡγήσατο and ἀλλὰ ἑαυτὸν ἐκένωσεν leaves τὸ εἶναι ἴσα θεῷ "hanging." It would probably have been more natural to leave the entire thought (οὐχ ἁρπαγμὸν ἡγήσατο τὸ εἶναι ἴσα θεῷ) together.

---

[65] Schenk, *Philipperbriefe* 190.

[66] Bligh, "Review" 128.

The center section of the hymn in 2:7b-8 creates the greatest problems for both Bligh and Manns. Bligh is forced to resort to interlocking chiasms that divide the text differently depending on the relations he is trying to establish (e.g., J'-H' vs. L), with such proposed chiasms resulting in forced parallels (e.g., J and J'). Neither of the parallels in Manns's scheme is readily apparent. The arrangement suggested earlier in this study is at least as persuasive, given the verbal parallels that it acknowledges:

ἀλλὰ <u>ἑαυτὸν ἐκένωσεν</u> μορφὴν δούλου λαβών,
ἐν <u>ὁμοιώματι ἀνθρώπων</u> γενόμενος·
καὶ <u>σχήματι</u> εὑρεθεὶς ὡς <u>ἄνθρωπος</u>
<u>ἐταπείνωσεν ἑαυτὸν</u> γενόμενος ὑπήκοος μέχρι θανάτου . . .

There is clearly something special about Phil 2:6-11. The question as to whether it is possible to establish a "definitive" arrangement of these verses is, perhaps, unanswerable. In any case, it goes beyond the concerns of the present study.

Lund has proposed three extended arrangements within Philippians. The first is that of 2:1-11:[67]

εἴ τις οὖν παράκλησις ἐν Χριστῷ,   2:1
εἴ τι παραμύθιον ἀγάπης,
εἴ τις κοινωνία πνεύματος,
εἴ τις σπλάγχνα καὶ οἰκτιρμοί, πληρώσατέ μου τὴν χαρὰν   2:2

     ἵνα τὸ αὐτὸ φρονῆτε,
A   τὴν αὐτὴν ἀγάπην ἔχοντες, σύμψυχοι,
     τὸ ἓν φρονοῦντες,

μηδὲν κατ' ἐριθείαν μηδὲ κατὰ κενοδοξίαν,   2:3
ἀλλὰ τῇ ταπεινοφροσύνῃ ἀλλήλους ἡγούμενοι ὑπερέχοντας ἑαυτῶν,
μὴ τὰ ἑαυτῶν ἕκαστος σκοποῦντες, ἀλλὰ καὶ τὰ ἑτέρων ἕκαστοι.   2:4
τοῦτο φρονεῖτε ἐν ὑμῖν ὃ καὶ ἐν Χριστῷ ᾿Ιησοῦ,   2:5

ὃς ἐν μορφῇ θεοῦ ὑπάρχων   2:6
οὐχ ἁρπαγμὸν ἡγήσατο τὸ εἶναι ἴσα θεῷ,
ἀλλὰ ἑαυτὸν   2:7
ἐκένωσεν

     μορφὴν δούλου λαβών,
B   ἐν ὁμοιώματι ἀνθρώπων γενόμενος·
     καὶ σχήματι εὑρεθεὶς ὡς ἄνθρωπος

ἐταπείνωσεν   2:8
ἑαυτὸν
γενόμενος ὑπήκοος μέχρι θανάτου,
θανάτου δὲ σταυροῦ.

---

[67] Lund, *Chiasmus* 216. Lund's original scheme is printed in English. This representation uses the UBS Greek text.

διὸ καὶ ὁ θεὸς αὐτὸν ὑπερύψωσεν   2:9

   καὶ ἐχαρίσατο αὐτῷ   τὸ ὄνομα
                             τὸ ὑπὲρ πᾶν ὄνομα,
                             ἵνα ἐν τῷ ὀνόματι Ἰησοῦ   2:10

        πᾶν γόνυ κάμψῃ
        ἐπουρανίων
C   καὶ ἐπιγείων
        καὶ καταχθονίων,
        καὶ πᾶσα γλῶσσα ἐξομολογήσηται

    ὅτι   κύριος   2:11
          Ἰησοῦς
          Χριστὸς

εἰς δόξαν θεοῦ πατρός.

Much of what has been said in the examination of other schemes for 2:6-11 also applies to Lund's arrangement of these verses, and so comments here will be limited to his analysis of 2:1-5. First, the "central triplet" of A actually consists of four elements rather than the three shown. Second, it is difficult to see how σπλάγχνα καὶ οἰκτιρμοί is "antithetical" to κατ' ἐριθείαν μηδὲ κατὰ κενοδοξίαν, except in the general sense that virtues are antithetical to vices. Third, the way in which ἀλλὰ τῇ ταπεινοφροσύνῃ ἀλλήλους ἡγούμενοι ὑπερέχοντας ἑαυτῶν (the suggested parallel to κοινωνία πνεύματος) "mention[s] and describe[s] "fellowship"[68] is unclear. Fourth, "love" could be so defined as to be exemplified in nearly any positive action and does not represent a specific parallel to μὴ τὰ ἑαυτῶν ἕκαστος σκοποῦντες, ἀλλὰ καὶ τὰ ἑτέρων ἕκαστοι. Fifth, verse 5 seems to relate more naturally to what follows (2:6-11) than to what precedes (2:1-4). All in all, Lund's arrangement has little to do with oral patterning, and Black's understanding of 2:1-4 has more to commend it.[69]

Lund presents a similar arrangement for 2:12-18:[70]

ὥστε, ἀγαπητοί μου, καθὼς πάντοτε ὑπηκούσατε,   2:12

μὴ ὡς ἐν τῇ παρουσίᾳ μου μόνον
ἀλλὰ νῦν πολλῷ μᾶλλον ἐν τῇ ἀπουσίᾳ μου,
  μετὰ φόβου
  καὶ τρόμου
    τὴν ἑαυτῶν σωτηρίαν
    κατεργάζεσθε·

---

[68] Ibid. 217.

[69] See note 20 above.

[70] Lund, *Chiasmus* 221.

A	θεὸς γάρ ἐστιν	2:13
	ὁ ἐνεργῶν	
	ἐν ὑμῖν	
	καὶ τὸ θέλειν	
	καὶ τὸ ἐνεργεῖν ὑπὲρ τῆς εὐδοκίας.	
	πάντα ποιεῖτε χωρὶς γογγυσμῶν	2:14
	καὶ διαλογισμῶν,	
	ἵνα γένησθε ἄμεμπτοι	2:15
	καὶ ἀκέραιοι,	
	τέκνα θεοῦ	
	ἄμωμα	
B	μέσον γενεᾶς	
	σκολιᾶς	
	καὶ διεστραμμένης,	
	ἐν οἷς φαίνεσθε ὡς φωστῆρες ἐν κόσμῳ,	
	λόγον ζωῆς ἐπέχοντες,	2:16
	εἰς καύχημα ἐμοὶ	
	εἰς ἡμέραν Χριστοῦ,	
	ὅτι οὐκ εἰς κενὸν ἔδραμον	
	οὐδὲ εἰς κενὸν ἐκοπίασα.	
A'	ἀλλὰ εἰ καὶ σπένδομαι	2:17
	ἐπὶ τῇ θυσίᾳ	
	καὶ λειτουργίᾳ τῆς πίστεως ὑμῶν,	
	χαίρω καὶ συγχαίρω πᾶσιν ὑμῖν·	
	τὸ δὲ αὐτὸ καὶ ὑμεῖς χαίρετε καὶ συγχαίρετέ μοι.	2:18

Again, however, points of verbal correspondence and/or acoustic resonance are virtually absent from Lund's arrangement, and so comments here will be limited to several salient issues. First, the proposed arrangement does not handle well the basic text divisions (2:12-13; 2:14-16; 2:17-18).[71] Second, the parallels suggested are rather general (e.g., obedience to Paul; different frames of mind), without points of verbal correspondence. Third, as is frequently the case with Lund's outlines, it does not handle well the basic grammatical/syntactical units within the text. For example, the threefold division of 2:13a seems unnecessary: θεὸς γάρ ἐστιν / ὁ ἐνεργῶν / ἐν ὑμῖν. Fourth, the analysis of the central five lines of A as being "plainly chiastic"[72] is, perhaps, more of a reflection of the analytical processes of a literate culture than of the spontaneous "gestures" (to use Jousse's term) of an

---

[71] Even so, an alternate handling of 2:12b-2:14a would be just as apt:
μετὰ φόβου καὶ τρόμου
τὴν ἑαυτῶν σωτηρίαν κατεργάζεσθε·
θεὸς γάρ ἐστιν ὁ ἐνεργῶν ἐν ὑμῖν ...
πάντα ποιεῖτε
χωρὶς γογγυσμῶν καὶ διαλογισμῶν

[72] Lund, *Chiasmus* 221.

oral/rhetorical culture. "Plainly chiastic" in an oral/rhetorical culture would more likely be:

> τὴν ἑαυτῶν σωτηρίαν κατεργάζεσθε·
> θεὸς γάρ ἐνεργεῖ αὐτήν ἐν ὑμῖν.

The difference is subtle, but marked—and is the factor that weighs most heavily against many of Lund's analyses.

Lund's third arrangement encompasses 3:7-10a:[73]

	ἀλλὰ <u>ἄτινα</u> ἦν μοι κέρδη, ταῦτα <u>ἥγημαι</u>	3:7
	διὰ τὸν Χριστὸν	
	ζημίαν.	
A	ἀλλὰ μενοῦνγε καὶ <u>ἡγοῦμαι πάντα</u>	3:8
	ζημίαν εἶναι	
	διὰ τὸ ὑπερέχον τῆς γνώσεως Χριστοῦ ᾿Ιησοῦ τοῦ κυρίου μου,	
	δι᾿ ὃν τὰ <u>πάντα</u> ἐζημιώθην, καὶ <u>ἡγοῦμαι</u> σκύβαλα	
	ἵνα <u>Χριστὸν</u> κερδήσω καὶ εὑρεθῶ ἐν αὐτῷ,	3:9
	μὴ ἔχων ἐμὴν	
	δικαιοσύνην	
	τὴν ἐκ νόμου	
B	ἀλλὰ τὴν διὰ πίστεως <u>Χριστοῦ</u>,	
	τὴν ἐκ θεοῦ	
	δικαιοσύνην	
	ἐπὶ τῇ πίστει,	
	τοῦ γνῶναι <u>αὐτὸν</u> καὶ τὴν δύναμιν τῆς ἀναστάσεως αὐτοῦ	3:10

Here the possibilities are more promising because of the multiple occurrences of ἡγέομαι, ζημία, and δικαιοσύνη.

Lund's proposed structure, however, suffers from inconsistent divisions of the text. Why, for example, is ἀλλὰ ἄτινα ἦν μοι κέρδη, ταῦτα ἥγημαι kept together, while διὰ τὸν Χριστὸν is treated as a separate element and the single word ζημίαν treated as a third element?[74] Or why is μὴ ἔχων ἐμὴν separated from δικαιοσύνην? Rightly or wrongly, it is easy to draw the conclusion that the text has been divided in order to *create* rather than to *reflect* parallels. Another problem is the fact that verse 10a seems to go more naturally with what follows than with what precedes.[75] A further consideration is the potential parallel between κερδός and κερδαίνω, words that are relatively rare in Paul's letters.

---

[73] Lund, *Chiasmus* 218

[74] Especially when δι᾿ ὃν τὰ πάντα ἐζημιώθην, καὶ ἡγοῦμαι σκύβαλα is kept together as a single element.

[75] See the discussion of 3:10-11 above.

Schenk has suggested the following understanding of 3:8b-9:[76]

ἵνα
Χριστὸν
 κερδήσω
 καὶ
 εὑρεθῶ
 ἐν αὐτῷ,
 μὴ ἔχων ἐμὴν
 δικαιοσύνην
 τὴν ἐκ νόμου
 ἀλλὰ τὴν διὰ πίστεως Χριστοῦ,
 τὴν ἐκ θεοῦ
 δικαιοσύνην
 ἐπὶ τῇ πίστει,

This arrangement, however, seems overly complex, and can be reduced to the following basic elements:

Χριστὸν   κερδήσω
εὑρεθῶ   ἐν αὐτῷ,

ἐμὴν   δικαιοσύνην τὴν ἐκ νόμου
τὴν ἐκ θεοῦ δικαιοσύνην ἐπὶ τῇ πίστει,

With these insights taken into consideration, and with the entirety of 3:10-11 included, a more likely arrangement for 3:7-11 might be:

ἀλλὰ ἅτινα ἦν μοι <u>κέρδη</u>,
 ταῦτα <u>ἥγημαι</u> διὰ τὸν Χριστὸν <u>ζημίαν</u>.
  ἀλλὰ μενοῦνγε καὶ <u>ἡγοῦμαι πάντα ζημίαν εἶναι</u>
   διὰ τὸ ὑπερέχον τῆς γνώσεως Χριστοῦ Ἰησοῦ τοῦ κυρίου μου,
   δι᾽ ὃν <u>τὰ πάντα ἐζημιώθην</u>,
  καὶ <u>ἡγοῦμαι σκύβαλα</u>
 ἵνα Χριστὸν <u>κερδήσω</u>
 καὶ εὑρεθῶ ἐν αὐτῷ,
 μὴ ἔχων ἐμὴν <u>δικαιοσύνην</u> τὴν ἐκ νόμου
  ἀλλὰ τὴν διὰ πίστεως Χριστοῦ,
 τὴν ἐκ θεοῦ <u>δικαιοσύνην</u> ἐπὶ τῇ πίστει,
 τοῦ γνῶναι αὐτὸν καὶ τὴν δύναμιν τῆς <u>ἀναστάσεως</u> αὐτοῦ
 καὶ τὴν κοινωνίαν τῶν <u>παθημάτων</u> αὐτοῦ,
 συμμορφιζόμενος τῷ <u>θανάτῳ</u> αὐτοῦ,
 εἴ πως καταντήσω εἰς τὴν <u>ἐξανάστασιν</u> τὴν ἐκ νεκρῶν.

Admittedly, this arrangement does not have the tidy symmetry of Lund's. It does, however, recognize the verbal parallels in the passage, and it makes an effort to work with such conceptual parallels as are present.

---

[76] Schenk, *Philipperbriefe* 250. Cf. Silva, *Philippians* 185; O'Brien *Philippians* 394.

John Reumann has suggested the following arrangement of 3:20-21:[77]

ἡμῶν γὰρ τὸ πολίτευμα ἐν οὐρανοῖς ὑπάρχει,
  ἐξ οὗ καὶ σωτῆρα ἀπεκδεχόμεθα κύριον Ἰησοῦν Χριστόν,
    ὃς μετασχηματίσει τὸ σῶμα τῆς ταπεινώσεως ἡμῶν
    σύμμορφον τῷ σώματι τῆς δόξης αὐτοῦ
      κατὰ τὴν ἐνέργειαν τοῦ δύνασθαι αὐτὸν
      καὶ ὑποτάξαι αὐτῷ τὰ πάντα.

He argues that "its couplets exhibit a chiasmus, each line leading on to the next, moving from the heavens above to the parousia thence of Christ, then to his transforming action at the parousia, by analogy with what he has already experienced in his own body; the last two lines expand the horizon by moving back to Christ's active and potential power and the cosmic scope of his present and final work."[78]

This explanation is intriguing, but it is not readily apparent. The only verbal parallel present is the repetition of σῶμα, a repetition only to be expected in the transformation motif that Paul uses. A more natural arrangement is the "possible original form" Reumann suggests elsewhere in his article:[79]

ἡμῶν γὰρ τὸ πολίτευμα ἐν οὐρανοῖς ὑπάρχει,
  ἐξ οὗ καὶ σωτῆρα ἀπεκδεχόμεθα κύριον Ἰησοῦν Χριστόν,
  ὃς μετασχηματίσει τὸ σῶμα τῆς ταπεινώσεως ἡμῶν
  σύμμορφον τῷ σώματι τῆς δόξης αὐτοῦ
  κατὰ τὴν ἐνέργειαν τοῦ δύνασθαι αὐτὸν
    καὶ ὑποτάξαι αὐτῷ τὰ πάντα.

Schenk has identified a series of possible small-scale structures throughout Philippians. In general, these structures reflect literate analysis rather than oral/rhetorical composition. There are few verbal parallels, and the other parallels are often strained. They will be presented without further comment.

διὰ   1:19
  τῆς ὑμῶν
    δεήσεως
    καὶ
    ἐπιχορηγίας
  τοῦ πνεύματος

μενῶ   1:25-26
  καὶ παραμενῶ πᾶσιν ὑμῖν
    εἰς τὴν ὑμῶν προκοπὴν
    καὶ χαρὰν τῆς πίστεως,

---

[77] J. Reumann, "Philippians 3.20-21—A Hymnic Fragment?," *NTS* 30 (1984) 604.

[78] Ibid.

[79] Ibid. 598.

ἵνα τὸ καύχημα ὑμῶν
περισσεύῃ ἐν Χριστῷ ᾿Ιησοῦ
ἐν ἐμοὶ
διὰ τῆς ἐμῆς παρουσίας πάλιν πρὸς ὑμᾶς.

διὰ τὸ ἔργον Χριστοῦ   2:30
μέχρι θανάτου ἤγγισεν,
παραβολευσάμενος τῇ ψυχῇ
ἵνα ἀναπληρώσῃ τὸ ὑμῶν ὑστέρημα τῆς πρός με λειτουργίας.

τὸν πλεονάζοντα εἰς λόγον ὑμῶν.   4:17-18
ἀπέχω δε πάντα
    καὶ περισσεύω·
    πεπλήρωμαι
δεξάμενος παρὰ ᾿επαφροδίτου τὰ παρ᾿ ὑμῶν,
ὀσμὴν εὐωδίας, θυσίαν δεκτήν, εὐάρεστον τῷ θεῷ.

ὁ δὲ θεός μου   4:19
πληρώσει
    πᾶσαν χρείαν ὑμῶν
    κατὰ τὸ πλοῦτος αὐτοῦ
ἐν δόξῃ
ἐν Χριστῷ ᾿Ιησοῦ.

ἀσπάσασθε πάντα ἅγιον ἐν Χριστῷ ᾿Ιησοῦ.   4:21-23
ἀσπάζονται ὑμᾶς οἱ σὺν ἐμοὶ ἀδελφοί.
ἀσπάζονται ὑμᾶς πάντες οἱ ἅγιοι . . .
ἡ χάρις τοῦ κυρίου ᾿Ιησοῦ Χριστοῦ μετὰ τοῦ πνεύματος ὑμῶν.

Finally, Schenk has also suggested a concentric structure for 2:19-24:[80]

a   ἐλπίζω δὲ ἐν κυρίῳ ᾿Ιησοῦ Τιμόθεον ταχέως πέμψαι ὑμῖν,
        ἵνα κἀγὼ εὐψυχῶ γνοὺς τὰ περὶ ὑμῶν.

b   οὐδένα γὰρ ἔχω ἰσόψυχον ὅστις γνησίως τὰ περὶ ὑμῶν
        μεριμνήσει,

c   οἱ πάντες γὰρ τὰ ἑαυτῶν ζητοῦσιν, οὐ τὰ ᾿Ιησοῦ Χριστοῦ.

b'   τὴν δὲ δοκιμὴν αὐτοῦ γινώσκετε, ὅτι ὡς πατρὶ τέκνον σὺν
        ἐμοὶ ἐδούλευσεν εἰς τὸ εὐαγγέλιον.

a'   τοῦτον μὲν οὖν ἐλπίζω πέμψαι ὡς ἂν ἀφίδω τὰ περὶ ἐμὲ
        ἐξαυτῆς· πέποιθα δὲ ἐν κυρίῳ ὅτι καὶ αὐτὸς ταχέως
        ἐλεύσομαι.

---

[80] Schenk, *Philipperbriefe* 234.

As noted above, this paragraph is framed by the repetition of ἐλπίζω . . . ταχέως
. . . πέμψαι in 2:19 and 2:24. There are, however, no verbal parallels in 2:20-22,
and it is unlikely that this structure would have been readily apparent to the ear.

D. Summary

Oral patterns in Philippians are plentiful. Instances of chiasmus occur in 1:27;
3:3-4; 3:8-9; and 3:10-11. Inclusion brackets 1:12-26; 1:27-30; 2:1-18; 2:19-24;
2:25-30; 3:12-14; and 3:1-4:1. Alternation occurs in 1:15-17; 1:21-24; and 4:12.
Ring-composition reinforces the unity of 2:19-24 and 3:1-4:4. An ABA' structure on
the macro-scale occurs in 2:1-4:1, while 2:1-18 and 3:1-4:1 exhibit ABA'
argumentation. Micro-scale examples of inversion occur in 1:3-5; 1:27; 2:7-8; and
2:12; a larger inverted structure is present in 2:25-30. Word-chains are present in
1:3-8; 3:7-11; and 3:12-14. Although it is possible that the central portion of the letter
follows an ABA' pattern, the attempt to find an overall "chiastic" structure to the
letter cannot be sustained.

Chapter 11

1 THESSALONIANS

It is generally accepted that Paul wrote 1 Thessalonians from Corinth early in his missionary career. The letter is commonly dated c. A.D. 50, although Lüdemann's revised chronology would place it considerably earlier.[1] The integrity of 1 Thessalonians is generally accepted, with the exception of 2:13-16, which is often viewed as a non-Pauline interpolation.[2] Additional discussion has centered around the sequence of the letters, with a number of scholars arguing that 2 Thessalonians preceded 1 Thessalonians.[3]

The overall structure of 1 Thessalonians has been analyzed using a variety of methods.[4] Most recently, Charles Wanamaker has used classical rhetoric to arrive at an arrangement in which the two major sections of the letter, the Narratio (2:1-3:10) and the Probatio (4:1-5:22), are linked by a shorter Transitus (3:11-13):[5]

Epistolary prescript		1:1
Exordium		1:2-10
Narratio		2:1-3:10
First part of the Narratio	2:1-12	
Digressio	2:13-16	
Second part of the Narratio	2:17-3:10	

---

[1] Cf. Lüdeman, *Paul* 262-263; contrast Kümmel, *Introduction* 257.

[2] E.g., B. A Pearson, "1 Thessalonians 2:13-16: A Deutero-Pauline Interpolation," *HTR* 64 (1971) 79-94; H. Boers, "The Form-Critical Study of Paul's Letters: 1 Thessalonians as a Case Study," *NTS* 22 (1975-76) 140-158; D. Schmidt, "1 Thess 2:13-16: Linguistic Evidence for an Interpolation," *JBL* 102 (1983) 269-279. Cf. Schmithals, *Gnostics* 176-181, who views 1 Thessalonians as a composite letter.

[3] Most recently, C. A. Wanamaker, *Commentary on 1 & 2 Thessalonians* (Grand Rapids: Eerdmans, 1990) 37-45. See Kümmel, *Introduction* 263-264, for arguments supporting the traditional order.

[4] See Jewett for a summary list (*Thessalonian Correspondence* 216-221). For a detailed discussion of studies prior to 1972, see Hurd, "1 Thessalonians" 1-21.

[5] Wanamaker, *Thessalonians* 49.

Transitus	3:11-13
Probatio	4:1-5:22
Peroratio and Epistolary pstscript	5:23-28

It is interesting to compare this understanding of the letter with that resulting from epistolary analysis.

A. Epistolary Structure

The epistolary conventions found in 1 Thessalonians (disregarding vocatives) are distributed throughout the letter as follows:

1:1-2	Sender (1:1a), addressees (1:1b), greeting (1:1c), thanksgiving (1:2)
2:1-5	Disclosure formula (2:1), verb of knowing (2:2), verb of knowing (2:5)
2:11-13	Verb of knowing (2:11), thanksgiving (2:13)
2:18-3:6	Visit wish (2:18), dispatch of emissary (3:1), verb of knowing (3:3), verb of saying (3:4), dispatch of emissary (3:5), visit wish (3:6)
3:11-13	Wish-prayer (3:11-13)
4:1-6	Request formula (4:1), verb of knowing (4:2), verb of saying (4:6)
4:9-10	περὶ δὲ (4:9), writing statement (4:9), request formula (4:10)
4:13-15	Disclosure formula (4:13), verb of saying (4:15)
5:1-2	περὶ δὲ (5:1), writing statement (5:1), verb of knowing (5:2)
5:12-14	Request formula (5:12), request formula (5:14)
5:23-28	Peace-wish (5:23), greetings (5:26), grace-benediction (5:28)

The salutation (1:1) and the closing (5:23-28) are clearly identifiable units within the letter, including a peace-wish (5:23-25), greetings (5:26-27), and a grace-benediction (5:28). The thanksgiving begins at 1:2, and the disclosure formula in 2:1 may best be understood as introducing the letter-body.[6] The cluster of "visit" and "emissary" language in 2:18-3:6 suggests the presence of an apostolic parousia, and

---

[6] Paul's effusive expression of gratitude throughout 1:2-3:13 has led to some discussion as to how much of it, if not all, should be designated the thanksgiving. Schubert, for example, regarded the entire section as the thanksgiving (*Thanksgivings* 22). The scholarly consensus seems to be to limit the thanksgiving proper to 1:2-10 (e.g., White, *Body* 115-117; Jervis, *Romans* 91-94).

indeed, 2:17-3:13 is most commonly understood as such.[7] The emphatic request formula in 4:1 (λοιπὸν οὖν, ἀδελφοί, ἐρωτῶμεν ὑμᾶς καὶ παρακαλοῦμεν ἐν κυρίῳ Ἰησοῦ, ἵνα . . .) suggests the beginning of a new section of the letter, one that extends through 5:22. This extended paraenetic section may be subdivided into five subsections, each introduced by an epistolary convention: 4:1-8 (request formula), 4:9-12 (περὶ δὲ), 4:13-18 (disclosure formula), 5:1-11 (περὶ δὲ), and 5:12-22 (request formula).[8]

The resulting epistolary structure bears a marked resemblance to Wanamaker's rhetorical structure:

Salutation		1:1
Thanksgiving		1:2-10
Letter-body		2:1-3:13
Body-opening and middle	2:1-16	
Apostolic parousia	2:17-3:10	
Eschatological climax	3:11-13	
Paraenesis		4:1-5:22
Letter-closing		5:23-28

B. Readily Apparent Oral Patterns

Strong verbal parallels exist in 1 Thessalonians between 1:2-10 and 2:13-16. The most obvious parallel is the repetition of the εὐχαριστέω formula in 1:2 and 2:13:

εὐχαριστοῦμεν τῷ θεῷ . . . ἀδιαλείπτως . . .

ἡμεῖς εὐχαριστοῦμεν τῷ θεῷ ἀδιαλείπτως . . .

The parallel is strengthened by the repetition of ἀδιαλείπτως, a word used only four times in Paul's letters.[9] If these sentences stood alone, they would be classified as an instance of ring-composition.

The points of correspondence, however, are more numerous, for in each paragraph, the first sentence recalls how Paul's converts received the gospel: in power and the Holy Spirit (1:5-6) and as truly God's Word (2:13). As well, the second sentence in each paragraph uses similar wording to emphasize how the Thessalonians responded to the gospel (1:7; 2:14):

---

[7] E.g., Funk, "Apostolic Parousia" 254; White, *Body* 140-141; Jervis, *Romans* 114-116. White actually limits the apostolic parousia to 2:17-3:10 and views the wish-prayer of 3:11-13 as an eschatological climax (*Body* 119).

[8] Cf. Hurd, "Thessalonians, First Letter to the," *IDBSup* 900.

[9] The other two uses are 1 Thess 5:17 and Rom 1:9.

καὶ <u>ὑμεῖς μιμηταὶ</u> ἡμῶν <u>ἐγενήθητε</u> καὶ τοῦ κυρίου . . .

<u>ὑμεῖς</u> γὰρ <u>μιμηταὶ ἐγενήθητε</u>, ἀδελφοί, τῶν ἐκκλησιῶν τοῦ θεοῦ . . .

The triple use of λόγος in 1:5-8 corresponds to a similar cluster in 2:13.[10] The adverb πάντοτε occurs in both 1:2 and 2:16,[11] and each paragraph concludes with a reference to the wrath (ἡ ὀργή) that will come upon their opponents (1:10; 2:16). Thus, although the topics are developed differently in each paragraph, the similarities of sequence, the word-chains, and the introductory formulae in 1:2-10 and 2:13-16 are difficult to dismiss as being simply coincidental.

The intervening paragraph, 2:1-12, has a strong internal cohesiveness. It is framed by the occurrences of παράκλησις and παρακαλέω in 2:3 and 2:12. Four of the letter's seven occurrences of εὐαγγέλιον are found in 2:1-12, as are two of the three uses of δοκιμάζω (twice in 2:4). The only uses of μάρτυς (2:5, 10) and μαρτυρέω (2:11) occur in this paragraph. The chain οὐκ . . . οὐδὲ . . . οὐδὲ . . . οὐκ . . . οὔτε . . . οὔτε in 2:3-6 would have been difficult to ignore, and two sets of similarly worded phrases help bind the paragraph together:

| 2:2 | λαλῆσαι πρὸς ὑμᾶς τὸ εὐαγγέλιον τοῦ θεοῦ |
| 2:9 | ἐκηρύξαμεν εἰς ὑμᾶς τὸ εὐαγγέλιον τοῦ θεοῦ |

| 2:7 | ὡς ἐὰν τροφὸς θάλπῃ τὰ ἑαυτῆς τέκνα |
| 2:11 | ὡς πατὴρ τέκνα ἑαυτοῦ |

There are also connections between 1:2-10 and 2:1-12 that are reminiscent of the raft-building passage in Homer: (1) the mention of εὐαγγέλιον (1:5), which anticipates its repeated use in 2:1-12; and (2) the rare word εἴσοδος (1:9), which is repeated in 2:1.[12]

The overall pattern of 1:2-2:16 fits no specific category seen in either the Greco-Roman or OT writings surveyed. There are too many verbal parallels to call it simple inversion, but neither is inclusive or anaphoric ring-composition an accurate description.[13] Here, it appears, is another instance of the ABA' pattern in Paul's thought:[14]

---

[10] Surprisingly, λόγος occurs only three other times in the letter: 2:5; 4:15, 18.

[11] Among Paul's letters, the heaviest concentration of uses of πάντοτε occurs in 1 Thessalonians (1:2; 2:16; 3:6; 4:17; 5:15, 16).

[12] These are the only two occurrences of εἴσοδος in Paul's letters.

[13] Cf. F. F. Bruce: "It is better to recognize 2:13 as introducing a further thanksgiving: the opening words . . . are too emphatic to be merely resumptive . . . and the apologia of 2:1-12 is an integral part of the letter and no mere digression" (*1 & 2 Thessalonians* [Waco: Word, 1982] 43).

[14] Hurd ("1 Thessalonians" 25-29), Johanson (*Brethren* 99), and Ellis (*Letters* 15) all reach the same conclusion.

A	Thanksgiving for the Thessalonians	1:2-10
B	Paul's ministry in Thessalonica	2:1-12
A'	Renewed thanksgiving	2:13-16

The change from second person to first person, the use of the emphatic pronoun ἡμεῖς, and the vocative ἀδελφοί all signal a formal shift at 2:17. Funk and others have identified 2:17-3:13 as the "apostolic parousia" of 1 Thessalonians.[15] Its focus is Paul's desire to visit Thessalonica, and it is framed by statements concerning Christ's parousia (2:19; 3:13). These statements are actually the final two of three refrains introduced by ἔμπροσθεν that undergird all of 1:1-3:13:[16]

1:3	ἔμπροσθεν τοῦ θεοῦ καὶ πατρὸς ἡμῶν
2:19	ἔμπροσθεν τοῦ κυρίου ἡμῶν ᾿Ιησοῦ ἐν τῇ αὐτοῦ παρουσίᾳ
3:13	ἔμπροσθεν τοῦ θεοῦ καὶ πατρὸς ἡμῶν ἐν τῇ παρουσίᾳ τοῦ
	κυρίου ἡμῶν ᾿Ιησοῦ μετὰ πάντων τῶν ἁγίων αὐτοῦ

A definite cohesiveness exists within 2:17-3:13, which is created by the repetition of πρόσωπον (2:17 [twice]; 3:10), περισσεύω and cognates (2:17; 3:10, 12), στηρίζω (3:2, 13), ἔμπροσθεν (2:19; 3:9, 13), and χαίρω and cognates (2:19, 20; 3:9 [twice])—and which is reinforced by the repeated idea τὸ πρόσωπον ὑμῶν ἰδεῖν (2:17; 3:10).

It seems clear that the refrain of 2:19b, which is sandwiched between the question of 2:19a and answer of 2:20 is intended to mark the end of a subsection (2:17-20). Differences of opinion, however, exist regarding how 3:1-13 should be subdivided. Schubert argued that the phrase τίνα γὰρ εὐχαριστίαν δυνάμεθα τῷ θεῷ ἀνταποδοῦναι περὶ ὑμῶν (3:9) constituted a thanksgiving formula that introduced a third thanksgiving section,[17] and Hurd includes 3:9 as a transition point.[18] Both of these scholars divide 3:1-13 into two sections: 3:1-8 and 3:9-13. Johanson also breaks the passage at 3:9, but he properly notes the repetition of μηκέτι . . . στέγω . . . πέμπω and identifies it as an instance of inclusion around 3:1-5:[19]

---

[15] Originally Funk limited the apostolic parousia to 2:17-3:8 (Funk, *Language* 269). Later he expanded it to 2:17-3:13 (Funk, "Apostolic Parousia" 250, 254). White (*Body* 85), Doty (*Letters* 43), and Jervis (*Romans* 114-116) have followed his lead.

[16] The "improper" preposition ἔμπροσθεν is relatively rare in Paul's letters, appearing four times in 1 Thessalonians (1:3; 2:19; 3:9; 3:13) and only three times elsewhere (2 Cor 5:10; Gal 2:14; Phil 3:13).

[17] Schubert, *Thanksgivings* 17-27.

[18] Hurd, "1 Thessalonians" 20, 27. Hurd, however, also notes: "No doubt a few of these [transition] points are caused by the fact that Paul used some of the features we have listed not only to open sections, but also in the development of his argument" (ibid. 20).

[19] Johanson, *Brethren* 103.

Διὸ <u>μηκέτι στέγοντες</u> εὐδοκήσαμεν καταλειφθῆναι ἐν ᾿Αθήναις μόνοι, καὶ <u>ἐπέμψαμεν</u> Τιμόθεον, τὸν ἀδελφὸν ἡμῶν . . .

διὰ τοῦτο κἀγὼ <u>μηκέτι στέγων ἔπεμψα</u> . . .

He thus divides 3:1-13 into three sections: 3:1-5; 3:6-8; and 3:9-13.[20] It should be noted that the points of verbal and syntactical correspondence between 3:1-2 and 3:5 extend beyond those identified by Johanson, for each sentence continues with the sequence εἰς τὸ . . . infinitive . . . πίστις:

εἰς τὸ στηρίξαι ὑμᾶς καὶ παρακαλέσαι ὑπὲρ τῆς πίστεως ὑμῶν

εἰς τὸ γνῶναι τὴν πίστιν ὑμῶν

The question arises, however, as to whether 3:9 is the most appropriate place to see a break. One consideration is the presence of the wish-prayer in 3:11-13. These verses are introduced by the two *beracha* formulae of 3:11 and 3:12-13.[21] Concerning such doubled formulae Hurd comments: "Paul had a tendency to pair his transitional sentences at significant turning points in his writings."[22] The wish-prayer itself is characterized by the use of the optative mood (κατευθύναι . . . πλεονάσαι . . . περισσεύσαι), and it is closed by the ἔμπροσθεν refrain in 3:13. A final item to note is the presence of a word-chain in 3:1-10: five of the letter's eight uses of πίστις occur in these verses. For these reasons it seems wise to recognize 3:11-13 as self-contained unit and to view the apostolic parousia as consisting of four subsections: 2:17-20; 3:1-5; 3:6-10; and 3:11-13.

The first (2:17-20) and fourth (3:11-13) subsections of the apostolic parousia are roughly parallel. Both express Paul's desire to visit the Thessalonians (2:18; 3:11), and both close with the eschatological statements noted above (2:19; 3:13). Since 3:1-10 deals primarily with Timothy's visit (3:1-5) and his report on that visit (3:6-10), it is possible to see the whole section of 2:17-3:13 as another instance of the ABA' pattern:[23]

A	Paul's desire to visit Thessalonica	2:17-20
B	Timothy's visit to Thessalonica	3:1-10
A'	Paul's hope to visit Thessalonica	3:11-13

---

[20] Ibid. 150.

[21] Sanders ("Transition" 359), R. Jewett ("The Form and Function of the Homiletic Benediction," *ATR* 51 [1969] 20), and Hurd ("1 Thessalonians" 19) all note the presence of the two *beracha* formulae.

[22] Ibid.

[23] Hurd ("1 Thessalonians" 27), Johanson (*Brethren* 108), and Ellis (*Letters* 15) all see the same pattern, although all three posit a break at 3:9.

In the paraenetic section of 4:1-5:24 Paul addresses a number of issues facing the Thessalonian church. Clear formal divisions occur at the emphatic request formula of 4:1, the disclosure formula of 4:13, and the request formula of 5:12. Within these sections additional transitional formulae occur at 4:9 (περὶ δε), 5:1 (περὶ δε), and 5:14 (request formula). The paraenesis closes with a wish-prayer in 5:23-24 similar to that of 3:11-13.

As in the first half of the letter, a number of verbal parallels are present in 4:1-5:24. Perhaps the strongest are those between 4:1-2 and 4:10b-12:

Λοιπὸν οὖν, ἀδελφοί, ἐρωτῶμεν ὑμᾶς καὶ παρακαλοῦμεν ἐν κυρίῳ Ἰησοῦ, ἵνα καθὼς παρελάβετε παρ' ἡμῶν τὸ πῶς δεῖ ὑμᾶς περιπατεῖν καὶ ἀρέσκειν θεῷ, καθὼς καὶ περιπατεῖτε, ἵνα περισσεύητε μᾶλλον. οἴδατε γὰρ τίνας παραγγελίας ἐδώκαμεν ὑμῖν διὰ τοῦ κυρίου Ἰησοῦ.

παρακαλοῦμεν δὲ ὑμᾶς, ἀδελφοί, περισσεύειν μᾶλλον, καὶ φιλοτιμεῖσθαι ἡσυχάζειν καὶ πράσσειν τὰ ἴδια καὶ ἐργάζεσθαι ταῖς ἰδίαις χερσὶν ὑμῶν, καθὼς ὑμῖν παρηγγείλαμεν, ἵνα περιπατῆτε εὐσχημόνως πρὸς τοὺς ἔξω καὶ μηδενὸς χρείαν ἔχητε.

Not only is a request formula present in each set of verses, but several other verbal parallels exist. Three of the letter's four uses of περιπατέω occur in these verses, as do two of the three uses of περισσεύω. The only uses of παραγγελία and παραγγέλλω are found here, as are the only uses of μᾶλλον. These strong verbal parallels suggest that 4:1-12 should be viewed as a unit.[24] Within that unit, 4:3-8 is clearly set off by the presence of the word-chain that uses ἁγιασμός (4:3, 4, 7) and ἅγιος (4:8), and that is anticipated by the use of ἁγιωσύνη in 3:13.

The internal cohesiveness of 4:13-5:11 is supported by the repetition of οἱ λοιποί (4:13; 5:6), ζάω (4:15, 17; 5:10), and the similar wording that appears in 4:18 and 5:11:

ὥστε παρακαλεῖτε ἀλλήλους ἐν τοῖς λόγοις τούτοις.

διὸ παρακαλεῖτε ἀλλήλους καὶ οἰκοδομεῖτε εἰς τὸν ἕνα, καθὼς καὶ ποιεῖτε.

The individual paragraphs in this section (4:13-18 and 5:1-11) both exhibit the presence of word-chains, with a number of words appearing only in their respective paragraphs. Paul's only uses in 1 Thessalonians of κοιμάομαι (4:13, 14, 15) and περιλείπομαι (4:15, 17) are in 4:13-18. His only uses of κλέπτης (5:2, 4), καθεύδω (5:6, 7 [twice], 10), μεθύω (5:7 [twice]), and νήφω (5:6, 8) are in 5:1-11. This latter paragraph also has significant concentrations of ἡμέρα (4 of 6 uses) and νύξ (4 of 6 uses).

---

[24] If this conclusion is correct, then the περὶ δὲ of 4:9 may be viewed more as an internal transitional device than as a major section marker.

In 5:1-11 the basic contrast between ἡμέρα and νύξ is focused in the chiasmus of verse 5:[25]

πάντες γὰρ ὑμεῖς υἱοὶ <u>φωτός</u> ἐστε καὶ υἱοὶ <u>ἡμέρας</u>
οὐκ ἐσμεν <u>νυκτὸς</u> οὐδὲ <u>σκότους</u>

Although Hurd has proposed a larger structure encompassing 5:2-8,[26] more promising is his observation that "through the whole passage runs a steady alternation between words associated with 'day' and those connoting 'night'."[27] If "peace," "safety," "watch," and "be sober" are added to "day/light," and if "destruction," "sleep," and "be drunk" are added to "night/darkness," the sequence in 5:2-8 becomes:

A/B	αὐτοὶ γὰρ ἀκριβῶς οἴδατε ὅτι <u>ἡμέρα</u> κυρίου ὡς κλέπτης ἐν <u>νυκτὶ</u> οὕτως ἔρχεται.
A	ὅταν λέγωσιν, <u>εἰρήνη καὶ ἀσφάλεια</u>,
B	τότε αἰφνίδιος αὐτοῖς ἐφίσταται <u>ὄλεθρος</u> ὥσπερ ἡ ὠδὶν τῇ ἐν γαστρὶ ἐχούσῃ, καὶ οὐ μὴ ἐκφύγωσιν.
B	ὑμεῖς δέ, ἀδελφοί, οὐκ ἐστὲ ἐν <u>σκότει</u>,
A	ἵνα ἡ <u>ἡμέρα</u> ὑμᾶς ὡς κλέπτης καταλάβῃ·
A	πάντες γὰρ ὑμεῖς υἱοὶ <u>φωτός</u> ἐστε καὶ υἱοὶ <u>ἡμέρας</u>.
B	οὐκ ἐσμὲν <u>νυκτὸς</u> οὐδὲ <u>σκότους</u>·
B	ἄρα οὖν μὴ <u>καθεύδωμεν</u> ὡς οἱ λοιποί,
A	ἀλλὰ <u>γρηγορῶμεν καὶ νήφωμεν</u>.
B	οἱ γὰρ <u>καθεύδοντες νυκτὸς καθεύδουσιν</u>, καὶ οἱ <u>μεθυσκόμενοι νυκτὸς μεθύουσιν</u>·
A	ἡμεῖς δὲ <u>ἡμέρας</u> ὄντες <u>νήφωμεν</u> ἐνδυσάμενοι θώρακα πίστεως καὶ ἀγάπης καὶ περικεφαλαίαν ἐλπίδα σωτηρίας·

This entire passage is reminiscent of the alternation pattern seen in Greco-Roman and OT works. It is brought neatly to a conclusion in 5:10 with the statement: εἴτε <u>γρηγορῶμεν</u> εἴτε <u>καθεύδωμεν</u> ἅμα σὺν τῷ κυρίῳ ζήσωμεν.

It is particularly interesting to note how Paul in 5:1-10 moves back and forth between second, third, and first person plurals as a means of driving home his point. The positive affirmation of ὑμεῖς (5:1-2) gives way to a negative example stated in the third person plural (5:3), and then returns to the positive affirmation of ὑμεῖς (5:4-5a). The positive evaluation and subsequent exhortation directed toward ἡμεῖς (5:5b-6) again gives way to a negative example stated in the third person (5:7), before returning to a final exhoration for ἡμεῖς (5:8-10). Here, in minature, are two examples of the way in which Paul's argumentation "oscillates" in ABA' patterns.

---

[25] Cf. G. Milligan, *St. Paul's Epistles to the Thessalonians* (New York: Macmillan, n.d.) 67; Bruce, *1 & 2 Thessalonians* 108; Wanamaker, *1 & 2 Thessalonians* 183.

[26] Hurd, "1 Thessalonians" 23-24.

[27] Ibid. 24.

The miscellaneous nature of the final instructions in 5:12-22 is reflected in the scarcity of verbal parallels within these verses. The verb νουθετέω is repeated (5:12, 14), as is the adverb πάντοτε (5:15, 16). Otherwise there are no repetitions. There are, in fact, stronger ties to earlier portions of the letter. Johanson notes a number of words from 4:1-12 that reappear in 5:12-22: ἐρωτάω (4:1; 5:12), παρακαλέω (4:1,10; 5:14), τοῦτο γάρ ἐστιν θέλημα τοῦ θεοῦ (4:3; 5:18) πνεῦμα (4:8; 5:19), and ἀπέχω (4:3; 5:22).[28] The strongest of these elements is the phrase τοῦτο γάρ ἐστιν θέλημα τοῦ θεοῦ, along with the words ἐρωτάω and ἀπέχω that appear nowhere else in the letter.[29]

Although it is tempting to see an ABA' pattern in the three sections of 4:1-5:24,[30] the points of correspondence between 4:1-12 and 5:12-22 are not nearly as strong as those between, say, 1:2-10 and 2:13-16. Probably the similarities between 4:1-12 and 5:12-22 have more to do with the ethical instructions contained in these two sections than with any sort of oral patterning. It seems best, therefore, to see Paul as working his way through a series of issues loosely-grouped under various general headings:

4:1-12	Ethics
4:1-8	Sexual purity
4:9-12	Brotherly love
4:13-5:11	Eschatology
4:13-18	The dead in Christ
5:1-11	Times and seasons
5:12-22	Church life
5:12-13	Recognition of leaders
5:14-15	Relations with others
5:16-22	Summary advice

One final set of verbal parallels occurs in the opening and closing sections of 1 Thessalonians. It will be recalled that two of the uses of ἀδιαλείπτως appear in the thanksgiving formulae of 1:2 and 2:13. The third use of ἀδιαλείπτως occurs in 5:17. Interestingly enough, the words εὐχαριστέω (1:2), πάντοτε (1:2), and προσεύχομαι (1:2) also appear in the immediate context (5:16-17):

---

[28] Johanson, *Brethren* 143.

[29] These words are, in fact, rare in Paul's letters. His only other use of ἐρωτάω is in Phil 4:3. The verb ἀπέχω in the middle voice occurs only in these two verses, although the active voice is used in Phil 4:18 and Phlm 15.

[30] Bjerkelund (*Parakalo* 129-130), Johanson (*Brethren* 143), and Ellis (*Letters* 15) all see such a pattern, consisting of A (4:1-12), B (4:13-5:11), and A' (5:12-24/28). Hurd disagrees: "Here the sort of parallels that we have noted in the first three chapters are largely absent . . . It seems as though these last two chapters had an organizational principle which was different from that of the first three, although in a loose way one can speak of 4:13-5:11 as being a central panel within 4:1-5:22" ("1 Thessalonians" 28).

πάντοτε χαίρετε, ἀδιαλείπτως προσεύχεσθε, ἐν παντὶ εὐχαριστεῖτε· τοῦτο
γὰρ θέλημα θεοῦ ἐν Χριστῷ 'Ιησοῦ εἰς ὑμᾶς.

Although εὐχαριστέω, πάντοτε, and προσεύχομαι are common enough in Paul's
letter openings and closings,[31] ἀδιαλείπτως is relatively rare[32] and serves as a
reminder that Paul often ends his letters with language similar to that at the
beginning.

C. Other Suggested Structures

Hurd has proposed four "chiastic" arrangements within 1 Thessalonians
somewhat in the style of Lund.[33] The first expands Béda Rigaux's suggestion for
2:19-20:[34]

A	For what is our hope or joy
B	or crown of boasting—
C	is it not you—
D	before our Lord Jesus Christ
D'	at his coming?
C'	For you are
B'	our glory
A'	and joy.

The most prominent verbal parallel is the repetition of χαρά, which forms an
inclusion around the verses.

Yet a number of questions may be posed regarding this arrangement: (1) What
makes the second person pronoun a key element? Forms of ὑμεῖς occur five times
in 2:17-20. What makes these two occurrences special?[35] (2) If the repetition of the

---

[31] εὐχαριστέω is present in all six of Paul's opening thanksgivings, although it occurs only
twice at the end of his letters (Rom 16:4; 1 Thess 5:18). πάντοτε occurs in five of Paul's
thanksgiving sections, but only at the end of 1 Thessalonians. προσεύχομαι appears only in the
thanksgiving of Philippians, although the noun προσευχή appears in Rom 1:9; 1 Thess 1:2; and
Phlm 4. At the end of Paul's letters, the verb occurs twice (1 Thess 5:17, 25) and the noun occurs
once (Phlm 22).

[32] The adjective occurs twice in the NT, both times in letters ascribed to Paul. The adverb
occurs four times, again all in Paul's letters.

[33] It is interesting to note that neither Lund nor Welch chooses to discuss 1 Thessalonians.
Welch writes: "Paul's earliest letters, the two to the church in Thessalonika, appear to manifest
little internal structure . . . Although it can be said that these letters are composed of relatively
discrete sections, no indications are forthcoming from these texts themselves to the effect that
these sections were in any way intended to be read in parallel relationship with corresponding
sections in other portions of the writing" ("Chiasmus" 213).

[34] Hurd, "1 Thessalonians" 23.

[35] ὑμεῖς occurs 85 times in 1 Thessalonians. It is usually *rare* words, however, that are

second person pronoun is important, why is the repetition of the first person pronoun not given equal weight? Forms of ἡμεῖς occur four times in the same verses.[36] Would the listeners have noticed either of these words as key?[37] (3) Why are ἐλπίς and χαρά kept together while δόξα and χαρά are separated? (4) Why is the parenthetical phrase placed in parallel with the noun and verb of the answer rather than in parallel with the noun and verb of the question? In fact, are not the question, the parenthetical phrase, and the answer *all* parallel with one another?

Whatever is concluded regarding these matters, it still remains (1) that Paul's question and its answer are unbalanced by the presence of ἐλπίς in the question,[38] and (2) that the entire structure is unbalanced by the presence of the parenthetical phrase ἢ οὐχὶ καὶ ὑμεῖς. If the text were handled consistently, it might be arranged as follows—a scheme that is not quite as symmetrical as the initial proposal:

A	For what is
B	our hope
C	or joy
D	or crown of boasting—
A'	is it not you—
E	before our Lord Jesus Christ
E'	at his coming?
A"	For you are
D'	our glory
C'	and joy.

But if the grammatical structure of the verses is respected, the text is probably best represented as follows:

τίς γὰρ ἡμῶν ἐλπὶς ἢ χαρά ἢ στέφανος καυχήσεως
    —ἢ οὐχὶ καὶ ὑμεῖς—
ἔμπροσθεν τοῦ κυρίου ἡμῶν Ἰησοῦ ἐν τῇ αὐτοῦ παρουσίᾳ;
ὑμεῖς γάρ ἐστε ἡ δόξα ἡμῶν καὶ ἡ χαρά.

---

regarded as key elements in such a structure (cf. Blomberg, "2 Corinthians" 6). Johanson takes a similar stance: ". . . in order to safeguard the selection of verbal elements from becoming the means of an arbitrary imposition of structures foreign to the text, the selection of verbal elements and formulations will be almost totally restricted to those that occur not more than twice within the respective text-sequences where a pattern is established" (*Brethren* 148).

[36] ἡμεῖς in all four cases occurs 51 times in 1 Thessalonians. The nominative case occurs 7 times.

[37] Indeed, a number of textual variants apparently have arisen from scribes mishearing ἡμεῖς for ὑμεῖς and vice versa. Two of the most prominent examples are 2 Cor 6:16 and Gal 4:28. Two examples in 1 Thessalonians are 1:9 and 4:8.

[38] Hurd notes this shortcoming, but he apparently does not view it as a major drawback: "Except for that single element the passage is structurally perfect" ("1 Thessalonians" 23).

In either case, the question and answer are clearly parallel; the parenthetical phrase anticipates (and emphasizes) Paul's answer. The central position of the ἔμπροσθεν refrain keeps in the foreground the eschatological concern so evident throughout the letter. It seems likely that the repetition of χαρά would have been apparent to the ear, but recognition of the transposed relationship between στέφανος καυχήσεως and δόξα seems less likely.

Hurd's second chiastic arrangement is that proposed for 4:3-8:[39]

A	For this is the will of <u>God</u>, your <u>consecration</u>:
B	that you abstain from immorality;
C	that each of you know how to take a wife for himself in <u>consecration</u> and honor,
D	not in the <u>passion of lust</u> like the heathen
E	who do not know <u>God</u>;
F	that no man transgress and wrong his brother in this matter,
F'	because the Lord is an avenger in all these things as we solemnly forewarned you.
E'	For <u>God</u> has not called us
D'	for <u>uncleanness</u>,
C'	but in <u>consecration</u>.
B'	Therefore whoever disregards this, disregards not man
A'	but <u>God</u>, who gives his <u>Holy Spirit</u> to you.

This scheme, however, is again open to the criticism that two of the primary points of correspondence involve a word (ὁ θεός) that is quite common in Paul (427x). More promising is the repetition of ἁγιασμός, which is part of the word-chain in 4:3-8 and a word that is relatively rare in Paul's letters.[40] Furthermore, the suggested parallel between B and B' is unclear. And although F and F' (v.6) are clearly related as instruction and the grounds for obeying that instruction, it is unclear as to why they should be considered two elements rather than one.

Two possible parallels, it appears, have been overlooked in the above arrangement. The first is that between 4:3 and 4:7:

τοῦτο γάρ ἐστιν θέλημα <u>τοῦ θεοῦ</u>, ὁ <u>ἁγιασμὸς</u> ὑμῶν, ἀπέχεσθαι ὑμᾶς ἀπὸ τῆς <u>πορνείας</u>

οὐ γὰρ ἐκάλεσεν ἡμᾶς <u>ὁ θεὸς</u> ἐπὶ <u>ἀκαθαρσίᾳ</u> ἀλλ' ἐν <u>ἁγιασμῷ</u>.

Conceptually, these verses are virtually identical. The same three elements are present in each: (1) God's demand/expectation for the Christian is (2) holiness, (3) not sexual impurity. More important for this study, they contain points of verbal

---

[39] Ibid. 24-25.

[40] ἁγιασμός occurs only 6 times in Paul's letters, and nowhere else in 1 Thessalonians.

correspondence between ὁ θεός (if such a common word is included) and ἁγιασμός, as well as semantic correspondence between πορνεία and ἀκαθαρσία.[41] These observations raise the question as to why verse 7 has been placed parallel to verses 4 and 5 in the proposed arrangement, rather than in its more natural relationship as parallel to verse 3? Furthermore, why has verse 3 been divided into two parts while verse 7 has been divided into three parts? The following, it seems, would have been a more consistent arrangement:

A	τοῦτο γάρ ἐστιν θέλημα τοῦ θεοῦ,
B	ὁ ἁγιασμὸς ὑμῶν,
C	ἀπέχεσθαι ὑμᾶς ἀπὸ τῆς πορνείας,
A'	οὐ γὰρ ἐκάλεσεν ἡμᾶς ὁ θεὸς
C'	ἐπὶ ἀκαθαρσίᾳ
B'	ἀλλ' ἐν ἁγιασμῷ.

A second overlooked possible parallel seems to exist between 4:2 and 4:8:

οἴδατε γὰρ τίνας παραγγελίας <u>ἐδώκαμεν</u> ὑμῖν διὰ τοῦ κυρίου ᾿Ιησοῦ.

τοιγαροῦν ὁ ἀθετῶν οὐκ ἄνθρωπον ἀθετεῖ ἀλλὰ τὸν θεὸν τὸν καὶ <u>διδόντα</u> τὸ πνεῦμα αὐτοῦ τὸ ἅγιον εἰς ὑμᾶς.

Here, the conceptual parallel between the command given and the consequences of rejecting it is strengthened by the verbal repetition of δίδωμι, a word that appears only in these two verses of the letter.

When the above matters are taken into consideration, a revised arrangement similar to that of inversion may be proposed:

A	οἴδατε γὰρ τίνας παραγγελίας <u>ἐδώκαμεν</u> ὑμῖν διὰ τοῦ κυρίου ᾿Ιησοῦ.
B	τοῦτο γάρ ἐστιν θέλημα τοῦ θεοῦ, ὁ <u>ἁγιασμὸς</u> ὑμῶν, ἀπέχεσθαι ὑμᾶς ἀπὸ τῆς πορνείας,
C	εἰδέναι ἕκαστον ὑμῶν τὸ ἑαυτοῦ σκεῦος κτᾶσθαι ἐν ἁγιασμῷ καὶ τιμῇ, μὴ ἐν πάθει ἐπιθυμίας καθάπερ καὶ τὰ ἔθνη τὰ μὴ εἰδότα τὸν θεόν,
C'	τὸ μὴ ὑπερβαίνειν καὶ πλεονεκτεῖν ἐν τῷ πράγματι τὸν ἀδελφὸν αὐτοῦ, διότι ἔκδικος κύριος περὶ πάντων τούτων, καθὼς καὶ προείπαμεν ὑμῖν καὶ διεμαρτυράμεθα.

---

[41] Both have a connotation of sexual sin (J. P. Louw and E. A. Nida, eds., *Greek-English Lexicon of the New Testament Based on Semantic Domains* [New York: United Bible Societies, 1988] 770-771), and both are found in close context within the NT vice lists (2 Cor 12:21; Gal 5:19; Eph 5:3; Col 3:5).

B'   οὐ γὰρ ἐκάλεσεν ἡμᾶς ὁ θεὸς ἐπὶ ἀκαθαρσίᾳ ἀλλ' ἐν <u>ἁγιασμῷ</u>.

A'   τοιγαροῦν ὁ ἀθετῶν οὐκ ἄνθρωπον ἀθετεῖ ἀλλὰ τὸν θεὸν τὸν καὶ <u>διδόντα</u> τὸ πνεῦμα αὐτοῦ τὸ ἅγιον εἰς ὑμᾶς.

Although it is not as detailed as Hurd's proposal, this arrangement, it seems, better reflects the verbal (and conceptual) parallels within the passage, as well as respecting the grammatical structure. The focus of Paul's instruction in 4:4-6 thereby serves to emphasize marriage as the only proper sphere for sexual relations.

The single instance of chiasmus that is noted by Jeremias in 1 Thessalonians occurs in 4:15-18 with its contrasting pairs related to life and death:[42]

οἱ ζῶντες οἱ περιλειπόμενοι
τοὺς κοιμηθέντας
οἱ νεκροὶ ἐν Χριστῷ
οἱ ζῶντες οἱ περιλειπόμενοι

Hurd has arranged the entire paragraph as follows:[43]

A   For this we say to you by the <u>word</u>
B   of the <u>Lord</u>
C   that <u>we who are alive, who are left</u> until the coming of the <u>Lord</u>
D   shall not <u>precede</u>
E   <u>those who sleep</u>
F   For the Lord himself will descend from heaven
           with a cry of command,
           with the archangel's call, and
           with the sound of God's trumpet.
E'   And <u>the dead</u> in Christ
D'   will rise <u>first</u>
C'   then <u>we who are alive, who are left</u>, shall be caught up . . . to meet the <u>Lord</u> in the air
B'   and so we shall always be with the <u>Lord</u>.
A'   Therefore comfort one another with these <u>words</u>.

Commenting on this arrangement, Hurd notes that "some parallels are better than others."[44] He goes on, however, to say: "But the general sequence seems clear: spoken words, confidence in the Lord, those who live and remain to meet the Lord, the idea of precedence, the dead, the picture of the return of the Lord."

In support of this arrangement, it should be noted that there are clear parallels between C and C':

---

[42] Jeremias, "Chiasmus" 148.
[43] Hurd, "1 Thessalonians" 22.
[44] Ibid.

ὅτι ἡμεῖς οἱ ζῶντες οἱ περιλειπόμενοι εἰς τὴν παρουσίαν τοῦ κυρίου

ἔπειτα ἡμεῖς οἱ ζῶντες οἱ περιλειπόμενοι ἅμα σὺν αὐτοῖς ἁρπαγησόμεθα
ἐν νεφέλαις εἰς ἀπάντησιν τοῦ κυρίου εἰς ἀέρα

As well, given Paul's practice of referring to those who die as "asleep"
(κοιμάομαι),[45] the parallel between E and E' is a logical one, although the decision
to separate the subject and predicate of the ὅτι clause might be questioned. And
undoubtedly F is the eschatological focus of the paragraph.

It is the parallels in the outer panels, however, that are the weakest in Hurd's
arrangement of 4:15-18. The use of κύριος as an element on which to base a parallel
must be questioned, for this is a common word in Paul's letters.[46] So any number of
parallels could be proposed when it is singled out as a key element. Furthermore,
the decision to make the single word κυρίου a separate element (B) and to set it
parallel to an entire clause (καὶ οὕτως πάντοτε σὺν κυρίῳ ἐσόμεθα) must be
questioned.[47] Would it not have been more natural to keep τοῦτο γὰρ ὑμῖν λέγομεν
ἐν λόγῳ κυρίου—or, at least, ἐν λόγῳ κυρίου—together as a unit?

A less detailed approach would be to view the repetition of οἱ ζῶντες οἱ
περιλειπόμενοι as ring-composition that frames verses 15-17:

τοῦτο γὰρ ὑμῖν λέγομεν ἐν λόγῳ κυρίου, ὅτι ἡμεῖς οἱ ζῶντες οἱ
περιλειπόμενοι εἰς τὴν παρουσίαν τοῦ κυρίου οὐ μὴ φθάσωμεν τοὺς
κοιμηθέντας·

ὅτι αὐτὸς ὁ κύριος ἐν κελεύσματι, ἐν φωνῇ ἀρχαγγέλου καὶ
ἐν σάλπιγγι θεοῦ, καταβήσεται ἀπ' οὐρανοῦ, καὶ οἱ νεκροὶ
ἐν Χριστῷ ἀναστήσονται πρῶτον,

ἔπειτα ἡμεῖς οἱ ζῶντες οἱ περιλειπόμενοι ἅμα σὺν αὐτοῖς ἁρπαγησόμεθα
ἐν νεφέλαις εἰς ἀπάντησιν τοῦ κυρίου εἰς ἀέρα· καὶ οὕτως πάντοτε σὺν
κυρίῳ ἐσόμεθα.

The macro-structure of the passage is thereby revealed as ABA': A = the living in
Christ; B = the dead in Christ; A' = the living in Christ. Regardless of the level of
detail proposed, the verses function together as a clearly-delimited paragraph, with
their focus on the future prospects of those Christians who had already died prior
to the time of Paul's letter.

---

[45] Cf. 4:13, 14; also 1 Cor 11:30; 15:6, 18, 20, 51.

[46] κύριος occurs 25 times in 1 Thessalonians and a total of 194 times in Paul's letters; 129
of those 194 times the word is used—as it is here—absolutely, as a title.

[47] Cf. Johanson: "[Hurd's] method of mixing thematic and lexical elements in establishing
parallel elements is unsatisfactory" (*Brethren* 148). He believes that Hurd's arrangement of 4:15-
18 "provides a striking example of this weakness" (ibid. n.708).

One approach to 5:2-8 has already been set out above. As noted earlier, Hurd has proposed a structure for these verses as well:[48]

A   The <u>day</u> of the Lord will come
B   like a thief <u>in the night</u>.
C   When they say, "Peace" . . . then sudden destruction . . .
        There will be no escape.
D   But you are <u>not in darkness</u>
        for the day to surprise you like a thief.
E   For you are all sons of <u>light</u>
E'   and sons of the <u>day</u>.
D'   We are <u>not of the night</u> or of <u>darkness</u>.
        So let us not <u>sleep</u> as others do,
C'   but let us keep <u>awake</u> and be <u>sober</u>.
B'   For those who <u>sleep, sleep at night</u>,
        and those who get <u>drunk</u> are <u>drunk at night</u>.
A'   But, since we belong to the <u>day</u>, let us be sober.

This scheme does a good job of keeping thought units together—better, it seems, than was sometimes the case in Hurd's first three arrangements.

Yet three items need to be noted: (1) Although it is not readily apparent in the English translation above, elements A and B unnaturally divide verse 2b. The verb actually comes at the end of the sentence (ἡμέρα κυρίου ὡς κλέπτης ἐν νυκτὶ οὕτως ἔρχεται), so dividing it into two parts is not accomplished as cleanly as would appear to be the case. (2) Verse 5 (E + E' + the first line of D') has not been handled consistently. The clauses should be represented in one of two ways,

either: πάντες γὰρ ὑμεῖς υἱοὶ φωτός ἐστε καὶ υἱοὶ ἡμέρας.
         οὐκ ἐσμὲν νυκτὸς οὐδὲ σκότους·

or: πάντες γὰρ ὑμεῖς υἱοὶ φωτός ἐστε
         καὶ υἱοὶ ἡμέρας.
         οὐκ ἐσμὲν νυκτὸς
         οὐδὲ σκότους·

(3) Elements D' and C' divide the text somewhat awkwardly. Verse 6 is a conclusion (ἄρα οὖν) drawn from verse 5b and is held together grammatically by the strong contrast of μὴ . . . ἀλλά. If the grammar of verses 5b and 6 is respected, it might be better represented as:

D'   οὐκ ἐσμὲν νυκτὸς οὐδὲ σκότους·

C'   ἄρα οὖν μὴ καθεύδωμεν ὡς οἱ λοιποί
      ἀλλὰ γρηγορῶμεν καὶ νήφωμεν.

---

[48] Hurd, "1 Thessalonians" 23-24.

There are numerous verbal repetitions in these verses, including a number of synonymns. The difficulty comes in determining which elements with corresponding words are parallel to one another. For example, the word κλέπτης appears in combination with νύξ in B; it reappears in D in combination with σκότος, a synonym for νύξ. Yet B in Hurd's proposal is set in parallel with B' where κλέπτης is notably absent but νύξ is repeated twice. What was the controlling factor in making the decision to choose B' over D? Another example is the use of ἡμέρα. This word appears four times in the scheme. Twice (A and A') it is made the key point of correspondence. Once (E) it is set parallel to its synonym φῶς (E'). Once (D) it is ignored. Why is the use of synonyms (ἡμέρα and φῶς) more significant than the repeated combination of ἡμέρα and κλέπτης that appears in both A/B and D?[49]

The difficulty arising from the abundance of repetitions and synonyms suggests that Hurd is correct in calling attention to "steady alternation" as the most prominent characteristic of the passage. An analysis of his scheme in terms of key words and their connotations—with E and E' combined for the sake of consistency—highlights that alternation:

A .	day	positive
B	night	negative
C	[no words underlined]	positive (suggested by the parallel with C')[50]
D	darkness	negative
E	light/day	positive
D'	night/darkness/sleep	negative
C'	awake/sober	positive
B'	sleep/night/drunk	negative
A'	day/sober	positive

Although this pattern of alternation differs somewhat from that identified earlier, it nonetheless supports the view that alternation might be a more appropriate understanding of this passage than either inversion or concentric symmetry.

1 Thessalonians closes with a wish prayer in 5:23-24, a prayer request in 5:25, greetings in 5:26-27, and a grace benediction in 5:28. Included within the wish-prayer for the readers' entire sanctification is a final instance of chiasmus:

---

[49] Not to mention the synonymns νύξ and σκότος that also appear in the latter pair of sentences.

[50] It may be noted in passing that C creates a dilemma for Hurd's arrangement under any sort of analysis. The way in which it is parallel to C' is unclear, and the relationship between it and the rest of the scheme is ambiguous. It contains none of the key words or synonyms highlighted as structuring the passage. It begins on a positive note (εἰρήνη καὶ ἀσφάλεια), but it ends on a negative note (ὄλεθρος . . . οὐ μὴ ἐκφύγωσιν). The scheme under examination apparently views it as a positive element, but an equally strong case could be made to view it as a negative element.

αὐτὸς δὲ ὁ θεὸς τῆς εἰρήνης <u>ἁγιάσαι</u> ὑμᾶς <u>ὁλοτελεῖς</u>,
καὶ <u>ὁλόκληρον</u> ὑμῶν τὸ πνεῦμα . . . <u>τηρηθείη</u>.

P. A. van Stempvoort has proposed an alternative approach that he believes is a simpler solution to the spirit, soul, body issue:[51]

αὐτὸς δὲ ὁ θεὸς τῆς εἰρήνης ἁγιάσαι
    <u>ὑμᾶς ὁλοτελεῖς</u> καὶ
    <u>ὁλόκληρον ὑμῶν τὸ πνεῦμα</u>.
καὶ ἡ ψυχὴ καὶ τὸ σῶμα ἀμέμπτως ἐν τῇ παρουσίᾳ τοῦ
κυρίου ἡμῶν Ἰησοῦ Χριστοῦ τηρηθείη.

Bruce correctly notes, however, that "this is an unnatural way to divide the sentence."[52]

D. Summary

Repeated wording plays a prominent role in the composition of 1 Thessalonians, whether that repeated wording is understood as inclusion, ring-composition, or the ABA' pattern. The ABA' pattern appears to structure at least chapters 1-3, and at a micro-level it characterizes Paul's argument in 5:1-10. Word-chains are common and often provide the key to understanding the micro-structure of passages. Refrain undergirds chapters 1-3. Alternation appears to be the best way of understanding 5:2-8. Examples of chiasmus are limited, as are examples of inversion and concentric symmetry.

---

[51] P. A. van Stempvoort, "Eine stilistische Lösung einer alten Schwierigkeit in 1 Thess. v.23," *NTS* 7 (1960-61) 262-265

[52] Bruce, *1 & 2 Thessalonians* 128.

Chapter 12

PHILEMON

Philemon is the shortest of Paul's letters, and the most personal. The letter's authenticity has never been seriously questioned, nor has its integrity. The place and date of writing are commonly linked to those of Colossians, for many of the same people are named in both letters. Since Paul writes as a prisoner (vv.1, 9, 10, 23), suggestions for the place of composition include Ephesus, Caesarea, and Rome.[1] Proposed dates vary with the suggested place of Paul's imprisonment, and range from A.D. 56 through A.D. 60.[2]

Philemon has served as the test case for a variety of critical methods applied to Paul's letters. White, for example, used Philemon as "a point of departure" for epistolary analysis.[3] Church used it as a test case in the early development of rhetorical analysis.[4] And Petersen chose to analyze it in his pioneering work in the area of sociological analysis.[5] Three reasons, it seems, stand behind this frequent choice of Philemon: (1) its integrity and Pauline authorship are undisputed; (2) its length corresponds closely to the length of non-literary papyri letters; and (3) its brevity makes it easy to handle.

A. Epistolary Structure

There are two clusters of epistolary conventions in Philemon:

v.1-7   Sender (v.1a), addressees (v.1b-2), greeting (v.3), thanksgiving (v.4), joy expression (v.7), vocative (v.7)

---

[1] Cf. Kümmel, *Introduction* 346-349, for a concise summary.

[2] Ibid. 348.

[3] J. L. White, "The Structural Analysis of Philemon: A Point of Departure in the Formal Analysis of the Pauline Letter," in *SBLSP* (1971) 1:1-48.

[4] Church, "Rhetorical Structure" 17-33.

[5] Petersen, *Rediscovering Paul.*

| v.19-25 | Writing statement (v.19), vocative (v.20), confidence formula (v.21), writing statement (v.21), greetings (v.23), grace-benediction (v.25) |

This distribution of conventions suggests that Philemon follows closely the basic structure of the standard Greek letter of the day:

Standard Greek Letter[6]		*Philemon*	
Salutation		Salutation	v.1-3
Health wish	=	Thanksgiving	v.4-6
Body		Body	v.7-22
formulaic transition		joy expression[7]	v.7
travel plans		apostolic parousia[8]	v.21-22
Greetings		Greetings	v.23-24
Prayer sentence	=	Grace-benediction	v.25

B. Readily Apparent Oral Patterns

The relative brevity of Philemon limits the scope for oral patterning in the letter. There are, however, several items to note. The first is the presence of verbal correspondences between the letter opening and closing: (1) a form of συνεργός appears in both verse 1 and verse 24; and (2) references to prayer (προσευχή) appear in both verse 4 and verse 22.

Second, a form of inclusion frames the entire letter-body. The combination of ἀναπαύω and τὰ σπλάγχνα appears immediately following the joy expression that introduces the letter-body (v.7) and immediately preceding the confidence formula that opens the apostolic parousia (v.20). This combination is reinforced by the vocatives (ἀδελφέ) that also appear in these verses. Paul has used inclusion to delimit his plea on behalf of Onesimus in a way similar to that seen in some papyrus letters (e.g., P.Hib. 1:41; Ep. Diog. 41).

The result of these parallels is that the body of the letter is framed by the opening and closing epistolary elements:

A	Salutation	(v.1-3)	συνεργῷ ἡμῶν
B	Thanksgiving	(v.4-6)	ἐπὶ τῶν προσευχῶν μου
C	Opening of the letter-body	(v.7)	ὅτι τὰ σπλάγχνα τῶν ἁγίων ἀναπέπαυται διὰ σοῦ
C'	Closing of the letter-body	(v.20)	ἀνάπαυσόν μου τὰ σπλάγχνα ἐν Χριστῷ
B'	Apostolic parousia	(v.21-22)	διὰ τῶν προσευχῶν ὑμῶν
A'	Greetings and benediction	(v.23-25)	οἱ συνεργοί μου

---

[6] Cf. Doty, *Letters* 14.

[7] Cf. White (*Body* 76-79) and Jervis (*Romans* 100-101).

[8] Cf. White (*Body* 98-108) and Jervis (*Romans* 118-119).

Since a letter's opening and closing are intended to re-establish and maintain personal relations with the recipients, it is only natural that similar language will appear in both places.

Within the letter-body itself several key words are repeated, most notably παράκλησις and παρακαλέω (twice) in verses 7-10 and ὀφείλω and προσοφείλω in verses 18-19.[9] The threefold repetition of παρακλη- heightens the request Paul is making, and the repetition of -οφείλω artfully turns Philemon's potential concern over material debt (v.18) into a reminder of his spiritual debt to Paul (v.19).

Homoeoteleuton and word play are apparent in the sequence Ὀνήσιμον . . . ἄχρηστον . . . εὔχρηστον in verses 10-11, and homoioteleuton is present in verse 16: οὐκέτι ὡς δοῦλον ἀλλὰ ὑπερ δοῦλον, ἀδελφὸν ἀγαπητόν. These devices, that lay emphasis on Onesimus's changed status, would have appealed to the ear. Thus even in such a brief and personal a letter as Philemon, oral patterning informs Paul's composition and reinforces his message.

C. Other Suggested Structures

The single instance of chiasmus in Philemon, which has been frequently noted, is found in verse 5:[10]

ἀκούων	σου		τὴν ἀγάπην
		καὶ	τὴν πίστιν
	ἣν ἔχεις		πρὸς τὸν κύριον Ἰησοῦν
		καὶ	εἰς πάντας τοὺς ἁγίους

Philemon's love is directed toward "all the saints," and his faith is directed toward "the Lord Jesus." Here, however, the chiasmus is purely conceptual. It bears little relation to acoustic resonances heard by an original audience or to oral patterns incorporated into a letter by a writer. And since these latter issues are the principal concerns of this study, the treatment of this verse will be left for others.[11]

Thomas Boys suggested that Philemon actually consists of a nine-part inverted system similar to concentric symmetry.[12] Welch built on Boys's analysis to arrive at the following ten-part structure:[13]

---

[9] Note also δέσμιος/δεσμός in verses 9-13 and πολλὴν in verses 7-8.

[10] See P. T. O'Brien for a list of scholars who have drawn attention to the chiasmus (*Colossians, Philemon* [Waco: Word, 1982] 278).

[11] E.g, M. J. Harris *Colossians & Philemon* (Grand Rapids: Eerdmans, 1991) 250.

[12] T. Boys, *Tactica Sacra* (London: Hamilton, 1924) 65-66.

[13] Welch, "Chiasmus" 225.

A	Epistolary	1-3
B	Paul's prayers for Philemon	4
C	Philemon's love, faith, and hospitality	5-7
D	Paul could use his authority	8
E	But prefers to make supplication	9-10
F	Onesimus a convert of Paul's	10
G	Paul has made Onesimus profitable	11
H	Receive Onesimus as Paul's own bowels	12
I	Paul retained Onesimus as Paul's minister in the bonds of the Gospel	13
J	Without Philemon's willing consent Paul will not require Philemon to take Onesimus back	14
J'	Perhaps the reason Onesimus left was so that Philemon could take Onesimus back forever	15
I'	Not as a servant but as a brother in the Lord	15
H'	Receive Onesimus as Paul's own self	17
G'	Paul will repay any wrong Onesimus has done	18-19
F'	Philemon indebted as a convert to Paul	19
E'	Paul makes supplication to Philemon	20
D'	Although he could ask for obedience	21
C'	Paul requests hospitality of Philemon	22
B'	Philemon's prayers for Paul	22
A'	Epistolary	23-25

Given the natural affinities between opening and closing sections of a letter, it is not surprising to find that Welch's scheme has strong verbal connections in the outer panels. It grows steadily weaker, however, as it moves toward the center. The "epistolary" elements (A, A') are related by the word συνεργός, and elements B and B' are related by the repetition of προσευχή. Welch's titles for C and C' suggest that hospitality is the common theme in both sections. The concept of hospitality, however, appears only in verse 22 (ἐτοίμαζέ μοι ξενίαν), with no point of correspondence—verbal or conceptual—in verses 5-7. In fact, the combination of ἀναπαύω and τὰ σπλάγχνα in verses 7 and 20 seems to argue against the correspondence proposed by Welch.

Some degree of conceptual correspondence exists between elements D/E and D'/E', but the same concept—i.e., that of asking rather than demanding—also appears in verse 14 and permeates the entire letter. Again, some degree of correspondence may be acknowledged between the concepts conveyed in the figurative language of F and F', but the stronger connection seems to be between ὀφείλει and προσοφείλεις in verses 18-19. As well, the correspondence suggested between G and G' is not readily apparent. In fact, the verb ὀνίνημι in verse 20 has the specific connotation of joy, benefit, or profit, and it might have been seen to have a stronger oral/aural connection to verse 11. There is a natural connection between sending (ἀναπέμπω) in verse 12 (H) and receiving (προσλαμβάνω) in verse 17 (H'), but the precise way in which I and J correspond to I' and J' is unclear. Furthermore, since

verses 12-17 are the heart of Paul's appeal on behalf of Onesimus, it seems
somewhat artificial to sub-divide the argument as Welch has done.

Lund has also refined Boys's outline, reducing it to a simpler, five-part
system:[14]

A	Salutation	1-3
B	Philemon's conduct toward all the saints. He is the object of Paul's prayer.	4-6
C	Paul had experienced much joy in the past, because his brother had refreshed the hearts of the saints.	7
D	Paul refrains from pressing his claims on Philemon and prefers to ask a favor of him.	8-11
E	Paul and Onesimus: He is beloved of Paul.	12-15
E'	Paul and Onesimus: Philemon should love him also.	16-17
D'	Paul offers to reimburse Philemon, though he might have pressed his claims on him.	18-19
C'	Paul expects much joy in the future in that his own heart will be refreshed through his brother.	20
B'	Philemon's conduct toward Paul, who is an object of the prayers of the saints.	21-22
A'	Salutation	23-25

This scheme accurately reflects the verbal parallels in the outer panels of the
letter (v.1-7 and v.20-25). The proposed parallel between D and D', however, is less
compelling, for it is built solely on the repetition of Paul's name. Paul had a habit,
it seems, of using his name to urge compliance (2 Cor 10:1; Gal 5:2), to affirm his
sincerity (1 Thess 2:18), and to close his letters (1 Cor 16:21). Building a parallel
on the use of his name alone, therefore, is tenuous. Furthermore, although Paul
appeals rather than commands in both paragraphs, that particular feature runs
throughout the letter (e.g., v.14). It seems unwise, therefore, to limit such a
significant theme only to these verses. A much stronger case could have been made
if the key words of verses 7-10 (παράκλησις and παρακαλέω) had reappeared
in verses 18-19.

Lund also sees a "strophic arrangement" that creates "definite limits to the
separate sections in which the letter is written."[15] One of the samples that he offers
comprises verses 12-15:[16]

> ὃν ἀνέπεμψά σοι, αὐτόν,
> τοῦτ' ἔστιν τὰ ἐμὰ σπλάγχνα·
>   ὃν ἐγὼ ἐβουλόμην πρὸς ἐμαυτὸν κατέχειν,
>   ἵνα ὑπὲρ σοῦ μοι διακονῇ ἐν τοῖς δεσμοῖς τοῦ εὐαγγελίου,
>   χωρὶς δὲ τῆς σῆς γνώμης

---

[14] Lund, *Chiasmus* 219.

[15] Ibid. n.4.

[16] Ibid. 220. The UBS text has been segmented according to Lund's English outline.

οὐδὲν ἠθέλησα ποιῆσαι,
ἵνα μὴ ὡς κατὰ ἀνάγκην τὸ ἀγαθόν σου ᾖ
ἀλλὰ κατὰ ἑκούσιον.
τάχα γὰρ διὰ τοῦτο ἐχωρίσθη πρὸς ὥραν
ἵνα αἰώνιον αὐτὸν ἀπέχῃς,

Apart from the notorious difficulty of identifying "strophic arrangements" in the NT, Lund's proposal for these verses has several weaknesses. First, although it may be conceded that verses 12-15 (as well as verses 16-17) focus on Paul and Onesimus, the entire letter is concerned with Paul, Onesimus, and Philemon. The discussion of Onesimus actually begins in verse 10, a fact that Lund's scheme ignores in that it detaches the relative clause of verse 12 from its main clause (v.10-11). Second, verse 15 seems to go more naturally with verses 16-17 than with verses 12-14. This connection is especially strong in that verses 15 and 16 comprise a single idea, consisting of a number of contrasts (hour-eternity, servant-brother, me-you, flesh-Lord). Third, the title given to this element sacrifices content for correspondence. Although limiting verses 12-15 (or, better, 12-14) to the subject of Paul's love for Onesimus certainly captures the tone of verse 12, it ignores the content of verses 13-14. Finally, the parallels that Lund proposes are tenuous at best and lack any points of verbal correspondence.

Both Welch's and Lund's proposals reflect the points of verbal correspondence between the epistolary opening and closing. Each, however, has weaknesses at its center. Neither is particularly compelling. It seems, therefore, wisest to adopt a somewhat less rigidly structured understanding of the letter-body.

D. Summary

Inclusion frames the letter-body of Philemon. Two small-scale examples of word-chain appear within the body. Homoeoteleuton and word-play are also present. The single instance of chiasmus is conceptual rather than oral/aural. Although three key words in the letter opening appear in inverted order in the closing, attempts to impose inversion or concentric symmetry on the entire letter cannot be sustained. The letter contains no examples of alternation, ring-composition, or refrain.

Chapter 13

PAUL'S USE OF ORAL PATTERNS

The survey of the data in Chapters 6-12 has highlighted numerous examples of oral patterning in Paul's letters. They range from patterns within individual clauses to patterns that organize whole sections of a particular letter. There are many similarities to patterns seen in the extrabiblical materials and in the OT. There are also, however, significant differences. The task in this present, final chapter will be to examine those similarities and differences more closely.

A. The Categories Delineated

Chapters 3-5 identified eight categories of oral patterning found in Greco-Roman rhetoric and literature and in the OT. Characteristic features were noted, and criteria for recognizing examples established. A brief review of those findings is here in order:

1. *Chiasmus* is the transposition of corresponding words or phrases at the sentence level. The words or phrases transposed are usually identical, synonymous, or antonymous. Chiasmus functions in three ways: (a) to reinforce a point, (b) to make a comparison, and (c) to sharpen a contrast.

2. *Inversion* refers to the reversal of the order in which two or more topics are introduced and subsequently discussed. In most cases the topics are reintroduced by name, often accompanied by the particles μέν and δέ. Inversion plays an important role in learning and memory skills.

3. *Alternation* has as its central characteristic the interplay between two alternate choices or ideas. The interplay may involve the repetition of words, the use of synonymns, the discussion of results, or the listing of specific examples. Alternation serves at least two functions: (a) it defines the issues at stake, and (b) it involves the listener/reader in the decision-making process.

4. *Inclusion* is the use of the same word(s) to begin and end a discussion. Exact correspondence must be sought; synonyms or antonyms are not acceptable. This pattern is clearest when the words are used infrequently in the immediate context. The primary purpose of inclusion is to delimit discrete topics in extended discussions.

5. *Ring-composition* refers to the correspondence in wording between sentences that frame a section. In either case, similar wording is used in both sentences. Anaphoric ring-composition sets off a section of a discussion; inclusive ring-composition resumes a train of thought.

6. *Word-chain* is defined as the frequent repetition of a given word and its cognates within a clearly delimited context. The repetition often emphasizes or gives color to the topic under discussion.

7. *Refrain* is the use of repeated wording or formulaic phrases to open and/or close sections of a discussion. Although this pattern is close to ring-composition, it differs in that an opening statement may not be balanced by a closing statement, or vice versa. Refrain serves both to mark the beginning (or ending) of successive sections and to unify extended portions of a work.

8. *Concentric symmetry* involves multiple correspondences that occur over an extended passage and have a single element at the center. The point of correspondence should be verbal and grammatical, rather than purely conceptual. Verbal parallels should involve central or dominant terminology not regularly found elsewhere in the structure. Concentric symmetry tends to focus attention on the central element of the structure, which usually has some degree of significance. A simpler variation of concentric symmetry is the ABA' pattern.[1]

Paul uses all of the oral patterns found in the Greco-Roman and OT materials investigated, but he does not use all of them with the same frequency. As might be expected, Paul's longer letters have more instances of oral patterning than are present in his shorter letters. In fact, the descending sequence of total oral patterns (from high to low) follows almost exactly the canonical sequence of the letters (from long to short). Galatians is the exception, having the second lowest total of oral patterns even though it is the fourth longest letter. Chiasmus and word-chain are the only two patterns that are present in all seven letters. Inversion, inclusion, ABA', ring-

---

[1] Since the ABA' structure plays such a significant role in Paul's letters, it has been listed as a separate pattern in the charts that follow.

composition, and alternation form a "second tier," appearing relatively frequently (16-33x) and in at least five of the letters. Concentric symmetry (9x) and refrain (5x) are the least frequently used patterns, both in number of occurrences and in number of letters (four each). The following chart sets out their frequency:

	Rom	1 Cor	2 Cor	Gal	Phil	1 Thess	Phlm	Total
Chiasmus	24	12	11	9	4	3	1	64
Word-Chain	19	11	5	5	4	7	2	53
Inversion	8	10	4	2	8	1	0	33
Inclusion	9	4	7	0	5	2	2	29
ABA'	4	11	2	0	2	4	0	23
Ring-Comp.	6	3	4	0	3	3	0	19
Alternation	4	4	2	2	3	1	0	16
Conc. Sym.	2	3	3	1	0	0	0	9
Refrain	2	1	1	0	0	1	0	5
Total	78	59	39	19	29	22	5	251

When the extent of oral patterns in the letters is examined, however, a different distribution results. The table that follows is based on the number of lines in the UBS GNT that a given pattern encompasses. For example, chiasmus—as defined in this study—commonly occurs in either one or two lines; inversion, on the other hand, might encompass four lines or forty lines, depending on the specific construction.

	Rom	1 Cor	2 Cor	Gal	Phil	1 Thess	Phlm	Total	%
Word-Chain	281	377	193	152	29	112	11	1155	53.3
ABA'	177	361	159	0	107	132	0	936	43.2
Conc. Sym.	246	163	282	11	0	0	0	702	32.4
Refrain	248	158	124	0	0	151	0	681	31.4
Inclusion	85	79	56	0	183	38	24	465	21.5
Ring-Comp.	58	10	323	0	50	9	0	450	20.8
Inversion	42	229	12	22	39	12	0	356	16.4
Alternation	26	21	19	42	15	12	0	135	6.4
Chiasmus	45	23	20	13	7	11	2	121	5.6

From this chart, it is clear that, although chiasmus is the most frequently used oral pattern in Paul's letters, it is the least extensive, comprising only 5.6% of the total text of the seven letters examined. Word-chain, which is second in frequency, is first in total extent (53.3%), although it commonly involves sections of moderate length (21.8 lines per occurrence). ABA' (40.7 lines per occurrence), concentric symmetry (79.1 lines per occurrence), and refrain (136.2 lines per occurrence) all tend to organize larger sections of Paul's letters. This latter fact is confirmed when such examples as 1 Cor 12-14 (ABA'), 2 Cor 1-7 (concentric symmetry), and Rom 5-8 (refrain) are taken into account. Inclusion, ring-composition, and inversion tend to organize smaller sections, although the inversions of 1 Cor 1:13-4:13 and 9:1-27, the ring-composition of 2 Cor 1:12-7:6, and the inclusion of Phil 1:27-4:9 are obvious exceptions.

One additional set of figures to note is the percentage of each letter that is affected by oral patterning. The table that follows is based on the number of lines in the UBS GNT. For each letter the data is listed first by oral pattern, then in terms of total lines for the entire letter.

	Rom	1 Cor	2 Cor	Gal	Phil	1 Thess	Phlm
Word-Chain	31.9	46.3	34.3	55.1	14.5	60.2	26.8
ABA'	20.1	44.3	28.2	0	53.5	71.0	0
Conc. Sym.	28.0	20.0	50.1	4.0	0	0	0
Refrain	28.2	19.4	22.0	0	0	81.2	0
Inclusion	9.7	9.7	9.9	0	91.5	20.4	58.5
Ring-Comp.	6.6	1.2	57.4	0	25.0	4.8	0
Inversion	4.8	28.1	2.1	8.0	19.5	6.5	0
Alternation	3.0	2.6	3.4	15.2	7.5	6.5	0
Chiasmus	5.1	2.9	3.6	4.7	3.5	5.9	4.9
Oral Patterns	650	629	438	184	161	162	24
UBS Text	880	815	563	276	200	186	41
% of Letter	73.8	77.2	77.8	67.4	80.5	87.1	58.5

Interestingly, Romans, 1 Corinthians, and 2 Corinthians have very similar percentages of their text touched by oral patterning. Galatians is, again, lower than might be expected, while Philippians and 1 Thessalonians both show somewhat higher percentages. Philemon is the least "oral" of the seven letters, a fact that is not surprising given its brevity.

B. Comparisons and Contrasts

Going beyond matters of definition, frequency, and extent, the use of oral patterning in Paul's letters needs to be treated. In particular, matters concerning comparisons and contrasts in Paul's usage vis-à-vis that found in the Greco-Roman treatments and the OT must here be discussed.

Chiasmus. As seen in the first chart above, Paul uses chiasmus frequently. Most often he repeats at least one word in each line (e.g., Rom 6:3; 1 Cor 6:13; Gal 6:13). Only rarely does he use synonyms (e.g, 1 Thess 5:5). Occasionally, the use of antonyms heightens a contrast (e.g., Rom 6:10; Gal 3:3). Periodically, a combination of elements occurs (e.g., Phil 3:3-4). Paul's use of chiasmus is probably to be attributed principally to his familiarity with the OT rather than to his knowledge of Greco-Roman rhetoric or literature. As well, it is worth noting that he consistently reproduces the chiastic structure of OT texts when he quotes them (e.g., Rom 10:19; 14:11; 15:9; 1 Cor 1:19).

Paul uses chiasmus in ways comparable to what appears in the OT, as well as in Greco-Roman rhetoric and literature. First, chiasmus serves to make statements memorable. This use is seen most clearly in Paul's Corinthian correspondence where he combats the rhetorical skills of the "super-apostles" and deals with a church enamored with slogans[2] (e.g., 1 Cor 6:13; 2 Cor 9:6; 10:12). Second, chiasmus can be used to sharpen contrasts, and so is especially well suited to Paul's antithetical style of argumentation (e.g., 1 Cor 14:22; Gal 6:8). Finally, Paul uses chiasmus for emphasis. By transposing elements in a sentence, repeated words are pushed to opposite ends or pulled together at the center. In so doing, Paul disrupts the expected word order and emphasizes the words that have been displaced (e.g., Rom 6:3; 2 Cor 5:21; Gal 2:20).

Inversion. Inversion of the more complex type, as seen in some Greco-Roman speakers and writers, occurs infrequently in Paul's letters. Paul has nothing, for instance, to compare with the intricate question and answer sequence that appears in Homer's *Odyssey* between Odysseus and his mother's ghost. The OT, however, uses inversion on a more limited scale, and there are a number of examples of inversion in Paul's letters that compare well with the OT usage.

The clearest example of inversion in Paul's letters is 1 Cor 1:13-4:13. Here he asks three rhetorical questions (1:13) and then answers them in reverse order (1:14-4:13): in 1:14-17 answering the third question (re: baptism); in 1:18-2:16 addressing at length the second question (re: the cross); with the first question being related directly to the problem of σχίσματα, which is characterized by the statements in 1:12. The repetition of two of these statements in 3:4 makes it evident

---

[2] For a discussion of the slogans appearing in 1 Corinthians, see Hurd, *I Corinthians* 67-68, 120-123.

that Paul has returned to the topic of σχίσματα in 3:1-4:13. So in 1 Cor 1:13-4:13, as noted earlier in Chapter 7, the overall structure is similar to Quintilian's discussion of physics, ethics, and dialectic (*Institutio Oratoria* 12.2.10-23).

A less clear example of inversion is 1 Cor 9:1-27, primarily because Paul asks four questions in rapid succession (9:1). It would be natural, given the pattern of 1:13-4:13, to expect him to address the four topics of these questions in the verses that follow. In fact, however, the third and fourth questions constitute the beginning of Paul's answer to the second question, an answer that encompasses 9:1b-2. The remainder of chapter 9 goes on to address the issue of Paul's freedom, first in terms of his "rights" as an apostle (9:3-18), then in terms of his willingness to surrender those rights for the progress of the gospel (9:19-23), and finally in athletic terms that illustrate his point (9:24-27).

On a smaller scale, Paul often inverts the order of two of the items that he takes up. His discussion of "vessels for honor and dishonor" in Romans 9 is one example. The contrast is established in 9:21; then in 9:22 Paul answers his own question, using slightly different terms in inverted order. The same pattern continues in Rom 9:24-29. The Jew-Gentile order of 9:24 is inverted in the OT quotations that follow in 9:25-29, although again in different terms.

This tendency toward inversion is also evident in the ABBA structures found in Paul's letters. In its basic antithetical form, Rom 2:7-10 fits into this category. Several passages in 1 and 2 Corinthians also fit the ABBA pattern (1 Cor 3:10-11; 6:15-17; 15:12-13; 15:15-16; 2 Cor 1:3-4). Paul occasionally uses μέν and δέ to reintroduce paired topics not mentioned by name in a manner reminiscent of Greco-Roman writings (e.g., 2 Cor 2:15-16).

Despite attempts to analyze larger sections of Paul's letters using this pattern, it seems best to conclude that Paul used inversion on an extended scale only occasionally. On the other hand, inversion on a smaller scale occurs within Paul's letters frequently and in ways similar to what can be found in the other writings surveyed. As well, it needs to be noted that Paul often uses rhetorical questions as part of his practice of inversion.

Alternation. Paul often expresses himself in antitheses, so it is not surprising that examples of alternation can be found in his letters. Nor, given his propensity for inversion, is it surprising that his discussion of alternatives commonly takes the form of an inverted or partially-inverted arrangement.

A relatively simple example occurs in 1 Cor 4:10, where, as is often the case, the final two elements are inverted to signal the end of the discussion. Another, longer example from 1 Corinthians appears in 1:22-25, where the structure is more complex because of the interplay of the terms "sign/power/strength" associated with the Jews and "wisdom" associated with the Gentiles. Rom 10:8-13 contains a well-balanced example, although attention is most often focused on the chiasmus of the central verses. Later in the same letter there is a slightly longer example in 14:7-9.

One of the most complex examples of alternation to be found in Paul's letters is that of 1 Cor 7:12-16. Within the basic ABBAABBA pattern of the passage is a smaller ABCDDCBA pattern found in 7:12-14.

In Paul, therefore, alternation sets the issues at stake in sharp contrast to one another. Although this pattern is rare in the OT materials surveyed, Paul's use of alternation reflects his Jewish background, for he exhibits a tendency to include a final "twist" at the end of the discussion to bring it to a memorable conclusion. This rhetorical feature is not seen in Greco-Roman speakers and writers. Probably it became a part of Paul's discourse as a result of his study of the OT.[3]

Inclusion. If inclusion is defined as the exact correspondence between words that are used infrequently in a given discussion,[4] then this particular pattern occurs less often in Paul's letters than might be imagined. One example that happens to coincide with a conventional epistolary section is found in the salutation of Romans (1:1-7). The use of inclusion to delimit the letter-body of Philemon has been noted. This pattern may be seen frequently in Paul's Corinthian correspondence (1 Cor 10:23-33; 11:17-22; 12:4-11; 2 Cor 1:12-14; 4:1-16; 10:1-11; 10:12-18; 13:1-10), and several interesting uses of inclusive/resumptive wording occur in Rom 14:1-15:13.

In both the OT and in extrabiblical works, the purpose of inclusion seems to have been to delimit discrete topics in an extended discussion. Interestingly, Paul's clearest uses of inclusion are found in 1 Corinthians, where is it widely agreed that he is addressing a series of discrete topics. One example is 11:17-34: whereas forms of ἐσθίω occur repeatedly in 11:17-34, συνέρχομαι occurs only at the beginning and end of the discussion. Similarly, the first paragraph of this section (11:17-22) is framed by inclusion using ἐπαινῶ.

Ring-Composition. Bassler's analysis of Rom 1:16-2:29 has drawn attention to the potential presence of ring-composition in Paul's letters. Although this rhetorical pattern is not pervasive, it is found in a number of places. Smaller-scale instances occur, for example, in Romans (e.g., 8:35-39), 1 Corinthians (e.g., 14:1-5), and 1 Thessalonians (e.g., 3:1-5; 4:1-10). In each case, Paul frames a discussion with inclusive ring-composition. The Romans example is especially memorable because Paul holds the repeated wording to the end of the paragraph and then expands it from τῆς ἀγάπης τοῦ Χριστοῦ to the more formal τῆς ἀγάπης τοῦ θεοῦ τῆς ἐν Χριστῷ Ἰησοῦ τῷ κυρίῳ ἡμῶν. In the last three examples the repetition actually begins rather than concludes the final sentence of the paragraph.

---

[3] For a discussion of this sort of pattern in the OT, see A. Mirsky, "Stylistic Device for Conclusion in Hebrew," *Semitics* 5 (1977) 9-23; cf. Parunak, "Oral Typesetting" 159-160.

[4] This statement is a combination of two criteria: (1) exact correspondence between words should be sought, and (2) the recurrence of seldom-used words is significant. See Chapter 5 above.

In 1 Cor 5:13 Paul uses an OT quotation found five times in Deuteronomy to close his discussion. The wording is not precisely the same as that of 5:2, but the similarities are strong enough to consider it an instance of inclusive ring-composition.[5] On a larger scale, Paul uses repeated wording to make transitions between sections of his argument. The relationship between 2 Cor 2:12-13 and 7:5-6 is an important example. Rather than viewing the similarities between 2:12-13 and 7:5-6 as evidence that a later redactor has inserted the intervening material, it is probably preferable to see these similarities as indicating anaphoric ring-composition. Paul, as noted earlier, is normally quite careful with his transitions.

1 Corinthians 12-14 is a more complex instance. The new topic of spiritual gifts is introduced with a disclosure formula in 12:1. Paul uses anaphoric ring-composition in 12:31a and 14:1 to frame the "digression" about love in chapter 13. The latter verse also serves as part of inclusive ring-composition framing 14:1-39. In a related pattern, it is possible to see 11:34b and 14:40 serving as a form of inclusion that links chapters 12-14 to the preceding discussion of church order in 11:2-34.

The preceding examples make it clear that Paul used ring-composition in his letters, although he did not use it with the formal consistency of, say, Herodotus. Paul's use was more varied. The framing might be inclusive, anaphoric, or both at once. It might also be resumptive or concluding. Regardless, the correspondences in wording would have helped the reader/listener find his/her way through the argument, thereby serving as a form of oral patterning.

Word-chain. A phenomenon closely related to Paul's use of inclusion and ring-composition is his fondness for word-chains and link-words. Fischer has observed how certain words tend to dominate portions of Paul's letters:

> Certain words recur in most passages as though they were a planetary train, all circling around in complex fashion to produce a simple motion at the last . . . it should be noted how these frequently used words tend to be keynotes and spin off into word-chains by synonyms, puns, word-plays and antithetical expressions.[6]

1 Cor 9:20-21 provides an intriguing micro-scale example of such a "planetary train": the noun νόμος (4x) gives way to ἄνομος (4x) which, in turn, is played off the rare cognate ἔννομος.[7]

Fischer argues that a change in a word-chain is a stronger indication of a new topic than inclusion is.[8] Paul's use of word-chains ís especially evident in Romans

---

[5] Talbert views it as inclusion (*Corinthians* 12).

[6] Fischer, "Literary Forms" 212.

[7] The only other NT use of ἔννομος is in Acts 19:39.

[8] Ibid. 214. Furthermore, he argues that such a change is a stronger indicator than opening formulae.

(e.g., ch. 5-8, 9-11, 14-15) and 1 Corinthians (e.g., ch. 5-6, 8-10), where they often help delimit sections that resolve into ABA' patterns. The frequency with which Paul uses word-chains and the way in which he uses them to unify sections of his letters reflects a form of oral patterning characteristic of Hebrew literature.[9] A comparable pattern, however, is not seen in the Greco-Roman speeches and writings surveyed earlier.

Refrain. Paul uses repeated wording in other ways as well. In Rom 14:1-2 and 15:1 he repeats forms of the ἀσθεν- word group to begin parallel sections. Strictly speaking, this is neither ring-composition nor inclusion. The word group, however, appears nowhere else in chapters 14-15,[10] and its repetition in 15:1 undoubtedly would have functioned to clue the listener to the resumption of a topic addressed earlier.

A similar use of resumptive wording occurs in 1 Thessalonians. The parallel organization of 1:2-10 and 2:13-16 has been discussed previously. It is sufficient here to note that similar wording begins the first and second sentences in each paragraph. Once again, Paul gives the listener/reader oral clues that he has returned to a topic begun earlier in the letter.

Such oral clues may be used to indicate the ends of sections as well. This kind of pattern is seen most clearly in Romans 5-8, where Paul uses similar wording to close each of his major sections (5:11, 21; 6:23; 7:25; 8:39). Interestingly, he also uses the phrase in the opening verse of chapter 5, thereby creating a form of inclusive ring-composition not only for 5:1-8:39 but for 5:1-11 as well. In this latter construction, the pattern is reinforced by the relative pronoun that follows in each sentence (δι' οὗ) and by the homoeoteleuton of τὴν προσαγωγὴν and τὴν καταλλαγὴν. This use of repeated wording to begin and/or end sections is similar to the use of refrain seen in the OT.

Concentric Symmetry. Concentric symmetry is rare in Paul, especially as the phenomenon was defined in Chapter 5: "multiple inverse correspondences that extend over a considerable expanse of material and have a single element at the center." The preceding statement is true despite numerous attempts to find elaborate concentric structures in his letters. In fact, the occasional examples that occur are mostly on a relatively small scale, such as those found in 1 Cor 11:8-12 and 2 Cor 8:16-23.

Paul actually displays a tendency toward more balanced structures. The frequent occurrence of ABBA patterns was noted above. There are also a number of ABCCBA patterns in his letters. These structures generally occur on a small scale

---

[9] Two additional examples from Ezekiel will reinforce this point: (1) זנה occurs 20 times in Ezekiel 16, 18 times in Ezekiel 23, and only 4 times elsewhere in the book; (2) רעה, although it is a common word elsewhere in the OT, occurs 15 times in Ezekiel 34 and only once in the other chapters.

[10] Cf., however, the textual variants at 14:21.

(e.g., 1 Cor 15:39-41; 2 Cor 12:7-9; Gal 4:4-6), although there is a longer example in Gal 3:7-14.

There are, it is true, a few instances of concentric symmetry that appear to structure larger sections of Paul's letters. The discussion of headcoverings in 1 Cor 11:2-16 is one example. Blomberg's suggestion for 2 Cor 2:14-4:6 is another example, as is his more complex proposal for 2 Cor 1-7.

In terms at least of their basic outlines, Paul's discussion of the problem of Israel in Romans 9-11 and his instruction on spiritual gifts in 1 Corinthians 12-14 are also possible examples of concentric symmetry. In each case, there is an "oscillation" in the word-chain from B to C to B', with the central panel being readily discernable. In neither case, however, is the connection between A and A' quite as clear. In both passages, the overall discussion could, perhaps, be resolved into an ABA' pattern. In fact, given Paul's fondness for the ABA' pattern, it might be preferable to view both Romans 9-11 and 1 Corinthians 12-14 in those terms.

Paul uses the ABA' pattern with much greater frequency than he does concentric symmetry. He uses it occasionally on a small scale (e.g., Rom 5:15-17). More commonly, however, he uses it at a larger scale. The details of the following examples have been discussed in previous chapters, and so only the references need to be included here: Rom 14:1-15:13; 1 Cor 5:1-6:20; 11:17-34; 12:4-31; 2 Cor 8:1-9:15; 1 Thess 1:2-2:16; 2:17-3:13.

Summary. In terms of oral patterning, Paul was neither a slavish imitator nor a groundbreaking pioneer. He was, rather, a creative user of those features that he found helpful. Some of his compositional techniques can be traced to his Jewish background; others, perhaps, were adopted from Greco-Roman rhetoric. Paul used oral patterns, regardless of their source, much as he used the Hellenistic letter form: in an almost unconscious manner as the most effective means of communicating his message.

C. Exegetical Insights

What remains in the investigation of oral patterning in Paul's letters is to see how the recognition of this phenomenon can assist in understanding and explaining the content of those letters. The present section, therefore, will summarize some of the more salient ways in which an analysis of oral patterns sheds light on Paul's message and the form in which that message was communicated. The letter to Philemon has been omitted because of the limited number of oral patterns present in it.

Romans. Oral patterning is helpful in tracing out the line of Paul's argument in Romans. One of the oral patterns that aids in understanding the function of Romans 5 in Paul's argument, for example, is that of word-chain. An analysis of the word-chains found in and around Romans 5 highlights that chapter's transitional nature and suggests that it is better not to pursue a sharp break either before, in the middle of, or at the end of the chapter. Romans 5 is transitional: 5:1-11 looks both backward to chapters 1-4 and forward to chapters 6-8; similarly, 5:12-21 has "connections in both directions." Paul's discussion of the life of faith flows naturally out of his discussion of justification by faith. Rhetorically, at least, the transition that takes place in Romans 5 is a smooth one.

Chapter 5 is not the only place in Romans where studying Paul's use of word-chains is helpful. Words that assume special prominence in 3:21-31 continue in Romans 4 and serve to clarify the three subdivisions within that chapter. Interestingly—after dominating 3:21-4:25 and then fading out in chapters 5-8—the δικαι- and πιστ- word groups take center stage again in Rom 9:30-10:21, this time at the center of an ABA' pattern. Here, as in other places, Paul uses the ABA' pattern to look at an issue from different perspectives. The discussion of righteousness by faith at the heart of chapters 9-11 demonstrates that these chapters are not an appendix or excursus, but are, in fact, directly related to what precedes—especially chapters 1-4.

Recognizing a shift in the word-chains within Rom 14:1-15:13 also helps resolve these chapters into an ABA' pattern. The shift in the word-chains is reinforced by a modified form of ring-composition in which repeated forms of the ἀσθεν- word group begin parallel sections (14:1-2; 15:1), and so cue the listener to the resumption of a topic addressed earlier. The center panel of the ABA' pattern is framed by inclusion and sets out Paul's basic teaching in these chapters: the strong brother (defined in 14:1-12) is to determine (κρίνω, 14:13) not to cause the weak brother to stumble (5x in 14:13-23) and thus stand condemned (κατακρίνω, 14:22-23) by his/her own conscience.

High concentrations of key words in portions of Romans 5-8 lend support to understanding these chapters as either an inverted structure or an ABA' pattern. Verbal parallels between 5:1-11 and 8:18-39 effectively frame the chapters, and a repeated refrain serves to unify them. Whether the overall structure of chapters 5-8 is seen as inverted or ABA', the effect is still the same: it focuses attention on the center of the section and its handling of the problems of sin and the law.

From another perspective, the repeated refrain that undergirds Romans 5-8 emphasizes the theological truth that the key to the problems of sin and the law—and, indeed, the key to the entire Christian life—is a life lived in and through "our Lord Jesus Christ." Similarly, on a smaller scale, the repeated refrain of 1:24, 26, 28 both ties together Paul's discussion of the revelation of God's wrath (1:18-32) and emphasizes the theological truth that mankind's desperate condition is directly tied to God's judicial "handing over" of those men and women who refuse to acknowledge his true status.

Elsewhere in Romans, ring-composition and the ABA' pattern help clarify the complex and seemingly disjointed argument of 5:12-21. Ring-composition also helps the listener/reader focus on the heart of Paul's teaching regarding indwelling sin (7:8-11, 17-20) in the midst of the complex argumentation of Romans 7. A combination of chiasmus and alternation in 10:8-13 reinforces the involvement of the entire person in responding to the gospel message.

1 Corinthians. Similarly in 1 Corinthians, oral patterning is helpful in understanding the train of Paul's argument. The way in which 1 Cor 6:12-20 relates to what precedes it, for example, presents a challenge. In some ways, this paragraph is similar to Rom 5:1-11 serving as a transition between major sections of the letter. Hurd has identified important points of contact between 6:12-20 and the main themes of chapters 7-15.[11] At the same time, 6:12-20 is clearly related to 5:1-11 by its use of the πορν- word-group, and so forms part of an ABA' pattern that encompasses chapters 5-6. This ABA' pattern sheds some light on the relation of 6:12-20 to its immediate context.

Generally, the central panel of an ABA' pattern is crucial to Paul's discussion in the outer panels. Such is the case, for example, in Romans 9-11 where the issue of Israel's apparent rejection is brought into contact with their response to the gospel of justification by faith (9:30-10:21). It is also true in Rom 14:1-15:13 where the discussion of strong and weak believers is given a very practical focus in the appeal to pursue peace and edification rather than putting obstacles in one another's way (14:13-23).

In 1 Corinthians 5-6 the central panel of 6:1-11 deals with lawsuits and believers' competency to judge issues within the church (6:2). The link-word in these verses is κρίνω, a word that also appears in 5:3, 5:12, and 5:13 related to church discipline of the incestuous man. The list of 6:9 clearly declares other sexual vices off-limits for believers and, by logical extension, worthy of disciplinary judgment. The Corinthians might believe that "all things are lawful" (6:12), but they are wrong: "The body is not for immorality, but for the Lord" (6:13). They must use the insight available to them ("Do you not know . . .?" 6:15) to make proper moral decisions that will result in glory to God (6:20). Although he does not explicitly use the word, Paul, in effect, is asking the Corinthians to exercise "judgment" in the use of their liberty. So here, liberty is limited by the specific sanctions of a vice list; later in 8:1-11:1 it will be limited by considerations of love for other believers (cf. 10:23).

Similar analyses can be made of 1 Corinthians 8-11 and 12-14. In both sections, what appears to be a "digression" is essential to Paul's argument: chapter 9 gives an extended example of how the principles of love limit liberty; chapter 13 reminds the Corinthians that love is the key to the exercise of spiritual gifts. These examples highlight the fact that Paul's thought is not as "disjointed" as it sometimes appears, and they support the contention that the ABA' pattern in 1 Corinthians 5-6 is the key to following Paul's argument in these chapters.

---

[11] Hurd, *I Corinthians* 86-89.

Two further instances of the ABA' pattern should be noted: in both 11:2-16 and 11:17-34, the central panel is the key to understanding the basis for Paul's position. In the first passage, the central panel (11:8-12) consists of a tightly-constructed argument related to the creation order. In the second passage, the central panel (11:23-26) invokes a piece of church tradition. In these adjoining sections, we see confirmed what may be inferred elsewhere in Paul's letters: that he sought validity for his instruction in both the OT and the tradition of the early church.

An understanding of the pattern of inversion is also useful in following the train of Paul's argument. Recognition of the inverted construction of 1:13-4:13 helps identify the issues that Paul is addressing and isolates those that he deems most important. Similarly, recognition of the inverted construction of 9:1-27 highlights the fact that Paul's discussion is focused on the way in which he limits his liberty, not on his rights as an apostle.

Paul uses alternation several times in 1 Corinthians, including the intricate discussion of 7:12-16. In each case, the pattern serves to contrast opposing attitudes (1:22-25; 4:10) or to work through the implications of a complex situation (7:2-4, 12-16). Recognizing the basic pattern of alternation helps the present-day reader identify the underlying issues and analyze the thrust of Paul's argument.

In conjunction with the alternating patterns present in chapter 7, Paul ties together his argument with repeated wording (7:7, 17, 20, 24) and focuses his primary point with chiasmus (7:22). Noting the latter two patterns is especially important if the basic thrust of Paul's thinking is to be kept in view. A more extensive use of repeated wording—whether it is considered ring-composition or refrain—is found in chapters 12-14, where Paul is careful to repeat similar words and phrases as he makes the transitions between the major sections of his argument. In each of these instances, correctly noting Paul's use of oral patterns helps keep in focus both the unity and the progression of the discussion.

2 Corinthians. As is true with respect to epistolary analysis, oral patterning likewise offers few answers to the question regarding whether canonical 2 Corinthians was originally more than one letter. An analysis of oral patterns within 2 Corinthians does, however, support the integrity of each of the three acknowledged sections within the letter (1-7, 8-9, 10-13).

If Blomberg's concentric arrangement is accepted, the unity of chapters 1-7 is confirmed. Furthermore, Paul's discussion in these chapters is given focus by the centrality of 5:11-21, a section that is held together by a word-chain and uses chiasmus (5:17, 21) to emphasize the new life made possible by Christ's substitutionary death. Similarly, recognition of either an ABA' or an ABBA pattern in chapters 8-9 confirms their unity and argues against the theory that these chapters combine fragments of two separate letters.

At a more detailed level, ring-composition offers an alternative to the partition theories that are often proposed to explain the "digression" of 2:14-7:4. The abrupt changes of topic at 2:14 and 7:5 and the apparent continuity between 2:13 and 7:5 have led some scholars to suggest that 2:14-7:4 is an interpolation. It is possible, however, that 2:12-13 and 7:5-6 represent an instance of anaphoric ring-composition. 2 Cor 7:5-6 is particularly well integrated with its surrounding context. The themes of tribulation (θλῖψις) and encouragement (παράκλησις) connect not only to the opening blessing section, but also to 7:4. In fact, παρακαλέω and παρακλήσις occur seven times in chapter 7 and constitute part of the word-chain that unifies 7:2-16. So here, two oral patterns lend support to the integrity of chapters 1-7. The possibility that Paul deliberately repeated himself as an oral cue for his listeners/readers must be given at least as much credence as the suggestion that a later redactor "pulled apart" 2:13 and 7:5 in order to insert 2:14-7:4.

Within 2:14-7:4, oral patterning offers a similar solution to the problem of 6:14-7:1. The points of verbal correspondence between 6:11-13 and 7:2-3 suggest the possible presence of either anaphoric ring-composition or an ABA' pattern. Such a suggestion, of course, does not answer the question of whether or not 6:14-7:1 reflects wording from a previous letter. Nevertheless, given Paul's use of repeated wording elsewhere, the possibility that this section was part of 2 Corinthians from the beginning must be accorded at least as much credence as the theory that a redactor inserted it later.

Oral patterns also play an important part in structuring 2 Corinthians 10-13. Inclusions using ἄπειμι and πάρειμι bracket both 10:1-11 and 13:1-10, thereby setting off the opening and closing paragraphs of the section. The phrase εἰς οἰκοδομὴν καὶ οὐκ εἰς καθαίρεσιν is repeated in both of these paragraphs as well (10:8; 13:10). In addition, 10:12-18 is framed by the phrase "commend ourselves" (συνίστημι + ἑαυτούς). Furthermore, the unity of 11:1-12:13 is reinforced by the eightfold repetition of ἄφρων/ἀφροσύνη[12] and the repetition of ὑστερηκέναι τῶν ὑπερλίαν ἀποστόλων in 11:5 and 12:11. Within chapters 10-13 there are a number of examples of chiasmus and concentric symmetry (10:11, 12; 12:7, 9, 20; 13:3). In fact, the frequency with which such oral patterns occur and the skill with which he uses them seem to run counter to Paul's statement (11:6) that he is "unskilled in speech" (ἰδιώτης τῷ λόγῳ). Although he was not a trained orator, Paul could use the common techniques of rhetorical composition when they served his purposes.

Galatians. Paul uses oral patterning in Galatians in two ways: (1) to focus his arguments, and (2) to sharpen the contrasts inherent in his polemic. The first use may be seen clearly in the inverted structure of 4:4-6, where Paul focuses on Jesus's saving activity vis-à-vis the Mosaic law. The repetition of ἐξαπέστειλεν ὁ θεὸς and τὸν υἱὸν αὐτοῦ frames the passage. The four short participial and ἵνα clauses stand in sharp contrast to the longer opening and closing lines. The repetition of γενόμενον and ἵνα catch the attention of the listener, as does the repetition of ὑπὸ

---

[12] 11:1, 16 (twice), 17, 19, 21; 12:6, 11.

νόμον. Whether or not these verses are a confessional formula drawn from the early church, as some suggest,[13] Paul uses them to good effect in his argument (3:18-4:11) that Jesus's incarnation brought to an end the law as the religious system that governs the life of believers.[14]

Paul uses inversion to focus his argument again in chapter 3, this time in a longer passage (3:7-14). At the heart of the structure, two OT quotations (Hab 2:4; Lev 18:5) contrast living ἐκ πίστεως (3:11) and living ἐξ ἔργων νόμου (3:12). This contrast is central to Paul's argument (3:1-18) against seeking righteousness by keeping the law.[15]

Paul also uses oral patterns to sharpen his polemic. Word-chains involving antithetical pairs run throughout chapters 3-4. In 3:1-14, the contrast drawn is between law and faith. After a section in which seed and promise come to the fore (3:15-22), law and faith reappear in 3:17-26. The subsequent discussion in 3:28-4:11 is dominated by the contrast between slave and heir.

The antithesis of flesh and Spirit is another prominent theme in Galatians. Paul repeatedly uses chiasmus to sharpen the contrast between these conflicting lifestyles (e.g., 3:3; 5:17; 6:8). A longer pattern of alternation in 5:16-25 places these same lifestyles in sharp contrast yet again. Flesh and Spirit might be in conflict (5:17), but Christ's death on the cross (5:24) has made believers alive to follow the Spirit. Paul concludes this section in 5:25 with a chiastically-framed summary statement that makes his point in a memorable way and encourages the behavior he wants the Galatians to adopt.

Philippians. The significance of understanding 1:3-5 as having an inverted structure is that τῇ μνείᾳ ὑμῶν would then point to the *Philippians'* remembrance of *Paul* (rather than the reverse), perhaps a monetary remembrance. Scholarly discussion of these verses has been extensive. Much of that discussion has focused on the interpretation of ἐπὶ πάσῃ τῇ μνείᾳ ὑμῶν. On the one hand, advocates favoring an objective genitive commonly formulate their arguments in terms of the use of ἐπί with the dative and Paul's use of μνεία.[16] On the other hand, O'Brien has addressed these issues from a perspective that views ὑμῶν as a subjective genitive.[17]

---

[13] E.g., Longenecker, *Galatians* 166.

[14] Longenecker labels this section "The Believer's Life not 'under Law' but 'in Christ': Against Nomism" (ibid. 135).

[15] Longenecker: "Righteousness Apart from the Law: Against Legalism" (ibid. 98).

[16] Cf. Hawthorne, *Philippians* 16; Silva, *Philippians* 48. It is interesting to note Silva's comment on 1:5 that ἐπί "is used to express the grounds of thanksgiving only here and in 1 Cor 1:4" (ibid. 50). This statement seems to weigh against his argument for 1:4 as temporal, especially since in the parallel passages "the construction is different" (ibid. 48). If Paul is capable of using ἐπί in a causal sense in verse 5, why must verse 4 be temporal?

[17] O'Brien, *Philippians* 58-61.

If the discussion is framed only in terms of the passage's linguistic possibilities, interpretation has resulted in a draw. If Paul's tendency toward inversion is acknowledged, however, the subjective genitive becomes more of a possibility, especially given Paul's practice of "telegraphing" the contents of his letters in the thanksgiving sections. Correspondence between the thanksgiving of 1:3-11 and the closing "thank you note" of 4:10-20, therefore, must be seen as going beyond the theme of thanksgiving to include also the *reason* for giving thanks: the Philippians' monetary gift.

Correctly acknowledging the presence of inclusion, alternation, and inversion, makes it possible to avoid the common error of subdividing 1:12-26, for the way in which these oral patterns are used suggests that 1:12-26 is a unit. Furthermore, paying careful attention to the oral patterns that are present suggests that the focus of the passage is 1:18-20, the precise verses where a break is commonly made.

A key pattern for a proper understanding of 1:12-26 is that of inclusion. It is this very pattern that occurs most frequently in Philippians and gives definition to other portions of Paul's letters (e.g., 1:27-30; 2:19-24; 2:25-30; 3:12-14). It has been proposed earlier, in Chapter 10, that the entirety of 1:27-4:9 is framed by inclusion. If this proposal is accurate, it confirms the unity of the larger portion of the letter.

Also supporting the integrity of Philippians is the presence of what may well be a modified form of ring-composition in 3:1 and 4:4. One argument offered for viewing the letter as a composite is that the similarities between verses 3:1 and 4:4 reflect wording that was originally contiguous but later pulled apart by a redactor who inserted a fragment of another letter (3:2-4:3). An alternate view is that Paul, in 4:4, repeated himself in order to bring his listeners back to where he had broken off at 3:1. Such a use of repeated wording would be in keeping with the rhetorical practices seen elsewhere in his letters.

Not only does the proposed inclusion around 1:27-4:9 support the unity of 1:1-4:9, it also offers a starting point for an understanding of the unusual position of the apostolic parousia (2:19-30). As discussed in Chapter 10 above, the numerous similarities between 2:1-18 and 3:1-4:1 suggest the presence of an ABA' pattern. The central panel of such a pattern would be 2:19-30. In this way, the apostolic parousia—and its glowing commendation of Timothy and Epaphroditus—is sandwiched between sections that call the listener/readers to humility (2:1-18) and the rejection of human accomplishment (3:1-4:1).

1 Thessalonians. Hurd and Johanson have shown how ring-composition and the ABA' pattern contribute to a proper understanding of the structure and argument of 1 Thessalonians. Both of these oral patterns are particularly prominent in the first three chapters. Two additional patterns must be highlighted: word-chain and refrain. Word-chain is helpful in determining both the extent and the focus of the ABA' patterns, while refrain sounds the important themes of looking for Christ's return

(1:3; 2:19; 3:13) and encouraging one another (4:18; 5:11) in the expectation of that return.

Reminiscent of the modified ring-composition seen in Rom 14:1-15:13 is the resumption in 1 Thess 2:13-14 of the topic addressed in 1:2-10. Similarly, 2:17-20 and 3:11-13 are roughly parallel and serve to frame the intervening verses. Hurd is correct in stating that the theme of 3:1-10 is "faith." Five of the eight occurrences of πίστις are found in these verses.[18] So here, as elsewhere in Paul's letters, a word-chain helps clarify an ABA' pattern.

The word-chain is somewhat less clear in 1:2-2:16. The evidence, however, seems to run counter to Hurd's suggestion that the theme of 2:1-12 is "love." Hurd correctly notes the use of ἀγαπητός in 2:8, but the only other occurrences of that word group in chapters 1 and 2 are ἀγάπη in 1:3 and ἀγαπάω in 1:4.[19] In contrast, words related to *speaking* "the gospel" and *receiving* "the word" are concentrated primarily in these chapters. Again, recognition of an ABA' pattern and the related word-chains helps to clarify Paul's thinking and focus his message. In 1:2-2:16 his emphasis is on the beginning of the *gospel* in Thessalonica; in 2:17-3:13 his concern is the continuance in *faith* of the Thessalonian believers.

If any word can be said to "structure" chapters 4 and 5, it would be παρακαλέω. This word occurs five times in these chapters, once in each of the major sections and at important places in each of those sections. In the sections on sexual purity (4:1-8) and brotherly love (4:9-12) Paul "encourages" the Thessalonians to "abound more" (περισσεύειν μᾶλλον; 4:1,10). He "encourages" them (5:14) to take certain actions in relation to church life (5:12-22). In both of the eschatological sections (4:11-18; 5:1-11), he closes with the admonition to "encourage one another" (παρακαλεῖτε ἀλλήλους; 4:18; 5:11). Also, the repetition of ἐλπίς in 4:13 and 5:8 might be a use of inclusion to frame these latter two sections.[20] In fact, the strategic placement of these two key words suggests that the focus of chapters 4 and 5 is on *encouragement* in Christian living (4:1-12; 5:12-22) and *hope* for the future (4:13-5:11).

Summary. Paul used different oral patterns depending on the rhetorical exigencies he faced.[21] The contrast between Galatians and 2 Corinthians 10-13, for example, is sharp. In both instances his writing is emotionally charged. That emotion, however, is channeled in different ways. To the Galatians he wrote in "black and white," sharpening the contrast between their thinking and his own through the use of chiasmus and alternation and focusing his arguments against legalism and nomism

---

[18] 3:2, 5, 6, 7, 10. The other uses are in 1:3, 8; 5:8.

[19] ἀγάπη also occurs in 3:6, 12; 5:8, 13; ἀγαπάω in 4:9.

[20] ἐλπίς occurs elsewhere in the letter only at 1:3 and 2:19.

[21] This conclusion agrees with Spencer's finding that Paul varied his writing style so that it was appropriate for the audience (cf. *Literary Style*).

through inversion. In writing to the Corinthians he framed the sections of his argument carefully, using inclusion and ring-composition and giving them a special polish that was, perhaps, intended to compare favorably with the rhetoric of the "super-apostles." To the Romans, whom he had never met, Paul wrote with care, making smooth transitions and using ABA' patterns to examine every aspect of an issue. 1 Corinthians reveals a similar use of the ABA' pattern in addressing the specific concerns of that congregation.

To the Philippians, probably his favorite congregation, Paul wrote a far-ranging "family letter" with an extended exhortation in 3:1-4:3 that is unified by the theme of "joy" and held together structurally by a liberal use of inclusion and a more restrained use of ring-composition. Paul's joyous response to Timothy's report on the Thessalonians' progress is reflected in 1 Thessalonians by the movement of thought from their reception of the gospel (1:2-2:16), to their continuance in faith (2:17-3:13), to their further growth and hope for the future (4:1-5:22)—a movement that is brought into sharper focus by examining Paul's use of ABA' patterns and word-chains.

Giving attention to oral patterning in Paul's letters is helpful on several levels. In some cases it uncovers evidence that must be considered in addressing issues of integrity. In other cases it helps clarify the line of Paul's argument. It can also help delimit the extent of certain passages and avoid subdividing thought units arbitrarily. Similarly, it can give clues to the focus of Paul's concern in a given passage and help clarify the relation of that concern to the surrounding context. In sum, it may be said that oral patterning offers an additional body of "formal" evidence that can be used in conjunction with other exegetical methods to help "fine-tune" the interpretation of Paul's letters.

CONCLUSION

Paul wrote letters. Because the finished product is literary, the natural tendency is to view the production of those letters from the perspective of a literate culture. Practitioners of epistolary analysis seek to isolate the "standard Pauline letter form" and make decisions regarding the integrity of certain letters based on how well they fit that literary form. Practitioners of rhetorical analysis seek to identify the ways in which Paul's letters conform to the parts of rhetorical discourses, frequently within the context of their literary composition. Scholars pore over Paul's letters in silence, applying literary techniques facilitated by our electronic age of computers and sophisticated software, ignoring the predominant orality of the culture within which those letters were produced. Only recently have scholars begun to acknowledge the way in which the rhetorical culture of the first century affected the composition of the NT writings.

Paul wrote letters because a letter was the most personal means available for communicating over a distance. Letters, however, had no narrative to assist the listener in following their organization. The listener required clues to that organization. One means of providing those clues was the use of epistolary conventions. But how did the listener follow the train of the argument in places where there were no epistolary conventions? This question is especially crucial for Paul's letters, for his letters are twice as long as Seneca's and ten times as long as Cicero's. The answer is that other compositional devices were used.

Rhetorical categories and figures were part of the culture of Paul's day. Rhetoric was "in the air, " and Paul was a creative user of the rhetorical features that he found helpful in communicating his message. Among those features were compositional devices that provided the listener with clues to the organization of longer discourses. Since those devices were patterns readily apparent to the ear and related to the oral dictation of Paul's letters, the term "oral patterning " has been used in this study to describe them.

A survey of selected Greco-Roman speakers and writers, coupled with a study of selected OT writings, has uncovered a number of frequently used oral patterns.

Further analysis (1) organized those patterns into the eight categories of chiasmus, inversion, alternation, inclusion, ring-composition, word-chain, refrain, and concentric symmetry, and (2) identified criteria for recognizing examples of each pattern. The purpose in the analysis of these categories and criteria has been to provide a foundation for the examination of oral patterning in Paul's letters.

The study of seven Pauline letters has identified numerous examples of oral patterning in Paul's letters, patterns that ranged from those within individual clauses to those that organized whole sections of particular letters. Of the patterns observed in the Greco-Roman and OT materials, all eight were found in Paul's letters. Yet Paul does not seem to have used these oral patterns with the same frequency, and the use he made of them differed depending on the rhetorical exigencies he faced. In addition, the ABA' pattern appears with some regularity in Paul's letters.

Exegetically, the examination of Paul's letters has suggested that giving attention to oral patterning can be used, in conjunction with other methods, to sharpen the interpretation of those letters. It can help uncover evidence that should be considered in addressing issues of integrity. It can shed new light on interpretive difficulties. It can help clarify the line of Paul's argument. It can help identify the focus of a given passage and clarify the relation of that passage to its context.

Homiletically, recognizing the presence of oral patterns in Paul's letters can be helpful as well. Major turning points can be identified, with the extent of particular thought patterns then clarified. If, for example, Paul intended Phil 1:12-26 to be taken as a unit (as has been suggested above), we do a serious disservice to Paul's message by subdividing this section into two or three parts. Giving careful attention to the oral patterns present in the passage can inform our understanding of both the content and the communication of that message.

On another level, the study of oral patterning in Paul's letters should challenge anyone seriously concerned with communicating the NT message effectively. As Boomershine has noted, the end of the twentieth century is experiencing another "paradigm shift": the shift from print media to electronic media. In terms of the "cultures" discussed earlier in this study, it might be characterized as a shift from a literate culture to an aural-visual culture. People read less and are entertained more. Sight and sound dominate popular culture. This is the age of the satellite dish and the hand-held television. A household without a computer, a compact disc player, and a video cassette recorder is considered "behind the times." The average television commercial lasts fifteen to thirty seconds, with the images changing at least once per second. Sound and motion hardware for computers is becoming commonplace, and time spent "surfing the internet" is rapidly overtaking time spent in front of the television. Sales of home video games are skyrocketing. Experiments in virtual reality seek to integrate input for all five of the senses into a single entertainment package. Although literacy is still important, popular communication has moved off the printed page and away from silent documents to interactive technology and "talking books." In a very real sense, oral communication is again moving to the forefront.

What was it about Paul's letters that led his opponents to say, "His letters are weighty and strong" (2 Cor 10:10)? Could it be that part of the answer lies in his use of oral patterning? Could it be that we can learn not only from Paul's theology but also from his rhetoric? Could it be that part of the solution to the challenges of communication in our aural-visual culture lies in an analysis of oral patterning and the application of principles derived from that analysis? These questions, of course, are beyond the scope of this study. Pursuing their answers, however, is well worth the time and effort required.

BIBLIOGRAPHY

A. Biblical Texts

Biblica Hebraica Stuttgartensia. Ed. K. Ellinger, W. Rudolph. Stuttgart: Deutsche Bibelstiftung, 1983.

Deuteronomium. Ed. J. W. Wevers. Göttingen: Vandenhoeck & Ruprecht, 1977.

Genesis. Ed. J. W. Wevers. Göttingen: Vandenhoeck & Ruprecht, 1974.

The Greek New Testament. 3rd ed. Ed. K. Aland, M. Black, C. M. Martini, B. M. Metzger, and A. Wikgren. New York: United Bible Societies, 1975.

Isaias. Ed. J. Ziegler. Göttingen: Vandenhoeck & Ruprecht, 1939.

Novum Testamentum Graece. 26th ed. Ed. E. and E. Nestle, B. Aland, K. Aland, M. Black, C. M. Martini, B. M. Metzger, and A. Wikgren. Stuttgart: Bibelgesellschaft, 1979.

B. Greco-Roman Literature

Aristotle. *Works*. 3 vols. Eds. Academia Regia Borussica. Berlin: de Gruyter, 1960.

Aristotle [Ps]. *Rhetorica ad Alexandrum*. Trans. H. Rackham. Cambridge, MA: Harvard University Press, 1937.

Augustine. *Christian Doctrine*. Trans. M. Dods. A Select Library of the Nicene and Post-Nicene Fathers of the Christian Church. Grand Rapids: Eerdmans, 1979.

_____. *City of God*. Trans. J. F. Shaw. A Select Library of the Nicene and Post-Nicene Fathers of the Christian Church. Grand Rapids: Eerdmans, 1979.

Chrysostom. *Homilies on Romans*. Trans. J. B. Morris and W. H. Simcox. A Select Library of the Nicene and Post-Nicene Fathers of the Christian Church. Grand Rapids: Eerdmans, 1989.

_____. *Homilies on First and Second Corinthians*. Trans. T. W. Chambers. A Select Library of the Nicene and Post-Nicene Fathers of the Christian Church. Grand Rapids: Eerdmans, 1989.

_____. *Homilies on Philippians, Colossians, and Thessalonians*. Oxford Translations Revised. A Select Library of the Nicene and Post-Nicene Fathers of the Christian Church. Grand Rapids: Eerdmans, 1979.

Cicero. *De Inventione*. Trans. H. M. Hubbell. Cambridge, MA: Harvard Univesity Press, 1949.

_____. *De Oratore*. Ed. K. F. Kumaniecki. Leipzig: Teubner, 1995.

_____. *Letters to Atticus*. 3 vols. Trans. E. O. Winstedt. Cambridge, MA: Harvard University Press, 1919.

_____. *Orator*. Ed. R. Westman. Leipzig: Teubner, 1980.

Cicero [Ps]. *Rhetorica ad Herennium*. Ed. G. Achard. Paris: Société d'Edition "Les Belles Lettres," 1956.

The Cynic Epistles. Ed. A. J. Malherbe. Missoula, MT: Scholars Press, 1977.

Demetrius. *On Style*. Trans. W. R. Roberts. Cambridge, MA: Harvard University Press, 1927.

Demosthenes. *Orations*. 3 vols. Ed. S. H. Butcher. Oxford: Clarendon, 1903.

Dio Chrysostom. *Orations*. 2 vols. Ed. G. de Budé. Leipzig: Teubner, 1916.

Epictetus. *Discourses*. 2 vols. Trans. W. A. Oldfather. New York: Putnam, 1926.

Epicurus: The Extant Remains. Trans. C. Bailey. Oxford: Clarendon, 1926.

Eusebius. *Ecclesiastical History*. 2 vols. Trans. K. Lake (vol 1) and J. E. L. Oulton (vol 2). Cambridge, MA: Harvard University Press, 1969, 1975.

Herodotus. *Histories*. 2 vols. Ed. C. Hude. Oxford: Clarendon, 1908.

The Hibeh Papyri. 2 vols. Trans. B. P. Grenfell, A. S. Hunt, E. G. Turner, and M. -Th. Lenger. London, Egypt Exploration Society, 1906, 1955.

Homer. *Works*. 4 vols. Eds. D. B. Morris, and T. W. Allen. Oxford: Clarendon, 1902.

Isocrates. *Discourses*. 4 vols. Eds. G. Mathieu and E. Brémond. Paris: Société d'Edition "Les Belles Lettres," 1956.

Methodius. Trans. W. R. Clark. The Ante-Nicene Fathers. Grand Rapids: Eerdmans, 1978.

The Oxyrhynchus Papyri. 44 vol. Trans. B. P. Grenfell, A. S. Hunt, et al. London: Egypt Exploration Society, 1898-1976.

Petronius. *Satryicon*. Trans. M. Heseltine. London: Heinemann, 1969.

Plato. *Works*. 5 vols. Eds. I. Burnet, et al. Oxford: Clarendon, 1901.

Pliny. *Letters and Panegyricus*. 2 vols. Trans. B. Radice. Cambridge, MA: Harvard University Press, 1972.

Quintilian. *Institutio Oratoria*. 2 vols. Ed. M. Winterbottom. Oxford: University Press, 1970.

Seneca. *Epistulae Morales*. 3 vols. Trans. R. M. Cummere. Cambridge, MA: Harvard University Press, 1970.

_____. *Moral Essays*. 3 vols. Trans. J. W. Basore. Cambridge, MA: Harvard University Press, 1970.

C. Commentaries, Monographs, and Articles

Achtemeier, P. J. *"Omne Verbum Sonat*: The New Testament and the Oral Environment of Late Western Antiquity." *JBL* 109 (1990) 3-27.

Aland, K. and Aland, B. *The Text of the New Testament*. Trans. E. F. Rhodes. Grand Rapids: Eerdmans, 1987.

Aletti, J. N. "La présence d'un modèle rhétorique en Romains: Son rôle et son importance." *Bib* 71 (1990) 1-24.

_____. "La *dispositio* rhétorique dan les épîtres pauliniennes: Propositions de méthode." *NTS* 38 (1992) 385-401.

Alexander, L. "Hellenistic Letter-Forms and the Structure of Philippians." *JSNT* 37 (1987) 87-101.

Allo, E. B. "Le défaut d'éloquence et le style oral de Saint Paul." *RSPT* 23 (1934) 29-39.

Amphoux, C. -B. "Le Style oral dans le Nouveau Testament." *ETR* 63 (1988) 379-384.

Aune, D. E. Review of *Galatians* by H. D. Betz. In *RelSRev* 7 (1981) 323-328.

Bahr, G. J. "Paul and Letter Writing in the Fifth [*sic*] Century." *CBQ* 28 (1966) 465-477.

_____. "The Subscriptions in the Pauline Letters." *JBL* 87 (1968) 27-41.

Bailey, K. E. "Recovering the Poetic Structure of I Cor i.17-ii.2." *NovT* 17 (1975) 265-296.

_____. *Poet and Peasant*. Grand Rapids: Eerdmans, 1976.

Barrett, C. K. *A Commentary on the First Epistle to the Corinthians*. New York: Harper and Row, 1968.

Bassler, J. M. *Divine Impartiality: Paul and a Theological Axiom*. SBLDS 59. Chico, CA: Scholars, 1982.

Bauer, K. L. *Logica Paullina*. Halle, 1774.

_____. *Rhetoricae Paullinae*. Halle, 1782.

Baumgarten, S. J. *Auslegung der beiden Briefe St. Pauli and die Corinthier*. Halle: Gebauer, 1761.

Beare, F. W. *A Commentary on the Epistle to the Philippians*. New York: Harper & Row, 1959.

Belleville, L. L. "Continuity or Discontinuity: A Fresh Look at 1 Corinthians in the Light of First-Century Epistolary Forms and Conventions." *EvQ* 59 (1987) 15-37.

_____. "A Letter of Apologetic Self-Commendation: 2 Cor 1:8-7:16." *NovT* 31 (1989) 142-163.

_____. *Reflections of Glory: Paul's Polemical Use of the Moses-Doxa Tradition in 2 Corinthians 3.1-18*. JSNTSup 52. Sheffield: JSOT Press, 1991.

Bengel, J. A. *Gnomon Novi Testamenti*. 2 vols. n.p., 1742.

Berchman, R. M. "Galatians (1:1-5): Paul and Greco-Roman Rhetoric." In *Judaic and Christian Interpretation of Texts: Contents and Contexts*, eds., J. Neusner and E. Frerichs, 1-15. New York: University of America, 1987.

Berger, K. "Apostelbrief und apostolische Rede: Zum Formular frühlicher Briefe." *ZNW* 65 (1974) 190-231.

Betz, H. D. *Der Apostel Paulus und die sokratische Tradition: Eine exegetische Untersuchung zu seiner 'Apologie' 2 Kor 10-13*. Tübingen: Mohr-Siebeck, 1972.

_____. "2 Cor 6.14-7.1: An Anti-Pauline Fragment?" *JBL* 92 (1973) 88-108.

_____. "The Literary Composition and Function of Paul's Letter to the Galatians." *NTS* 21 (1975) 353-379.

_____. *Galatians: A Commentary on Paul's Letter to the Churches in Galatia*. Philadelphia: Fortress, 1979.

_____. "The Problem of Rhetoric and Theology according to the Apostle Paul." In *L'Apôtre Paul*, ed. A. Vanhoye, 16-48. Leuven: Peeters/Leuven University, 1986.

_____. *2 Corinthians 8 & 9*. Philadelphia: Fortress, 1985.

Bjerkelund, C. J. *Parakalo: Form, Funktion, und Sinn der parakalo-Sätze in den paulinischen Briefen*. Oslo: Universitetsforlaget, 1967.

Black, C. C. "Rhetorical Criticism and the New Testament." *PEGLMBS* 8 (1988) 77-70.

_____. "Rhetorical Criticism and Biblical Interpretation." *ExpTim* 100 (1989) 254-255.

_____. "Rhetorical Questions: The New Testament, Classical Rhetoric, and Current Interpretation." *Dialog* 29 (1990) 62-70.

Black, D. A. "Paul and Christian Unity: A Formal Analysis of Philippians 2:1-4." *JETS* 28 (1985) 299-308.

_____. "The Pauline Love Command: Structure, Style, and Ethics in Romans 12:9-21." *FilNeot* 2 (1989) 3-22.

Black, E. *Rhetorical Criticism: A Study in Method*. New York: Macmillan, 1965.

Blass, F. *Die Rhythmen der asianischen und römischen Kunstprosa*. Leipzig: Deichert, 1905.

Bligh, J. *Galatians in Greek: A Structural Analysis of Paul's Epistle to the Galatians*. Detroit: University of Detroit Press, 1966.

_____. Review of *Carmen Christi*, by R. P. Martin. In *Bib* 49 (1968) 127-129.

_____. *Galatians—A Discussion of Paul's Epistle*. London: St. Paul, 1969.

Blomberg, C. L. "The Structure of 2 Corinthians 1-7." *CTR* 4 (1989) 3-20.

Boers, H. "Form Critical Study of Paul's Letters. 1 Thessalonians as a Case Study." *NTS* 22 (1976) 140-158.

Boobyer, G. H. *'Thanksgiving' and the 'Glory of God' in Paul*. Borna/Leipzig: Noske, 1929.

Boomershine, T. E. "Biblical Megatrends: Towards a Paradigm for the Interpretation of the Bible in Electronic Media." *SBLSP* (1987) 144-157.

Botha, P. J. J. "Mute Manuscripts: Analysing a Neglected Aspect of Ancient Communication." *TE* 23 (1990) 35-47.

_____. "The Verbal Art of the Pauline Letters: Rhetoric, Performance and Presence." In *Rhetoric and the New Testament: Essays from the 1992 Heidelberg Conference*, eds. S. E. Porter and T. H. Olbricht, 409-428. JSNTSup 90. Sheffield: JSOT Press, 1993.

Bowman, G. "Noch einmal Römer 1,21-32." *Bib* 54 (1973) 413-414.

Bowra, C. M. *Homer*. London: Duckworth, 1972.

Boys, T. *Tactica Sacra*. London: Hamilton, 1924.

Bradley, D. G. "The *Topos* as a Form in the Pauline Paraenesis." *JBL* 72 (1953) 238-246.

Brandt, W. J. *The Rhetoric of Argumentation*. New York: Bobbs-Merrill, 1970.

Breck, J. "Biblical Chiasmus: Exploring Structure for Meaning." *BTB* 17 (1987) 70-74.

Brinsmead, B. H. *Galatians—Dialogical Response to Opponents*. SBLDS 65. Chico, CA: Scholars, 1982.

Brown, M. T. "The Interpreter's Audience: A Study of Rhetoric and Hermeneutics." Ph.D. dissertation, Graduate Theological Union, 1978.

Bruce, F. F. *Commentary on Galatians*. Grand Rapids: Eerdmans, 1982.

_____. *1 & 2 Thessalonians*. Waco: Word, 1982.

Brunot, A. *La génie littéraire de Saint Paul*. Paris: Cerf, 1955.

Bühlmann, W. and Scherer, K. *Stilfiguren der Bibel*. Freiberg: Herder, 1973.

Bullinger, E. W. *Figures of Speech Used in the Bible Explained and Illustrated*. London: Eyre and Spottiswood, 1898. Reprint edition, Grand Rapids: Baker, 1968.

Bultmann, R. *Der Stil der paulinischen Predigt und die kynische-stoische Diatribe*. Göttingen: Vandenhoeck & Ruprecht, 1910.

_____. *History of the Synoptic Tradition*. Trans. J. Marsh. New York: Harper and Row, 1963. First German edition, 1921.

_____. *Theology of the New Testament*. 2 vols. Trans. K. Grobel. New York: Charles Scribner's Sons, 1951, 1955.

_____. *Existence & Faith: Shorter Writings of Rudolf Bultmann*. Trans. S. M. Ogden. New York: Meridian, 1960.

Bünker, M. *Briefformular und rhetorische Disposition im 1. Korintherbrief*. Göttingen: Vandenhoeck & Ruprecht 1983.

Burton, E. deW. *A Critical and Exegetical Commentary on the Epistle to the Galatians*. Edinburgh: T & T Clark, 1921.

Burke, K. *A Rhetoric of Motives*. New York: Braziller, 1955.

Campbell, D. A. *The Rhetoric of Righteousness in Romans 3:21-26*. JSNTSup 65. Sheffield: Academic Press, 1992.

Ceresko, A. "The Chiastic Word Pattern in Hebrew." *CBQ* 38 (1976) 303-311.

_____. "The Function of Chiasmus in Hebrew Poetry." *CBQ* 40 (1978) 1-10.

Champion, L. "Benedictions and Doxologies in the Epistles of Paul." Dissertation. Ruprecht-Karls Universität, Heidelberg, 1933.

Chevallier, M. A. "L'Argumentation de Paul dans 2 Corinthiens 10 á 13." *RHPR* 70 (1990) 3-15.

Church, F. F. "Rhetorical Structure and Design in Paul's Letter to Philemon." *HTR* 71 (1978) 17-33.

Clanchy, M. T. *From Memory to Written Record: England, 1066-1307*. Cambridge, MA: Harvard University Press, 1979.

Clark, D. J. "Criteria for Identifying Chiasm." *LB* 35 (1975) 63-72.

Clark, D. L. *Rhetoric in Greco-Roman Education*. New York: Columbia University Press, 1957.

Cosby, M. R. "Paul's Persuasive Language in Romans 5." In *Persuasive Artistry: Studies in New Testament Rhetoric in Honor of George A. Kennedy*, ed. D. F. Watson, 209-226. JSNTSup 50. Sheffield: Academic Press, 1991.

Coetzer, W. C. "The Literary Genre of Paraenesis in the Pauline Letters." *TE* 17 (1984) 36-42.

Collange, J -F. *The Epistle of Saint Paul to the Philippians*. London: Epworth, 1979.

Collins, J. J. "Chiasmus, the 'ABA' Pattern and the Text of Paul." In *Studiorum Paulinorum Congressus Internationalis Catholicus*, 2:575-583. AnBib 18. Rome: Pontifical Biblical Institute, 1963.

Colson, F. H. "Μετασχηματισα 1 Cor iv 6." *JTS* 17 (1915-16) 379-384.

Conzelmann, H. *1 Corinthians*. Trans. J. W. Leitch. Philadelphia: Fortress, 1975.

Corbett, E. *Classical Rhetoric for the Modern Student*. New York: Oxford University Press, 1965.

_____., ed. *Rhetorical Analysis of Literary Works*. New York: Oxford University Press, 1965.

Craddock, F. B. *Philippians*. Atlanta: John Knox, 1985.

Craigie, P. C. *The Book of Deuteronomy*. Grand Rapids: Eerdmans, 1976.

Cranfield, C. E. B. *The Epistle to the Romans*. 2 vols. Edinburgh: T & T Clark, 1975.

Creed, R. P. "Studies in the Techniques of Composition of the *Beowulf* Poetry in British Museum MS. Cotton Vitellius A. xv." Ph.D. dissertation. Harvard University, 1955.

_____. "*Beowulf* 2231a: sinc-fœt (sōhte)." *PQ* 35 (1956) 206-208.

_____. "The *andswarode*-System in Old English Poetry." *Speculum* 32 (1957) 523-528.

_____. "On the Possibility of Criticizing Old English Poetry." *Texas Studies in Literature and Language* 3 (1961) 97-106.

_____. "The Singer Looks at His Sources." *CompLit* 14 (1962) 44-52.

_____. "The *Beowulf*-Poet: Master of Sound-Patterning." In *Oral Traditional Literature: A Festschrift for Albert Bates Lord*, ed. J. M. Foley, 194-216. Columbus, OH: Slavica, 1981.

_____. "Sound-Patterning in Some Sung and Dictated Performances of Avdo Medjedović." *Canadian-American Slavic Studies* 15 (1981) 116-121.

Crosby, R. "Oral Delivery in the Middle Ages." *Speculum* 11 (1936) 88-110.

Crumpacker. M. "Headship and the Equality of the Sexes (1 Cor 11:2-16)." Paper presented at the annual meeting of the Evangelical Theological Society, Washington, D.C., 16-18 November, 1993.

Culley, R. C. "An Approach to the Problem of Oral Tradition." *VT* 13 (1963) 113-125.

_____. *Oral Formulaic Language in the Biblical Psalms.* Toronto: University of Toronto Press, 1967.

_____. "Oral Tradition and the OT: Some Recent Discussion." *Semeia* 5 (1976) 1-33.

_____. *Studies in the Structure of Hebrew Narrative.* Missoula, MT: Scholars, 1976.

_____. "Oral Tradition and Biblical Studies." *OrT* 1 (1986) 30-41.

Cuming, G. J. "Service-endings in the Epistles." *NTS* 22 (1975) 110-113.

Dahl, N. A. *Studies in Paul.* Minneapolis: Augsburg, 1977.

Dahood, M. "Chiasmus." In *IBDSup*, ed. K. Crim, 145. Nashville: Abingdon, 1976.

Daube, D. "Rabbinic Methods of Interpretation and Hellenistic Rhetoric." *HUCA* 22 (1949) 239-264.

Davies, W. D. Review of *Galatians* by H. D. Betz. In *RelSRev* 7 (1981) 310-318.

Deissmann, A. *Light from the Ancient East: The New Testament Illustrated by Recently Discovered Texts of the Graeco-Roman World.* Trans. L. R. M. Strachan. London: Hodder & Stoughton, 1909.

Denniston, J. D. *Greek Prose Style.* Oxford: Clarendon, 1952.

Dewey, A. J. "A Re-Hearing of Romans 10:1-15." *SBLSP* (1990) 273-282.

Dewey, J. "The Literary Structure of the Controversy Stories in Mark 2:1-3:6." *JBL* 92 (1973) 394-401.

_____. "Oral Methods of Structuring Narrative in Mark." *Int* 43 (1989) 32-44.

di Marco, A. "Der Chiasmus in der Bibel." *LB* 36 (1975) 21-97; 37 (1976) 49-68; 39 (1976) 37-85; 44 (1979) 3-70.

Dobschütz, E. von "Zum Wortschatz und Stil des Römerbriefs." *ZNW* 33 (1934) 51-66.

Dockx, S. "Lieu et date de l'épître aux Philippiens." *RB* 80 (1973) 230-246.

Doty, W. G. "The Epistle in Late Hellenism and Early Christianity: Developments, Influences, and Literary Form." Ph.D. dissertation. Drew University, 1966.

_____. "The Classification of Epistolary Literature." *CBQ* 31 (1969) 183-199.

_____. *Letters in Primitive Christianity*. Philadelphia: Fortress, 1973.

Driver, S. R. *Introduction to the Literature of the Old Testament*. 6th ed. New York: Scribner's, 1897.

Duggan, J. J. *The Song of Roland: Formulaic Style and Poetic Craft*. Berkeley: University of California Press, 1973.

Dunn, J. D. G. *Romans*. 2 vols. Dallas: Word, 1988.

Düntzer, H. "Über den Einfluss des Metrums auf den homerischen Ausdruck." *Jahrbücher für classische Philologie* 10 (1864) 673-694.

_____. "Zur Beurtheilung der stehende homerischen Beiwörter." In *Homerische Abhandlungen*, 507-516. Leipzig: Hahn'sche Verlagsbuchhandlung, 1872.

Ellendt, J. E. *Über den Einfluss des Metrums auf der Gebrauch von Wortformen und Wortverbindungen*. Königsberg: Programm Altstädtisches Gymnasium, 1861.

Elliot, N. *The Rhetoric of Romans: Argumentative Strategy and Constraint and Paul's 'Dialogue with Judaism'*. JSNTSup 45. Sheffield: JSOT Press, 1990.

Ellis, E. E. *Paul's Use of the Old Testament*. Grand Rapids: Eerdmans, 1957.

_____. *Pauline Theology, Ministry and Society*. Grand Rapids; Eerdmans, 1989.

Ellis, P. F. *Seven Pauline Letters*. Collegeville, MN: Liturgical Press, 1981.

Exler, F. X. J. "The Form of the Ancient Greek Letter: A Study in Epistolography." Ph.D. dissertation. Catholic University of America, 1923.

Farrell, T. J. "Early Christian Creeds and Controversies in the Light of the Orality-Literacy Hypothesis." *OrT* 2 (1987) 132-145.

Faw, C. E. "On the Writing of First Thessalonians." *JBL* 71 (1952) 217-225.

Fee, G. D. *The First Epistle to the Corinthians*. Grand Rapids: Eerdmans, 1987.

Feuillet, A. "Le Règne de la Mort et le Règne de la Vie (Rom. V, 12-21)." *RB* 77 (1970) 481-521.

Finnegan, R. *Limba Stories and Story-Telling*. Oxford: Clarendon, 1967.

_____. *Oral Literature in Africa*. Oxford: Clarendon, 1970.

_____. "How Oral is Oral Literature?" *BSOAS* 37 (1974) 52-64.

_____. "What is Oral Literature Anyway? Comments in the Light of Some African and Other Comparative Material." In *Oral Literature and the Formula*, eds. B. A. Stolz, R. S. Shannon, 127-166. Ann Arbor, MI: Center for the Coördination of Ancient and Modern Studies, 1976.

_____. *Oral Poetry: Its Nature, Significance, and Social Context.* Cambridge: Cambridge University Press, 1977.

Fiore, B. "Romans 9-11 and Classical Forensic Rhetoric." *PEGLMBS* 8 (1988) 117-126.

Fischer, J. A. "Pauline Literary Forms and Thought Patterns." *CBQ* 39 (1977) 209-233.

Fitzmyer, J. A. "Memory and Manuscript: The Origins and Transmission of the Gospel Tradition." *TS* 23 (1962) 442-457.

_____. *Romans: A New Translation with Introduction and Commentary.* New York: Doubleday, 1993.

Foley, J. M. *Oral-Formulaic Theory and Research: An Introduction and Annotated Bibliography.* New York: Garland, 1985.

_____. *The Theory of Oral Composition: History and Methodology.* Bloomington, IN: Indiana University Press, 1988.

Forbes, C. "Comparison, Self-Praise and Irony: Paul's Boasting and the Conventions of Hellenistic Rhetoric." *NTS* 32 (1986) 1-30.

Forbes, J. *The Symmetrical Structure of Scripture.* Edinburgh: T & T Clark, 1854.

_____. *Analytical Commentary on the Epistle to the Romans, Tracing the Train of Thought by the Aid of Parallelism.* Edinburgh: T & T Clark, 1868.

Fox, E. "The Samson Cycle in an Oral Setting." *Alcheringa Ethnopoetics* 4 (1978) 51-68.

Funk, R. W. *Language, Hermeneutic, and the Word of God.* New York: Harper and Row, 1966.

_____. "The Apostolic Parousia: Form and Significance." In *Christians History and Interpretation: Studies Presented to John Knox*, eds. W. R. Farmer, C. F. D. Moule, R. R. Niebuhr, 249-268. Cambridge: University Press, 1967.

Furnish, V. P. *II Corinthians.* Garden City: Doubleday, 1984.

Gamble, H. *The Textual History of the Letter to the Romans.* Grand Rapids: Eerdmans, 1977.

Garland, D. E. "The Composition and Unity of Philippians: Some Neglected Literary Factors." *NovT* 27 (1985) 141-173.

Geoffrion, T. C. *The Rhetorical Purpose and the Political and Military Character of Philippians: A Call to Stand Firm.* Lewiston, NY: Edwin Mellen Press, 1993.

Gerhardsson, B. *Memory and Manuscript: Oral Tradition and Written Transmission in Rabbinic Judaism and Early Christianity*. Lund: C. W. K. Gleerup, 1961.

Gesemann, G. *Studien zur südslavischen Volksepik*. Reichenberg: Verlag Gebrüder Stiepel, 1926.

Gevirtz, S. *Patterns in the Early Poetry of Israel*. Chicago: Chicago University Press, 1963.

Gilliard, F. "More Silent Reading in Antiquity: *Non Omne Verbum Sonabat*." *JBL* 112 (1993) 689-694.

Girardin, B. *Rhétorique et théologie. Calvin, Le commentaire de l'Epître aux Romains*. Paris: Beauchesne, 1979.

Gitay, Y. "Deutero-Isaiah: Oral or Written?" *JBL* 99 (1980) 185-197.

Goody, J. and Watt, I. "The Consequences of Literacy." In *Literacy in Traditional Societies*, ed. J. Goody, 27-84. New York: Cambridge Unversity Press, 1968.

Grant, R. M. "Hellenistic Elements in 1 Corinthians." In *Early Christian Origins*, ed. A. Wikgren, 60-66. Chicago: Quadrangle, 1961.

Gray, B. "Repetition in Oral Literature." *JAF* 84 (1971) 289-303.

Greenwood, D. "Rhetorical Criticism and Formgeschichte: Some Methodological Considerations." *JBL* 89 (1970) 418-426.

Grobel, K. "A Chiastic Retribution Formula in Romans 2." In *Zeit und Geschichte: Dankesgabe an Rudolf Bultmann zum 80. Geburtstag*, ed. E. Dinkler, 255-261. Tübingen: Mohr, 1964.

Grotius, H. *Annotationes in Novum Testamentum*. 3 vols. Paris, 1641-50.

Gunkel, H. *Genesis*. Göttingen: Vandenhoeck & Ruprecht, 1910.

Gunn, D. M. "Narrative Patterns and Oral Tradition in Judges and Samuel." *VT* 24 (1974) 286-317.

_____. "The 'Battle Report': Oral or Scribal Convention?" *JBL* 93 (1974) 513-518.

_____. "Traditional Composition in the 'Succession Narrative'." *VT* 26 (1976) 214-229.

_____. *The Story of King David: Genre and Interpretation*. JSOTSup 6. Sheffield: JSOT Press, 1978.

Hall, R. G. "The Rhetorical Outline of Galatians: A Reconsideration." *JBL* 106 (1987) 277-287.

Hansen, G. W. *Abraham in Galatians: Epistolary and Rhetorical Contexts*. JSNTSup 29. Sheffield: JSOT Press, 1989.

Harris, M. J. *Colossians & Philemon*. Grand Rapids: Eerdmans, 1991.

Harrison, R. K. *Introduction to the Old Testament*. Grand Rapids: Eerdmans, 1969.

Havelock, E. A. *Preface to Plato*. Cambridge, MA: Harvard University Press, 1963.

_____. "Preliteracy and the Presocratics." *ICSB* 13 (1966) 44-67.

_____. "Thoughtful Hesiod." *YCS* 20 (1966) 61-72.

_____. "Dikaiosune: An Essay in Greek Intellectual History." *Phoenix* 23 (1969) 49-70.

_____. "Prologue to Greek Literacy." In *University of Cincinnati Classical Studies II*, 331-339. Norman, OK: University of Oklahoma Press, 1973.

_____. *Origins of Western Literacy*. Toronto: Ontario Institute for Studies in Education, 1976.

_____. "The Preliteracy of the Greeks." *NLH* 8 (1977) 369-391.

_____. "The Alphabetization of Homer." In *Communication Arts in the Ancient World*, eds. E. A. Havelock, J. P Herschbell, 3-21. New York: Hastings House 1978.

_____. "The Ancient Art of Oral Poetry." *Philosophy and Rhetoric* 12 (1979) 187-202.

_____. "The Oral Composition of Greek Drama." *Quaderni Urbanati di Cultura Classica* 35 (1980) 61-113.

_____. *The Literate Revolution in Greece and Its Cultural Consequences*. Princeton: Princeton University Press, 1982.

_____. "The Linguistic Task of the Presocratics." In *Language and Thought in Early Greek Philosophy*, ed. K. Robb, 7-82. LaSalle, IL: Monist Library of Philosophy, 1983.

_____. "The Orality of Socrates and the Literacy of Plato." In *New Essays on Socrates*, ed. E. Kelly, 67-93. Washington, DC: University of America Press, 1984.

_____. "Oral Composition in the *Oedipus Tyrannus* of Sophocles." *NLH* 16 (1984) 175-197.

_____. "The Alphabetic Mind: A Gift of Greece to the Modern World." *OrT* 1 (1986) 134-150.

_____. *The Muse Learns to Write: Reflections on Orality and Literacy from Antiquity to the Present*. New Haven: Yale University Press, 1986.

_____. "The Cosmic Myths of Homer and Hesiod." *OrT* 2 (1987) 31-53.

Hawthorne, G. F. *Philippians*. Waco: Word, 1983.

Hays, R. B. *The Faith of Jesus Christ: An Investigation of the Narrative Substructure of Galatians 3:1-4:11*. SBLDS 56. Chico, CA; Scholars, 1983.

Heinrici, C. F. G. *Das zweite Sendschreiben des Apostels Paulus an die Korinthier*. Berlin: Hertz, 1887.

Hendrickson, G. L. "Ancient Reading." *CJ* 25 (1929) 182-196.

Herder, J. G. "Vom Erlöser der Menschen: Nach unsern drei ersten Evangelien." In *Herders Sämmtliche Werke*, ed. B. Suphan, XIX:135-252. Berlin: Weidmannsche Buchhandlung, 1880.

Hermann, G. "De Iteratis apud Homerum." Dissertation. Leipzig, 1840.

Hester, J. D. "Rhetorical Structure of Galatians 1:11-2:14." *JBL* 103 (1984) 223-233.

_____. "The Use and Influence of Rhetoric in Galatians 2:1-14." *TZ* 42 (1986) 386-403.

Hillers, D. R. *Covenant: The History of a Biblical Idea*. Baltimore: Johns Hopkins, 1969.

Hodge, C. *An Exposition of the First Epistle to the Corinthians*. Reprint. Grand Rapids: Eerdmans, 1972.

Hooker, M. D. "Philippians 2:6-11." In *Jesus und Paulus. Festschrift für Werner Georg Kümmel zum 70. Geburtstag*, ed. E. E. Ellis and E. Grässer, 151-164. Göttingen: Vandenhoeck & Ruprecht, 1978.

Houston, J. P. *Fundamentals of Learning and Memory*. 4th ed. New York: Harcourt, Brace, Jovanovich, 1991.

Howes, R. F. *Historical Studies of Rhetoric and Rhetoricians*. Ithaca, NY: Cornell University Press, 1961.

Hübner, H. "Der Galaterbrief und das Verhältnis von antiker Rhetorik und Epistolographie." *TLZ* 109 (1984) 241-250.

Hughes, F. W. *Early Christian Rhetoric and 2 Thessalonians*. JSNTSup 29. Sheffield: JSOT Press, 1989.

Hughes, P. E. *Paul's Second Epistle to the Corinthians*. Grand Rapids: Eerdmans, 1962.

Humphries, R. A. "Paul's Rhetoric of Argumentation in 1 Corinthians 1-4." Ph.D. diss., Graduate Theological Union, 1979.

Hurd, J. C., Jr. *The Origin of I Corinthians*. London: SPCK, 1965.

_____. "Concerning the Structure of 1 Thessalonians." Paper presented at the annual meeting of the Society of Biblical Literature, Los Angeles, CA, 1-5 September 1972.

_____. "First Letter to the Thessalonians." In *IDBSup*, ed. K Crim, 900. Nashville: Abingdon, 1976.

_____. "Concerning the Authenticity of 2 Thessalonians." Paper presented at the annual meeting of the Society of Biblical Literature, Dallas, Texas, 19-22 December 1983.

_____. "Outline of Paul's Life." Photocopied handout, n.d.

_____. "Good News and the Integrity of 1 Corinthians." In *Gospel in Paul: Studies on Corinthians, Galatians and Romans for Richard N. Longenecker*, eds. L. A. Jervis, P. Richardson., 38-62 JSNTSup 108. Sheffield: Academic Press, 1994.

Immerwahr, H. R. *Form and Thought in Herodotus*. Cleveland, OH: Western Reserve University Press, 1966.

Jackson, K. and Kessler, M., eds. *Rhetorical Criticism: Essays in Honor of James Muilenburg*. PTMS 1. Pittsburgh, Pickwick Press, 1974.

Jason, H. "The Story of David and Goliath: A Folk Epic?" *Bib* 60 (1979) 36-70.

Jebb, J. *Sacred Scripture*. London: Cadell & Davies, 1820.

Jennrich, W. A. "Classical Rhetoric in the New Testament." *CJ* 44 (1948-49) 30-32.

Jeremias, J. "Zur Gedankenführung in den paulinischen Briefen." In *Studia Paulina in Honorem J. de Zwaan*, eds. J. N. Sevenster and W. C. van Unnik, 146-154. Haarlem: E. F. Bonn, 1953.

_____. "'Flesh and Blood Cannot Inherit the Kingdom of God' 1 Cor 15:50." *NTS* 2 (1956) 151-159.

_____. "Chiasmus in den Paulusbriefen." *ZNW* 49 (1959) 145-156.

Jervis, L. A. *The Purpose of Romans: A Comparative Letter Structure Investigation*. JSNTSup 55. Sheffield: JSOT Press, 1991.

Jewett, R. "The Epistolary Thanksgiving and the Integrity of Philippians." *NovT* 12 (1970) 40-53.

_____. "Romans as an Ambassadorial Letter." *Int* 36 (1982) 5-20.

_____. *The Thessalonian Correspondence: Pauline Rhetoric and Millenarian Piety*. Philadelphia: Fortress, 1986.

_____. "Following the Argument of Romans." In *The Romans Debate: Revised and Expanded Edition*, ed. K. P. Donfried, 265-277. Peabody: Hendrickson, 1991.

_____. "Numerical Sequences in Paul's Letter to the Romans." In *Persuasive Artistry: Studies in New Testament Rhetoric in Honor of George A. Kennedy*, ed. D. F. Watson, 227-245. Sheffield: JSOT Press, 1991.

Johanson, B. C. "Tongues, A Sign for Unbelievers? A Structural and Exegetical Study of I Corinthians XIV. 20-25." *NTS* (1979) 180-203.

_____. *To All the Brethren: A Text-Linguistic and Rhetorical Approach to 1 Thessalonians*. Stockholm: Almqvist and Wiksell, 1987.

Jousse, M. Le Style oral rhythmique et mnémotechnique chez le Verbo-moteurs. Paris: Beauchesne, 1925.

Judge, E. A. *The Social Pattern of Christian Groups in the First Century.* London: Tyndale, 1960.

_____. "The Early Christians as a Scholastic Community." *JRH* 1 (1960/61) 4-15, 125-137.

_____. "Paul's Boasting in Relation to Contemporary Professional Practice." *AusBR* 16 (1968) 37-50.

_____. "St. Paul and Classical Society." *JAC* 15 (1972) 19-36.

Karris, R. J. "The Function and Sitz im Leben of the Paraenetic Elements in the Pastoral Epistles." Ph.D. dissertation. Harvard University, 1971.

Käsemann, E. "Zum Verständnis von Römer 3,24-26." *ZNW* 43 (1950/51) 150-154.

_____. *Commentary on Romans.* Trans. G. Bromiley. Grand Rapids: Eerdmans, 1980.

Keck, L. E. "Oral and Independent or Literary and Interdependent?" In *The Relationships Among the Gospels: An Interdisciplinary Dialogue*, ed. W. O. Walker, Jr., 93-102. San Antonio: Trinity University Press, 1978.

Kelber, W. "Walter Ong's Three Incarnations of the Word: Orality—Literacy—Technology." *Philosophy Today* 23 (1979) 70-74.

_____. "Mark and Oral Tradition." *Semeia* 6 (1970) 7-55.

_____. *The Oral and Written Gospel: The Hermeneutics of Speaking and Writing in the Synoptic Tradition, Mark, Paul and Q.* Philadelphia: Fortress, 1983.

_____. "From Aphorism to Sayings Gospel and from Parable to Narrative Gospel." *Foundations & Facets Forum* 1 (1985) 23-30.

_____. "The Authority of the Word in St. John's Gospel: Charismatic Speech, Narrative Text, Logocentrism, Metaphysics." *OrT* 2 (1987) 108-131.

Kennedy, G. A. *The Art of Persuasion in Greece.* Princeton: Princeton University Press, 1961.

_____. *The Art of Rhetoric in the Roman World: 300 B.C.-A.D. 300.* Princeton: Princeton University Press, 1972.

_____. *Classical Rhetoric and Its Christian and Secular Tradition from Ancient to Modern Times.* Chapel Hill, NC: University of North Carolina Press, 1980.

_____. *New Testament Interpretation through Rhetorical Criticism.* Chapel Hill, NC: University of North Carolina Press, 1984.

Kenyon, F. G. *Books and Readers in Ancient Greece and Rome.* Oxford, 1932; reprint, Chicago: Ares, 1980.

Kessler, M. "A Methodological Setting for Rhetorical Criticism." *Semitics* 4 (1974) 22-36.

Keyes, C. W. "The Greek Letter of Introduction." *AJP* 56 (1935) 28-44.

Kikawada, I. M. "Some Proposals for the Definition of Rhetorical Criticism." *Semitics* 5 (1977) 67-91.

Kim, C. -H. *Form and Structure of the Familiar Greek Letter of Recommendation.* SBLDS 4. Missoula, MT: University of Montana Press, 1972.

_____. "Index of Greek Papyrus Letters." *Semeia* 22 (1981) 107-112.

Kinoshita, J. "Romans—Two Writings Combined." *NovT* 7 (1964) 258-277.

Kiparsky, P. "Oral Poetry: Some Linguistic and Typological Considerations." In *Oral Literature and the Formula*, eds. B. A Stolz, R. S. Shannon, 73-106. Ann Arbor, MI: Center for the Coordination of Ancient and Modern Studies, 1976.

Kirk, G. S. "Homer and Modern Oral Poetry: Some Confusions." *CQ* 10 (1960) 271-281.

_____. *The Songs of Homer.* Cambridge: Cambridge University Press, 1962.

_____. "Studies in Some Technical Aspects of Homeric Style." *YCS* 20 (1966) 76-152.

_____. "Homer: The Meaning of an Oral Tradition." In *Literature and Western Civilization: The Classical World*, eds. D. Daiches, A. Thorlby, 155-171. London: Aldus Books, 1972.

_____. *Homer and the Oral Tradition.* Cambridge: Cambridge University Press, 1976.

Kirkpatrick, P. G. "Folklore Studies and the Old Testament." Ph.D. dissertation. Oxford, 1984.

Kline, M. G. *The Treaty of the Great King: The Covenant Structure of Deuteronomy.* Grand Rapids: Eerdmans, 1963.

Knox, J. *Chapters in a Life of Paul.* Nashville: Abingdon, 1950.

König, E. *Stylistik, Rhetorik, Poetik in Bezug auf die biblische Literatur.* Leipzig: Weicher, 1900.

Koskenniemi, H. *Studien zur Idee und Phraseologie des griechischen Briefes bis 400 n. Chr.* Helsinki: Suomalaisen Kirjallisuunden Kirjapaino Oy, 1956.

Kraftchick, S. J. "Ethos and Pathos in Galatians Five and Six: A Rhetorical Analysis." Ph.D. dissertation, Emory University, 1985.

Kselman, J. S. "Semantic-Sonant Chiasmus in Biblical Poetry." *Bib* 58 (1977) 219-223.

Kümmel, W. G. *Introduction to the New Testament.* Trans. H. C. Kee. Nashville: Abingdon, 1975.

Lang, M. L. *Herodotean Narrative and Discourse.* Cambridge, MA: Harvard University Press, 1984.

Lanham, R. A. *A Handlist of Rhetorical Terms: A Guide for Students of English Literature.* Berkeley, CA: University of California Press, 1968.

Lausberg, H. *Handbuch der literarischen Rhetorik: Eine Grundlegung der Literaturwissenschaft.* 2 vols. Munich: Heubner, 1960.

_____. *Elemente der literarischen Rhetorik.* 2nd ed. Munich: Heubner, 1963.

Lentz, T. M. *Orality and Literacy in Hellenic Greece.* Carbondale, IL: Southern Illinois University Press, 1989.

Liebreich, L. J. "The Compilation of the Book of Isaiah." *JQR* 46 (1956) 259-277.

_____. "The Compilation of the Book of Isaiah." *JQR* 47 (1956) 114-127.

Lieu, J. L. "'Grace to You and Peace': The Apostolic Greeting." *BJRL* 68 (1985)   161-175.

Lightfoot, J. B. *The Epistle of St. Paul to the Galatians.* London: Macmillan, 1865.

Lohfink, N. "Darstellungskunst und Theologie in Dtn 1,6-3,29." *Bib* 41 (1960) 105-134.

Lohmeyer, E. "Probleme paulinischer Theologie I: Briefliche Grussüberschriften." *ZNW* 26 (1927) 158-173.

_____. *Kyrios Jesus: Eine Untersuchung zu Phil 2,5-11.* Heidelberg: Winter, 1928.

Lohr, C. H. "Oral Techniques in the Gospel of Matthew." *CBQ* 23 (1961) 403-435.

Long, T. *Repetition and Variation in the Short Stories of Herodotus.* Frankfurt am Main: Athenäum, 1987.

Longacre, R. E. *The Grammar of Discourse.* New York: Plenum, 1983.

Longenecker, R. N. "Ancient Amanuenses and the Pauline Epistles." In *New Dimensions in New Testament Study*, eds. R. N. Longenecker and M. C. Tenney, 281-297. Grand Rapids: Zondervan, 1974.

_____. *Galatians.* Dallas: Word, 1990.

Longman, T., III. *Literary Approaches to Biblical Interpretation.* Grand Rapids: Zondervan, 1987.

Lord, A. B. "Homer and Huso I: The Singer's Rests in Southslavic Heroic Song." *TAPA* 67 (1936) 106-113.

_____. "Homer and Huso II: Narrative Inconsistencies in Homer and Oral Poetry." *TAPA* 69 (1938) 439-445.

_____. "Homer and Huso III: Enjambement in Greek and Southslavic Heroic Song." *TAPA* 79 (1948) 113-124.

_____. "Homer, Parry, and Huso." *AJA* 52 (1948) 34-44.

_____. "Composition by Theme in Homer and Southslavic Epos." *TAPA* 82 (1951) 71-80.

_____. "Yugoslav Epic Folk Poetry." *IFMJ* 3 (1951) 57-61.

_____. "Homer's Originality: Oral Dictated Texts." *TAPA* 84 (1953) 124-134.

_____. "Avdo Medjodović, Guslar." *JAF* 69 (1956) 320-330.

_____. "The Role of Sound Patterns in Serbocroatian Epic." In *For Roman Jakobson*, eds. M. Halle, H. G. Lunt, H. McLean, C. H. Van Schooneveld, 301-305. Hague: Mouton, 1956.

_____. "The Poetics of Oral Creation." In *Comparative Literature: Proceedings of the Second Congress of the International Comparative Literature Association*, ed. W. P. Friedrich, 1-6. Chapel Hill, NC: University of North Carolina Press, 1959.

_____. *The Singer of Tales*. Cambridge, MA: Harvard University Press, 1960.

_____. "The Gospels as Oral Traditional Literature." In *The Relationships Among the Gospels: An Interdisciplinary Dialogue*, ed. W. O. Walker, Jr., 33-91. San Antonio: Trinity University Press, 1978.

_____. "Words Heard and Words Seen." In *Oral Tradition and Literacy: Changing Visions of the World*, eds. R. A. Whitaker and E. R. Sienaert, 1-17. Durban, South Africa: Natal University Oral Documentation and Research Center, 1986.

_____. "The Merging of Two Worlds: Oral and Written Poetry as Carriers of Ancient Values." In *Current Issues in Oral Literature Research: A Memorial for Milman Parry*, ed. J. M. Foley, 53-64. Columbus, OH: Slavica, 1986.

Louw, J. P. *A Semantic Discourse Analysis of Romans*. Pretoria: University of Pretoria, 1979.

Lüdemann, G. *Paul, Apostle to the Gentiles: Studies in Chronology*. Trans. F. S. Jones. Philadelphia: Fortress, 1984.

Lund, N. W. "The Presence of Chiasmus in the New Testament." *JR* 10 (1930) 74-93.

_____. "The Presence of Chiasmus in the Old Testament." *AJSL* 46 (1930) 104-126.

_____. "The Influence of Chiasmus upon the Structure of the Gospel according to Matthew." *ATR* 13 (1931) 405-433.

_____. "The Influence of Chiasmus upon the Literary Structure of the Gospels." *ATR* 13 (1931) 27-48.

_____. "The Literary Structure of Paul's Hymn to Love." *JBL* 50 (1931) 266-276.

_____. "Chiasmus in the Psalms." *AJSL* 49 (1933) 281-312.

_____. *Chiasmus in the New Testament*. Chapel Hill, NC: University of North Carolina Press, 1942.

_____. "The Significance of Chiasmus for Interpretation." *Crozer Quarterly* 20 (1943) 105-123.

Lundbom, J. R. *Jeremiah: A Study in Ancient Hebrew Rhetoric*. SBLDS 16. Missoula, MT: Scholars, 1975.

Mack, B. L. *Rhetoric and the New Testament*. Minneapolis: Fortress, 1990.

Magoun, F. P., Jr. "Recurring First Elements in Different Nominal Compounds in *Beowulf* and in the *Elder Edda*." In *Studies in English Philology*, eds. K. Malone and M. B. Ruud, 73-78. Minneapolis: University of Minnesota Press, 1929.

_____. "The Oral-Formulaic Character of Anglo-Saxon Narrative Poetry." *Specululm* 28 (1953) 446-467.

_____. "Bede's Story of Caedman: The Case History of an Anglo-Saxon Oral Singer." *Speculum* 30 (1955) 49-63.

_____. "The Theme of the Beasts of Battle in Anglo-Saxon Poetry." *Neuphilologische Mitteilungen* 56 (1955) 81-90.

Malherbe, A. J. "The Beasts at Ephesus." *JBL* 87 (1968) 71-80.

_____. "'Gentle as a Nurse': The Cynic Background of 1 Thess 2." *NovT* 12 (1970) 203-217.

_____. "Ancient Epistolary Theorists." *OJRS* 5 (1977) 3-77.

_____. "Medical Imagery in the Pastoral Epistles." In *Texts and Testaments: Critical Essays on the Bible and Early Church Fathers*, ed. W. E. March, 19-35. San Antonio: Trinity, 1980.

_____. *Socials Aspects of Early Christianity*. 2nd ed. Baton Rouge: Lousiana State University Press, 1983.

_____. "Exhortation in First Thessalonians." *NovT* 25 (1983) 238-256.

_____. "Self-Definition Among Epicureans and Cynics." *In Self-Definition in the Greco-Roman World*, eds. E. P. Sanders, B. F. Meyer, 46-59. Jewish and Christian Self-Definition, vol 3. Philadelphia: Fortress, 1983.

_____. "'In Season and Out of Season': 2 Timothy 4:2," *JBL* 103 (1984) 235-243

_____. *Moral Exhortation: A Greco-Roman Sourcebook*. Philadelphia: Fortress, 1986.

_____. *Paul and the Thessalonians*. Philadelphia: Fortress, 1987.

Man, R. E. "Chiasm and the New Testament." Th.M. thesis, Dallas Theological Seminary, 1982.

_____. "The Value of Chiasm for New Testament Interpretation." *BSac* 141 (1984) 146-157.

Manns, F. "Un hymne judéo-chrétien: Philippiens 2,6-11." *Euntes Docete* 29 (1976) 259-290.

Marrou, H. I. *A History of Education in Antiquity*. Trans. G. Lamb. New York: Sheed and Ward, 1956.

Martin, R. P. *Carmen Christi. Philippians ii.5-11 in Recent Interpretation and in the Setting of Early Christian Worship*. Cambridge: University Press, 1967.

_____. *Philippians*. Greenwood, SC: Attic Press, 1976.

_____. *2 Corinthians*. Waco: Word, 1986.

Martin, W. W. "The Fallacy of the Structural Formula." *TAPA* 96 (1965) 241-253.

Marxsen, W. *Intoduction to the New Testament: An Approach to its Problems*. Trans. G. Buswell. Philadelphia: Fortress, 1968.

Matlin, M. M. *Cognition*. New York: Holt, Rinehart and Winston, 1983.

McArthur, H. K. "Computer Criticism." *ExpTim* 76 (1965) 367-370.

_____. "Καὶ Frequency in Greek Letters." NTS 15 (1969) 339-349.

McCarthy, D. M. *Treaty and Covenant: A Study in Form in the Ancient Oriental Documents and in the Old Testament*. Rome: Pontifical Biblical Institute, 1763, 1978.

_____. "Covenant in the Old Testament: The Present State of Inquiry." *CBQ* 27 (1965) 217-240.

_____. *Old Testament Covenant: A Survey of Current Opinions*. Oxford: Blackwell, 1969.

McEvenue, S. E. *The Narrative Style of the Priestly Writer*. AnBib 50. Rome: Pontifical Biblical Institute, 1971.

McGuire, M. R. P. "Letters and Letter Carriers in Ancient Antiquity." *CW* 53 (1960) 148-153, 184-185, 199-200.

Meecham, H. G. *Light from Ancient Letters: Private Correspondence in the Non-Literary Papyri of Oxyrhynchus of the First Four Centuries, and its Bearings on New Testament Language and Thought*. London: George Allen & Unwin, 1923.

Meeks, W. Review of *A Commentary on Paul's Letter to the Churches in Galatia* by H. D. Betz. In *JBL* 100 (1981) 304-307.

Meillet, A. *Les Origines indo-européennes des mètres grecs*. Paris: Presses Universitaires de France, 1923.

Mendenhall, G. E. "Covenant Forms in Israelite Tradition." *BA* 17 (1954) 50-76.

Metzger, B. M. *A Textual Commentary on the Greek New Testament*. New York: United Bible Societies, 1971.

Meyer, B. F. "The Pre-Pauline Formula in Rom 3:25-26a." *NTS* 29 (1983) 198-208.

Meyer, P. W. Review of *Galatians* by H. D. Betz. In *RelSRev* 7 (1981) 318-323.

Milligan, G. *St. Paul's Epistles to the Thessalonians.* New York: Macmillan, 1908.

Mirsky, A. "Stylistic Device for Conclusion in Hebrew." *Semitics* 5 (1977) 9-23.

Mitchell, M. M. "Concerning 'peri de' in 1 Corinthians." *NovT* 31 (1989) 142-163.

_____. *Paul and the Rhetoric of Reconciliation: An Exegetical Investigation of the Language and Composition of 1 Corinthians.* Louisville, KY: Westminster/John Knox, 1993.

Moffatt, J. *An Introduction to the Literature of the New Testament.* 3rd ed. Edinburgh: T & T Clark, 1918.

Moo, D. J. *Romans 1-8.* Chicago: Moody, 1991.

Morris, L. *1 Corinthians.* Gand Rapids: Eerdmans, 1985.

Morton, A. Q. and McLeman, L. *Christianity in the Computer Age.* New York: Harper & Row, 1965.

Moulton, R. G. *The Literary Study of the Bible.* London: Isbister & Co., 1896.

Mowinckel, S. "Die Komposition des deuterojesajanischen Buches." *ZAW* 49 (1931) 87-112.

Muilenburg, J. "Form Criticism and Beyond." *JBL* 88 (1969) 1-18.

Müller, D. H. *Die Propheten in ihrer ursprünglichen Form.* Wien: Hölder, 1896.

Müller, G. *De Aeschyli Supplicum temporum atque indole.* These de Halle, 1908.

Mullins, T. Y. "Petition as a Literary Form." *NovT* 5 (1962) 46-54.

_____. "Disclosure: A Literary Form in the New Testament." *NovT* 7 (1965) 44-60.

_____. "Greeting as a New Testament Form." *JBL* 87 (1968) 418-426.

_____. "Formulas in New Testament Epistles." *JBL* 91 (1972) 380-390.

_____. "Ascription as a Literary Form." *NTS* 19 (1973) 194-205.

_____. "Visit Talk in the New Testament Letters." *CBQ* 35 (1973) 350-358.

_____. "Benediction as a New Testament Form." *AUSS* 15 (1977) 59-64.

Murko, M. "Die Volksepik der bosnischen Mohammedaner." *Zeitschrift des Vereins für Volkskunde* 19 (1909) 13-30.

_____. *Bericht über phonografische Aufnahmen epischer, meist mohammedanischer Volkslieder im nordwestlichen Bosnien im Sommer 1912*. Vienna: Alfred Hölder, 1912.

_____. *Bericht über eine Bereisung von Nordwestbosnien und der angrenzenden Gebiete von Kratien und Dalmatien behufs Erforschung der Volksepik der bosnischen Mohammedaner*. Vienna: Alfred Hölder, 1913.

_____. *Bericht über eine Reise zum Studium der Volksepik in Bosnien und Herzegowina im Jahre 1913*. Vienna: Alfred Hölder, 1915.

_____. *Bericht über phonografische Aufnahmen epischer Volkslieder im mittleren Bosnien und in der Herzegowina im Sommer 1913*. Vienna: Alfred Hölder, 1915.

_____. "Neues über südslavische Volksepik." *Neue Jahrbücher für das klassische Altertum, Geschichte und deutsche Literatur* 22 (1919) 273-296.

_____. "L'Etat actuel de la poésie populaire épique yougoslave." *Le Monde slave* 5 (1928) 321-351.

_____. *La Poésie populaire épique en Yougoslavie au début du XXe siècle*. Paris: Librairie Ancienne Honoré Champion, 1929.

_____. "Auf den Spuren der Volksepik durch Jugoslavien." *Slavische Rundschau* 3 (1931) 173-183.

_____. "Nouvelles observations sur l'état actuel de la poésie en Yougoslavie." Revue des études slaves 13 (1933) 16-50.

Murphy-O'Connor, J. *1 Corinthians*. Dublin: Veritas, 1979.

Myres, J. L. *Who were the Greeks?* Berkeley, CA; University of California Press, 1930.

_____. "The Last Book of the 'Iliad'." *JHS* 52 (1932) 264-296.

_____. "The Pattern of the Odyssey." *JHS* 72 (1952) 1-19.

_____. *Herodotus. Father of History*. Oxford: Clarendon, 1953.

_____. "The Structure of the 'Iliad' Illustrated by the Speeches." *JHS* 74 (1954) 122-141.

Nielsen, E. *Oral Tradition. A Modern Problem in Old Testament Introduction*. Chicago: Alec R. Allenson, Inc, 1954.

Norden, E. *Die antike Kunstprosa vom VI. Jahrhundert v. Chr. bis in die Zeit der Renaissance*. 2 vols. Leipzig: Teubner, 1898.

Notopoulos, J. "Parataxis in Homer." *TAPA* 80 (1949) 1-23.

_____. "Continuity and Interconnexion in Homeric Oral Composition." *TAPA* 82 (1951) 81-101.

_____. "Homer and Cretan Heroic Poetry: A Study in Comparative Oral Poetry." *AJP* 73 (1952) 225-250.

_____. "Homer as an Oral Poet in the Light of Modern Greek Heroic Oral Poetry." In *Yearbook of the American Philological Society*, 249-253. Philadelphia: American Philological Society, 1954.

_____. "Homer and Geometric Art: A Comparative Study in the Formulaic Technique of Composition." *Athena* 61 (1957) 65-93.

_____. "Modern Greek Heroic Oral Poetry and Its Relevance to Homer." Text accompanying Folkways Record FE 4468, *Modern Greek Heroic Oral Poetry*. New York: Folkways, 1959.

_____. "Homer, Hesiod, and the Achaean Heritage of Oral Poetry." *Hesperia* 29 (1960) 177-197.

_____. "The Homeric Hymns as Oral Poetry: A Study of the Post-Homeric Oral Tradition." *AJP* 83 (1962) 337-368.

Nyberg, H. S. *Studien zum Hoseabuche*. Uppsala: Lundequistska Bokhandeln, 1935.

O'Brien, P. T. "Thanksgiving and Gospel in Paul." *NTS* 21 (1974) 144-155.

_____. *Introductory Thanksgivings in the Letters of Paul*. Leiden: Brill, 1977.

_____. *Colossians, Philemon*. Waco: Word, 1982.

_____. *Commentary on Philippians*. Grand Rapids: Eerdmans, 1991.

Olbricht, T. H. "An Aristotelian Rhetorical Analysis of 1 Thessalonians." In *Greeks, Romans, and Christians*, eds. W. Meeks, D. Balch, E. Ferguson, 216-236. Minneapolis: Fortress, 1990.

Olson, S. N. "Epistolary Uses of Expressions of Self-Confidence." *JBL* 103 (1984) 585-597.

_____. "Paul's Expressions of Confidence in His Readers." *CBQ* 47 (1985) 282-295.

Ong, W. Review of *The Singer of Tales* by Albert Lord. In *Criticism* 4 (1962) 74-78.

_____. Review of *Preface to Plato* by Eric A. Havelock. In *Manuscripta* 7 (1964) 179-181.

_____. "Oral Residue in Tudor Prose." *PMLA* 80 (1965) 145-154.

_____. *The Presence of the Word*. New Haven: Yale University Press, 1967.

_____. "Oral Culture and the Literate Mind." In *Minority Language and Literature*, ed. D. Fisher, 134-149. New York" Modern Language Association of America, 1977.

_____. *Interfaces of the Word: Studies in the Evolution of Consciousness and Culture*. Ithaca, NY: Cornell Univeristy Press, 1977.

_____. "Literacy and Orality in Our Times." *ADE Bulletin* 58 (1978) 1-7.

_____. *Orality and Literacy*. London: Mithuen, 1982.

_____. "The Psychodynamics of Oral Memory and Narrative: Some Implications for Biblical Studies." In *The Pedagogy of God's Image: Essays on Symbol and the Religious Imagination*, ed. R. Mason, 55-73. Chico: Scholars, 1982.

_____. "Oral Remembering and Narrative Structures." In *Georgetown University Round Table on Languages and Linguistics 1981*, ed. D. Tannen, 12-24. Washington, DC: Georgetown University Press, 1982.

_____. "Orality, Literacy, and Medieval Textualization." *NLH* 16 (1984) 1-12.

_____. "Writing is a Technology that Restructures Thought." In *The Written Word: Literacy in Transition*, ed. G. Baumann, 33-50. Oxford: Clarendon, 1986.

Otterlo, W. A. A. van. *Untersuchungen über Begriff, Anwendung und Entstehung der Griechischen Ringkomposition*. Amsterdam: N.V. Noord-Hollandsche Uitgevers Maatschappij, 1944.

Parker, T. H. L. *Commentaries on the Epistle to the Romans 1532-1542*. Edinburgh: T & T Clark, 1986.

Parry, Adam. "The Language of Achilles." *TAPA* 87 (1956) 1-7.

_____. "Have We Homer's *Iliad*?" *YCS* 20 (1966) 177-216.

_____. "Language and Characterization in Homer." *HSCP* 76 (1972) 1-22.

_____., ed. *The Making of Homeric Verse: The Collected Papers of Milman Parry*. New York: Oxford University Press, 1987.

Parry, Anne A. "The Gates of Horn and Ivory." *YCS* 20 (1966) 3-57.

_____. "Homer as Artist." *CQ* 65 (1971) 1-15.

_____. *Blameless Aegisthus: A Study of AMYMΩN and Other Homeric Epithets*. Leiden: Brill, 1973.

Parry, M. "A Comparative Study of Diction as One of the Elements of Style in Early Greek Epic Poetry." M.A. thesis. University of California, 1923.

_____. *L'Epithète traditionnelle dans Homère: Essai sur un problème de style homérique*. Paris: Société Editrice "Les Belles Lettres," 1928.

_____. *Les Formules et la métrique d'Homère*. Paris: Société Editrice "Les Belles Lettres," 1928.

_____. "The Homeric Gloss: A Study in Word-sense." *TAPA* 59 (1928) 233-247.

_____. "The Distinctive Character of Enjambement in Homeric Verse." *TAPA* 60 (1929) 200-220.

_____. "Studies in the Epic Technique of Oral Verse-Making, I: Homer and the Homeric Style." *HSCP* 41 (1930) 73-147.

_____. "Studies in the Epic Technique of Oral Verse-Making, II: The Homeric Language as the Language of Oral Poetry." *HSCP* 43 (1932) 1-50.

_____. "The Traditional Metaphor in Homer." *ChP* 28 (1933) 30-43.

_____. "Whole Formulaic Verses in Greek and Southslavic Heroic Songs." *TAPA* 64 (1933) 179-197.

_____. "The Traces of the Digamma in Ionic and Lesbian Greek." *Language* 10 (1934) 130-144.

_____. "About Winged Words." *ChP* 32 (1937) 59-63.

Parunak, H. V. D. "Oral Typesetting: Some Uses of Biblical Structure." *Bib* 62 (1981) 153-168.

Peabody, B. *The Winged Word: A Study in the Techinque of Ancient Greek Oral Composition as Seen Principally through Hesiod's "Works and Days"*. Albany, NY: State University of New York Press, 1975.

Pearson, B. A. "1 Thessalonians 2:13-16: A Deutero-Pauline Interpolation." *HTR* 64 (1971) 79-94.

Perelman, C. and Olbrechts-Tyteca, L. *The New Rhetoric*. Trans. J. Wilkinson and P. Weaver. South Bend, IN: Notre Dame University Press, 1971.

Perkins, P. "Christology, Friendship and Status: The Rhetoric of Philippians." *SBLSP* (1987) 509-520.

Perry, A. M. "Epistolary Form in Paul." *Crozer Quarterly* 25 (1948) 48-53.

Petersen, N. R. *Rediscovering Paul*. Philadelphia: Fortress, 1985.

Pohlenz, M. *Herodot, der erste Geschichtsschreiber des Abendlandes*. Berlin: Teubner, 1937.

Pollard, T. E. "The Integrity of Phlippians." *NTS* 13 (1966) 57-66.

Poole, M. *Annotations upon the Holy Bible*. 2 vols. London, 1688.

Radday, Y. T. "Chiasmus in Hebrew Biblical Narrative." In *Chiasmus in Antiquity*, ed. J. W. Welch, 211-249. Hildesheim: Gerstenberg, 1981.

Radlov, V. V. *Proben der Volksliteratur der nördlichen türkischen Stämme*. Vol 5. *Der Dialect der Kara-Kirgisen*. St. Petersburg: Commissionäre der Kaiserlichen Akademie der Wissenschaften, 1885.

Ramsay, W. M. *A Historical Commentary on St. Paul's Epistle to the Galatians*. London: Hodder & Stoughton, 1900.

Reumann, J. "The Gospel of the Righteousness of God: Pauline Reinterpretation in Romans 3.21-31." *Int* 20 (1966) 432-452.

_____. "Philippians 3.20-21—A Hymnic Fragment?" *NTS* 30 (1984) 593-609.

Roberts, C. H. "Books in the Graeco-Roman World and in the New Testament." In *Cambridge History of the Bible*, eds. P. R. Ackroyd, et al, 1:48-66. 3 vols. Cambridge: Cambridge University Press, 1970.

Roberts, J. H. "Pauline transitions to the letter body." *BETL* 73 (1986) 93-99.

_____. "Transitional techniques to the letter body in the *corpus Paulinum*." In *A South African perspective on the New Testament. Essays by South African New Testament scholars presented to Bruce Manning Metzger during his visit to South Africa in 1985*, eds. J. Petzer, P. J. Hartin, 187-201. Leiden: Brill, 1986.

_____. "The Eschatological Transitions to the Pauline Letter Body." *Neot* 20 (1986) 29-35.

_____. "θαυμαζω: An expression of perplexity and some examples from papyri letters." *Neot* 25 (1991) 109-122.

_____. "Paul's expression of perplexity in Galatians 1:6: The force of emotive argumentation." *Neot* 26 (1992) 329-338.

Robbins, C. J. "Rhetorical Structure of Philippians 2:6-11." *CBQ* 42 (1980) 73-82.

Robbins, V. K. and Patton, J. H. "Rhetoric and Biblical Criticism." *Quarterly Journal of Speech* 66 (1980) 327-350.

_____. Review of *New Testament Interpretation through Rhetorical Criticism* by George A. Kennedy. In *Rhetorica* 3 (1985) 145-149.

_____. "Writing as Rhetorical Act in Plutarch and the Gospels." In *Persuasive Artistry: Studies in New Testament Rhetoric in Honor of George A. Kennedy*, ed. D. F. Watson 142-168. JSNTSup 50. Sheffield: JSOT Press, 1991.

_____. "Progymnastic Rhetorical Composition and Pre-Gospel Traditions. A New Approach." In *The Synoptic Gospels: Source Criticism and the New Literary Criticism*, ed. C. Focant, 111-147. BETL 110. Leuven: Leuven University Press, 1993.

Rolland, P. "La Structure littéraire de la Deuxieme Epître aux Corinthiens." *Bib* 71 (1990) 73-84.

_____. *A l'écoute de l'Epître aux Romains*. Lire la Bible. Paris: Cerf, 1991.

Roller, O. *Das Formular der paulinischen Briefe. Ein Beitrag zur Lehre vom antiken Briefe*. Stuttgart: Heidelberg, 1934.

Rosenberg, B. A. *The Art of the American Folk Preacher*. New York: Oxford University Press, 1970.

_____. "The Formulaic Quality of Spontaneous Sermons." *JAF* 83 (1970) 3-20.

_____. "The Psychology of the Spiritual Sermon." In *Religious Movements in Contemporary America*, eds. I. I. Zaretsky and M. P. Leone, 135-149. Princeton: Princeton University Press, 1974.

_____. "The Message of the American Folk Sermon." *OrT* 1 (1986) 695-727.

Russell, R. "Pauline Letter Structure in Philippians." *JETS* 25 (1982) 295-306.

Russo, J. A. "A Closer Look at Homeric Formulas." *TAPA* 94 (1963) 235-247.

_____. "The Structural Formula in Homeric Verse." *YCS* 20 (1966) 219-240.

_____. "Is 'Oral' or 'Aural' Composition the Cause of Homer's Formulaic Style?" In *Oral Literature and the Formula*, eds. B. A. Stolz, R. S. Shannon, 31-54. Ann Arbor, MI: Center for the Coördination of Ancient and Modern Studies, 1976.

Sampley, J. P. "Paul, His Opponents in 2 Corinthians 10-13 and the Rhetorical Handbooks." In *The Social World of Formative Christianity and Judaism*, ed. J. Neusner, 162-177. Philadelphia: Fortress, 1988.

Sanders, J. T. "The Transition from Opening Epistolary Thanksgiving to Body in the Letters of the Pauline Corpus." *JBL* 81 (1962) 348-362.

_____. "First Corinthians 13: Its Interpretations Since the First World War." *Int* 20 (1966) 181-187.

Schäfer, R. "Melanchthons Hermeneutik im Römerbrief-Kommentar von 1532." *ZTK* 60 (1963) 216-235.

Schenk, W. *Die Philipperbriefe des Paulus: Kommentar*. Stuttgart: Kohlhammer, 1984.

Schlier, H. *Der Römerbrief*. Freiburg: Herder, 1977.

Schmidt, D. "1 Thess 2:13-16: Linguistic Evidence for an Interpolation." *JBL* 22 (1975-76) 140-158.

Schmithals, W. *Gnosticism in Corinth*. Trans. J. E. Steely. Nashville: Abingdon, 1971.

_____. *Paul and the Gnostics*. Trans. J. E. Steely. Nashville: Abingdon, 1972.

_____. *Der Römerbrief als historisches Problem*. Gütersloh: Mohn, 1975.

Schneider, N. *Die Rhetorische Eigenart der paulinische Antithese*. Tübingen: Mohr, 1970.

Schubert, P. *Form and Function of the Pauline Thanksgivings*. Berlin: Töpelmann, 1939.

_____. "Form and Function of the Pauline Letter." *JR* 19 (1939) 365-377.

Schussler-Fiorenza, E. "Rhetorical Situation and Historical Reconstruction in 1 Corinthians." *NTS* 33 (1987) 386-403.

Scroggs, R. "Paul as Rhetorician: Two Homilies in Romans 1-11." In *Jews, Greeks, and Christians*, eds. R. Hammerton-Kelly and R. Scroggs, 271-298. Leiden: Brill, 1976.

Sedgwick, W. B. "Reading and Writing in Classical Antiquity." *ContRev* 135 (1929)   90-94.

Shoemaker, T. P. "Unveiling Equality: 1 Corinthians 11:2-16." *BTB* 17 (1987) 60-63.

Siegert, F. *Argumentation bei Paulus gezeigt an Röm 9-11*. Tübingen: Mohr, 1985.

Silva, M. "Betz and Bruce on Galatians," *WTJ* 45 (1983) 371-385.

_____. *Philippians*. Chicago: Moody, 1988.

Slusser, M. "Reading Silently in Antiquity." *JBL* 111 (1992) 499.

Smit, J. "The Letter of Paul to the Galatians: A Deliberative Speech." *NTS* 35 (1989)   1-26.

Spencer, A. B. *Paul's Literary Style: A Stylistic and Historical Comparison of II Corinthians 11:16-12:13, Romans 8:9-39, and Philippians 3:2-4:13*. Jackson: ETS, 1984.

Stanford, W. B. *The Sound of Greek: Studies in the Greek Theory and Practice of Euphony*. Berkeley, CA: University of California Press, 1967.

Stark, R., ed. *Rhetorika: Schriften zur aristotelischen und hellenistischen Rhetorik*. Hildesheim: Olms, 1968.

Steen, H. A. "Les clichés epistolaire dans les Lettres sur Papyrus Grecque." *Classica et Mediaevalia* 1 (1938) 119-176.

Stempvoort, P. A. van. "Eine stilistische Lösung einer alten Schwierigkeit in 1 Thess. v.23." *NTS* 7 (1960-61) 262-265.

Stirewalt, M. L. "Paul's Evaluation of Letter Writing." In *Search the Scriptures*, ed. J. M. Myers, et al, 179-196. Leiden: Brill, 1969.

_____."The Form and Function of the Greek Letter-Essay." In *The Romans Debate*, ed. K. Donfried, 175-206. Minneapolis: Augsburg, 1977.

Stock, A. "Chiastic Awareness and Education in Antiquity." *BTB* 14 (1984) 23-27.

Stowers, S. K. *The Diatribe and Paul's Letter to the Romans*. SBLDS 57. Chico, CA: Scholars, 1981.

_____. *Letter Writing in Greco-Roman Antiquity*. Philadelphia: Westminster, 1986.

Swift, R. C. "The Theme and Structure of Philippians." *BSac* 141 (1984) 234-254.

Sykutris, J. "Epistolographi," In *PW* 186-220.

Talbert, C. H. "The Problem of Pre-existence in Philippians 2.6-11." *JBL* 86 (1967) 141-153.

_____. *Reading Corinthians*. New York: Crossroads, 1987.

Thomson, I. H. *Chiasmus in the Pauline Letters*. JNSTSup 111. Sheffield: Academic Press, 1995.

Thraede, K. *Grundzüge griechisch-römisher Brieftopik*. Münich: Beck, 1970.

Thrall, M. E. "*The* Problem of II Cor. VI.14-VII.1 in Some Recent Discussion." *NTS* 24 (1977) 132-148.

Titus, E. L. "Did Paul Write I Corinthians?" *JBR* 27 (1959) 299-302.

Van Seters, J. *Abraham in Tradition and History*. New Haven: Yale University Press, 1975.

_____. *In Search of History*. New Haven: Yale University Press, 1983.

Vouga, F. "Römer 1,18-3,20 als narratio." *TGl* 77 (1987) 225-236.

Walker, W. O., Jr., ed. *The Relationships Among the Gospels: An Interdisciplinary Dialogue*. San Antonio: Trinity University Press, 1978.

Wanamaker, C. A. *Commentary on 1 & 2 Thessalonians*. Grand Rapids: Eerdmans, 1990.

Ward, R. F. "Paul and the Politics of Performance at Corinth." Ph.D. dissertation, Northwestern University, 1987.

_____. "Pauline Voice and Presence as Strategic Communication." *SBLSP* (1990) 283-292.

Watson, D. F. *Invention, Arrangement, and Style: Rhetorical Criticism of Jude and 2 Peter*. SBLDS 104. Atlanta: Scholars, 1988.

_____. "The New Testament and Greco-Roman Rhetoric: A Bibliography." *JETS* 31 (1988) 465-472.

_____. "A Rhetorical Analysis of Philippians and Its Implications for the Unity Question." *NovT* 30 (1988) 57-88.

_____. "The New Testament and Greco-Romans Rhetoric: A Bibliographical Update." *JETS* 33 (1990) 520-523.

Watters, W. R. *Formula Criticism and the Poetry of the Old Testament*. Berlin: de Gruyter, 1976.

Watts, J. D. W. *Isaiah 34-66*. Waco: Word, 1987.

Weima, J. A. D. *Neglected Endings: The Significance of the Pauline Letter Closings.* JSNTSup 101. Sheffield: JSOT Press, 1994.

_____. "Preaching the Gospel in Rome: A Study of the Epistolary Framework of Romans." In *Gospel in Paul: Studies on Corinthians, Galatians and Romans for Richard N. Longenecker*, eds. L. A. Jervis and P. Richardson, 337-366. JSNTSup 108. Sheffield: Academic Press, 1994.

Weiser, A. *Introduction to the Old Testament.* Trans. D. M. Barton. London: Darton, Longman & Todd, 1961.

Weiss, J. "Beiträge zur paulinischen Rhetorik." In *Theologische Studien*, ed. C. R. Gregory, 165-247. Göttingen: Vandenhoeck & Ruprecht, 1897.

Welch, J. W. "Chiasmus in the New Testament." In *Chiasmus in Antiquity*, ed. J. W. Welch, 211-249. Hildesheim: Gerstenberg, 1981.

Wendland, P. "Die urchristlichen Literaturformen." In *HNT* 1.3. Tübingen: Mohr/Siebeck, 1912. 341-343.

Wenham, G. *Genesis 1-15.* Waco: Word, 1987.

Whallon, W. "Formulaic Poetry in the Old Testament." *CompLit* 15 (1963) 1-14.

_____. *Formula, Character, and Context: Studies in Homeric, Old English, and Old Testament Poetry.* Cambridge, MA: Harvard University Press, 1969.

White, J. L. "Introductory Formulae in the Body of the Pauline Letter." *JBL* 90 (1971) 17-33.

_____. "The Structural Analysis of Philemon: A Point of Departure in the Formal Analysis of the Pauline Letter." *SBLSP* (1971) 1:1-48.

_____. *The Form and Function of the Body of the Greek Letter: A Study in the Letter-Body in the Non-Literary Papyri and in Paul the Apostle.* SBLDS 2. Missoula, MT; University of Montana Press, 1972.

_____. *The Form and Structure of the Official Petition.* SBLDS 5. Missoula, MT: University of Montana Press, 1972.

_____ and Kensinger, J. L. "Categories of Greek Papyrus Letters." *SBLSP* (1976) 79-92.

_____. "Epistolary Formulas and Chichés in Greek Papyrus Letters." *SBLSP* (1978) 289-319.

_____. "The Ancient Epistolography Group in Retrospect." *Semeia* 22 (1981) 1-14.

_____. "The Greek Documentary Letter Tradition Third Century B.C.E. to Third Century C.E." *Semeia* 22 (1981) 89-106.

_____. "Paul and the Apostolic Letter Tradition." *CBQ* 45 (1983) 433-444.

_____. "New Testament Epistolary Literature in the Framework of Ancient Epistolography." *ANRW* Series II.25.2 (1984) 1730-1756.

_____. *Light from Ancient Letters*. Philadelphia: Fortress, 1986.

_____. "Ancient Greek Letters." In *Greco-Roman Literature in the New Testament*, ed. D. E. Aune, 85-106. Atlanta: Scholars, 1988.

Whitman, C. H. *Homer and the Heroic Tradition*. Cambridge, MA: Harvard University Press, 1967.

Whittaker, M. "A. Q. Morton and J. McLeman." *Theology* 69 (1966) 567-568.

Wilder, A. N. *The Language of the Gospel: Early Christian Rhetoric*. New York: Harper & Row, 1964.

Wiles, G. P. *Paul's Intercessory Prayers*. SNTSMS 24. Cambridge: University Press, 1974.

Wilke, C. G. *Die neutestamentliche Rhetorik: Ein Seitenstück zur Grammatik des neutestamentlichen Sprachidioms*. Leipzig: Arnold, 1843.

Wire, A. *The Corinthian Women Prophets. A Reconstruction through Paul's Rhetoric*. Minneapolis: Fortress, 1990.

Wittig, S. "Formulaic Style and the Problem of Redundancy." *Centrum* 1 (1973) 123-136.

Wolf, F. *Prolegomena ad Homerum sive (de) Operum Homericorum Prisca et Genuina Forma Variisque Mutationibus et Probabili Ratione Emendande*. Halle: Saxonum, 1975.

Wuellner, W. "Paul's Rhetoric of Argumentation in Romans: An Alternative to the Donfried-Karris Debate Over Romans." *CBQ* 38 (1976) 330-351.

_____. "Greek Rhetoric and Pauline Argumentation." In *Early Christian Literature and the Classical Tradition*, ed. W. R. Schödel and R. L. Wilken, 177-188. Paris: Beauchesne, 1979.

_____. "Paul as Pastor: The Function of Rhetorical Questions in First Corinthians." In *L'Apôtre Paul*, ed. A. Vanhoye, 49-77. Leuven: Peeters/Leuven University Press, 1986.

_____. "Where is Rhetorical Criticism Taking Us?" *CBQ* 49 (1987) 448-463.

Yoder, P. B. "A-B Pairs and Oral Composition in Hebrew Poetry." *VT* 21 (1971) 470-489.

Young, E. J. *Who Wrote Isaiah?* Grand Rapids: Eerdmans, 1958.

Zakovitch, Y. "From Oral to Written Tale in the Bible." *JSJF* 1 (1981) 9-43.

Zmijewski, J. *Der Stil der paulinischen 'Narrenrede'*. Bonn: Hanstein, 1978.

INDICES

INDEX OF ANCIENT REFERENCES

Greco-Roman Literature

Old Testament

New Testament

INDEX OF AUTHORS